Foreign Affairs

1. *The Seven Years War (1756–1763).* This relieved the colonies of the French menace from Canada, but the financial burdens it entailed helped to bring on the American Revolution.

2. *The Pinckney Treaty (1795).* It gave the United States the right of deposit at New Orleans and paved the way for American expansion into the Mississippi Valley.

3. *The Louisiana Purchase (1803).* A major step in expanding the domain of the United States across the continent of North America.

4. *The Transcontinental Treaty (1819).* The Floridas became an acknowledged part of the United States, and Spain relinquished all claim to the Oregon country.

5. *The Webster-Ashburton Treaty (1842).* This brought an end to a period of tense relations between the United States and Great Britain.

6. *The Oregon Treaty (1846).* It established the title of the United States to the Far Northwest below the 49th parallel.

7. *The Mexican War (1846–1848).* It added California and the Southwest to the Union, but this brought in its turn conflict over the extension of slavery.

8. *French Intervention in Mexico (1862–1867).* This attempt to foist a monarchy on Mexico was foiled by the opposition of the Mexican people and the astute diplomacy of Secretary of State Seward.

Supreme Court Rulings

1. *Marbury v. Madison (1803).* Established the precedent for judicial review of Congressional legislation.

2. *McCulloch v. Maryland (1819).* A great exposition of the doctrine of implied powers. It was nationalistic in intent.

3. *Dartmouth College v. Woodward (1819).* Upheld the sanctity of contract, placing property rights above popular or legislative will.

4. *Cohens v. Virginia (1821).* Maintained the doctrine of the supremacy of the federal government.

5. *Gibbons v. Ogden (1824).* Established federal control over interstate and foreign commerce.

6. *Charles River Bridge v. Warren Bridge (1837).* Upheld the power of a state to regulate corporations in the public interest.

7. *Dred Scott v. Sanford (1857).* Asserted that Negro slaves and their descendants could not become Federal citizens and that Congress could not prohibit slavery in the territories of the Union.

8. *Ex Parte Milligan (1864).* Military tribunals declared illegal where the civil courts were open. This angered the radicals, who cowed the Court.

The United States of America:

A HISTORY

Volume I: To 1876

Dexter Perkins

UNIVERSITY PROFESSOR EMERITUS, CORNELL UNIVERSITY
PROFESSOR EMERITUS, THE UNIVERSITY OF ROCHESTER

Glyndon G. Van Deusen

RESEARCH PROFESSOR OF HISTORY, EMERITUS
THE UNIVERSITY OF ROCHESTER

Volume I

THE

United States

OF

America:

A HISTORY

To 1876

SECOND
EDITION

The Macmillan Company, New York
Collier-Macmillan Limited, London

TO OUR STUDENTS,

who, during our many years of teaching, have given us hope for the future of the country whose past we have studied together.

Preface
to the Second Edition

Vigorous action and dramatic development are the chief characteristics of the American story and as such have to dominate its narration. At the same time, the tellers of the tale have to keep in mind factual accuracy and sound interpretation. The absence of serious criticism encourages us to believe that we have come measureably close to the achievement of these goals.

In preparing the second edition of this work, we have brought the bibliographies up to date, made some corrections and additions in the body of the narrative, and have added a new chapter that carries the history of the United States in the twentieth century well into the administration of Lyndon B. Johnson. We submit the result to teachers and students, believing that it will meet with their approval, and hoping that they will profit by its use.

D. P.

G. G. V. D.

Preface
to the First Edition

JOHN DONNE said, "No man is an island," and certain it is that no man lives to himself. Similarly, no man belongs only to his own time. He is the heir to the past and the maker of the future. It is essential, therefore, that he see himself against the larger background. That is what history is about, to make the past more intelligible and to illuminate the present with an eye to meeting the future more effectively.

The development of the United States from a disparate group of struggling colonies into the most powerful nation in the world is an impressive story. We believe that understanding this story is essential to good citizenship. Because of this, we have given substantial weight to the political narrative which ties the story together, gives it convenient unity, and makes understanding easier for the student. Emphasis has been placed on economic forces and their vital relationship with politics. Attention has also been paid to the social and intellectual developments, in due recognition of the significant part they have played in American life. Particular attention has been given to foreign policy— a course which hardly needs to be argued today when the United States is allied with nations on four continents and when decisions involving life and death impend in the international sphere. We have also sought to recreate the salient personalities in our history. Men learn best, perhaps, from the example of the great figures and even when they do not so learn they are fascinated by them. We have tried to keep this fact in mind.

We have sought to tell the story simply, without overwhelming the reader with detail, bearing in mind that most of the hundreds of thousands of students who wish to understand the American past presumably will never become specialists in the field. Our hope is to stimulate the student to further interest, and to arouse in him a sense of social responsibility.

D. P.

G. G. V. D.

A Bibliographical Introduction

EVERY SERIOUS STUDENT of history will wish to go beyond the textbook. In order to help him do so, we have put in each of our two volumes this bibliographical introduction. In addition, Suggested Readings follow each chapter, pointing out works of special value on the topics covered in the text.

Essential to further study is *The Harvard Guide to American History* (1954), edited by Oscar Handlin, Arthur Meier Schlesinger, Samuel Eliot Morison, Frederick Merk, Arthur Meier Schlesinger, Jr., and Paul Herman Buck. This massive volume covers virtually all works of importance published before December, 1950. Further, it groups together various types of material, such as biographies, works on special subjects, sources, and the like. It contains useful hints on such matters as the methods of note-taking, the mechanics of citation, and history as a literary art. No one should attempt research, even of a limited kind, without this guide. It should, however, be added that it does not evaluate the immense mass of materials with which it deals, and that it necessarily omits the most recent works.

Another volume particularly useful to both teachers and students deals in large part with more recent publications. This is William H. Cartwright and Richard L. Watson, Jr., *Interpreting and Teaching American History* (1961), the Thirty-First Yearbook of the National Council for the Social Studies. It contains not only advice and suggestions regarding the teaching of history, but also chapters by qualified scholars indicating the modern trends in historical interpretation and giving valuable bibliographical information. These chapters cover the whole range of American history, beginning with the colonial period and ending with the aftermath of World War II and the ideas and culture of the twentieth century.

For those who seek less detailed sources of information, the best course of action (outside the consultation of a library card catalogue) is to go to the bibliographies in the various historical series. An old series, still valuable for bibliographical purposes, is *The History of American Life* (13 Vols., 1927–1948), edited by Arthur M. Schlesinger and Dixon Ryan Fox. The sweep of these volumes is so great that one can hardly do without them. They stop at 1941, however. Another old series is *The Chronicles of America* (50 Vols., 1918–1921), edited by Allen Johnson, with six supplementary volumes (1950–1951) edited by Allan Nevins. More recent, and of excellent quality, is *The New American Nation Series,* edited by Henry S. Commager and Richard B. Morris. This series is still in preparation, but the following volumes have been published: Wallace Notestein, *The English People on the Eve of Colonization, 1603–1630* (1954); Louis B. Wright, *The Cultural Life of the American Colonies, 1607–1763* (1957); Lawrence H. Gipson, *The Coming of the Revolution, 1763–1775* (1954); John R. Alden, *The American Revolution, 1775–1783* (1954); Russell B. Nye, *The Cultural Life of the New Nation, 1776–1830* (1960); John C. Miller, *The Federalist Era, 1789–1801* (1960); Glyndon G. Van Deusen, *The Jacksonian Era, 1828–1848* (1959); Louis Filler, *The Crusade Against Slavery, 1830–1860* (1960); Ray A. Billington, *The Far Western Frontier, 1830–1860* (1956); Harold U. Faulkner, *Politics, Reform and Expansion, 1890–1900* (1959); Foster R. Dulles, *America's Rise to World Power, 1898–1954* (1955); George E. Mowry, *The Era of Theodore Roosevelt, 1900–1912* (1958); Arthur S. Link, *Woodrow Wilson and the Progressive Era, 1910–1917* (1954); John D. Hicks, *Republican Ascendancy, 1921–1933* (1960). The student should also consult William E. Leuchtenberg, *Franklin D. Roosevelt and the New Deal, 1932–1940* (1963); Clement Eaton, *The Growth of Southern Civilization: 1790–1860* (1961); Francis S. Philbrick, *The Rise of the New West: 1754–1830* (1965); A. Russell Buchanan, *The United States and World War II* (1964); and George Dangerfield, *The Awakening of American Nationalism, 1815–1828* (1965).

Useful, too, is the *Chicago History of American Civilization,* edited by Daniel J. Boorstin. The following volumes have been published: Herbert Agar, *The Price of Power: America Since 1945* (1957); Robert H. Bremner, *American Philanthropy* (1960); Marcus Cunliffe, *The Nation Takes Shape, 1789–1837* (1959); Richard M. Dorson, *American Folklore* (1959); John T. Ellis, *American Catholicism* (1956); Nathan Glazer, *American Judaism* (1957); Samuel P. Hayes, *The Response to Industrialism* (1957); Maldwyn A. Jones, *American Immigration* (1960); William E. Leuchtenberg, *The Perils of Prosperity: 1914–1932* (1958); Robert G. McCloskey, *The American Supreme Court* (1960); Edmund S. Morgan, *The Birth of the Republic, 1763–1789* (1960); Howard H. Peckham, *The War for Independence, A Military History* (1958); Henry Pelling, *American Labor* (1960); Dexter Perkins, *The New Age of Franklin Roosevelt, 1932–1945* (1957); Charles P. Roland, *The Confederacy* (1960); Otis A. Singletary, *The Mexican War* (1960).

This series also includes Harry L. Coles, *The War of 1812* (1965); John

Hope Franklin, *Reconstruction: After the Civil War* (1961); William T. Hagan, *American Indians* (1961); Winthrop Hudson, *American Protestantism* (1961); Howard H. Peckham, *Colonial Wars, 1689–1762* (1963); John B. Rae, *American Automobiles* (1965); John F. Stover, *American Railroads* (1961); and Bernard A. Weisberger, *The American Newspaperman* (1961).

Since 1957 the American Historical Association has published a series of brief pamphlets dealing with various topics, American and European. A list of those that deal with the United States follows: Alexander De Conde, *New Interpretations in American Foreign Policy;* Otis A. Singletary, *The South in American History;* Hal Bridges, *Civil War and Reconstruction;* Edmund S. Morgan, *The American Revolution: A Review of Changing Interpretations;* Ray A. Billington, *The American Frontier;* Charles G. Sellers, Jr., *Jacksonian Democracy;* George E. Mowry, *The Progressive Movement, 1900–1920: Recent Ideas and New Literature;* Harry R. Stevens, *The Middle West;* Louis B. Wright, *New Interpretations of American Colonial History;* Frank Freidel, *The New Deal in Historical Perspective;* Harvey L. Carter, *The Far West in American History;* Ernest R. May, *American Intervention: 1917 and 1941;* W. Burlie Brown, *United States History: A Bridge to the World of Ideas.*

This pamphlet series also includes John D. Hicks, *Normalcy and Reaction, 1921–1933: An Age of Disillusionment;* C. Vann Woodward, *The Age of Reinterpretation* (1961); Chase C. Mooney, *Civil Rights: Retrospect and Prospects* (1961); Keith B. Berwick, *The Federal Age, 1789–1829: America in the Process of Becoming* (1961); Susan S. Burr, *Money Grows Up in American History* (1962); Stanley Elkins and Eric McKitrick, *The Founding Fathers: Young Men of the Revolution* (1962); Richard C. Brown, *They Were There: A Guide to Firsthand Literature for Use in Teaching American History* (1962); Albert A. Blum, *The Development of American Labor* (1963); William T. Hagan, *The Indian in American History* (1963); W. Stull Holt, *The Historical Profession in the United States* (1963); Arthur A. Ekirch, Jr., *American Intellectual History,* 2nd ed. (1963); Gilbert C. Fite, *American Agriculture and Farm Policy Since 1900* (1964); Louis R. Harlan, *The Negro in American History* (1965); Edwin S. Gaustad, *American Religious History* (1966).

A word should also be said about the topical histories in various fields, though these can be discovered grouped in the *Harvard Guide.* In the field of constitutional history, A. H. Kelly and W. A. Harbison, *The American Constitution* (rev. ed., 1955), and C. B. Swisher, *American Constitutional Development* (rev. ed., 1954) survey the whole field. In diplomatic history, T. A. Bailey, *A Diplomatic History of the American People* (rev. ed., 1958); S. F. Bemis, *A Diplomatic History of the United States* (rev. ed., 1955); and J. W. Pratt, *A History of United States Foreign Policy* (1955) are the best known works, and are excellent from the bibliographical point of view. In the field of economic history, a general survey is H. U. Faulkner, *American Economic History* (rev. ed., 1960). Also one should use E. C. Kirkland, *A History of American*

Economic Life (rev. ed., 1951), and Howard R. Smith, *Economic History of the United States* (1955). For the relation of economic thought to historical development, Joseph Dorfman, *The Economic Mind in American Civilization* (5 Vols., 1946–1959) is important. A fundamental work in the history of American literature is R. E. Spiller, and others, *Literary History of the United States* (rev. ed., 1953). It has an excellent bibliography and *Bibliography Supplement* (1959). For intellectual history, Merle Curti, *The Growth of American Thought* (rev. ed., 1951) is of high importance, as is also R. H. Gabriel, *The Course of American Democratic Thought* (rev. ed., 1956).

Other works covering a less wide field, but useful for the more restricted subjects with which they deal, will be found in the Suggested Readings.

Teachers who are interested in learning what books are available in paperbacks should consult the catalogue published quarterly by R. R. Bowker Company, *Paperbound Books in Print,* 62 West 45th Street, New York 36, New York. Text editions of books of the type mentioned above or in the Suggested Readings are starred in the Bowker catalogue.

Finally, for works published relatively recently, the review sections of the *American Historical Review* and the *Mississippi Valley Historical Review* should be consulted.

Table of Contents

THE DAWN OF AMERICAN CIVILIZATION
[1492–1783]

THE YOUNG REPUBLIC
[1783–1815]

GROWTH AND CHANGE
[1815–1860]

EXPANSION AND DISCORD
[1840–1860]

DIVISION AND REUNION
[1860–1876]

Maps and Charts

The United States of America:

A HISTORY

Volume I 〖 TO 1876 〗

THE DAWN

John Winthrop (1587–1649)

The first governor of Massachusetts Bay.
A good Puritan, on occasion he could be
stern and unyielding, but he had
great administrative
ability and was an
outstanding leader.

{[1492-1783]}

OF AMERICAN
CIVILIZATION

1 ⋅ Europe Discovers a New World

IN THE YEAR 1492, the continent of North America lay remote, unknown, and secure, guarded by vast ocean spaces from contact with either Europe or Asia. A few thousand Indians, descendants of primitive Asiatic peoples who, many generations before, had moved across the Bering Strait into Alaska and then down into the continent, were scattered across its eight

The Lonely Continent—Its Geographical Features

million square miles of territory. They had long since lost all connection with their Asiatic cousins. About 1000 A.D., Norsemen had spent several seasons on the North Atlantic coast, but the vast reaches of the North Atlantic had been too perilous for even those hardy Vikings. Their occasional visits ceased, and

Europe went on about its business, leaving the Indians in undisturbed possession of this new world.

This land, so thinly peopled by its Indian tribes, was a treasure house. The warm currents of the Pacific Ocean and the Gulf Stream helped to give it a climate that (excluding the frozen North) varied from temperate to subtropical and made possible a wide diversity of agricultural products. There was a generally adequate rainfall, save in the Great Plains region and in a considerable area west of the Rocky Mountains, as well as an abundance of rich soil and water power and vast stores of mineral deposits. Over 800 million acres of forest below the forty-ninth parallel, and the Great Lakes, lay ready and waiting for the woodman's axe. The long, indented coast lines had many fine harbors, and the Atlantic coast not only offered harborage but also gave easy access through and around the Appalachian chain to the vast plain lying between those mountains and the Rockies. Nature was opening the way for settlement in America, making easy the expansion of settlement from east to west. If the colonists who were to come had landed on the west coast, penetration to the middle of the continent would have been a much more difficult undertaking.

The Background of Discovery

The discoveries that led to colonization, however, came from the European world that lay across the Atlantic. There, as early as the thirteenth century, a civilization that had had to contend with the collapse of Roman authority, with waves of barbarian invasion, and with internal violence, had gradually been stabilizing itself. The feudal system of society had developed, bringing order in its train, towns had sprung up, trade and commerce had increased, and better cultural conditions had been established. By the close of the fourteenth century, Europe was at the dawn of a new era.

One of the manifestations of this European stability had been the rise of a considerable traffic with the Orient. Knowledge of the East, gained through the twelfth-century crusades and the voyages of Marco Polo (1254–1324) and other medieval travelers, together with a growing appetite among Europeans for Eastern luxury goods such as spices, dyes, perfumes, and drugs combined to make for an increase of communications and trade between Western Europe and the cities of Persia, India, and China. The West was acquiring capital, and as it did so, it sought means of making life more pleasant.

There were difficulties, however, in this Oriental trade. The only trade routes that Europe knew lay through the eastern Mediterranean and then by overland caravan to cities with such alluring titles as Bokhara and Samarkand. Italy was strategically placed for controlling this commerce, and Italian merchants and bankers had established over it a monopolistic control. Their charges were high; in consequence, Western Europe paid heavily for the goods it so much desired. Then, too, the goods furnished by the West in

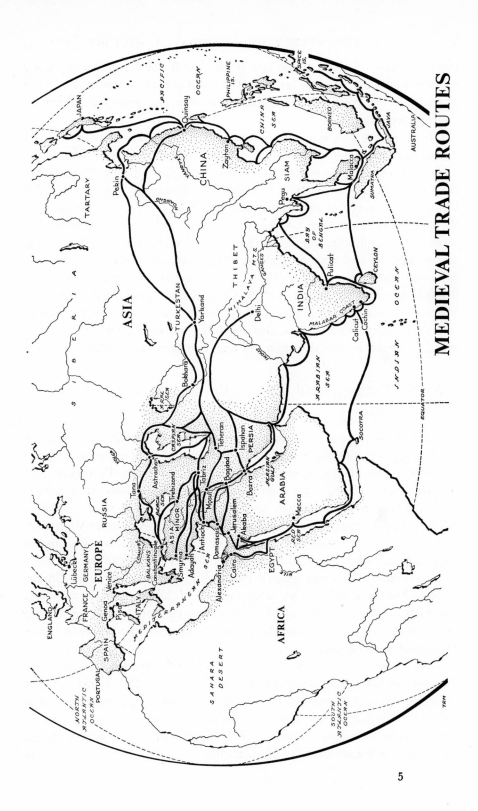

MEDIEVAL TRADE ROUTES

this trade were relatively coarse and crude, and brought considerably lower prices than did the Oriental luxuries. The result was an unfavorable balance of trade for the West, a balance that grew more and more burdensome as the years went on.

Obviously, the best way out of Western Europe's dilemma was to find a new and cheaper route to the East. Portugal sought it in the fifteenth century, pushing down along the west coast of Africa until Bartholomew Diaz reached the Cape of Good Hope in 1486. Spain sent the Italian navigator Christopher Columbus in search of this route, sailing with a fleet of three small ships, the largest not much over 100 tons burden. Columbus sailed westward for seventy days and when he sighted San Salvador (October 12, 1492) was certain that he had reached Cathay. When two other Italians, John and Sebastian Cabot, reached the North American mainland a few years later, it was in search of the territories of the Great Khan. In one sense, Portuguese Vasco de Gama had better luck than Columbus, since he found the sought-for eastern route when he rounded the Cape of Good Hope in 1498 and sailed on across the Indian Ocean to Calicut on the coast of Malabar.

Early Trading and Exploring Activities

The success of these ventures into the unknown intensified the exploring and trading activities of the western nations. Portugal's new passage to India broke the Italian monopoly on the eastern trade, giving the Portuguese control over that very profitable commerce until, a century later, their hold in turn was broken by the Dutch and the English. The West redoubled its efforts to find a western route to the East Indies. Pope Alexander VI grandly divided the world between Portugal and Spain (1493) by drawing an imaginary line which gave all the New World, save Brazil, to Spain, an act of munificence which was ignored by the English and drew from Charles VIII of France a desire to see what the will of Adam, the first man, had really left to the Spaniards. The French monarch's comment shows that the attention of Europe was already beginning to center on the new found lands of the western hemisphere.

More was soon discovered about these lands in the West. Columbus made four voyages to the New World. On the third of these (1498–1500) he began exploring the eastern coast of South America, although, ironically enough, he went to his death a few years later believing that he had only discovered parts of Asia. Amerigo Vespucci (1451–1512) furthered South American exploration to some extent, and was unduly immortalized when a contem-

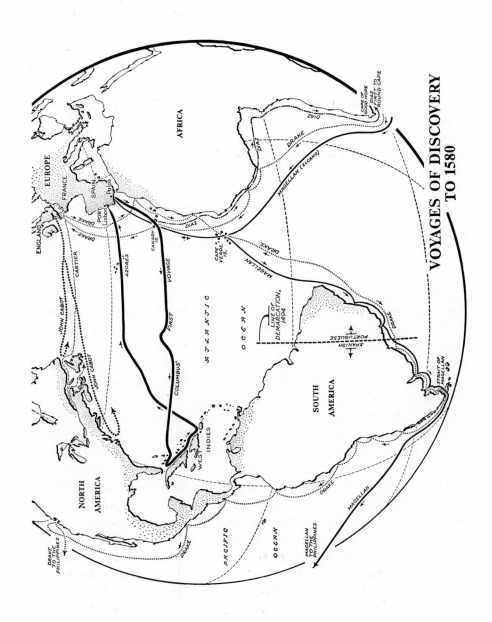

VOYAGES OF DISCOVERY
TO 1580

porary German professor identified the New World with his name. In 1500 Pedro Cabral took possession of Brazil in the name of Portugal. Diego Velasquez conquered Cuba in 1511. The Spaniards tightened the grip on the West Indies that had been established by Columbus and began looking further afield. In 1512, Ponce de Leon, the governor of Porto Rico, set foot on Florida, and a year later Vasco Nunez de Balboa crossed the Isthmus of Panama and stood on the shore of the Pacific.

Exploration of the western hemisphere was an ever-swelling tide which soon began to sweep over the native peoples that stood in its way. The majestic extent of South America became apparent as Magellan, a Portuguese in the service of Spain, passed the straits at its southern tip, bound on a three-year voyage round the world. The Portuguese made good their claim to Brazil. Spanish Hernando Cortez overran Mexico (1519–1521), setting up Spain's authority in that beautiful land. Ten years later, Pizarro conquered the Peruvian Incas and took possession of their vast stores of gold and silver. Before the sixteenth century was half over, Spain had an empire in the New World, an empire which furnished hundreds of millions in specie to fortify the Spanish Hapsburgs' power.

Emboldened by the successes of Spanish captains in South and Central America, other Spanish *conquistadores* probed into North America during the first half of the sixteenth century. De Soto, Narvaez, and Coronado, with great daring and greater cruelty, stormed, stole, and murdered their way across the wild lands north of the Gulf of Mexico, or up from Mexico itself into the mesa country of New Mexico in search of the legendary Seven Cities of Cibola whose streets were supposed to be paved with pure gold. De Soto discovered the Mississippi, died beside it, and was buried under its waters. The others found much peril and hardship, little gold. But they established Spain's claim to the Floridas and to New Mexico, and a claim to Louisiana as well, although that was to be superseded by the fact of French control.

France lagged behind the Spaniards in establishing its title to New World possessions. Distracted by internal civil and religious disturbances, and plagued by foreign wars, the French, perforce, centered their attentions at home while Spain built its empire. To be sure, Jacques Cartier explored the lower reaches of the St. Lawrence in 1540 and France laid claim to Canada as a result, but little was done to make good this claim. Some twenty years later, a feeble attempt to establish a French Protestant colony in Florida ended when the Spaniards massacred its garrison, alleging that this was not because they were French but because they were Lutherans (a compliment that the French repaid a few years later by massacring the Spaniards—not, of course, because of their nationality, but because they were robbers and murderers).

The real French push in the New World came a couple of generations later when, at the beginning of the seventeenth century, driven by a hunger for gold and spices, fish and furs, Samuel de Champlain, the Sieur de Monts, and others pushed into the Bay of St. Lawrence and explored the Atlantic coast as far south as Cape Cod. Gradually French fur traders, missionaries, and explorers like Father Hennepin and the Sieur de La Salle carried the French flag into the Great Lakes and Mississippi valley region. In this way the control of France, though tenuous, was stretched in a great arc from the Gulf of St. Lawrence out to Lake Superior and down the Mississippi to the Gulf of Mexico.

There was one piece of great bad luck that attended this expansion of French power. When, on an expedition into New York in 1609, Champlain and some Algonquin Indians attacked a band of Iroquois, the French earned the ill-will of that powerful confederacy. This hatred of the Iroquois for the French, though it had its low as well as its high points during the ensuing years, was very helpful to the English and the Dutch in their later colonizing efforts, for it was an effective means of checking French expansion south of Montreal.

CHAMPLAIN AND THE ALGONQUINS FIGHTING THE IROQUOIS (1609)

This drawing was made by Champlain. The defeat of the Iroquois, due largely to the superiority of French arms, made relations between the French and the Iroquois confederacy difficult.

COURTESY OF THE NEW YORK PUBLIC LIBRARY

The Spaniards and the French were empire-builders more interested in exploration, furs, the precious metals, and missionary work than they were in colonizing their own nationals in foreign parts. The Dutch and the English also were at first more concerned with "settlements" as bases for trade and exploration than they were in actual colonization. The English, however, were confronted not only by the difficulty of keeping such trading settlements supplied from overseas, but also by a number of other circumstances that pushed them into the serious business of peopling the New World from the Old.

The Origins of English Colonization

The awakening of English interest in the New World was due to the English seamen of the sixteenth century: to Hawkins, Drake, Frobisher, and their like—buccaneers, slave traders, swashbuckling adventurers who killed their enemies in the name of the Virgin Queen and the Lord Jesus. As the attention of Englishmen centered upon the exploits of these ravagers of the Spanish Main, it also centered upon the stories that began to circulate about the riches to be found in the North American lands not pre-empted by Spain. Interest in those lands prompted Sir Humphrey Gilbert and Sir Walter Raleigh to attempt the establishment of settlement outposts—one in Newfoundland, the other in Virginia—during the latter part of the sixteenth century.

The efforts of Gilbert and Raleigh failed for want of steady supplies, and that fact, coupled with Spanish predominance in the New World and Spanish power in the Old, at first kept English colonizing efforts at a low ebb. There soon came, however, a turn in the tide of national power. Philip II of Spain (1556–1598) spent treasure like water in an attempt to dominate Europe. His great effort to conquer England went down to disaster when the Spanish Armada (1588) was badly beaten by Drake's sea-dogs in the English Channel and many of the remaining Spanish galleons were wrecked off the coast of Ireland. Eight years later, Sir Francis Drake sailed into the Spanish harbor of Cadiz and lay there for days, plundering the Spaniards of an immense treasure. These events spelled out the weakness that had come to Spain from an overextension of its strength, and at the same time raised English pride to a pitch never known before. The time was now ripe for a serious English attempt to colonize the lands beyond the seas.

Various factors over and above Spanish weakness and English confidence lay back of the English colonizing efforts of the early seventeenth century. English merchant adventurers, by vigorous trading efforts abroad, had amassed a considerable store of wealth which they were anxious to invest for further profits. There was much poverty among the English lower and middle classes. This made for unrest, as did certain violent differences in religious belief. There was a widespread conviction that England was over-populated, and that the transfer of a portion of its population overseas would be good for the country and for the individuals concerned. The circumstances were propitious, and a number of English merchant capitalists determined to take advantage of them.

Sir Walter Raleigh's patent had been granted by Queen Elizabeth I in 1584, and the land had been named Virginia in honor of the Virgin Queen. Under Elizabeth's successor, James I, Raleigh was accused of high treason and his patent was forfeited. His right of settlement was transferred in 1606 to a group of capitalists interested in searching for gold and a western passage to India, and also attracted by the glowing reports of the New World that had been brought back by some of Raleigh's would-be colonizers. This group of capitalists was known as the Virginia Company of London.

The Settlement of Virginia and Massachusetts

On May 13, 1607, a band of 100 colonists sent out by the London Company established themselves on the coast of Virginia in a settlement that was called Jamestown in honor of the English King. This was the first permanent English settlement in what was later to become the United States.

At first the settlement languished. The colonists, accustomed to a land of open countryside and thickly populated towns, found themselves confronted by all the problems and dangers of a forested frontier scantily peopled by strange beings known as Indians. The discontent of the settlers was augmented, too, by the fact that the London Company regarded them as its servants, out of whose labor profits were to be made. During the first three years, the colonists managed to exist chiefly by reason of the strenuous exertions of Captain John Smith, who organized their efforts and helped them establish trade with the Indians. Even so, they were always in danger of starvation. In the years that followed, massacre by the Indians, epidemics, and crop failures reduced them at times to desperate straits. But gradually they pushed the Indians back and found increasing profits in the culture of a New World plant known as tobacco. By 1630, Virginia colony was securely established.

James I had issued another patent in 1606 to a group of promoters living mainly in Plymouth and known as the Virginia Company of Plymouth.

These had the right to make settlements along the more northerly Atlantic coast, but no successful effort was made in that direction until 1620. In that year, the efforts of the promoters were crowned with success because a group of English men and women had fallen into difficulties with their country's Established Church and with the English Crown.

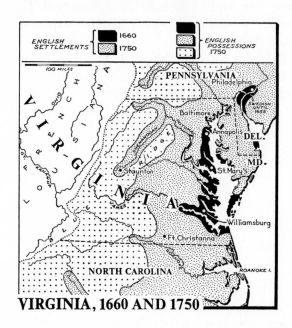

VIRGINIA, 1660 AND 1750

When Henry VIII, at the beginning of the sixteenth century, had broken with the Catholic church and set up the Episcopal establishment as the official English church, it might have been thought that any ensuing religious difficulties would be between the Catholic and the English Episcopal churches. There were plenty of such difficulties, but, in addition, others developed within the body of English Protestantism itself. This was an age in which great stress was laid upon creed and form of worship, violent controversy sometimes developing over what, to the twentieth century, would seem to be forms of belief and practice that are either unimportant or are such as should be left to the individual's judgment. By the latter part of the century there had arisen in the English church a body of dissidents who objected to parts of the Anglican church service, particularly because it allowed no opportunity for participation by the ordinary members of the congregation and because it maintained such Roman Catholic practices as kneeling at the communion service and making the sign of the cross on a child's head at baptism. These dissenters further believed that reform was needed in such matters as the meager salaries paid to parish priests and the common practice of high church officials holding more than one office in order to enhance their incomes. They also looked with a critical eye upon the general manners and morals of the time, which they felt were lax and much in need of improvement. The Church, they felt, should be leading the way in a reforming movement and the Church was showing no disposition to undertake such leadership. These critics of the Anglican church were known as Puritans.

As the sixteenth century wore on, the Puritans became more and more objectionable to the Established Church and to the English government itself. Queen Elizabeth I wanted all pastors to deliver officially prepared sermons. She objected to individual sermons as apt to be destructive to church doctrine. The Puritans insisted upon such sermons, and as the Anglican bishops attempted to punish the recalcitrants, the Puritans began denouncing the bishops. They also began to favor the Presbyterian form of church government set up in Scotland by John Knox, which gave great authority to the individual churches, whereas in the Anglican church the administrative authority was chiefly lodged in the King and the archbishops.

Even more objectionable to the government and the Anglican church was a small group of religious zealots known as Separatists. They believed in each individual's worshiping God according to the dictates of his own conscience. They liked the idea of a multiplicity of churches, each with its own organization; and since the Established Church opposed freedom of worship, the Separatists felt that they had to withdraw from it. In religious matters the Separatists were boldly denying the authority of the national government.

Puritans and Separatists alike were under heavy disfavor of the government during the last years of Elizabeth. The Queen died in 1603, and the Stuarts who followed her—James I (1603–1625) and Charles I (1625–1649) —were even more intolerant of these dissenters. Their leaders were fined and imprisoned, whipped and branded, and their followers were persecuted in similar fashion. But, despite persecution by Church and Crown, Puritanism grew to be a great power in England. Puritans such as Oliver Cromwell, John Pym, John Hampden, and John Milton, were among the most distinguished men of their day. The Puritan movement underlay the first English revolution of the seventeenth century (1642–1648) in which King Charles I lost his head. The Puritans were themselves intolerant of those who differed with them, but their defiance of King and Established Church, and their insistence upon setting up their own standards of conduct exalted principles of liberty and freedom that were to take root in America.

First of these dissenters to come to America were the Separatists. Persecuted at home, and hearing that Holland was a land of religious freedom, a little band of them had slipped over to that country during the years 1607–1609. There they had found life hard and had felt themselves among an alien people. Some of them decided to try Virginia. The Virginia Company of London gave them permission to form a colony there, and James I, more from a desire to get religious nonconformists as far away as possible than from any feeling of compassion or magnanimity, agreed not to interfere with them if they lived in a peaceable manner. They obtained financial aid from the Virginia Company and a minority of them, together with a number of others picked up in England, some Separatists, and some "strangers," organized a colonizing effort.

This little band of about 100 people was led by the cheerful postmaster of Scrooby Manor, William Brewster, and by a pious young farmer, honest and straightforward, whose name was William Bradford. Their tiny ship was the *Mayflower*. Bradford's account indicates that they headed for the mouth of the Hudson, but the winds were contrary, and they finally cast anchor, after a voyage of sixty-five days, in what is now Provincetown Harbor. A month or more was spent exploring the coast and then, in December, 1620, or early January, 1621, the whole party landed at Plymouth, and settlement began in earnest.

Plymouth was outside the Virginia Company of London grant, but the Council of New England, as the Virginia Company of Plymouth was now called, gave the Pilgrims permission to stay on the site they had chosen. Then began the hard business of wresting a living from the none too fertile soil and from the waters off the rockbound New England coast. Forty years later, there were less than 1,000 people in Plymouth plantation. It remained a separate colony until united with the Massachusetts colony in 1691.

The Massachusetts colony was, in its origin, a commercial venture. By the decade of the 1620s, English fishing fleets were frequenting the New England waters and a fishing settlement had been made at Cape Ann near Gloucester Harbor. This settlement had been financed by a company of Puritan merchants, clergymen, and country gentry who called themselves the Dorchester Adventurers. It was not successful as a simple fishing venture, but one of the settlers, Roger Conant, became convinced that a permanent establishment could be effected. He was supported by pastor John White of Dorchester, England, one of the leading spirits in the Dorchester Adventurers. Conant and some fellow enthusiasts started a settlement at what is now Salem. This was under the auspices of the Adventurers, who had reorganized as "The New England Company for a Plantation in Massachusetts Bay." In 1628 the New England Company was again reorganized, and some London merchants of substance (Matthew Cradock, Sir Richard Saltonstall, and others) were brought into the venture. A royal charter with a most generous land grant was obtained in 1629 for what was now known as the Massachusetts Bay Company.

It is impossible to say just when the idea of making the colony a Puritan asylum was born. It may have been in the minds of men like John White and Roger Conant, though of this there is no certain evidence. At any rate, the founders of the colony were Puritans; stern Captain John Endicott, governor of the colony, was a Puritan, the great bulk of the settlers belonged to that persuasion; and as the persecution of Puritans in England grew more severe, the colony became a refuge for those of the Puritan faith. In fact, the very able John Winthrop and the imperious Thomas Dudley, leaders of the first sizeable Puritan migration in 1630, had this idea much in mind. Approximately 1,000 settlers, chiefly Puritans, came over with Winthrop and Dudley in 1630. Within thirteen years the population of Massachusetts Bay numbered over 16,000 souls. This influx is known as the Great Migration. Economic influences and the spirit of adventure played a part in this and other Puritan migrations, but the primary purpose was to make New England an experiment in the Puritan way of life.

It may be that Winthrop, Dudley, and the other Puritan leaders had some thought of making the Massachusetts settlement one of large landed estates tilled by tenants, in the fashion of the English manor. But in New England, where, as in Virginia, land was plentiful, settlers hardy enough to brave the dangers of the New World had no disposition to play the role of tenant. The form the settlement took bore no relation to those twin enemies of democracy, feudalism and hereditary privilege. It was rather that of the town, composed of freeholders who worked for no lord but themselves. At first the chief pursuit was agriculture, but the soil was rocky and none too fertile, and the livelihood gained from it was hard and dour. Agriculture remained the chief pursuit throughout the colonial period, but by the 1640s Massachusetts was also looking to the sea as a means of livelihood—to fishing, to trading with the West Indies, and to the building of her own ships with the oaks of her own forests.

The Spread of Settlement in New England

As Massachusetts colony became a going concern, other Puritan settlements were established in New England. Two Puritan noblemen, Lord Say and Sele and Lord Brooke, established Saybrook in 1635 at the mouth of the Connecticut River. At about the same time, emigrants from Massachusetts inspired by visions of the fertile lands along the Connecticut, and also by political differences with Governor Winthrop, came with their pastor, the Reverend Thomas Hooker, to Hartford. This was the origin of Connecticut colony.

NEW ENGLAND SETTLEMENTS 1660

Rhode Island was founded as the result of religious differences. Its founder, Roger Williams, had come to Massachusetts in 1631, only to find himself at odds with Winthrop and John Cotton. Winthrop believed that the authority of the magistrates came from God rather than from the people and profoundly distrusted what he called "mere democracy." Cotton believed in government by church members only, where great power would be exercised by the ministers of God's church on earth, since they were those who most surely knew the Divine Will. These men were representative of an age of intolerance and conformity, when religious and political rule from above was still the order of the day in the western world.

Roger Williams, on the other hand, was a rebellious spirit. He was an ardent apostle of tolerance. In an era which accepted the class structure of society, he abhorred class privilege and said so openly. At a time when political absolutism ruled in the western world, he was not afraid to declare that a government responsible to the people was infinitely superior to a government based on the divine right of kings; that the governors of society are merely the agents of those who govern; and that the state should have only enough power to serve the ends of justice, never enough to enable it to limit liberty of thought and opinion. Williams was the first great American exponent of that principle of liberty of action and of thought which is one of the bases of American democracy.

Williams was expelled from Massachusetts in 1635 because of his views on religious toleration and because he denied the King's right to grant land that he did not in reality own. Williams settled Providence in 1636 with a collection of men and women of widely variant religious and social ideas, who found it impossible to live under the rigidly theocratic government of Massachusetts. This was the beginning of Rhode Island colony, which was to develop into a state only forty miles square but whose charter, granted in 1663, upheld the great principle of religious freedom.

New Hampshire, the other New England colony of this early period, was founded between 1623 and 1640 on land granted by Charles I to John Mason, an English adventurer, colonizer, and businessman. Anglicans, Puritans, and religious dissidents from Massachusetts settled Exeter and the other towns that went to make up this colony. Massachusetts annexed them all, 1641–1643, but in 1677 this step was disallowed in England. In 1679, New Hampshire became a royal province.

Foundation of the Middle Colonies

The Middle Colonies (New York, Pennsylvania, New Jersey, Delaware, and Maryland) came into being for a variety of social and economic reasons. New York was founded by the Dutch West India Company, an organization established in 1621 to plunder the Spaniards and the Portuguese, as well as to engage in more legitimate trade and commerce. The first permanent settlers from Holland landed on the island of Manhattan in 1626. They bought the island from the Indians for $24.00 (the Dutch were always shrewd traders) and proceeded to build the busy agricultural and trading colony of New Netherland. This was conquered by the English in 1664 and given to James, Duke of York, the brother of King Charles II. Thereafter it was known as New York colony.

A Swedish trading company established settlements along the Delaware River (1628–1643), which were conquered by the Dutch in 1655 and made a part of New Netherland. When the Duke of York was given New Netherland, he gave the region along the Delaware to his friends and servants, John, Lord Berkeley, and Sir George Carteret, governor of the island of Jersey. In honor of Sir George, this area was named New Jersey.

Maryland was settled in 1634. Sir George Calvert and his son Cecilius meant to make money by its establishment and also intended the colony to be a refuge for persecuted English Catholics. The Calverts did not turn up their noses, however, at sturdy Protestant settlers. Indeed, the latter constituted a majority of the first settlers, and it was not long before Protestant-Catholic dissension was rife in the colony.

Pennsylvania was founded in 1681 by the eminent and wealthy Quaker William Penn. In part it was a money-making proposition, but Penn also intended it to be a refuge for Quakers and a community where men could live together as brothers, secure in the possession of both property and liberty.

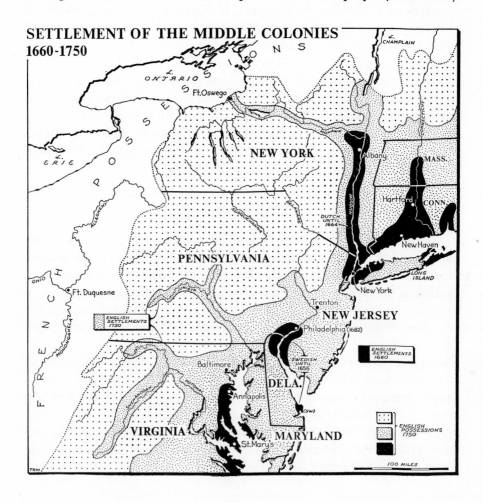

SETTLEMENT OF THE MIDDLE COLONIES
1660-1750

NORTH AMERICA, 1689

A portion of this Pennsylvania "province" was split off in the early eighteenth century to form the colony of Delaware with a separate colonial assembly, although for a long time the Penns continued to act as its proprietors.

The South Beyond Virginia

The settlement of the Carolinas came during the latter part of the 17th century. Anthony Ashley Cooper (later the Earl of Shaftesbury), Arthur Hyde, Earl of Clarendon, George Monck, Duke of Albemarle, and some others, were very influential at the court of King Charles II. They sought to realize profits from the King's grant to them of the province of Carolina, a vast tract lying between the twenty-ninth parallel and the later famous line of 36′30′. Aristocrats all, they believed that it would be feasible to transfer the feudal system of landholding to which they were accustomed in England to the New World. Their intent was to sell part of their hundreds of thousands of acres in the Carolinas, retaining the right to collect from the purchasers yearly payments known as quit rents. They would also profit from the cultivation of their own estates. Their tenants would raise tropical and semi-tropical products and naval stores. The noble lords meant to establish in the New World what seemed to them the only good social order—an aristocratic, manorial, agricultural society composed of nobility, tenantry, and yeoman farmers.

Settlement of the Carolinas began in 1670. There were two centers, one on Albemarle Sound, the other at Charleston. These were the origins of what developed into the separate colonies of North and South Carolina.

Georgia, granted by George II to James Oglethorpe and others in 1732, was partially the result of the growth in eighteenth-century England of a benevolent and humanitarian spirit. Its proprietors meant it to be an asylum for imprisoned debtors, and by the terms of its charter they could not take profits from the enterprise. The intent of the English government was some-

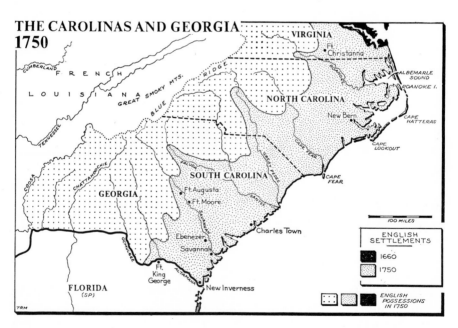

THE CAROLINAS AND GEORGIA 1750

what less altruistic. It intended Georgia to serve as a buffer against the Spanish colonies to the South, and as a means of relieving the cost of maintenance of the English poor.

The Motives of English Settlement

A variety of motives lay back of English colonization in America. Religious difficulties were important in the settlement of New England, Maryland, and Pennsylvania. There was altruism in the planning of William Penn and James Oglethorpe. Economic profit was a factor in the establishment of all the colonies, whether it was sought by trade, the discovery of precious metals, fishing, farming, or real estate operations.

The settlement of the Carolinas is the best example of a particular economic motive that also affected the settlement of New Hampshire, Maryland, New Jersey, and Pennsylvania. During the seventeenth and eighteenth centuries, England was changing from an agricultural to a mercantile economy. Though the price of land was falling, other prices were rising, and the tenants on the manorial estates were finding life more and more difficult. They looked longingly toward the New World. So, too, did the landed proprietors, who constituted the heart and center of the English nobility, and who were having a hard time to maintain their incomes and their social positions. For this reason, men like John Mason, Sir George Carteret, the Calverts, and Penn, sought to find wealth in America through the sale of land or the setting up of vast estates worked by tenants who, the great ones felt, would be willing to work for them across the Atlantic. This was an effort of the English landed aristocracy to perpetuate itself by a new establishment across the sea. The only trouble with this ambition was that an Old World order based on closed landholding and the medieval principle of obedience to the lord of the manor could not be transferred successfully to a New World where land was abundant, authority was weakened by frontier conditions, and freedom was in the very air of the wilderness.

Whatever the combinations of motive that lay back of colonization, the effect was the transfer not only of people but of methods of thinking and ways of living into the wilderness beyond the sea. Each colony was a center where the life that had been lived in Europe was starting up in different surroundings from any it had known before. It was the beginning of a transit of civilization, from an old to a new environment, just as some day in the not far distant future the forms and institutions of our own society may be transferred to some planet among the stars.

The early years of all the colonies were years of hardship, toil, and danger. At first the colonists were very much dependent upon supplies from home, and these sometimes failed or were long delayed. They had to learn from the Indians about such fundamentals as corn planting. The Indians were sometimes hostile. Privation and disease, as well as the rigors of New England winters, took a heavy toll. But, despite the difficulties which beset them, the colonies took root and grew.

In 1625, there were approximately 1,980 colonists in what was to be the United States of 1790. Of these, 1,800 were in Virginia, and the remaining 180 were at Plymouth. By 1700 this total had swelled to 250,000 inhabitants. Sixty years later, the best estimates (there was no census until 1790) show 1,695,000 inhabitants, of whom 1,385,000 were white and 310,000 were Negroes.

There were various sources of this population increase. Colonial life demanded much manual labor, and the labor supply was scarce. In consequence, colonial families were large. Even though mortality was high, this meant a considerable increase in the number of souls. Beginning with a Dutch importation of twenty "Negars" into Virginia in 1619, Negro slaves were another source of population, although slavery did not spread with any rapidity for some sixty years. Very significant, of course, was the continued influx of white settlers from overseas.

A majority of this constant stream of new arrivals were Englishmen of the middle and lower classes, men and women whose lives in the old country were drab and in whom the love of adventure was sufficiently strong to make them willing emigrants. These, as well as less desirable citizens—paupers and criminals, "lewd fellows of the baser sort"—were urged or forced into migration by an English government which felt that the homeland was overcrowded, and that a good way to get rid of criminals was to send them overseas. Finally, a number of non-English peoples found it desirable, for one reason or another, to pull up stakes and come to the New World. These helped, almost from the beginning, to make America a congeries of nationalities.

Settlers Other Than the English

Some of the non-English additions to this American population were of a minor character, so far as numbers were concerned. Here and there in the colonies appeared a few Jews, Irish, Welsh, and Scots. A few score Swedes and Finns established themselves in "New Sweden" along the Delaware. A thousand or so French Huguenots, sober, thrifty traders and commercialists, came to the colonies, seeking better economic conditions and escape from religious persecution. Peter Faneuil, the Bowdoin family, John Jay, and the Pintards of South Carolina were among the distinguished descendants of these French settlers. Between 7,000 and 10,000 Dutch were in New Netherland when it was conquered by the English in 1664. These hardy commercial people were frugal and industrious, but they also introduced such sports as sleighing, skating, bowling, and golf to the New World. Van Cortland, Van Rensselaer, and Schuyler, among others, are Dutch names that have had long and honorable association with American history.

The largest elements of non-English population in the colonies were the Germans and the Scotch-Irish. Economic difficulties and religious persecution in the Germanies of the seventeenth and eighteenth centuries, together with propaganda by ship owners and colonial proprietors, such as William Penn, started a German immigration that assumed significant proportions. In 1709, some 13,000 people from southwest Germany and Switzerland landed in England. They were not welcome there, and over 7,000 of them came to America. The larger part of these settled in east-central New York, under contract to produce naval stores. This project collapsed, and, after squabbles with the government of New York colony and various land speculators, those who did not migrate into Pennsylvania were allowed to purchase land of the Indians along the Mohawk River. Thereafter, the German immigrants shunned New York, going rather into the frontier areas of Pennsylvania and regions further south, where land was plentiful. By 1760, they numbered some 170,000 people. Deeply religious, they brought Lutheranism to America, along with a multiplicity of such sects as the Amish, the Dunkards, the Mennonites, and the Moravians. Mainly thrifty farmers and mechanics, they built stone houses and sometimes stone barns, tended their lands well, and contributed an interest in folk art and music that has survived in fine embroidery, beautiful wood carving, and such musical events as the Bach festival at Bethlehem, Pennsylvania. These Germans had no reason to love England or monarchical government, and were therefore the more ready to support the movement for independence and republican government when it finally came.

Even more numerous than the Germans were the Scotch-Irish. Early in the eighteenth century these Scotch Presbyterian inhabitants of Ulster county in northern Ireland began coming to the colonies, impelled to migrate because they disliked the established Anglican church, and because they were subjected to high rents by absentee landowners and to injurious trade restrictions by the English government. By 1760, there were 280,000 Scotch-Irish in America. Scattered in some 500 settlements, all the way from New England to Georgia, they were especially numerous in New Hampshire, Pennsylvania, and along the southern frontier. Hardy, bold, and self-reliant, it has been well said of them that, wherever they went, "they made free with property rights, encroaching upon the manors that had been reserved and showing a general opposition to the payment of rents." They also brought with them a hearty contempt for England, and became a leaven of discontent with Great Britain during pre-Revolutionary times. Andrew Jackson and Woodrow Wilson were to come of this Scotch-Irish stock.

These various nationalities met and slowly began to mingle in the New World and to create a new society. A Frenchman who settled in America, J. Hector St. Jean Crèvecoeur (he married a certain Mehitable Tippet of Yonkers in 1769) wrote in the latter part of the eighteenth century that he knew a family whose grandmother was English, the wife Dutch, the son's wife French, and in the next generation four sons married to four wives of different nationalities. These Americans, by reason of their novel environment, he remarked, were largely uninhibited by ancient traditions, and so were free to build a new civilization on their heritage from Europe. Once they had been scattered all over Europe, but now, said Crèvecoeur, "Americans are the western pilgrims, who are carrying along with them that great mass of arts, sciences, vigour, and industry which began long since in the east; they will finish the great circle."

The Darker Side of America's European Heritage

The American colonists did, indeed, carry with them from Europe a manifold heritage. Some of it was brought deliberately, some unthinkingly, but all of it was deeply woven into the natures of the men and women who crossed the Atlantic in search of a new home. Part of this heritage was dark and somber in character. Part of it was well worth preservation and development. Taken as a whole, it furnished a complex of traditions and motivations that powerfully influenced thought and action in colonial America. An understanding of this European background is essential to an understanding of America, past and present.

One of the darker aspects of the European heritage was bigotry and superstition. The Protestant Reformation, which came at the beginning of the sixteenth century, threw the European religious world into turmoil and bred a hatred between Catholics and Protestants that made the period from 1550 to 1700 one of the most intolerant eras in the history of Western civilization. The colonists brought violent religious prejudices with them across the ocean.

On many occasions, as has already been shown, they demonstrated their own intolerance in matters of religious faith and practice.

Europe in this period was not only intolerant; it was also cruel and superstitious. Most Europeans, particularly in the seventeenth century, were firm believers in witchcraft and sorcery. Popular imagination had many a poor soul in league with the devil and his angels, and Europe often ran red with blood as a result of witchcraft trials and persecutions. Cruelty was also the order of the day. The death sentence was inflicted for such misdemeanors as stealing a loaf of bread. Cropping, branding, and whipping were the usual punishments for a host of minor crimes; hanging, drawing, and quartering for those of a graver nature. Torture was used by the courts to obtain confessions. Slave trading was an accepted practice. Bear-baiting was a popular sport in England. Inhuman treatment of the feeble-minded and the insane was customary. The eighteenth century saw some alleviation of these barbarities, but the great bulk of the colonists brought over with them cruel and superstitious habits and beliefs which help to explain the harsh treatment of the Indians, the Salem witchcraft trials of 1692, and the ready acceptance, even by the God-fearing Puritans of the practice of enslaving the Indians.

Another unpleasant characteristic of European life in the colonial period was the predominance of arbitrary authority in government. Truly representative government was unknown. Kings were regarded as necessary to the safety of states. They claimed to rule by divine right. On the continent they were unencumbered by anything like representative legislatures. In England itself the revolutions of 1648 and 1688 limited the power of the crown, but even there truly representative government was not established until the nineteenth century. Colonists from all countries were accustomed to rule from above, and frequently to misrule, for the monarchs were seldom governed by high motives. Europe was a blood bath of international war in the seventeenth and eighteenth centuries, due to the greed and faithlessness of the European dynasts, while in internal affairs justice was frequently subordinated to the king's will. These circumstances help to explain both the loyalty with which the colonists long regarded the English crown, and the increasing repugnance which they held for the English government as its authority came to clash with their own interests.

Arbitrary authority, cruelty, and intolerance were not the only evil features of life in Europe during the colonial period. As has been indicated before, economic hardships blighted the lives of many Europeans. These hardships increased as the flood of gold and silver from the New World poured into the coffers of the Old, for it produced a veritable revolution in prices. Between 1500 and 1750, prices of goods in Europe doubled and sometimes tripled. The small European middle class, made up chiefly of local traders and merchant adventurers, profited as a result of this price rise. But as the cost of living increased, life grew difficult for the landed aristocracies and was grim indeed for that great mass of citizens who seldom saw the glint of crowns or ducats or doubloons. As these people were pushed by economic hardship into migrating to America, they brought with them a lively recollection of the grim character of European life.

The Positive European Contributions

But if Europe had some hard lessons to give its emigrants, it also had some great gifts to bestow. This same war-torn, despotically governed, hardship-ridden world was also manifesting a vitality, a resourcefulness, and a richness of thought and culture that was of immense value as part of the American heritage.

The period from 1500 to 1750 in Europe witnessed the development of a great scientific revolution. This had begun in the Middle Ages, and it gathered force in the colonial period. Copernicus gave it impetus with his demonstration that the sun and not the earth was the center of the universe. Galileo, Kepler, Boyle, and a host of others contributed epoch-making scientific discoveries. Newton crowned the whole with his theory of gravitation, demonstrating that the universe operated under a system of natural law. Under this impact, false conceptions of the nature of the world and of man—such as the belief that the world was flat, that it was the center of the cosmos, that a man could command the sun to stand still—were slowly and painfully cleared away. Experimentation joined with abstract reasoning to create new and fruitful hypotheses, and great bodies of knowledge—physics, chemistry, geology—took form. Even medicine showed signs of advance along experimental lines in physiology, pathology, and hygiene. It was the dawn of a new day.

The life of a pioneer did not give much time for reflection or experimentation. But knowledge of the scientific revolution was bound to reach the New World, either through word of mouth or in the books that reached the sparsely furnished library shelves. As will be shown later on, there was considerable colonial interest in science and scientific discoveries.

During this same era, European economic institutions entered a field of dynamic change. The rise of nation-states, with their relative security of condition; the great wealth that came as a result of the explorations and discoveries; and a steadily rising stream of inventions, from lead pencils (1565) to the flying shuttle and the power loom of the eighteenth century, produced a transformation of European society. A bourgeois class developed, and the medieval craft and merchant gilds gave way to the industrial and merchant capitalist. Joint-stock companies formed. Factory methods of production appeared. Speculative manias developed and Europe turned more and more to trading ventures far afield. A vast increase in national wealth and productive capacity opened men's eyes to opportunities for profit and power, while it bred a demand for greater individual freedom in the pursuit of gain. This was the heyday of the bourgeois class, the merchants and traders who, long before *Wilhelm Meister* was written, could have said with Goethe:

> Keep not standing fixed and rooted,
> Briskly venture, briskly roam;
> Head and hand, where'er thou foot it,
> And stout heart are still at home.
>
> In what land the sun does visit,
> Brisk are we, whate'er betide;
> To give space for wandering is it,
> That the world was made so wide.

The American colonists brought the spirit and many of the forms of this rising capitalism to the New World. From the beginning, they were imbued with the profit motive. When hampered in their pursuit of profit by the hard soil of New England, the Puritans turned to commerce and shipbuilding, and a variety of other occupations. As will be shown later on, one of the great features of colonial life was its steadily maturing capitalistic economy, based on the desire for individual gains that would make life more pleasant.

European thought and culture, like European science and the European economy, was full of life and movement during the colonial period. Religious leaders, from Luther and Calvin to the Wesleys; a brilliant galaxy of philosophers, from Bacon and Descartes to Hume; and scores of writers, artists, and musicians attested the vitality of European civilization. It was, indeed, a center of cultural development that had a profound effect upon the colonies.

There was nothing static about the religious life of the Europeans. The Protestant revolt of Luther, Calvin, and Zwingli was answered by a Catholic Counter Reformation. Despite itself, the Anglican church nurtured Puritanism within its bosom. There were still other movements of religious reform. Jansenism was a French Catholic counterpart of Puritanism, as Pietism was in the church founded by Martin Luther. The Anglican Methodism of John and Charles Wesley, out of which before the end of the eighteenth century emerged today's Methodist Episcopal church, was a similar protest against the lack of spirituality of the "two-bottle orthodox" Anglican clerics, and against bishops and rectors who regarded the forms of religion more highly than the substance.

Puritanism, Jansenism, Pietism, and Methodism were essentially reforming movements. All save Jansenism became fundamental parts of American life. Puritanism profoundly affected the history of New England and spread far beyond the borders of that area. Pietism developed centers of influence in Pennsylvania and in various sections of the frontier. Methodism became in time one of the most powerful religious bodies in the United States.

Another development that affected both religious and secular thought and practice was to be of great consequence on both sides of the Atlantic. This was the great rationalist movement that began in the seventeenth and reached its high point in the eighteenth century. One of the most important of its forms was religious rationalism, or, as it is sometimes called, deism.

The religious rationalism that reached its apex in eighteenth-century Europe was bred partly of the scepticisms that grew as explorers and men of science demolished many of the medieval concepts held in the Christian faith. It was also a manifestation of a growing confidence in human reason, a belief, stimulated by the widening of the bounds of knowledge, that man could, indeed, become the master of his own destiny. This deistical movement accepted belief in God "the Clockmaker," who had created the world and then left it to run by itself, but it was critical of Christian orthodoxy, particularly of those aspects, such as miracles, that transcended the ordinary processes of nature. It attacked superstition, wherever found. It defended tolerance. It exalted science and the scientific method of reasoning as the best approach to a solution of life's mysteries. It prided itself upon a broadly cosmopolitan and humanitarian outlook, though it would accept any national patriotism that was humanitarian and peaceful in character. It exerted an increasingly powerful influence upon eighteenth-century thought. The British philosopher David Hume and that Frenchman of many talents, Voltaire, are the best examples of this type of rationalism.

Rationalist concepts of politics vied with rationalist religious ideas in swaying the eighteenth-century climate of opinion. Divine right and political absolutism came under heavy attack. The English philosopher John Locke (1632–1704), in his *Second Treatise on Government* (1690), declared that men had rights which government could take away only in punishment for crime; that government should be responsible to the people; that majority rule was infinitely preferable to royal absolutism; and that the rule of law was a far safer guide than the whims of a despot.

Shortly after Locke, the French philosopher Baron de Montesquieu (1689–1755) asserted that the best laws and the best government are those that develop out of the character of a nation's people and are suited to its climate and topography. Montesquieu also praised the idea of having divided powers in a government, believing that this would be an effective bar to tyranny. These widely circulated concepts of Locke and Montesquieu had an enormous influence upon eighteenth-century thought.

Other rationalists of the time of Locke and Montesquieu also turned their attention to the role of government in economic life. Nation-states in that period practiced what is known as mercantilism. This meant that each state regulated and controlled industry and commerce. Subsidies, honors, exemptions, and monopolies stimulated industrial and commercial developments favored by the government; the state determined the quantity and quality of goods produced, and the ways in which they were marketed; high tariffs protected home industry and hampered the trade of foreign countries; colonies were used as sources of a state's raw materials and as markets for its manufactured goods. In these ways each government tried to establish a favorable balance of trade for its state, a condition that meant a steady increase in the nation's supply of gold and silver. The ultimate object was national power, this to be achieved by exploiting one's colonies and draining the resources of other states. The inevitable result of mercantilism was a condition of chronic international warfare, which was always economic and often military in character. Another result was the creation of a huge number of bureaucratic controls over business and businessmen.

The constant warfare of the period and the burdensome and often injurious regulations of economic activity produced a rising clamor for reform. "Laissez-faire, laissez-passer," said a French merchant, Le Gendre, to Louis XIV's minister of finance, Colbert, in the seventeenth century, and this demand for freedom from economic control became an important part of eighteenth-century rationalistic thought. It reached a high point in Adam Smith's *An Inquiry into the Nature and Causes of the Wealth of Nations* (1776), a book which emphasized the importance of self-help and attacked governmental interference with the operation of economic law. These same ideas were also propagated by a group of French thinkers known as the Physiocrats.

Rationalism in all its aspects was a part of the eighteenth-century climate of opinion, and as such it inevitably became a part of American life and thought. American philosophers such as Benjamin Franklin were familiar with the writings of Hume and Voltaire. They knew Locke by heart, quoting him in their differences with England, and there is every reason to believe that they fully appreciated the criticism of mercantilistic practices that had become such a prominent feature of European thought. In fact, as will appear later on, the American argument against British economic policies in the period just before the Revolution was distinctly rationalistic in character.

There were many other aspects of European intellectual and cultural life that became a part of the American heritage. The Puritans brought with them an interest in Bible reading which made elementary education a practical necessity. The same was true of most of the Protestant sects. This, coupled with a marked development in education that was taking place in England, and with a very natural determination that children should not grow up like savages in a wilderness, explains the early appearance in the colonies of elementary education, a movement in which New England took the lead. In the realm of higher education, Harvard (1636), William and Mary (1693), and Yale (1701) were started in an endeavor to reproduce the type of university education then prevalent in England. In architecture the colonists brought with them types of building they had known in Europe —the high stoops and high-gabled houses of the Dutch, the Swedish notched-log cabins (gradually adopted by the other settlers) and, in the eighteenth century, the English architectural style known as Georgian. Colonial furniture and household decorations were enriched by oriental designs characteristic of the "Chinoiserie" that became the rage in Europe, made popular by the East India Company's imports of Oriental wares. Dutchmen brought with them paintings by the great Dutch artists of the seventeenth century. From 1650 on, the more affluent colonials had their portraits painted in England, and in this way the colonial vogue of such painters as Hogarth, Gainsborough, Reynolds, and Romney was spread.

One aspect of European thought that bore fruit somewhat later than the colonial period was humanitarianism. Beccaria's *An Essay on Crimes and Punishments* (1764), inveighing against the harsh penal systems of the day, was to have significant repercussions on American thought and practice in the early nineteenth century. The interest in international peace evidenced by such writings as those of Grotius, Pufendorf, the Abbé Saint-Pierre, and Immanuel Kant, was always dear to the hearts of the Quakers and bore fruit in early nineteenth century America in the formation of the American Peace Society (1828) and the peace efforts of Elihu Burritt, "The Learned Blacksmith," who spoke, or at least read, some twenty languages.

Since England itself was the chief source of the settlers of the thirteen colonies, an understanding of the European background of America requires some knowledge of English political institutions in the colonial period. Englishmen professed loyalty, and indeed felt it, to the English King, but government in the tight little island did not derive simply from royal edicts. The members of the English court system, from the justices of the peace in the counties to the white-wigged judges who sat on the great courts of the King's Bench and Common Pleas, were appointed by the king and were removable at his will. The justice they dispensed, however, derived not from his pleasure but from the great fabric of national law, a fabric slowly and painfully woven through centuries of English history. Particularly important in its pattern was the common law, which guaranteed jury trial and the right to life, liberty, and property, unless the defendant was deprived thereof by due process in the courts.

Another limitation in the King's power was the authority of Parliament. This ancient and honorable body was bicameral in character. Its House of Lords represented the greater nobility, and the bishops of the Established Church. In its House of Commons sat the representatives of the freeholders (gentry and yeomen farmers) and a scattering representation of the town merchants. The franchise under which the Commons were elected was very limited in scope. In fact, it was more or less of an historical accident, but even so it symbolized the great principle of representative government.

The principle of representation was defended more and more strongly by the country gentry and the merchants during the latter part of the reign of Queen Elizabeth I, the last of the Tudor line. It became a burning issue under the House of Stuart, which succeeded the Tudors in 1603 in the person of James I, and which was very much inclined to insist upon its divine right to rule. The conflict that ensued resulted in the beheading of Charles I in 1649 and the dethroning of James II in the so-called "Glorious Revolution" of 1688. This latter event established Parliamentary supremacy in the government, even though that government remained far from being genuinely representative in character.

The English colonists in America brought with them a lively understanding of the importance of the English struggle for the right of self-government and an abiding sense of the superiority of a government of law over one imposed by the will of one man. The vast majority of these colonists, however, were neither political nor economic radicals or revolutionaries. On the contrary, they were hardheaded, practical-minded men, and their general outlook was conservative.

It was only natural that practical men should bring familiar forms of local government over to the New World settlements. England was administered locally by county, parish, and (in the cities) borough organizations, all under the supervision of the King's Council. The most important part of the county governmental system was the office of justice of the peace. Appointed by the King, the justices acted as individual judges and also on occasion sat as a court. They fixed wages for the county. They also levied taxes and in this and other ways acted much as do our own county boards of supervisors. The county also had a sheriff, to say nothing of a lord lieutenant. Landowners served on juries. The parish vestry was partly religious and partly civil in its functions. It levied the poor tax and took care of the poor within the parish borders. The parish meeting house was a center of local life, both religious and secular. Each parish had its own constable. The town boroughs also had a limited form of self-government. As in the case of the principles that underlay English law and English representative government, these English forms of local government were transferred to the New World by the English colonists.

Such was the European background of the American settlements. The hardships and misery which characterized European life were stimuli to colonization, and the migrants who came from Europe to the New World certainly did so with a lively memory of the social, economic, and political conditions that they had left behind them. But it is also important that the colonists, especially those with some education and cultural background, brought with them a rich and varied cultural tradition which was peculiarly European, and which was constantly reinforced by continued contacts with the Old World. This had to be the case, for pioneer conditions made American culture slow in development, and the intellectual colonists were linked to Europe by practically every book on their shelves. It was inevitable that European customs, fashions, institutions, and habits of thought and opinion should become the basis of American civilization. The fact that they did so is one of the keys to an understanding of much that has happened in American history.

And so, quite suddenly, with the voyage of Christopher Columbus, a new world had swum into the ken of mankind. Its discovery was speedily followed by exploration and settlement.

Some of the consequences of discovery and exploration were bad. America excited greed and envy as nations struggled to secure the New World, or to plunder those who had secured it. International war became very much the order of the day; European cruelty, bigotry, and superstition spread into the new lands of the West.

But the record of what followed the discoveries was by no means entirely black. Though greed, and cruelty, and intolerance had been given greater scope, Europe had also begun the transplanting of its finer qualities to the New World—concepts of justice, tolerance, and fair dealing, boundless energy, artistic achievement, and the scientific approach to life.

New World Gifts to Europe

And as Europe gave its political and social ideals, its science and arts to America, so it began receiving from the West gifts that enriched its own life. New plants and animals appeared on the European scene, new words enriched the European vocabulary, new business forms, such as the joint-stock trading company, were created to cope with trading ventures overseas. Most important of all, perhaps, the European mind was stimulated and its imagination fed by the information (and misinformation) that poured in, through the spoken and the written word, about the vast wilderness beyond the sea. Milton's conception of the world in which he lived was far grander than that which Dante had held 400 years before. Slowly, painfully, with many errors and false steps, mankind was broadening its vision, increasing its knowledge and its power.

Suggested Reading

The geography of North America and its relation to American history is examined in Ellen C. Semple and C. F. Jones, *American History and Its Geographic Conditions* (1933). J. E. Gillespie, *A History of Geographical Discovery, 1400–1800* (1933), and J. B. Brebner, *The Explorers of North America, 1492–1806* (1933) are excellent on European discovery and exploration, and there are interesting accounts by some of the early explorers in Vilhjamur Stefannson, ed., *Great Adventures and Explorations* (1947). H. I. Priestly, *The Coming of the White Man, 1492–1848* (1929) is also useful, and S. E. Morison, *Admiral of the Ocean Sea* (2 vols., 1942) is by far the best biography of Columbus.

The English settlement of the New World is dealt with in authoritative and interesting fashion in Wallace Notestein, *The English People on the Eve of Colonization, 1603–1630* (1954); T. J. Wertenbaker, *The Middle Colonies* (1938), *The Old South* (1942), and *The Puritan Oligarchy* (1947); C. M. Andrews, *The Fathers of New England* (1919), and W. F. Craven, *The Southern Colonies in the Seventeenth Century, 1607–1689* (1949). French and Spanish colonization efforts are described in G. M. Wrong, *The Rise and Fall of New France* (2 vols., 1928), and E. G. Bourne, *Spain in America, 1450–1580* (1905). Francis Parkman, *Pioneers of France in the New World* (rev. ed., 1885) is fascinating, and F. A. Kirkpatrick, *The Spanish Conquistadores* (1934) has much of interest, as has Paul Horgan, *Conquistadores in North American History* (1963).

Good biographies of English founders are Bradford Smith, *Captain John Smith: His Life and Legend* (1953); P. L. Barbour, *The Three Worlds of Captain John Smith* (1964); E. S. Morgan, *The Puritan Dilemma: The Story of John Winthrop* (1958), and O. E. Winslow, *Master Roger Williams* (1957).

For the European background and heritage, see E. P. Cheyney, *The European Background of American History, 1300–1600* (1904) and *The Dawn of a New Era, 1250–1453* (1936); Max Savelle, *The Foundations of American Civilization* (1938); and W. C. Abbott, *The Expansion of Europe* (1938). Various aspects of rationalism are examined in R. V. Sampson, *Progress in the Age of Reason: the Seventeenth Century to the Present Day* (1956); L. G. Crocker, *An Age of Crisis* (1959); and F. E. Manuel, *The Eighteenth Century Confronts the Gods* (1959).

2 ′ The Framework of Colonial Government

T HE CHARTER GRANTED to the Virginia colony by James I declared that the settlers had "all liberties, franchises, and immunities within any of our other dominions, to all intents and purposes as if they had been abiding and born within this our realm of England or any other of our said dominions." This statement established a precedent for the English colonies, marking them off from those of other nations.

Political Beginnings and Types of Government

The settlers who bore with them the flags of the continental countries were considered by their governments to be outside the rights and privileges of the citizens who remained at home; the English settlers took the rights and privileges of Englishmen with them. And this was not because the king graciously willed it, but rather by virtue of the principles of English government and English law. The Virginia charter was not simply a royal dispensation. It was a recognition of long-established customs and institutions that, as Professor Edward Channing has said, "mark off English colonization from all other colonization, ancient and modern."

The seventeenth-century English colonist might logically claim the protection of the law against tyrannical authority and the right of appeal to the English courts from the English Crown as among his privileges. He could not, however, claim self-government as an inherent right, for it had not yet been clearly set up as one of the basic institutions of monarchical England. And yet the principle of self-government was soon very firmly established in England's North American colonies. This was partly because English trading companies and other corporations had enjoyed the privilege of governing themselves, and the men of the London and Plymouth companies were therefore familiar with the idea. When the arbitrary and monopolistic forms of governmental control which the companies first tried in the colonies did not work, they naturally turned to letting the settlements try the business of ruling themselves. The local governments then set up took a representative form because scattered settlements made general assemblies of the freemen impossible. In doing so, they naturally adopted the system used in the English Parliament of sending deputies to represent local towns or boroughs.

When, in 1624, the London Company went to pieces and the English Crown took over the administration of Virginia colony, the representative government there established might well have been destroyed by the arbitrary-minded Stuarts. But James I and his successor Charles I allowed it to continue. In this way a precedent was set up for the self-government of even royal colonies. This was a fortunate thing for the development of American democracy.

By the late seventeenth century, three types of colonial government had been established in North America: "the charter colonies," "the proprietary colonies," and "the royal colonies." Typical charter colonies were Connecticut and Rhode Island. They possessed charters, granted by the Crown, guaranteeing the right of self-government and the traditional rights of Englishmen. In both of these colonies, the voters elected the governor and both branches of the colonial legislature. Pennsylvania and Maryland are the best examples of the proprietary colonies. There the proprietors held by patents or charters, emanating from the king. The Maryland charter was granted in 1632, that of Pennsylvania fifty years later. These patents, together with the rights and privileges granted by the proprietors to the colonists, established a framework of government. In each case, the proprietor appointed the governor, an appointment that had to be ratified by the Crown, and the governor appointed the upper house (council) of the colonial legislature. The voters elected the assembly. The royal colonies, such as New York and Virginia, had governments that were directly subject to written instructions from the Crown, though customs and concessions made to them from time to time formed what may be called traditional constitutions or charters. In these colonies, the governor and his council were appointed directly by the Crown, the assemblies being elected by the voters.

As the seventeenth century merged into the eighteenth, charter and proprietary colonies tended to disappear while royal colonies became the order
of the day. A chronic need for more effective administration, coupled with
difficulties between Crown and charter colony, proprietors and Crown, or
proprietors and colonists, led to the Crown's taking over more and more of
the business of directing colonial affairs. By the middle of the eighteenth
century, Massachusetts, New Hampshire, New Jersey, New York, Virginia,
North Carolina, South Carolina, and Georgia all were royal colonies.

Even in the seventeenth century, the colonial governments had certain
characteristics in common. All had a governor, a council, and an assembly.
Each colonial assembly was elected by the voters of the colony, and each
assembly became accustomed to initiating legislation. Through the assemblies,
representative government was firmly and solidly established in all the colonies as an American institution.

Suffrage in the Colonial Period

The meaning of "representative government" during the colonial period
was far from government by the majority of the people. Suffrage, by custom
and specific regulation, was restricted to males who were twenty-one and
over. At the beginning of the colonial settlements, any adult male who could
qualify as a freeholder, in some instances simply as a free man, could cast
his ballot at the polls; but as the seventeenth century wore on, a variety of
limitations were imposed upon the franchise. Religious qualifications became
customary in New England, with church membership a common requirement. Quakers, Baptists, Roman Catholics, and Jews were excluded from
the polls. The New England colonies frequently required good-character
qualifications as well. Some colonies established residence requirements.
Property qualifications were everywhere—either general, as in Rhode Island,
which required the ownership of "competent estates," or specific, as in the
requirement that a voter possess real estate from which he derived a forty-
shilling income. Sometimes a voter had to own property that was taxable,
or that had a certain value, or was of a certain extent, this last usually being
fifty to 100 acres of land. Occasionally, personal property would serve as a
basis for enfranchisement.

These colonial suffrage qualifications were very similar to those existing in
the English towns, boroughs, and counties of the period. To them were added
other limiting and distinctively American factors, such as scattered settlements, large election districts, and lack of party organization to get out the
vote.

By the middle of the eighteenth century, there had been some changes in voting qualifications, not all of them in the liberal direction. The requirement of church membership had gradually disappeared in New England as secular interests and the number of non-Puritan inhabitants increased. New Haven permitted nonmembers of the church to vote as early as 1662, and the same privilege appeared in the Massachusetts charter of 1691. The taxpaying feature of the suffrage had disappeared, save in South Carolina. On the other hand, the southern colonies began restricting the vote to their white citizens, a practice followed by other colonies as well. Limitations on Catholic voting became more rigid than they had been 100 years before; residence requirements were everywhere enforced; and property qualifications were everywhere retained and in some instances increased. The net result by 1760 was that from one-sixth to one-fiftieth of the population of the various colonies were qualified to go to the polls, while on election days only from 2 to 10 per cent of the population voted.

These percentages were not as extreme as might be imagined. In those days of large families, one-sixth of the population probably meant 85 per cent of the adult males. Recent investigation indicates that Massachusetts, on the eve of the Revolution, had an effective, middle-class democracy, where the property qualifications for the franchise could be easily met and only a small number of adult males could not qualify to vote. Suffrage in the eighteenth century was not as democratic as it was to become in later years, but neither was it harshly restrictive. And the percentage of enfranchised adult males who actually voted was probably not a great deal smaller than the percentage of enfranchised voters who go to the polls today.

Local Government in the Colonies

Local government in the colonies derived from English models, with variation due to colonial conditions. In the South, the chief local political unit was the county. The voters of the county elected the men who represented them in the colonial assembly. The county court was the chief organ of local administration. This court consisted of the justices of the peace, usually eight in number, customarily appointed by the governor, though they were sometimes elected. The county court nominated a list of three candidates, from whom the governor chose a county sheriff. The court also tried all petty offenders. It selected the constables, the coroner, and the surveyor, and had charge of highway construction, bridges, and ferries.

A subdivision of the county was the parish. Administratively, this subdivision was both political and ecclesiastical. It was controlled by a vestry of twelve men. The vestry was at first elective, but it became a closed corporation which filled its own ranks. The vestry saw to poor relief. It also levied church taxes, appointed church wardens, and supervised the general morals of the parish.

In these southern counties and parishes, the appointive rather than the elective principle was predominant. It was a system of government which, if the appointments were well made, brought to the front the ablest and most intelligent members of the community. And it harbored enough of the elective idea so that, without too much difficulty, it could be modified into a more democratic form of government.

New England also had county government, with county sheriffs and justices of the peace, but its chief political subdivision was the town. There was a variety of reasons for this. Many of the first New England settlers came over as church societies and tended to settle as close social units. New England's soil was not suited to the growing of one great staple, such as tobacco. This tended to promote a system of small farms and more compact settlements. New Englanders soon found that they could not live by the land alone, and, as they promptly turned to commerce, fishing, and shipbuilding, town settlements on the seacoast and along the rivers were a logical development.

The most significant feature of the New England town was the town meeting. This institution probably owed its origin to memories of the English parish and, like the parish, it had both political and ecclesiastical aspects. Politically, it consisted of all citizens recognized as freemen. In its annual meetings, it chose the members of the colonial assembly, selected its own militia company, appointed the magistrates and other local officials, and made land grants. Also responsible to it were the selectmen, who were chosen to carry out the policies laid down in the annual meeting. When it met as an ecclesiastical body, with "sinners"—that is to say, nonchurch members—excluded from its ranks, it operated as a church society, choosing its own ministers and other church officials, and regulating its own religious life.

The town meeting was not an example of pure democracy. Not every citizen was eligible for membership. But for its day it was remarkably democratic. It gave an opportunity for a large number of men to participate in the government of the community and was, therefore, a nursery in practical political education and a training school for those who would go on to positions of larger responsibility. Not without reason, Thomas Jefferson called these town meetings "little republics."

The middle colonies had both county and town governments. These had the chief characteristics of both forms, but with the counties more democratically organized than in the South and with the towns more representative and less democratic in form than in New England.

Local colonial government, with its transference from overseas of so many political forms, bore witness to the strength of the English heritage. It was self-governing to a remarkable degree, in view of the times in which it operated. Most significant of all, perhaps, was the extent of its independence of England's control, for this independence was conducive to the growth of a self-reliant spirit.

Seventeenth-Century Freedom from British Control

While the principle of representative government, with some tincture of democracy added, was being solidly established in the seventeenth-century colonies, little attempt at establishing control over them was being made by the king's government in London. Committees of the king's council were set up to control navigation and trade, but up to 1650 little had been accomplished by these bodies. Cromwell's government, after the execution of Charles I, put colonial control in the hands of the Council of State, and it appointed a subcommittee to deal with matters of trade and commerce. Under the Restoration, there appeared a Board of Trade which had colonial commerce under its jurisdiction. Finally, in 1674, a body designed to handle some of the internal as well as the external affairs of the colonies, the Lords of Trade, was established. From time to time, also, colonial domestic matters came under the surveillance of the King's Privy Council, a body of lords, clergy, and commoners possessed of much governmental power.

These various administrative units, however, exercised little authority, for the colonies were in truth a long way off. The Lords of Trade and the Privy Councillors, a majority of whom worked hard and meant well, were appalled by how little reliable information there was about the colonial affairs with which they were supposed to deal. The net result was that, like the earlier councils, they bothered little with matters colonial, except for commercial problems that were closely tied to English policy. Often these, too, received only scant attention. The colonists were very much left alone for over half a century.

That the seventeenth-century colonists were pretty much left to "gang their own gait" was demonstrated by the English attitude toward laws passed by the colonial legislatures. No colony was supposed to make laws contrary to those of England, but, at first, no colony was required to transmit its laws to England for acceptance or rejection. Only beginning with Penn's charter in 1681 did the British government demand transmission of colonial laws to the Privy Council for examination, and then only within five years of their passage. The Massachusetts charter of 1691 shortened the period to three years, with the express statement that the Privy Council was free to accept or reject the laws as it saw fit.

Englishmen at home in England did not question the supremacy of English over colonial law, but the specific establishment of this supremacy was another matter. The difficulty of enforcing English law 3,000 miles away among a people who had themselves been granted the right of legislation staggered the boldest imagination. According to the reasoning of the government in London, it was much better to trust to the loyalty of these British subjects, and to the influence of the royal officials in the colonies, as a means of preventing unwarranted divergence from the laws of the English Parliament.

The attitude of the seventeenth-century colonials toward English law was equivocal. Generally speaking, they accepted the right of Parliament to make laws for them, although occasionally in New England, when political or religious tempers flared, bold spirits asserted that the colonists were not bound to obey laws from overseas. There never was any general agreement in the colonies as to whether English law or colonial law had precedence. But there was never any official denial of the right of Parliament to legislate for them, nor did they deny their dependence on the Crown. The colonists had too lively a sense of what Crown and Parliament could do for them in the way of protection against the Spaniards, the French, and the Dutch, and they were themselves as yet too immature, to challenge directly the authority of England. They did not contest the legality of such Parliamentary acts as applied to them. They were always glad, moreover, to invoke the aid of Parliament when such aid seemed necessary. But they were equally ready to evade what seemed to them unnecessary or hurtful Parliamentary laws, and they demonstrated real skill in developing evasion tactics.

As England, about the middle of the seventeenth century, began seriously to regulate colonial trade, evasion tactics multiplied, and by 1680 the colonials, especially in New England, were demonstrating in a number of ways a decidedly independent spirit. Yankee merchants broke acts regulating commerce as they sought to redress the unfavorable balance of their direct trade with England, and in consequence England's revenue from its colonial trade failed to come up to expectations. Quarrels between royal officials and the assemblies increased in number. Massachusetts was so contemptuous of royal authority that its charter was annulled in 1684. Furthermore, the colonies were continually bickering among themselves. Under these circumstances, the Privy Council decided to establish a more uniform colonial administration, and to bring the colonies more under subjection to the Crown. The Council had the enthusiastic support of James II (1685–1688), who was particularly intent upon destroying the liberties of the New England colonists.

England Attempts to Control the Colonies, 1686–1713

The Council's plan called for a drastic revision of administration in all the proprietary and charter colonies. A Dominion of New England, extending from Delaware Bay to Nova Scotia, was to take the place of the separate colonies. It was to be ruled by a royal governor and his appointed council, without the benefit of any representative assembly. On May 16, 1686, Sir Edmund Andros, an upright and faithful servant of the King, but humorless and intolerant, was made governor-general of this new dominion of the Crown.

The Andros regime lasted from December, 1686, to April, 1689. During that time, the governor brought Massachusetts, Plymouth, Connecticut, and Rhode Island under his sway, imposing and collecting taxes with only the approval of his appointed council. The colonists chafed under this arbitrary government, and when news came of the English Revolution of 1688 deposing James II, the citizens of Boston arose and overthrew Andros. Connecticut and Rhode Island thereupon resumed their old charters; Massachusetts, however, had played too obstreperous a role to be allowed such independent action, and its revised charter, granted in 1691, made it a royal colony with a governor appointed by the king and armed with the right of veto. The charter also contained express provision for an ultimate royal veto of colonial laws, and for the right of appeal from the colony's courts to the Privy Council. Plymouth and the settlements in Maine also were joined to Massachusetts by this charter.

During the period from 1689 to 1713, which spanned the reigns of William and Mary and Queen Anne, the nature of the English government shifted from one of strong executive to one of strong Parliamentary control, and the English merchant class assumed a more and more commanding influence with the government. In consequence, the colonists found their freedom of action circumscribed in a variety of ways. The royal veto disappeared in England, but Parliament insisted upon maintaining this curb over colonial legislation. The Board of Trade and the Privy Council kept watch over colonial legislation, and at their instance the ruling monarch vetoed acts that encroached upon the royal prerogative, that injuriously

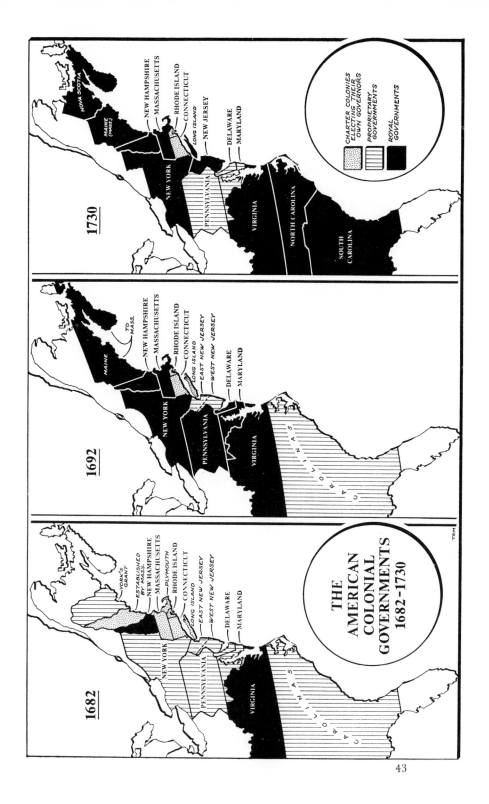

THE
AMERICAN
COLONIAL
GOVERNMENTS
1682-1730

43

affected the material interests of the Crown, or that were inconsistent with English law. Furthermore, it was expected that laws passed in the royal colonies would be promptly presented for approval, while in the charter and proprietary colonies the time limit for presentation was curtailed, now ranging from six months to three years. At the same time, the number of royal colonies increased, New Jersey becoming a royal province in 1702 and the Carolinas suffering the same fate a few years later. In all save the charter colonies of Connecticut and Rhode Island, the governor and his council were now subject to some degree of royal control.

"Salutary Neglect," 1721–1760

The years between 1721 and 1760 saw the dominance in English politics of Sir Robert Walpole, who was prime minister from 1721 to 1742, and of ministers trained by him. During these years, British officialdom continued to scrutinize the acts of the colonial legislatures, and royal governors were given careful instructions as to their attitudes toward laws passed by the colonial assemblies. Parliamentary legislation regulated colonial iron manufacturing, colonial coinage and paper money issues, and numerous aspects of colonial trade and commerce. The general attitude of the British government toward the colonies was restrictive.

Despite such evidences of control, however, this period has been described, with some justice, as one of "salutary neglect" of the colonies by the British government. Walpole was no fervid supporter of overenthusiastic schemes for snuffing out the independent spirit of the colonies, and plans for destroying colonial liberties died a-borning while he was in command of the British government. Disallowance of colonial acts decreased considerably during these forty years. Efforts at control from England continued to be hampered by distance, periods of warfare, and lack of regular means of communication. And control from England by means of the royal governors ran head-on into the determined resistance of the colonial assemblies.

Colonial Legislatures vs. Royal Governors

By the eighteenth century, the colonial assemblies had established for themselves wide prerogatives. They enjoyed an undisputed right to initiate all laws passed in the colonies. They also had the right to determine what bills should be brought forward for passage, what projects should be financially supported, and what colonial government policies should be sanctioned by legislation. English officials, in general, conceded that the colonies could be taxed only by Parliament, or by their own assemblies; and as no comprehensive scheme of Parliamentary taxation was devised before 1763, the colonists came more and more to look upon taxation as their own peculiar right. It was only natural, in view of these circumstances, that they should become intent upon increasing their prerogative at the expense of the royal governors sent over from England.

The royal governors represented the Crown, and the powers of the Crown were being gradually taken away by the House of Commons. It was the misfortune of the eighteenth-century colonial governors that they had to keep the royal prerogative unimpaired in the colonies during the time it was disappearing at home. The colonial assemblies claimed that their prerogatives were similar to those of the House of Commons and obstinately resisted the authority of these royal appointees. In fact, the assemblies claimed that the King could do nothing in the colonies that he could not do in England. The consequence was a chronic state of conflict between the governors and the elected representatives of the people.

The occasions of this conflict were well-nigh infinite. Governors and assemblies quarreled over control of colonial funds, control of the governor's salary, methods of appropriation, the manner and character of appointments, and a host of other things. The governors came to the fray armed with numerous weapons: they could veto bills; they could prorogue and dissolve assemblies; they could refuse to approve salary grants to agents of the assemblies. But the assemblies were even better equipped for the struggle. They adopted the expedient of passing only short-term revenue bills, and they paid the governor his salary year by year. They made appropriations with detailed and specific instructions as to how they should be employed. They attached riders to money bills that were essential to the conduct of the government, and they refused to accept amendments from the councils. And they kept enlarging their appointment of executive officers until in several of the colonies the executive power was largely in the hands of commissioners appointed by the legislature.

The trump card in this struggle between the royal governors and the colonial assemblies was the power of the purse, and this power was held by the colonists. In consequence, the governors fought a losing battle. And as the assemblies saw the increase of their own strength and the loosening of control from England, it became more natural for them to feel that such English control as remained was being permitted by them, rather than being imposed from overseas.

By the middle of the eighteenth century, the American colonies stretched from New England to the northern frontier of Florida, and from tidewater to the foot of the Appalachian range. Their population numbered some 200,-000. Both in numbers and in territorial extent, they had reached a condition that might well justify them in forming a nation of their own. A variety of factors operated to prevent such a development, and still other factors were preparatory to the establishment of a loose sort of national unity.

Factors Which Kept the Colonies Apart

One of the outstanding characteristics of seventeenth-century colonial life was its fragmented character and, as a consequence, the prevalence of a spirit of provincialism. Among the influences that kept these early colonists from achieving any consciousness of national unity was the topography of the land in which they dwelt. New England—with its rocky hillsides, its many rivers, and its excellent harbors—invited the planting of town settlements, the establishment of shipping and other manufactures, and considerable dependence upon oceangoing commerce and fishing as a means of livelihood. The southern colonies—with their broad acres of fertile soil—were ideally suited to scattered settlement and to agricultural pursuits. The topography of the middle colonies inclined them to both ways of living, since they had some fine harbors, mountainous areas where mineral wealth was found, and much good farm land, especially in the river valleys.

Thus each section, by the nature of its environment, tended to develop along lines that were wholly or partly dissimilar from those of the other areas. The consequence was that New England fishermen and Virginia tobacco growers developed divergent interests and needs, and quite different ways of life. Even in the Carolina grant, marked differences of environment, north and south, produced different sets of interest, and the people of the two regions soon manifested an independence of spirit that promoted the establishment of separate colonies.

Differences in environment, among other factors, naturally led to variations in the character of landholding. Virginia, with a plentiful supply of land at its disposal, evolved a generous system of land grants. There "headrights" of fifty acres, with additional amounts of land granted to those who brought relatives and servants to the colony, resulted in scattered settlements and individual farms, with the eventual appearance of plantations of hundreds and even thousands of acres. New England, on the other hand, where fertile land was less plentiful and where settlers tended to band together as church groups, evolved the system of the town grant. This was much smaller than the Virginia grant, being at first only from twenty to thirty acres for the individual settler.

These differences in landholding, together with climatic differences, inevitably produced differences in agricultural output and marketing needs that were scarcely conducive to a community of thought and action. The New Englander concerned with the price of fish or the cost of shipping looked on indifferently as the Pennsylvanian anxiously watched a decline in the price of wheat or as the Virginian groaned over a glut in the tobacco market. The aloofness of South Carolina from the other colonies was more marked after rice became the staple product of the country around Charleston. Such differences were all the more clearly defined because there was very little trade between the early northern and the southern colonies on the North American continent. Both found commerce with Europe and the West Indies more lucrative than commerce with their immediate neighbors.

Another economic variation that was anything but conducive to a community of political interest lay in the various types of money that circulated in the colonies. The colonists all used the terms "pound," "shilling," and "pence," but the pieces so designated varied in value from Massachusetts to Georgia and nowhere had the same value as English coins of like denomination. Using the coin of a distant colony was often, therefore, a frustrating experience. Paper money in various forms was also used by most of the colonies from time to time, there being no prohibition by the home government until the middle of the eighteenth century. The paper money issues were of different and often uncertain values, and the depreciated paper of one colony would often invade and disrupt the currency of a neighbor, causing much hard feeling.

There were still other factors than topography and economics that stood as obstacles to the development of colonial unity. One of these was the wide variety of national strains with which the colonies were populated. The colonials of the middle eighteenth century were still pretty much of a hodgepodge of nationalities. Even with intermarriage, and intermarriage began early, the variation of custom and tradition here represented could not help but be a barrier to the establishment of unity of interest or a common mores. And this barrier was made the more formidable by a considerable measure of national segregation. The Dutch remained concentrated chiefly in New York colony, and the Scotch-Irish and Germans found it economically advisable to settle up and down the frontier, rather than spreading themselves more evenly from the tidewater to the Appalachian range. The development of an American nationality which Crèvecoeur saw in the 1780s was at best a slow process.

Rather closely linked to this variety in national strains, with its divisive effects, was a wide variety in religious faiths. The colonists placed great emphasis on religious doctrine. The New England Puritans were chiefly Congregationalists, but early seventeenth-century differences in theology led to the persecution of Quakers and the expulsion of Roger Williams and Anne Hutchinson from Massachusetts Bay Colony, events that by no means indicated a happy community of spirit among the parties concerned. The Dutch Reformed and Presbyterian Churches, like the Congregationalists, owed much to the teachings of John Calvin of Geneva, but, even so, there was plenty of room for doctrinal divergence and consequent dispute between Yankees, Dutchmen, and Scotch-Irishmen. Much more was this the case when Calvinists of the Scotch-Presbyterian variety met Anglicans or Pennsylvania Quakers, or Maryland Catholics. Diversity of religious conviction flared into open resentment when non-Anglicans in the southern colonies were forced to pay taxes in support of the established Anglican church or had to go to an Anglican rector in order to be legally married. More than one good couple, on the banks of the Yadkin or in some other outlying district many miles away from the nearest Anglican cleric, "went it alone" rather than making the arduous trip required for compliance with a law for which they had no respect. Religious differences were a barrier to the growth of an American spirit.

Distance in colonial times, perhaps as much as any other factor, limited the growth of a community of interest. Lack of easy communication among colonists could be as effective as religious bigotry and boundary quarrels among colonial governments to foster prejudice and bad feeling. The dislike of New Englanders for New Yorkers was notorious, and it was heartily returned. Quaker settlers of Pennsylvania were unpopular in the other colonies. People from the southern colonies were often looked on askance in New England, while New Englanders were frequently held in contempt in the South. William Byrd of Virginia, an eighteenth-century planter and one of the more cultured men of his day, recorded it as his conviction that the New Englanders were peculiarly proficient in living up to the letter but evading the spirit of the law.

Much of this prejudice was due to ignorance of how the people in other colonies thought and acted. It is startling in the twentieth century to realize, from John Adams' letters to his wife in 1775, how many of the New England delegation to the First Continental Congress in Philadelphia were traveling away from home for the first time, and how much they found that was new and strange in their eyes. As a matter of fact, the average colonial felt closer to the English homeland and more loyal to the King than he did to the people in a colony 100 miles from his abode—people whom he had never seen and about whose manner of life he was almost wholly ignorant.

Last but by no means least among the barriers to colonial unity were the disputes that broke out continually between the colonies. Differences over boundaries were chronic. Colonial tariffs produced retaliatory duties from the provinces that considered themselves injured, and the rapid multiplication of these conflicts was only avoided by the disallowance in England of such tariff legislation. In the repeated wars that took place between England and France, the colonists remote from the scene of action took small interest in the fray and, in repeated instances, the "bread colonies" (particularly Pennsylvania and New York) insisted on continuing their trade with the French. At one time, New York sent so much flour to the West Indies that it was difficult to provision the British forces operating against Canada, a fact which enhanced New York's unpopularity with the New England colonists.

Factors Which Drew the Colonies Together

Such were the various factors that made for disunity among the colonies. Unchecked, these forces would have prevented the development of anything like a national spirit, and would have made cooperation in a movement for independence from Great Britain nearly impossible.

But by the end of the seventeenth century a variety of influences began to appear that gave the colonials a number of common interests and common aims. One of these factors was increased communication between the colonies. While the great majority of the colonials still stayed closely at home, intercolonial travel had a considerable development. Coastal trading, practically the sole means of contact in the seventeenth century, grew steadily in the decades before the Revolution. Internal trade developed as main highways were opened between Boston and New York and from New York to Philadelphia and Baltimore, while lesser roads fanned out from Philadelphia through York, Pennsylvania, and Frederick, Maryland, into Virginia and the upcountry of the Carolinas. Connecticut Yankees and New Jerseyites traded with New York. A few New Yorkers went to southern colonies to live and New York families intermarried with Bostonians and Philadelphians. The Germans and the Scotch-Irish drifted along the frontier line. And as all these movements took place, they were necessarily accompanied by a gradual lessening of that prejudice which springs so easily from ignorance of one's fellow men.

If colonial unity was fostered by an increase of intercolonial trade and travel, it was also promoted by improvement in another means of communication. Better roads led to the development of a postal service. Massachusetts and Connecticut blazed the way by establishing local postal systems in the seventeenth century, and their example was followed by New York, Pennsylvania, and New Jersey. In 1710, Parliament established a General Post Office for the Dominions, with a Postmaster General in London and offices in New York and other colonial towns. This facilitated the delivery of letters and such few newspapers as there were, although the cost was high, the service intermittent, and the mail scanty indeed. From 1753 to 1774, Benjamin Franklin was Postmaster General for the colonies, an office in which he performed very useful service by increasing the frequency and efficiency of mail deliveries.

Along with an increase in direct contacts between the colonies came the gradual development of more intangible ties. The colonials shared a hardiness of spirit that was a heritage of the migratory movement, as well as a product of life in a frontier society. They were emigrants who had had the courage to uproot themselves and start a new life in a new world, or the sons and daughters of emigrant families. This fact was common knowledge, and it is not unlikely that the colonials thought of themselves and of each other as, on the whole, a little better than those who had stayed at home. Puritan William Stoughton's remark, "God sifted a nation that he might send choice grain into the wilderness," was applicable to colonial thinking far beyond the confines of Massachusetts Bay.

Another bond, intangible but real, derived from the presence of the red man. All the colonies, at one time or another, had trouble with the Indians. Colonists generally knew something of the perils of tomahawk and scalping knife, and heard with mingled feelings of pity, terror, and relief about raiding parties and burned and desolated frontier villages. They knew, too, the cost of campaigns such as that of King Philip's War (1675–1676), which destroyed the power of the Narragansetts at vast expense to the New Englanders, or the Yamasee War (1715), which crushed the Indians of South Carolina at a heavy price to the settlers of that region. As the years went on, the need for common action against the Indian menace became a pressing concern.

Stronger ties than those formed as a result of increasing communication or a common recognition of peril on the frontier were produced by the prevalence of English forms and English institutions. The colonists of the first half of the seventeenth century were (save for the Dutch) almost wholly English. They established precedents, and those who followed after, themselves in large part of the same nationality, found English law, traditions, and forms of government in possession of the field. Thus was set up a common standard of life to which all men more or less willingly repaired, a font from which, even though mingled with streams from other sources, a common nationality could flow.

The standard of nationality that was thus being created was by no means a mere copy of English forms. Other nationalities, as has been shown, brought their peculiar contributions in ways of living and thinking. But as the new environment brought new developments in thought and institutions, Americans gradually became aware that their modes of thought and action were diverging from those on the other side of the Atlantic.

The spirit of liberty and humanity, a spirit stifled in the Old World, was in the air of America. This was significantly shown when both Virginia and New England—the one Anglican, the other Puritan—manifested a common dislike for arbitrary control by a priestly hierarchy. It was also shown in their practice of hiring their ministers instead of submitting to their being imposed from above. It was shown in American penal laws, which, framed with due regard for the scarcity of labor and the fact that the colonial governments were closer to the people than was the national government of England, were definitely milder in character than were those of the mother country. Here were some of the rudiments of an American tradition. There were others as well, particularly in the political field.

The growing attitude of independence, so far as the royal governors were concerned, demonstrated a similarity of interest in a weak executive power that was destined to become one of the traditions of American political life. The New England town meeting was a development that had no parallel in the Old World. The colonists generally showed a marked disposition to improve upon the synthetic system of local representation that was in vogue in England. There was a definite tendency toward local representation in the eighteenth-century colonial assemblies: paying for the services of colonial representatives had long been a common practice; written ballots speedily found acceptance throughout the new country; and franchise qualifications in taxes and property holdings rested on laws that were of a similar character throughout the colonies. In fact, the colonies were establishing similarities of political conduct that could not but smooth the path toward national unification.

Indeed, political unity of a still more concrete sort was distinctly logical. The amalgamation of scattered settlements into colonies took place as though by inexorable law. Why should not the colonies thus formed also band together? The way to this was pointed out in 1643, when Massachusetts Bay,

Plymouth, Connecticut, and New Haven formed the New England Confederation. The idea appeared again, and more forcefully, in the Albany Plan of Union.

The Albany Congress of 1754

In 1754, the British government urged the formation of an alliance between the British colonies and the Indian tribes south of the Great Lakes, for the purpose of ending intertribal wars and unifying opposition to the threat of French aggression. Prominent colonials supported the project, and seven colonies (New York, New Hampshire, Massachusetts, Connecticut, Rhode Island, Maryland, and Pennsylvania) sent delegates to a congress at Albany.

While the avowed purpose of this meeting was to coordinate plans of defense, larger ideas were very much in the air. Governor Shirley of Massachusetts, and the Massachusetts assembly as well, hoped that the conference would result in a defensive league or confederation. Benjamin Franklin of Pennsylvania had the same idea, and on the way to the conference he showed to several delegates a plan for uniting the colonies.

At the first meetings of the Albany Congress, it was unanimously agreed that some sort of intercolonial organization was necessary for security purposes, and a plan of union was adopted. This was to be put into operation by act of Parliament. The plan drawn up by Franklin provided for a president-general, appointed by the Crown, and a general council, chosen every three years by the colonial assemblies. This body would have power over Indian affairs and others which primarily concerned the frontier regions.

The council agreed upon at Albany never came into being. It found small favor in the colonies—in part because the colonial councils felt slighted, and partly because the colonial assemblies feared it might result in limiting their own freedom of action. Governor Shirley opposed it strenuously, preferring a plan of union that would give Parliament much more power of control and would recognize the principle of parliamentary taxation. The British government objected to it because it gave the colonies power that should be lodged in London.

But even though the plan drawn up by the Albany Congress was stillborn, it remained a significant proposal. On the one hand, its reception in the colonies indicated the strength of the forces that kept the colonies separate and distinct from one another; on the other, it showed that some sort of colonial union was very much in the air. And Franklin, in his defense of the plan and his opposition to Shirley's idea of parliamentary taxation, took ground very similar to that which was to be taken a few years later by the leaders of the American Revolution.

By the middle of the eighteenth century, the colonial governments had clearly established representative government as one of their basic principles and had also achieved a very real measure of independence from British control. They had gone far toward achieving political maturity. And as the colonies came of age politically, they moved—slowly, it is true, and with halting steps—toward a condition of life that made the establishment of some sort of political union more and more a possibility.

Suggested Reading

The· basic histories for a study of colonial government are, Edward Channing, *A History of the United States* (6 vols., 1912–1925), vols. I and II; Herbert L. Osgood, *The American Colonies in the Seventeenth Century* (3 vols., 1904–1907) and *The American Colonies in the Eighteenth Century* (4 vols., 1924); and Charles M. Andrews, *The Colonial Period of American History* (4 vols., 1934–1938).

For additional examination of political institutions, the student should consult L. W. Labaree, *Royal Government in America* (1930); E. B. Greene, *The Foundations of American Nationality* (1922) and *Provincial America* (1905); L. G. Tyler, *England in America, 1580–1652* (1904); C. M. Andrews, *Colonial Self-Government* (1904), and Ella Lonn, *The Colonial Agents of the Southern Colonies* (1945).

Political relations between England and the Colonies are authoritatively treated in the following books: L. H. Gipson, *The British Empire before the American Revolution* still incomplete (12 vols., 1936–1965); O. M. Dickerson, *American Colonial Government, 1696–1765: A Study of the Board of Trade in its Relation to the American Colonies* (1912); A. H. Basye, *The Lords Commissioners of Trade and Plantations, 1748–1782* (1925); J. P. Greene, *The Quest for Power: The Lower Houses of Assembly in the Southern Royal Colonies* (1963), and L. A. Harper, *The English Navigation Laws: A Seventeenth Century Experiment in Social Engineering* (1939). By no means to be neglected are the volumes by G. L. Beer: *The Old Colonial System, 1660–1754* (1912), *The Origins of the British Colonial System, 1578–1660* (1908), *British Colonial Policy, 1754–1765* (1907), and *The Commercial Policy of England toward the American Colonies* (1893). British administrative policy in the colonies is examined in briefer compass in the scholarly and interesting C. P. Nettels, *The Roots of American Civilization* (1938); though it is weighted on the economic side, this book is still the best one-volume treatment of the colonial period.

3 · The Colonial Economy

THE ECONOMIC ACTIVITIES of the North American colonists during the early periods of settlement were almost wholly agricultural in character. This was due to the uncertainty of food supplies from overseas and the stubborn fact that gold-hunting and even commercial fishing were unsatisfactory substitutes for bread and meat. As the colonies increased in population and stability, other forms of economic activity—trade, commerce, industry—appeared, but at the end of the colonial period agriculture remained the pursuit of approximately 90 per cent of the inhabitants. One reason for this was the abundance of land, and the attractiveness of that independence which is always a hoped-for accompaniment of land ownership. Equally important was the general character of the colonial economy, which was too poor and in which labor was too scarce to permit the ready expansion of effort into more highly developed forms of economic activity.

A Primitive Economy

Colonial agriculture was decidedly primitive in character. At first there was even a lack of European-made tools, which, crude as they were in this period, would have been more than welcome to pioneers hard-pressed to scratch a living from the soil. Only heavy, hand-made implements—mattocks, spades, sickles, and flails—were available. The Pilgrims went twelve years without a plow; at the time of the founding of Harvard College (1636), there were only thirty-six plows in all New England; and as late as the middle of the seventeenth century, there were only 150 plows in Virginia. These early sodbreakers were large and cumbersome. Drawn by four to six oxen and guided by two men, they scratched a furrow some three inches deep. Most of them were not even iron-tipped before 1700, iron being scarce and thought to poison the soil.

The colonial farmer could scarcely develop a high degree of efficiency with such primitive tools. He worked under other handicaps as well. Little or nothing was known about crop rotation or fertilization. Scientific animal breeding, which became important in eighteenth-century England, scarcely affected American livestock before the Revolution. Labor on the farm or plantation was hard drudging work that brought only low returns in terms of purchasing power. Farmers had to work long hours to make a living, and the customary farm day lasted from sunrise to sunset.

The Products of the Land

Crops and animals were partly imported from England and were partly indigenous. The settlers brought with them most of the small grains, the clovers, common garden vegetables, hops, most of the larger varieties of fruit, and all the common farm animals except the turkey. They found Indian corn, white and sweet potatoes, tobacco, watermelons, strawberries, and the bird that was to be so closely associated with the American Thanksgiving.

The colonists not only found new crops in the New World; they had valuable aid from the Indians in producing them. The red man taught the Europeans how to plant corn with a fish as fertilizer in each hill, how to grow tobacco, how to make maple syrup, and how to dry meat. Without such Indian aid, the difficulties of survival would have been markedly increased.

Climate and soil dictated, to a considerable extent, the character of the crops grown in different parts of the colonies. Almost from the beginning, corn was the mainstay of life in all but the Middle Colonies, and it made livestock profitable everywhere. Tobacco soon became the great cash crop of the South. By 1680, the South was exporting about twenty million pounds of tobacco a year, and this amount quintupled by 1775. The South also came to raise considerable quantities of rice and indigo.

Small grains were grown from Pennsylvania northward and became great articles of export in the northern colonies. Wheat eventually made Pennsylvania the richest colony in the North. Livestock were raised in all the colonies. They were especially a back-country industry, for cattle, hogs, and sheep were more easily transportable to market than the crops they ate. Along with livestock and corn, New England raised rye (eventually exporting a small quantity), potatoes, and the usual garden vegetables. The New Englanders also raised considerable numbers of cattle and sheep.

Government Controls of Agriculture

One of the interesting features of colonial agriculture was the control over it which was exercised, or attempted, by the colonial governments. The seventeenth century, in particular, was an era that considered extensive regulation of the economy an indispensable function of government, and colonial records of that period are cluttered with such legislation. Bounties were offered repeatedly for growing hemp, flax, and silk. Under pressure from the British government, legislatures from time to time passed laws ordering, or prohibiting, the production of this or that crop. Price-fixing for beef, pork, and other products was frequently used, and in time of glut in tobacco production the tobacco colonies attempted to restrict acreage. These controls were sporadic, lacked uniformity, and aroused little enthusiasm among the planters and farmers. They probably worked fairly well in times of dire necessity, only to be disregarded as conditions improved. At least they demonstrate that governmental regulation of agricultural production appeared early on the American scene.

Industrial Beginnings

Agriculture was the principal business of the colonies, but they soon developed other forms of economic activity. One of these was manufacturing, which began to appear for a variety of reasons. There was abundant raw material, especially wood, and by the eighteenth century there were considerable supplies of both iron and copper. The colonists needed manufactured goods and, being mainly poor, had little money with which to buy expensive foreign manufactures. English goods sold in the colonies for about double their price in England. In the eighteenth century, when the colonies dabbled with depreciated currencies in the form of paper money, the colonial importer would protect himself by hiking the price of his imports as much as seven times above the English price. The colonists also needed finished goods with which to expand a favorable balance of trade with the West Indies markets. The logic of the situation pushed the colonials inexorably toward industrial development.

Lumbering was one of the earliest of these industrial activities. Good timber was in great demand in Europe, and the woodsmen and sawmills of

New England—where pine and oak abounded—supplied it in growing amount. The ring of the axe and the whine of the saw were heard in all the other colonies as well. There was an insatiable market for this product at home and in England, Spain, Portugal, and the West Indies. Lumbering was the colonial industry favored above all others by Great Britain.

Colonial shipbuilding, likewise favored by Britain, early came into vogue. Governor Winthrop's *Blessing of the Bay,* launched on the Mystic River in 1631, may be said to have started the American merchant marine. By 1676, Massachusetts alone had 430 ships of between thirty and 250 tons burden.

Lumbering and shipbuilding were industries of great potential significance, but by far the greatest manufacturing development of the seventeenth century was in the realm of household industry. This was from necessity rather than choice. Bad transportation and the consequent uncertainty and costliness of supplies, whether these came from abroad or from the interior of the country, were formidable obstacles to the setting up of manufacturing shops or plants of large-scale proportions. The scarcity of capital and labor were other factors in the situation. It was only natural, under these circumstances, that farmers, with scant supplies of cash and in need of winter work that would keep the family employed, should turn to manufacturing in the home. The same was true of planters, especially when the price of tobacco was low and one had to pinch pennies to buy the equipment and clothing needed on the plantation. Consequently, the great bulk of the manufactured products used in seventeenth-century colonial America—clothing, boots, shoes, farm implements, and the like—were produced in the home or in small shops that depended to a large extent upon family labor.

Household manufacturing was often drudgery. It was, however, a vital supplement to agriculture. Despite the monotony of carding, spinning, nail-making, and the like, the variety of occupation that it meant for the rural population kept life on the farm from being unutterably dull during the winter months. When it could be made into a form of social activity, such as the spinning bee, it was an important element in community living. And it did encourage habits of diligence and perseverance, skillful economy, and that ingenious resourcefulness in meeting constantly changing situations that has often been labeled an American characteristic. Today, classes in manual training, domestic science, and the household arts are trying to give students those skills which were provided in the homes of the colonial period.

As significant as any contribution made by household manufacturing to American life was the part it played in the Revolution. It was then everywhere an important aspect of economic activity, vigorous and well-developed in all the colonies. It kept the economy of every area self-sufficient to a remarkable degree. Without it, and under the stress of the British blockade and occupation of important areas of the country, colonial resistance would have had to crumble. Domestic manufacturing was essential to obtaining independence.

Fishing and whaling were other forms of industrial activity that developed to significant proportions, though in the latter part of the colonial era. By the time of the Revolution, New England fisheries employed 10,000 men, yielded a product worth some $2 million yearly, and kept 350 ships busy carrying fish to Europe and the West Indies. Whaling, too, became a considerable industry in the eighteenth century, stimulated by inventions for extracting whale oil on shipboard. American whalers ranged from the Arctic Ocean to the southern seas. By 1774, some 360 ships, principally from New England, were engaged in this perilous business, and families such as the Macys, the Folgers, and the Coffins were growing affluent on the proceeds.

By the middle of the eighteenth century, iron manufacturing had gained a foothold in New England and the middle colonies. "Bloomeries," forges, and slitting mills had been set up, and the colonials were producing bar and pig iron of excellent quality and in such amount that after supplying domestic needs they still had a small quantity for export.

A considerable number of other industrial activities, ranging from tanneries to pottery shops and brick kilns, had sprung up in all the colonies. There was even, here and there, a printing establishment.

The American newspaper industry, for so it may be called, was started in colonial times. The first North American news sheet, and the tenth in the world, was published in Boston by one Benjamin Harris in 1690. It was called *Publick Occurrences both Forreign and Domestick* and was a single sheet, folded in four to a size of eleven by seven inches—with the fourth page left blank. *Publick Occurrences* had only one issue, for some of the observations it contained aroused the ire of the governor and council of the colony. The second paper, the Boston *News-Letter,* was started in 1704 and continued until 1776, when, being Tory in sympathy, it gave up the ghost just before the British evacuation of Boston. By 1765, there were twenty-three newspapers in the colonies. They were all weeklies, and, by modern standards, poor affairs, but American newspaperdom had nevertheless started on its long career.

Trade and Commerce

The colonists felt the need of industrial development at an early stage in their existence, but far more pressing was the necessity for trade and com-

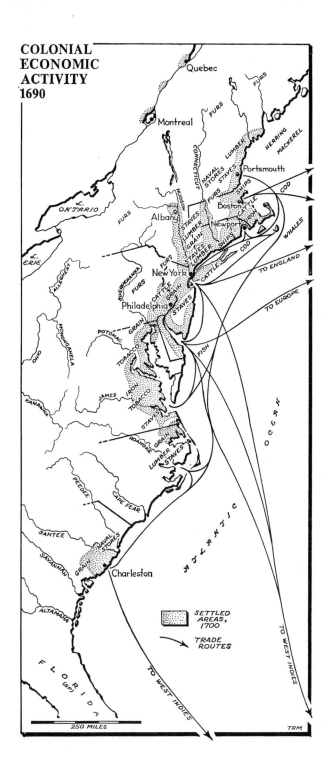

COLONIAL
ECONOMIC
ACTIVITY
1690

Quebec

FURS

FURS

Montreal

FURS

HERRING

MACKEREL

CONNECTICUT

NAVAL
STORES

LUMBER

STAVES

HUDSON

FURS

Portsmouth

SHIPS

COD

L. ONTARIO

FURS

Albany

LUMBER

STAVES

GRAIN

STAVES

Boston

Newport

CATTLE

IRON

WHALES

L. ERIE

SUSQUEHANNA

ALLEGHENY

FURS

New York

LUMBER

SHIPS

COD

CATTLE

TO ENGLAND

FURS

CATTLE

GRAIN

TO EUROPE

Philadelphia

STAVES

POTOMAC

OHIO

MONONGAHELA

GRAIN

TOBACCO

FISH

JAMES

IRON

TOBACCO

KANAWHA

STAVES

ROANOKE

GRAIN

LUMBER
STAVES

OCEAN

PEEDEE

CAPE FEAR

SANTEE

SAVANNAH

NAVAL
STORES

GRAIN

ATLANTIC

Charleston

ALTAMAHA

SETTLED
AREAS,
1700

FLORIDA
(SP)

TRADE
ROUTES

TO WEST INDIES

250 MILES

TO WEST INDIES

TRM

merce. This budding capitalistic society needed profits, and more profits, if it was to grow and become strong. These could not be obtained in isolated cells of economic activity. Then, too, as the colonists produced more and more tobacco, rice, wheat, and naval stores, each community felt a stronger need for outlets that would take care of its surplus. Another stimulus to commerce was the chronic want of specie, which could only be obtained in trade. In response to this complex of urges, colonial commerce steadily increased in amount.

Seventeenth-century commercial activity, as it slowly spread beyond the bounds of each colony, was chiefly intercolonial in character. It was in part an inland trade along tidewater and between tidewater and frontier, carried on principally by peddlers and fur traders. There was also a rising trade along the coast which collected cargoes for export and "sea-peddled" imports and local commodities such as rum, tinware, breadstuffs, and tobacco. From about 1700 on, however, trade with the Old World and with the West Indies became an important part of the colonial economy.

The eighteenth-century colonies were dependent upon trade with foreign parts to a degree never since equalled in American history. England was a market for colonial goods that ranged from naval stores and furs to grain and tobacco. The West Indies market was almost as important. By 1750, one-half of the total commerce of the northern colonies and one-eighth of that of those in the South was with the West Indies, either directly or by triangle trades such as the famous exchange of New England rum for African

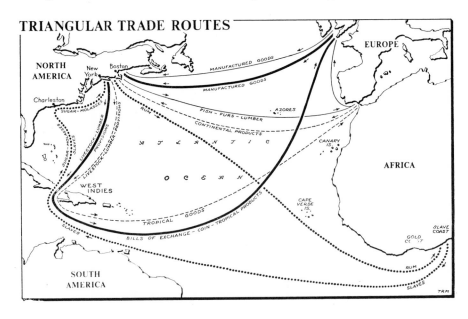

TRIANGULAR TRADE ROUTES

slaves for West Indies sugar and molasses. An eighteenth-century colonial skipper might take on a cargo of New England livestock, lumber, and provisions, trade it for West Indian tropical products, and then trade these in turn for English manufactured goods or Continental products to be brought back to the colonies. Southern Europe was a market for colonial fish and lumber. As the years went by and the colonial vision expanded, Yankee traders pushed into all the seven seas in search of profits, often in blithe disregard of English trade regulations.

A most important impetus to the expansion of colonial commerce was the unfavorable balance of trade with England. This was the result of the exchange of colonial raw materials, such as lumber and naval stores, for English manufactured goods. It particularly affected the northern colonies, whose staple agricultural products (such as wheat, salted beef, pork, and bacon) were cut off from English import after 1660 by British commercial regulations favoring the English landed proprietors. Northern merchants, therefore, were forced to ship these products to the West Indies, to southern Europe, and to Africa in order to get specie or bills of exchange with which to right their balances in England and so enable them to continue purchase of the prized furniture, clothing, tools and other articles that were available on the English market.

The unfavorable balance of the trade of the northern colonies with England had other effects than that of driving those colonies into a utilization of West Indian and European markets. It was a constant stimulus to the diversification of the northern economy, which was constantly pushed into manufacturing goods for home use in order to maintain a viable and prosperous economic life. It also helps to explain why the unsavory but very profitable business of slave trading became a prominent feature of eighteenth-century northern economic activity.

The Slave Trade

The New England slavers were ships of about sixty-tons burden. They carried crews of six or seven men, including the officers. The value of ship and cargo outward bound from Salem, Newburyport, or some other New England haven ranged from £750 to £1,000; the profits of such a voyage in the triangle trade might be as much as 33 per cent over and above all costs, plus a depreciation allowance of one-third the value of the ship. This meant not only wealth for the traders, but the ability to draw favorable bills of exchange on the West Indies for the payment of balances in London.

Slavery was not regarded as a sin by the Puritans, any more than it was by the southern planters. The residents of Massachusetts enslaved Indians, until the practice proved unprofitable (due to the red man's propensity for dying in bondage or escaping to his kinfolk), and it was customary to start the voyage of a slaver toward the African coast with prayers for its success. Little attention was paid to the horrors of the "Middle Passage," where from 8 to 10 per cent of the slaves on every trip died, or to the way in which the Negroes were chained, branded, and beaten, or shot down in cold blood to prevent escape. It was a brutal age—and slave-trading brought handsome returns. Peter Faneuil, the eighteenth-century Boston merchant—careful, generous, benign, a doer of good deeds and held in great repute in Boston— engaged in this traffic. One of his ships was a snow, the *Jolly Bachelor*. William B. Weeden, the historian of New England, asks:

> did Peter slap his fair round belly and chuckle
> when he named the snow Jolly Bachelor? This must
> be merely the sad irony of fate, that the craft
> deliberately designed to be packed with human pains
> and to echo with human groans should in its very name
> bear the fantastic image of the luxury-loving chief
> owner. If these be the sources of profits and property,
> where is the liberty of Faneuil Hall, where the charity of
> good Peter's alms?

Economic Problems of the Southern Colonies

The tidewater South had a favorable balance in its traffic with England. Since there were substantial profits in growing tobacco, rice, and indigo, the South was free from any great temptation to look to nonagricultural pursuits for its economic livelihood. But by the middle of the eighteenth century the South was having its own economic difficulties.

British merchants reaped great profits from the trade of the southern colonies. It was carried largely in the ships of the merchants, and the freight and insurance charges were substantial enough to yield a handsome return over and above all losses. The merchants bought the goods the planter needed. These goods were purchased on commission and often, the planters thought, with little attention to their best interests. The merchants advanced funds to the planters at high interest rates, for the purchase of goods and slaves. In these ways, the profits of the planters were constantly being drained away by charges, and these charges were not one whit abated in times of war or overproduction. As the eighteenth century went on, the indebtedness of the planters to the merchants increased, and so did their dissatisfaction with the way in which they were being treated. This planter-merchant relationship was one of the factors preparing colonial America for the break with Great Britain.

British Mercantilistic Policies— The Navigation Acts

The attitude of the British government toward both commerce and industry in the colonies was in line with the mercantilistic ideas of the age. Britain's primary aim was to build up the power of the state, with the center of that power in England itself. But the British government's policy toward colonial industry, even though based on statist considerations, was not, at first restrictive. Seventeenth-century England was not as yet a manufacturing country on a large scale and hence had little reason to dislike the meager industrial efforts of the colonists. Some of the early colonizing companies even undertook to export workers in wood, textiles, and other materials to the New World, hoping thereby to build up the manufacture of tar, pitch, glass, and other products. Even during the eighteenth century, when the Whig merchants rose to ascendancy in Parliament and British manufacturers became conscious of the possibility of American competition, England continued to encourage lumbering and shipbuilding, and the manufacture of naval stores and crude iron, products of which Britain was in short supply. Concerning other products that offered competition to British merchants and traders, however, eighteenth-century Parliamentary legislation took on a forbidding aspect.

The Woolens Act of 1699, aimed at the Irish but including the colonies, prohibited the shipment of woolen yarn and cloth from the colony of origin, and forbade intercolonial trade in raw wool. In 1732, a similar prohibition was laid on trade in beaver hats. In the year 1750, the colonists were forbidden to build any more plating forges, slitting mills, or steel mills. These acts were passed at the behest of English interests and were thoroughly in keeping with the government's mercantilistic policy. They were proof that Parliament meant to exercise its right to legislate for the colonials, a claim that was not exactly soothing to those colonists who wished to build up their own industries.

England's paramount interest in the regulation of colonial economic life was not, however, the control of industry. Even in the eighteenth century, colonial industrial development never threatened British manufacturers with a serious rivalry, either in English or in world markets. By and large, the colonies remained to the end what they were supposed to be in mercantilistic theory—sources of raw materials and markets for British manufactured goods. Britain's primary interest lay in controlling and directing colonial trade to England's maximum advantage, and, as a result, the laws known as the Navigation Acts were passed by Parliament.

Between 1650 and 1673, six sets of Acts were passed by Parliament regulating colonial trade. These were all clarified and summarized in the Act of 1696, and they were supplemented by the Molasses Act of 1733. The overall design of these Acts was to make the colonies profitable to England and to keep the profits of English and English-colonial commerce from falling into the hands of foreigners.

The Navigation Acts imposed a variety of restrictions upon colonial trade. Ships that engaged in colonial commerce had to be built and owned in Britain or in the colonies, and 75 per cent of the crews had to be British subjects. Then there were the "enumerated articles"—colonial goods that had to be sent directly to England, either because England needed them or so that England could profit by levying a duty on them before they reached the European continent. The list of these goods, first made up in 1651, included tobacco, sugar, cotton, indigo, ginger, and dyewoods. It was expanded in the eighteenth century to include molasses, rice, naval stores, copper, and furs. In 1766, all exports from the colonies were required to go to England unless destined for a port south of Cape Finisterre—a concession to the colonial trade in fish with southern Europe. By these Acts, England sought to keep control over the products of the North American continent, and over those of the West Indies as well.

The Navigation Acts were meant to control colonial imports as well as exports. Practically all imports from the European continent had to be brought to England and then transshipped, the same being true of the returned cargoes. The Molasses Act of 1733 levied a duty of six pence a gallon, collected by British officials at colonial ports, on non-British molasses, and similar duties on non-British sugar and rum. This Act was a double-barreled weapon, designed to aid the British planters in the West Indies at the expense of the North American colonies and to injure France by disrupting the trade of her West Indian subjects.

Effects of the Navigation Acts

The Acts affecting colonial industry and commerce had a mixed effect upon American economic life. There were some definitely hurtful aspects. As has been shown, tobacco was an increasingly important part of the colonial foreign trade. In 1750, tobacco exports from the North American mainland approximated 50 per cent of the total value of colonial exports to England. In that year, Virginia and Maryland exported about eighty-five million pounds of tobacco, of which four-fifths was reshipped to the continental countries. The Navigation Acts thus deprived the colonists of the profit of direct shipment to the continent, to say nothing of colonial dissatisfaction with the way in which transshipment was handled by English agents. The same was true of the transshipment of indigo, a colonial product which Britain could by no means consume in its entirety in the eighteenth century. It is also possible, although here the evidence is by no means conclusive, that British regulation had a retarding effect upon shop or factory textile production in the colonies.

But it is easy to overemphasize the damage to the colonial economy caused by British regulation. Had all the regulatory Acts been rigidly enforced, the colonists would have been grievously hurt. The fact is, however, that most of the Acts were either not enforced or their harsh effects were mitigated by remedial action. The duties on tobacco and other goods reshipped from England were, to a very considerable extent, offset by drawbacks. The colonists speedily became adepts at smuggling and evasion; and Britain, its attention centered on domestic problems and foreign wars, was loath to use extreme measures to enforce its statutes 3,000 miles from the scene of their enactment. This was particularly significant in connection with the Molasses Act, which, by itself, could easily have ruined the colonies' West Indian trade; this Act was a dead letter from the start.

British commercial regulations were irritating to the colonials because, even if not enforced, they hung like the sword of Damocles over the heads of His Majesty's distant subjects. But, irritating though they were, they had to be weighed against the advantages that accrued to the colonials from being a part of the British realm—advantages that were both numerous and considerable. Shipbuilders and ship merchants profited from the prohibition of foreign-built ships in Britain's trade. Colonial goods shipped to British markets were often given preference over the goods of would-be competitors in other nations. In England tobacco growing was forbidden. Furthermore, British attempts at regulating colonial industry prompted colonial acts stimulating both home and shop manufacturing. Most important of all, in that age of chronic warfare, being in the British Empire meant having the protection of the British fleet and army, a shield and buckler of no mean value against the Canadian French and Indians. Taking all such factors into consideration, it must be concluded that, until 1763, British regulation of colonial industry and commerce was not a serious handicap to colonial development and that its disadvantages were more than offset by the advantage of being part of the British imperial system.

It is important to note that, by the middle of the eighteenth century, the handling of imperial affairs was presenting the British government with some complex and difficult problems. It had to satisfy diverse economic groups— the English and especially the London merchants, whose commitments centered around the home market, a landed gentry concerned with the maintenance of prices for English-grown farm products, capitalists and traders deeply involved in commercial activities that girdled the globe, the planters of the West Indies, and the colonists in North America.

The conflict of interest that arose in the eighteenth century between the West Indian planters and the North American colonists illustrates the type of difficulty that had to be dealt with in formulating British policy. The Molasses Act of 1733 was an effort to placate the West Indian sugar planters by cutting off the trade of the northern colonies with the French West Indies in sugar and molasses. It failed because of systematic evasion, which the British government made no serious attempt to check. Some twenty years later, the British West Indies planters tried hard to secure passage of a law that would prohibit all commerce between the North American colonials and the French West Indies. The British government was still reluctant to wreak such havoc on the North American trade. The law did not pass, and smuggling continued to flourish. It is not too much to say that British policy, until 1763, was marked by an effort to evolve a systematic plan of imperial administration and a course of action that would leave the Empire viable in all its parts. This was a complex and delicate undertaking.

The Colonial Labor Supply

As the colonies grew in population and in wealth, as their agricultural output increased and their trade and commerce expanded, the acquisition of an adequate supply of labor was an ever-present problem. What is thought of today as a free laboring class was practically nonexistent from the beginning of colonization to the time of the Revolution. Here and there farm laborers who worked for wages could be found, but they were extremely scarce. There was a scattering of free laborers in the towns, and some itinerant workers who moved from place to place as one job failed or a more attractive one beckoned. Craftsmen such as shoemakers, ironworkers, glasscutters, and carpenters were in short supply, especially in the seventeenth century. Localities would sometimes give them bonuses and other special concessions to get them to settle permanently in a community. A seventeenth-century Virginia law forbade certain types of craftsmen to till the fields, so important was it that they stick to their jobs. Promises of high wages and steady employment were made to attract the immigration of skilled artisans; with the growth of urban centers in the eighteenth century, they did become more plentiful, but free labor, skilled or unskilled, was in great demand throughout the colonial period.

The reasons for this scarcity of free labor are clear. Land was abundant and cheap; often it cost nothing. Farming, save in New England, was generally profitable, and the farmer could consider himself a person of dignity. The freedom of farm life, the feeling of being lord of what one surveyed, was attractive. It was no wonder that the great majority of colonists chose life on the farm rather than the uncertainty and low prestige of the laborer's status. The laboring man, skilled or unskilled, also had to face the fact that money with a value equivalent to specie was scarce and frequently unavailable for the payment of wages. Most important of all, in keeping the labor supply scarce, was the lowly position of European labor. In 1610, an English ploughman had a wage, plus food, of 60s. a year, and it cost from £6 to £10 to get from England to America; the free laborer's difficulties in transporting himself to the colonies are therefore obvious.

One consequence of the labor scarcity was the development of the jack-of-all-trades in American life. The average farm family led a life that was largely self-sufficient, and a farm boy as he grew up learned a wide variety of skills. The village smith not only shoed horses; he made his own nails and horseshoes, and often heated and hammered bog iron into wrought iron on his anvil. The peddler who wanted to be popular with his customers was a tinker and a general repair man as well. Ingenuity and inventiveness were at a premium in such an economy.

Free labor could not well transport itself, as such, to America, but there were plenty of Europeans who were anxious to come to the New World, even if it meant working for others. Those who were oppressed, those who were of an adventurous disposition, and those who saw no hope of bettering their condition at home, to say nothing of a number of scoundrels who needed to get out of their own country, constituted a very considerable body of people ready and willing to break their home ties and travel into foreign parts.

Four main factors energized this motley mass into migration. The first was a desire for change of condition or status. The second was the demand of would-be colonial employers for labor which, especially in the South, was essential to the making of real profits. The third was the profits that could be made by the shipowners from the business of transportation. The fourth was the fact that, at least until the latter part of the seventeenth century, England considered itself overpopulated and sought to rid itself of a labor supply that eighteenth-century English opinion came to regard as very valuable at home.

Indenture and Redemption

Since there was a considerable amount of labor anxious to come to America and free to do so, and since shipowners were eager to transport it, some means had to be found for financing its transportation. The systems that evolved were those of indenture and redemption.

Indentured servants were penniless migrants who, as individuals, literally sold themselves for limited terms of service, usually three to five years, in order to pay for their passage. The conditions of service and the agreement to finance the passage were written in duplicate on a single sheet, which was then separated into two parts by a jagged tear, or "indent." Fitting the two sheets together was proof of the validity of the contract. The indenture was usually to a merchant, a ship's captain, or an emigrant agent. On arrival in America, the indentured persons were brought on deck and auctioned off to the highest bidders among the planters or other would-be purchasers who came on board, and the contracts were then assigned to their new masters. The seventeenth-century English emigrants who came to America without means came almost exclusively as indentured servants.

The eighteenth century saw a new class of bound servants appear in America—the redemptioners, people who had some money before they started migrating, but not enough to get them to America. They gave this money to a merchant or emigrant agent, who, in turn, put them on shipboard and guaranteed passage. Another distinguishing feature of redemptioners was that they traveled as families, one or two members of the family often serving as guarantors for the rest. Once they were in America and their services contracted, their status was exactly like that of the indentured servants. Redemption appeared at the beginning of the eighteenth century. The German immigrants generally came as redemptioners, as did many eighteenth-century English colonists.

By no means were all of the immigrants who signed articles binding them to years of service honest and full of virtue, nor did all of them come willingly to America. Some were kidnapped by shipmasters and sold, willy-nilly, at the end of the voyage. Some were criminals, sent over to get them out of the mother country, their sentences commuted into years of servitude that ranged from fourteen years for the death sentence to shorter periods of indenture for minor crimes. These criminals were so considerable in number that, in 1751, Benjamin Franklin proposed in his *Gazette* to exchange rattlesnakes for the felons sent over by the English government. Some of the poor people in America sold themselves into short terms of servitude for a lump sum that would be paid to them when they had fulfilled their part of the bargain. Some prisoners in American jails were sold into servitude at the end of their sentences in order to pay for their room and board in prison.

The American colonies were populated to a considerable extent by indentured servants and redemptioners. Probably half of the white immigrants of the seventeenth century belonged in the former category. Between 1635 and 1705, some 100,000 indentured servants came to Virginia alone. Three-fourths of the white population of Pennsylvania, Virginia, and Maryland in 1776 came of this stock.

The indentured servant, per se, did not contribute a great deal to the character of the American population. Some, to be sure, did well. In 1629, seven out of the forty-four members of the Virginia House of Burgesses had been bond servants five years before. Matthew Thornton, who signed the Declaration of Independence, came over to America as an indentured servant. So did the eminent eighteenth-century Maryland lawyer Daniel Dulany. So did Mary Morrils, Benjamin Franklin's maternal grandmother, who was bought for £20 on her arrival, and married her purchaser. The great majority of the indentured servants, however, were poor, shiftless people at home, and remained poor and shiftless after they arrived in America. Perhaps one out of five became a respectable and useful citizen. The remainder died in servitude, returned to England, or joined the lower and more shiftless elements of the population. The eighteenth-century redemptioners who came over in families as settlers were a considerably more valuable part of the population.

The life of the bound servant in the American colonies was not an easy one. There was plenty of injustice and cruelty. Some immigrants who were paying their own way were bound into indenture by callous ship captains who made them sign agreements to be responsible for the fares of those who died on the journey overseas. There were cases of families separated by the sale of their members after landing. Masters sometimes cruelly exploited their bond servants, the exploitation increasing toward the end of the period of service, with intent to provoke flight and thereby relieve the master of the outfitting or other compensation that the servant should receive at the close of the indenture. Servants could not marry without the consent of the master, and they were whipped for gross disobedience or for running away.

Generally, however, the colonies sought by legislation to guarantee to the indentured person food, clothing, lodging, a modicum of decent treatment, and a little money and an outfit of clothing at the end of the term of service. Some colonies—Maryland and North Carolina, for example—gave fifty acres of land to those who completed their contracts. As for immigrants who came with only verbal agreements instead of written indentures—and there were many—the colonies quickly evolved rules concerning their treatment that had the force of law and that afforded protection both to the servant and his employer in the carrying out of the contract.

It is only fair to remember that, while some employers were hard task-masters, some servants were rascals, with no sense of responsibility to those who held their bonds. The irate planter who advertised that he would give a reward of one old shoe and no thanks for the return of his runaway servant was one among a good many who felt that they had entered into contracts that were very bad bargains indeed.

Indenture was often harsh and brutal, but it was a part of harsh and brutal times, when the rights of the individual were not as respected in America as they were to be in later years. Nevertheless, the indentured serv-ant possessed of ability and ambition had a better chance of getting ahead in America than he had in the Old World, and the system under which he labored was the only practicable system of getting over to America the labor and the settlers of which that pioneer country was so much in need.

Wages of Free Labor—Wage and Price Regulation

The indentured servant of either category received no wage, and statistics are scanty about the wages of free labor in colonial times. Connecticut, in 1660, paid farm labor 2s. a day, and 2s.6d. to carpenters. Such wages were regarded as high. A century later, farm laborers were getting some £12 a year in the middle colonies and £20 a year in the South. Slave labor usually cost the southern planter about £8 a year, counting all costs of maintenance. One writer on the period estimates that free labor in the colonies was paid from 40 to 70 cents for a sixteen-hour day. It is a safe generalization that the real wages of an American workman were from 30 to 100 per cent above those of a contemporary English workman.

Since economic freedom for the individual was not a ruling concept in this period of history, it is not surprising that efforts to regulate both wages and prices were common in all the colonies. These were especially prevalent dur-ing the seventeenth century. When needed woodworkers, masons, or tailors who were dissatisfied with their wage status showed a disposition to wander off into other occupations, colonial legislatures were wont to pass laws forbidding such action. High wages were viewed askance by all save the laborer. The Puritans in particular looked upon high wages with dislike, for they believed that modest living and long hours of work were good for the soul, and the Puritan colonies passed a variety of laws that were designed to promote the spiritual well-being of the laborer by keeping his income at a modest level.

The efforts made at regulating wages and conditions of labor in the seventeenth century proved increasingly ineffective. During the eighteenth century, they were gradually abandoned, and the worker found himself more and more of a free agent in determining the mode of his livelihood and in bargaining with his employer about conditions of work. The fact that labor generally continued to be in short supply made this breakdown of governmental controls a blessing rather than a handicap for the worker.

This eighteenth-century movement toward a free economy, so far as labor was concerned, was paralleled by a corresponding relaxation of colonial attempts at control over prices and industrial activity. Gradually the idea gained ground that a free society could not be forcefully constituted, that freedom was the very essence of a dynamic economy, and that perhaps the greatest social good could be obtained by leaving a man at liberty to carve out his own destiny. It is significant that this change in the climate of opinion and in internal economic practice was well on the road to development when the colonies were faced by the prospect of rigid external controls imposed by Great Britain.

Slavery in Colonial Times

There was one aspect of the colonial economy in which the idea of control remained predominant. Slavery early became a social and economic institution in the colonies, and that institution could scarcely be tempered with freedom.

Slavery has appeared again and again in the story of mankind, during all periods of great and prolonged labor scarcity, and colonial times were no exception to the rule. Slavery began in the colonies and was retained and expanded because of the crying need for labor, and because men believed it to be cheaper than free labor, which it was. It certainly enabled the southern planter, when tobacco was cheap, to survive competition with the slave labor of the West Indies.

Slavery appeared in the colonies at an early date. The Puritans thought nothing of enslaving the Indians. In 1637, Massachusetts Bay, Plymouth, and Connecticut exterminated the Pequots as a tribe, kept the women and girls as slaves, and sold the men and boys to the West Indies. Ten years later, New England was seizing whole Indian villages, sometimes on account of petty offences by individuals, and trading the prisoners to the West Indies in exchange for Negro slaves. As late as 1706, Massachusetts sold Indian children under twelve taken in war. Some Indians were also enslaved in the South. In 1708, South Carolina had 1,400 Indian and 4,100 Negro slaves.

But Indian slavery did not flourish. The Indians were too scarce and too hard to catch to interest the professional slave traders. Furthermore, they were not good slaves by temperament, being prone to sulk and grow sullen under captivity. Negro slavery was not subject to these disadvantages in anything like the same degree.

Negro slaves were introduced to the New World by the Spaniards, and slavery first took root in South and Central America and in the West Indies. In 1619, a Dutch man-of-war brought twenty "Negars" to Jamestown. A few years later, Negro slaves began to appear in the North. By 1690, the southern colonies had a little over 5,000 Negro slaves. This was not many more than there were in the North. Southerners would undoubtedly have liked more, for the planters who obtained them profited by their labor. Their high price was discouraging, however, and Latin America and the West Indies absorbed most of the available supply.

About the year 1690, a considerable increase in the importation of Negro slaves began. The development of rice cultivation in the Carolinas was one factor in this increase, the Negro being better able than the white man to withstand the malaria that abounded in the lowlands where rice was best grown. As indigo culture developed into an important industry, the cultivation of both rice and indigo became a year-round affair that made the employment of gangs of Negro slaves increasingly profitable. The profits resulting from the employment of slave labor in the round-the-year job of tobacco growing had already been clearly demonstrated. Then, too, as England in 1713 obtained the Asiento (a monopoly on the slave trade with the American colonies of Spain), more slaves appeared on the English colonial markets, and they became cheaper in price. This stimulated an importation that, by 1861, had brought some 500,000 slaves from Africa to the North American mainland.

As early as 1765, there were 90,000 slaves in the Carolinas, and leading southerners were beginning to have fears for "white supremacy." Slavery had by then become firmly entrenched in the tobacco-growing colonies of Maryland, Virginia, and North Carolina, the slaves in those colonies outnumbering those in the lower South by four to one.

The legal status of slavery in the colonies was at first dubious. Slavery had no status in England until 1729, when it was given, at best, a quasi-legality by a judicial ruling that slaves coming into Great Britain and Ireland from the West Indies were not free and might be compelled by their master to return to the plantation. Only in 1772, in the Somerset case, did Lord Mansfield rule for the whole English bench that a slave became free by setting foot on the British Isles. Since, however, this did not decide the status of slavery in the British colonies, they were left free to deal with it as they saw fit.

Slavery was instituted in the North American colonies, and in the British West Indies as well, not by law but by force and custom. It was officially legalized in New England as early as 1641, and in Virginia about 1660. The other colonies followed these examples. All set up what came to be known as "slave codes." These were designed to guarantee the property rights of masters in the slaves, and in the children of slaves; to establish clearly the master's absolute authority, even to death, over the slave; to safeguard the personal property of the master against theft by the slave; and to set up measures, such as a curfew law and prohibition of the carrying of arms, designed to prevent slave insurrections. These codes illustrate both the arbitrary character of slavery and a lack of regard for the rights of the Negro as a human being.

Negro slavery increased in the North, although more slowly than it did in the South. More slaves were owned in eighteenth-century New York than in any other northern colony. There were some 20,000 slaves in New York by 1776, about one-seventh of the population of the colony. But no New England colony had this ratio of Negro slaves to free men. This was not because of moral or ethical considerations. The Puritans were no more prejudiced against enslaving Negroes than they were against enslaving Indians. They held the Negro fit for involuntary servitude because he was not of the elect, and Cotton Mather felt that his prayer to God for a servant had been answered when his congregation brought him a Negro slave. The number of slaves was smaller simply because slavery was not so profitable in New England as it was in New York.

The North was no better and no worse than the South in its treatment of slaves, and in its attitude toward the institution of slavery. But slavery was less useful, and therefore less vital, in the North than in the South. Slave labor was best in gangs of twenty to thirty men, watched over by an overseer. Northern agriculture did not accommodate so well to the use of gang labor. Also it had no year-round employment. Nor did slaves work out particularly well as fishermen, or as sailors in New England coastal waters. As the increase in the North's population gradually lessened the labor scarcity, the northern demand for slaves withered. In these ways, the North was being prepared to accept the belief that all men, white and black, were created equal, and that, for the Negro as for the white, life, liberty, and the pursuit of happiness were unalienable rights. But as late as Revolutionary times, neither North nor South saw any inconsistency in keeping slaves and at the same time denouncing as "slavery" Great Britain's interference with the economic practices of the American colonists.

Contrasts, 1630–1750

By the middle of the eighteenth century, the American colonies presented a marked contrast to the scattered settlements strung out along the Atlantic coast 125 years before. Instead of two or three thousand settlers, there were now some two million inhabitants, white and black. Earlier all had been rural, and the economy was hand to mouth. Now there were small cities— New York, Philadelphia, and Boston, each with twenty to thirty thousand inhabitants—and Charleston, South Carolina, was a thriving town of ten thousand people. The economy, too, was far removed from the primitive character of its early days. Its activity had expanded greatly, and it was diversified to a considerable degree.

One of the causes of this change was that, by dint of the use of indentured servants and Negro slaves, the colonists had provided themselves with a labor supply which greatly enhanced the production of all kinds of goods. Another favorable factor had been the character of British control over colonial economic activity. This, though irritating at times and in principle disquieting, had presented no serious impediments to colonial development and, in the favors it had granted and the protection it had afforded, often stimulated colonial production. Other factors were the abundance of land and resources and the favorable opportunities enjoyed by the colonists for engaging in commercial activity. In consequence, the people in the urban centers, in the rural village communities, and on the frontier were working hard and producing some remarkable results.

By 1750, American agriculture, household industry, shops, and factories were supplying the colonies' economic necessities, as well as raw materials and goods for a thriving export trade. The thirteen colonies had an iron industry, centered largely in Pennsylvania, that was producing more bar and pig iron than Great Britain itself, and a small amount of this colonial iron was being exported. American shipyards were producing three-quarters of the ships that carried the commerce of the colonies under colonial registry and more than one-quarter of the ships that sailed the seven seas under British registry. These ships were pouring a flood of American products into British and European markets.

American rice was of such a prime quality that it obtained premium prices abroad, and 100,000 barrels were exported yearly from Charleston. American tobacco controlled the market in England and on the continent as well. The middle colonies were producing great quantities of wheat, flour, beef, and pork for export. Governor Morris of Pennsylvania declared in 1775 that

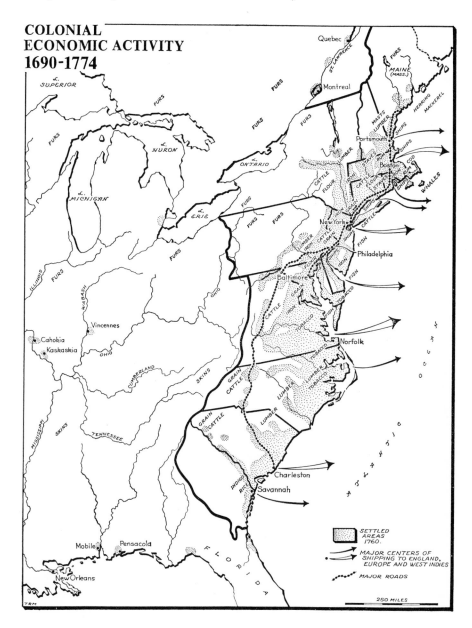

COLONIAL ECONOMIC ACTIVITY 1690-1774

Pennsylvania alone could export each year enough food for 100,000 people. Naval stores, deerskins, and muskrat and beaver furs to the value of hundreds of thousands of pounds were annually exported. The colonies produced vast quantities of rum to moisten the throats of the home population, and for sale abroad. Massachusetts alone was producing for export two million gallons of rum a year. New England fishing fleets, their home bases close to the sources of supply, were doing such a business with Europe and the West Indies that they were driving the English fishing fleets off the Banks of Newfoundland. By 1776, Philadelphia was the second city of the British Empire, and Boston had become the largest shipping center in the Empire outside the British Isles.

The economy of the thirteen colonies had by no means reached a plateau by the middle of the eighteenth century. Economic activity was expanding. New opportunities for profit were constantly opening up. In consequence, colonial society was filled with aspiration, with hope for and confidence in a still better future. It was a situation that made the colonials determined to protect both their accomplishments and their hopes from interference by statesmen on the other side of the Atlantic.

Suggested Reading

Valuable information on the economic history of the colonies is to be found in C. P. Nettels, *The Roots of American Civilization,* already cited, and his *The Money Supply of the American Colonies Before 1720* (1934); E. A. J. Johnson, *American Economic Thought in the Seventeenth Century* (1932); William B. Weeden, *Economic and Social History of New England, 1620–1789* (2 vols., 1890), and P. A. Bruce, *Economic History of Virginia in the Seventeenth Century* (2 vols., 1896).

Two authoritative works dealing with colonial agriculture are P. W. Bidwell and J. I. Falconer, *History of Agriculture in the Northern United States, 1620–1860* (1925), and L. C. Gray, *History of Agriculture in the Southern United States to 1860* (2 vols., 1933), vol. I. See also Lyman Carrier, *The Beginnings of Agriculture in America* (1923).

On colonial industry, see R. M. Tryon, *Household Manufactures in the United States, 1640–1860* (1917); V. S. Clark, *History of Manufactures in the United States, 1607–1860* (rev., three-vol. ed., 1929), vol. I; and A. C. Bining, *Pennsylvania Iron Manufacture in the Eighteenth Century* (1938) and *British Regulation of the Colonial Iron Industry* (1933). Carl Bridenbaugh, *The Colonial Craftsman* (1950) is interesting and authoritative.

On trade and commerce, see the works cited in the previous chapter. Important also are S. E. Forman, *The Rise of American Commerce and Industry* (1927) and Bernard Bailyn, *The New England Merchants in the Seventeenth Century* (1955). The student should also consult F. B. Tolles, *Meeting House and Counting House* (1948), which treats of the activities of the Quaker merchants in Philadelphia.

The colonial labor supply is examined in A. E. Smith, *Colonists in Bondage* (1947); M. W. Jernegan, *Laboring and Dependent Classes in Colonial America* (1931); and R. B. Morris, *Government and Labor in Early America* (1946). Special studies of slavery in colonial times are to be found in L. J. Greene, *The Negro in Colonial New England* (1942) and J. C. Ballagh, *A History of Slavery in Virginia* (1902). The curious reader might also wish to consult U. B. Phillips, *American Negro Slavery* (1929) and W. E. B. DuBois, *The Suppression of the American Slave Trade* (1896).

4 ⋅ The Colonial Way
of Life

ABOUT 65 PER CENT of the American colonists of the middle eighteenth century were English in origin. Some 10 per cent were of German and 16 per cent of Scotch and Scotch-Irish ancestry. Dutch, French, and Swedish parentage accounted for perhaps 5 per cent of the whole. A sprinkling of other nationalities, such as Finns, Swedes, and Jews, made up the remainder. By and large, it was a busy, hard-working people, ingenious and aggressive in seeking wealth and comfort. In the urban centers, the more well-to-do elements in the population laid considerable stress on luxury and refinement. In the back country, men and women concentrated, perforce, on the hard business of making a living and improving the family property.

Social Status in the Colonial Period

Colonial society had early developed signs of social stratification. The concept of a stratified society had been brought over from Europe, where there were distinct cleavages between the nobility and the commoners, to say nothing of gradations within each of these main groups. There was never any immigration of the English nobility, but in the seventeenth century men of means from England and planters from the Barbadoes had begun coming into the colonies. These men had assumed leadership in political and in social and economic affairs. Together with other energetic, ambitious, and capable

78

individuals who rose from the ranks, they had started the development of a colonial aristocracy that was based primarily on economic achievement. Below this top rank, other social groups had become well defined by the eighteenth century.

At the top of the eighteenth-century social ladder were the gentry or the "Better Sort," as the colonial newspapers phrased it in their society columns. These were the people of distinction. The well-to-do merchants and ship-owners of New England, the wealthy merchants and landowners of New York and Philadelphia, the lordly great planters and mercantile gentry of the Chesapeake region and the Carolina lowlands, and everywhere a sprinkling of professional people—clergymen, lawyers, doctors, a few retired English naval officers—constituted the membership of this class. They were addressed as "Honorable," or "Excellency," or, at the very least, as "Mr.," "Mrs.," or "Miss." All of middle-class origin, they were that new order of being, the American gentry.

Next on the social ladder came the American middle class itself. Its elements were the yeomen farmers, the tradespeople, craftsmen, and artisans, in the main hard-working, respectable folk. Save for the Carolina lowlands, where there was no considerable social group between the planters and the shiftless white folk who were at the bottom of society, this middle class constituted the great bulk of the population. The more prosperous among them might even be titled "Mr." or "Mrs." The rest, especially in those families where the man did not enjoy the franchise, were more apt to be known as "Goodman Smith" or "Goodwife Jones," the latter appellation being frequently shortened to "Goody."

The third and fourth orders of society consisted of the unskilled but free laborers, who were usually addressed familiarly by their given names— "John," "Jim," or "Martha"—and the indentured servants, slaves, and free Negroes, who were also addressed in familiar terms.

Each of these social groups had distinguishing traits and characteristics. Pride in wealth and family characterized the wealthy merchants and the great planters. For these, wealth guaranteed status, and their status was one of privilege and power. They were common members of the privileged class, but there were considerable differences in their outlook on life.

The great planters felt themselves to be above the common run; sometimes they were even scornful of the lesser planters. Many of them cultivated the manners of English rural society. Conspicuous spenders, they drank and gambled and were much addicted to hunting and horse racing. They also had a penchant for military life, and were prominent in the local militia. They were independent in spirit, proud of their position as lords of their own domain, and impatient with outside interference in the affairs of their plantations. Accepting the obligations of *noblesse oblige,* they willingly served without pay as the political and judicial leaders of their communities. In religion, they were chiefly Anglican, though they were none too faithful in church attendance. Their genius lay in the cultivation and care of their estates—and in politics, where they possessed a liberality of outlook that made it easy for them to follow Washington, accept the political theories of Jefferson and Madison, and thus move easily from monarchy to republicanism.

The merchants led lives that were more sedentary than those of the planters. They had a high regard for law and contracts and, if they had a gambling instinct, exercised it in trade and land speculation rather than at the card table or race track. The demands of business made them more prone to travel than the planter, and more cosmopolitan in their outlook. They had generally a wider knowledge of world affairs than had the lordlings of the South.

The great middle class, North and South, was chiefly made up of the small farmers and planters, whose efforts in the fields seldom got much above the subsistence level. Some were shiftless, but more were thrifty and hard-working people. They were conscious of status, according respect to those of their own class who "got ahead," and more still to the gentry. Often debtors, with the psychology of debtors, the majority were more interested in making ends meet than in social advancement, although there were always those who were anxious to rise in the social scale. Narrow in outlook, and quick to resent exploitation or any other kind of interference in their affairs, they were also sociable, simple-minded, neighborly, and imbued with the belief that, fundamentally, they had as much right to respect and a decent life as any man on earth.

The small minority of tenants, journeymen, farm hands, dock hands, and sailors worked hard, though often fitfully, and drank hard when they were in funds. They showed little or no interest in the accumulation of means or property. In the main shiftless and unstable, they made little constructive contribution to colonial society.

The Negro slave was on the lowest rung of the social ladder, but even among the slaves there were social gradations. The personal or house servant was in the highest slave rank. He was usually well treated and was looked up to by the other slaves. The next in order was the plantation artisan—carpenter, bricklayer, or wheelwright—who was also accorded a measure of good treatment. The great mass were the field workers, their lot tolerable in the tobacco regions, often hopeless and pitiful in the rice and indigo areas. More tractable than the Indian, the slaves could not be termed happy in their servile status. The picture of the plantation Negroes as a happy, joking, banjo-playing, carefree lot is largely myth. There were numerous runaways, and the fear of slave revolt was ever present among the southern whites.

Unable to take any positive role in the direction of society, the slaves nevertheless profoundly affected almost every aspect of southern life. Slavery stimulated that proneness to force and mastery which characterized the planter class. It steadily widened the gulf between the planter and the small freeholder. It kept the plantation aristocracy from attaining its cherished ambition of becoming a replica of English rural society. It influenced speech and custom and helped to shape the legal codes of the South. In the long run, it profoundly affected southern views of natural rights and the equality of man.

The Fluidity of Colonial Society

If colonial society had distinct consciousness of social status and clear-cut social gradations, it also had a real degree of fluidity. Mention has already been made of the way in which individuals rose from indentured servants to membership in early Virginia's House of Burgesses. This was paralleled by similar improvements in status in every colony. It was not difficult for a young man possessed of energy, brains, and ambition, to rise from the ranks, either by his own efforts or by a fortunate marriage, or by a combination of both. John Hull of Boston, a seventeenth-century goldsmith and mintmaster, was the son of a blacksmith. William Pepperell, a fisherman, married the daughter of a prosperous New Englander and became a merchant. He and his son William, who was born in 1696, built up a prosperous business and became large landed proprietors. In 1730, the younger Pepperell was made Chief Justice of Massachusetts. He commanded the expedition which captured Louisburg in 1745 and in consequence became the first American baronet. Young Benjamin Franklin, coming as a penniless lad to Philadelphia in 1723, soon rose to fame and fortune. The distinguished planter, merchant, and patriot leader Henry Laurens (1724–1792) of South Carolina was the son of a Huguenot saddler. The fluidity of colonial society was one of its most striking characteristics, and the belief that America was the land of opportunity for the hard-working and ambitious man became an American tradition.

The Independent Spirit

Colonial society was not only fluid; it was impatient of injustice and of restraints upon its freedom. The never-ending conflict between the colonial assemblies and the royal governors gave evidence of these qualities, as did

SIR WILLIAM PEPPERELL
(1696–1759)

Wealthy colonial merchant, shipbuilder, real-estate operator, and soldier. A power in Massachusetts court before he began to study law.

COURTESY OF THE ESSEX INSTITUTE, SALEM, MASS.

the activities of the smugglers and other evaders of the Navigation Acts. Still further proof lay in the conflicts that were perpetually cropping up between colonials and proprietors in the proprietary colonies. Between 1660 and 1689 there were five revolts in Maryland against Lord Baltimore, for reasons varying from religious differences to the veto power of the governor and the high quit rents. Similar outbreaks of violence marred the relations between settlers and proprietors in New Jersey and the Carolinas. There were also conflicts between the small farmers and workers of the frontier and the merchant-landed proprietor upper classes of the tidewater regions in seventeenth-century Virginia, New York, and New Jersey, and in the eighteenth-century Carolinas. These help to explain the growing unpopularity of the proprietary governments and their gradual transformation into royal colonies. They were also a part of those struggles for privilege and preferment that are deeply imbedded in the history of the colonial period. Three of these—Bacon's Rebellion, the Zenger trial, and the Regulator movement in the Carolinas—deserve special mention.

Bacon's Rebellion (1676–1677) was the result of a complex of causes. In part it was due to discontent engendered by the irascibility and arbitrary conduct of Virginia's royal governor, Sir William Berkeley, who kept the same colonial assembly for fifteen years, suborned and corrupted some of its members, and allowed land-grabbing by a favored few. More directly and significantly, it was the result of restlessness and bitterness on the part of the frontier planters, who were harried by a variety of economic hardships—such as the low price of tobacco, high taxes, and English commercial restrictions—and who were also angered because the governor would not support their ruthless attempts to exterminate the Indians on the frontier.

The revolt was headed by Nathaniel Bacon, a twenty-nine-year-old Henrico county planter, arrogant and headstrong, whose chief aim was not political reform but wholesale slaughter of the Indians. The governor was forced to flee from Jamestown, which Bacon put to the torch. The revolt collapsed when Berkeley obtained help from England and Bacon died of a fever. The old governor took a bloody revenge for this sadly mismanaged and misdirected uprising against his authority.

Bacon's Rebellion was primarily a manifestation of the turbulent passions that early came to characterize the American frontier. The Zenger trial (1734–1735) was directly the outcome of malfunction by an autocratic government. Governor Cosby of New York was a pompous, avaricious, dictatorial bureaucrat, bent on enriching himself at the expense of the colony. All save a privileged few became bitterly opposed to him, and influential New York citizens set up the New York *Weekly Journal,* edited by John Peter Zenger, to publicize the governor's defects. The articles in the *Journal* on freedom of the press, trial by jury, and kindred subjects were filled with uncomplimentary allusions to Cosby and his friends. When, in 1734, the election of councilmen and aldermen went against Cosby's group, the governor had Zenger arrested for libel. He was defended by Andrew Hamilton of Philadelphia, a man nearly eighty years old but still the best lawyer in America. The jury's verdict of "not guilty" was a milestone in establishing the freedom of the press in America. It was also, as the cheering crowd in the court room bore witness, a manifestation of that dislike of arbitrary and tyrannical controls that was already an American characteristic.

The Regulator movements in the Carolinas, which occurred in the 1760s, were revolts of the back country against tidewater policies in colonial affairs. In North Carolina, the Regulators rose against insolence and venality on the part of colonial officials, the collection of church tithes and quit rents, and the perhaps necessary restrictions on freedom that arose from the extension of the authority of the colonial government into the Piedmont areas. In

South Carolina, the chief difficulty was the lack of government in the back country, and the indifference of the colonial assembly to the pleas of the upland folk for protection against desperadoes and for the establishment of courts, hospitals, and justices of the peace. In both cases, there was protracted feuding and fighting between tidewater and frontier. When the Revolution came and the tidewater gentry, in the main, sided with the rebellious colonies, it was only natural that the embittered interior should remain largely loyal to the British king.

The Importance of the Family

The conditions of colonial life made for a social structure that was at once stratified and fluid, a structure composed of restless human elements that were quick to defend their rights and privileges against oppression. The overwhelmingly rural and dispersed character of colonial society likewise made it inevitable that the family should be the most important single feature of the social organization. Individual families were customarily large, twenty to thirty people frequently being gathered together under one roof. Servants and dependent relatives were frequently part of such a brood, but its size was chiefly due to the number of children. A family of ten or twelve children was common, and twenty to twenty-five was not at all a phenomenal number. Patrick Henry was one of nineteen children. One Massachusetts man who died just before the Revolution left 157 descendants, including five great-grandchildren. The skyrocketing of population, however, was impeded by the high mortality rate. It was not at all unusual for three or four out of a family of ten children to die before the age of sixteen. A Plymouth gravestone reads, "Here lies ———— ———— with twenty small children."

The family was created through marriage, which came at an early age in the colonies. The majority of young people were married before they were twenty, and marriages at sixteen or even earlier were common. Chief Justice Marshall fell in love with his bride-to-be when she was fourteen, and two years later their troth was plighted. William Byrd II (1674–1744) referred to his twenty-year-old daughter Evelyn as an "antique virgin." Love was, of course, a factor in bringing men and women into the holy bonds of matrimony, but property, industry, and efficiency in the conduct of business or household affairs were also important considerations.

Unmarried men were looked upon with disfavor, and "spinster" was a term of reproach. Both, Colonel Byrd declared, were "as scarce among us and reckoned as ominous as a blazing star." Women were, indeed, at a premium, for more men than women migrated to America, and the need for a helpmate in a pioneer land was great. And women played important roles, other than those of wife and mother. There are many records of their participation in their husbands' business affairs. Some managed plantations, and others were successful newspaper editors. Woman's status in America, despite the hardships of continuous childbearing and of life on the frontier, was considerably superior to the status of women in Europe.

Amusements and Avocations

The hardships of colonial life were counterbalanced, to a considerable extent, by amusements and avocations. The theatre was a joy to many. Puritans and Quakers regarded it as sinful, and it was handicapped in the seventeenth century by the absence of urban centers, but in the eighteenth century the drama became well established in all the cities except Boston, where it was prohibited. Americans, however, showed little talent, either as playwrights or as actors. Where the theatre was not available, Punch and Judy shows, waxworks, trapeze artists, a few lions and elephants, and, in the eighteenth century, shows popularizing science traveled across the country.

Thespians, peripatetic or otherwise, furnished only one form of amusement. On election and muster days, and when the county court met, the local citizenry were wont to make merry with contests of strength and skill and much quaffing of the bowl. Horse racing, fox hunting, and cock fighting were popular sports in the South. Even parsons went to cock fights. In some sections, social clubs were popular. Hunting and fishing were universal pastimes, and bear and bull baiting—both very cruel sports—were not uncommon. Dancing was enjoyed even in Puritan New England, where the Puritan clergy inveighed bitterly against it. Music was popular everywhere; it ranged from fiddling, jigs, and ballads to the development of orchestral music and, in the eighteenth century, the enjoyment of Bach, Haydn, Mozart, and other composers dear to the hearts of the German immigrants.

As music became a more and more important part of colonial life, it enlisted the interest of a considerable number of amateur devotees. The same was true of painting, which was frequently an avocation of those who made their livings in other occupations. In the eighteenth century, as the currents of rationalism were wafted across the Atlantic, amateur scientists were to be found in all the colonies. The southern gentry, in particular, also developed a real interest in architectural design. These avocations, like the amusements of the times, played an important part in making colonial life attractive.

Colonial Religion—Puritans and Puritanism

Religion was another aspect of colonial times that did much to relieve the hardships and drudgery of daily living. A powerful and compelling force in the seventeenth century, it felt the impact of secular forces as time went on, while still remaining a most important social influence. The character of this influence varied with the sects and denominations, and these increased in number as nationalities other than the English were added to the colonial population. Of all the religious groups, the New England Puritans played the greatest role in colonial life.

New England Puritans inherited from their English forebears two forms of church organization, the Presbyterian and the Congregationalist. The Presbyterian Puritans believed that the church should be governed by a series of representative assemblies, or "synods." The Congregationalist Puritans held that each church should be a self-governing unit. New England Puritanism was Congregational, the more democratic of the two forms.

New England Puritanism has often been described as harsh and unlovely in its mode of life, and there is considerable justification for this point of view. The Puritans were credulous and superstitious people. They used horoscopes to discover the nature of ailments. They continually read the heavens for signs and omens. They believed in witchcraft and supernatural visitations, and this belief was responsible for the terrible Salem delusion of 1692. In that year, a group of hysterical young girls in Salem Village began accusing certain women of bewitching them. A frenzy of excitement followed, as confessions and accusations multiplied. A special court of magistrates was appointed by the governor to investigate the charges, and this court became infected with the excitement. Before it adjourned, fifty persons had confessed to being witches; nineteen people and two dogs had been hung; and one man, Giles Corey, had been pressed to death with great weights for refusing to plead, a stand that he took in order to save his property for his family. It was only when the highest families in the colony began to be involved that the stabler intellects took a hand. They prevailed upon the governor not to call the special court together again, and the hysteria gradually died down.

The early Puritans were as prone to antidemocratic ways as they were to superstitious practices. Their seventeenth-century leaders wanted to establish a society in which the primary duties of the citizen would be to those above them—to God, the king, and the magistrates of the colony—and in which the church would exert a compelling influence on the government. They were in a fair way of realizing these aims in early Massachusetts Bay Colony. The gentry were given special privileges in dress and the best seats in the meetinghouse. A servant who spoke disrespectfully of the magistrates was in danger of having his ears cropped. In 1649, there was only one "Mr." to fourteen "Goodmen" in the colony. And the government was theocratic in character. In early Massachusetts, only church members could vote in the town meetings. As late as 1691, four-fifths of the adult males could not vote for the magistrates or the deputies to the general court because they were not church members. All citizens had to pay taxes for the support of the Congregational church. Quakers, Anne Hutchinson, Roger Williams, and other people who did not agree with the doctrines of the ruling Puritans were driven from Massachusetts. The Quakers were warned to stay away on pain of death. Some of them persisted in disregarding this warning, however, and in the 1650s five were executed in Boston.

The Puritan conception of God and of man's relationship to Him was as narrow and bigoted as their attitude toward the unorthodox. They regarded the Most High as an austere deity, bent upon securing His own glory. He damned honorable but unconverted men, and reprobate infants, and took delight in consigning the wicked to the flames of hell. As Michael Wigglesworth wrote in his poem, *The Day of Doom:*

> They cry, they roar for anguish sore,
>   and gnaw their tongues for horrour.
> But get away without delay,
>   Christ pitties not your cry:
> Depart to Hell, there may you yell,
>   and roar Eternally.

The Puritans lived in perpetual fear of offending this awesome God, and continually sought to propitiate and honor Him. They would have nothing to do with religious music, painting, and sculpture, regarding these as Papist extravagances rather than as true manifestations of the religious spirit. They also abjured dancing and the theatre. They spent Sunday in meditation and in going to church for morning and afternoon sermons that were sometimes two or three hours in length. Michael Wigglesworth once let his neighbor's stable door bang itself to pieces in a high wind rather than break his Sabbath meditation by going out and shutting it.

Such was the sterner side of Puritanism. Out of it has come a picture of the Puritans as whining, canting bigots, morbid killjoys whose lives were harsh, dull, and drab, hypocrites who set up impossible standards of virtue from which they themselves backslid. It took a Puritan saint, so the saying went, to find the easiest way through a penal statute. There is, however, another side to the shield.

The Puritans were intolerant and superstitious, as the record amply proves, but in this they were not unique. The age in which they lived was superstitious and intolerant. If they persecuted the Quakers, so did others, and the Puritans themselves were harshly persecuted in England. Again, the belief in witchcraft was a common delusion of the day, and it is worthy of note that, while the Salem witchcraft trials were the last that took place in New England, similar trials went on in Europe throughout the eighteenth century.

The Puritans did lead strict and sober lives by modern standards, but they were far from being killjoys. Both men and women smoked and drank. They liked and used rich stuffs of fine design in furnishing their homes, and the well-to-do appeared on occasion adorned with lace and arrayed in such colorful garments as violet cloaks and turkey-red grogram suits. Boston supported a dozen goldsmiths before it had a single lawyer. Much has been made of the fact that the Puritans cut down the Maypole erected at Merrymount by Thomas Morton, but this was done not because Morton and his comrades engaged in dancing and frivolity but because they were selling liquor and firearms to the Indians. Puritanism was often sober and severe, but it was far from drab.

Neither was Puritanism a rigid, unbending way of life. The rigid theocracy of its early days slowly gave way as non-Puritan elements became more and more a part of New England's life, and as the interest of New England society in the material aspects of living constantly increased. In 1662, the Halfway Covenant allowed what was a "frightful inroad" to the hard-shelled Puritans—the baptism of the children of pious parents who had yet had no definite religious experience. In 1691, public opinion in Massachusetts supported the new charter, which established a representative assembly based, not on church membership, but on property holdings and which guaranteed religious freedom for all Protestants. And, even though the Puritan ideal society was aristocratic and theocratic, the self-government of the Congregational churches and the town meetings promoted the development of democratic principles.

The Puritans also had faith in the power of reason. They believed, as Cotton Mather said, "that the light of reason is the law of God." This, in itself, forced them to face the existence of a changing material environment and a changing climate of opinion and kept them from becoming mere stick-in-the-mud conservatives.

The basic Puritan aim was improvement of themselves and others. They were dissatisfied with the past—ready to break with it and to discipline themselves in order to make a better life prevail. They were moralistic, self-righteous, narrow, and quick at name-calling and invective, but in these things they mirrored their age. In their zeal to create a better life, and in their willingness to sacrifice comfort and convenience and endure tribulation in order to make that better life prevail, they were in advance of their age.

The influence of Puritanism has been widespread. New England was its center, but migration swept it into the other colonies and out along the frontier. It has had something to do with the passage of laws for the improvement of society, from Sunday observance to prohibition. Its emphasis on work well done as evidence of at least an inclination toward Godliness has probably aided in the development of that glorification of wealth that is so characteristic of American society today. The high value that Puritanism placed upon education, as a means of giving the individual access to God's Word and as a preparation for life, had much to do with the creation of the New England educational system. And the Puritan insistence upon moral standards, the supremacy of law, the authority of conscience, and the responsibility of the individual to God has been woven into the fabric of American life. Puritanism bears a large measure of responsibility for whatever is distinctive in American life today.

The Anglican Church and Other Denominations

If Puritanism was the chief religion of New England, Anglicanism was pre-eminent in the South, especially in the tidewater regions. Because of vigorous promotion from England, especially by the Society for the Propagation of the Gospel in Foreign Parts, the Anglican church was established in Maryland, Virginia, and the Carolinas, and its congregations increased in number throughout the North, even in New England. But, though it could number some 500 churches by the middle of the eighteenth century, it was not a strong religious organization. Everywhere it met the bitter opposition of the dissenting groups, which feared its propensity to restrict their freedom and resented being taxed for its support. The fact that there was no bishop in America, which meant that local ministers had to go to England to be ordained, the large size of the parishes in the South, and the small salaries granted by the legislatures of the colonies where it was established kept outstanding colonials from entering its service and attracted only those English rectors who had failed to get ahead at home. In consequence, the Anglican ministry varied from mediocre in New York to disgraceful in Virginia and never showed evidence of any marked improvement.

Weak though it was, however, the Anglican church made two important contributions to colonial life. It furnished, especially through its missionary activities, a considerable stimulus to education and to the life of the spirit. And though, as became an established church, it preached the doctrine of nonresistance to authority, distance from England had the effect of making the Anglican parishes in the South almost as independent in practice as the Congregational parishes of New England. In its way, even Anglicanism helped to furnish a seed bed for democracy.

Numerous other sects and denominations had obtained a firm foothold in the colonies by the middle of the eighteenth century. The Quakers were distinguished by their use of "thee" and "thou" in speech and by their sitting in silence in their meetings until the spirit moved someone to speak. They were active missionaries, and a network of Quaker meetings was spread from Maine to South Carolina. They had some 300 congregations in all, with their center of strength in Pennsylvania and New Jersey. Like the New England Puritans, they glorified labor as a means of doing God's Will on earth. The Baptists, exponents of complete separation of church and state and of baptism by immersion, had grown rapidly in New England and in the southern colonies. Despite persecution by Episcopalians and others who believed in a state church, there were nearly 500 Baptist congregations by 1750. The German Pietists (Mennonites, Moravians, and others) had over 250 churches. Extremely devout and putting much emphasis upon religious experience, they were of fundamental importance in the development of revivalism in America. German and Dutch Lutherans, zealous in their adherence to orthodox Protestant Christianity, had about 100 congregations scattered from the middle colonies to Georgia, but mainly centered in Pennsylvania. Some fifty churches and from 4,000 to 7,000 communicants marked the extent of Catholic influence, which was chiefly confined to Maryland.

The Growth of Tolerance

Intolerance in varying degrees marked the relations of the Christian faiths with one another throughout the colonial period. The planters of the South felt that, while there were probably other roads to heaven, no gentleman would go there save by the Anglican church. That church would have liked to see all the colonists compelled to pay taxes for its support. The New England sects were jealous and fearful of Anglican inroads, and the Anglicans were scornful of the New England church system, since it was not founded, like their own, on the apostolic succession. The Presbyterians, Baptists, Quakers, German Reformed, and Lutherans of the back country were intolerant of one another, and especially of the Church of England. All the Protestants disliked Catholicism and favored political restrictions for Catholics.

The eighteenth century brought the slow increase of a more tolerant spirit on the part of the various denominations. Protestantism was, in its origin, a revolt against authority, and it was only natural that this revolt should continue. It was aided and abetted by the pressure of economic interest and by the scepticism and humanitarianism of the rationalist movement. Even the Congregationalists and the Anglicans saw that it was necessary to accept some measure of dissent, although they both continued to feel that toleration should be distinctly limited in character.

The appearance of a more tolerant spirit was accompanied by a decrease in religious devotion throughout the colonies. Church attendance lessened. A heretical belief known as Arminianism—a doctrine which declared in part that any man could be saved who believed in Christ and by works continued to merit salvation—made considerable headway among the faithful.

This "falling away," as the orthodox termed it, was due to a variety of factors. The influx of non-Puritans in New England and the growth of interest in secular pursuits made for worldlymindedness. So did the worldliness of the Anglican clergy, and a growing belief that the ministers of the established churches were insisting on doctrines that no longer met the needs of the day. The rising tide of European religious rationalism was also beginning to make itself felt in the colonies. In consequence, the pastors and the orthodox devout in general became seriously alarmed about the state of religion. The outcome of this condition of affairs was a revivalist movement that is known as the Great Awakening, which took place in the decade from 1735 to 1745.

The Great Awakening, 1735–1745

The man directly responsible for the beginning of the Great Awakening was Jonathan Edwards (1703–1758), the deeply religious pastor of a church in Northampton, Massachusetts, and one of the most profound minds that America has produced. He was the grandfather, curiously enough, of that great Don Juan Aaron Burr. Edwards told his congregation that God was dreadfully provoked by this stiff-necked generation. In a graphic phrase, he described mankind as dangling, precariously as a spider, over the flaming pit of hell. He declared that a spiritual awakening on the part of the individual could be taken as evidence from on high of predestination for a life of heavenly bliss, and emphasized the overwhelming importance of being "born again." His sermons had great emotional power, and within a year there were 300 conversions in Northampton.

The Great Awakening spread sporadically from its Northampton beginnings throughout New England and into the rest of the colonies. Other preachers of grace and conversion added fuel to the fire. Gilbert Tennent of New Jersey (1703–1764) was one of these, but the greatest of them all was the English evangelist George Whitefield (1714–1770). During his life he visited America seven times, spending almost six years in the colonies between 1737 and 1748. Whitefield worked zealously with all the evangelical sects, and his marvelous eloquence spread revivalism from Georgia to Maine.

The Great Awakening had some significant results. There was considerable bitterness and even schism in the various denominations between the "New Lights," who favored zealous and emotional preachers, whether or not they were educated, and the "Old Lights," who stressed the importance of an educated clergy and deplored the emotional excesses that often accompanied revivals. The Boston ministry divided over revivalism, Anglicans joining the "Old Lights" in their opposition to it. "I am sorry to see you here," said an Anglican, Timothy Cutler, to George Whitefield on a Boston street. "So is the Devil," was the reply. Throughout the Congregationalist and Presbyterian churches of the colonies, the "Old Light," "New Light" struggle was waged with varying degrees of bitterness.

Because of the Awakening, the dissenting sects rapidly increased in size. Since many Anglicans were also affected by the movement, it was one of the sources from which, later in the century, that offshoot of Anglicanism known as the Methodist Episcopal church was to spring. The boldness of the revivalists, who went into any church that would receive them, regardless of creed, was a unifying force that broke down provincial barriers and helped to make evangelical Protestantism a basic characteristic of American society. Finally, the Great Awakening helped to create more cultural unity in the colonies, since it stimulated the founding of four colleges: Princeton (1746), Brown (1764), Rutgers (1766), and Dartmouth (1769). These were established primarily, but by no means exclusively, to educate ministers of the gospel.

The Fine Arts and Education

Colonial interest in religion was one measure of the state of culture in the colonies, if culture is defined as the effort to develop, intellectually and morally, the search for truth, beauty, and virtue. Another measure was interest in the fine arts, which was certainly not extensive. The colonies produced no first-rate genius in either music or sculpture. Painting was worse than mediocre until, toward the close of the colonial period, there appeared painters of such considerable merit as Boston-born John Singleton Copley, Benjamin West, who came from near Philadelphia, and Maryland's Charles Willson Peale. Architecture was the principal colonial contribution to the fine arts, as is attested by the beauty of such seventeenth-century New England homes as the House of the Seven Gables and the Paul Revere house in Boston, the Georgian architecture that succeeded that of the Puritans and the Dutch in New England and New York, the Quaker and later Georgian architecture of Philadelphia, and the stately Georgian homes of the eighteenth-century merchants and planters from Maryland to Charleston.

Still other measurements of culture are provided by the colonial interest in education, reading, and literary production—what may be called the intellectual life. There was not much of this in any seventeenth-century North American colony, but the Puritans, more than any others, kept alive the great classical traditions that had become such a fundamental part of the European heritage. This was best shown in the field of education, where respect for the classics was combined with more utilitarian concerns.

It was the Puritan intent to use education in making their children good Puritans and good citizens. For those purposes, the Massachusetts Act of 1647 provided that every Massachusetts town of fifty or more families should appoint a schoolmaster, whose wages should be paid either by the parents or the town, and that every town of 100 families or more should establish a grammar school where there would be sound training in Latin and Greek. Connecticut copied this law in 1650, and by 1672 all New England, except Rhode Island, was theoretically under a system of compulsory education. Actually, the New England educational system was neither compulsory nor free. A small tuition fee was generally required from all who could afford it, and by no means all the communities established the schools required by law. Nevertheless, here was a beginning of the state-supported school systems of a later day, as well as an origin of another of America's great traditions— state-directed social activity for the common good.

In addition to its public and grammar schools, New England had a number of private schools to which were sent the sons of the well-to-do. There was also considerable tutoring. And college training was not neglected. Harvard College, founded by act of the Massachusetts legislature in 1636, was firmly established by 1650, with a curriculum similar to that of Oxford and Cambridge. Yale was established in 1701 by a group of self-sacrificing ministers of the gospel.

New England led all the colonies in education. This was due in part to the Puritan impulse, in part to New England's more compact town life, in part to a widespread recognition of individual and civic responsibility for education, and in part to the influence of an educated leadership. Massachusetts Bay colony, among all the others, had the highest proportion of university graduates among its leaders.

The educational achievements of the other colonies varied widely, both in quality and quantity. Rhode Island and New York under the English had no school system or compulsory education laws in the colonial period, education in those colonies being carried out almost wholly by tutoring or in private schools. Pennsylvania showed more interest in education but never succeeded in making it a public responsibility. The southern colonies were slow to develop public schools, although the southern well-to-do were zealous in the education of their children. In the schools of Boston, New York, and Philadelphia, just before the Revolution, there was some tendency to stress

THE FAIRBANKS HOUSE AT DEDHAM, MASSACHUSETTS

Built in 1636 and now occupied by the eighth generation of the Fairbanks family. Known as the most picturesque landmark in America, this is, save for the shell and adobe houses of Florida and California, the oldest house now standing in America.

COURTESY OF THE NEW YORK PUBLIC LIBRARY

THE CRAIGIE OR LONGFELLOW HOUSE (1759)

Home of the poet Henry Wadsworth Longfellow in Cambridge, Massachusetts. It is a fine example of eighteenth-century New England colonial architecture.

COURTESY OF THE LIBRARY OF CONGRESS

WESTOVER
CHARLES CITY COUNTY
VIRGINIA

Home of William Byrd (1674–1744), planter, author, colonial official, and a representative of the Virginia aristocracy; fond of elegance and luxury, he was often in debt. Westover is a fine example of eighteenth-century Georgian colonial architecture.

95

the student's place in society rather than genteel training. In consequence, vernacular and vocational education began to find a place along with such classical and theoretical subjects as Latin, Greek, mathematics, and philosophy. The southern back country had to rely mainly on church schools, some of which were good, some bad. The South had one college, William and Mary, founded in Virginia in 1693; the sons of the planters usually went there or to England for their higher education.

All the colonial colleges were founded under the auspices of religious groups. Harvard, Yale, and Dartmouth were Congregational, William and Mary was Episcopalian, Princeton was Presbyterian, Brown was Baptist, and Rutgers was Dutch Reformed. Even the most secular of these institutions, King's College (1754, later Columbia), and the College of Philadelphia (1755, later the University of Pennsylvania) were "shared and fought over," as one authority has it, by the Anglicans and the Presbyterians. All, however, were primarily liberal arts colleges rather than religious seminaries. Clergymen were a steadily decreasing minority of their graduates, and none of the colleges required adherence to a particular creed as a condition of admission. All save one of the colleges founded around the middle of the eighteenth century had interdenominational boards of control. In varying degrees, the hold of the religious groups on higher education was weakening before the inroads of rationalism and the practical need of toleration. The college curricula, on the other hand, remained virtually unchanged throughout the colonial period. They were basically classical, with mathematics, philosophy, and a smattering of science thrown in during the last two years.

Colonial Literature

Colonial reading was necessarily restricted by the scarcity and expensiveness of books. It was, nevertheless, considerable in amount, especially in the northern and middle colonies. Many of the colonists were conscious of their English cultural heritage and sought to use it in their new life. They brought with them useful books, such as medical treatises, law books, and books on the art of government. The classics that were held in high regard in England as a result of the Renaissance and its development of a humanistic tradition had an honored place, as did historical subjects and (most popular of all) works on divinity. Some colonists—such as John Winthrop, Jr., the seventeenth-century governor of Connecticut, and William Byrd II of Virginia—read scientific treatises. The poetry of Shakespeare, Spenser, and George Herbert was widely read. The colonist liked to combine pleasure and profit in his reading, but the primitive conditions of society continually accented the importance of books that were on the practical side.

Libraries multiplied in the eighteenth century. The Harvard College library, largest in the colonies, had 5,000 volumes, and other colleges had respectable collections. Under the influence of Franklin and others, circulating libraries came into vogue, and the amount of secular literature provided for public use steadily increased. New York City's first public library opened for use in the same year that instruction began at King's College. Another indication of the increasing interest in literature was the appearance, in the generation just before the Revolution, of no less than 119 booksellers' shops in the four principal cities of the colonies. These shops carried the works of such writers as Locke, Pope, Milton, Shakespeare, Swift, and Voltaire.

There was a considerable amount of writing in the colonies, but little of it could be called literature. Most of it, especially in New England, was didactic, published sermons predominating over all else. A good deal was historical and descriptive, following the precedent set by Captain John Smith in such valuable works as *The General History of Virginia* (1624) and *A Description of New England* (1616). The New England writings of John Winthrop, Edward Johnson, Increase and Cotton Mather, and others, were voluminous; Cotton Mather alone published 450 printed works. The primary purpose of these authors was to show God's providence toward the Puritans and to point out the "fact" that Puritan New England was a kind of culmination in God's plan for the world. Sober and largely objective accounts of happenings in New England, such as William Bradford's *Of Plymouth Plantation, 1620–1647,* were rare. Many New Englanders kept diaries, and *The Diary of Samuel Sewall, 1674–1729* and the *Diary of Cotton Mather, 1681–1724* provide valuable information about conditions in colonial New England and about the Puritan attitude toward life. Not until the eighteenth century did the rationalist influence begin to creep into New England literature, and its effect was not significant until just before the Revolution. It is a far cry from the Mathers to Thomas Hutchinson's *The History of . . . Massachusetts Bay (1764–1828).*

The middle colonies produced mainly histories and descriptive writings. In the southern colonies, there was little writing in the seventeenth century, though Virginia produced some respectable history and personal narrative. The output of such productions increased somewhat in the eighteenth century. Especially revealing are the diaries of William Byrd of Westover (1674–1744), with their description of the life and loves of a rich Virginia planter. And the correspondence of leading Virginia statesmen, such as Washington, Jefferson, George Mason, and Peyton Randolph, has genuine literary quality.

Of belles-lettres there was little indeed in colonial times, and what there was came chiefly from New England. Most of this was in the category of Michael Wigglesworth's *Day of Doom* (1662), a work possessing small literary merit, though it gives a lively account of the terrors of the Judgment Day. New England's Anne Bradstreet (c. 1612–1672) was the one outstanding American poetess before Emily Dickinson. New England's ablest poet of the colonial period, Edward Taylor (1642–1729), was not published, partly because of his own wish, until the twentieth century.

The hardships attendant upon colonial life, the lack of time for ease and gracious living, and the scarcity of printing facilities help to explain the small quantity and mediocre quality of colonial literature. Such literature as there was showed, in its general trend, the influence of the religious spirit and the importance to the American mind at that early day of writings that would be conducive to self-improvement, salvation, and the promotion of colonial settlement.

Science in the Colonies

Interest in science is another measure of the status of colonial culture. The New England Puritans, imbued with respect for reason and convinced that the wonders of the natural world only confirmed the truth of Puritan theology, were as ready as other parts of Western civilization to accept the scientific revolution. John Winthrop, Jr., deeply interested in science and its practical application, was the first colonial Fellow of the London Royal Society, which was founded in 1662. Increase Mather (1639–1723) and others founded the first offshoot of the Royal Society, a short-lived scientific club in Boston in 1683. Copernican astronomy, which destroyed the belief that the earth was the center of the universe, had rough going in Christian countries for two hundred years, but it had gained a substantial foothold in New England by the beginning of the eighteenth century. Cotton Mather (1662–1727), Increase Mather's son, was one of its outstanding exponents; a member of the Royal Society, he was deeply interested in New England fauna and was a fervent supporter of Zabdiel Boylston (1679–1766), the first colonial physician to practice inoculation for smallpox.

Scientific interest was by no means confined to New England. The College of William and Mary early undertook to teach mathematics and natural philosophy. Philadelphia became the eighteenth-century center of scientific investigation, thanks largely to the efforts of Benjamin Franklin, who in so many ways typified the spirit of the rationalist enlightenment. The University of Pennsylvania, of which Franklin was the real founder, established the first chair of botany and natural history in the colonies, and also the first systematic instruction in medicine. Franklin's Junto, a society formed to promote interest in science, merged in 1769 with a similar organization to form the American Philosophical Society, with Franklin as its first president.

As everyone knows, Franklin's kite experiment identified lightning as an electrical discharge. This and his deep interest in the whole field of scientific research brought him honor after honor in England, where he was given the Copley medal (1753), was made a Fellow of the Royal Society (1756), and received honorary degrees from three British universities. Other distinguished Philadelphia scientists were the botanist John Bartram (1699–1777), the astronomer David Rittenhouse (1732–1796), and physician Benjamin Rush (1745–1813).

Some southern planters were also patrons of science. Numerous eighteenth-century Virginians found it a fascinating subject. William Byrd of Westover devoted considerable time to botanical observations, as did John Clayton (c. 1685–1773) and Dr. John Mitchell (d. 1768). In South Carolina, Dr. Alexander Garden (c. 1730–1791), among others, made extensive researches in botany and zoology. He became a member of the Royal Society of Upsala and the London Royal Society, and the famous Swedish natural scientist Linnaeus named the gardenia in his honor. The first history museum in America was founded in Charleston.

Colonial interest in science was both utilitarian and theoretical. Mather, Boylston, Franklin, and others, were as much concerned with the usefulness of their scientific discoveries as they were with adventures into curious and unknown fields. America, with its new fauna and flora, and its opportunity for the utilization of fresh natural resources, was an excellent field for scientific development, and Americans earned a respectable place in the scientific world.

Colonial society on the eve of the Revolution had developed some clearly defined ideals and loyalties. It aspired to a happy life, whether this was the life of the spirit or simply one of improved material condition. It still accepted as fact that man was part of the divine plan and that he must seek to find happiness, here and hereafter, through seeking God's will and striving to make it his own. But the interests of the society had become increasingly materialistic as economic opportunity increased, and the Americans who composed this society also believed that real happiness could be achieved through industry, the conquest of nature, and the building of a good life on the western shores of the Atlantic.

Freedom, Optimism, and Conservatism

The quest of the colonials for happiness was made all the more natural by what one German traveler called the colonial "conviction of freedom." This was felt by the merchant aspiring to affluence through evasion of the Navigation Acts and by the planter lording it over his own domain. Nowhere was it more clearly felt than among the ordinary farmers and workers of the colonies as new lands opened up and trades and jobs multiplied on every hand.

It was inevitable that this sense of freedom should be closely allied to colonial optimism. The eighteenth-century American colonist, rich or poor, believed that he lived in a country with a future, one in which any man worth his salt could "get ahead." This was possible by individual effort, but it could also be through cooperation, for the grim necessities of frontier living and the human need for companionship produced cooperative social activity that ranged from log rollings to gentlemen's clubs and governmental intervention in economic affairs. But, whether alone or in partnership with others, progress was regarded as inevitable. High and low could echo with fervor the pronouncement of Judge William Allen of Philadelphia—"You may depend upon it that this is one of the best Poor Man's Countries in the World." The colonial optimist was also a pragmatist. The constant struggle with soil, forest, and climate and the multiple needs of a primitive society committed these early Americans to a practical, utilitarian attitude toward life. Uprooted from one environment and flung into another of such a different character, it was inevitable that they should be flexible in their attitudes, not at all disposed to cling blindly to time-honored customs and traditions. It was what one could do that counted in this new country, and since accomplishment was the measure of success, its method became of secondary importance.

But, though achievement took precedence over tradition, the colonials were far from being radicals, either politically or socially. From its beginning, America oriented itself around a middle-class norm. The colonists, stemming primarily from the bourgeois elements of Europe, accepted the social codes and the economic principles of a competitive, capitalistic society. They modified these codes and principles under pressure of necessity, but they always resisted departure from the norm, whether that departure was toward a communistic or a feudal form of society. They accepted social gradation, manifesting a marked respect for status as long as that status was fluid and not fixed. They did not question the right of the King to rule over them, or of Parliament to make laws for them. The innovations in government or society that were consciously made were dictated by practical not theoretical considerations.

The Trend Toward a National Life

One change in colonial life that was made unconsciously but was significant was the movement toward a uniform civilization. Slowly, travel and trade broadened the perspective of the upper classes. Intermarriage in these same upper levels gave the great families intercolonial influence. England was the arbiter of elegance for all, and English fashions came to all ports. Eighteenth-century colonial culture had a real degree of uniformity architecturally, in reading, in styles of furniture, even (save for Boston) in the theatre. It is a striking fact that New York City, which in 1700 was distinctly Dutch in its houses, shops, goods, and religious services, was so bombarded by other colonial, and English, influences that on the eve of the Revolution it had acquired much more of the general appearance and outlook of its sister commercial cities, Boston and Philadelphia.

Accompanying this trend toward uniformity was a trend toward the creation of a true American nation. Nothing that can be called American nationalism existed in colonial times. But out of the colonial awareness of strength and freedom, out of an increasing economic well-being, out of the growing uniformity of custom and culture, and—perhaps most of all—out of a transplanted English national consciousness and Locke's concepts of natural rights and the Enlightenment's emphasis on the dignity of the individual, there was emerging a colonial America that would soon become a new nation and evolve its own credo of nationalism.

Suggested Reading

There is a wealth of material on the social and cultural life of the colonies. Perhaps the best general treatment of this subject is L. B. Wright, *The Cultural Life of the American Colonies, 1607–1763* (1957). C. Bridenbaugh's *Cities in the Wilderness: the First Century of Urban Life in America, 1625–1742* (1938) is also excellent, as is the same author's *Myths and Realities: Societies of the Colonial South* (1952). T. J. Wertenbaker, *The Golden Age of Colonial Culture* (1942) is worth examination, as are also W. E. Dodd, *The Old South* (1937) and J. T. Adams, *Provincial Society, 1690–1763* (1927). See also M. Kraus, *The Atlantic Civilization* (1949) and C. L. Ver Steeg, *The Formative Years, 1607–1763* (1964).

Woman's status in colonial times is dealt with in A. W. Calhoun, *A Social History of the American Family, from Colonial Times to the Present* (3 vols., 1917–1919), vol. I, and A. M. Earle, *Colonial Dames and Goodwives* (1895) contains some interesting information, as does E. S. Morgan, *Virginians at Home* (1952) and Julia Spruill, *Women's Life and Work in the Southern Colonies* (1938).

One aspect of intellectual trends is examined in L. W. Labaree, *Conservatism in Early American History* (1948). S. E. Morison, *The Intellectual Life of Colonial New England* (1956) is spirited and informative.

Religious trends and developments are dealt with in W. W. Sweet, *Religion in Colonial America* (1942); E. S. Gaustad, *The Great Awakening in New England* (1957); W. M. Gewehr, *The Great Awakening in Virginia* (1930). Puritanism is analyzed in Perry Miller, *The New England Mind: the Seventeenth Century* (1939) and *The New England Mind: from Colony to Province* (1953). Mark Van Doren, ed., *Samuel Sewall's Diary* (1927) is an abridgment which gives a graphic picture of an outstanding Puritan leader. M. L. Starkey, *The Devil in Massachusetts* (1949) is a study of the Salem witchcraft episode. O. E. Winslow, *Jonathan Edwards* (1940) is a good biography of that remarkable divine.

T. J. Wertenbaker's *Torchbearer of the Revolution* (1940) and W. E. Washburn's *The Governor and the Rebel: a History of Bacon's Rebellion in Virginia* (1958) give quite different interpretations of the role of Nathaniel Bacon.

Bernard Bailyn, *Education in the Forming of American Society* (1960) examines colonial education. R. Hofstadter and W. P. Metzger, *The Development of Academic Freedom in the United States* (1955) examines that subject in the colonial as well as in other periods. Daniel J. Boorstin, *The Americans* (1958) emphasizes the utilitarian aspects of colonial life. For the roots of American nationalism, see Hans Kohn, *American Nationalism: an Interpretative Essay* (1957). Brook Hindle, *The Pursuit of Science in Revolutionary America, 1735–1789* (1956) is interesting and informative. On colonial medicine, see O. T. Beall, Jr. and R. H. Shyrock, *Cotton Mather, First Significant Figure in American Medicine* (1954), and John Duffy, *Epidemics in Colonial America* (1953).

5 ˒ Enemies Within and Without

THE ENGLISH COLONISTS in North America were faced by more problems than those involved in bringing European civilization across the Atlantic and establishing it in the wilderness. They had to face hostile opposition, first from the natives in the New World and then from England's Old World rivals, who were also interested in colonizing ventures. The first and, for the time being, most serious threat came from the American Indians.

The Indian Problem

No one knows how many Indians there were in the Atlantic coastline areas during the early seventeenth century. There were probably around 5,000 warriors in all New England, and perhaps as many more in the region that lay between New England and the Florida frontier—a total of between 25,000 and 30,000 red-skinned inhabitants.

The red man had a form of social organization that differed markedly from that of the white. Indian society was centered first about the clan, or family, and secondly in the tribe, which was composed of several clans. A variety of tribes were scattered along the eastern seaboard. A congeries of these tribes, speaking the same language and known as the Algonquin Indians, occupied the region from Virginia and Maryland to Maine and in some areas stretched west to the Mississippi. Another group, known as the Iroquois, lived on both sides of the St. Lawrence River, surrounded Lake Erie, and covered all central Pennsylvania and New York except for the lower Hudson.

The Indians along the Atlantic coastline planted some crops, especially corn, but they were still in the hunting stage of social organization. Though their customs varied, certain qualities and characteristics were common to all. They were sociable, emotional, virile, and—though not unintelligent— ignorant and superstitious. They were physically dirty and physically brave, apt to have a sense of humor, and prone to vanity. They practiced monogamy and loved their children. They held animistic beliefs, certain that magic powers existed in objects, animals, and even men and were anxious to establish harmonious relations with these powers. Their concept of justice was limited, being chiefly confined to taking revenge on those who inflicted what they considered a wrong. They held their lands as possessions of the clan and had no comprehension of the English system of private land ownership. This was a serious obstacle to good relations with the whites, particularly since the Indians were in possession of the land when the whites arrived.

The principal New England Indian tribes were the Penacooks, Massachusetts, Wampanoags, Narragansetts, Pequots, and Mohicans. The Indians in eastern Massachusetts at the time of the Puritans' arrival, having been decimated by a pestilence, were few and weak. At first they were helpful to

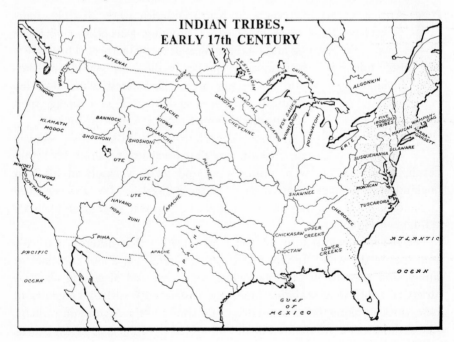

INDIAN TRIBES, EARLY 17th CENTURY

the newcomers, showing them where and how to plant and trapping and guiding for them. But as time went on there were some Indian, and undoubtedly some white, outrages. Furthermore, the Indians were certainly not God's chosen people, at least in Puritan eyes. By the middle 1630s, the magistrates and ministers of Massachusetts Bay colony decided upon a policy of an eye for an eye, and more where the red man was concerned. This meant that when Indian outrages occurred the Puritans put to death the men in the offending village and carried off the women and children to be sold into slavery. When this stern procedure was inflicted upon the Pequots, they promptly leagued with the Narragansetts for defense and offense. This ominous union was broken up by the intercession of Roger Williams with the latter tribe, a negotiation undertaken at the request of the Massachusetts officials who had banished him from their colony.

The Pequots undertook to revenge themselves on the whites singlehanded. The result was the Pequot War in 1637. The tribe was decimated, some 500 men, women, and children being roasted alive in a palisaded town, while the Puritan forces captured or shot down those who tried to escape. Those captured were sold into slavery, despite the pleas of Roger Williams. After this application of frightfulness, there was no more serious Indian warfare in New England for nearly forty years.

But during this peaceful period, relations between the Indians and the whites gradually deteriorated. More and more, the New Englanders obtained land by outright seizure or by the use of fines inflicted by their courts. More and more, the lands of the Indians came to be regarded as temporary reservations from which the red man could be removed to suit the white man's need. The Indians' friend, Roger Williams, declared that land had become "one of the gods of New England." Lust for land and conviction of the Indian's inferiority made the Puritans look upon him as an underling— a dependent, who had to be held under strict control. There were more and more laws forcing Indians to go to church, forbidding them to hunt on Sunday, and fining them as much as twelve days' labor for drunkenness.

The Indian sense of outrage deepened as these developments occurred. Massasoit, sachem of the Wampanoags and a determined friend of the whites, died in the winter of 1660–1661. His son Philip, the new sachem, was harshly dealt with for "disloyalty" by the Massachusetts authorities, who acted out of the conviction that they were dealing justly with him and with the Indians in general. Finally, in 1675, Philip and the Wampanoags took to the warpath and began looting and murdering along the frontier. The Narragansetts, and other tribes as well, were drawn into the struggle, and the scalping knife and tomahawk became symbols of dread throughout Plymouth, Massachusetts, and Connecticut. During this period of terror, Deerfield was burned and Springfield destroyed. Colonial forces captured the Narragansetts' principal fort in December, 1675, and hundreds of Indian men, women, and children were killed, but the war dragged on. The Indian cause, never very bright, was weakened by Philip's ineptitude as a leader and by the death of the able Narragansett sachem Canonchet. Philip was killed on August 12, 1676, and hostilities dwindled, coming to an end some two years later.

King Philip's War was a cruel affair. Many Indians, including Philip's wife and his nine-year-old son, were sold into slavery in the West Indies. Whites were fiendishly tortured and murdered in cold blood. The war was also very costly to the colonists. One out of every sixteen white men of military age in New England had been killed; at least twenty towns had been destroyed or abandoned; the whole frontier had been laid waste. Plymouth, Massachusetts, and Connecticut reported war expenditures of over £80,000. But the major Indian menace to the New England colonies was now a thing of the past. From this point on, the Indians of New England became a subsidiary factor in the great struggle for empire that developed between England and France.

Indian relations in the colonies outside of New England were of a mixed character. The Dutch, and later the English, fought with the tribes around Manhattan, and eventually the remnants of these tribes were dispossessed and forced to leave. On the other hand, the Dutch established with the powerful Iroquois confederacy relations that meant trade for the white man and firearms for the Indians. When the English took over New Amsterdam, they followed this same policy and sought to extend trade with the Indians further west, much to the annoyance of the French. The Quakers had good relations with the Susquehannas and the Delawares, due in part to Penn's fair dealing and in part to the fear these Indians had of the Iroquois. Further south, however, the relations of Indians and whites were anything but cordial.

The Indians in Virginia, usually known as the Powhatan confederacy, resented the colonists from the beginning, but the capture of Pocahontas, daughter of Chief Powhatan, and her subsequent marriage in 1614 to John Rolfe was followed by a peace that lasted for some eight years. Powhatan died in 1618 and his successor, Opechancanough, resented the continual white encroachments on lands that the Indians regarded as their own. In 1622, the Indians attacked the white settlements, killing 357 Virginians. The Virginians replied with fire and sword, and hostilities continued for three years, during which the Indian cornfields were systematically destroyed and their fighting strength greatly weakened. An uneasy twenty years of truce ensued. Then, in 1644, Opechancanough, old and blind, organized an attack in which 500 white settlers were massacred. Once again the red man's corn fields were laid waste and his warriors beaten in combat. Governor Berkeley's forces captured Opechancanough, but the governor's plan to send the chief to England as a present to King Charles I came to nought when the chief was shot by a revengeful soldier. Peace followed, the Indians acknowledging the sovereignty of the English king and ceding to the English all the tidewater lands that lay between the York and James rivers.

The peace that came with Opechancanough's demise lasted until 1676. Then the Susquehannas, forced south by the more warlike Senecas of the Iroquois confederacy, began raiding and murdering the settlers on the Virginia frontier. These attacks, coupled with Governor Berkeley's determination to trust in forts and friendly Indians to stop the depredations, were factors in Bacon's Rebellion. Once more the Indians were severely chastised, even though in the process Bacon found himself fighting with the governor as well. The weakened tribes of the Powhatan confederacy fell further back into the wilderness as the process of expulsion and extermination went on its way.

Indian troubles were by no means unknown in the areas south of Virginia. In 1711, a new Swiss settlement in North Carolina excited the jealousy of the Tuscaroras. Hostilities broke out and lasted for about two years, Virginia and South Carolina giving assistance to the North Carolinians. Many of the Tuscaroras were captured or killed; the remainder fled to New York, where they became the sixth tribe in the Iroquois confederacy. As warfare with the Tuscaroras died down, bad treatment by English traders and some Spanish instigation induced the Yemassee Indians in South Carolina to take up arms. Several hundred settlers were killed before South Carolina, aided by North Carolina and Virginia, put down the revolt.

Colonial Indian relations followed a general pattern. As the white settlers increased in numbers, difficulties multiplied. Sometimes these were disposed of peacefully, the Indians yielding before superior strength, or the whites assuming a diplomatic role where, as in the case of the Iroquois, the Indians were strong. In the last analysis, the Indian faced one of three fates: he was exterminated, sold into slavery, or eventually forced to move back into the wilderness as the whites took triumphant possession of his lands. And with regrettable frequency he was debauched and degraded in the process by the white man's liquor and the white man's diseases, to both of which he was peculiarly susceptible.

The Indian story was not altogether one of conflict, cruelty, and injustice. Some Indians learned to live on amicable terms with the whites. Some were converted to Christianity. Some white captives, women and children, became accustomed to life in an Indian village and refused to return to white civilization. But peaceful coexistence of the two races was probably impossible, all circumstances considered, and it would be difficult to argue that the march of civilization would have been better served if the Indians had been left in undisturbed possession of what is now the United States. The record of Indian-white relations in colonial times remains a tragic story.

The Struggle for Empire— Holland's Brief Role

Indians were not the only enemies of the British colonists in North America. There was bad feeling between the Spaniards in Florida and the colonists to the north. English claims to territory on the North Atlantic seaboard overlapped those of the Dutch and the French, which was a source of friction from the beginning of the settlements. In 1613, at the request of the governor of Virginia, Captain Samuel Argall raided Acadia, destroying Port Royal and all other settlements there. Other raids followed, the French in return harrying the English and colonial fisheries. No love was lost between the English and the French colonists from the beginning. The same could be said about the English and the Dutch, for the New Englanders pressed in on New Amsterdam, taking possession of lands on the Connecticut and Delaware rivers and on Long Island that the Dutch claimed as their own. These events were the North American harbingers of the great struggle for empire between England, France, and Holland, a struggle into which the English colonies were drawn as irresistibly as if it were some vast whirlpool.

For the colonies were, at the beginning, pawns in the game that started when the New World and the new sea lanes to the East were opened up. Gradually nations of western Europe became seapower conscious. Richelieu, Louis XIII's great minister, started a French navy in the 1630s. The Dutch, impelled by their desperate struggle for independence from Spain, had begun to build a navy even earlier. In the first half of the seventeenth century, Holland was the greatest sea power in Europe, for Spain's control of the oceans had vanished with the destruction of the Armada in 1588. The threat to English security posed by the Dutch and the French led Cromwell's government to begin an English navy and to war with Holland. This same policy, continued under Charles II, brought the capture of New Amsterdam in 1664 and, together with French attacks upon Holland, fatally weakened Dutch power.

Colonial Background of the Second Hundred Years War

While Holland, attacked on both land and sea, was wasting itself in futile efforts to maintain its world position, France had been expanding on the North American continent. Spurred on by the lure of adventure, the profits of the fur trade, and the desire of the Jesuits and Sulpicians to christianize the natives, priests, explorers and traders pushed out along the Great Lakes and down the Mississippi. Louis Jolliet, Father Marquette, and Greysolon Duluth opened up Wisconsin to the efforts of the missionaries and to trade. Father Hennepin explored the upper reaches of the Mississippi. Pierre Gaultier de la Verendrye and others reached the Rocky Mountains. The proud and haughty Robert Cavelier, Sieur de la Salle, a man of driving determination, explored the Ohio River and pushed down the Mississippi to its mouth. There, on April 9, 1682, contemptuous of Spanish claims, he proclaimed Louisiana and the whole Mississippi basin possessions of Louis XIV. The government of New France under the leadership of resolute men like Jean Talon and Louis de Buade, Comte de Frontenac, established forts at strategic points from Lake Ontario to the Gulf of Mexico. French traders and even a few French settlers pushed into the West.

While New France extended its hold on the North American continent, Louis XIV set all Europe in turmoil. His warfare with the Dutch alarmed the English, for the French King was driving toward the Channel ports, thus threatening English trade routes and even raising the specter of invasion that Philip of Spain had raised a century before. When the Sun King undertook to extend his territories to the Rhine in the 1680s, most of Europe leagued against him; and England—where his sworn foe, William of Orange, became King after the Glorious Revolution of 1688—joined the fight. This automatically brought the French and the English colonies into the struggle. It was North America's first taste of world war and the beginning of what has sometimes been called the Second Hundred Years War. In the colonies the succeeding aspects of this struggle were known as King William's War (1689–1697), Queen Anne's War (1701–1713), King George's War (1740–1748), and the Seven Years War or the French and Indian War (1756–1763).

King William's War (1689–1697)

The French had elaborate plans, approved by Louis himself, for driving the English out of America, and an overland expedition was organized at

HUDSON   BAY   COMPANY

Ft. La Tourette

L. SUPERIOR

Ft.
Radisson

St. Ignace

Xavier

L. MICHIGAN   L. HURON

Ft. St. Joseph

Ft. Crèvecour

L. ERIE

Ft. Prudhomme

Ft. Arkansas

LOUISIANA

N E W   F R A N C E

Quebec

Montreal

Ft. Frontenac

L. ONTARIO

MISSOURI

OHIO

NEW-
FOUNDLAND
(BR)

A C A D I A

Port Royal

MAINE
(MASS.)

NEW YORK   N.H.   Portland

MASS.   Boston

CONN.

R.I.

PA.   New York

N.J.

MD.   DELA.

VIRGINIA

ROANOKE I.

N.C.

S.C.

GA.

Charleston

THE THIRTEEN COLONIES

A T L A N T I C   O C E A N

FLORIDA
(SP)   St. Augustine

G U L F
O F
M E X I C O

ENGLISH
POSSESSIONS

FRENCH
POSSESSIONS

SPANISH
POSSESSIONS

EASTERN
NORTH
AMERICA
1690

500 MILES

Havana

B A H A M A S
(BR)

YUCATAN
(SP)

CUBA
(SP)

JAMAICA
(BR)

HAITI
(FR)

SANTO
DOMINGO
(SP)

PUERTO
RICO
(SP)

ST. CROIX
(FR)

ST. MARTIN
(FR)

ANTIGUA
(FR)

GUADELOUPE
(FR)

DOMINICA
(FR)

MARTINIQUE
(FR)

ST. LUCIA
(FR)

ST. VINCENT
(FR)

GRENADA
(FR)

BARBADOS
(BR)

TOBAGO
(BR)

TRINIDAD

CURAÇAO (NETH.)

HONDURAS
(SP)

C A R I B B E A N   S E A

Puerto Bello

Cartagena

Caracas

Panama

NEW GRANADA   CARACAS

TRM

110

Quebec to capture New York. Help from France failed, however, and the plan fell through. The New Englanders, for their part, sought to destroy that haunt of French privateers, Port Royal, and hoped to seize Quebec. Port Royal was taken in 1690 and held for a year, but a New York plan to invade Canada by land petered out, and Frontenac held Quebec against the weak efforts of Sir William Phips, who had made his way up the St. Lawrence with a fleet of thirty-one sails. Thereafter the English were unable to use their superiority at sea to any good advantage, and the war, so far as the colonials were concerned, became a series of raids by the French and Indians, who spread death and terror along the New England frontier. The Peace of Ryswick (1697) restored the status quo in the New World, and accomplished practically the same thing in Europe.

A breathing space of five years followed the Peace of Ryswick. Then the witless Spanish King, Charles II, willed his throne to the Duke of Anjou, grandson of Louis XIV. It was promptly accepted for the boy by the Sun King, who began occupying the Spanish Netherlands and recognized the Stuart Pretender to the English throne as "James III." Louis also took over control of the Asiento and prepared to freeze the English out of trading privileges they had acquired in the Spanish empire. France was obviously moving in on the rich Spanish-American trade. In the face of these menacing events, England promptly joined Holland and Austria in an alliance against France, and the War of the Spanish Succession began. It lasted for twelve years, from 1701 to 1713.

Queen Anne's War (1701–1713)

In the North American theatre, this war resolved itself mainly into a series of hit-and-run expeditions by the opposing forces. English settlements in Newfoundland were pillaged, and the principal town, St. John's, was captured in 1708 by the French. The French and Indians harried New England, Deerfield was captured and burned, and Haverhill attacked. Almost every hamlet on the Massachusetts and New Hampshire frontiers was raided, and the colonists, striving desperately to fend off these attacks by means of militia cordons and the offer of rewards for scalps, found defense so difficult that it cost close to £1,000 in colonial currency to kill an Indian. Meanwhile, New York remained deaf to New England's cry for help, and Boston merchants, regardless of frontier horrors, vigorously traded food and arms for the beaver skins of the French Acadians. The one bright feature of the war was that in 1710, after several futile and humiliating attempts, a British naval force aided by colonial military contingents succeeded in capturing

Port Royal, Nova Scotia, thus destroying a nest of French privateers and opening the way for an attack on Quebec.

Before the capture of Port Royal, the British government had been reluctant to weaken the home fleet for the sake of colonial operations. But by 1709, the French fleet was no longer formidable, and the English Tory government, jealous of Marlborough's victories on the European continent, saw in an operation against Quebec a means of dimming the great general's popularity. Seven of his best regiments were taken for the expedition, and a powerful squadron was assembled, including some eighty-gun ships of the line. The colonial governments of New England, New York, New Jersey, and Pennsylvania somewhat tardily organized support for the British force and assembled, under Colonel Francis Nicholson, a land expedition for the conquest of Montreal.

The British squadron, under the command of the amiable but incompetent Sir Hovenden Walker, reached Boston in June, 1711, with 5,000 British regulars, who were subject to the orders of the equally incompetent Brigadier Jack Hill. Bungling and procrastination ensued; furthermore, the colonials found the British regulars offensive. Prices for supplies mounted to exorbitant heights as the thrifty New Englanders sought to make money out of the expedition. Finally, in the late summer, the fleet sailed from Boston, its military force augmented by nearly 1,500 colonials. Nicholson, with 2,300 colonial militia and Indians, started overland from Albany for Montreal.

The rest was tragedy and farce. Incompetently officered, without good pilotage, eight transports and a sloop piled upon the rocks not far from Gaspé, and nearly 1,000 men were lost. The attempt to reach Quebec by water was then abandoned, and there was nothing for Nicholson to do but to return in rage and humiliation to Albany, where he disbanded his little army. No further attack was made upon Quebec during the remainder of the war.

The War of the Spanish Succession ended with the Peace of Utrecht in 1713. England was intent upon concessions that would bolster its growing world trade, and France, weary and defeated, had to accept the terms offered. France agreed to dismantle the fortifications and fill up the harbor of Dunkirk, across the Channel from England. It was also agreed that the crowns of France and Spain should never rest upon the same head. Britain took Gibraltar and the island of Minorca from Spain, thus achieving naval supremacy in the Mediterranean. Britain also wrested from Spain the Asiento, in this way gaining a thirty-year monopoly on the slave trade in South America, and obtained other trading privileges as well. In the New World, the British gained Newfoundland, Nova Scotia (which included Port

Royal), and Hudson's Bay. The breakup of the French empire in Canada had begun.

The War of the Spanish Succession demonstrated the growth of British power, but it was significant in other ways as well. It showed that cooperation between the colonials and Great Britain in a joint military effort was difficult but possible. It demonstrated the lack of any sense of union among the thirteen colonies and the ease with which, even in wartime, colonial merchants could place profits above patriotism. It also showed that England regarded colonial interests as distinctly secondary to those that were closer to home. While the British navy did provide some escorts for the carrying trade in the North Atlantic and two fleet concentrations toward the close of the war, its principal theatre of operations was in the Mediterranean. London obviously viewed the interests of New England as being of small account.

King George's War (1740–1748)

After Utrecht, a generation of peace, save for Indian troubles, settled upon North America, but the steady expansion of international trade and the increase of commercial rivalries set the stage for the next conflict. The Family Compact of 1733 between the Bourbons of France and Spain allied those countries in an effort to curb British power. Spain bound itself to take away from Britain the trading privileges in the Americas given at Utrecht. France promised Spain aid in recovering Gibraltar. Britain feared that the resurgence of French trade and commerce menaced its own commercial future, and viewed askance the expansion of French interest in the East and West Indies, the Newfoundland fisheries, and the Canadian fur trade. All the principal statesmen of the eighteenth century felt that control of world commerce was essential to the stability of empire, and that colonies were essential parts of any commercial pattern. The so-called War of Jenkins' Ear between England and Spain began in 1739 out of commercial rivalries between the two countries. By 1744, it had merged into the war between England and France, known in the colonies as King George's War. This broke out in part over a quarrel as to who should succeed to the Austrian throne, a question that involved the balance of power on the European continent, but its origins also lay in commercial and colonial rivalries.

The English colonies in America were inevitably entangled in this international struggle for commercial empire. War or peace, so far as they were concerned, depended in considerable measure upon decisions made at Paris or London, but the fervor with which war was made in colonial quarters also depended, at least to a large extent, upon the colonists' sense of injury, or upon their belief that there was an advantage to be gained. And the New England colonists certainly had a mounting sense of grievance against the French.

French-inspired Indian raids had by no means ceased at the close of Queen Anne's war. The Maine Abenaki Indians, inspired by the Jesuit Father Râle and angered by the swift increase of New England settlers in Maine harassed the New England villages. Other raids were perpetrated by the Micmacs from Acadia, and the enraged New England governments did not hesitate to pay £100 for an Indian scalp. France had lost Port Royal, but French privateers and semipirates had continued their robbing and destroying tactics in Newfoundland and all along the New England coast. New England merchants were angered by their losses and were anxious to diminish competition in the fisheries and the fur trade. They also looked fearfully toward the new French stronghold of Louisbourg on Cape Breton Island, which the French had established as their naval outpost for Canada after the loss of Port Royal. It would be all too easy for a French fleet to come down from Louisbourg on Boston. The New Englanders were therefore easily aroused to hostile action against French Canada. Their attention centered upon Louisbourg, which, according to reliable reports, was highly vulnerable.

The governor of Massachusetts at this time was William Shirley, an able man, astute, tactful, and possessed of vision. He believed Nova Scotia to be the key to British power in North America. Shirley was a close friend of the powerful Duke of Newcastle, with whose assistance he urged the importance of an expedition against Louisbourg. The British government hesitated, for the French under Marshal Saxe were winning victory after victory on the European continent, even occupying Ostend, Britain's potential base for any invasion of Europe. Shirley succeeded in organizing a colonial expedition that had the support of New Hampshire and Connecticut and, to a limited extent, of Rhode Island as well. New York, New Jersey, and Pennsylvania, importuned for assistance, gave some needed financial support, but that was all. Britain, on receiving the news that this project was afoot, finally sent a fleet to support the colonial militia. The latter were under the command of William Pepperell, a firm and tactful Maine merchant who had some military background as a militia colonel.

The expedition against Louisbourg was a success. Pepperell's army of some 4,000 fishermen and farmers showed both courage and determination. On June 16, 1745, after a siege of forty-seven days, it captured a fortress garrisoned by 1,300 men and built according to the best engineering principles of the day. It was a victory that put England in control of the French fisheries, deprived France of its one naval bastion in North America, and opened the way to Quebec.

The colonists felt constant anxiety about a French counterstroke, but at the end of the war France had been unable to recapture either Port Royal or Louisbourg. France had won victories on the European continent, however, and at Aix-la-Chapelle (October 18, 1748), in a reciprocal surrender of conquests that dislodged the French from the Low Countries across the English Channel, Louisbourg was given back to its former masters. It was, perhaps, a fair exchange, but with the New England colonials who had spent their blood and treasure on the Louisbourg expedition it was not a popular peace. England, they felt, was altogether too willing to yield gains in America for European equivalents.

Colonial Background of the Seven Years War

During the uneasy years of truce that followed the close of the War of the Austrian Succession, England built up Halifax, the best port in Nova Scotia, as a fortress and naval base and sent settlers there at the cost of the British government. This was done, at least in part, to placate the New Englanders for the abandonment of Louisbourg. It was a move little relished by France.

Both France and England claimed all the territory east of the Mississippi, but their methods of implementing the claims were essentially different. France accepted only Frenchmen in Canada; the traders who came outnumbered the settlers, and French occupancy, easily stretched out by means of canoe transport along the lakes and rivers, established only a tenuous hold upon the country. The English welcomed people of all nationalities, and the large numbers that responded came for the purpose of settlement. In contrast to French expansion, that of the English colonies was much more in the nature of a compact mass, building roads and holding with power what it advanced to seize. By 1750, New France had less than 100,000 white men in all the vast territory it claimed, while the English settlers numbered close to two million.

And by the 1750s the French, with growing alarm, saw the English advance as an ever-increasing menace. New England and New York were pressing their frontiers ever closer to Canada. Pennsylvania and Virginia were expanding westward toward lands on the Ohio that France claimed and was resolved to hold. In 1749, the Ohio Company, a band of Virginia speculators, received from King George II the grant of 200,000 acres beyond the Alleghenies and the promise of 300,000 acres more.

The French were alarmed, but not dismayed. The restoration of Louis-bourg stimulated their aggressive spirit. In the same year that the Ohio Company obtained its grant, a French expedition to the Ohio formally claimed the basin of that river in the name of Louis XV and told the Indians that the advancing English were no better than robbers. The French built a string of forts in the Ohio country and took steps to drive the English from Oswego and central New York, their efforts there being countered by Sir William Johnson, a trusted friend of the Iroquois, who was in charge of a great tract of land in the Mohawk Valley.

The Marquis de Duquesne became governor of New France in 1752, with orders to drive the English from the Ohio. Duquesne was a strict disciplinarian who commanded respect by his drive and efficiency, and under his direction the French assumed the aggressive in the Ohio region. They wooed the Indians, spurred them on to massacre the English frontier settlers, and ejected those who escaped the tomahawk.

Virginia claimed the lands in the Ohio Valley, and the lieutenant-governor of Virginia, Robert Dinwiddie, who ran the province in the name of the absentee governor, began mustering the colony's militia and sent a young surveyor and major in a Virginia militia regiment out into the West with orders for the French to leave. George Washington, then twenty-one years old, made his way to Fort Le Boeuf on French Creek, a tributary of the Allegheny River. He reached it in December, 1753, and delivered his message. The French listened and refused the command, and Washington reported their determination to drive the English out of the whole western country.

Dinwiddie now redoubled his efforts to raise troops and strove, without much success, to arouse the other colonies. The Virginians started a fort where the Monongahela and the Allegheny join to form the Ohio. It was seized by the French, completed, and called Fort Duquesne.

Again Washington was sent into the West, this time with the Virginia regiment. His instructions were to relieve the English in the contested fort. He never reached it, but met the French near a place called Great Meadows close by the Youghiogheny River. He acted like a man determined to attack, and the French gave small evidence of having come out simply to warn him to go back to Jamestown. Each side later claimed that the other had fired the first shot. When the "charming" sound of bullets, as Washington put it, had ceased, ten Frenchmen and one Englishman had been killed, and the French and Indian War had begun.

The immediate sequel to this skirmish was anything but "charming." Washington threw up entrenchments at what he called Fort Necessity, in the

Great Meadows. There the French attacked him in overwhelming force. On July 3, 1754, he surrendered, being allowed to march out with the honors of war but agreeing to retire from the Ohio region. He and his little force returned to Virginia on foot, and the western Indians started going over to the French in droves. The alarm that thinking men in the colonies felt was symbolized by the cartoon in Franklin's *Gazette* of a snake divided into thirteen pieces, captioned "Join or Die." But the Albany Congress, held that summer, with representatives present from seven colonies, produced no positive results.

Both Britain and France held that a state of war existed in America, and each blamed the other for the situation. Great Britain authorized military operations in America and ordered the British fleet to attack French ships bound for the general area of operations. When, in 1755, France sent a fleet and 3,000 men to Canada, they were intercepted on the high seas, and, although the convoy managed to reach Canada, two French men-of-war were captured. The British, too, were girding for the fray, and 1,500 regulars were sent to Virginia under the command of Major-General Edward Braddock, with orders to capture Fort Duquesne.

The commander of this British force was short, stout, and sixty years of age. He was also hot-tempered, profane, a martinet, and contemptuous of the colonial militia and of colonials in general. He reached Virginia in February, 1755, eager for action. Week followed week, and Braddock became increasingly impatient with the lack of colonial cooperation, especially the high prices charged for supplies and the slowness with which they were gathered. But at length, in May, he set out across the mountains with his 1,500 regulars and 450 Virginia militia.

Braddock's force met the French and Indians some seven miles from Fort Duquesne. It was not a style of fighting to which the British regulars were accustomed. The main body of the French attacked in the open. The Indians, whooping and yelling, fired with deadly effect from behind trees and tufts of grass. Some of the colonials used Indian tactics, but Braddock held the main body of his troops in mass formation. They huddled blindly together, firing at random and often shooting their own men. The slaughter ended with Braddock mortally wounded and two-thirds of the British regulars either killed or wounded. The expedition against Fort Duquesne had been destroyed. George Washington took a major part in leading its remnants back to the seaboard and safety.

Braddock's defeat overshadowed the other events of the war in 1755, but these were far from insignificant. A French invasion down the Lake Champlain route was thrown back. The English hold on Acadia was also strength-

THE BRADDOCK EXPEDITION

The solid ranks of infantrymen were an easy prey for ambush. Note the Indian scout lurking in the left foreground.

ened, and a start was made in the forcible removal of from 6,000 to 10,000 Acadians from their homeland. As a war measure, they were scattered among the English colonies, a sad and tragic business that later furnished the inspiration for Henry Wadsworth Longfellow's poem *Evangeline*.

The Seven Years War (1756–1763)

These events had taken place without a declaration of war on either side. At last, on May 18, 1756, Britain declared war against France. By that time, the famous Reversal of Alliances had taken place. In the war of the Austrian Succession, Prussia and France had fought against England and Austria. Now for a variety of reasons, some legitimate and some contemptible, the British were leagued with Frederick the Great of Prussia, and France, Austria, and Russia were committed to crushing Frederick the Great and partitioning his dominions. But as always in the Second Hundred Years War, which in its worldwide aspects was a duel for empire, the fighting found England and France on opposite sides.

The French and Indian War, or the Seven Years War as it was called in

Europe, had opened inauspiciously for the British, and the French continued to hold the upper hand during the next two years. A French fleet seized Minorca. French reinforcements reached America, and the cultured and able Marquis de Montcalm was put in charge of French military operations in the American sphere. Montcalm reached Canada in the spring of 1756 and proceeded to win some brilliant military successes.

The French captured Oswego in the summer of 1756. This was a major achievement, although it did alarm the Iroquois and lead them to make a firm alliance with the English. Other Indians, however, flocked to Montcalm's camp, and the New England frontier, again beset by raiding parties, became a place of terror. In 1757, Montcalm moved down Lake Champlain and captured Fort William Henry, on Lake George, together with its garrison of 2,000 men. A year later, with 3,000 men, he held Fort Ticonderoga, between Lake George and Lake Champlain, against 16,000 British regulars and colonials. Europe rang with his praises.

But, despite Montcalm's victories, a change had become apparent by 1758 in the fortunes of this great world struggle. William Pitt the elder (1708–1778)—the "Organizer of Victory"—and the so-called Great Ministry of which he was the guiding genius came into power in July, 1757. Arrogant and proud, Pitt was also vigorous, eloquent, honest, a fine administrator, and a devoted English patriot. The tide of world battle had already begun to turn, for over in India, Clive, in January, 1757, had beaten the French at Plassey and then won Bengal. Pitt accelerated the tide. As Secretary of State for War, he gave heavy subsidies to Prussia, and these, together with Frederick the Great's military genius enabled the Prussian king to move with vigor against the French on the European continent. Pitt also gave the English army a new spirit by weeding out incompetents and threatening even high officers with impeachment, and he was quick to discover and promote military talent. He gave Geoffrey Amherst the chief military command in America; Amherst, though slow and careful to a fault, was a splendid organizer and brought regulars and colonials into harmony.

In 1757, Pitt's attention was also attracted to a young quartermaster-general who was showing great energy and initiative—James Wolfe (1727–1759). Wolfe came of a military family. At sixteen he was a veteran with fighting experience. At twenty-two, he was a lieutenant-colonel who read poetry and philosophy as well as works on the art of war. Highly emotional, proud, burning with desire to achieve some great deed, he was also popular with his men. Like most of the British regulars, he was contemptuous of the colonial militia, but he tried to treat everyone fairly, down to the lowest subaltern.

Pitt made America a scene of major operations in the Seven Years War. He planned in 1758 to send 7,000 men, commanded by Brigadier General Forbes, against Fort Duquesne and a fleet and 14,000 regulars to take Louisbourg and then Quebec. The ill-fated expedition against Fort Ticonderoga that Montcalm turned back was to have been the third arm of a three-pronged attack designed to wipe out French power in America.

The rebuff at Fort Ticonderoga delayed the attack on Quebec and Montreal in 1758, but all was not lost in that year. Oswego was recaptured in August, and with it military stores intended for Fort Duquesne. On November 25, 1758, the French at Fort Duquesne, lacking supplies and confronted by Forbes' carefully organized force, blew up that stronghold and retired to the West. The fort and the tiny settlement around it were renamed Pittsburgh by the victorious English. Meanwhile on July 27, 1758, Louisbourg, along with 6,000 men, had fallen. Since Wolfe had played a prominent part in this victory, Pitt put him in command of the army that was ordered to storm Quebec in 1759.

As the spring of 1759 came on, Amherst with 11,500 men was ordered to advance on Montreal by way of Lake Champlain, and a fleet of 250 ships with 8,500 British regulars and 17,000 sailors and marines moved on Quebec. The fleet safely negotiated the treacherous tides and shoals of the St. Lawrence and on June 26 the troops began disembarking on the island of Orleans, just below the city. Wolfe had started on his last glorious campaign.

Quebec was an almost impregnable fortress, protected on every side by natural obstacles. The mile-wide river, with its swift currents and strong tides, together with the steep cliffs that guarded the city, made storming an almost impossible operation. Wolfe occupied the island of Orleans and the cliffs on the opposite shore from the city. He raided the countryside on both sides of the river below Quebec, and the guns of the fleet bombarded the citadel, spreading death and destruction in the town. The fleet guarded itself against the storms that swept the river and fended off the fire rafts that were sent down upon it. But Montcalm's defensive strategy was excellent, and weeks went by before the proper opportunity for assault presented itself.

On July 31, an effort to land in force east of the city ended in dismal failure and the loss of between 400 and 500 men. The French were overjoyed and the British dismayed. Fort Niagara fell into British hands, but this did not weaken Montcalm's position at Quebec; and Amherst, always slow and methodical in his movements, was giving Wolfe no aid. While the summer was moving toward its close, the best that the British could do was to continue the bombardment of the city and the ravaging of the countryside.

"DEATH OF GENERAL WOLFE"—PAINTED BY BENJAMIN WEST (1771)

Wolfe and Montcalm died in the same battle on the Plains of Abraham. Both were able leaders, but one had gained and the other lost an empire.

At length a way was discovered to reach the heights above Quebec. A narrow, winding road, not strongly guarded, led up the cliffs, about a mile and a half to the west of the city to a plateau called the Plains of Abraham. Near this road was a path, steep and difficult. On the night of September 12, twenty-four volunteers worked their way up this path. They surprised and overpowered the guard at the top of the road, which was then cleared. Men and a few field pieces were brought up and by eight o'clock on the morning of September 13, 1759, some 4,500 British troops were drawn up on the Plains of Abraham, within a mile of Quebec.

Fortune now continued to favor the British. Montcalm rushed troops to meet them, but his orders for reinforcements were countermanded by the Marquis de Vaudreuil, governor of the province, who regarded himself as a strategist and tactician superior to Montcalm. Vaudreuil and the men under his own command did not move, though they were almost within sight of the battle. Field guns that Montcalm asked for were refused by the commandant of the city. Montcalm also acted precipitately in offering battle with only 4,000 men, when a short delay would have enabled him to gather a force that would have far outnumbered the British. Montcalm ordered the force that he had assembled to charge, but the charge broke before a devastating British fire and countercharge. The French then retreated in disorder. In the melee, both commanders fell, mortally wounded. Five days later, Quebec surrendered.

The fall of Quebec was not the last French disaster in 1759. France had made desperate preparations for the invasion of England, but, two months after Quebec was taken, Admiral Hawke destroyed the French fleet that had been assembled in Quiberon Bay to transport the French army across the English Channel. England was on the verge of victory over its great rival.

During the next year, the English closed in on Canada. Amherst was at Lake Champlain, threatening Montreal, and marched another force to Oswego on Lake Erie. A last French attempt to send a naval squadron to the rescue of its Canadian forces ended in disaster. Montreal surrendered on September 8, 1760, and with it the remnants of the army of Montcalm. Canada was no longer in French hands.

The war in Europe and on the sea continued, but in those theatres also the tide ran in favor of England and Prussia. The English navy won victory after victory, and on the continent the alliance against Frederick the Great fell apart.

Pitt wanted to go on fighting until France was prostrate, but George II, the great minister's supporter, died in 1760. King George III was determined on peace, and the heavy expenditures resulting from Pitt's massive war efforts were potent arguments in favor of ending hostilities. Pitt resigned (October 5, 1761) because his colleagues would not support him in declaring war against Spain, which had concluded a new Family Compact with France. When negotiations with Spain failed, war was declared against that country in January, 1762, but at the same time England began to turn toward peace.

The Peace of Paris (1763)

The articles of a general pacification were signed early in 1763, that between England and France being called the Peace of Paris (February 10, 1763). Britain returned to France the rich sugar islands of Guadeloupe and Martinique, together with fishing rights and the small islands of St. Pierre and Miquelon off Newfoundland. Havana, which had been taken from Spain, was given back to that country, but in exchange Spain ceded Florida

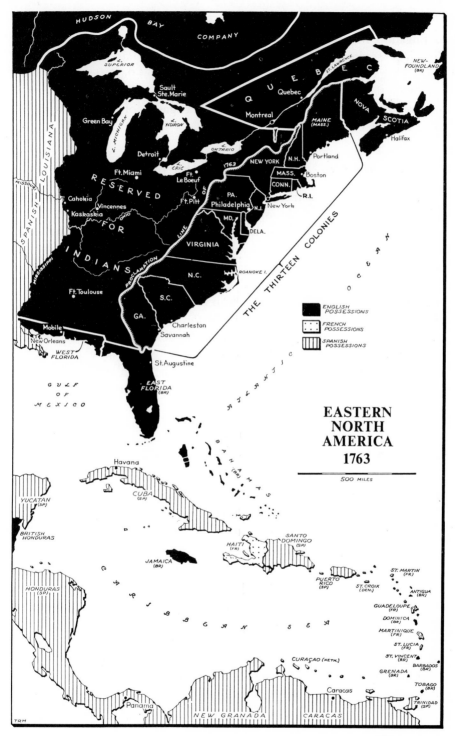

HUDSON BAY COMPANY

L. SUPERIOR

Sault
Ste. Marie

Green Bay

L. MICHIGAN

L. HURON

Detroit

L. ERIE

Ft. Miami

R E S E R V E D

Cahokia

Vincennes

Kaskaskia

F O R

Ft. Pitt

OHIO

I N D I A N S

Ft. Toulouse

SPANISH — LOUISIANA

MISSOURI

MISSISSIPPI

Mobile

New Orleans

WEST
FLORIDA

L. ONTARIO

1763

Ft.
Le Boeuf

PROCLAMATION

LINE

OF

QUEBEC

ST. LAWRENCE

Quebec

Montreal

MAINE
(MASS.)

NOVA SCOTIA

NEW-
FOUNDLAND
(BR.)

Halifax

Portland

N.H.

NEW YORK

MASS.

CONN.

Boston

R.I.

PA.

Philadelphia

N.J.

New York

MD.

DELA.

VIRGINIA

N.C.

ROANOKE I.

S.C.

GA.

Charleston

Savannah

St. Augustine

THE THIRTEEN COLONIES

ATLANTIC OCEAN

GULF
OF
MEXICO

EAST
FLORIDA
(BR.)

ATLANTIC OCEAN

ENGLISH
POSSESSIONS

FRENCH
POSSESSIONS

SPANISH
POSSESSIONS

Havana

BAHAMAS
(BR.)

**EASTERN
NORTH
AMERICA
1763**

500 MILES

YUCATAN
(SP.)

CUBA
(SP.)

BRITISH
HONDURAS

HAITI
(FR.)

SANTO
DOMINGO
(SP.)

ST. MARTIN
(FR.)

JAMAICA
(BR.)

PUERTO
RICO
(SP.)

ST. CROIX
(DEN.)

ANTIGUA
(BR.)

HONDURAS
(SP.)

GUADELOUPE
(BR.)

DOMINICA
(BR.)

MARTINIQUE
(FR.)

ST. LUCIA
(FR.)

CURAÇAO (NETH.)

ST. VINCENT
(BR.)

BARBADOS
(BR.)

GRENADA
(BR.)

TOBAGO
(BR.)

Caracas

TRINIDAD
(SP.)

Panama

NEW GRANADA

CARACAS

CARIBBEAN SEA

TRM

123

to England. France yielded Canada to England, together with all other French possessions east of the Mississippi. France retained Louisiana, but Louis XV gave it to Spain in recompense for the losses the latter had suffered in making the Family Compact. This open-handed generosity of the French monarch has few parallels in history. The navigation of the Mississippi was to be free for both England and Spain.

Significance of a Century of Warfare

The Peace of Paris marked the end of an epoch in the history of Great Britain, for by it the British government chose the path of empire. Britain had destroyed French power in India, and in the ensuing years English influence reigned supreme in that vast area. England was dominant on the North American continent. There had been some talk in Britain of taking the French sugar islands and returning New France to Louis XV. "Some are for keeping Canada; some Guadeloupe; who will tell me which I shall be hanged for not keeping," William Pitt had asked the House of Commons while he was still in power. Pitt had declared that the destruction of French power in North America was the great aim of the war. Not to have kept Canada would have provoked an explosion of wrath in the colonies far greater than that which had flamed up over the return of Louisbourg to the French in 1748. And Canada, like India, meant empire.

The enlargement of the British imperial domain by the conquest of Canada had great significance for the thirteen colonies. It meant that they were now free from the French menace on their northern borders. Their expanding economy, with its insatiable thirst for land was also free, or so it seemed, to push into the areas beyond the Alleghenies. But the raising of the Union Jack in Canada and the West was to produce problems that were not evident in 1763 to either the government in London or the colonists in North America.

Suggested Reading

For the red man and his relations with the colonists, the following books offer important material: C. T. Foreman, *Indians Abroad, 1493–1938* (1943); Clark Wissler, *The American Indian* (rev. ed., 1938); R. M. Underhill, *Red Man's America: A History of Indians in the United States* (1953); R. H. Pearce, *The Savages of America:*

A Study of the Indians and the Idea of Civilization (1953); and Paul Radin, *The Story of the American Indian* (1957).

H. H. Peckham, *The Colonial Wars, 1689–1762* (1964) is excellent.

British imperial policy in the struggle for empire is examined in L. H. Gipson, *The British Empire Before the American Revolution,* previously cited, vols. VII and VIII. Important also is G. M. Wrong, *The Rise and Fall of New France* (2 vols., 1928), and a brilliant interpretation of this great clash between the Powers is to be found in Francis Parkman, *A Half Century of Conflict* (2 vols., 1910). Useful also is John Tebbel, ed., *The Battle for North America* (1948), which is an abridgment of Parkman's *France and England in North America.* Background for the culminating phases of the American conflict is furnished in W. L. Dorn's *Competition for Empire, 1740–1763* (1940) and A. T. Mahan's *The Influence of Sea Power Upon History, 1660–1783* (1894).

Some special studies and biographies give valuable information on the Anglo-American push into the territories claimed by France. The student should consult A. T. Volwiler, *George Croghan and the Westward Movement, 1741–1782* (1926); C. A. Vandiveer, *The Fur Trade and Early Western Exploration* (1929); and J. E. Bakeless, *Daniel Boone, Master of the Wilderness* (1955). O. A. Sherrard, *Lord Chatham* (3 vols., 1952–1958) is excellent. On Washington's role, see D. S. Freeman, *George Washington* (7 vols., 1948–1957), vols. I and II, and C. H. Ambler, *George Washington and the West* (1936).

6 ⋅ The Break with Britain

THE SEVEN YEARS WAR and its victorious conclusion in 1763 created a series of financial and political problems for England and the thirteen colonies. The appearance of these problems at a time when the practice of self-government and a marked degree of economic maturity had become firmly established in the colonies further complicated the situation.

A Clash of Viewpoints

This conjunction of circumstances produced one crisis after another in the relations of the colonies with the British government.

One difference of viewpoint between England and the colonies was the direct consequence of the magnificent territorial gains that had come at the end of the war. Britain was bound to think about the administration of Canada and the region west of the Alleghenies as an imperial problem—one in which the interests of the Indians, the colonials, the British merchants and fur traders and, indeed, the Empire as a whole had to be duly weighed. On the other hand, the colonies—where pioneers were already exploring the trans-Allegheny regions and American land speculators were eagerly seeking grants of western lands—were bound to view policy concerning the disposition of the West from a distinctly provincial point of view. These differing approaches to a common problem were certain to produce disagreement.

Another instance of differing viewpoints lay in the area of trade regulation. British control of colonial trade had been for many years loose and easily evaded, but now a new spirit was abroad in British Parliamentary circles. George Grenville, as Chancellor of the Exchequer and First Lord of the Admiralty, became head of the British ministry in April, 1763. Both he and the powerful British merchant class in Parliament were devotees of the belief that England should be the economic center of the Empire and that the colonies should serve as economic adjuncts to England's greatness. These men looked with horror on the smuggling and illegal trading of the colonials. The colonists, on the other hand, regarded such practices as necessary means of redressing their unfavorable balance of trade with England, of obtaining the specie that was needed in their currencies, and of lining their own pockets with the profits of an immensely lucrative trade with foreign nations.

Closely allied to trade regulation in the thinking of the British ministry was the problem of raising revenue. Britain's national debt had been nearly doubled by the Seven Years War. It stood in 1764 at £129,586,789. Taxes in England had increased as a result of the war by over £3,000,000—the land tax alone, in 1763, standing at four shillings to the pound—and the discontent of English taxpayers was stridently vocal. But still more money would have to be raised, for Britain faced the cost of administering and preserving peace in Canada and the West. This prospect was brought grimly home when, in 1763, the Ottawa chieftain Pontiac, under the influence of French fur traders, attacked and destroyed all the British posts west of Niagara except Detroit and was subdued only after months of campaigning. The cost of governing the new lands was estimated at £300,000 yearly. Nothing was more logical, from the British point of view, than that the colonials should defray from one-third to one-half of this expense. The colonists, however, who had been reluctant to furnish requisitions by the British government even during the Seven Years War, and who felt that their own taxes were onerous, had no enthusiasm whatever for any additional financial burdens.

Grenville's Program

Grenville—a tactless, vain, tiresome individual, but a demon for efficiency, economy, and a balanced budget—developed his program for colonial administration between the years 1763 and 1765. The Proclamation of October 7, 1763, temporarily reserved the West for the Indians. This was meant in part to reassure the Indians, who had been suddenly transferred from French to British sovereignty. It also pleased the British fur traders, but it deprived

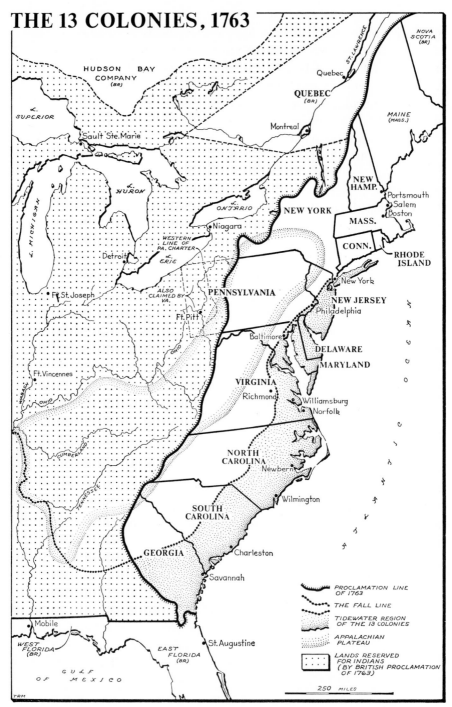

THE 13 COLONIES, 1763

HUDSON BAY COMPANY (BR)

L. SUPERIOR

Sault Ste. Marie

L. HURON

L. MICHIGAN

QUEBEC (BR)

Quebec

Montreal

ST. LAWRENCE

NOVA SCOTIA (BR)

MAINE (MASS.)

NEW HAMP.

Portsmouth
Salem
Boston

NEW YORK

MASS.

CONN.

RHODE ISLAND

Niagara

L. ONTARIO

WESTERN LINE OF PA. CHARTER

Detroit

L. ERIE

PENNSYLVANIA

New York

NEW JERSEY

Philadelphia

Ft. St. Joseph

ALSO CLAIMED BY VA.

Ft. Pitt

OHIO

Baltimore

DELAWARE

MARYLAND

Ft. Vincennes

WABASH

OHIO

VIRGINIA

Richmond

Williamsburg
Norfolk

CUMBERLAND

TENNESSEE

NORTH CAROLINA

Newbern

Wilmington

SOUTH CAROLINA

GEORGIA

Charleston

Savannah

Mobile

WEST FLORIDA (BR)

EAST FLORIDA (BR)

St. Augustine

GULF OF MEXICO

PROCLAMATION LINE OF 1763

THE FALL LINE

TIDEWATER REGION OF THE 13 COLONIES

APPALACHIAN PLATEAU

LANDS RESERVED FOR INDIANS (BY BRITISH PROCLAMATION OF 1763)

250 MILES

TRM

128

the colonies of any control over their western land claims. Next, provision was made for strict maintenance of the Navigation Acts. The Royal Navy was ordered to help enforce the customs regulations. The Admiralty courts, whose judges tried smuggling cases without the benefit of a jury, were given such grievous powers as the right to take cases to Halifax for trial, thus compelling the owner of the goods in question to follow at his own expense. Another mercantilistic procedure used by Grenville was the enactment of a series of new trade regulations that were designed to aid English merchants at the expense of their colonial brethren. Still another was the Currency Act of 1764, which forbade the colonies to issue paper money and in this way protected the investments of English merchants and other men of means in the colonial area.

The Proclamation of 1763 and tightening mercantilistic regulations might help the merchants and fur traders of the tight little island but did little to ease the strain on the British taxpayers. Grenville therefore, shepherded three other acts through Parliament. The first of these, the Sugar Act of April 5, 1764, was specifically designed to produce revenue through customs duties. The duty of 6d. a gallon on foreign molasses (French and Spanish) was reduced to 3d. in order to lessen the temptation to smuggle; duties were laid on silks, wines, and other articles; and stringent provision was made for enforcement. Another measure, the Quartering Act, passed early in 1765, directed the colonials to supply barracks or other accommodation, some provisions, and part of the money cost of quartering the 10,000 troops that it was estimated would be needed for the maintenance of peace and order in the colonies. The third measure, the Stamp Act of March 22, 1765, was open and unabashed direct taxation. It required stamps on all legal and commercial paper and on newspapers as well. Even marriage licenses would have to be stamped. This act alone was estimated to be worth at least £60,000 a year to His Majesty's government.

Grenville had first proposed the Stamp Act a year before it was passed. The colonial agents in London, Franklin among them, had protested, and Grenville had agreed to give the colonies time to suggest ways in which revenue could best be raised among them. The only suggestion that the colonials made was the use of requisitions. These had been tried before; had been easily evaded, and were utterly unacceptable to Grenville.

William Pitt, a bitter political opponent of Grenville, did not like the Stamp Act. Colonel Barré, a Pitt supporter, spoke against the Act, apostrophizing the Americans as Sons of Liberty who were filled with the spirit of freedom. Even these critics, however, did not question the right of Parliament to legislate for the colonies. The Stamp Act passed by a huge majority in the House of Commons, and George III signed it gladly, declaring that it was wise legislation.

Development of Colonial Opposition

Parliament did not foresee any substantial American resistance to the Stamp Act, and yet two incidents had only recently occurred—one in Boston, the other in Virginia—that could have been taken as warnings of what might happen if the British government tried to tighten its control over the colonies.

Boston had witnessed a stirring protest by lawyer James Otis against the practice of issuing Writs of Assistance, general search warrants that were exceedingly useful against smugglers. The judges before whom the argument was made had upheld the Writs, but John Adams said later that those who heard Otis' impassioned defense of the rights of Englishmen "went away ready to take up arms." In Virginia, the legislature, when tobacco was high in price, had transmuted the Anglican clergy's salaries from 17,000 pounds of the weed into two pence a pound, whereby the clerics were greatly outraged. The Act was disallowed in England and a member of the clergy brought suit against the Virginia assembly for damages. When the case had come to trial in 1763 the jury, swayed by the eloquence of Patrick Henry, who denounced the disallowance of the Tobacco Act as an infringement of English liberty, had given the plaintiff one penny. The colonists were obviously sensitive on the subject of tighter controls from overseas.

In varying degrees, the colonists disliked all parts of the Grenville program. They were suspicious of a standing army of British red coats being established in their midst. They were indignant over the denial of the right of trial by jury that characterized the enforcement of the Navigation Acts and the Sugar Act. The outlawry of paper money was a hardship, especially since the Sugar Act curtailed the colonists' best supply of specie, that which came from the trade with the French and Spanish West Indies. These grievances might have been borne, though reluctantly and with ill grace, for long-established precedent had given Parliament the right to disallow colonial laws, to quarter troops, and to regulate trade. But the Stamp Act was clearly and specifically direct taxation by Parliament. This was an innovation. It came, moreover, when times were hard in the colonies, when real estate values were declining, trade was languishing, and the hard money with which the stamps would have to be purchased was at a premium. It was on the Stamp Act, therefore, that the colonials centered their resentment.

The Stamp Act Congress

Patrick Henry and James Otis precipitated the colonial discontent into action. Henry—an eloquent, ambitious, twenty-nine-year-old lawyer of the Virginia frontier—was in the Virginia House of Burgesses, where, like other young members, he was restive under the control of the older tidewater aristocracy. In May, 1765, after many of the members had left for their homes, Henry rose and, with a ringing speech that drew the charge of treason, pushed through the House resolves stating that Americans had all the rights of Englishmen; that one of these rights was no taxation without representation; and that taxation of Virginians should be by their own representatives. James Otis, less spectacularly but more constructively, proposed in the Massachusetts House of Representatives that an intercolonial congress be called to consider what steps might be taken regarding the Stamp Act.

The Massachusetts assembly rose to Otis' appeal, and invitations were sent out for a meeting in New York. The invitations met a mixed reception. Many feared that such a gathering might take hasty and ill-considered action. A few radicals welcomed it as according an opportunity for vigorous pronouncement on the rights of Englishmen. Conservative fears and opposition from the Crown ("Ministerial monkery," said John Adams) kept Virginia, Georgia, North Carolina, and New Hampshire from accepting the invitation, but in October, 1765, the representatives of the other nine colonies gathered in New York.

The deliberations of the Stamp Act Congress resulted in a series of resolutions that were moderate in character. They acknowledged the duty of the colonials to "His Majesty's person and government." They also acknowledged that Parliament had a right to legislate for the colonies. As for the Sugar Act, they contented themselves with declaring that it was grievous and hard to bear. In regard to smuggling trials and taxation, they were more outspoken, asserting that trial by jury was the inherent right of every British colonial and that only their own legislatures, where they were represented, could constitutionally impose taxes upon them. The resolutions ended by humbly supplicating for the repeal of the Stamp Act and of the other acts which extended the power of the Admiralty and restricted American commerce.

The Stamp Act Congress had great historical significance. As the first intercolonial assembly that was entirely spontaneous, it was a milestone on the road to independence. Accepting the supremacy of the Crown over the colonies, it nevertheless placed the case of the colonies squarely on the fundamental rights of Englishmen, and foremost among these rights it placed the great principle of no taxation without representation. British statesmen could and did claim that the colonies had virtual representation in Parliament; that they were as well represented as Leeds, or Birmingham; that members of Parliament sat for the whole British realm, rather than for any particular constituency. But the colonists, quite logically, refused to see themselves as represented anywhere except in their own assemblies. This difference in viewpoint as to political rights was as fundamental as the difference of opinion over the levying of monetary contributions in the colonies for the benefit of the British government.

The First Crisis Comes and Goes

The meeting in New York during those October days of 1765 gave formal representation to American discontent. More forceful representations appeared elsewhere. The merchants of Boston, New York, Philadelphia, and Charleston refused to do business requiring stamps; in consequence, English

BOSTONIANS PAYING THE EXCISEMAN

The Liberty Boys are treating the tax collector with some indignity. The placard bearing the hated words "Stamp Act" has been turned upside down and tacked to the tree of liberty.

trade with the colonies went into a precipitous decline. Bands of men and boys styling themselves Sons of Liberty and often encouraged by merchants and other men of substance, rioted and pillaged in Boston and other towns, burning the effigies of royal officials and driving the appointed stamp collectors into hiding. Some stamps were destroyed by the mobs, bales of them never appeared on the market, and very few were sold. The colonial uproar was prodigious. Even Franklin, who had counseled acceptance of the Stamp Act, once it was passed, was amazed at the violent reaction of the populace.

The crisis would have been prolonged and might even have resulted in bloodshed had it not been for a change of ministry in England, where the Parliamentary situation was fluid. The Whigs were dominant, the Tories of this period not even constituting a party, but the Whigs were split into factions. There were the Bedfordites, sometimes known as the "Bloomsbury Gang," the Grenvilleites, the Old Whigs, the Pittites, the King's Friends, and still other groups. There was also George III, who, though accepting the fact that King and Parliament must act in conjunction as governors of the Empire, was as anxious to play an important role in the government as the Whigs were to maintain Parliamentary supremacy. This fluidity of political organization, not the impact of colonial discontent, explains the changes in the British ministry that took place in the fifteen years before the Revolution. These ministerial shifts produced shifts in policy that were determined more by the situation in London than by that in the colonies.

The king was bored by Grenville, who lectured him on his duties and was so parsimonious that he tried to curtail expenditures at Buckingham Palace. In July, 1765, the monarch took advantage of factional intrigues that had deprived Grenville of majority control in Parliament and turned to the Old Whigs for a ministry. Their leader was the Duke of Rockingham, an honest and well-meaning individual, but a mediocrity more devoted to horse racing than he was to the arduous business of politics.

Rockingham faced a difficult situation as head of the new ministry. The English merchants were complaining because their yearly trade with America had fallen from £3,000,000 to £1,500,000. They had great influence in Parliament, and they demanded action. William Pitt, the great Organizer of Victory in the Seven Years War, had always opposed the Grenville program, and Rockingham needed Pitt's support. Pitt and Edmund Burke argued for repeal of the Stamp Act on the ground that it was taxation without representation. Benjamin Franklin, questioned on the American attitude before the bar of the House of Commons, gave a soothing and diplomatic picture of Americans' fundamental loyalty to Crown and Parliament. Faced by a situation over which he had little control, Rockingham finally obtained the King's reluctant consent to a change in policy toward the colonies. In the spring of 1766, the Stamp Act was repealed and the Sugar Act was modified to a duty of 1*d*. a gallon on all British and foreign molasses imported into the colonies.

The news of this shift in the attitude of the British government was greeted with enthusiasm in the colonies. The merchants applauded, and the Sons of Liberty celebrated, sometimes in riotous fashion. Better than 500 sermons were preached in commendation of the repeal. No one seemed to notice that the retreat of the Rockingham ministry in actual taxation had been accompanied by a Declaratory Act that was much more popular in Parliament than was the repeal of the taxes; this Act asserted in unequivocal fashion the full right and power of the Crown and Parliament to make laws and statutes for the colonies "in all cases whatsoever." His Majesty's government had retired a considerable way in practice, but it had not abandoned one iota of principle.

The repeal of the Stamp Act was followed by a period of relative calm in the relations of the colonies with the mother country. There were a few minor disturbances. The New York assembly proved obdurate about providing quarters for British soldiers and in consequence was dissolved by the royal governor of the colony. Bostonians quibbled and delayed about providing compensation for those royal officials whose property had been damaged by the Stamp Act rioters. But such difficulties were in keeping with a long record of colonial obstinacy and intransigence in matters where the colonial purse was involved. The only real problem that remained was that of the British government's finances. They were in a low state, but the colonists refused to regard this as a matter for their concern.

The Second Crisis

Rockingham's ministry, which never had more than the feeblest majority, soon fell, and in August, 1766, the King called William Pitt to head the government. Pitt was not the man he once had been. Suffering from the gout and some other mysterious malady that impaired his reason, his brilliant mastery of Parliament during the war was now conspicuous by its absence. More and more he absented himself from the House of Commons, but not before he had made Mr. Charles Townshend the Chancellor of the Exchequer.

A brilliant, erratic, unpredictable *bon vivant* (his nickname was "Champagne Charley"), Townshend faced the government's deficit in debonair fashion. His views on taxation of the colonies had not been made crystal clear by his record, since he had voted for the Stamp Act and also for its repeal. In January, 1767, he announced that he once again favored the Stamp Act but subsequently agreed not to press the point, since the colonials seemed so upset about direct taxation. He therefore proposed to raise the revenue so necessary for the relief of English taxpayers by external taxation alone—that is to say, through the revenues of the customs at American ports.

The Duty Act of 1767 was framed and passed in accordance with Townshend's desires. It levied duties on paper, lead, glass, paint, and tea brought into the colonies. Townshend also took steps to strengthen the customs service. He provided more Writs of Assistance and smaller revenue cutters that could chase smugglers into shallow bays and inlets. Furthermore, certain royal officials were now to be paid out of the fines and judgments levied against the colonists, thus weakening the hold that colonial assemblies had on the salaries of royal officials in general. English regulation of colonial trade was now in a way to become really effective. Townshend estimated that £40,000 of revenue from the colonies would flow into the British treasury. As a matter of fact, from 1768 to 1774, the American customs did bring in an average of some £30,000 annually, at a cost of only £13,000. External taxation really seemed to work.

But the Townshend Acts fanned the smoldering flame of colonial discontent. They not only made smuggling more difficult; they also brought up again the question of taxation without representation. Townshend was clearly raising taxes in the guise of customs regulations. The protest against this in 1765 had been overshadowed by the Stamp Act storm, but the protest had been there. Now that internal taxation was not at issue, what had been minor became a major matter in colonial eyes. This became apparent in John Dickinson's *Letters of a Pennsylvania Farmer* (1768), and in a Circular Letter sent out by the Massachusetts assembly at the instigation of Samuel Adams to the other colonial legislatures.

Dickinson, an immensely influential figure in Pennsylvania, declared that the colonies were dependent on Great Britain, but only as much as "one perfectly free people can be on another." Parliament, he said, could lay duties on American trade if they were laid for the purpose of regulation. It could not lawfully collect customs for the purpose of raising revenue, for no free people could be taxed without its consent. Samuel Adams, in the Massachusetts Circular Letter and in other writings, argued that Parliamentary law was subordinate to "the law of God and Nature" which, in turn, was the basis of the British constitution. According to the law of God and Nature, said Adams, all taxation should be levied by truly representative assemblies;

therefore, Parliament could not constitutionally tax the colonies. Such an argument did not represent the ultimate in logic, but it was so effective that the Massachusetts assembly was dissolved for sending out the Circular Letter and the Virginia assembly for receiving it.

Colonial opposition to the Townshend Acts gradually mounted. The merchants of the principal cities, though somewhat hesitantly, entered into non-importation agreements, and the import of British goods once again markedly diminished. The Massachusetts Circular Letter asked for concerted action by discussion and petition against Parliamentary taxation, and this was supported with considerable effect by James Otis and Josiah and James Warren in Massachusetts, Patrick Henry in Virginia and the influential merchant and planter Christopher Gadsden in South Carolina. The Sons of Liberty again became active, rioting and breaking windows and driving the Commissioners of the Customs in Boston into the harbor's Castle William in fear of their lives. The Commissioners asked the British government for help, and on September 28, 1768, there arrived in Boston two regiments of the line.

The British redcoats stationed in Boston behaved reasonably well, but irritating incidents occurred. British troops would march with a great roll of drums past Puritan churches where Sunday services were being held. British officers insulted colonial civilians. One officer struck James Otis on the head with the flat of his sword. Civilian discontent with the presence of the "bloody-backs" increased. The climax came on March 5, 1770, with the "Boston Massacre." When a group of men and boys pelted with snowballs a sentry outside the Custom House, he called out the guard. A crowd gathered and began to jeer and threaten. After a soldier was knocked down and another hit with a club, the soldiers fired into the mob, and it ran for cover, leaving four citizens dead in the street. Blame rested on both sides for this unfortunate affair, but it is clear that the soldiers fired only under intense provocation. When, seven months later, some of their number were tried before a Boston jury, they were defended by John Adams and Josiah Quincy. All were acquitted, save two, who escaped with branding in the hand for manslaughter.

The Boston Massacre roused popular feeling to fever heat. Under pressure from the citizenry, led by Sam Adams, the regiments were moved from the city to Castle William. But if the Boston mob responded eagerly to Adams' leadership, the more conservative citizens of the colonies were alarmed by the affair. They felt that the movement of protest against British policy was in danger of passing out of the hands of the merchant class into those of irresponsible political theorists like Sam Adams and the "illiterate Mechanicks" who thronged into the Sons of Liberty. This reaction to the events in Boston, coupled with the fact that Great Britain was once again retreating in its effort to tax the colonies, soon reduced the "Massacre" to the status of an incident.

End of the Second Crisis— The Quiet Years

On the same day that colonial citizens had lain dying on the snow-covered streets of Boston, Lord North had risen in the House of Commons to propose partial repeal of the Townshend Acts. His Lordship, a "booby-looking" man but a skillful Parliamentarian, had emerged as Chancellor of the Exchequer and the principal figure in a ministry that had been disrupted by Townshend's death in the fall of 1767 and by Pitt's increasing disability. North and Lord Hillsborough, an Irish peer of small wisdom who was made Secretary of State for the colonies in 1768, now controlled colonial policy. Facing the opposition of English merchants to customs duties that were stimulating the development of colonial manufactures, and recognizing that colonial discontent was increasing the cost of collecting these same duties, North developed a plan of strategic retreat. He proposed repeal of all the Townshend duties except for the tax on tea, which was the only one that produced a sizeable revenue. The right to tax and, largely, the revenue were still upheld, but the Acts that hurt British business interests were abandoned. North also hoped that this procedure would divide and weaken colonial opposition to British policy. Parliament accepted his proposals, and news of this reached the colonies by the middle of May, 1770.

Colonial opinion was divided as to how North's policy should be received. Radicals like Sam Adams and Patrick Henry urged continued resistance, coupled with the demand that all obnoxious British acts passed since 1763 be repealed. On the other hand, the New York merchants abandoned nonimportation, save for tea. The merchants of the other principal towns soon followed suit, and this action put a damper on resistance to British controls. The second crisis in British-colonial relations was over.

Though the period from 1770 to 1773 is known as that of the "Quiet Years," it was not a time of perfect serenity. Tea smuggling continued on a broad scale. Colonial resentment over customs regulations resulted in the burning of the revenue vessel *Gaspee* at Providence in 1772. Samuel Adams, Patrick Henry, and another young Virginian with a taste for radical political theory—Thomas Jefferson—developed what the Tory pamphleteer Daniel Leonard called "the foulest, subtlest, and most venomous serpent ever hatched from the egg of sedition." This was committees of correspondence, local and intercolonial, that kept the discontented in the different colonies aware of common grievances and alert to challenge any revitalization of British coercion. In general, however, calm prevailed. The merchants no longer clubbed together for purposes of boycott. Trade increased, and John Adams, dining with John Hancock, drank "green tea from Holland I hope but don't know."

The Third and Final Crisis

This period of happy relations was shattered by the passage of the Tea Act of 1773. This Act, ironically enough, was not the result of any desire to coerce the colonies, financially or otherwise. It was, rather, the result of an effort by Parliament to cope with an economic crisis that promised great harm to the Empire. The British East India Company, a mammoth commercial organization, had been corruptly managed and was on the threshold of bankruptcy. If it went down in ruin, the scandal would be immense, the British government would suffer a serious loss of prestige, and Britain's hold on India would be seriously weakened. The Tea Act was the British government's effort to avert such a catastrophe.

By this fateful act, the government loaned the East India Company £1,400,000 and gave it permission to ship tea directly to the colonies, where it would be sold by the Company's special agents. This eliminated the former procedure of bringing the tea to England, where it had paid duty and had then been sold to middlemen who, in turn, had sold it to merchants in America. The customs duty of 3d. a pound at American ports was left in force, but so advantageous to the Company was this new arrangement that it could sell its tea in America at prices lower than those the smugglers charged for the tea they brought in from Holland.

The Tea Act seemed innocuous enough to the members of Parliament. The Company would be saved, and the colonials would get tea cheaper than they had ever had it before. But out of this Act arose the third crisis in eight years over British policy in America. The merchants of Philadelphia, New York, and Boston held protest meetings, for they saw ruinous competition looming, not only in tea but in wines and silks and Heaven knew what else. The smugglers were furious. The radicals saw in this act a nefarious attempt by the British government to entice Americans into accepting taxation without representation. It was, they declared, the beginning of a movement that would end in destroying American political liberties and that would make the colonies into the economic serfs of the mother country.

With some trepidation of spirit, in view of the rising colonial excitement, the officials of the British East India Company shipped 1,253 chests of tea valued at between £40,000 and £50,000 to the four principal colonial towns. Not an ounce of it reached the consignees, for everywhere the most ominous preparations had been made for its reception. Some was kept aboard ship, some was stored in warehouses, and in Boston a mob disguised as Indians and spurred on by John Hancock and Sam Adams swarmed on to the tea ships and dumped the hated article into the harbor. This was the Boston Tea Party of December 16, 1773—a party that, as one wag put it, provided tea for all the codfish off the Banks of Newfoundland.

The Boston Tea Party provoked a serious reaction among sober-minded colonials who had theretofore been sympathetic with the opposition to British policy. Benjamin Franklin called it "an act of violent injustice." The merchants especially were shocked at this wanton destruction of property. This revulsion in colonial opinion bade fair to be a serious handicap to the radicals bent upon establishing American freedom from British controls. Fortunately, from their point of view, Britain decided to meet force with force.

The Intolerable Acts

London was highly indignant over what had happened in Boston. A universal cry arose at the British capital for harsh disciplinary action. The time had come, Britons thought, when their government must either exert its authority over the colonies or write them off as lost to its control, but the latter alternative was unthinkable. On March 25, 1774, Lord North put through the House of Commons the Boston Port bill, closing the port until Boston paid for the tea it had destroyed. Two months later, the Massachusetts Government Act drastically remodeled the Massachusetts charter. This Act prohibited town meetings unless approved by the governor and provided for appointment by the Crown of many officials formerly chosen by the colonials. Another Act made specific provision for quartering troops in Massachusetts towns, and still another provided for transfer to England of murder trials in law enforcement cases. This legislation made it clear that the British government was committed to a policy of coercion in the colonies.

News of the Boston Port bill produced a violent reaction throughout the colonies. If Britain forced Boston into submission, all the rights and privileges that Americans regarded as their own would be endangered, perhaps lost forever. New England rallied to the support of the beleaguered town. Other colonies promised aid, especially provisions, that had to be brought overland to a people who were stubbornly holding out against Lord North's blockade.

THE BOSTONIANS IN DISTRESS

Besieged Bostonians in a cage suspended from the Tree of Liberty are being fed by Marblehead men with codfish in contribution boxes. This cartoon shows the economic hardships suffered as a consequence of the Boston Port bill.

In New York, a committee of fifty-one solid citizens proposed a Continental Congress, and this move gained wide support in the other colonies. The calling of the Congress was hastened by still another Parliamentary Act, passed on June 22, 1774—the Quebec Act, which made British policy in regard to Canada and the West a further source of grievance and of fear as to the designs of Britain in the New World.

Ever since 1763, the British government had been fumbling with the formulation of a policy regarding the western lands. Some wished settlement there permanently restricted, so that the fur trade would continue to flourish. Many colonials, and some Englishmen as well, wanted the western lands opened up for speculation and settlement. Virginia, by its charter of 1609, claimed vast stretches of western territory, and Connecticut and Massachusetts also had extensive western land claims. George Washington was deeply involved in western land speculation. Patrick Henry, another land speculator, termed the West his hobbyhorse. Colonial land companies staked out claims to over a million acres west of the Alleghenies, claims based on Indian treaties, colonial grants, and hoped-for validation by the government in London.

British policy in regard to the West had begun to crystallize in 1773. In that year, the Privy Council had taken significant action in regard to the lands south of the Ohio river. It ordered survey before any land grants; the survey was in lots running from 100 to 1,000 acres, which were to be sold at public auction. This indicated that land policy in the West would be controlled from London rather than from the colonies, and that the government was not interested in validating the claims of speculators. More significant still were the provisions of the Quebec Act in regard to the lands north of the Ohio.

The Quebec Act extended the boundaries of the royal province of Quebec south and west to the Ohio and the Mississippi, thus wiping out the claims of the colonies in that region and jeopardizing all land claims based on colonial grants and Indian treaties. It produced a violent repercussion in America. Virginia protested, colonial speculators raged, and colonial fur traders were bitter at the prospect of their activities being controlled by royal officials at Montreal.

The Quebec Act roused colonial resentment from still another point of view. Framed as an honest effort to deal justly with the French inhabitants of that region, it provided that Roman Catholics in the province should be allowed the free exercise of their religion, and that French law forms, which

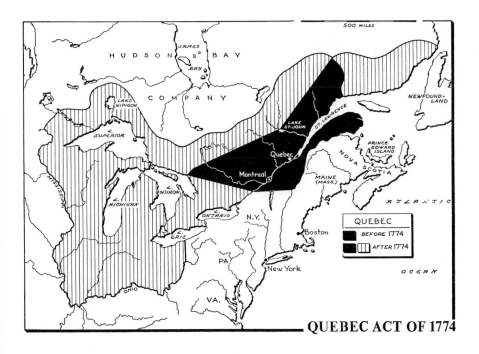

QUEBEC ACT OF 1774

did not provide trial by jury, should prevail in cases under civil law. For a variety of reasons, the excited colonies felt that these provisions were indeed sinister.

Rivalry between Dissenters and Anglicans had, in varying degrees, marked the history of all the colonies. New England had been and still was fearful of an Anglican establishment that would force the Puritans to pay taxes for the support of the Episcopal church. Partly because of this, the New England ministry had ranged itself on the colonial side in the recent disputes with Britain. Congregational pulpits had thundered against the Stamp and Townshend Acts, pastor John Lothrop had preached on "Innocent Blood Crying to God from the Streets of Boston," and many another patriot divine had staunchly upheld the patriot cause. Now Puritan clergy and laity alike felt that the Quebec Act was another evidence of England's nefarious designs, a menace to Protestantism in the colonies. Both John and Samuel Adams believed that the barriers against "Popery" were being let down. Puritan mobs carried banners inscribed "No Popery." Such feelings, to a lesser degree, were echoed in the colonies further south.

The popular mind joined the Quebec Act with the Boston Port bill and the Massachusetts Government Act as "The Intolerable Acts." They furnished a telling argument with all classes as to the iniquity and diabolical schemes of the English government.

The First Continental Congress

While the Intolerable Acts were stirring colonial resentment against Britain to a fever heat, the Continental Congress passed from the realm of ideas into that of action. All shades of opinion welcomed the gathering of this assemblage. Conservatives felt that in such a body sane counsels would prevail and steps leading to reconciliation with Great Britain would be taken. Radicals hoped to use the Congress in forging weapons against British policy. The Virginia House of Burgesses, led by Patrick Henry and Richard Henry Lee, believed that the Congress could be used to support beleaguered Massachusetts—where Suffolk County, with Boston its capital, was attempting to govern itself in defiance of the newly appointed governor, General Gage, and the four regiments he had brought with him to Boston. When the Virginia Assembly issued a call for the Congress, the other colonies fell into line. Philadelphia was chosen as the most central meeting place, and there all save Georgia sent delegates to gather in Carpenter's Hall early in September, 1774.

The First Continental Congress was a motley body. John Adams described it as one-third Whig, one-third Tory, and the rest mongrel. It had come into being by diverse procedures, some of its delegates being chosen by colonial assemblies, others by committees of correspondence and other local authorities, official and quasi-official. Radical members (Samuel and John Adams are good examples), wanted the Congress to take a strong stand against all British controls. Conservative members, like Joseph Galloway of Pennsylvania, were anxious to see the Congress adopt a conciliatory point of view toward the mother country. Many of the delegates came to Philadelphia without any definite plan of action. The Congress was a reasonably fair sample of colonial opinion as it stood in the fall of 1774.

Disregarding the large body of citizens that had no clear ideas about the course that the colonies should pursue in their dispute with Great Britain, there were two bodies of public opinion, the radical and the conservative. The radicals were a mixed group, socially and geographically, and they operated from a mixture of motives. Debtors, men of wealth and position, political theorists, planters, small farmers, tradesmen, fishermen, mechanics, representatives of the tidewater, and representatives of the frontier were all to be found in the radical ranks. Some were fearful of British taxation; others opposed British mercantilistic practices as stifling colonial initiative and limiting colonial prosperity; and still others took their stand on the great principle of the right to self-government. In some but by no means all of the colonies, the radicals represented frontier elements that were resentful of controls exerted by tidewater merchants and aristocrats, controls which meant underrepresentation in colonial assemblies, inequitable taxation, and lack of appropriations for internal improvements and protection against the Indians on the frontier. The radicals moved slowly, and the great majority of them regretfully, toward a complete break with the mother country.

Conservative public opinion was made up chiefly of those who had a stake in the existing scheme of things. Church of England clerics, especially in the middle and northern colonies, belonged to this group. So did officeholders in general, those who reverenced royalty, and sticklers for legality who could cite a host of precedents as to the paramount authority of Crown and Parliament. Finally, some prominent families took the conservative side almost automatically when families with which they were in close rivalry became identified as colonial extremists. When the Livingston family in New York espoused the radical cause, the De Lanceys, who had also protested British tyranny, moved into the loyalist camp.

Thanks to the British acts of coercion, the Continental Congress faced a situation in which the controversy over taxation was now overshadowed by the conflict over political rights and political control. Here the radical political theorists were in their element, and during the weeks of wrangling it became apparent that they held the balance of power. A Suffolk County convention had adopted resolutions known as the Suffolk Resolves, declaring that no obedience was due to the Parliamentary acts of 1774; that military preparations should be made against the possibility of attack by the troops in Boston; and that seizure of patriot leaders by the British should be answered by the imprisonment of royal officials. On September 17, 1774, the Congress approved these resolves. It then proceeded to adopt a Declaration of Rights and Grievances, which asserted that taxation should be only in local assemblies and declared that Parliament had the right to regulate external commerce, but not for purposes of taxation.

The Congress also set up a "Continental Association" providing a series of nonimportation and nonconsumption agreements. In view of the withdrawal of the merchants from the boycott of 1770, Congress put enforcement of these agreements in the hands of locally chosen "Committees of Safety and Inspection" which, presumably, would be controlled by patriots whose probity and determination were beyond question. Finally, the delegates passed a resolution that a subsequent Congress should be called in May, 1775, if by that time grievances were not redressed.

The Outbreak of Hostilities

The proceedings of the First Continental Congress showed that men were now being controlled by the onrushing course of events. Many delegates who thought the Suffolk Resolves altogether too extreme voted for them rather than leave Massachusetts unsupported and give an impression of American disunity. Many delegates were for a "British-American Parliament" proposed by Joseph Galloway, which was defeated by a margin so narrow that the vote of one colony tipped the balance. This plan was then expunged from the record, again because of the necessity of presenting a united front. The situation demanded bold and decisive action, and the Congress turned reluctantly to a boycott enforced by patriots. That Britain would yield to such pressure was highly doubtful. Many believed with John and Samuel Adams that the result would be war, but few had any joy in such a prospect.

During the winter of 1774–1775 the Committees of Safety and Inspection busied themselves with enforcing the nonimportation and nonconsumption agreements. They also gathered stores of powder and arms and started the drilling of militia. These committees were especially active in the Boston area, where Governor Gage, with 5,000 troops and many ships of war, was main-

THE BATTLE OF LEXINGTON, 1775—FROM A PRINT (1798)

This contemporary engraving from a drawing by E. Tisdale shows the colonials rallying to attack the British grenadiers. It emphasizes the destruction being caused by the British.

taining an uneasy control. On April 19, 1775, Gage sent out a force of 1,000 redcoats under the command of Lieutenant Colonel Francis Smith to destroy stores that had been collected at Lexington and Concord, some eighteen miles from Boston, and to arrest Hancock and Sam Adams. The countryside had been aroused by Paul Revere and others, and the British found colonial militia drawn up on Lexington Common. There the Revolution started in earnest, although which side fired the first shot has always been a matter of dispute. The militia took shelter, Indian fashion, behind stone walls and trees, and the British pushed on to Concord, where they met another band of patriots at Concord bridge. By now the whole countryside was aroused, militia were pouring in from all directions, and Smith ordered a retreat that was harassed on all sides by the punishing fire of riflemen, many of whom could hit a squirrel at 100 yards. Before the British reached Boston, 273 of their men had been killed or wounded; the colonial loss was ninety-five killed and wounded. Each side loudly accused the other of committing atrocities.

Increased military action followed Lexington and Concord. Colonial militia under Ethan Allen and Benedict Arnold seized Crown Point and Fort Ticonderoga, opening the way for an invasion of Canada. Other colonial forces invested Boston. They were driven off the commanding height of Breed's Hill in the so-called Battle of Bunker Hill (June 17, 1775), although at fearful cost to the British regulars. The colonials and Great Britain were now in open conflict, a fact which was dramatized the following fall and winter when Brigadier General Richard Montgomery succeeded with a few

MILITARY ACTIVITY, 1775–EARLY 1776

hundred men in capturing Montreal (November 13, 1775) and then joining Benedict Arnold in a desperate but unsuccessful attempt to take Quebec.
The attack on Canada ended with the retreat of the Americans from Canadian soil in the spring of 1776, but time had been purchased against a
possible British invasion down the Champlain route, and the bravery and
hardihood of the American commanders and their men had been amply
demonstrated.

The Second Congress and the Declaration of Independence

When the Second Continental Congress met in the State House at Philadelphia May 10, 1775—the day that Benedict Arnold seized Fort Ticonderoga—the delegates found the city full of preparation for armed resistance
to "British tyranny." This Congress was more radical than its predecessor
had been. Those who shrank from warfare with Great Britain, however, were
still in the majority, and an "Olive branch" petition, framed by John Dickinson, John Jay, Benjamin Franklin and others was forwarded to King George
III. At the same time, the Congress began raising a Continental Army of
20,000 men and appointed George Washington commander-in-chief. The
wisdom of this became apparent when the King not only ignored the petition
but, on August 23, 1775, issued a Proclamation of Rebellion.

During the following year, Congress slowly and cautiously moved toward
a complete break with the British government. This delay was due to a number of factors. Lack of unity among the colonials was a barrier to swift and
drastic action. Loyalty to King and Crown died hard, and with thousands it
never did die. Many who were not moved by sentimental ties feared that
commercial ruin and governmental anarchy would be the result of separation.
Others lived in constant expectation of a change in British policy. During
this period, Washington kept referring to the British army as "the ministerial
troops," and there were continued appeals from "the King badly advised" to
"the King better advised."

But as the months went by, a variety of circumstances pushed the colonists
toward a complete breach with the mother country. Certain British military
procedures—the employment of 30,000 mercenaries from west and south
Germany, the burning of the New England towns of Charlestown and Fal-
mouth, the incitement of the Iroquois in central New York against the colonials—produced a deepening sense of resentment. Thomas Paine's pamphlet
Common Sense, published in January, 1776, was a clever appeal to colonial

self-interest. It called for resistance to tyranny, and invoked the blood of the slain and the rights of man. It was unthinkable, said Paine, that a continent should be ruled by an island. The time had come for independence. Washington called Paine's argument "sound doctrine and unanswerable reason." *Common Sense* sold over 100,000 copies.

Still another source of encouragement to the colonists was their success at Boston, which General William Howe, successor to General Gage, was forced to evacuate in the early spring of 1776. Most important of all was the growing conviction that, alone and unaided, the colonists would never be able to conquer the armies and the mighty fleet that England could throw into the fray. Foreign aid was essential to the patriot cause, but it was most unlikely that such aid would be forthcoming unless the colonists burned their bridges behind them and committed themselves with finality to independence.

During the spring of 1776, resolutions in favor of independence began to appear throughout the colonies. These symbolized a growing demand for action that became evident in Congress itself. There, on June 7, 1776, Richard Henry Lee of Virginia, in obedience to instructions from the Virginia convention, introduced a resolution that "these United Colonies are, and of right ought to be, free and independent states. . . ." Since some still felt that the move was premature, there was considerable debate, but on July 2, 1776, twelve colonies voted for the resolution. A week later, the New York delegates, having now received proper instructions, added their vote to the list.

In the meantime, a committee had been appointed to draft a declaration. Jefferson, as chairman, framed the document, with the aid of Franklin and John Adams. It was then debated in Congress. Changes were suggested, and some phrases were struck out and others added, while Jefferson twisted and winced at these alterations of his handiwork. The result, however, was in all essentials the product of Jefferson's mind and pen. The final draft of the document was adopted on July 4. Most of the members signed it on August 2, those who were then absent signing it at a later date.

The Declaration of Independence was much more than an assertion that the colonies had separated themselves from Great Britain and had become free and independent states. Its stately, measured phrases presented a bill of political and economic grievances suffered at the hands of George III. It declared that these indicated the King's intent to establish an absolute tyranny over the colonies. The latter had suffered these injuries patiently and had repeatedly petitioned both King and Parliament for redress, but in vain. Independence, therefore, had become a necessity. This independence was not merely the consequence of wrongs endured, but was necessary because

CONGRESS VOTING INDEPENDENCE—PAINTED BY PINE AND SAVAGE (1785)

The members of Congress were aware, as they cast their votes, that they had taken a step from which there was no turning back. They were now, in British eyes, rebels who would suffer the extreme penalty if the Revolution failed.

connection with Great Britain made it impossible to establish a good society in America.

Men, the Declaration asserted, are created equal. They have unalienable rights, among which are life, liberty, and the pursuit of happiness. Governments are instituted for the protection of these rights, and legitimate government rests upon the consent of the governed. When government no longer safeguards man's unalienable rights, the people have the right of revolution. Such was the situation which had been brought about by British tyranny.

These doctrines of the Declaration have their roots in ideas advanced by the Greeks and Cicero, in the writings of medieval theorists, and especially in the works of such seventeenth- and eighteenth-century philosophers as Hooker, Hobbes, and Locke. Jefferson never claimed any originality for his handiwork, and the inspiration he derived from Locke's *Second Treatise on*

Government is plain and unmistakeable. But if the argument in the Declaration derived from the thought of the past, the document itself looked to the future, to the founding of a society of free men.

Taken as a statement of historical fact, the Declaration is vulnerable. The impression it gives of the colonists as patient and long-suffering is decidedly exaggerated. The King was no more to blame than Parliament for the acts of which complaint was made. The people of the colonies were by no means as united in their determination to throw off the British yoke as Jefferson assumed they were. The Declaration is a skillful justification of the act of revolution.

But if the Declaration was in part specious, its practical significance was great. It made the break with Britain definite. In furnishing a creed to which all patriots could repair, it crystallized the distinction between patriot and loyalist in the colonies. It was essential for obtaining foreign aid, for it demonstrated that the colonists were now determined, not to reform the British Empire, but to remove themselves from it. Above and beyond all this, it associated the foundation of the United States with those great principles of human freedom for the realization of which men must always strive if democracy itself is to endure.

Suggested Reading

There is a voluminous literature on the period from 1763 to 1775, and the following list is very selective.

Two excellent books on the immediate background of the Revolution are John C. Miller, *Origins of the American Revolution* (1943), a well-written and balanced treatment, and Clinton Rossiter, *Seedtime of the Republic* (1953), which is brilliant, incisive, and challenging. Carl Bridenbaugh, *Cities in Revolt* (1955) gives new information on urban attitudes toward the Revolution, and O. M. Dickerson, *The Navigation Acts and the American Revolution* (1951) is an important study of British trade policy and its effect on America. Edmund S. Morgan, *The Birth of the Republic* (1956) is a fresh and stimulating treatment of the crucial years. C. H. Van Tyne, *The Causes of the War of Independence* (1922) is not original in interpretation but is well written and clear in outline.

For an English viewpoint on the Revolution, see L. B. Namier, *England in the Age of the American Revolution* (1930); H. E. Egerton, *The Causes and Character of the American Revolution* (1923); and W. E. H. Lecky, *The American Revolution, 1763-1783* (1914) which, though old, is a classic.

Carl Becker, *The Eve of the Revolution* (1921) is full of the author's dry humor and shrewd insight, and his *The Declaration of Independence* (1951) is the classic study of the document. E. S. and H. M. Morgan, *The Stamp Act Crisis: Prologue to Revolution* (1953) is scholarly and authoritative. Dumas Malone's *Jefferson the Virginian* (1948) and *Jefferson and the Rights of Man* (1951) are valuable for insights on the Revolutionary period from the point of view of a rising statesman.

Also to be consulted are, Bernard Knollenberg, *Origin of the American Revolution* (1960); L. H. Gipson, *The Coming of the Revolution* (1954); C. W. Alvord, *The Mississippi Valley in British Politics* (1916); T. P. Abernethy, *Western Lands and the American Revolution* (1937); J. M. Sosin, *Whitehall and the Wilderness* (1961); Edward Dumbauld, *The Declaration of Independence and What It Means Today* (1950); and David Hawke, *A Transaction of Free Men: The Birth and Course of the Declaration of Independence* (1964).

7 ⸱ The American Revolution

THE DECLARATION OF INDEPENDENCE committed the colonials to a contest in which the odds were against them. They lacked anything remotely resembling a regular army, and of their military leaders only Washington, Horatio Gates, Daniel Morgan, and Philip Schuyler had had any real experience in the field. Equipment was woefully short; Washing-

The Balance of Forces

ton had to count heavily on foreign sources for powder and even for woolen goods, and such sources of supply were both irregular and inadequate. Finances were never in good shape, despite the fact that over $7 million in specie was eventually obtained from abroad. Congress had to rely chiefly on state requisitions, which were always in arrears, and on repeated issues of Continental paper currency, which depreciated in value until by 1781 it took $1,000 in paper to equal a dollar in specie and the term "not worth a Continental" became a byword.

The erstwhile colonies were tardy in supplying men as well as money, and the American army was an unstable quantity. It consisted of the Continental Line, which was usually enlisted for three years or for the duration of the war, and of state militia. By 1777, Washington had a sound nucleus of Continental veterans, sometimes as many as 8,000–10,000 men, but the majority of his troops always consisted of militia, enlisted for three-, six- or nine-month periods, and of volunteers who came out when danger threatened a locality and disappeared when the crisis was past. He never had over 22,000

152

militia in his army, and never more than 18,000 militia in any one battle. By contrast, the British commanders who opposed Washington had at their command 30,000 mercenaries, generally known as Hessians, some 15,000 regulars, and the support of various bands of Tories and Indians. On the sea, the colonials had no navy and at first no prospect of outside naval support, the revolutionary government having to rely upon privateers which did considerable damage to British commerce but were an annoyance rather than a counterpoise to the British fleet.

Colonial weakness was striking, but there were also factors that operated in favor of the patriots. The British government faced a formidable opposition in Parliament to the war, an opposition that became more vocal as the war went on. The distance between London and the scene of military operations led, perforce, to delay and inefficiency in formulating plans of campaign and putting them into execution. The redcoats found the New World's climate trying, especially in the North, and they had to fight over terrain that was much more familiar to the colonials than to themselves. The British fleet, even at the beginning of the struggle, had to make its dispositions with a view to the possibility of French attacks. It is also entirely probable that expectation of an early colonial collapse kept the British leadership at home and in America from nerving itself for an immediate all-out war effort that would have been hard indeed to meet. Finally, the "military honor" of the forces already in America forbade making the war one of strangulation, which might easily have been done, and led to one fruitless campaign after another. British commanders felt that, for the sake of their reputations, they must have victories on the field of battle.

The Campaign of 1776

The British plan of campaign in 1776 was devised by Lord George Germain, Secretary of State for the colonies. Ten thousand trained and well-equipped troops were sent to Canada, and General Guy Carleton, who was there in command, was told to move south toward Albany. General William Howe's army, which had been stationed at Halifax after its evacuation of Boston, was built up to 30,000 men, and Howe was ordered to take New York. General Henry Clinton, with 3,000 men, was detached from Howe's main force with instructions to strike in the Carolinas, where it was supposed that he could enlist much Tory and Indian aid. Squadrons of the British fleet supported these operations. Faced by these formidable preparations, the colonials busied themselves drilling troops and concentrating such forces as they possessed in the threatened areas.

Had the British concentrated all their forces in one mighty attack upon New York and New England, the campaign of 1776 might have been disastrous for the patriots. As it was, the colonials were able to thwart two of the three British offensives. North Carolina patriots scattered a Loyalist force of Highland Scots and up-country Regulators at Moore's Creek Bridge (February 27, 1776), and when Clinton arrived in the area, he found no Loyalist support worthy of the name. The Carolina patriots devastated Cherokee towns and kept the Indians in check. A naval assault on Charleston failed when the British cannon balls harmlessly imbedded themselves in the soft palmetto logs of the fort on Sullivan's Island commanded by Colonel William Moultrie. Clinton lingered in southern waters for weeks, but by midsummer, completely frustrated, he gave up the attack and sailed to rejoin Howe in New York.

The projected invasion from Canada had no better success than that which attended Clinton's southern expedition. When Carleton and "Gentleman Johnny" Burgoyne attempted to seize Fort Ticonderoga in October, 1776, stubborn opposition by the patriots, under Benedict Arnold, thwarted their efforts. In the area around New York, however, the colonials found themselves hard pressed.

Washington was in personal command of the American forces in the New York region, which he rightly judged would be the scene of the principal British offensive. The American commander-in-chief was cold and reserved by nature, resentful of criticism, and sometimes jealous of other American generals. He was not a professional soldier and in his inexperience sometimes made mistakes that might well have had fatal results for the American cause. But his mistakes became less frequent as the war went on, and his courage, integrity, selfless devotion, and balanced judgment were of enormous value to the patriots. As a commander and a leader he had no equal on either side of the struggle.

General William Howe and his elder brother, Admiral Lord Howe, occupied undefended Staten Island in July, 1776. Some weeks were then spent in preparing for an offensive campaign and in vainly offering pardon to rebels who would lay down their arms. It was not until August that Howe began to move against Washington, whose troops were inferior, both in numbers and quality, to those of his opponent. Washington made mistakes in the disposition of his forces that might have proved fatal to the patriot cause, had it not been for the slow movements of his adversary. Defeated at the battle of Long Island (August 27, 1776), the Americans abandoned New York, narrowly escaping disaster in the process. On October 28, Washington was defeated again at White Plains, and the following month he lost 3,000

GENERAL WASHINGTON

The commander-in-chief of the American forces. The artist—Charles Willson Peale—has caught the dignity, authority, and forcefulness that characterized Washington throughout the Revolution.

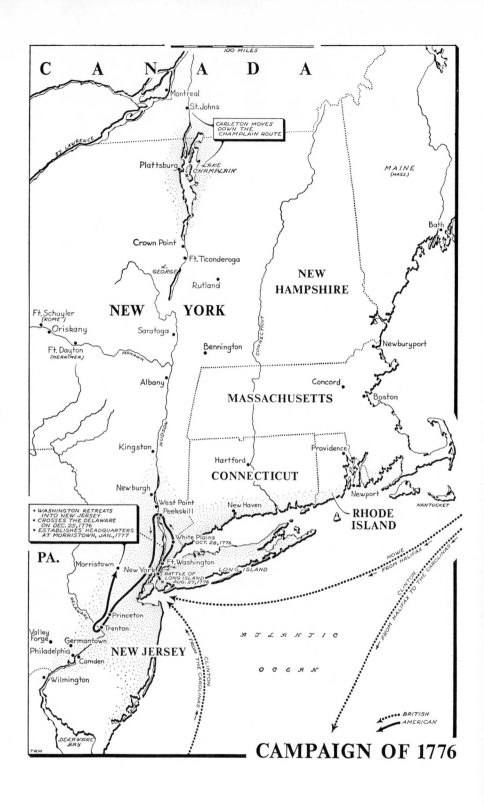

CAMPAIGN OF 1776

men who were forced to surrender at Fort Washington on upper Manhattan island. Pursued by Howe, the American general retired into New Jersey with the remnant of his forces. Howe drove him across the Delaware river but then went into winter quarters, with outposts on the east bank of the Delaware.

The patriot cause seemed desperate, but Washington now executed a brilliant stroke. Reinforced by regulars and militia from the Hudson area and from Philadelphia, he crossed the Delaware with 2,400 men on the night of December 25, 1776, surprising and capturing 1,000 Hessians at Trenton under the command of Colonel Rall. This coup, and subsequent campaigning in the Princeton area, left Washington in control of West Jersey, and he went into winter quarters at Morristown.

Howe was knighted for his victory in New York, but the American army remained very much in being. A campaign that had verged on complete disaster ended with successes that gave the patriots much needed hope.

The Tide Turns in Earnest (1777)

Howe formulated three plans of campaign for 1777. Germain approved one of these, by which Howe would move the main body of his forces by land into Pennsylvania while he left garrisons at Newport and New York. Germain also approved a plan formulated by General Burgoyne, who had superseded Carleton in the Canadian area. Burgoyne proposed a three-pronged offensive centering on Albany. He would lead an army from Canada down through the Champlain area, an auxiliary force under Lieutenant-Colonel Barry St. Leger to come from Oswego down along the Mohawk, and the forces left in New York city to advance up the Hudson to Burgoyne's support; they were to meet at Albany, and New England would then be cut off from the other rebellious areas.

The difficulties of communication across the Atlantic, and perhaps Howe's jealousy of Burgoyne, now raised havoc with British plans. Howe decided to move into Pennsylvania by sea instead of by land. When Germain heard of this change of procedure, he sent a despatch urging that it should not preclude major support for the army driving down from Canada; but when Howe received this communication (August 16, 1777), he was at sea with the great bulk of his forces, en route to Chesapeake Bay. It was then too late for any change in his movements, and he had not even ordered the troops left in New York to cooperate with "Gentleman Johnny."

The results of this failure to synchronize the British plans of campaign were soon to become apparent, but at first all seemed to be going well. Howe

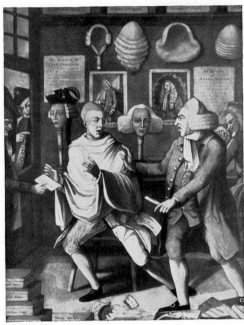

A CARTOON OF THE
REVOLUTION

*Many of the inhabitants of
New York and Philadelphia
cooperated willingly with the
British during the occupation
of those cities. This barber who
refused to shave Captain Crozer
of one of His Majesty's ships
represents the patriotic element.*

COURTESY OF THE NEW-YORK HISTORICAL SOCIETY, NEW YORK CITY

landed at the head of Chesapeake Bay toward the end of August with 15,000 troops. Washington had taken a position at Brandywine Creek with 11,000 men, 8,000 of whom were Continentals, but he was beaten back by a combination of flanking movements and frontal attack, and the British occupied Philadelphia, September 25, 1777. Howe then placed 9,000 men at Germantown, seven miles from the city. Washington's move against this detachment on October 4 was repulsed, and, after some further ineffective campaigning, the Americans went into winter quarters at Valley Forge. The British general settled down for a winter of such conviviality as to lead to Benjamin Franklin's comment that Philadelphia had taken Howe, but the Tory aid which the British commander had confidently expected was disappointingly small, and he shortly heard of a major disaster suffered by British arms in the North.

While Howe was campaigning in Pennsylvania, the northern campaign had got underway. Burgoyne, with an army of 9,500 men that included some 1,000 Canadians, Indians, and Tories, pushed south from Quebec into the Champlain region, while St. Leger with a mixed force of 900 troops and some 1,000 Indian allies moved into the Mohawk valley. Opposed to Burgoyne was a patriot army of some 5,000 men, approximately half of whom were Continentals, commanded at first by Philip Schuyler and subsequently by Horatio Gates. Lying at Fort Schuyler on the Mohawk, near the site of the present city of Rome, were several hundred colonials under Colonel Peter Gansevoort and Lieutenant-Colonel Marinus Willett.

At first fortune seemed to favor the British. Burgoyne, issuing one boastful proclamation after another, took Fort Ticonderoga and moved slowly southward. St. Leger invested Fort Schuyler and demanded the instant surrender of the colonials. But then one mishap after another descended upon the

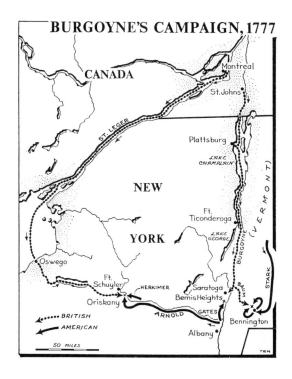

BURGOYNE'S CAMPAIGN, 1777

British commanders. The patriot army before Burgoyne was augmented by militia from surrounding areas, while his force was weakened in a series of engagements, especially John Stark's destruction of a British foraging expedition under Colonel Baum that had been sent in force to Bennington, Vermont. The Tories and Indians began deserting Burgoyne's standard. Worse still, the expected support from the Mohawk region and from New York did not appear.

There was good reason why the whoops of St. Leger's Indians were not heard on the lower Mohawk. Gansevoort and Willett most obstinately and contumaciously refused to surrender Fort Schuyler. Nicholas Herkimer with colonial militia moved up to the relief of the fort. In the ensuing engagement at Oriskany, the colonials were repulsed and Herkimer was mortally wounded, but St. Leger's forces were roughly handled in the process. A second relief expedition of 1,000 men next appeared. Benedict Arnold, its commander, offered to spare the life of a half-witted Tory captive, Hon Yost, if the latter would go into St. Leger's camp and tell of a mighty army that was coming to the relief of the fort. Yost joyfully accepted the offer. He told a hair-raising tale, and the Indians, who took his word as gospel because he was a madman, at once deserted. St. Leger was forced by this defection to retreat to Oswego.

Deprived of St. Leger's support and unaided from the New York direction, Burgoyne's position became desperate. The colonials stopped his forward thrust at Freeman's Farm (September 19, 1777), and three weeks later he was badly mauled at Bemis Heights. He thereupon retreated to Saratoga. There, outnumbered and surrounded, on October 17, 1777, he surrendered his remaining force of 5,000 men.

Burgoyne's surrender had far-reaching effects. The patriots were immensely spirited, while British morale sank to a low point and Lord North began to talk about resignation. Parliament repealed the Townshend tea duty and the Massachusetts Government Act and sent commissioners to America who vainly tried to woo the patriots with a promise of home rule. Most significant of all was the impact of Saratoga on the international situation.

The French Alliance

France and Spain, desirous of weakening Britain's power, had been furnishing assistance to the patriots since early in 1776 in the form of munitions. These had been shipped to the colonies by a French agent, Caron de Beaumarchais, who organized for this purpose a bogus mercantile concern, Rodrigue Hortalez and Company. The patriots sent Silas Deane, Benjamin Franklin, and Arthur Lee to the French court, late in 1776, to obtain more aid and recognition of American independence. Franklin made a great impression on the French, who regarded him as typical of those children of nature, the Americans, a point of view that Franklin did his best to encourage. France had hesitated to recognize American independence, lest the revolt peter out, but when the news of Saratoga reached Paris Vergennes, the French Foreign Minister, promised recognition. The result was two treaties with France, signed on February 6, 1778, which recognized the United States of America, opened the ports of each nation to the other's commerce, bound the colonials not to lay down their arms before independence was achieved, and guaranteed French possessions in the New World and American territory as it should be determined at the close of the war. France was now a full-fledged partner in the revolutionary struggle.

Over and beyond French participation in the war, Vergennes' influence and the French example were largely responsible for Spain's entering the lists against Great Britain in 1779, for Holland's participation a year later, and for the formation of the Armed Neutrality of the North which, in the early 1780s, assumed an ominous attitude toward Britain's interference with the neutral commerce of Scandinavian countries and of Russia. After Saratoga, Britain not only found itself more and more isolated from the rest of Europe but also forced to contend with an increasing number of foes. The turning point of the Revolution, faintly visible after the British failure to crush the revolt in 1776, had been reached with the French alliance of 1778.

Despite the stimulus provided by Saratoga, the winter of 1777–1778 was one that tried the souls of patriots. Washington's army, in winter quarters at Valley Forge, scarcely twenty miles from Philadelphia, suffered badly from the frigid weather and from a breakdown of the commissariat. The toll of dead and maimed was heavy, and there were many desertions. Congress was chagrined over the loss of Philadelphia, and many Congressmen were critical of Washington's leadership. There was some sentiment for replacing him by Gates, but this never developed into anything like a plot or cabal. Hope revived, however, with news of the French alliance, and spring enlistments raised Washington's force to nearly 10,000 men. It was, moreover, well equipped and reasonably well disciplined, the latter being due in some part to the efforts of General von Steuben, a German soldier of fortune who— like the "Baron" De Kalb and the Poles Kosciusko and Pulaski—rendered valuable service to the American cause.

The New British Strategy

The British plan of campaign for 1778 and the years that followed was, save for the South, defensive in character. Howe had resigned, and Clinton, who replaced him, was ordered to evacuate Philadelphia and to marshal forces for a descent on Georgia; meanwhile, he ravaged the New England coast and also furnished troops for attacking the French in the West Indies. In June, therefore, Clinton sent part of his force to New York by sea and started overland with 10,000 men for the same destination. Washington moved toward him from Valley Forge, and the two armies made contact at Monmouth on June 28, 1778. A stubbornly fought conflict ensued with about 300 casualties on either side, but it left Clinton free to pursue his way to New York.

Clinton's subsequent movements were limited by the appearance on the American coast of a French fleet of twelve ships of the line and five frigates under Count d'Estaing. This force rendered ineffective the British blockade and enabled hundreds of American privateers to slip out of harbor and prey on British commerce. These privateers were the patriots' chief contribution to war on the sea, save for the brilliant sea duel in which the *Bon Homme Richard* under John Paul Jones captured the British warship *Serapis* in September, 1779.

After ineffectual land and naval maneuvers against British positions in Rhode Island, d'Estaing sailed for the West Indies, where he remained for most of the next three years. The British evacuated Newport but still largely controlled the sea approaches to that town and to New York. Another Frenchman, however, Admiral de Grasse, was able to land a French army of 6,000 men under the Count de Rochambeau in Rhode Island during the summer of 1780. This army was destined to play a very important part in the campaign that ended the war.

Subsequent to the 1778 campaign, British efforts in the North were confined to blockade, local raiding operations, and attempts to seduce prominent patriots. These last succeeded in one major instance. Benedict Arnold—married to a beautiful and luxury-loving Philadelphia belle, Margaret Shippen, heavily in debt, smarting under slights by Congress and Pennsylvania civil authorities, and, as a Protestant New Englander with poignant memories of the French and Indian wars, loathing the French alliance—fell a prey to British wiles. For months he supplied Clinton with valuable information about troop and naval movements and then, in 1780, sought, as commander of West Point, to surrender that fortress to the British. Arnold's treason was discovered, and his coadjutor, Major John André, captured within the American lines when dressed in civilian clothes, was executed as a spy. Arnold escaped to the British, who gave him sizable rewards for his treachery. Save for the loss of a brave and brilliant leader, no great damage resulted to the American cause.

The War in the West and in the South

While the war in the northern and middle colonies dragged its slow length along the seaboard, there were military operations of consequence on the northern and northwestern frontiers. The Iroquois and other Indian tribes had ravaged the New York, Pennsylvania, Virginia, and Kentucky frontiers, massacring settlers in these outlying districts. The forays in the Wyoming

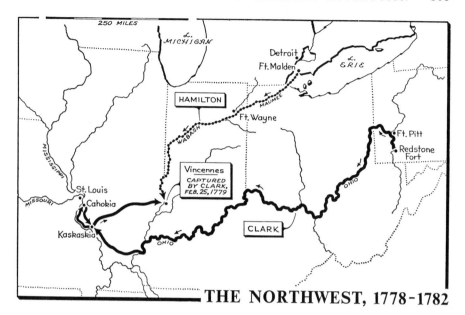

THE NORTHWEST, 1778-1782

Valley of Pennsylvania and the Cherry Valley of New York were especially bloody. In 1779, General John Sullivan scourged the Indian towns in central New York, decimating Iroquois military strength. Just previously, George Rogers Clark had moved into the Ohio Valley, where he punished the Indians allied with the British, captured Vincennes and a British force stationed there, and by his efforts strengthened the American claim to what was to become known as the Old Northwest.

The main object of British attack in these years was the South, where Clinton, lured on once more by the expectation of Tory and Indian support, hoped to re-establish British control. After 3,000 troops sent from New York and 2,000 from the British post at St. Augustine, Florida, had established control over Georgia in a brief winter campaign, 1778–1779, Congress sent General Benjamin Lincoln into the South; he succeeded in gathering a force of 6,000 men, chiefly militia. Lincoln failed to reconquer Georgia and soon found himself confronted by a new peril, for early in 1780, Clinton, with a fleet and 8,000 troops, appeared off Charleston. Lincoln tried to defend the city, was trapped by the British commander, and on May 12, 1780, Charleston, and an American army of 5,000 men and 300 cannon, surrendered. Flushed with triumph, Clinton returned to New York, leaving the British forces in the South under the command of Charles, Lord Cornwallis.

It looked as though South Carolina's fate was sealed, but the patriots in both South Carolina and Georgia turned to partisan warfare under the leadership of Francis Marion (the "Swamp Fox"), Thomas Sumter, and other daring commanders. During the summer of 1780, Washington sent some 1,500 Continentals south under Baron De Kalb, who was soon replaced by Horatio Gates. Reinforced by some 2,000 militia, Gates attempted to seize Camden, South Carolina, on August 16, 1780, but was badly defeated by Cornwallis. Two days later, Sumter's partisans were severely handled by the dragoons of Colonel Banastre Tarleton. Once again the patriot cause in South Carolina appeared to be in eclipse, and Cornwallis felt free to carry the war into North Carolina. There, however, at King's Mountain (October 7, 1780) 900 patriot backwoods riflemen destroyed a force of 1,200 Tories under Major Patrick Ferguson and, weakened by this defeat, Cornwallis judged it prudent to go back to South Carolina.

The struggle for North Carolina was resumed in 1781. Cornwallis moved again into that state, only to be confronted by a strengthened American force under General Nathanael Greene, who was ably supported by General Daniel Morgan. At Cowpens, South Carolina, on January 17, 1781, Morgan's riflemen routed Tarleton, giving a decided boost to American morale. Cornwallis sought in vain to force a decisive combat in which he could meet and crush the elusive Americans. At Guilford Court House in North Carolina (March 15, 1781), the Britisher won a victory over Greene; though this brought no decisive results, Cornwallis felt that the situation was favorable enough for him to move into Virginia. He fortified himself at Yorktown and waited for reinforcements from the North, while the British troops left in the Carolinas kept up a running fight with Greene's army. They made no progress in subduing the countryside, and at the end of the war held only Charleston, Savannah, and the immediately surrounding areas.

Yorktown

Cornwallis, at Yorktown, urged Clinton to send aid and in turn was told to move into Pennsylvania and cooperate there with Clinton or else send most of the men under his command to New York. The two British commanders were at cross purposes, and, as a result, Cornwallis with over 7,000 men remained at Yorktown. American forces under Steuben, "Mad Anthony" Wayne, and the Marquis de Lafayette (who had come to America to fight for liberty in 1777 and had become one of Washington's trusted officers) began gathering in Virginia.

Suddenly, Cornwallis found himself trapped. In response to appeals from Washington, a French fleet of twenty ships of war under Admiral De Grasse arrived on the Atlantic coast and, temporarily, held command of the sea in

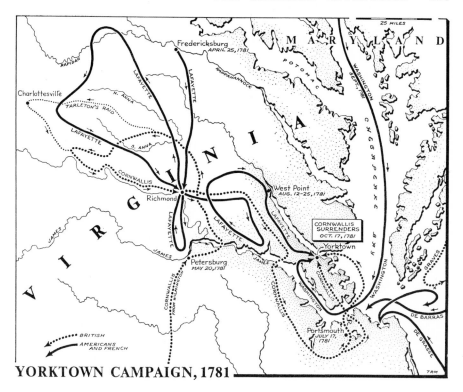

YORKTOWN CAMPAIGN, 1781

the New York-Virginia area. Washington, persuaded by Rochambeau to move against Cornwallis rather than attack New York in force, left only a few regiments to mask Clinton in New York and led 5,000 French and 2,000 American troops across Pennsylvania into Virginia. He moved so swiftly that he was past Philadelphia before Clinton learned of his whereabouts. De Grasse commanded the approaches to Chesapeake Bay, bringing in more French troops and making impossible the relief of Cornwallis by sea. Since 16,000 men invested Yorktown by land, there was no escape. Cornwallis and 7,000 men surrendered on October 19, 1781. There is evidence that as the British troops marched in surrender between the French and American armies, the British bands played a tune called "The World Turned Upside Down." The catastrophe was scarcely of that order, but, practically speaking, the surrender at Yorktown meant the end of the war.

The Peace of Paris (1783)

The surrender of Cornwallis brought a decisive change in British policy toward the Americans. George III wished to continue the effort to subdue the patriots, and the pliant Lord North bent to his will, but Parliamentary opposition to the King's power and to the war itself steadily increased. In April, 1780, Parliament had passed a declaration "that the influence of the Crown has increased, is increasing, and ought to be diminished." Now, on March 4, 1782, a motion to abandon the struggle in America passed the Commons. North resigned, and a new ministry, headed by Rockingham, took over the government and put out feelers for peace. Rockingham himself and some of the other Whigs still hoped that America might be saved for the Empire.

The conferences that now ensued admirably illustrate the difficulties inherent in international negotiations where the stakes are high. Vergennes remained firm in seeking the independence of the United States, but he was not so much interested in America's welfare as he was in securing advantages for France and Spain. He supported Spanish claims to Florida and to other large amounts of territory east of the Mississippi. The Spanish Foreign Minister, Count Floridablanca, was suspicious of American aspirations and sought to keep the new country as weak as possible. He was perfectly willing to leave New York, Charleston, and other key points in British hands. The American Congress was determined that the Mississippi on the west and the thirty-first parallel on the south should be the boundaries established in any treaty of peace. Suspicion of French and Spanish designs was rife in America, and the American peace commissioners were instructed to make recognition of independence the focal point of their efforts. At the same time, prudence dictated that they work closely with France.

The peace was negotiated at Paris. The American commissioners were Franklin, John Adams, John Jay, and Henry Laurens. Franklin played the leading role at first, with Adams and Jay later taking an important part in the proceedings. The Sage of Philadelphia was seventy-six years old in 1782, but his mind was clear and his powers of persuasion were undiminished. Richard Oswald, Alleyne Fitzherbert, and others acted for the British government.

At first the British agents sought to entice the Americans into separate discussion of peace terms. Though Franklin did violate his instructions to the extent of secret talks with Oswald, he insisted that negotiations with England should be carried on simultaneously by France and America, and he took pains to maintain friendly relations with Vergennes. In his talks with the British, Franklin cannily expressed the hope that some time and in some way America and Great Britain might be reunited, a point of view that was distinctly pleasing to Oswald.

As talks between the various countries proceeded, Jay became increasingly suspicious of France and Spain. He found it easy to persuade Franklin and Adams to join him in suggesting to the British that America might accept a separate peace treaty. The British responded positively, and negotiations now assumed a more rapid tempo. Any vague hopes the Americans had entertained of acquiring Canada were abandoned for British support of American claims to the trans-Appalachian region. At one stage, the Americans proposed that the two countries establish a mutual freedom of trade and navigation throughout their dominions. Such an agreement would have had tremendous consequences, but British mercantilists would have none of it.

The British and American commissioners signed the treaty of peace between their two countries on September 3, 1783. It accepted as the boundary between Canada and the United States a line ambiguously defined that sup-

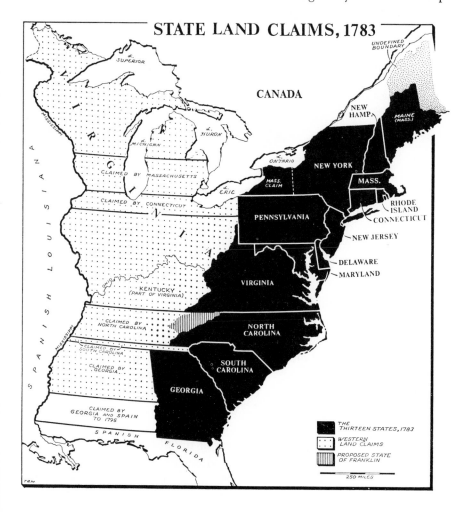

STATE LAND CLAIMS, 1783

"EVACUATION DAY"

This lithograph by E. P. and L. Restein shows Washington's triumphal entry into New York City (November 26, 1783). It was a fitting triumph for the man who had played the leading role in bringing the Revolution to a successful conclusion.

posedly followed the St. Croix river in Nova Scotia and the highlands south of the St. Lawrence to the forty-fifth parallel of latitude, and then a river-Great Lakes boundary to the Lake of the Woods and the Mississippi. It asserted that the western boundary of the United States was the Mississippi River as far south as the thirty-first degree of latitude. The treaty validated American private debts. It agreed that Congress would recommend to the states the restitution of confiscated Tory estates. It secured for the United States fishing rights in the Newfoundland area and in the Gulf of St. Lawrence and agreed that the navigation of the Mississippi should be open to both countries. As a result of valor and determination, foreign aid, and Britain's willingness to give generous terms so that the ties between the United States and France might be weakened, the patriots had ended their struggle with the mother country with a peace that could scarcely have seemed possible in 1776. Congress ratified the treaty January 14, 1784.

Franklin diplomatically assuaged Vergennes' anger over the separate negotiation of peace between Britain and the United States, and the French Foreign Minister indicated his forgiving spirit by helping the Americans secure a loan of six million livres from France. He had the more reason to be magnanimous, since the Anglo-United States treaty did not become official until France also made peace.

Negotiations between England on the one hand and France and Spain on the other came to a head shortly after the conclusion of the Anglo-American agreement, Britain ceding the island of Tobago to France and the Floridas to Spain. This latter cession gave America a weak southern neighbor and opened the way for securing the thirty-first parallel as the southern boundary of the United States.

The Revolution and Political Change

The American Revolution was far more than a struggle for freedom from Great Britain. The act of separation and the war itself inevitably produced far-reaching political, economic, social, and cultural changes within American society. Of these, the first to appear were changes in political conditions.

After Lexington and Concord, the royal governors fled to England, and the colonies undertook to carry on their governments by means of provincial congresses. Some colonies—Virginia was one—petitioned Congress for advice as to the kind of permanent governments they should set up, but the best advice Congress could give was that they should construct such governments as would "best produce the happiness of the people." Left to themselves by this ambiguous counsel, the colonies tackled the job.

There were actually two forms of permanent government to be established—one provincial, the other national—and there was much discussion of both. It took some years to bring the national government into being, but the governments of the "states," as the Declaration of Independence called the former colonies, were an immediate and pressing matter. During 1776, a number of state governments were created, and by 1780 all the state constitutions had been framed and put into operation. All were new save those of Rhode Island and Connecticut, which continued to use their old charters with some minor revisions.

A number of considerations, some theoretical and some practical, shaped the formation of the new state constitutions. Locke and Montesquieu, revered by this generation, were looked to as useful guides. Experience had shown the unwritten British constitution to be dangerously susceptible to diverse interpretations, and so the colonists regarded written constitutions as absolutely essential. Conflict with the executive power of the Crown, as wielded by the royal governors, had imbued the patriots with a hearty fear of executive authority and a determination to limit its prerogatives. Finally, some of the men who framed these constitutions were political liberals and others were conservatives. The constitutions themselves were inevitably a compromise between those who shrank from drastic change and suspected the intelligence and emotional stability of the masses and those whose foremost goals were freedom and equality of opportunity for all men.

The new state constitutions were drawn up for the most part by the provincial congresses, or by legislatures elected at a time when constitution-making was not an issue. Some of them were hastily drafted in times of stress and danger. In general, however, the work was well done; in two instances, Massachusetts and New Hampshire, the documents were the result of state constitutional conventions called by the legislatures and were submitted to the voters for ratification. This was an American contribution to political theory and practice, and it set a pattern for framing subsequent charters of government in the United States.

Generally speaking, the liberals had the upper hand in the framing of these state documents, for when the makeshift governments had come into being, the suffrage had been considerably widened and known Tories had been excluded from the polls. It is not surprising, therefore, that the preambles of the state constitutions declared the people to be the source of all political power and provided freedom of speech, press, and petition, and the rights of habeas corpus and of trial by jury. Although tax, property, and sometimes religious qualifications for voting and officeholding remained, the constitutions widened the suffrage of colonial days. In many states, redistricting curbed the power of the seaboard urban areas and increased that of the frontier. The constitutions made government officials and judges elective and centered power in the legislatures, especially in the lower house.* The state governors, indeed, emerged largely as figureheads; they had no power of patronage, and in eleven states they had no veto and were subject to impeachment. Montesquieu's concept of a balance of powers—executive, legislative, and judicial—had influence with the state constitution makers, but they were not interested in establishing an even balance between these three branches of government. This same point of view became even more apparent when Congress undertook to frame a charter for the national government.

---

* Ten of the state legislatures were bicameral. Pennsylvania, Georgia, and Vermont each had one house.

From the beginning of the Revolution, the patriots agreed that a national government was a necessity. They felt, as Franklin had once said, that they must continue to hang together or they would hang separately. In addition, the existence of a contiguous territory, and of common enemies in the French, Spaniards, and Indians, and the possession, for the most part, of a common language and common historical traditions emphasized the practicality and, indeed, the necessity of creating a common nation with a central government. The existence of the Continental Congress and the responsibilities it assumed in organizing armed forces, making treaties, issuing currency and establishing a postal service gave ample proof of the importance of such an authority, if America was to emerge from the war as a nation rather than a motley group of weak and independent states.

If the states were to unite as a nation, it was obvious that the latter would have to have a constitution, and in 1776 the Continental Congress entrusted to a committee of thirteen (one from each state) the work of drawing up such a plan of national organization. At this point, state jealousies and fear of centralized power began to enter into the picture.

There were a number of divisive influences that weighed upon the thinking of the committee of thirteen and upon that of the Congress as a whole. Representatives of states with large populations felt that representation in the national legislature should be proportioned to state population, while the small states upheld the principle of equal representation. How to provide for the expenses of the national government was a subject of lengthy dispute. All agreed that the states must contribute to the support of the central government, but some wanted such contributions based on the wealth of the states, others on the basis of population, and the southern states wanted contributions based on population only if slaves were excluded from enumeration. Another source of division was whether or not Congress should have control over the lands west of the Appalachians. Massachusetts, Connecticut, Virginia, the Carolinas, Georgia, and even New York had more or less valid claims to lands in the West. The other states held that such claims should be relinquished, their chief argument being that this was essential for equality of opportunity in obtaining land grants.

John Dickinson was the chief author of the plan entitled "The Articles of Confederation" that was drawn up by the committee of thirteen, submitted to Congress, and, after considerable debate and a few changes, adopted on November 15, 1777. It declared that "The Stile of this confederacy shall be 'The United States of America' " and that it would be a "league of friendship." It provided a unicameral legislature, the delegates thereto being chosen annually by the states. The delegates would vote by states on legislative measures. Each state would contribute to the expenses of the United States in proportion to the value of the improved lands in the state, the taxes providing for these contributions to be levied by the states themselves (the old principle of requisition, carried over from colonial times). There was no attempt to set the western boundaries of any state. The Congress was given authority over foreign and Indian affairs. It could regulate the coinage, borrow money, establish a postal service, build and equip a navy and raise an army, and adjudicate disputes between states. All powers not specifically given to Congress were reserved to the states, which, the document stated, would retain their "sovereignty, freedom, and independence."

As events were to prove, the Articles of Confederation formed a workable instrument, but one which had great defects. It did not provide for either a national executive or a national judiciary. Congress had no control over commerce or taxing power, and many of its powers could not be exercised without the consent of nine states. Perhaps worst of all, the Articles could not be amended unless the states gave their unanimous consent. Such a constitution would be absolutely unworkable in the United States of today, but it was probably the best that could have been expected, in view of the problems involved in its making, and American inexperience in forming anything like a central government.

Ratification of the Articles began in 1778, but some of the states quibbled and delayed. Maryland, New Jersey, and Delaware were especially recalcitrant because of the failure to give Congress authority to establish western boundaries for the states with trans-Appalachian land claims, the contention centering around the lands lying north and west of the Ohio River. Delaware and New Jersey finally ratified in the winter of 1778–1779, but Maryland held out. The Virginia delegation proposed establishing the Confederation without Maryland, but this was frowned upon as dangerous to the whole experiment. As the months went by, sympathy for Maryland's attitude increased, especially among the so-called landless states. Land speculators who had purchased from the Indians and feared that the states would not recognize their titles helped on the agitation for putting the western lands in a national domain. Gradually the states with western claims moved toward surrendering those claims to the central government. New York, whose claims were the most shadowy of all, led the way, followed by Virginia, and then the other states fell into line. By January, 1781, the demand that the states give up their claims beyond the Ohio River had been largely met.

The giving up of state claims to the western lands had two important consequences. It led to Maryland's ratification of the Articles in February and, consequently, the formal announcement of the Confederation on March 1,

1781. It also resulted in the creation of a great national domain, the organization and settlement of which had a profound and lasting influence upon national politics and policies, and, indeed, upon the character of American life.

The Revolution and Economic Change

Economic changes, as well as political developments, characterized the revolutionary era. There was, as always in wartime, considerable burning and pillaging of property. Foreign trade was disrupted, especially in finished goods, and great scarcities resulted. On the other hand, there was a marked rise in household manufacturing, which was systematically aided and encouraged by the revolutionary government and without which the war could hardly have been won. Since urban labor was at a premium, its wages rose; but price inflation tripled and quadrupled where wages doubled, and the lot of the town worker was hard indeed.

Price and wage inflation led to attempts, especially in New England, at price and wage controls, and to laws requiring the use of state currencies as legal tender. These evidences of the continued prevalence of mercantilistic thought provoked widespread evasion by the business class and were abandoned before the end of the war. On the whole, the war weakened the principle of governmental control and strengthened economic individualism in America. It is interesting that this happened just as Adam Smith, in *The Wealth of Nations* (1776), was forcefully expounding the doctrine that the individual's pursuit of self-interest would result in maximum social gain. The concept of laissez faire was moving into its heyday.

Certain elements in all classes sought to make profit out of the war. Not a few merchants continued to carry on trade with England, or with the British forces occupying New York and Philadelphia, despite the efforts of Congress to prevent such traffic. Others sought wealth at the expense of the French forces. Congressman Samuel Chase, for example, a signer of the Declaration of Independence and later a judge on the United States Supreme Court, took part in an effort to corner the supply of flour on news of the approach of the French fleet. Such profiteering was not confined to farmers and businessmen. A group of sailors, asked in 1777 to remain in the service of Virginia, replied, "Country here or Country there damn my eyes and limbs but I'll serve them that give the best wages."

Of course, many of the profits made in the war were entirely legitimate. Despite the havoc wrought by marching armies, many farmers prospered as a result of the wartime demand for farm produce. Privateering reaped large returns, and men like John and Andrew Cabot and Elias Hasket Derby made fortunes in the business. Sutlers, and army contractors such as Jeremiah Wadsworth of Connecticut, Robert Morris of Philadelphia, and Philip Schuyler of Albany (who sold provisions to the army in which he was a major general) made money out of the war.

If the war profited some individuals, it caused grievous loss to others. British blockades ruined the whale oil and candle business and brought the fishing industry almost to a standstill. Not only the town laborers, but also the clergy, public officials and others on fixed salaries suffered badly from the wartime inflation. The Continental army, both officers and men, was hard hit from the same quarter. The army was resentful over arrears in pay at the end of the war, but Washington managed to soothe the discontented and Congress tardily made suitable pay arrangements so that the soldiers finally went home in peaceful fashion.

The great majority of the Tories suffered grievous economic loss in the war. They were harshly treated, especially after considerable numbers began to take up arms in the latter part of the struggle. Millions of pounds worth of Tory property was confiscated and between 70,000 and 100,000 Tories went into exile. The distress of these wanderers was only partially alleviated by pensions and other forms of assistance from the British government.

The war meant hardship to some forms of business and many individuals, but the lessons and demands of war, coupled with increasing prospects of a return to more normal economic activity, stimulated two forms of business organization that were to have great influence upon the character of the American economy. The rise of American banking began with the organization of the Bank of North America, established in 1782 as an aid to the war effort, followed two years later by the Bank of New York. The chartering of eleven banking and business corporations between 1781 and 1785 began a development of the corporate form of business activity which was to become a vital part of American economic life.

The Revolution and Social Change

The Revolution produced social as well as political and economic changes in American society. The emigration of the Tories—among whom aristocratic conservatism was prevalent—obviously gave society a more liberal tinge. Plenty of men conservative in religion and politics and possessed of culture and wealth were numbered in the patriot ranks, however, and class distinctions remained substantially as they had been in the colonial period.

The suffrage, already largely democratic because it was based chiefly on land that was easy to obtain, was expanded. But there were still some tax and property limitations; property qualifications for officeholding made it practically impossible for a poor man to become either a state senator or a governor. Sceptics, agnostics, and often Catholics were still deprived of all chance for political preferment.

An antislavery movement appeared, hastened in part by the equalitarian dogmas of the Revolution. There was some manumission of slaves, and all the states save South Carolina and Georgia barred the importation of slaves from abroad. Pennsylvania in 1780, Massachusetts in 1783, and other northern states where slavery was unprofitable, either abolished slavery or provided for gradual emancipation. On the other hand, the Revolution did nothing to better the condition of indentured servants. Those remnants of feudal aristocracy, entail and primogeniture, had largely fallen into the discard before the Revolution, but they were formally abolished during the Revolutionary period. The confiscation of Tory estates did something to democratize the ownership of land, as did the freeing of western lands from the restrictions on settlement imposed by the British government, but these same developments opened the path to land ownership by speculators and wealthy merchants and planters. On the whole the Revolutionary impact had a democratizing effect, but it can scarcely be described as drastic in character.

The Revolution and American Culture

There remains for consideration the influence of the Revolution upon American culture. This was in part destructive. The burning of Charleston library, its 7,000 volumes being at that time the largest collection of books in America; the closing of seven of the nine colleges in the country and the destruction of college property; the demoralization of religious life by wartime conditions; the popularization of duelling by French officers; the 100 to 200 per cent profits made by Boston speculators in woolen goods while Washington's soldiers were dying at Valley Forge; the loss of Loyalist brains and talents—these could scarcely be counted as cultural gains. On the other hand, the war did make, directly and indirectly, some cultural contributions. Joel Barlow's *Vision of Columbus* and President Stiles's election sermon on *The United States Elevated to Glory and Honor* demonstrate the undoubted growth of national pride, and histories of various states appeared, showing a similar development at the state level. Religious freedom and the postwar spread of liberal theologies was fostered by the disestablishment of the Episcopal church, which occurred as a direct outcome of the war. The widespread reorganization of American churches on a national basis fostered the development of national unity and national patriotism, and encouraged the establishment of at least eight new colleges by various religious denominations.

Education in America was also stimulated in a variety of secular ways by the Revolution. The exigencies of war time promoted improvements in medicine and medical education, and in the science of engineering. Americans learned the value of pamphleteering, à la Tom Paine, as a means of influencing public opinion. Hessian officers made investigations that contributed to American scientific knowledge. Most significant of all was the impact of French influence.

The general American conception of the French as savage, diminutive, immoral infidels, with frizzled hair and painted faces, faded as a result of contact with such Frenchmen as La Fayette, Berthier (later Napoleon's chief of staff), Henri de Saint Simon, and the well-behaved and effective French army. In that army were engineers, doctors, and dentists who contributed to the scientific knowledge of the New World, and Major L'Enfant, architect and engineer, who planned the national capital. Such contacts, together with the presence of French aid and the hope of support from French Canada, brought some improvement in the legal status of Catholics and a more tolerant attitude toward that church than there had been in colonial America.

Suggested Reading

In addition to the works cited in the previous chapter, the student should use Howard Peckham, *The War for Independence* (1958); Christopher Ward, *The War of the Revolution* (2 vols., 1952); J. R. Alden's *The American Revolution, 1775–1783* (1954) and J. C. Miller's *Triumph of Freedom, 1775–1783* (1948), all excellent treatments. The Revolution is studied from an English viewpoint in Eric Robson, *The American Revolution, 1763–1783* (1955) and Piers Mackesy, *The War for America* (1964). Herbert Butterfield, *George III and the Historians* (1957) is enlightening; and C. P. Nettels, *George Washington and American Independence* (1951) is scholarly and informative. Lynn Montross' *The Reluctant Rebels* (1950) and E. C. Burnett's *The Continental Congress* (1941) are important studies. See also W. H. Nelson, *The American Tory* (1962) and P. H. Smith, *Loyalists and Redcoats* (1964).

There are some excellent biographies of Revolutionary leaders. The works of Freeman and Malone on Washington and Jefferson have already been cited. J. C. Miller's *Sam Adams: Pioneer in Propaganda* (1936) and Carl Van Doren's *Benjamin Franklin* (1938) are well worth reading, as are S. E. Morison, *John Paul Jones: A Sailor's Biography* (1959) and Clarence Ver Steeg, *Robert Morris* (1954). Robert D. Meade, *Patrick Henry* (1957) carries Henry's career up to the Revolution and promises to be a definitive biography.

The social and economic history of the Revolution is treated in a variety of works. Very useful are R. A. East, *Business Enterprise in the American Revolutionary Era* (1938) and Rolla M. Tryon, *Household Manufactures in the United States, 1640–1860* (1917). R. E. Brown, *Middle-Class Democracy and the Revolution in Massachusetts, 1691–1780* (1955) is a challenging interpretation of American democracy as it existed in Massachusetts before and during the Revolution. In this connection, see also R. J. Taylor, *Western Massachusetts in the Revolution* (1954). J. F. Jameson, *The American Revolution Considered as a Social Movement* (1940) is an important though outdated study of the social effects of the Revolution. In connection with it, the student should use F. B. Tolles, "The American Revolution Considered as a Social Movement: a Re-Evaluation," *The American Historical Review,* LX (Oct., 1954), 1–12, which is a succinct analysis of Jameson's study in the light of more recent historical investigation.

Cultural and intellectual aspects of the revolutionary period are treated in Adrienne Koch, *The Philosophy of Thomas Jefferson* (1943); Hesketh Pearson, *Tom Paine, Friend of Mankind* (1937); H. M. Jones, *America and French Culture, 1750–1848* (1927); and in the charming essay "Culture in Knapsacks" in D. R. Fox, *Ideas in Motion* (1935).

The role of the Negro is treated in Benjamin Quarles, *The Negro in the American Revolution* (1961).

On the diplomatic side, see E. S. Corwin, *French Policy and the American Alliance* (1916) and S. F. Bemis, *The Diplomacy of the American Revolution* (1935).

THE YOUNG

Thomas Jefferson (1743–1826)

*Jefferson was not quite fifty-eight
years old when he became President. This
portrait was painted from life in 1805
by Rembrandt Peale.*

[1783-1815]

REPUBLIC

8 ⋅ The Confederation and the Constitution, 1783-1789

URING THE YEARS immediately following the Revolution, economic conditions in the United States were in a state of flux. The farmers (and it must be remembered that some 90 per cent of the American population lived on the land) at first had good prices for tobacco, wheat, and corn. After 1785, however, a fall in prices, together with heavy taxes and rigorous demands by creditors for the payment of debts, brought harder times, and the rural popula-

Social and Economic Conditions During the 1780s

tions of the states besieged their state governments with demands for relief. For the commercial classes, the situation was somewhat different. Peace meant the opening of American markets to foreign goods, which were eagerly welcomed by a population sick of the rigors of wartime. Specie became scarce as it moved into the hands of foreign creditors, however; the market became glutted, and in 1784–1785, especially in New England, there developed a commercial depression. Then times became better for the merchants and shippers, as trade with France, with Holland, and with the Orient increased. The British West Indies were closed to American shipping, but even there

American goods in considerable quantities were smuggled in or brought in foreign bottoms. By 1787 the commercial depression was over.

Manufacturing had a pattern that varied somewhat from that of both farming and commerce. The dumping of British goods in the early 1780s hit the manufacturing interests hard, and their immediate condition was precarious in the extreme. Many of the states then proceeded to establish protective tariffs against foreign imports. These saved American manufacturing from collapse under British competition, and a real development in the manufacture of iron, glass, textiles, and other products ensued. At the same time, societies for the promotion of manufacturing appeared in most of the northern and middle states.

In general, after the initial depression that hit first manufactures and then

THE UNITED STATES IN 1783

commerce, there was improvement in both these branches of the economy, but the lot of the farming population became harder as that of commerce and industry improved.

Opening Up the West

The difficulties experienced by agriculture in the latter 1780s did not prevent but rather stimulated the movement of Americans into the West. Lured on by the rich lands beyond the Appalachians, thousands of settlers crossed the mountains into Kentucky, Tennessee, and the valleys of the rivers

NEWLY CLEARED LAND
IN AMERICA

This tells a graphic story of labor on the forested frontier west of the Alleghenies. As manual labor pushes back the forest, cultivation of the soil takes place around and between tree stumps; logs are split so that the rail fence can be built.

COURTESY OF THE NEW YORK PUBLIC LIBRARY

running south into the Gulf of Mexico. There was a similar surge into the region north and west of the Ohio River. This movement made more and more needful the clear delimitation of the national domain, and the development of a land policy that would regularize settlement and make land titles authentic.

The states with land claims in the West had agreed to surrender them to the national government, but it took some time to work out details and make the final transfers. The Virginia agreement to cede had been made with the proviso that land titles established through previous purchase from the Indians should be void, and the speculators from Maryland and Pennsylvania who had made such purchases fought hard against the carrying out of this provision. Then again, Virginia and other "landed" states had issued to soldiers of the Revolution land bounties in the West that had to be honored, and the states concerned reserved land for that purpose in western New

York and in eastern Ohio. By 1786, with the exception of such reserves, the Northwest had passed under the control of the United States. South of Virginia, however, the states were still reluctant to cede their lands, because they wanted to use them in recouping the expenses of the war.

North Carolina, in 1783, had opened the Tennessee country to settlers who relied upon the state for protection against the Indians. When it appeared in 1784 that the state would cede that region to the national government, land speculators like John Sevier and William Blount and the actual settlers on the frontier decided to organize their own government and seek admission to the Union as a state. The result was the creation by Sevier and others of a semi-independent state named "Franklin." This was largely a speculators' pawn, and it had a precarious existence until just before 1789, when North Carolina definitely ceded its Tennessee lands to the Union. South Carolina ceded its claims in 1787, but Georgia, fascinated by the prospect of profits from land sales, became involved in dubious land speculation schemes and did not finally surrender its claims until 1802.

In New England, a controversy between New York and New Hampshire over land in the Connecticut valley region resulted in the settlers organizing their own government. There, as in the southwest, land speculation complicated the situation. New York finally surrendered its claims in 1790, and the state of Vermont was admitted to the Union in 1791.

The Great Land Ordinances

While the states were reluctantly giving up their pretensions to the western lands, Congress developed its land policy. This was a twofold business, involving both the method of land sales and the establishment of a plan of government.

The first definitive step in land policy defined procedures of survey and sale. After much discussion and conflict of opinion between those who favored settlement by the New England town method and those who wanted settlement to proceed at the initiative of the individual settler, Congress finally adopted the Ordinance of 1785. This established the bases of the public land system as it existed until the Homestead Act of 1862.

The Ordinance of 1785 applied to all government lands. It provided for survey of the public domain into townships six miles square, which, in turn, would be subdivided into sections one mile square—that is to say, 640 acres in extent. The land was to be sold alternately by township and by section. Sales were to take place after due notice, by auction in the already existing states, and the minimum price would be $1.00 per acre in specie or its equivalent. Four sections in each township were reserved for future sale, and the sixteenth section in each township was to be used for public school maintenance. After a specified amount of land had been surveyed, the area would be opened for sale and settlement.

The authors of this first great land ordinance attempted to emphasize order in settlement, rather than speed and immediate government income. Purchasers bought only after the land was surveyed, rather than moving out into the wilderness and marking out their plots for themselves. But the ordinance also made it difficult for bona fide settlers to buy land, even at the minimum price per acre. Few, save the speculators, had the $640 to pay for a section. This, coupled with the fact that survey was a slow process, stimulated "squatting" on unsurveyed land. The provisions of the act regarding price and the manner of sale bear witness to the hold which land speculation had on the imaginations and the pocketbooks of various members of Congress.

Interest in land speculation now rose to fever pitch. One of its products was the Ohio Company, organized in Boston by Brigadier General Rufus Putnam and friends in 1786. The agent of this company, Reverend Manasseh Cutler, a cleric with a gift for salesmanship, asked Congress for a grant of one and a half million acres in the area west of Virginia. He was told that he could have his grant if he would apply for five million acres more for the Scioto Company—a group of Congressmen, government officials, and businessmen who felt that, on account of their positions, they could not openly engage in a giant land speculation. Cutler fell in with their plans and obtained both grants from Congress. The Ohio Company's land cost the company $.08 an acre. The Scioto Company was a failure, and after its settlers had suffered much hardship because of its false promises, its lands went back to the government.

The speculator was usually an evil influence on the frontier. He bought up huge tracts which he held for sums that ranged from triple to sixty times his purchase price, and the settlers who bought of the speculators were often burdened by debt in consequence of the excessive prices paid for their farms. Land speculation fostered both mortgages and tenantry. Horace Greeley, a sound authority on western lands, wrote in 1847 that "the mischiefs already entailed on the industry and business of the country by land speculation are incalculable. . . ." On the other hand, the speculators furnished a ready market for public lands and sometimes were an asset to the settlers, providing them with credit and helping them to build towns that later developed into some of the West's great cities. Moses Cleaveland did this for the town that came to bear his name. The Ohio Company was of real help to the first settlers who came out under its auspices from New England, and the Reverend Manasseh Cutler's activities in Congress were to a considerable extent responsible for the Ordinance of 1787, one of the great legislative acts in American history.

The Ordinance of 1787 was the result of two things, the situation in the West and Cutler's skillful lobbying in Congress. The pioneers who moved into the West felt that they should be left to run their own affairs. That the squatters, and the more legitimate settlers as well, were of no mind to be bossed by the East was evidenced by the state of "Franklin" and the Vermont tangle. Similar separatist movements developed in western Pennsylvania and in Kentucky during the 1780s, and it became increasingly clear that the West would never accept colonial status or governmental dictation by eastern legislators.

In 1784, Jefferson proposed that the Mississippi valley east of the river be divided into fourteen self-governing districts that eventually would be admitted to the Union "on an equal footing with the . . . original states." This proposal contained details that both the West and the East disliked; though adopted, it was not put into effect and was still being debated in Congress when the Ohio and Scioto Company land deals went through. Cutler, as agent of the Ohio Company, then threw his influence into the scales with a petition that a governmental system be speedily established in the West as an aid to land sales. The interest that congressmen had in the western lands gave point to his petition and on July 13, 1787, Congress passed an ordinance for the government of lands northwest of the Ohio.

The Ordinance of 1787 provided that the region beyond the Ohio should be temporarily organized as territory, with a governor, secretary, and three judges appointed by Congress. It was to be subdivided into not less than three or more than five territories, each with its appointed governor. When any one of these had a population of 5,000 "free males, of full age," it would still have a governor with absolute veto power, but it would elect a legislature whose powers would be shared with a council of five appointed by the governor and Congress. It could also send a delegate to Congress with power to debate but not to vote. When the territory reached 60,000 population, it could frame a constitution and ask for admission to the Union as a full-fledged and equal state. The Ordinance included a bill of rights guaranteeing to the inhabitants habeas corpus, jury trial, security of private contracts, proportional representation, and freedom of worship. It prohibited slavery in the whole Northwestern region. It limited the suffrage under territorial status. Voters had to own fifty acres of land and officeholders 200 acres.

This Northwest Ordinance had both defects and virtues. Framed by easterners interested in preserving their section's control of Congress and in preserving speculative opportunity for themselves, it limited and delayed self-government by the authority given to the appointed territorial governors and by the property qualifications imposed on the suffrage. In effect, it also fostered speculation, for under it the provision in the Ordinance of 1785 for survey before settlement was simply disregarded. This opened the way for such men as John Cleves Symmes of New Jersey and Colonel Duer of the Scioto Company to move into the Ohio region with grants, and the prospect of grants, that resulted in clouded titles and often the mulcting of honest but misguided settlers.

But, in spite of these limitations, the Ordinance of 1787 was of great positive significance. Those who wished to go West no longer feared that they would lose their political privileges by doing so, the result being a great increase in the westward drive of population. The Ordinance made it certain that the nation's westward expansion would be in the form of equal states, rather than as a series of colonial dependencies. This assurance was vital to the preservation of the Republic as it had emerged (a group of equal states) from the Revolution.

Frontier Problems

Frontier aspirations, coupled with the ever-present Indian problem and Spain's control of the lower Mississippi, brought the West very much into the international limelight under the Confederation. Britain held stubbornly to a series of frontier posts that included Oswego, Niagara, and Detroit, despite her having agreed to surrender them in the treaty of 1783. Convinced that they were important for control of the fur trade, and that they would be of great strategic value if the American union broke up, the British government refused to honor its promise of surrender on the ground that America was also violating the treaty by permitting the states to hinder British creditors in collecting debts owed them in America. Britain also began organizing the Indians for resistance to American settlement in the West.

As land-hungry frontiersmen poured across the Appalachians, the American government cajoled the Indians, or bulldozed them by show of military force, into treaties of cession. The red man was resentful of such treatment, and British agents such as Sir John Johnson, Joseph Butler, and the Mohawk chief Joseph Brant succeeded in organizing the Iroquois, the Miamis, the Chippewas, and other tribes in a confederacy designed to check the cession of Indian lands and to insist on the creation of an Indian buffer state on the Ohio. The Indian confederation was loose and full of conflicting desires, but

Kentucky frontiersmen viewed it with anxiety and animosity. They promptly began raiding Indian villages in the Ohio region, and by 1789 the Northwest was on the verge of an Indian war.

Britain not only helped the Indians of the Northwest to organize, but also showed a disposition (though no actual steps were taken) to foster separatist movements in Vermont and Kentucky. The British government obviously had little faith in the viability of the new nation. And it was certain that the Confederation was not sufficiently powerful to control the frontier and protect it against Indian raids.

Like the northwestern frontier, that on the south and southwest was a center of international friction. There 120,000 Americans in Kentucky, Tennessee, and Georgia were pressing on the Spanish borders in the Floridas and Louisiana, where some 25,000 Spaniards, Greeks, and other Europeans and 50,000 to 60,000 Cherokees, Creeks, Chickasaws, and Choctaws lived under Spanish rule. Spanish colonial government at this time was strong and efficient, its best means of controlling its American neighbors being its possession of the mouth of the Mississippi. It not only held New Orleans, but also occupied—and stubbornly refused to give up—Natchez on the east bank of the Mississippi. Only when there seemed to be prospect of an Anglo-American alliance did the Spaniards assume a conciliatory attitude toward their neighbors.

In 1784, the Creeks, Choctaws, and Chickasaws, alarmed by the land hunger of the Georgians, formed an alliance with Governor Esteban Miró of Louisiana against American traders, but American pressure on the Indians continued and in 1785 precipitated a war between the Creeks and the state of Georgia. The United States tried to negotiate a settlement of this war, into which it seemed likely Spain would be drawn, but the efforts of the American government were in vain. It was equally luckless in negotiations with Spain over the Spanish-American boundary in the West.

Diplomatic Negotiations

On June 26, 1784, the Spanish Foreign Minister, Count Floridablanca, closed the Mississippi to United States navigation. He then sent Don Diego de Gardoqui to the United States to obtain a treaty recognizing Spanish control of the Mississippi, and Spain's right to practically all of Alabama and Mississippi and parts of Tennessee, Kentucky, and Georgia—an area to which Spain claimed title by reason of conquests during the Revolution.

In negotiation with Gardoqui, John Jay, Secretary of Foreign Affairs in the Confederation, refused to countenance Spain's territorial demands and stood staunchly for the thirty-first parallel (the Spaniard demanded the thirty-fifth parallel) as the boundary between Spanish and American territory. But, influenced by eastern desires for expanded foreign trade, Jay was willing to give up for twenty-five years the right to navigate the Mississippi in return for trade privileges with Spain that were desired by eastern commercialists. A tentative agreement drawn up along these lines was vetoed in Congress by the votes of the five southern states, whereupon the negotiations broke down. When, in 1788, Spain reopened the river to American navigators, they still had to pay duty at New Orleans.

The West was wild with anger at the news of Jay's willingness to give up navigation rights on the Mississippi and the apparent acceptance of such an arrangement by the northeastern states. Between 1786 and 1789, there was much western talk of separation from the Union, and General James Wilkinson and others were involved in a conspiracy to set up a western republic that would have free use of the Mississippi under the protection of Spain. Miró was receptive to this idea. The Spanish government was cool to it, however, and most American frontiersmen felt that they could neither go it alone nor endure close association with autocratic Spain.

America's failure to free itself from the British incubus on the Canadian frontier and its inability to achieve a satisfactory settlement with Spain were only two indications of the Confederation's weakness in the field of foreign relations. Jefferson, who succeeded Franklin as Minister to France in 1785, found the court of Louis XVI a school of humility. He was able to obtain only limited concessions for American trade with the French West Indies and with France itself. John Adams, as Minister to England, expected to accomplish great things in the way of commercial arrangements and harmonious relations in general, but was sadly disappointed. The British government looked upon the United States more as a rival in the New World than as a potential ally. Relations with the Barbary pirates of the Mediterranean were still worse. The colonies, under the protection of the British navy, had had a flourishing trade in the Mediterranean, but the British flag no longer covered American commerce. In 1786, the Sultan of Morocco was bribed into granting a commercial treaty. Algiers, Tunis, and Tripoli, on the other hand, found it more profitable to levy tribute on American shipping and enslave captured Americans, while Secretary Jay looked on in wrathful impotence. Jay wrote to Jefferson in 1787, "To be respectable abroad, it is necessary to be so at home; and that will not be the case until our public faith acquires more confidence, and our government more strength."

Weakness of the Central Government

The Confederation's difficulties in the field of diplomacy were due more to the nation's lack of economic power and of an army and navy than to its form of government, but such leaders as Washington, Madison, Jay, and John Adams were becoming convinced that America would never be a great nation, either politically or economically, with such a weak and ineffectual government. There was increasing evidence in America's domestic affairs to support this point of view. There disturbing signs appeared right and left. The states were disposed to run their affairs without regard to any national policy. They were lackadaisical about sending their representatives to Congress, waged war with the Indians on their own account, and ignored agreements with foreign powers. Some even built their own navies. Since they were lax about fulfilling the monetary requisitions of the Congress, that body was chronically without funds and tried in vain to get an amendment to the Articles of Confederation that would allow the United States to levy and collect a 5 per cent duty on imports. This move required unanimous approval by the states, and New York, under the leadership of Governor George Clinton and other strong supporters of state sovereignty, refused its consent.

Disregard of the national government's welfare by the states was not the only disquieting feature of the national situation. Debtor-creditor relationships within the states, as these developed between 1783 and 1789, were ominous for the stability of the republic. The states had emerged from the Revolution with heavy debts. The debt certificates had depreciated in value during the war, and many of them had been bought up by speculators. State governments under the influence of the conservatively minded, who were often creditors as well, undertook to pay off their obligations and taxed heavily for that purpose. This brought loud outcries for relief from the debtor elements, which were chiefly agrarian, and a demand for paper money issues which would inflate the currency and make for easier payments. Seven of the thirteen states responded with issues of paper money. Most of them did this in controlled fashion, and the results were not particularly damaging to creditor interests, but in some states the situation was grim. Rhode Island's paper depreciated steeply in value, and the country was treated to the spectacle of creditors fleeing from their debtors and being fined for not accepting the state's legal tender in payment of debts. Massachusetts, which had a debt of $11 million in 1780, pursued an opposite course. The state's government was controlled by the mercantile-creditor interest, and it undertook to liquidate the debt without the benefit of a paper money issue. Taxation was heavy, specie became scarce, debtors crowded the jails, and in 1786 an uprising occurred in the Worcester-Springfield area under the leadership of Daniel Shays, a veteran of the Revolution. This "rebellion" was beaten down by state militia under General Benjamin Lincoln, acting under orders from Governor Bowdoin, but public opinion was sympathetic with the rioters. The governor was badly defeated when he came up for re-election, and none of the rebels were punished.

Men who valued order in the affairs of the nation and who had a high regard for the sacredness of private property and of contracts were disturbed by the spread of paper money issues and by the events in Rhode Island and Massachusetts. Washington wrote to a friend that "there are combustibles in every state which a spark might set fire to." The government of the Confederation, as all could see, was impotent to act in quelling disturbances within the various states. Even in Massachusetts, where the federal arsenal at Springfield had been attacked by the insurgents, Congress had refrained from coming to the assistance of the state authorities. Many leaders of public opinion began to turn toward the idea of reorganizing the national government so that it might function more effectively in ridding the nation of foreign and domestic embarrassments.

Moving Toward Governmental Reform

Out of the widespread dissatisfaction felt with the existing central government came recommendations for specific action. Pelatiah Webster of Pennsylvania, one of the ablest thinkers of his day, proposed revamping the Articles of Confederation so that the states would surrender part of their sovereignty to the central government. James Madison, Jefferson's learned young counselor and friend in Virginia, felt that something must be done along the same line and suggested giving the national government a veto on the acts of the state legislatures. These and similar ideas were very much in the air when, in 1785, a situation developed that brought them into focus.

Maryland and Virginia were interested in obtaining a common understanding about navigation on the Potomac. Commissions from the two states met at Mount Vernon in 1785, drew up resolutions, and asked the cooperation of Pennsylvania. With this as a beginning, Madison pushed through the Virginia legislature a resolution appointing a commission to meet with men appointed by the other states to consider the trade of the union and the need for a uniform system of commercial regulations. The Virginia commission, of which Madison was a member, invited the other twelve states to send delegates to a convention at Annapolis.

In response to the Virginia invitation, delegates from five states met at Annapolis on September 11, 1786. Madison was there for Virginia, and New York was represented by Alexander Hamilton, a brilliant young lawyer who had been Washington's aide and secretary in the Revolution and was a firm advocate of a strong national government. Delegates from four other states had been appointed, but after three days had gone by they had not appeared. On the third day, the delegates already at Annapolis adopted a report drawn up by Hamilton proposing a meeting of delegates from all the states at Philadelphia the following May. There, the report declared, they were to devise ways of making "the Federal Government adequate to the exigencies of the Union; and to report such an Act for that purpose to the United States in Congress assembled, as when agreed to by them, and afterwards confirmed by the Legislatures of every State, will effectively provide for the same."

Hamilton's resolution seemed harmless enough. It spoke only of revising the Articles of Confederation, and that with the consent of the states. It was sent to the states and to Congress. The latter paltered and delayed, but finally called a convention to meet in Philadelphia in May, 1787. Twelve states—all but stiff-necked and suspicious Rhode Island—chose delegates, and in the spring these state representatives moved on horseback, by stage, or by sailing ship to Philadelphia. They had been selected, ostensibly, to revise the Articles of Confederation, but they ended by creating the Constitution of the United States.

Jefferson, over in Paris, at first termed the fifty-five men who gathered in the State House at Philadelphia an "assemblage of demi-gods." He later modified this opinion, but it is certain that it was a distinguished gathering. Forty-one of its members had served in Congress, twenty-six in state legislatures, and seven as state governors. Thirty-seven had studied in institutions of higher learning, either at home or abroad. Washington, Madison, and Edmund Randolph were there from Virginia, and Hamilton shone in the New York delegation. There were Roger Sherman from Connecticut, Franklin, and Gouverneur and Robert Morris from Pennsylvania, John Dickinson from Delaware, Elbridge Gerry and Rufus King from Massachusetts, the Pinckneys and John Rutledge from South Carolina. "Doctor" Franklin, as the other delegates called him, was eighty-one years old and suffering from gout and the stone; he attended as often as his health would permit, however, and his tolerance and kindly spirit helped to calm more than one heated debate. Washington served as presiding officer. Perhaps because of a painful rheumatic condition in his shoulder, but chiefly because of a badly fitting set of false teeth, he seldom spoke; nevertheless, all looked up to him and his presence contributed greatly to the dignity of the proceedings. It was a gathering of strong men who had energetically supported the idea of a convention and therefore who had been chosen by the state legislatures almost as a matter of course. Most of them had been warned before they left home that they had no right to do more than amend the Articles of Confederation.

A great majority of the fifty-five had for a long time been prominent in economic as well as political affairs. Some of them owned personal property that included the depreciated securities of the national government. Even more owned real estate. They may have expected, and probably did expect, to benefit personally from a change in the form of government. But Madison's notes on the convention (the best record of its proceedings) show that their views and aims were by no means narrowly personal or strictly economic in character. The intent of the Founding Fathers, as they later came to be called, was to create a better national government, one that would benefit all classes of society, one which the wise and the honest could accept with sincerity and enthusiasm.

The Creation of the Constitution

A scattering of delegates met in the State House on the morning of May 14, 1787, but it was not until May 25 that representatives of a majority of the states were in attendance. On that day, Washington was unanimously elected President of the Convention. Four days later, Edmund Randolph presented a series of resolutions that became known as the Virginia Plan.

Randolph's project showed that the Virginians at least sought much more than a revision of the Articles of Confederation. It proposed a national legislature consisting of two branches, the first chosen by the people of the several states and the second elected by the members of the first branch, both of which could initiate legislation. Representation in this legislature should be proportional either to the quotas of contribution from or to the numbers of free inhabitants in the various states. There would be a Chief Executive, selected by the legislature, and a national judiciary with limited jurisdiction. The plan provided for the admission of new states and for the amendment of the "Articles of Union" without the assent of the national legislature. It also provided that alterations in the Articles of Confederation should be submitted for approval to constituent assemblies chosen by the people of the various states. This followed the precedent set in establishing the state constitutions of Massachusetts and New Hampshire.

After the presentation of the Virginia Plan, the Convention got down to work as a Committee of the Whole. It approved the creation of a national government with an executive, a national judiciary, and a two-chambered legislature. It adopted (temporarily, as it proved) Randolph's proposal for election of the chief executive, although there was strong sentiment for his popular election. In fact, much of the Virginia Plan had been accepted by the middle of June. But, at the same time, marked dissension had developed in the Convention. The center of the contention was the Virginia Plan's proposal for proportional representation in the new Congress.

The small-state delegates, such as William Paterson of New Jersey, declared that proportional representation would endanger the very existence of the smaller states, and would allow Virginia, Massachusetts, and Pennsylvania to control the new government. Paterson asserted that New Jersey would "rather submit to a monarch, to a despot, than to such a fate." Large-state delegates, on the other hand, held it unreasonable for a state like New Jersey to have the same rights or influence as Pennsylvania or Virginia. For days the debate continued, often in heated fashion, while Franklin did his best to maintain a spirit of harmony and good feeling.

On June 14, Paterson forced the issue between the contending forces by presenting a New Jersey Plan. Instead of a new form of government, this proposed amendment of the Articles of Confederation so that Congress might levy duties and regulate trade. It provided for a plural executive and for a national judiciary. It also declared that Acts of Congress and treaties should be the supreme law of the respective states, and gave the federal executive the right to call out the power of the Confederated States "if necessary to carry such acts and treaties into execution." This plan increased the prerogatives of the central government, but under it the powers of the states would be, to a great extent, preserved. The small states rallied to it as a means of side-tracking the Virginia Plan.

In the debate that followed the introduction of the New Jersey Plan, Madison argued for proportional representation in Congress and for a strong national government. Hamilton said that even the Virginia Plan was not strong enough. He proposed a President and Senate chosen for life or during good behavior, with state governors appointed by the national government.

The New Jersey Plan was defeated on June 19, but the fears of the smaller states remained as strong as ever. In the face of an increasingly critical situation, the large-state party began to make concessions. Its members agreed to adopt the term "United States," instead of the word "National" to describe the central government's organization. This was scarcely a major concession, so tempers continued to run high, and Franklin vainly proposed opening the morning sessions with prayer. Finally—following the suggestion that first came from Sherman of Connecticut and was then urged by Franklin—the delegates agreed to representation proportional to population in the lower house and equal representation of the states in the upper house. This "Great Compromise," reached on July 16, 1787, prevented the dissolution of the Convention.

On July 24, the Convention chose a Committee on Detail to take up the resolutions voted so far and draft them into a constitution. While the Committee worked on the draft, the Convention took a ten-day recess. Washington and Robert and Gouverneur Morris went trout fishing near Valley Forge, and numerous other delegates went on fishing trips and sightseeing excursions.

On August 6, the Convention again convened and began examining the printed draft prepared by the Committee on Detail. Certain changes had been made by that Committee. In place of broad general powers, the national legislature was given a set of enumerated powers specifically limiting its authority. The power of the executive and judicial branches was similarly limited. The chief executive was called "the President," the legislature "the Congress," and the two branches of the legislature were titled the "House of Representatives," and the "Senate."

During the remainder of August and the first two weeks of September, the Convention discussed the Committee draft, item by item. Much of it was accepted, but some parts were modified. It was decided that there should be no property qualifications for legislators, and that any person privileged to vote in a state might vote in a federal election. The Senate would be elected by the state legislatures, and the members of the House of Representatives would be elected by the people and would be paid out of the federal treasury, rather than by the states. Provision was made for an army and navy. Religious tests for public officers were defeated, and state coinages were banned. Some wanted a single seven-year term for the President, but, after lengthy discussion, it was decided that he should have a four-year term of office and should be eligible for re-election.

Some of the major aspects of the Constitution were the result of compromises between powerful bodies of opinion. The "Great Compromise," which has already been discussed, was one of these adjustments. Another, of equal if not of even greater importance, was the product of conflict over the relative importance of state and national sovereignty. Some of the delegates wished to give the national government power to coerce the states, while others were resolutely opposed to such action. The solution finally reached had been first suggested in the New Jersey Plan, which would have made national laws and treaties the supreme law of the states. The Convention now made the Constitution "the supreme law of the land," binding on all branches of the central government, and also binding on state officers and state judges. This, together with the provisions that specified the powers of the national legislature and certain limitations on the states (Article I, sections 8–10) provided a solution of the problem of conflicting state and national authorities, by putting both governments under the rule of law as interpreted by the courts. This ingenious contribution to political theory made the constitution a workable instrument and, as events were to prove, gave the new government a solid foundation.

The establishment of the Constitution as the "supreme law," under which both state and national governments would function, made clear the principle of dual citizenship. Every citizen would be under two governments, each with its own powers. Recognition of this dual status was essential to the successful operation of a federal union.

Still other compromises were found to be necessary during the course of the Convention. The South favored and the North opposed counting slaves in proportioning representation in the House. It was finally agreed that five slaves should be counted as three white persons in apportioning both direct taxes and representation in Congress. Another clash of opinion, chiefly between southern and northern delegates, came over the regulation of commerce and the importation of slaves, for many of the southern delegates feared that navigation acts, such as the restriction of American exports to American ships, might be imposed at the behest of the commercial states. At the same time, there was much southern insistence on the right to import slaves, but other delegates were anxious to prohibit slave importations and to establish the control of Congress over commerce; as a result, congressional control over commerce was maintained and the importation of slaves was declared not subject to prohibition before the year 1808.

There was also a protracted difference of opinion as to the proper method of electing the President. It was finally decided that he should be chosen by presidential electors, who were to be chosen by each state in such way as its legislature might direct and to be equal in number to its entire membership in Congress. Each elector would vote for two persons. The one receiving the highest number of votes, if it was a majority, would be President, and the one with the second highest number of votes, Vice President. If there was a tie majority vote, a choice between the two candidates would devolve upon the House, and if no one had a majority, the House would choose from among the five highest. In either case where the House elected the President, each state would have only one vote.

Despite the fact that great effort was made by the Convention to accommodate differences of opinion, a number of the delegates were dissatisfied with the final result. Hamilton signed the Constitution reluctantly and only on the ground that its "chance of good" was preferable to "anarchy and Convulsion." Gerry and Randolph declined to sign, as did Luther Martin of Maryland. In fact, only thirty-nine of the fifty-five members affixed their signatures to the document. The division of opinion here indicated prompted Franklin to propose and the convention to adopt, in its own ratification procedure, the statement that it was "Done in Convention by the unanimous consent of the States present." In this way, the majority hoped to win reluctant signers and also give the people the impression that the document had unanimous approval.

The Struggle over Ratification

The Constitution was signed on September 17, 1787. It was then sent to Congress, which, rather reluctantly, forwarded it to the states. Since it contained the statement that when the ratifying conventions of nine states had approved it, the organization of the new government would begin, a furious struggle between the proponents and opponents of ratification immediately ensued.

The advocates of the Constitution called themselves "Federalists." They argued that only with a stronger national government could the United States command respect among the nations of the world, and pointed to the need of a strong and unified policy for dealing with internal problems such as the establishment of a uniform currency and the pacification of the frontier. They declared that without effective union the country would be forced into the wasteful and inefficient maintenance of thirteen different nations and national policies and asserted that economic strife between different sections of the country could be dealt with only by a strong union. They emphasized the failure of the states to comply with the requisitions of the government under the Articles of Confederation; the ways in which states trespassed on one another's rights; the lack of any guarantee for the states under the Confederation against internal violence; and the injury to the nation's "dignity, interest, and revenue" that arose from the lack of federal control over commerce.

The most famous of the arguments in favor of the Constitution are those which came from the pens of Madison, Hamilton, and Jay. In a series of eighty-five essays, originated in New York by Hamilton as a counter to Governor Clinton's powerful opposition to the Constitution, the Federalist position was brilliantly developed. These papers were later collected under the title of *The Federalist*. They probably had little influence on the average voter, but their clear exposition of the principles of political theory and practice makes them vital for an understanding of the thought that underlay the making of the Constitution.

The opponents of the Constitution stressed two main arguments. The Constitution contained no bill of rights and therefore left unguarded the fundamental liberties of the people. It created a national rather than a federal form of government, one altogether too large to permit the proper functioning of democratic government. These Antifederalists (as they rather illogically called themselves) agreed that the national government should be strengthened, especially in regard to trade regulations and the collection of revenue, but they felt that the Constitution makers had gone far beyond such necessary reforms. They had created a behemoth with such control over taxation that it would annihilate the state governments, would be a source of intolerable expense, and would be used by the wealthy and powerful to prey upon the poor. Patrick Henry, who had been opposed to the Convention from the start, declared that under the Constitution an established religion would be set up and that the Kentuckians would lose for all time the power to navigate the Mississippi. Other critics invoked the specters of double taxation and tariffs for the benefit of the northeastern part of the country. Many planters were alarmed lest adoption of the Constitution open the way for the collection of the debts owed to British creditors.

Economic interest was undoubtedly a factor in rallying support for or against the Constitution, for many a poor man, many a debtor, was fearful of its consequences to his pocketbook. On the other hand, the majority of businessmen and reasonably well-to-do agrarians undoubtedly felt that under a stronger national government there would be not only greater security of property, but also an expansion of business opportunity through the establishment of a national market and national regulation of commerce. Such men valued the Constitution because it would mean freedom from control of their economic activities by the states.

But economic interest did not align all the poor against the Constitution, nor all the affluent on its side. There was no clear line of cleavage throughout the country, in the struggle over ratification, between the well-to-do owners of personalty such as public securities, and the small farmers and debtors. The small farmers constituted such a huge majority of the population that they could easily have defeated ratification, but they were by no means a unit in opposition to the document. The Antifederalists, in general, had very little to say about the states being forbidden to coin money, emit bills of credit, issue paper money, or impair the obligation of contract—provisions that were distinctly favorable to propertied interests. It is also significant that many solid men of means—such as Patrick Henry, James Monroe, Luther Martin, George Clinton—were on the Antifederalist side.

There was really no clear-cut division in the struggle over ratification of the Constitution. Political as well as economic lines were blurred. The Antifederalists were no more positive than were the Federalists about the infallibility of majority rule. They advocated neither a broader suffrage nor the direct election of Senators and of the President. Both Federalists and Antifederalists thought generally in middle-class terms, believing that self-interest was man's dominating motivation in politics and that political machinery should be so constructed as to prevent those in power from abusing their power. They differed only in their concepts of how to achieve those objectives.

Ratification moved swiftly at first. Between December 7, 1787, and January 9, 1788, five states (Connecticut, Delaware, Georgia, New Jersey, and Pennsylvania) approved the Constitution. In the first four states there was no serious opposition, but in Pennsylvania the constitutional convention was summoned by the legislature only after a Federalist mob had dragged two opposing members to the State House and held them there to form an involuntary quorum. The Pennsylvania convention, however, was safely Federalist.

The Massachusetts convention appeared to be Antifederalist, but the Federalists won over John Hancock by promising to support him in the next gubernatorial election. His proposal to ratify and at the same time to recommend a set of amendments to the Constitution won over enough delegates so that the convention ratified on February 6, 1788, by a vote of 187 to 168. Maryland ratified in April, South Carolina in May, and New Hampshire in June. Both of the latter states recommended amendments.

Virginia was a key state. If it refused to ratify and New York followed its example, the establishment of a smoothly working national government would be difficult indeed. Patrick Henry was denouncing the Constitution up and down the land, and Edmund Randolph, who feared that it provided insufficient safeguards for personal liberty, was in milder opposition. But Madison was a tower of strength in its support; the eminent lawyer George Wythe and Edmund Pendleton were also for it; and Washington, though not a delegate to the convention, was known to be its supporter. Much to the disgust of the Antifederalists, Randolph finally changed sides, coming out in support of ratification with recommendation of amendment. The final vote in the Virginia convention was eighty-nine to seventy-nine.

Virginia was the tenth state to ratify. In the New York convention, the Antifederalists were in the majority, but the news of Virginia's action, brought by express riders arranged for by Hamilton, was decisive. It would not do, the delegates felt, for New York to remain outside the new union. New York ratified on July 26, 1788, with recommendation of amendment, by a vote of thirty to twenty-seven.

Only two states were now left outside the fold. North Carolina still hesitated, at first refusing to ratify until a second federal convention should consider its proposed amendments; final action was not taken until November 19, 1789, after the new government had been set up. Rhode Island, last of all, waited until May, 1790, to ratify, and then did so only after the United States Senate had passed a bill severing commercial relations between Rhode Island and the United States. At last all the thirteen states were in the new Union.

Historical Significance of the Constitution

The Founding Fathers demonstrated both conservatism and radicalism in their work at Philadelphia. They were conservative in establishing a balance of power in the new government that would prevent the influence of gusts of popular opinion from dominating the national councils. This was accomplished partly by providing a four-year term for the President, a six-year term for the Senate (with one-third of that body to be elected every two years), and a two-year term for the House of Representatives, and partly by establishing a national judiciary removed as far as possible from popular control (that is, appointed by the President with the consent of the Senate, to serve for life or during good behavior). The founders also acted conservatively in establishing practically every safeguard of property that was asked for by property interests.

But if the Convention displayed conservatism in framing the Constitution, it demonstrated its radicalism in its attitude toward changing the form of government. The delegates had come together with instructions to amend the Articles of Confederation and to submit those amendments to the state legislatures for their approval. The Articles of Confederation provided that such amendments, to be binding, must receive the unanimous consent of the states. The men at Philadelphia, however, disregarded these limitations on their authority. They created a new government, arbitrarily deciding that it should be submitted, not to the state legislatures, but to state constitutional conventions. They put in the Constitution a statement that when nine states had ratified, it should be put in operation. Such procedures were not those of minds altogether respectful of precedents and existing authority.

The Constitution framed at Philadelphia was by no means a perfect instrument. Under it, the executive and legislative powers were separated to an extent that has sometimes impaired the efficient conduct of government. The Constitution was also deficient in provisions guaranteeing the equal rights of citizens, for its framers had no vision of the Industrial Revolution, with its development of masses of urban laborers and its enormous concentrations of economic power. It made no provision for the development of the party system of government. The democratization of government and society that has taken place since 1787 has required twenty-two amendments of the original charter, and amendment is a slow and painful process. Jefferson always believed that the Constitution was too inflexible to be an ideal instrument of government.

But, even with its defects, the Constitution remains an admirable and a remarkable document. It established a new federal framework under which both the states and the nation could function effectively and live at peace with one another. It based the government of the United States upon law and upon the sovereignty of the people, the foundations of any truly democratic society. It provided specific powers for the three branches of government, but in such a way as to leave wide latitude in the exercise of those powers. Even though difficult to amend, it has proven sufficiently adaptable to changing needs and national desires to enable it to survive as the charter of a nation that, weak and puny when the Constitution was adopted, has achieved the highest standard of living on the globe and has become the leader of the free world. The Constitution was not perfect, but it was a milestone on the long, hard road to freedom and equality for all mankind along which nations with democratic ideals must find their way.

Omens for the Future

The years from 1783 to 1789 were eventful ones in the history of the United States. Economically, the nation manifested both ability to withstand the shocks resulting from war conditions and a capacity for growth. Commerce and industry improved, and the surge of land-hungry pioneers into the West indicated an expansive vitality that augured well for the future of the nation, if it could be ordered and controlled. Politically, much was achieved. A land policy had been established that, despite the favors it conferred upon speculators, laid the basis for westward expansion upon the principle of political equality. Alarmed by the weakness of the government under the

Articles of Confederation, national leaders had framed and the people had approved a better form of government. The Constitution, despite its defects, demonstrated that Americans possessed political skill, a genius for compromise, and a society in which middle-class ideals, rather than those of an aristocracy or a proletariat, were paramount. Though these six years were full of trials, they were also full of happy omens for the future.

Suggested Reading

Useful works for the period of the Confederation are those by E. C. Burnett and Lynn Montross cited in the previous chapter. John Fisk, *The Critical Period of American History, 1783–1789* (1892) has had great influence, and its interpretation is in part supported by Broadus Mitchell, *Alexander Hamilton* (1957), vol. I. That the 1780s were not so critical is a point of view maintained in Merrill Jensen, *The New Nation: A History of the United States During the Confederation, 1781–1789* (1950).

Andrew C. McLaughlin, *The Confederation and the Constitution* (1905) is an old study, partly superseded by later investigation, but one that still contains valuable analyses and interpretations of the period. E. S. Morgan, *The Birth of the Republic, 1763–1789* (1956) has some perceptive comments on both the Confederation and the Constitution.

On the formation of the Constitution, an indispensable work is that of Charles A. Beard, *An Economic Interpretation of the Constitution of the United States* (new ed., 1949). This brilliant and provocative analysis is subjected to severe criticism in Robert E. Brown, *Charles Beard and the Constitution* (1956). Forrest McDonald's *We the People: the Economic Origins of the Constitution* (1958) is another critical examination of the argument that economic factors were all-important in the making of the Constitution. Fred Rodell, *Fifty-five Men* (1936) is popular in style and somewhat outdated, but it is suggestive in treatment. The first two chapters of Arthur N. Holcombe's *Our More Perfect Union* (1950) constitute an excellent examination of the political principles of the Constitutional Convention. Irving Dilliard, *Building the Constitution* (1950) is an interesting account of the Convention in the form of news "despatches."

Carl Van Doren's *The Great Rehearsal* (1948) is a careful and well-written account of the making and ratification of the Constitution. Cecilia M. Kenyon, "Men of Little Faith," *William and Mary Quarterly,* third series, XII (Jan., 1955), 3–43, is a scholarly analysis of the struggle over ratification of the document. Also useful are Irving Brant, *James Madison: The Nationalist, 1780–1787* (1938) and James Madison: *Father of the Constitution, 1787–1800* (1950); C. P. Smith, *James Wilson: Founding Father, 1742–1798* (1956); J. T. Main, *The Antifederalists: Critics of the Constitution* (1961), and Clinton Rossiter, *1787—The Grand Convention* (1966). For studies of state politics in the period of the Confederation, see T. C. Cochran, *New York in the Confederation* (1932) and R. L. Brunhouse, *The Counter-Revolution in Pennsylvania, 1776–1790* (1942).

9 ⸰ The Heyday of Federalism, 1789-1796

THE CONSTITUTION went into effect over a nation of some four million people, only 200,000 of whom lived in towns or cities of 2,500 or more population, and only 3 per cent in towns of 8,000 or more inhabitants. The country was, therefore, overwhelmingly rural in character. In 1790, the first national census indicated that there were 750,000 Negroes in the land, some 60,000 of these being freemen and the rest slaves.

Social Aspects of the New Nation

Life for the great majority of this population was simple and rigorous, but there were amusements for all classes of society. The well-to-do gave festive dinners where port and madeira flowed freely and politics and religion were customary topics of conversation. All classes enjoyed hunting and fishing. Horse racing was taboo in Puritan New England but very popular in the South. Dancing attracted ladies of high and low degree, and the quilting party was a rural institution. Drinking was fashionable and common, if not universal. Liquor was served in prisons and at funerals, and there were 1,500 grog shops in New York City alone. Duelling, known and practiced before the Revolution, was now more common than ever, with pistols at ten paces for the aristocracy, and gouging, slashing, no-holds-barred contests of brute strength on the frontier.

A colonial aristocrat on his way to a dance or a horse race was a striking figure, for the dress of the upper classes was colorful and gay. Men wore knee breeches, long-backed coats with silver buttons, brightly colored vests, and pointed shoes with huge silver buckles. Their hair was tied in a queue and, until 1794, heavily powdered. Women rustled in taffetas and brocades, with chintz for every day. Their hats varied from mountainous creations topped with feathers to muskmelon bonnets and caps. Powder and rouge for the ladies were much in style.

The dress of the lower classes—artisans, day laborers, and small farmers—was of the simplest sort. The women wore cheap stuffs, such as osnaburgs and linsey-woolsey, and their dresses were coarse and ill-fitting. The men wore yellow buckskin or leather breeches, red flannel jackets, clumsy shoes, and often leather aprons well-greased, like the breeches, to keep them soft and pliable.

Transportation for high and low was almost as difficult as it had been in colonial times. Travel from Charleston to New York or Boston was a major undertaking. If winds were contrary, it might take a week to go from New York to Providence by way of Long Island Sound. There were few good roads anywhere, and almost no bridges in the South and West. Clumsy ferries on northern rivers were endangered by masses of floating ice in winter and early spring. A stagecoach called in admiration the "Flying Machine" made the trip from New York to Philadelphia in two days.

The problems of travel made communication, whether by the printed or the written word, difficult. There were 106 newspapers in the country by 1790, and dailies were just beginning to appear in Philadelphia and New York, but daily and weekly papers alike were small, poorly printed affairs. They carried out-of-date foreign news, domestic politics, shipping intelligence, poetry, history, miscellaneous tidbits of information, and appeals to subscribers to pay their bills. There were but seventy-five postmasters in the entire country in 1789. Eleven years later there were 900 post offices, but postage was high ($.08 for transporting a letter thirty miles), and high charges for newspapers and pamphlets limited their circulation outside the urban centers.

Hygiene was even more primitive than the state of communications. New York and Boston were full of alleys, lanes, and unpaved streets, choked with dust or mud, and lined with miserable, flimsy habitations. New York had open sewers along and across the streets, where filth and refuse collected and droves of malodorous hogs acted as scavengers. Slaughter houses were located within city limits, and the blood of the slaughtered animals ran into the streets. Water supplies were often contaminated, and milk with a low bacterial count was unheard of. Only in Philadelphia, the great social center of America, were there well paved and lighted streets, good drainage, and an effective water system.

Americans were as harsh in their treatment of criminals and the insane as they were indifferent to hygienic precautions. There were a few so-called lunatic asylums, though these were little better than almshouses for the feeble-minded. It was widely believed that the insane were accursed of God. Harmless morons and idiots were allowed to roam at large, subject to the jokes and ridicule of the neighborhood men and boys. The violent were cooped up in asylums, jails, attics, cellars and outhouses. When in frenzy, they were strait-jacketed or beaten into silence.

Ordinary lawbreakers were treated in ways that bore slight relationship to the high principles of the Declaration of Independence. Penalties for minor crimes were largely corporal, and the lash, the pillory, and the branding iron were in daily use. Prisons were often filthy and bug-infested, and the inmates were usually thrust into a common pen, regardless of age, sex, or the severity of the offense. Pennsylvania, in 1790, overhauled its criminal code, establishing what was in effect a state prison with solitary confinement for felons and some effort at vocational training. This was definitely a pioneer effort in American—and, for that matter, world—penology.

If the science of penology was in its infancy, natural science was in a somewhat better state. It had achieved considerable stature in the colonial period, and wartime needs and conditions had stimulated its development. Philadelphia, the home of Franklin's Philosophical Society, was its American center. There Benjamin Rush, a celebrated doctor of medicine and "father of American chemistry," taught at the University of Pennsylvania. Joseph Priestley, discoverer of oxygen, driven out of England in 1794 because of his sympathy with the French Revolution, spent a few months of every year in Philadelphia until his death in 1804, and Benjamin Silliman, chemist and authority on natural history, came to study there. But other scientific centers and scientists of note also graced the American scene. The American Academy of Arts and Science was established at Boston in 1780, the Connecticut Academy of Arts and Science at New Haven in 1799. New England's Nathaniel Bowditch was working on his *American Practical Navigator*, which was published in 1802 and became known as the "Bible of the Sea." Alexander Wilson (1766–1813) came to the United States in 1794 and before his death nineteen years later had composed the first truly American ornithology.

There was some advance in medicine as well as in natural science. By 1800 there were four medical schools of importance: Yale, the University of

Pennsylvania, Harvard, and the Columbia College of Physicians and Surgeons (founded in 1768, ruined by the Revolution, and reorganized in 1792). America could boast three or four hospitals, two medical societies, and some 100 doctors with degrees from abroad, chiefly from Edinburgh. There were also outstanding names in American medicine: Benjamin Rush (1745–1813) and Philip Syng Physick (1768–1837) of Philadelphia; Ephraim McDowell (1771–1830) of Danville, Kentucky; and John Warren (1735–1815) of Boston and Harvard. These men performed successful operations, even ovariotomies and hip and shoulder amputations.

Medical science, however, was still sadly primitive. In those days before the germ theory had been developed bacteria had been discovered, but their function was unknown. Blistering, cupping, purging, and bleeding were sovereign remedies for all diseases. Terrific doses of calomel, ipecac, opium and mercury drove the sick to patent nostrums, and quackery flourished. Surgery and dentistry were in their infancy, the dentist primarily relying on extraction. Neither anesthesia nor antisepsis existed, and the mortality rate in surgical operations was fearfully high. The great contributions of American medicine to human welfare were still to come.

Inauguration of the New Government

The government of this new nation, where the customs and traditions of European civilization were mixed and blended with the primitivism of the frontier, was supposed to assemble in New York on March 4, 1789. Congress had been elected, with comfortable majorities committed to support the Constitution; and the presidential electors had unanimously chosen George Washington for President, with John Adams, next highest on the list, as Vice President. But storms, mud, and contrary winds were obstacles to promptness, and by March 4 only eight Senators and seventeen members of the House had gathered at the mouth of the Hudson. It was not until April 6 that Congress assembled for the official counting of the electoral ballots. Eight days later, Washington was formally notified at Mount Vernon. He left for New York on April 16. Traveling slowly overland, applauded everywhere, receiving ovations in Baltimore and Philadelphia, he reached New York and a tumultuous welcome on April 23. A week later, arrangements were complete for his inauguration.

On April 30, 1789, in Federal Hall, which had been remodeled under the direction of Major L'Enfant, Washington took the oath of office and in a low voice read his inaugural address. His honesty and simplicity were never more apparent. These qualities, the memories of times past, and the deepening lines and wrinkles of his face, moved those who saw and heard him.

New York, center of the national government, was a busy city in 1789. Business was good, the wharves were crowded, and an air of prosperity and

THE FIRST INAUGURATION OF AN AMERICAN PRESIDENT

Washington took the oath of office standing on a balcony of Federal Hall in New York City. The President's Oath was here administered for the first time: "I do solemnly swear that I will faithfully execute the Office of the President of the United States, and will to the best of my ability preserve, protect, and defend the Constitution of the United States." Washington replied, "I swear—so help me God."

optimism pervaded the business district at the harbor's edge. John Jacob Astor, a young man from Waldorf, Germany, who had come to New York in 1784 and was trafficking in flutes and furs, bought his first real estate in 1789 on Bowery Road near Elizabeth Street. Lower Broadway and Wall Street were residential centers and the "Three Hundred" of high society flaunted its elegance and aristocratic notions at its dinners, balls, and teas, and in such brilliant drawing rooms as those of Mrs. Hamilton and Mrs. Henry Knox. The aristocratic note even appeared in Congress with the suggestions, quickly overborne, that the President be given the title of "His

Elective Highness" and the Sergeant at Arms be called the "Usher of the Black Rod."

Congress momentarily considered high-sounding titles, but it speedily got down to more sober business. James Madison, a leader in the House, pushed through a tariff ranging from 5 to 15 per cent ad valorem that was intended to produce revenue and also to protect and stimulate the domestic production of such articles as iron manufactures, glass, hemp, and cordage. Bills creating the State, Treasury, and War Departments were passed during the summer, and in September a Judiciary Act organized the federal court system, providing for a Supreme Court of six members, together with four circuit and thirteen district courts. This Act gave the Supreme Court the power to review state courts' decisions as to the constitutionality of statutes, and was a forerunner of judicial review of both state and national legislation. Finally —and this was no mean task—seventy-eight constitutional amendments proposed by the states were examined, and twelve were finally recommended to the states by Congress. Ten of these—guaranteeing freedom of religion, speech, press, petitions, and the right of jury trial, and reserving to the states and the people all powers not expressly delegated to Congress or prohibited to the states—became the Bill of Rights in the Constitution.

Precedents in Government

In addition to setting up governmental machinery and the first ten amendments to the Constitution, Congress and the President established certain precedents. The House of Representatives and the Senate made it clear that they would not allow members of the President's Cabinet to appear on the floor in defense of their departmental proposals. Washington repulsed the French Minister Comte de Moustier for attempting to open communication directly with him, instead of through the State Department. In setting up relationships between the executive and the legislative departments, Hamilton's reports to Congress established executive leadership in the legislative process. Had it not been for the opposition of Madison and Jefferson, Hamilton would probably have been asked to report in person to the House, and, with this as a beginning, something like the British Cabinet system might have developed in the United States.

So far as the President personally was concerned, Washington held that Congress had control over legislation, and he would interfere with lawmaking only where he deemed a veto necessary. He did veto a bill apportioning representation in Congress, and there was one unfortunate effort to consult personally with the Senate about Indian negotiations. On this occasion, amidst noise and confusion on the Senate floor, the Senators sought delay, and Washington, feeling that the conference had been fruitless, never repeated the experiment. Thereafter he avoided even a consultative relationship with the Senate. But Washington was, nevertheless, an able administrator. Conscious that he was setting precedents, he was energetic, firm, systematic, and efficient in his conduct of the presidency. He demonstrated the importance of these qualities in a chief executive, and left them as models for his successors.

Washington had two strong and two mediocre men in his official family. Henry Knox, a long-time friend, was not a man of superior talents and had an undistinguished career in the War Department. Edmund Randolph was a satisfactory but not outstanding figure as Attorney General. Washington's appointments of Hamilton as Secretary of the Treasury and Jefferson, summoned from Paris, in the State Department were first-class, since both were strong and capable men, whose virtues more than counterbalanced the fact that each was to become a leading figure in opposing political camps.

Political groupings were not long in putting in an appearance. Divergencies of view on governmental policy soon manifested themselves, and storm clouds rapidly gathered, with Hamilton as the center of the storm.

Hamilton's Character and Philosophy

Alexander Hamilton was a native of the island of Nevis in the West Indies, were he had been born January 11, 1755. He was the illegitimate child of a Scotch father and a French Huguenot mother. His precocity early attracted attention, and he was sent to New York, where he studied at Columbia (then King's College). Short of stature (he was five feet, seven inches tall), he was handsome, with clear-cut features, reddish-fair hair, and eyes so dark as to be almost violet-blue in color. His gaze was intent and severe, but his mouth was smiling and generous. A man of aristocratic tastes, he moved in the best society and married Elizabeth Schuyler, daughter of the wealthy Hudson lord of the manor, General Philip Schuyler.

Hamilton's reputation as writer, speaker, reasoner, grew during the Revolutionary period and in the struggle over the ratification of the Constitution. He was thirty-two when he became the Secretary of the Treasury. An honest, ambitious, immensely energetic, and by nature affectionate and generous man, he was also obstinate, vain, and apt to be intolerant of opposition and of mediocrity, and he possessed little or no knowledge of frontier conditions.

Hamilton's attitude toward government and society was pre-eminently that of a conservative. He had full appreciation of the value of stability and the importance of authority. He respected leadership, whether in government or in business, and suspected the masses as being full of ignorance, prejudice, and unbridled impulses. People with ability to "get ahead" he held in high regard, believing that, as the driving force in the nation's economy, they should be given every opportunity to utilize their talents. The resultant national prosperity, he felt, would trickle down upon the general populace.

Government, Hamilton felt, should be a constructive force left in the hands of men of talent. He distrusted democracy. Though he was willing to accept enough of it to keep the people quiet, his whole instinct was for a government in which large measures of control were vested in the few.

The Hamiltonian System

Hamilton's aim, as Secretary of the Treasury, was to build national prosperity. To that end, he sought to establish the credit of the government on a firm basis, to attract investment in government funds by moneyed men (who would thus be given a stake in the established order), and to stimulate the prosperity of the industrial and commercial elements so that the United States would have a better balanced economy.

As means to these ends, Hamilton proposed a number of measures. In his *First Report on the Public Credit* (1790), he urged the assumption of all the old government debts, state and national, at the face value of the debt

ALEXANDER HAMILTON
(1757–1804)

The brilliant, profound and intolerant architect of the federal economic system was only thirty-two years of age when he became Secretary of the Treasury.

certificates. This meant the assumption of a debt which, with accrued interest, amounted to nearly $85,000,000. Hamilton also asked Congress to increase the nation's fluid capital by allowing certain classes of government securities to circulate like currency, by establishing a national bank with a capital of $10 million and a note circulation of $7.5 million, and by setting up a national mint. He also requested Congress to pass an excise law that would help provide for the running expenses of the government and a protective tariff that would foster the growth of the nation's industrial power.

Men who feared the creation of a strong national government disliked and feared Hamilton's plans. So did agrarians suspicious of urban business interests and idealists intent upon upholding the principle of equality and therefore opposed to special favors for creditors and the business class. On the other hand, his proposals had a strong appeal for businessmen and for those who saw, regardless of their own immediate interests, the importance of soundness and stability in governmental affairs.

The Attack on Hamilton's System

A series of assaults were made on Hamilton's program. Madison led the attack on assuming the debts of the old national government, arguing that many of these debt certificates, which had depreciated to one-fifth or less of their face value, had passed out of the hands of the original holders, often into the hands of speculators. This was true, but there was no way of determining when or how many times they had changed hands. Madison proposed to distinguish in assumption between the original and the present holders of the certificates. The former would be given the difference between what they had obtained for the certificates and their face value, and the present holders would be given only the highest market price that had prevailed since their time of purchase. This plan proved inoperable because of the inadequate records of sale, and Hamilton's plan was adopted.

An attack upon the assumption of state debts came closer to success. States that had paid off most of their debts were naturally opposed to the idea and states'-rights advocates were hostile to a transfer of the allegiance of the wealthy from the states to the nation. Once again, justice seemed to indicate that speculators should not be allowed to reap exorbitant profits. On the other hand, states with large debts, the speculators, and the supporters of Hamilton's financial policy rallied to assumption. The contest was close, but Hamilton finally made a bargain with Madison and Jefferson (who had just arrived from Paris) placing the capital in Philadelphia for ten years and then in a district ten miles square on the Potomac. The South was anxious to secure the capital, and this agreement as to the site of the present city of Washington carried the day for Hamilton's proposal.

Hamilton had won the great argument over assumption. His victory was important for the stability of the new government. It also put an estimated $40 million profit in the hands of the speculators in government securities.

Hamilton's national bank proposal also produced division among the nation's leaders. Jefferson and Madison both opposed it, since they were suspicious of all banks. They felt that a national bank would give moneyed interests an undue hold on the government and believed that there was no explicit warrant in the Constitution for such a creation. This latter argument became the center of the attack on the bank bill. It was used by all those fearful of an expansion of federal power at the expense of the states.

The bank bill passed Congress, but when Washington, stirred by the argument over its constitutionality, consulted his Cabinet, it split evenly. Jefferson and Randolph opposed and Knox and Hamilton favored the bill. Hamilton pointed out that it abridged no right of any state or individual. Every power vested in a government, he declared, includes "a right to employ all the means requisite and fairly applicable to the attainment of the ends of such power, and which are not precluded by restrictions and exceptions specified in the Constitution, or not immoral, or not contrary to the essential ends of political society." With the Cabinet split, Washington accepted the advice of the members who sponsored the measure, and the bank bill became law. By his act, the President helped establish the theory of broad construction, which has ensured the flexibility of the Constitution and provided room for national growth and development.

All the measures that Hamilton proposed, with the exception of the protective tariff, were enacted into law. They put the new government on a sound financial footing, promoted business confidence, and stimulated economic growth. The violent conflicts of opinion that they engendered inevitably influenced political thought and activity. By the close of 1791, lines of political battle were beginning to appear in Congress. And Thomas Jefferson, by virtue of his fame, his service to the country, and his own convictions, was a natural leader for the growing opposition to Hamilton and his policies.

Jefferson's Character and Philosophy

Jefferson was in many ways a striking contrast to his great opponent. He was over six feet tall, loose-jointed, shy and gentle, with a mild countenance, red hair and blue eyes. He was by nature cautious, disliked open controversy, and never engaged in a personal quarrel. His father was a middle-class Virginia farmer, who lived near the Blue Ridge, and his mother was a Randolph, one of Virginia's aristocracy.

Jefferson was born on April 13, 1743, in Albemarle county on the fringe of the frontier. He attended William and Mary, where he studied law and political philosophy. Like Hamilton, a successful lawyer, he was in Virginia politics from the age of twenty-six. Member of the Continental Congress, author of the Declaration of Independence, Governor of Virginia during the Revolution, Minister to France from 1785 to 1789, he had already had a distinguished career when he became Secretary of State. His political ideas derived from English rather than French sources, but in France he had become intimately acquainted with and appreciative of French liberal thought. He was a Deist in religion and also an ardent admirer of the Christian system of morals. At forty-eight, a polished man of the world, he was to be a tower of strength for those who distrusted Hamilton and his ideas.

Jefferson's ideal was freedom. He was a devotee of civil and religious liberty and of freedom of thought and expression. Politically, he advocated a suffrage land qualification so small as to give practically every farmer a vote. At the same time, he believed (as did most of the politicians on both sides of the political fence) in government under a system of checks and balances that would limit and restrict the actual operation of majority rule. He was as fearful of the tyranny of the majority as any Hamiltonian; the difference was that his attitude was based on a compassionate understanding of the frailties of human nature, rather than on a contempt for the mob. He felt that government had to be based on the will of the people, but it was a will that needed leadership and, sometimes, control.

Jefferson's emphasis on liberty shaped his conception of the scope of government. His belief that there should be as much government as was necessary, but that it should be kept to a minimum, was a concept widely held in a day when Western civilization was stirring in protest against the exercise of arbitrary governmental authority. The Industrial Revolution had begun, and middle-class entrepreneurs wanted elbow room. Jefferson's attitude toward government, however, did not derive from sympathy with business-class aspirations. He had no desire for an Industrial Revolution in the United States. His ideal society would be composed largely of small, land-owning farmers. He distrusted the working classes of the cities as an inevitably debased proletariat, out of place in a democracy of virtue. This agrarian ideal was accepted by the majority of those who followed Jefferson's leadership.

Because Jefferson had ideals of government, he did not conceive of it as static. He believed profoundly in the flexibility of governmental forms and institutions. He thought the procedure for constitutional amendment was altogether too difficult. Viewed from Paris, he described Shays Rebellion as "honorably conducted . . . God forbid we should ever be twenty years without such a rebellion. . . ." He realized that the governmental problem must be solved anew by each generation, and he had faith that an intelligent and informed people would work out its political salvation.

Division over Foreign Affairs

The lines of division in domestic affairs between the followers of Hamilton and Jefferson were clearly drawn in the conflict over Hamilton's program. By 1792, the two groups were also taking opposite sides in regard to foreign relations.

The French Revolution had begun in 1789. At first it had met with general approval in America, but as it moved from the moderate reform aspect of its early days toward violence within and war without—as Danton, Robespierre, and Marat began coming to the fore and personal and property rights came increasingly under attack—Americans divided in their attitude toward events in France. Merchants, traders, and men of property, Hamiltonian in their viewpoint, drew back from France in disgust. Their model was England, where freedom slowly broadened down "from precedent to precedent." There lay the major part of their trade and financial connections, and England was becoming increasingly hostile to the great experiment that was being carried on across the Channel. Jefferson and his supporters, however, continued to be sympathetic with the French revolutionists. In their opinion, France was following America's example in raising the standard of liberty, and the French should be encouraged in their effort to hasten the dawn of a new day in Europe. Americans, too, had shed blood in the name of freedom. Jefferson was on record as believing that "the tree of liberty must be refreshed from time to time with the blood of patriots & tyrants. It is its natural manure." A considerable gulf was fixed between men who held such ideas and conservative merchants and traders.

The Beginnings of Political Parties

It was inevitable with the appearance of strong and ambitious leaders and growing divergences of public opinion over foreign and domestic matters that major political parties should take form and grow. Their first manifestations were congressional groups that supported either Hamilton or Madison. Only in the later 1790s did they develop clearly defined outlines of state and national organization. In the early 1790s, the parties were still fluid, but even then there were signs of the appearance of two great political groups, violent in their convictions and eager to control the nation's government and its policies.

The stronghold of the supporters of Hamilton's system, the men who were already beginning to call themselves Federalists, was in the North and East. There the men of means and the businessmen who looked for great economic development along industrial and commercial lines, men who admired English governmental forms or were tied to England by economic interest, rallied behind Hamilton, John Adams, and such southern leaders as Thomas Pinckney of South Carolina. Those agricultural regions which exported their products and were therefore tied to the commercial interests—the tobacco and wheat-growing regions especially—were apt to be Federalist in sympathy. A considerable number of urban laborers, men who voted to protect their jobs, were Federalists. Episcopalians and New England Congregationalists were apt to be found in the Federalist ranks. Federalism attracted those who believed that the national government should cater to the men of business and property. The traditionalists, the cautious, the lovers of stability, the selfish possessors of this world's goods, the people who looked upon the masses with fear and contempt, naturally gravitated into the Federalist party.

The Jeffersonian Republicans were strongest in the South and West. Their great strength lay in the small landholding class, the farmers of the Piedmont and frontier regions. Those southern planters who disliked Hamilton's funding scheme because it fostered speculation in public securities became Republicans. Dissenters and evangelical church members, especially those on the frontier, tended to vote the Republican ticket. Debtors, increasing numbers of town laborers, states' righters, sympathizers with the French Revolution, rallied under the Republican banner. Those who were by nature radical in their opinions, and those envious of the possessors of wealth and property, found Jeffersonian Republicanism congenial to their taste.

The ideological core of Jeffersonian Republicanism consisted of those who accepted the agrarian thesis of Jefferson's friend, John Taylor of Caroline. His argument was that America, for its own best interests, should remain a land of small farmers; that the farms, rather than industry and commerce, produced the nation's wealth; and that agrarian interests were in constant danger of being exploited by urban capitalism for its own selfish advantage.

As for government, Taylor held that it should function as little as possible. "The utmost favor which it is possible for a government to do for us farmers and mechanics," he said, "is neither to help nor hurt us."

The Election of 1792

As has been said, only the dim outlines of this party division were visible in 1792. It was clear, however, that Hamilton and his friends were in disagreement with Jefferson and Madison, and the election arguments of that year centered around the Hamiltonian system. Jefferson's defender, Philip Freneau, editor of the *National Gazette,* and Hamilton's friend, John Fenno, editor of the *United States Gazette,* traded savage blows. The Federalists pointed to Hamilton's success in putting the national government on a sound financial basis. They did not find it so easy to explain a disastrous defeat of General Arthur St. Clair by the Indians of the Northwest Territory (November 4, 1791), a defeat which brought criticism down on the head of Hamilton's friend, Secretary of War Knox. They were also hampered by a sharp financial depression, the aftermath of rampant speculation in securities. This depression came on early in 1792 and sent stock in the national bank from 120 to seventy-four, and 6 per cent government bonds from 130 to 106. Hamilton's critics hammered away on these points and on the "menace" to liberty and Republicanism that was implicit in Hamilton's policies.

There was no contest over the presidency in 1792. Washington was unchallenged, but a bitter contest did develop between Adams and Governor George Clinton of New York over the vice presidency. Adams emerged the victor, with seventy-seven votes in the electoral college to fifty for Clinton, but Hamilton's critics won a majority in the House of Representatives.

The election over, political excitement temporarily subsided. The nation's attention turned to the Indian situation that had developed in the Northwest, and to diplomatic relations with England, France, and Spain.

Opening Ohio for Settlement

Indian affairs in the Northwest remained in turmoil for some time after St. Clair's defeat. The Indians were supplied with arms and munitions by British traders, and scalping parties terrorized the frontier. A council at Sandusky in 1793 was barren of results. Washington then sent General "Mad Anthony" Wayne into the Ohio territory with an efficient fighting force. The British attitude was most disquieting: British officials assured the Indians that war between Britain and the United States was inevitable and British troops built a fort on the Maumee River, sixty miles south of Detroit. Washington told Wayne to reduce the fort if it stood in his way. At the battle of Fallen Timbers (August 18, 1794) Wayne soundly whipped a small army of Indians and Canadian volunteers, who fled to the fort, just two miles from the battlefield, for protection. "Mad Anthony," however, showed discretion; instead of attacking the fort, where British soldiers stood with flaming torches ready to fire a loaded cannon, he decided to waste the Indian towns and fields. This was done so effectively that the Indians, who now looked in vain for British aid, were forced to come to terms. By the treaty of Greenville (1795), the Indians opened practically all of what is now the state of Ohio to undisturbed settlement by the United States.

America and Neutral Rights

The Indian problem was to some extent tied up with the larger question of America's attitude toward the warring nations of Europe. There the French Revolutionists threw down the gauntlet to Austria and Prussia in 1792 and declared war on England early in 1793. Once in the maelstrom, England added the search and seizure of American ships and the impressment of American seamen to its provocative policy on the frontier. It looked as though America might once again become involved in a conflict with Great Britain.

The Federalists, under the leadership of Hamilton, John Adams, and John Jay, were increasingly critical of the French Revolution and friendly toward England. Despite English provocations, they felt that America, without a navy and faced by plenty of difficulties at home, should remain aloof from the European conflict. They also knew that trade with England, which was more than triple in value that with France, was important to the continuance of American prosperity. Republican leaders, however, remained sympathetic with the French, while they became increasingly critical of England and its policy toward neutrals. When, in the late fall of 1792, France was declared a republic and won important victories against Austria and Prussia, Jeffersonian Republican mass meetings and barbecues were held in celebration. This enthusiasm was momentarily dampened by the guillotining of Louis XVI (January 21, 1793) but when the news came that France had declared war on England and Spain, the pro-French enthusiasm of Jefferson's followers reached fever pitch. Republican clubs passed resolutions praising France, and laborers, college students, and street mobs tore down relics of royalty in the towns. Tom Paine, who had written the *Rights of*

Man in defense of the French Revolution, was ecstatically praised by Republican orators. When Citizen Genêt, newly appointed French Minister to the United States, landed at Charleston, South Carolina, on April 8, 1793, he was received with such adulation that he confidently began attempts to make America a base for French operations against England on the sea and against the Spanish possessions of Florida and Louisiana as well.

It was obvious that America would have to define its attitude toward the warring nations, and Washington turned to his Cabinet for advice. He found his counselors once more evenly divided, Knox and Hamilton against Randolph and Jefferson. Hamilton favored a proclamation of neutrality, while Jefferson argued that this would be of great assistance to Great Britain. As to whether the treaties of 1778 with France were binding, Hamilton said no and Jefferson, yes. On the question of whether Genêt should be received, both said yes, but Hamilton added that the Frenchman should be given notice that the United States did not hold itself bound by the treaties of 1778.

Washington tended to follow Jefferson's advice. Genêt was received unconditionally, an implicit recognition that the treaties were still in force. A proclamation was issued (April 22, 1793), but, out of consideration for Jefferson, the President did not use the word "neutrality." He simply stated the intent of the United States to remain "friendly and impartial" toward the belligerents and urged American citizens to follow this same course. Neutrality was obviously the government's policy.

Genêt's subsequent conduct was a blow to the friends of France. Affronted by the Neutrality Proclamation, he was insolent toward Washington, referring to him as "the old man," and talked of appealing to the people over the head of the President. He armed the "Little Sarah," a prize sent into Philadelphia by a French cruiser, renamed it *La Petite Démocrate,* and—against the express warning of the American government—sent it out as a privateer. The country was affronted, and Washington demanded and obtained Genêt's recall. By this time a change of government in France endangered his life, and he went to New York instead of Paris. Congress, on June 5, 1794, passed a neutrality law.

The Neutrality Act was the first attempt by a modern nation to define actions that would violate its neutrality, to incorporate these acts in its criminal code, and to enforce them. The offenses it listed were mainly those that Genêt had committed or tried to commit, such as arming ships for belligerents in American ports, or organizing armed expeditions against a friendly foreign power. Together with the Neutrality Proclamation, it established a policy toward warring nations that remained basically unchanged for nearly 150 years. As it was stated in these early years, it was not a manifestation of indifference to world affairs, but rather the result of a consciousness of weakness and of being sheltered by an ocean barrier 3,000 miles wide.

The foolishness of Genêt caused popular feeling to swing in favor of Washington and Hamilton. The Jeffersonian Republicans were hurt, and Jefferson himself, covered with abuse and disgusted by Hamilton's meddling in foreign affairs, resigned. His place was taken in January, 1794, by Edmund Randolph, who gave way in August, 1795, to Timothy Pickering, a staunch and bitter Federalist. Hamilton left the Treasury (January 31, 1795) to practice law and mend his private fortunes. The Cabinet of the Talents had at length gone to pieces, but it was to Washington's credit that he had kept it together for so long a time.

The Jay Treaty (1794)

Washington was determined not only to keep America out of war, but also to improve relations with England and with Spain. In April, 1794, he decided to send Jay to England, in order to seek fulfillment of the Treaty of 1783 and obtain respect for America's rights on the high seas. Fully as important for the United States was the maintenance of peace, for the Hamiltonian financial structure depended largely upon the revenues from customs. If there was war with England, these revenues would be cut off, and the government's credit badly, perhaps irreparably, damaged.

Hamilton indiscreetly informed George Hammond, the British Minister at Philadelphia, that the United States would not join the new armed neutrality of the northern European countries that was being formed in response to Britain's highhanded actions on the sea. This removed from Jay's armory one of his principal weapons. The treaty, which was signed November 19, 1794, was far from being an American triumph.

By the terms of the Jay Treaty, the British agreed to surrender the frontier forts by June 1, 1796. The treaty set up commissions of adjudication to settle the claims of the two parties over American debts owed to English creditors, British injuries to American commerce, and the damage done to England by Genêt's activities in America. As a result of these clauses, the United States paid England $2,807,428 and received $11,656,000 from the British government. Trade with the British East Indies was opened on satisfactory terms. These were real achievements. On the other hand, Jay could get no agreement about Indian relations or disarmament on the Great Lakes; he failed to obtain any recognition of America's rights as a neutral; and the concessions granted to American trade with the British West Indies were so slight and so humiliating that the Senate rejected that part of the treaty. Southerners were outraged by the prohibition of cotton exports to British ports. Though such exports were small, for the cotton gin had been invented only two years before, most of the debts to British creditors were owed in the South, and the planters felt that the treaty discriminated against them. Finally, the French were angered by a clause giving British ships the right to bring prizes into American ports.

The treaty had stormy going in Congress, and in the country Jeffersonian Republican orators had a field day, denouncing the agreement and its author. Jay had been presented at the British court and was reported to have kissed the Queen's hand. One Republican editor declared that he had "prostrated at the feet of Her Majesty the sovereignty of the people . . . he richly deserved to have his lips blistered to the bone." Jay was burned in effigy scores of times, and in New York Hamilton was stoned for defending him and the treaty. The document was barely approved in the Senate. When the House Republicans attempting to defeat it called for the papers connected with the negotiations, Washington refused them on the ground that the negotiation of a treaty was outside the province of the House and that they contained matters that ought not to be revealed. The necessary appropriation for carrying out the treaty was passed in Committee of the Whole by the deciding vote of the Speaker of the House.

Jay's treaty was unsatisfactory in many respects, but without it the danger of war would have been great. Had the United States gone to war in the 1790s, the consequences for the struggling young republic could easily have been disastrous.

The Pinckney Treaty (1795)

On October 27, 1795, less than a year after the Jay Treaty was signed, Thomas Pinckney in Madrid put his signature to a treaty that was of great importance to the American future, for Spain had decided to end the ambiguous and provocative situation on its North American frontier.

The Spanish government viewed with disquiet the ever-increasing pressure of the American frontiersmen on its Florida borders and along the lower Mississippi. It saw in the Indians only uncertain allies. Uneasily joined with England in the war against revolutionary France, Spain was moving toward peace with the latter country. Peace with France might well mean war with England, and the specter of an Anglo-American attack upon their colonies in North America haunted the dreams of the Spaniards. They were more than ever alarmed by news of the Jay Treaty negotiations. The conviction grew in Madrid that the best way to safeguard Spanish possessions in America was to give in to American demands.

By the terms of the Pinckney Treaty, the thirty-first parallel of latitude was made the boundary of West Florida from the Mississippi to the Chattahoochee River. Americans were given free navigation of the Mississippi, and the right of deposit of goods at the mouth of the river with only a "fair price" for storage. The Mississippi was recognized as the boundary between the United States and Spanish Louisiana. Both nations agreed not to use the Indians as a means of harming one another.

The Pinckney Treaty gave the United States all that it asked. Spanish garrisons north of the thirty-first parallel were withdrawn. Even though this was not done until 1798, the danger of Spanish intrigue and western treason was ended and the way was paved for the expansion of the United States into the Mississippi Valley. The Treaty was a definite indication that Spanish power in North America was on the wane. Within less than a generation, Spain was to be forced out of Louisiana and out of its holdings east of the Mississippi.

Political Maneuverings

While the Jay and Pinckney Treaties were being negotiated, the political pot, which had never ceased simmering, again began to boil. Party organization became more and more apparent in Congress, and interstate cooperation developed among political leaders. Jefferson kept in touch with leading Republican politicians in the various states while he was in Philadelphia. After his retirement, the national leadership in organizing the Republicans was taken over by Madison.

Republican state leaders took on prominent party roles. Samuel Adams and John Hancock ruled Massachusetts Republicanism, and dour Senator William Maclay helped to marshal the Republican host in Pennsylvania. George Clinton, Edward Livingston, and Aaron Burr were a mighty triumvirate in New York. Republican political clubs, known as "Democratic Societies," mushroomed—among them Tammany Hall, which was led by Jefferson's admirer John Pintard—until there were thirty-five such clubs in 1795.

The Republican leaders used anti-British propaganda as one of their main weapons. They denounced British policy on the high seas, accused Hamilton and John Adams of aristocratic leanings, and damned the Jay Treaty as servile truckling to Great Britain. Everywhere they preached that Federalism was unfavorable to a democracy and a republic; that the existing government was being run for the few; that Hamilton was at heart a monarchist; that the Federalists were destroying the Constitution by loose construction;

and that the Federalists equated opposition to their policies with disloyalty to the country. The Federalists, in turn, characterized the Republicans as dangerous and unprincipled men, the natural friends and supporters of violence and disorder.

The "Whiskey Rebellion"

Federalist and Republican attacks and counterattacks were given impetus by the so-called Whiskey Rebellion of 1794. The cause of this disturbance was the excise law sponsored by Hamilton. Its tax on whiskey stills was resented by frontier farmers from Pennsylvania to Georgia. Whiskey was a popular drink on the frontier, especially among the Scotch-Irish, and it was also the cheapest and easiest way of transporting frontier corn to the eastern markets. Taxation of these stills took away from the farmers part of what little cash they could command. Jefferson termed the excise "an infernal law," and as early as 1791 Western appeals were made for its nonobservance —appeals reminiscent of earlier protests against the Stamp Act and the duty on tea.

Concerned over the unrest that the excise produced in the western countries, the federal government removed the tax on the smallest stills. Resistance to the collection of the excise continued, however, and some bold spirits in the Pittsburgh region began raising a western militia. Some rioting occurred.

There was obviously an explosive situation in western Pennsylvania. On August 7, 1794, Washington issued a proclamation against the rioters and called for 15,000 militia. He also sent commissioners into the disturbed area. Negotiations with the rioters dragged on and the troops marched, Hamilton going along as a sort of unofficial observer. In the face of this armed force, resistance melted away. Hamilton, however, feeling that the government must display its authority, insisted upon arrests. One hundred and fifty persons were seized, and eighteen tattered prisoners were paraded through the streets of Philadelphia with papers in their hats marked "Insurgent." Two were finally convicted of treason and sentenced to death, only to be pardoned by Washington.

Considerable political furor rose out of this "Rebellion." The Federalists strove to link the disturbances with the Republican democratic clubs and to besmirch, as implicated in revolt, James Madison and a rising Pennsylvania Republican of Swiss birth named Albert Gallatin. The Republicans indignantly repelled these charges, accused Hamilton of despotic and tyrannical conduct, and castigated the government for precipitate military action. Jefferson warned against making another Tea Act out of the excise law.

AN INCIDENT OF THE WHISKEY REBELLION

In the West, tar and feathers entered politics again in 1794. Here a group of Whiskey Rebels escorts a federal tax collector from his burning home.

The Campaign of 1796

As 1796 came on, the political fires burned with a hotter flame. Washington now had a completely Federalist Cabinet, with Timothy Pickering in the State Department, Oliver Wolcott in the Treasury, James McHenry as Secretary of War, and Charles Lee as Attorney General, and he also continued to ask Hamilton's advice on matters of state. The Republicans responded to this situation with more and more violent attacks upon the President. Such attacks embittered his last days in office, and it was at least in part because of Republican assaults upon his integrity that he announced he was not a candidate for re-election.

The Republican candidate for President in 1796 was Thomas Jefferson, with Aaron Burr of New York the most popular choice as his running mate. The Federalists had some difficulty in selecting a candidate, due to the fact that Hamilton disliked John Adams and felt that his own influence in the government would be diminished by Adams' election. Hamilton's favorite was Thomas Pinckney of South Carolina, who had negotiated the Pinckney Treaty with Spain. Hamilton wanted to see Pinckney run even with Adams so that when the electoral college voted, a few ardent Hamiltonians could throw away their ballots for Adams. Pinckney, with a majority, would then become President, and Adams would have second place. During the campaign, however, it became clear that Adams was the Federalist choice for President and Pinckney for Vice President.

WASHINGTON REPELLING A FRENCH INVASION

This Federalist cartoon shows President Washington opposing a brave front to the landing of French liberals, portrayed as "cannibals." Jefferson and his supporters are trying to block the President's progress. A dog lifts its leg on a Republican newspaper.

During the summer and fall of 1796, each side belabored the other. The Federalists were denounced as spendthrift monarchists, supporters of consolidation. The Jeffersonians were charged with catering to lawlessness and quailing before the unruly passions of the mob. The Federalists were the pawns of Britain, and the Republicans dupes of France. Adams was a foe of the people. Jefferson was the head of a French party that was determined to alter the whole system of American government.

Once the campaign was at full heat, Hamilton worked for the election of

Adams as well as that of Pinckney, but several of the New England electors, suspicious of Hamilton's schemes, refused to vote for the South Carolinian. Adams had seventy-one votes in the electoral college, while Pinckney had only fifty-nine. Jefferson, with sixty-eight, was second and therefore became Vice President. Adams was "President by three votes," a fact that always

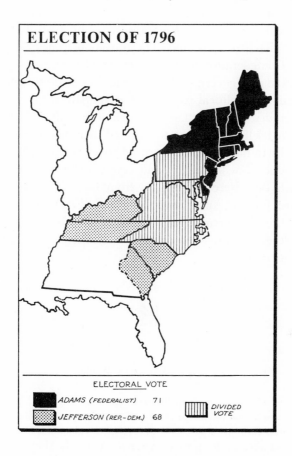

ELECTION OF 1796

ELECTORAL VOTE

ADAMS (FEDERALIST)   71

JEFFERSON (REP.-DEM.) 68

DIVIDED VOTE

caused him chagrin. He carried the North, with seven votes from Maryland. Jefferson carried the South and Pennsylvania, together with Kentucky and Tennessee.

Washington retired from the presidency abused and berated by the Republicans. In his Farewell Address, issued some three months before the electoral college met, he stressed the importance of national unity, warned against "the insidious wiles of foreign influence," and urged the nation to beware of "permanent alliances" and involvement in Europe's political affairs. Excited Republicans thought this part of the Address was directed against them, but there is no evidence that Washington was trying to influence the electoral college.

During the years between 1789 and 1796 America had prospered. It was still in many respects a primitive land, but it was already demonstrating that it had potential. Despite the difficulties that beset neutral traders, the demands of the warring nations had greatly stimulated American commerce. Indeed, the country as a whole had prospered and had also demonstrated stability as a national organization. The transition from government under the Articles of Confederation to that under the Constitution had been made smoothly, and the new government's credit had been firmly established. The gradual formation of political parties was accompanied by vituperative outbursts but proceeded in orderly fashion. Such violent altercation as there was did not translate itself into violent action, and there was every indication on all sides of loyalty to the republican form of government. Foreign policy, too, was being conducted with dignity and considerable success. The Indians, fortified though they were by supplies from Canada, were being pushed back; the British forts on American soil had been evacuated; and Spain had recognized the thirty-first parallel and the Mississippi boundary lines and had opened the Father of Waters to American commerce. The young country was off to a good start.

Suggested Reading

Social conditions at the beginning of the new era are well covered in J. A. Krout and D. R. Fox, *The Completion of Independence, 1790–1830* (1944). Elisabeth McClellan, *History of American Costume, 1607–1870* (1937) gives valuable information on American dress. The newspapers of the period are examined in F. L. Mott, *American Journalism* (1941) and William A. Dill, *Growth of Newspapers in the United States* (1928).

On the new federal government, see David M. Matteson, "Organization of Government," United States Sesquicentennial Commission, *Formation of the Union under the Constitution* (1941), which gives useful information on how the new government got under way. L. D. White, *The Federalists* (1948) is excellent for the development of the government's administrative machinery. E. S. Corwin, *The President* (1957) is informative regarding Washington's role as President and his concept of the extent of presidential powers.

There is much material on party organization and the early political leaders. Noble E. Cunningham, Jr., *The Jeffersonian Republicans* (1957) is a valuable account. C. A. Beard, *Economic Origins of Jeffersonian Democracy* (1915) is still indispensable for any analysis of Jeffersonian Republicanism. Claude G. Bowers, *Jefferson and Hamilton* (1925) is colorful and well written, but prejudiced in favor of Jefferson and the Jeffersonians. J. S. Bassett, *The Federalist System, 1789–1801* (1906) is an old but scholarly account of political and economic affairs. In vol. VI of D. S. Freeman, *George Washington*, previously cited, a graphic picture of Washington as President is given. J. C. Miller, *Alexander Hamilton: Portrait in Paradox* (1959) and Nathan Schachner's *Alexander Hamilton* (1946) and *Thomas Jefferson* (1951) are good biographies, perceptive and judicious in tone. Irving Brant, *James Madison* (5 vols., 1941–1956), vol. III, presents a detailed and sympathetic account of Madison's role during the period from 1787 to 1800. See also, J. C. Miller, *The Federalist Era* (1960); H. J. Ford, *Washington and His Colleagues* (1921); Joseph Charles, *The Origins of the American Party System* (1956). On the Whiskey Rebellion, see L. D. Baldwin, *Whiskey Rebels: The Story of a Frontier Uprising* (1939), and on the Bill of Rights, L. W. Levy, *Legacy of Suppression: Freedom of Speech and Press in Early American History* (1960), and R. A. Rutland, *The Birth of the Bill of Rights* (1955).

On foreign relations, S. F. Bemis, *The American Secretaries of State and Their Diplomacy* (15 vols., 1927–1966) is a standard work; vol. II contains Bemis's own account of Jefferson as Secretary of State. S. F. Bemis, *Jay's Treaty* (1923) and *Pinckney's Treaty* (1926) and Arthur P. Whitaker, *The Mississippi Question, 1795–1803* (1934) are essential for a study of foreign relations in this period, and Alexander De Conde, *Entangling Alliance: Politics and Diplomacy Under George Washington* (1958) is also important.

10 ⸳ The Downfall of Federalism, 1797-1801

JOHN ADAMS was sixty-one years old when he took the oath of office on March 4, 1797. A lawyer by profession, he had risen to prominence in Boston's legal circles by the time of the Revolution. From that time on, he had devoted himself mainly to public affairs, and his record was distinguished. He had been a leader in the movement for independence, a prominent figure in the Continental Congresses, a successful Minister to The Hague during the Revolution, one of the signers of the peace treaty with Great Britain, the nation's first Minister to London, and then for eight years Vice President of the United States.

John Adams, President

The new President was below middle height, stout and very bald, and his fat, round face habitually wore a cold, somewhat smug expression. Senator Ralph Izard of South Carolina, called Adams "His Rotundity." Senator William Maclay of Pennsylvania, a sharp-tongued Republican critic of Federalists in general, noted that Adams sometimes had a fatuous half-smile or simper, and nicknamed him "Bonny Johnny Adams." These were characterizations by political opponents, but it is certain that Adams was vain and open to flattery, obstinate, tactless, and sometimes violent of temper. It is equally beyond doubt that he was a fervent patriot, a disinterested servant of his country, and a man of high moral courage and of great intellectual power.

Adams believed that the source of the authority and power of government is the people, but he was far from idealizing the populace. Self-interest he believed to be the dominant human motivation and economic status the real basis of social distinctions. He was suspicious, if not contemptuous, of democracy, believing that absolute popular sovereignty leads inevitably to demagoguery and the spoliation of the rich. His *Discourses on Davila,* published as a series of articles in 1790–1791, bore witness to the low opinion he held of purely democratic forms, and long after his retirement he told John Taylor of Caroline that "there never was a democracy that did not commit suicide." But Adams was equally opposed to government by an oligarchy or aristocracy, believing that it would mean exploitation of the masses of the poor. The best government, in his opinion, would balance the rich against the poor in a two-chambered legislature, the rich being restricted to the Senate where they would have less power than if they were represented in and controlled both houses. The executive should have an absolute veto and hold the balance even between the two chambers.

Like Hamilton, Adams admired the British form of government. He thought of monarchy as an "Asylum against discord, Sedition and Civil War," and believed that eventually the United States might be impelled to seek its sanctuary. He liked the idea of an hereditary senate and executive, but would not have them established in America unless property became concentrated in a few hands or elections became full of violence and disorder. Regarding such hereditary forms as a last resort, he told Dr. Benjamin Rush in 1790 that he was "a mortal and irreconcilable enemy to monarchy" and "no friend to hereditary limited monarchy in America." He did not believe that the government established under the Constitution was the best in the world, but there is no real indication that he wished to abandon it in his time for a monarchical system.

Seeds of Dissension

Hamilton's distrust of Adams stemmed from fundamental differences in their social and economic philosophies. Hamilton regarded the men of means as the chief support of his system and wished to give them freedom of action. Adams distrusted the rich as much as he did the poor. He placed much more emphasis than did Hamilton on the importance of agriculture and the fisheries in the nation's economy. Again, in contrast to his rival for leadership among the Federalists, Adams feared the consequences of a large public debt and disliked taxes. He was also suspicious of bank note issues and bank discounts and had little more use for banks in general than had Jefferson and

Madison. In his economic views, Adams stood midway between the Hamiltonians and the Jeffersonians. He was the natural leader of the agricultural Federalists, and he had little patience with the proscriptive policies and domineering attitudes of the High Federalists who acknowledged Hamilton as their leader.

The seeds of trouble that were to sprout such a luxuriant crop in Adams' Administration had been sown before the inauguration. Trouble became inevitable when Adams retained Washington's Cabinet as his own. This he had to do, even though Pickering, McHenry, and Wolcott were all devoted to Hamilton and followed his leadership. At this time in the nation's history, there was no tradition of Cabinet members retiring from office with the President who appointed them. For Adams to have dismissed the Cabinet at the beginning of his administration would have been tantamount to a declaration of war on the Hamiltonians and would have riven the party, like the veil of the temple, from top to bottom. Adams, therefore, started his term of office with an official family that was devoted to his critic and rival for control of the Federalist party. During the first two years, however, party dissension was overshadowed by dramatic developments in foreign relations.

Trouble with France

The Jay Treaty angered the French. They regarded its failure to deal with search and seizure on the high seas and the permission it gave Britain to bring prizes into American ports as violations of the Franco-American treaties that had been signed and ratified in 1778. James Monroe, Minister to France, added fuel to the flame of French anger. He made his dislike of the Jay Treaty apparent and did nothing to explain or defend the document in Paris. The French government told Monroe that this agreement with Great Britain annulled the treaties of 1778, and the French began manifesting a more and more unfriendly attitude toward the American Minister, despite his sympathy with their reaction to the Treaty. French ships, privateers and others, began seizing American ships on the high seas. The government at Paris actually attempted to interfere in the election of 1796, its purpose being to promote the election of Jefferson.

Secretary of State Pickering recalled Monroe in 1796, and Charles Cotesworth Pinckney, a prominent South Carolina Federalist, was appointed in his place. When the latter reached France, the French government refused to receive him, and, after cooling his heels in Paris for a time, he left in a rage for Amsterdam.

The XYZ Affair (1797)

Relations with France had now deteriorated to a very low level indeed, but Adams decided to make an effort to improve them, a decision supported by Hamilton, the Cabinet, and Jefferson. A mission was appointed consisting of Charles Cotesworth Pinckney, John Marshall, leader of the Virginia Federalists, and Elbridge Gerry, a Massachusetts Republican who was also a friend of President Adams. It reached France in October, 1797.

The Administration accompanied this gesture toward France by a request to Congress for increased military appropriations and increased taxes. Republican opposition flared at once, and a congressional impasse resulted, marked by bitter debates between the followers of Jefferson and the High Federalists, who were determined upon an ambitious defense program.

While the members of Congress were quarreling over the defense build-up, the mission had rough going in France. Bonaparte's Italian campaign in the spring of 1797 had been brilliantly successful, and the Directory was busily gathering the spoils of war and surrounding itself in Europe with satellite states. The Directory itself was corrupt, and Talleyrand, its Minister of Foreign Affairs, was notoriously venal. His agents—later identified in the despatches of the American commissioners as Messieurs X, Y, and Z— told the Americans that the United States would have to pay a great deal of money for improved relations. Specifically, they indicated that a large loan and a gift of $240,000 to the Directory would smooth the path of negotiation. When the Americans refused, there ensued much talk and some threats to the effect that America might suffer the fate of the Venetian Republic whose independence had just been destroyed by Bonaparte. Still the Americans were obdurate. At last, as the Americans reported it, Monsieur X said:

> Gentlemen, you do not speak to the point; it is money: it is expected that you will offer money. We said that we had spoken to that point very explicitly: we had given an answer. No, said he, you have not: what is your answer? We replied it is no; no; not a sixpence.

The attitude of the French government made the negotiations fruitless, and Adams so informed Congress. That body asked to see the correspondence, and on April 3, 1798, Adams complied with the request. Congress was bitterly indignant at the way in which the commissioners had been treated. At its request the President published the XYZ correspondence, and popular indignation swiftly mounted. The slogan "Millions for Defense, but Not One

THE FRENCH GOVERNMENT DEMANDING MONEY

This cartoon, published in 1799, shows the French government (the Directory at the head of that government had five members; hence the five heads) demanding money from the American commissioners sent by Adams in 1797. The background shows the guillotine with a decapitated body, and Frenchmen bent on robbing one another. The whole illustrates the intense feeling aroused in the United States by the XYZ Affair.

Cent for Tribute" resounded throughout the land. Many sober-minded people believed that France was bent upon world conquest. The Republican friends of France were in high disfavor, President Adams was praised as the great defender of liberty, and the Federalist party enjoyed a popularity it had never known before. Jefferson and the Republicans were terrified by the prospect of war.

As a matter of fact, America and France were now, and for over two years continued to be, in a state of undeclared war. French decrees in 1798 ordered the seizure of neutral ships carrying British goods, and wholesale spoliation of American commerce ensued. Congress abrogated the treaties with France. Bills building up the army and navy, and providing taxes for that purpose, were passed and signed by the President. A series of combats ensued on the high seas, in one of which the thirty-six-gun frigate *Constellation* forced the surrender of the French frigate *L'Insurgente,* which had made itself obnoxious by seizing American merchantmen. In all, eighty-four French ships, mostly privateers, were captured by American commanders. The French did not attack American ships of war, but confined themselves to continued seizures of American merchantmen.

The High Federalists Become Persecutors

The High Federalists were delighted by this state of affairs, for it gave them an opportunity to persecute the Republicans on the ground that they were disloyal, if not actively treasonable, citizens of the republic. Such charges were false, but they were in keeping with the spirit of the times, and it must be said that the Federalists acted under a great deal of provocation. The newspapers and pamphlets of this period, both in Europe and America, were full of the most vicious personal attacks upon political leaders of all shades of opinion. The Federalists were suffering from the assaults of such leading Republicans as Franklin's grandson, Benjamin Franklin Bache—nicknamed "Lightning Rod Junior"—who denounced them in unmitigated fashion in the columns of his newspaper, the *Aurora.* Matthew Lyon of Vermont, a voluble, Irish-born member of Congress, was another extreme critic of the Federalists. Foreign-born pamphleteers, such as General Jean Baptiste Collot and Constantin François Volney and the English expatriates Thomas Cooper and the elder Joseph Gales, were also thorns in the flesh of the Federalist leadership.

This was also an era in which it was customary to place restrictions upon free speech and personal liberty when the national interest was deemed to be threatened. Most nations, including England, had laws against libels of a seditious character. In France, the nation most admired by the Republicans, an alien had to obtain a license permitting him to stay in the country, and political intolerance was and had for years been the order of the day. The Federalists did not feel that they were doing anything out of the ordinary in using legislation to strike at their persecutors.

The Federalists were prompted by other motives than a sense of injury in striking at their political opponents. A war that many of them desired appeared to be imminent, and it seemed only logical to deal harshly with the domestic friends of the foreign foe. Besides this, the Federalists had a marvelous sense of rectitude. Narrow and intolerant themselves, they believed, or professed to believe, that opposition to Federalist policies was factious opposition to the Constitution and to the basic principles of the American government. They dubbed their opponents "Jacobins," democratic extremists who would give full sway to the turbulent passions of the mob and deliver the country over to the French revolutionists. They undertook to save America from such a fate by passing restrictive legislation.

The Alien and Sedition Acts (1798)

The Federalist program for ensuring the safety of the nation took form in four acts passed by Congress during June and July, 1798. These were a Naturalization Act, an Alien Act, an Alien Enemies Act, and a Sedition Act. They were modeled largely upon contemporary English legislation and had the initial approval of President Adams. He was not, however, one of their most violent supporters and later declared that they originated with the Hamilton faction of the party. They best represented the attitude of the High Federalists.

The Naturalization Act had to do with the period of residence before a foreigner could become a naturalized citizen. Originally two years, and extended to five years in 1795, this period was now increased to fourteen years. This, it was hoped, would cut off the Republican party's supply of foreign-born voters and diminish the influence of alien pamphleteers who would be unable to obtain citizenship. The Alien Act, which was limited to two years' duration, gave the President power to arrest and deport undesirable aliens. Any such person advised to depart and failing to do so could be punished under this Act by imprisonment for up to three years and permanent ineligibility for citizenship. The Alien Enemies Act rendered liable to arrest and deportation in time of war or of actual or threatened invasion all alien males of age fourteen or over who were subjects of the hostile nation. All of these acts were clearly restrictive and punitive in character, but the Sedition Act went far beyond any of the rest in invading the rights and liberties of Americans.

The Sedition Act sought to punish anyone found guilty of certain broadly defined seditious activities. The culprit was made subject to a fine of up to $5,000 and imprisonment from six months to five years. Impeding the operation of any federal law, intimidating an officeholder in the performance of his duty, and advising an "unlawful assembly, or combination" were defined as seditious acts. It was further declared that writing or publishing, or caus-ing to be written or published, anything "false, scandalous and malicious" against the government of the United States, or against Congress, or against the President, with intent to defame them or to stir up sedition, should be punished by a fine of up to $2,000 and imprisonment not exceeding two years. The Act was to expire March 3, 1801.

Taken altogether, the Alien and Sedition Acts were designed to stigmatize the Republican party as tainted with disloyal, if not treasonable, sentiments. This, the High Federalists hoped, would insure Federalist control of the government and would destroy their political rivals. Such a result would aid the High Federalists in expanding the power of the central government and in establishing a standing army. They thought that such an army would al-ways be ready for use against foreign foes and would also be useful as a means of overawing, or even subduing, political opponents.

By establishing their unquestioned predominance in the federal govern-ment, the High Federalists also expected to clear the way for their grandiose foreign policy. Their aim, in short, was war with France and Spain, those countries now being in close alliance. Such a conflict would put an end to Republican attacks upon the Federalist party, and it would bring increased and advantageous commercial connections with Great Britain. It would also permit the conquest of Louisiana and the Floridas and even permit the United States, as Hamilton put it, "to squint at South America." This ex-pansion would be achieved through close cooperation, perhaps alliance, with Great Britain and with the South American revolutionary leader Francisco de Miranda. Hamilton was deeply interested in this imperialistic program. Always prone to dream of military glory, he thought of himself as leading an expedition that would at least conquer the Floridas.

The Federalist Program in Action

The Federalists had a program, and they undertook to put it into execu-tion. A separate navy department was created in 1798, the navy was en-larged, and an army of some 10,000 three-year volunteers was established. A direct federal property tax was instituted in 1799. The Federalists also set about enforcing the Alien and Sedition Laws.

Adams actually deported no one under the Alien Acts. Nevertheless, two boat loads of Frenchmen left the country in fear of deportation; one John D. Burke, an Irish expatriate, was driven into hiding; and an effort was made, with Adams' consent, to find three obnoxious Frenchmen, one of them being

234 THE UNITED STATES OF AMERICA: A HISTORY [VOL. I]

General Collot, and expel them from the country. Two of these men could not be found. Collot left the country before the Alien law could be used against him.

The Federalists used the Sedition Act to establish wholesale persecution of the Republicans. Prosecutions for seditious libel against the government, already begun under common law procedure before the passage of the act, were now increased. Adams took no direct part in this, but Secretary of State Pickering and federal judges, district attorneys, and marshals were zealous in enforcing the act. Federal Justice Chase was particularly active, charging juries in such a way as to encourage indictments and seeking everywhere to strike down Republicans. The four leading Republican newspapers in the country were attacked through their owners, editors, or principal writers, and several minor Republican sheets also came under the rod. A number of individual Republicans, prominent nationally or locally, were brought into court. Matthew Lyon was fined $1,000 and sentenced to four months in jail after a trial in which, as in other cases, there was grave suspicion of jury-packing. Dr. Thomas Cooper was imprisoned for six months and fined $400. A semiliterate Revolutionary veteran named David Brown, who had criticized the Federalists as tyrants seeking to enslave the people, was kept in jail for two years, being unable to pay a fine of $400 and costs. In New Jersey, a man who publicly wished that the wad of a cannon fired in salute of President Adams had hit the President in the seat of the pants was fined $100. In all, some twenty-five persons were arrested, eleven cases were brought to trial, and in ten cases the accused were pronounced guilty.

The Federalists justified the Alien and Sedition Acts and the prosecutions under them by charging that the country was full of plots and conspiracies against the nation. The government, therefore, should act in self-preservation against the conspirators. It had the right to act because the Constitution stated that the government was formed to "insure domestic tranquillity, provide for the common defense and promote the general welfare. . . ." But the Republicans had no intention of submitting tamely to the assaults of their political enemies.

The Virginia and Kentucky Resolutions (1798–1799)

Republican resentment over the charges leveled against them by the Federalists, and especially over the persecutions they endured under the Alien and Sedition Laws, resulted in the Virginia and Kentucky Resolutions of 1798–1799. The Virginia Resolutions were drafted by Madison and adopted by the Virginia legislature. Jefferson was the author of the Kentucky Resolutions. Both sets of resolves declared the Alien and Sedition Acts unconstitutional because they violated the Bill of Rights with its guarantee of freedom of speech, press, and petition. They expressed fear of a highly centralized government, asserting that the federal government was created by the states, rather than by direct action of the people, and that the states had the right to judge whether or not the federal government was exceeding its legitimate powers.

The Virginia and Kentucky Resolutions showed some variance of opinion as to what action should be taken when the federal government went beyond the bounds of its proper authority. The Virginia Resolutions declared that the states might "interpose" to right the wrong, without indicating the form of interposition. The Kentucky Resolutions declared the Alien and Sedition Acts to be "void and of no force," and called on the other states to unite with Kentucky in thwarting these unconstitutional proceedings. In 1799, Jefferson prompted the Kentucky legislature to pass an additional resolution declaring that where federal laws violated the Constitution, "nullification" by the states was "the rightful remedy."

It is altogether probable that both Madison and Jefferson meant these Resolutions to be used simply for focusing popular resentment against the Alien and Sedition Acts. Madison, writing in 1831, declared that this was the case; that they were not meant to be statements of constitutional doctrine. The fact remains, however, that the Resolutions put great emphasis on the compact theory of the Union, and in so doing utilized the concepts of "interposition" and "nullification." These ideas were to reappear in the nineteenth century and were to bear fruit which neither Madison nor Jefferson desired.

The Virginia and Kentucky Resolutions were sent out to the legislatures of the other states. The southern states did not respond, and the northern states, which were chiefly under Federalist control, replied unfavorably. Most of the latter declared that the Supreme Court and not the states was the final interpreter of the Constitution. From a political point of view, the Resolutions had little immediate effect. The elections for the Sixth Congress were begun in 1798 but extended into the spring of 1799. They were influenced more by the XYZ correspondence than they were by the Virginia and Kentucky Resolves, and the Federalists increased their majority in Congress by ten seats. The country as a whole was not disposed to weaken the newly formed Union, even though the Alien and Sedition Acts were unpopular in many quarters.

Federalist Troubles Multiply

Despite the fact that the Virginia and Kentucky Resolutions did not drastically damage the Federalists, the sorrows and miseries of that party multiplied. The Republican press flourished under persecution, and where there had been less than twenty such papers in 1798, by 1800 there were at least fifty supporting Jefferson for President. All the principal ones increased their circulation, and the barrage of assault upon the Federalists was wider spread and more violent than ever. Adams was berated, and Hamilton was besmirched. Worse still, from the point of view of political effect, the Federalists began openly quarrelling among themselves.

The new army furnished a subject for furious contention among the Federalists. Adams had not recommended and never liked the army increase provided by Congress and had signed the bill with reluctance. There was no question in anyone's mind as to who should be the general in command, and Washington accepted the post. His powers were rapidly failing, however, and the question of who would be second in command assumed great importance. Since Hamilton wanted the post, and Washington wanted him to have it, Adams gave in, but in bitterness of spirit. He then found himself thwarted in making subordinate army appointments. The President wished to appoint some moderate Republicans as officers, hoping in this way to conciliate Republican sentiment in such states as New York and Pennsylvania and perhaps bring the men into the Federalist camp. Hamilton and the High Federalists blocked this plan, and only Federalists received positions. As these differences developed, it became more and more apparent that Adams' Cabinet, especially Pickering and McHenry, were hostile to the President and were following Hamilton's leadership.

It was now evident that the Federalists were split into two wings: the ultras, who acknowledged Hamilton as their commander, and the moderates, who regarded Adams as the head of the party. The split became wider still, when Adams made the decision to reopen negotiations with France.

The French began making overtures to the American government in 1798. Talleyrand rather belatedly recognized that he had pushed America to the verge of war. He also learned of the Federalist project for an Anglo-American alliance with its threat to French and Spanish possessions in the New World. His determination to follow a conciliatory line was reinforced when Napoleon became the real ruler of France by the coup d'état of the 18th Brumaire (November 9, 1799). The latter was already dreaming of a great French empire in the New World with Louisiana as its center. He had no desire for hostilities with the United States, and one of the first things he did was to cause the French decrees of 1798 to be repealed.

Hamilton had no interest in peace with France, and Adams' Cabinet opposed sending another mission to that country, holding that France should send a mission to America, if such a move were made at all. Adams, however, was ready to meet the French more than halfway. In his message to Congress of December 8, 1798, he declared that American envoys would be named when it was evident that they would be accepted in Paris. He further offended the High Federalists by recommending no further army increase and only limited additions to the navy. Early in 1800, he appointed three commissioners with orders to proceed to the French capital, where they were graciously received. The ensuing negotiation produced the treaty of 1800, which nullified the treaties of 1778 and provided reasonable protection for American commerc...

When it became apparent that Adams would reopen negotiations with France, Hamilton and his followers were desolate at the turn of events. It was obvious that the President wanted peace, and Hamilton's dream of military glory and the conquest of the Floridas and Louisiana rapidly faded away. Peace sentiment gained ground in Congress, where a combination of Republicans and moderate Federalists passed a law in February, 1800, suspending enlistments in the army. Another cause of grievance for the High Federalists was that the elimination of the prospect of war made the Alien and Sedition Acts all the more unpalatable and deprived the Federalists of the campaign argument that the party which was most concerned about the safety of the country should be continued in power. Adams, however, was stubbornly content with his course. Years later, he declared that the only epitaph he desired was "Here lies John Adams, who took upon himself the responsibility of peace with France in the year 1800."

The Election of 1800

The presidential year 1800 opened with bright prospects for peace but with dimming hopes of Federalist victory. There was increasing discontent in the country over the cost of the war preparations that had been begun. Direct federal taxation on land and dwelling houses, which had been imposed by Congress, was very unpopular and exceedingly difficult to collect. The country's attention was shifting from France, which had stopped seizing American ships and was releasing captured American sailors, to England's policy of impressment, but at this juncture nobody wanted war with England. Worse still, from the Federalist point of view, internal faction in that party was becoming more and more violent. It was given a great impetus that spring, when Adams, convinced at last of the hostility of Pickering and McHenry, dismissed them from his Cabinet.

Congress adjourned May 13, 1800, but before it did so each party caucused and selected its candidates for President and Vice President. The Hamiltonian Federalists lacked an outstanding candidate for the presidency. They had wanted Washington to run again. This he had firmly refused to do, and his death (December 14, 1799) was a great loss to the Hamilton faction with which he had become closely identified. That element now accepted Adams' renomination but insisted upon Charles Cotesworth Pinckney, who had been a member of the XYZ mission to France, for Vice President. The Congressional caucus, urged by Hamilton, pledged equal support for both men. It was the hope of the High Federalists that a tie vote for Adams and Pinckney would result in the election going to the House of Representatives, and that there it might be possible to elect Pinckney President. The Republican caucus, without difficulty, chose Jefferson for President and Aaron Burr for Vice President, also pledging equal support for both men.

MAD TOM IN A RAGE

This Federalist cartoon shows the bitterness aroused by the election of 1800. Jefferson, assisted by brandy and the devil, is represented as attempting to destroy the federal government.

The campaign was no sooner fully launched than the dissension in the Federalist ranks broke into open warfare. Hamilton, furious at the dismissal of Pickering and McHenry made it abundantly clear that he wanted Pinckney elected President. The Adams Federalists, particularly strong in New

England, became openly and bitterly critical of Hamilton. Adams himself added fuel to the flame, for his attitude said plainly that the High Federalists were more dangerous than the Republicans to the well-being of the nation. He dubbed the Hamilton Federalists in Massachusetts the "Essex Junto," from the county in which their strength lay, and declared that they were a British faction. This remark was gleefully spread by the Republican press.

The Republican newspapers soon had an even juicier bit of news. Hamilton was determined to prevent Adams' re-election. He urged upon High Federalist leaders throughout the country the importance of choosing as electors in New England men who would surely vote for Pinckney as well as Adams, and asked for the choice of electors in the South one or two of whom would scratch Adams' name in the electoral college. Going even further, he collected a mass of information derogatory to the President and wrote a long letter entitled "The Public Conduct and Character of John Adams, Esq., President of the United States" for circulation among the New England and Maryland Federalists. This portrayed Adams as inordinately vain, jealous, egotistic, and bad tempered. It attacked his judgment and criticized him for dismissing Pickering and McHenry. Nevertheless, Hamilton asserted, he had "finally resolved not to advise the witholding from him of a single vote." If this attack, with its extraordinary conclusion, had any logic whatsoever, it was meant to take electoral votes away from Adams. Hamilton expressed the wish that "its circulation could forever be confined within narrow limits," but this was impossible. Aaron Burr obtained a copy and sent it to the Republican papers, who had it on the streets before the original copies reached the High Federalists for whom they were designed. The Republicans were elated, the Federalists confused and angry. The two Federalist factions were at open war, and the chance of a Federalist victory had gone glimmering.

The election of 1800 was a defeat not so much for Adams as for the Federalist party. Adams showed greater strength than he had in the election of 1796; excluding New York, he had six more electoral votes than he had had in the previous election. New York, which had given its vote to him in 1796, now went for Jefferson and Burr, but this was due to the latter's astuteness in presenting to the voters a very strong ticket of candidates for the legislature which, in turn, chose the presidential electors. Even in New York, however, the margin of Jefferson's victory was a narrow one. On the other hand, the turnover in Congress was decisive. The Republicans now had sixty-five seats in the House of Representatives, whereas in the preceding House the Federalists had had a majority of twenty. The Senate had switched from a Federalist majority of six to a Republican majority of four.

The Federalist defeat was the result of a number of factors. Internal dissension in the Federalist party was one cause of their downfall. As the danger of war lessened, people became more impatient of the persecutions under the Alien and Sedition Acts, and also of the taxation that had been sponsored by the commercial elements that constituted the nucleus of High Federalism. It was the agrarian Federalists who went over to Republicanism; with their going, the Federalists were doomed to the role of a minority party.

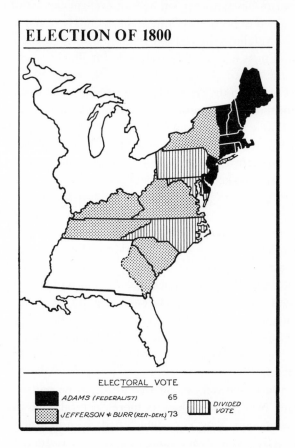

ELECTION OF 1800

ELECTORAL VOTE

ADAMS (FEDERALIST)   65

JEFFERSON & BURR (REP.-DEM.) 73

DIVIDED VOTE

But though the Republicans had won a signal victory, the election was not yet over. Since Jefferson and Burr each had the same number of votes in the electoral college, the choice of a President therefore devolved upon the old House of Representatives, where the voting would be by states. The Federalists not only had a majority of the members but also a majority of the states, so theirs was the decision as to whether Jefferson or Burr should become the third President of the United States.

At first, the Federalists in Congress were inclined to elect Burr as the more manageable of the two men and the one less disposed to weaken the power of the central government. Burr, however, had long been a bitter rival of Hamilton, in politics and before the bar, and the latter did his best to prevent Burr's election. At a dinner in New York, Hamilton gave as a toast, "May our government never fall a prey to the dreams of a Condorcet or the vices of a Catiline." It was clear that he had small use for a candidate who might be compared to the philosopher of the French Revolution, but he had far less for a man whom he considered dangerous and corrupt.

Hamilton's views undoubtedly carried weight with the members of Congress, but there were also other circumstances that contributed to the final result. Some of the Federalist leaders tried to make a deal with Burr safeguarding Federalist interests. When he had repulsed their advances, Jefferson was approached as to whether or not he would leave the public credit undisturbed and the increase of the navy in effect. He was also asked to promise that he would make no wholesale removals of the Federalists from subordinate civil offices in the government. He gave assurance that he would conduct the government in a moderate fashion, and the Federalists, on the thirty-sixth ballot in the House, gave him the election.

Thomas Jefferson was inaugurated on March 4, 1801, in the new, unfinished capitol at Washington. The ceremony took place in the little Senate chamber in the north wing, with Aaron Burr on his right hand and John Marshall, recently appointed by Adams as Chief Justice of the Supreme Court, on his left. There Jefferson read his inaugural address, in a voice so low as to be inaudible to the greater part of his audience. He pledged equal justice for all; respect for majority rule, together with solicitous regard for the rights of the minority; maintenance of the rights of the states—and of the nation; economy of administration; peace abroad; and no entangling alliances. It was an address aimed at healing the wounds of party warfare and uniting the thinking men of both parties behind his administration.

> We have called by different names brethren of the same principle [said Jefferson]. We are all Republicans, we are all Federalists. If there be any among us who would wish to dissolve this Union or to change its republican form, let them stand undisturbed as monuments of the safety with which error of opinion may be tolerated where reason is left free to combat it.

The night before Jefferson's inauguration, John Adams had worked until nine o'clock signing commissions of judicial appointees resulting from the passage by the Federalist Congress of the Judiciary Act of 1801, which created sixteen new federal judgeships and numerous additional marshals

THE CAPITOL IN 1800

This view of the east front shows that the capitol at Washington was still far from completed when Jefferson was elected. Between it and the President's "palace" where Jefferson was to live stretched over a mile of swampy land. Pennsylvania Avenue was merely a dirt road through the mud of the swamp.

and clerks. The need for this expansion of the judiciary had been generally recognized, and the lame-duck Federalist Congress pushed the bill through so Federalists could be appointed to this last stronghold of the party.

Adams did not go to bed that night. He packed up his last books and papers, and at four o'clock on the morning of March 4 his coach was rumbling along the Baltimore road. Sick and sore over his defeat, he had not had the heart to witness the triumph of his rival and erstwhile friend, though he must have heard the thunder of the guns that ushered in the inauguration day. The party of which he had been at least the titular head for four years had gone down to defeat with him as its principal candidate. Its place had been taken by a party that, in theory at least, was devoted to agrarian, rather than to commercial and industrial, interests.

The Federalist party had set up a strong government and a stable financial structure. It had also maintained the republican government that had been organized under the Constitution. Washington spoke truly when he said that there were not half a dozen men in the country who wished to substitute a monarchy for the republic. But the Federalists had acted in tyrannical fashion when the situation of the country did not call for action imperiling personal liberty or the freedom of the press; they had increased government spending and taxation, proceedings that were viewed askance by a large proportion of the electorate; they had fallen into faction and open quarrelling among themselves. Now the country had turned to Republicanism, and it was Jefferson's responsibility to guide the fortunes of the Union.

Suggested Reading

In addition to the books mentioned in the bibliography for Chapter 9, the following will be found useful.

Manning J. Dauer, *The Adams Federalists* (1953) is a careful study, well-documented and authoritative, of the Federalist party structure. Stephen G. Kurtz, *The Presidency of John Adams* (1957) is a scholarly account of the collapse of Federalism. Zoltan Haraszti, *John Adams and the Prophets of Progress* (1952) is a publication of Adams's notes on political and social problems, with commentary. Gilbert Chinard, *Honest John Adams* (1933) is a very good biography of the President, to some extent superseded by Page Smith, *John Adams* (2 vols., 1962).

On the Alien and Sedition Acts, see John C. Miller, *Crisis in Freedom, the Alien and Sedition Acts* (1951), a well-written account of their origin, character, and significance. F. M. Anderson, "The Enforcement of the Alien and Sedition Laws," in the *Annual Report of the American Historical Association, 1912* (1914), 115–126, is a succinct and scholarly account. See also J. M. Smith, *Freedom's Fetters* (1956).

On the Jeffersonian Republicans, in addition to C. A. Beard, *The Economic Origins of Jeffersonian Democracy*, previously cited, see Noble E. Cunningham, *The Jeffersonian Republicans* (1957), which is particularly useful for the study of party organization. Stuart G. Brown, *The First Republicans* (1954) is a thoughtful examination of the political philosophy and public policies of the founders of the party. William A. Robinson, *Jeffersonian Democracy in New England* (1916) is an admirable study of the growth of Republicanism during the 1790s and in subsequent years. E. D. Warfield, *The Kentucky Resolutions of 1798* (1887) is old but still useful. See also, E. P. Link, *Democratic-Republican Societies* (1942).

Republicanism in state politics is examined in D. H. Gilpatrick, *Jeffersonian Democracy in North Carolina, 1789–1816* (1931); W. R. Fee, *The Transition from Aristocracy to Democracy in New Jersey, 1789–1829* (1933); and H. M. Tinkcom, *The Republicans and Federalists in Pennsylvania, 1790–1801* (1950).

On the diplomatic activities of this period, see Bradford Perkins, *The First Rapprochement; England and the United States* (1955).

11 ʼ The Jeffersonian System, 1801-1809

THE REPUBLICAN TRIUMPH in 1800 seemed to the High Federalists little short of an utter catastrophe. The man who had said that America should have a Shays Rebellion every twenty years was now at the head of the government, flanked by James Madison, coauthor of the Virginia and Kentucky Resolutions, as Secretary of State, and by that

Federalist Forebodings

foreign-born politician who spoke with a French accent, Albert Gallatin, as Secretary of the Treasury. The Newark, New Jersey, *Gazette* had predicted that Jefferson's election would "destroy religion, introduce immorality and loosen all the bonds of society." In July, 1801, Theodore Dwight, a high priest of New England Federalism said in a speech at New Haven, "We have a country governed by blockheads and knaves; . . . Can the imagination paint anything more dreadful on this side of hell?" Such were the comments of partisan rancor. The cooler heads among the Federalists knew that Hamilton's judgment of Jefferson was more nearly correct when he said that the President was more revolutionary in theory than in practice and would pursue "a temporizing rather than a violent system."

244

Republican Conservatism

The new government did indeed begin functioning along distinctly conservative lines. Jefferson's inaugural had been a plea for harmony and cooperation in the conduct of affairs rather than a battle cry for radical departures. There were no startling proposals in the President's first message to Congress which was sent to the Capitol rather than being personally delivered, thereby inaugurating a practice that held until the time of Woodrow Wilson. As the months went by, it became increasingly obvious that the national bank, the basic features of the federal judicial system, and the powers and prerogatives of the executive branch of the government would all be left undisturbed. Nor was there any attempt to hand over to the states such parts of the federal administration as the collection of customs and excise taxes. Moreover—and this was the occasion of bitter mirth on the part of the Federalists—two aspects of that party's organizational procedure, both of which had been criticized by the Republicans during the 1790s, were taken over by the party which was now in power. The Republicans had viewed with alarm the way in which Hamilton influenced legislation, but now that Gallatin was in the Treasury, he was asked to make reports and give the House the benefit of his advice. The Republicans also took over from their opponents the device of the caucus and used it with great effect in establishing their legislative program. Exasperated though the Federalists were by both of these acts, they could not denounce their rivals for exhibiting a dangerous radicalism in legislative procedures.

There was some stir and argument in the matter of federal appointments to office. The clamor of Republicans for government positions was prodigious, and, as Jefferson ruefully remarked regarding vacancies, "those by death are few; by resignation, none." A number of Federalists were removed from office to make room for loyal party appointees. During the first term, there were 164 changes in 334 offices, and rare indeed were those occasions on which a member of the Federalist party profited thereby. But at least the Jeffersonians could declare with truth that there was no wholesale proscription of officeholders at the national level. Moreover, as time went on, tenure in office under Jefferson and his successors became as fixed and secure as it had been under the Federalists. Appointments were made, as they had been by the Federalists, from the ranks of gentlemen, the appointees had a reasonable expectation of holding their posts during life, and not a few were succeeded by their sons. What has been described as a "modest bureaucracy" began growing up under Republican auspices.

Marbury v. Madison, 1803

The only really radical movement undertaken by the Republicans was an attempted proscription of Federalist judges. John Pickering, a district judge in New Hampshire, was obviously unfit, by reason of habitual drunkenness or insanity, or both, to continue in office. The Republicans impeached and removed him from the bench. While this was going on, Chief Justice John Marshall delivered an opinion that filled the Republicans with fury and produced bitter attacks on the highest court in the land.

It must be remembered that this was a time when Republicanism and states' rights were in the ascendant everywhere save in New England, Delaware, and New Jersey. Centralization of power in the federal government had been checked, but it had not yet been determined where lay the power to declare acts of Congress unconstitutional. Outside of the exercise of such power by the states, Republicans generally held that Congress was the ultimate authority in determining the constitutionality of its own acts. This was why Marshall's decision in the case of *Marbury v. Madison* (1803) burst like a bombshell upon the Republicans.

Marbury had been one of the so-called midnight judges appointed by Adams in the closing hours of his administration, but Marbury's commission as a justice of the peace had not been delivered when Jefferson took office. It remained on Madison's desk, and Marbury moved in the Supreme Court for a writ of mandamus to compel its deliverance to him. Marshall's opinion held that Marbury had a right to the commission, but that the authority given the Supreme Court by the Judiciary Act of 1789 to issue writs of mandamus to public officers was unconstitutional, the reason being that the Supreme Court had no original jurisdiction in such cases. The heart of this decision—and it was developed at some length—was that the power to declare acts of Congress unconstitutional was vested in the Supreme Court of the United States.

Jefferson loathed this decision. He would have liked to move against Marshall, but for this he had no legal grounds. Instead, he urged the Republicans in Congress to proceed against another member of the Supreme Court, Judge Samuel Chase, the intemperate Federalist who had struck down Republicans under the Alien and Sedition Acts and was still thundering against them and their ways. Chase was impeached and tried before the Senate, but was acquitted. Had the impeachment succeeded, it is probable than an attack would have been made upon other members of the Supreme Court, perhaps even Marshall himself, by the impeachment process.

The Republican Program

The Republicans were interested in rooting out what they regarded as the obnoxious aspects of Federalism, but they also had a constructive program. Its objectives were peace, debt reduction, economy in government, and the maintenance of the rights of individuals and of the states. The realization of this program depended to a great extent upon Jefferson's leadership. Here he manifested great talent, maintaining such good personal relations with the officers of government and with prominent members of Congress that harmonious party policy was maintained during the first term. The President's leadership, combined with the party caucus, resulted in an effective development of legislative and executive policy.

First in order came the abolition of unpopular laws. Nothing had to be done about the Alien Act or the Sedition Act, which had expired by the time Jefferson took office, but other Federalist legislation was still on the books. One such measure was the Naturalization Act requiring a fourteen year period of residence; this was reduced to five years. The Federalist-imposed internal revenue taxes, including all excise levies, were repealed, and with them went a quarter of the government's patronage. For revenue Gallatin relied on land sales, customs, and postal services. The Judiciary Act of 1801 was also stricken from the books, after a bitter fight in Congress during which the Federalists charged Jefferson with destroying the Constitution. The Republicans thus rid themselves of laws against which they had made loud outcry, but all this was mild in comparison with what the Federalists had professed to fear.

As a matter of fact, Jeffersonian Republicanism in practice differed only in degree from Federalism. Like its rival system, it accepted a capitalistic order of society, leaving untouched the speculation in land that had gone merrily on under the Federalists. The Jeffersonians chartered state banks freely, especially to good Republicans. They made no attempt to widen the suffrage. The chief difference was that, whereas the Hamiltonians had governed in favor of commercialists and industrialists and had put the burden of taxation on the agrarians, the Jeffersonians lifted taxation from the agrarians and sought to leave everyone free to make headway in economic matters according to his talents. The Jeffersonian ideal was not regulation, but laissez faire.

The repeal of the internal revenue laws was a clear indication of Republican devotion to small and economical government, an ideal that Jefferson and Gallatin strove hard to realize. Under the latter's masterful leadership in the Treasury Department, policy was directed toward lowering expenditures and the reduction of the national debt. Military and naval costs were curtailed. Economies were effected by the abolition of the so-called "midnight judges," and by reform in some branches of the civil service. The consequence was reduction of the expenses of the national government, exclusive of the interest on the public debt, from some $7 million to about $3 million a year. These reductions enabled Gallatin to devote a considerable part of the government's income to paying off the national debt. The debt, which stood at approximately $83 million in 1801, had been lowered to $57 million by 1809; and Madison's administration, carrying on the same policy of economy, brought it down to $45 million in 1812.

War with the Barbary Pirates

Among the expenditures which Jefferson particularly disliked were those for the navy. The Federalist policy of building frigates was discontinued, and some of those already constructed were laid up in the Washington navy yard. Jefferson's idea of naval defense centered on gunboats, and some of these were constructed. They were scarcely seaworthy, and wags alleged that, after a storm, one or two of them were found high and dry in seaside corn fields. But the President saw little use in a seagoing fleet. His attitude toward international affairs was, in principle, isolationist. Shortly after his inauguration, he told Dr. George Logan that the United States had nothing to fear from European interests. "Our commerce," he declared, "is so valuable to them that they will be glad to purchase it when the only price we ask is to do us justice." This observation, like the policy of naval reduction, lost some of its force when the Administration turned to dealing with the Barbary pirates.

It had long been the practice of such states as Tripoli, Tunis, and Algiers to exact tribute from the commerce in the Mediterranean. The English navy had protected colonial merchantmen from such exactions, but this protection disappeared with American independence. The Washington and Adams Administrations paid $2 million for immunity from spoliation. This bribery was continued under Jefferson, but the appetites of the Barbary states were insatiable. The Dey of Algiers compelled the American ship that brought him tribute to hoist the Algerian flag and sail on an errand to the Sultan of Turkey. The Bashaw of Tripoli, dissatisfied with $80,000 tribute money, declared war on the United States by cutting down the flagstaff in front of the American consulate.

Jefferson's whole inclination was for peace, but where national honor was concerned he could become very wrathful indeed. He now proceeded to forceful action. Four squadrons were sent in succession to the Mediterranean, and in 1804 American warships repeatedly bombarded Tripoli. Such reprisals, together with the amazing exploits of a Yankee adventurer named William Eaton—who, with the pretender to the Tripolitan throne, organized a land expedition that overran half of Tripoli—forced the Bashaw to sue for peace. Such drastic procedures reduced the Mediterranean pirates as a whole to a state of tolerable respect for ships flying the American flag. The cost was heavy. A special $2\frac{1}{2}$ per cent import duty had to be created in order to relieve the Treasury burden, but this was more than counterbalanced by the gains for American commerce and the increase of American prestige in European eyes. A final treaty with Algiers in 1815 ended for all time the practice of giving tribute for the protection of American commerce and paying ransom for captured American seamen.

Louisiana

It was important to take action against the Barbary pirates, but a far more significant decision for the future of the United States confronted Jefferson during his first term in office. This concerned the vast region lying beyond America's western boundary, the region known as Louisiana.

France had ceded Louisiana to Spain in 1763 but on October 1, 1800, the day after the convention was signed which ended the undeclared war between France and the United States, Spain signed the secret Treaty of San Ildefonso giving Louisiana back to the French government. This cession, for which a quid pro quo was given in the shape of support for Spanish ambitions in Italy and the promise that Louisiana would never be disposed of to any other nation than Spain, was essential to a grandiose project that had taken form in the busy brain of the First Consul. Napoleon planned a great empire in the West with Louisiana as its center. In 1801, he sent his brother-in-law, General Le Clerc, with 20,000 men to subjugate the Negroes in Santo Domingo. That Caribbean island was to serve as the outer bastion of the projected empire, and once Santo Domingo had been pacified, Le Clerc's army was to be stationed in New Orleans.

The year following despatch of Le Clerc's army to Santo Domingo, the Spanish government suspended the right of deposit at New Orleans. This meant that Americans could no longer bring goods down the Mississippi to New Orleans and deposit them there for transshipment. The suspension of the right of deposit was done apparently without French pressure, but it fitted in very nicely with Napoleon's plans for expanding by cajolery or by force the area of his domain in the West. What the limits of that domain might be no man could say, but the implementation of Napoleon's policy could well mean French control of territories on both sides of the Mississippi, with the United States penned in east of the Alleghenies.

The actual transfer of Louisiana to France was delayed by negotiations over the benefits that Spain was to receive from the deal, but news of it leaked out. Jefferson, alarmed, wrote to Robert R. Livingston, United States Minister in Paris, that the possessor of New Orleans was the natural enemy of the United States and that if France took possession of the mouth of the Mississippi, "we must marry ourselves to the British fleet and nation." The assumption in Washington was that France was acquiring both New Orleans and the Floridas, and Madison told Livingston to inquire for what price France would sell both of these to the United States.

In November, 1802, news of the suspension of deposit at New Orleans reached the United States, together with a report that Spain had finally ordered the transfer of Louisiana to France. The western frontiersmen were mightily alarmed, and the Federalists in Congress urged immediate occupation of New Orleans, hoping to confront Jefferson with the dilemma of choosing between war with France and the loss of western political support. Jefferson was not to be rushed into precipitate action. He asked and obtained from Congress an appropriation of $2 million and sent James Monroe to France with specific instructions. Monroe was to help Livingston persuade Napoleon to sell New Orleans and the Floridas to the United States. If this were impossible, the Americans were to obtain a guarantee of the right of deposit. If France would grant nothing and had clearly hostile intentions toward the United States, Monroe and Livingston were to cross the Channel and seek a defensive alliance with Great Britain.

While Monroe was on his way to Paris, Livingston learned of a startling change in Napoleon's plans. Le Clerc's army had been decimated by fighting and yellow fever in Santo Domingo, and its general was dead. The outer bastion of the empire in the West had not been established. On receipt of this news, Napoleon abandoned his schemes for Louisiana, turning instead to renewal of war in Europe and a possible invasion of England. War with England might well mean British conquest of Louisiana, and he decided to sell the entire territory to the United States.

When, on April 11, 1803, Talleyrand asked Livingston if the United States would like to purchase Louisiana, Livingston replied that we wanted only New Orleans and the Floridas. He was then asked what the United States would give for Louisiana. The American, thunderstruck, asked time to consider, and to confer with Monroe. The latter arrived in Paris on the following day, and for three weeks the negotiators discussed terms. Agreement was reached, and the treaty of purchase was signed on May 2, 1803.

Louisiana cost the United States 60 million francs ($12 million) and the assumption of American claims against France up to 20 million francs more. For approximately $.08 an acre, the United States had acquired 865,000 square miles of magnificent country. Small wonder that, after the signing of the treaty, Livingston rose and shaking hands with the French negotiator Marbois and with Monroe, said, "We have lived long, but this is the noblest work of our lives."

The purchase of Louisiana ended the possibility which even Jefferson recognized that two American confederacies might develop—one in the East and the other in the West. It opened the way for America's becoming a world power of the first rank, but it was also in many respects a curious transaction. Livingston and Monroe had bought something that they had no authority to buy, from a French government that had no right to sell, and in the name of an American President who believed that the government had no constitutional right to make the purchase. Indeed, Jefferson began drawing up constitutional amendments that would make the transaction legal. Then, warned that delay would give Napoleon a chance to change his mind, the great exponent of strict construction of the Constitution decided to forget amendments and rely upon broad construction of that document in defending the acquisition. A further ironic touch was added by the method of payment, which was in 6 per cent United States government bonds that would be gradually redeemed after 1818. Napoleon sold these bonds to Baring Brothers in London and then used this British gold to finance the war that broke out between France and England in 1803. Finally, magnificent as the achievement was, neither the United States nor France had any clear idea of the extent of the empire that had been bought and sold. Pressed for information on this subject, Talleyrand could only say, "You have made a noble bargain for yourselves, and I suppose you will make the most of it." Future years were to prove the Frenchman a good prophet.

Expansionists, surprised but delighted by the acquisition of Louisiana, at once began pointing out how the vast resources of the region in forests, minerals, and fertile soil made for an economic development that would in time render America completely independent from Europe. On the other hand, some Federalists became gloomy as they foresaw New England dwarfed by an expanding South and West. In their minds, the acquisition of this vast area was bound to lead to confusion and disorganization. Fisher Ames declared that the country had some limits when the Mississippi was its bound-

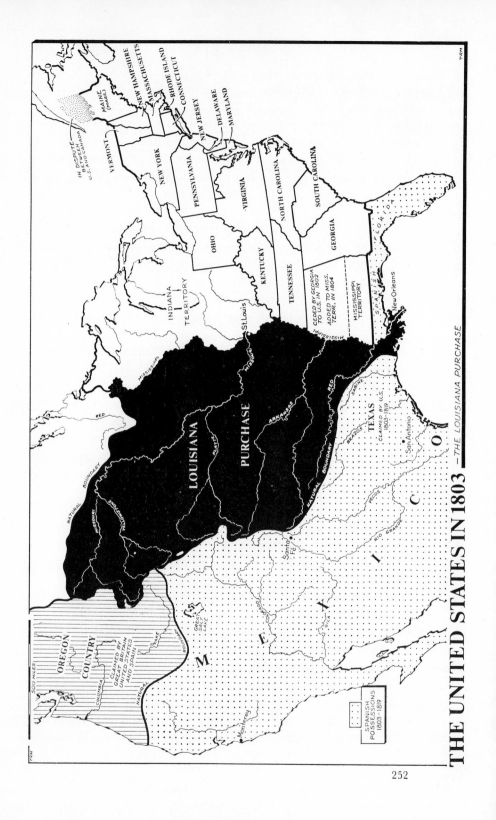

THE UNITED STATES IN 1803 —THE LOUISIANA PURCHASE

ary. "Now, by adding an unmeasured world beyond that river, we rush like a comet into infinite space."

Republicans generally had no such fears as those which afflicted the Federalists. For them the purchase of Louisiana opened far-reaching vistas of national development. Jefferson began dreaming of a great system of internal improvements. In 1805, he spoke of the desirability of a constitutional amendment that would permit setting aside each year a fund to be spent on roads, canals, river improvements, manufactures, education, "and other great objects within each state." Gallatin estimated that, by 1809, $3 million a year could safely be devoted to such a program, and in 1806 Congress authorized the construction of a national highway. This was the Cumberland road, stretching from Cumberland, Maryland, out to Illinois. Construction of this road, however, was not begun until 1811, and the whole problem of internal improvements at national expense became so complicated and so involved in politics that the plans Jefferson was revolving in his mind found no practical application for many years.

Exploration of the West

If Jefferson could not institute a far-reaching program of internal improvements, he could at least promote the exploration of America's new empire. He had been interested in the exploration of the West long before the purchase of Louisiana, and during his presidency the government moved energetically in that direction. In January, 1803, months before he thought of purchasing the territory, he asked Congress to appropriate money for a small military expedition that would explore Louisiana "in the interest of our external commerce" and would seek information about the animals and plants of the region. Congress was agreeable, despite the doubtful propriety of spying out the land of a friendly foreign power. The result was the Lewis and Clark expedition.

Meriwether Lewis, an adventurous Virginian who had been Jefferson's private secretary, and William Clark, the younger brother of George Rogers Clark of Revolutionary fame, together with a force of forty picked men, started from St. Louis in May, 1804. They went up the Missouri to its three forks, which they named Jefferson, Madison, and Gallatin. Still further to the west, they reached the three forks of the Jefferson, which they christened Philosophy, Philanthropy, and Wisdom—names that had no enduring popularity with the settlers (Philanthropy River became known as Stinking Water). From the upper courses of the Missouri, the expedition moved overland to a navigable tributary of the Columbia and then down that river to the Pacific Ocean. The return journey was made in 1806. During the whole trip one man had deserted, one had died, and one Indian was killed. This expedition gave the United States its best claim to the Oregon region and furnished the basis for a superb historical account written by a young Philadelphian who stood high in the estimation of President Jefferson. This was Nicholas Biddle, who was destined to play a conspicuous part in the later history of the United States.

While the Lewis and Clark expedition was under way, Lieutenant Zebulon Pike also journeyed into the West. He explored the headwaters of the Mississippi in 1805–1806 and a year later led another party of adventurous spirits up the Arkansas River and then by way of Colorado to the Rio Grande. This last trip was undertaken with a view to reconnoitering the country to which the United States had a more or less shadowy claim under the Louisiana Purchase. On viewing the peak in Colorado which bears his name, Pike wrote in his diary that it would never be climbed by mortal man; today there is a motor road to its summit.

The Election of 1804

Viewed from every aspect, Jefferson's first term was a great success. His domestic program had been validated by Congress, he had successfully upheld American interests in the Mediterranean, and the purchase of Louisiana brought him great popular acclaim. His renomination was a foregone conclusion, but in 1804 Burr was no longer at his side. Jefferson had come to distrust the affable New Yorker and had worked with Governor George Clinton in depriving Burr of his share of the New York state patronage. Though Clinton's mental powers were decidedly failing, he was in command of the New York state Republican machine, and he was made the candidate for Vice President.

The Federalists selected Charles Cotesworth Pinckney to run against Jefferson. It was a hopeless contest. Jefferson carried every state save Delaware and Connecticut, and the latter went Federalist by only a scant margin. The Republicans also controlled Congress by enormous majorities—twenty-seven to seven in the Senate and 116 to twenty-five in the House.

Jefferson's Time of Troubles

The election over, Jefferson looked forward confidently to an untroubled second term. Never was a man more completely disappointed. The smooth-running Republican political organization developed a multitude of rifts and dissensions during the next four years, difficulties with foreign nations multiplied, and even the decrepit Federalist party began showing signs of renewed strength. John Randolph of Roanoke—in an apt comparison—said that Jefferson's second term reminded him of the seven lean kine in Pharaoh's dream that rose from the river and devoured their seven fat predecessors.

One of the most spectacular signs of Republican trouble was the breakup of the Republican machine in New York State. There Burr was the great defector. Loathed by Jefferson, denied participation in the spoils of office, cast out of regular Republican circles by the Clintonians, he was still politically ambitious and politically dangerous. In 1804, a group of his friends in the New York state legislature nominated him for governor. The New York Federalists and certain New Englanders of the same party, enraged at the purchase of Louisiana—which they believed meant the permanent subjugation of New England by a combination of the West with "the lordlings of the South"—were revolving schemes for a New England confederacy that would include New York. When they sought assurance of Burr's cooperation, he cannily promised a "satisfactory" administration of the state if he were elected governor, and Federalist banquets rang with the toast to "Aaron's Rod . . . may it blossom in New York." Hamilton, however, threw his influence with telling effect against Burr, and Morgan Lewis, the regular Republican candidate, was elected. The sequel was Burr's challenge to Hamilton and the duel at Weehawken, New Jersey, July 11, 1804, where Hamilton fell mortally wounded.

Replaced by Governor Clinton on the Republican vice presidential ticket in 1804, Burr went on to develop with his unscrupulous friend, General James Wilkinson, grandiose plans for a western empire—plans that ended in the ruin of those he drew into the scheme and in his own trial for treason. He was acquitted, but this sequence of events robbed him of political power. Meanwhile, the Livingstons and Clintons had become involved in quarrels over the New York state leadership, and the formerly smooth-running New York Republican machine dissolved into a frenzy of factional strife that was reflected in congressional intrigues.

A situation similar to that in New York appeared in Pennsylvania, where quarrels between moderate and extreme Republicans over the scanty spoils of office and over the impeachment of state judges produced increasing acrimony and strife. Virginia was also a scene of Republican contention. Lack of federal patronage, Jefferson's broad construction of the Constitution in the purchase of Louisiana, and the forceful way in which the Administration pushed its programs through Congress aroused the discontent of John Taylor of Caroline and of John Randolph of Roanoke. These men were exponents of states' rights and of restraining the power of the executive branch of the national government. Their resentment was stridently expressed in Congress by John Randolph of Roanoke.

The open breach between Randolph and Jefferson became apparent when Jefferson, in 1805, asked Congress for $2 million with which he hoped to persuade France to extort West Florida from Spain and then give it to the United States. The tall, cadaverous congressman from Roanoke shrilled out a torrent of invective against an Administration that would "surrender the public purse to the first cutthroat who asked for it"; that would now try to buy what it had already bought two years before. The passage of the bill was delayed by such forays until Napoleon, who controlled Spanish policy, decided against selling West Florida, and Jefferson's scheme came to nought.

Yazoo

Randolph had an even more dramatic opportunity to attack the Administration in connection with the scandals over the Yazoo land sales. In 1797, the Georgia legislature had sold 50 million acres of the state's western land claims to the so-called Yazoo companies at a price averaging $.015 cents an acre. The whole transaction was steeped in fraud. The scandal broke into the open and an indignant electorate turned the rascals out of office. The next legislature rescinded the sale but made no provision for investors who, in good faith, had purchased Yazoo lands. These investors organized and sought relief from Congress and from the courts, and when the United States took over Georgia's western land claims in 1802 it inherited the controversy. Gallatin, Madison, and Levi Lincoln, all in Jefferson's Cabinet, devised a settlement which proposed using lands in Mississippi territory to satisfy the claims of the Yazoo purchasers, but Randolph now stepped into the picture. Any mention of the proposed transaction excited his rage. When he rose in Congress and, exclaiming in shrill tones "You are a Yazoo man," pointed his bony forefinger at a member of the House, that offending individual would cower in his seat. In Randolph's opinion, everyone connected with the affair was a scoundrel, including "St. Thomas of Cantingbury," as he called Thomas Jefferson. Supported by Nathaniel Macon of North Carolina and enthusiastically aided by the Federalist remnant, Randolph killed bill after bill for the relief of the Yazoo creditors. The situation was destined to be further complicated by Marshall's decision in *Fletcher v. Peck* (1810) that the Georgia act rescinding the Yazoo land sales was an impairment of contract and therefore unconstitutional. The Randolph faction, dubbed by their leader the "Tertium Quids," nagged Jefferson, spoiled Republican harmony, and delayed the relief bill until 1812, when it was finally passed under the succeeding administration.

The Difficulties of Neutrality

Far worse than domestic squabbles within Republican ranks were the problems that arose out of the battle of the giants being waged in Europe. In 1802, Napoleon had signed the Peace of Amiens with Great Britain, but this meant only a breathing space. The little Corsican's insatiable ambition and England's fear of his designs made inevitable a new outbreak of war between the two countries. It came in 1803, when England organized with Prussia and Austria the Third Coalition. Napoleon began gathering an army and a fleet of transports at Boulogne for an invasion of "perfidious Albion," and the struggle broke into the open in 1805, when Napoleon left his camp at Boulogne, marched swiftly into central Europe, and captured an Austrian army of 30,000 men at Ulm. Once again the tiger and the shark were linked in mortal combat, and once again neutral nations found themselves pawns in the struggle for world power.

Nelson's victory at Trafalgar (October 21, 1805) over the combined French and Spanish fleets broke the back of French naval power. It left Britain supreme on the sea, but it was an uneasy supremacy. French privateers were a constant menace. English merchants, too, viewed with alarm the rapid development of an American merchant marine that, even before the War of the Third Coalition broke out, was seizing a larger and larger proportion of world trade. The situation was further complicated by the great difficulties involved in manning the British fleet. This was the era of Captain Bligh and the famous mutiny on the *Bounty*. Discipline on England's ships of war was harsh and cruel, pay was low, and food was of poor quality. Desertion was common, and the navy constantly resorted to the press gang, which seized likely looking citizens on the streets and in the grog shops and forced them into His Majesty's service. Even this hated institution was only partially successful in filling the rosters of the navy with unwilling British sailors. The captain of a short-handed British warship often yielded to the temptation to stop a trim American merchantman, line up its crew, and take British deserters off its decks. The temptation was also strong to seize American seamen in the process, especially those whose naturalization papers were of recent date. The British contention was "once an Englishman, always an

Englishman.," a point of view all the more stubbornly held because, in some states, naturalization papers could be obtained well before the five-year limit of residence prescribed by the American Naturalization Act.

Impressment of American seamen had been a chronic source of difficulty between Britain and the United States, but it was by no means the only source of friction. The search and seizure of American ships—a bone of contention in the 1790s—soon became another sore point. This had given little trouble during Jefferson's first term, for the British admiralty courts had maintained the Rule of 1756, which declared that trade illegal in time of peace was illegal in time of war. In other words, if during peacetime France prohibited American ships from carrying goods between France and its West Indian colonies, Britain would regard such trade as illegal in wartime, despite French change of policy, and would hold the cargo as lawful prize. The British courts, however, in the case of the *Immanuel* (1799) and the *Polly* (1800) had laid down the rule that American merchantmen could carry goods from a French or Spanish colony to the mother country, provided the merchandise landed en route at a United States port and there passed through the customs. Under the "broken voyage" ruling American commerce had flourished. But a drastic change came in 1805, when, in the case of the *Essex*, admiralty judge Sir William Scott set up the theory that broken voyages were in the same category as continuous voyages and were therefore illegal. Under this ruling, British warships began seizing American merchantmen and confiscating their cargoes.

In 1806, Britain added to the woes of American merchants by declaring a blockade of all European ports from Brest to the Elbe River, and in 1807 the blockade was extended by an Order in Council to all the ports of France and its allies. Interference with American shipping and the impressment of American seamen now took a sharp upturn. In the period from 1783 to 1812, some 10,000 Americans were pressed into the British navy, three-quarters of them after the year 1803. This number was multiplied in the excited imaginings of the American public and the American press, where estimates ran as high as 50,000 gallant American tars, languishing in durance vile.

But Britain was not the only offender against what Americans regarded as their neutral rights. Napoleon's answer to the British blockade was the Berlin decree of 1806, which declared a paper blockade of Britain, and then the Milan decree of 1807, which characterized as enemies of France and subject to seizure all who submitted to the British Orders in Council. The French in their turn laid hold on American ships and confiscated their goods, so America found itself caught in the middle of this struggle of the titans.

Jefferson believed that free ships make free goods. That the rights of neutrals must give way to the convenience of foreign nations was to him a monstrous doctrine, the enforcement of which could not long be endured. "The day is within my time as well as yours," he wrote to a friend, "when we may say by what laws other nations shall treat us on the sea. And we will say it." Nevertheless, he felt that peace was a paramount necessity. The country must grow strong and get out of debt. Since he was also convinced that men's actions derived from convictions of self-interest, he came to the conclusion that pressure on the pocketbooks of the British and the French would secure respect for neutral rights.

The first American effort to play upon the self-interest of foreign nations came in 1806 with the passage of the Non-Importation Act. This prohibited the importation of British goods that could be obtained elsewhere or that could be produced in the United States. Passed in April, this Act was suspended until December, and meanwhile James Monroe, Minister to England, together with special agent William Pinkney, hung it over the heads of the British in an effort to get a favorable commercial treaty. Randolph dubbed this measure "a milk and water bill, a dose of chicken broth," and events proved he was right. Jefferson would not submit to the Senate the treaty that Monroe and Pinkney obtained with the bill as a weapon. Instead, he sent the document back to England.

The Chesapeake Affair

While the treaty was on its way back to its negotiators, an event occurred that produced great excitement in the United States. The American frigate *Chesapeake,* Captain Barron commanding, had been outfitting at the Washington navy yard for a Mediterranean cruise. It was behind schedule, and last preparations were hastily made. Finally the ship dropped down the Potomac to Portsmouth, where it took on heavy guns and stores, and (June 22, 1807) started out of Hampton Roads. On board were three American seamen who had been pressed on the British ship *Melampus* and had escaped, and also a bona fide British deserter named Jenkins Ratford. British ships in the vicinity of Hampton Roads, including the British frigate *Leopard,* knew that these men were on the *Chesapeake.*

As the *Chesapeake* stood out to sea, the *Leopard* ranged alongside and signaled that she had despatches for the American—not unusual procedure. When the *Chesapeake* hove to and a party of British officers came on board, the despatches proved to be an order to search the American ship for deserters. This Captain Barron refused, though he did not summon his men to quarters; and when the *Leopard,* on word of his refusal, poured three broadsides into the *Chesapeake,* only one gun could be fired in return and that by means of a live coal carried from the ship's galley by one of its officers. With twenty-one men killed or wounded, the *Chesapeake* struck her flag, the four "deserters" were taken off, and the American ship limped back into Hampton Roads.

When the news of this outrage broke, the country began clamoring for war. Jefferson promptly issued a proclamation excluding British warships from American waters, but his mood was not warlike. He told Monroe to demand an apology and the restoration of the four seamen. This was scarcely effectual, for the British promptly hung Jenkins Ratford, and did not make amends for seizing the Americans until five years had passed. But the President's recourse to negotiation did give time for tempers to cool.

The Embargo

The *Chesapeake* affair highlighted the need for a positive policy in defense of American rights, and Jefferson and his Cabinet began searching for a formula which would put the belligerent nations on an equal legal basis and at the same time permit the heaviest pressure to be exerted on the chief offender against American rights, Great Britain. The result was the Embargo Act of December 22, 1807, which prohibited commerce with any foreign port, whether in American or foreign vessels. American goods and American sailors were now to be kept at home.

The Embargo Act had a threefold purpose. It would prevent seizures of ships and men that, in Jefferson's opinion, were surely leading to war. Secondly, it would force British respect for American rights by the use of economic sanctions. This, like the Non-Intercourse Act, was a product of Jefferson's belief in the potency of self-interest. In 1807, United States exports amounted to $108 million, and it imported goods to the value of $138 million. Much of the export was in goods important to the British economy, and American imports were largely of English manufacture. Madison calculated in 1805 that 300,000 Englishmen would be thrown out of work, and that the British colonies would be reduced to utter chaos by the prohibition of all intercourse with Great Britain. Thirdly, the Administration also was convinced that the Embargo would reduce American economic dependence upon Great Britain and foster the growth of American manufactures. This last, in view of America's trouble with the nations overseas, both Jefferson and Madison were beginning to regard as a desirable achievement.

The Embargo had a mixed reception in Washington. Going through Congress smoothly enough, it was enacted into law four days after the President proposed it, but there were signs of trouble ahead. Gallatin was cool to it, foreseeing difficulties in enforcement. He preferred war to a long-standing trade interdict. Randolph, representing the "Quids," called it a servile yielding to Bonaparte. The Federalists predicted commercial disaster, even as their political hopes began to rise. Reactions throughout the country also differed. The South and West were loyal to the President and his policy,

OGRABME, THE AMERICAN SNAPPING TURTLE

This Republican cartoon by Alexander Anderson was meant to indicate that the Embargo was highly effective.

though deploring the hardships that were bound to be entailed by the disruption of trade. Opinion in the Middle Atlantic states was divided. Only in northern New York and among the major part of the New England states was there violent resentment and, as events proved, flagrant resistance to the Act.

Enforcement of the Embargo was, indeed, a major problem. Illicit commerce mushroomed, while the coastal trade suddenly assumed phenomenal proportions. Long lines of wagons crossed the sparsely guarded Canadian frontiers of New England and New York, and similar smuggling operations flourished on the borders of Florida. Massachusetts Federalists bitterly denounced Jefferson's "terrapin policy." They undertook a vigorous propaganda against it in the name of states' rights, throwing out dark hints of New England's secession from the Union. The President, they declared, was seeking to destroy New England's wealth; he wanted that section to become a satellite of the South and West.

Despite the actions and attitudes of critics and dissenters, the President moved vigorously and with the loyal cooperation of the Treasury and State Departments in the enforcement of the Embargo. The country witnessed the spectacle of the advocate of periodic rebellions and states' rights issuing a sweeping order for suppression of "the insurgents" in the Lake Champlain area, summoning reluctant state governors to enforce federal laws, and using the navy to crack down on seagoing exponents of individual freedom. Evasions continued. John Jacob Astor, for instance, used the bogus excuse of returning a "Mandarin" to China in getting clearance for a China-bound ship; the vessel was crammed with goods, and Astor realized a profit of $200,-000 on the voyage. Republican Governor Sullivan in Massachusetts winked at infractions of the law. In other quarters, however, the vigorous action of the federal government made the embargo reasonably effective.

The way in which the country as a whole stood back of Jefferson's experiment in economic sanctions was a genuine tribute to his hold on the respect and esteem of his countrymen. Despite the hardships endured because of the stagnation of tobacco exports, the South remained politically loyal. The West, too, suffered but endured, and the middle states wavered but in the end held firm. Only in New England was there a real rejuvenescence of Federalism.

The Election of 1808

The election of 1808 took place while the Embargo was in full swing. Jefferson refused a third term, thereby following Washington's example and establishing a long unbroken American tradition, but he named as his successor his long-time friend Secretary of State James Madison. Once again, Clinton was the Republican vice presidential candidate on a ticket set up by a congressional caucus. The Federalists named Charles Cotesworth Pinckney and Rufus King. By the twelfth amendment to the Constitution, ratified in 1804, the electors cast separate ballots for President and Vice President, thus eliminating the possibility of such intrigues as had been current in the election of 1800.

The election was at once proof of the Administration's hold on public opinion and of the way in which that hold was being tested. The nation went to the polls while the prohibition of foreign trade was in full force, with ships idling at the wharves, tobacco glutting the local markets, wheat plunging from $2.00 to $.75 a bushel, and land values in rapid decline. There was a welter of attack and defense of the Embargo, and of charges of bias toward England or toward France. Madison won by 122 electoral votes to forty-seven, but the Federalists carried Massachusetts, Connecticut, New Hampshire, Rhode Island, and Delaware and garnered two electoral votes in Maryland and three in North Carolina. Both houses of Congress remained Republican, but the Federalists made sweeping gains in the House of Representatives. Local as well as national factors were involved, but it was clear that the Embargo was a sore trial to the patience of the country.

Had the Embargo been effective in modifying the policies of the warring nations, Jefferson's plan would have paid off in handsome fashion. The truth was, however, that it had little effect upon the English and French governments. It damaged the English economy, but the use of the licensing system for British trade with the Continent, and the Spanish rebellion of 1808 against Napoleon with the accompanying prospect of great commercial opportunities in South America, strengthened the hand of the British Foreign Minister, George Canning, and disarmed his parliamentary critics. French policy also remained unaltered, and this lack of effective impact heightened American discontent.

Repeal of the Embargo

When Congress met in November, 1808, the Republicans were divided and uneasy over the Embargo, the Federalists belligerent in their hostility to the measure. The Administration, summoning all its forces, beat down a motion to repeal and passed a measure providing for more effective enforcement, but the triumph was short-lived. Movements looking to secession were gaining headway in New England, discontent with economic stagnancy was increasing in the middle states and in the South, and moderate Republicans long loyal to Jefferson but now confronted by his imminent retirement were ready to join the "Quids" in revolt. The result was an Administration retreat which took the form of a compromise. Congress repealed the Embargo, putting in its place nonintercourse with England and France alone; whenever either of the belligerents ceased to violate the commerce of the United States, trade with that nation would be resumed. This measure swept through both the Senate and the House; Jefferson signed it, although in great bitterness of spirit, on March 1, 1809, three days before Madison became President of the United States.

The new policy mollified popular resentment but at the same time weakened the pressure on the warring nations, for it served notice that Congress was backing away from a policy that hurt the country's pocketbook. Whether this scheme of offering at the same time a carrot and a stick would prove effective remained to be seen.

Jeffersonian Balance Sheet

Jefferson left the presidential mansion with relief akin to that of a prisoner freed from his chains. Leadership of the nation had proved increasingly burdensome, and he looked forward eagerly to devoting himself to scientific pursuits. But, despite the failure of the Embargo to achieve its objective and the growth of faction within Republican ranks, his presidency had been measurably successful. The transition from Federalist to Republican control had been accomplished with a minimum of friction, and had demonstrated the stability of the nation's institutions. The public domain had been magnificently expanded. Foreign policy had been conducted in a firm and dignified manner, and, if respect for American rights on the high seas had not been attained, at least the nation had not been led into a war for which it had little preparation. The task of devising a policy that would at once command national support and avoid truckling to the dynasts engaged in their struggle to the death, Jefferson left to his successor.

Suggested Reading

Aside from the works by Brant, Schachner, Chinard, Robinson, Fee, and Gilpatrick mentioned in the preceding bibliographies, the following are useful for a study of Jefferson's Administrations.

Henry Adams, *History of the United States of America* (9 vols., 1909–1931), a brilliant work, is still standard on both domestic and foreign affairs. It is corrected to some extent by Brant's *Madison*, previously cited, but the latter must be used with caution because of the author's bias in favor of his subject.

Regarding domestic matters, L. D. White, *The Jeffersonians* (1951) is excellent on administrative policy, and Stuart G. Brown, *The First Republicans* (1954) presents the political philosophy and public policy of the Republican party under Jefferson and

Madison in a favorable light. C. M. Wiltse, *The Jeffersonian Tradition in American Democracy* (1935) is a thought-provoking study. R. Hofstadter, *The American Political Tradition and Those Who Made It* (1948) contains some shrewd and penetrating comment on Jeffersonian theory and practice. S. H. Wandell and M. Minnigerode, *Aaron Burr* (2 vols., 1925) is a sympathetic treatment, and T. P. Abernethy, *The Burr Conspiracy* (1954), is the latest treatment of the subject.

Concerning foreign policy, A. L. Burt, *The United States, Great Britain, and British North America* (1940) is an important study, and Bradford Perkins, *The First Rapprochement; England and the United States, 1795–1805* (1955) throws new light on Anglo-American relations. J. F. Zimmerman, *Impressment of American Seamen* (1925) is the best treatment of the subject. On the embargo, see L. M. Sears, *Jefferson and the Embargo* (1927); W. W. Jennings, *The American Embargo, 1807–1809* (1921); and G. W. Daniels, "Cotton Trade under the Embargo," *American Historical Review,* XXI (Jan., 1916), 276–287. R. W. Irwin, *The Diplomatic Relations of the United States with the Barbary Powers* (1931) covers the subject in thorough fashion.

The student seeking further information should consult D. J. Boorstin, *The Lost World of Thomas Jefferson* (1948); Adrienne Koch, *The Philosophy of Thomas Jefferson* (1943) and *Jefferson and Madison: the Great Collaboration* (1950); Raymond Walters, *Albert Gallatin: Jeffersonian, Financier and Diplomat* (1957); N. E. Cunningham, Jr., *The Jeffersonian Republicans in Power* (1963); E. W. Lyon, *Louisiana in French Diplomacy* (1934); A. P. Whitaker, *The Mississippi Question* (1934); George Dangerfield, *Chancellor Robert R. Livingston of New York* (1960), and W. E. Hollon, *The Lost Pathfinder: Zebulon Montgomery Pike* (1949).

For Jefferson's interest in science, see E. T. Martin, *Thomas Jefferson, Scientist* (1952).

12 ⸱ The War of 1812

J AMES MADISON was fifty-seven years old when he became President of
the United States. Born of a well-to-do family long resident in Virginia,
he had graduated from Princeton (then the College of New Jersey) in
1771 at the age of twenty and, returning to Virginia, engaged almost at
once in a political career. He helped draft the constitution of Virginia in
1776 and then aided Jefferson in disestablishing re-
ligion in the state. In Congress (1780–1783), he
came out in favor of a strong central government,
and was a prime mover in the conferences that led to
the Philadelphia convention of 1787. Sponsor of the
Virginia Plan and coauthor of *The Federalist*, he helped carry ratification of
the federal Constitution in the Old Dominion. From 1789 to 1797, he was
prominent in Congress, the most formidable opponent that the Federalists
had in that body. He stood side by side with Jefferson in opposing the Alien
and Sedition laws, and after the Revolution of 1800 served ably for eight
years as Secretary of State.

*Madison
Tries to
Maintain Peace*

The new President was short of stature and frail in appearance, bald-
headed, with mild blue eyes and a weak voice. He spoke without passion or
oratory, almost as though talking to himself, and his manner in public was
diffident, formal, and precise. But this meek appearance was deceptive, for
he had a whimsical wit and on more than one occasion convulsed a dinner
table with his stories. At forty-four, Aaron Burr introduced him to Dolley

266

Payne Todd, and his marriage to this charming Philadelphia widow eighteen years his junior was a thoroughly happy one. A liberal for his day, a man of profound beliefs and a sweetness of disposition only occasionally marred by fits of petulance, he lived a life of uncommon virtue. He was indifferent to moneymaking but from childhood had a passion for knowledge and was well versed in history, political philosophy, and law. A man of great practical sense in the field of statesmanship, he was one of the most attractive and least spectacular of the Founding Fathers, and Jefferson loved him as though he were his son.

Madison delivered his inaugural address garbed in a suit of merino wool that had been raised in the United States—a symbol of his devotion to the American way of life. The inaugural itself emphasized his love of the Union, his regard for civil liberties, and his determination to carry on the general policies of his friend and predecessor. It was clear that the new President wanted peace, but it was equally clear that it had to be a peace which maintained American rights.

The most pressing need of the new administration was a settlement of the difficulties with England and France. Relations with the former were in a particularly bad way. Impressment and visit and search of American vessels were in full swing, and Britain had as yet made no satisfactory adjustment of the *Chesapeake* outrage. France, too, was seizing American ships and confiscating their cargoes, sometimes with the specious excuse that it was helping America to enforce the Non-Intercourse Act. Madison was most anxious for a way out of these difficulties. He went so far as to secretly inform each government that if it would relax its Orders or Decrees, he would ask for a declaration of war upon the other unless it, too, ceased its molestation of American commerce.

The British minister to the United States, David M. Erskine, had married an American wife and was to some degree sympathetic with the American point of view. His zeal for peace and good understanding between the two countries now proved most embarrassing to the President. Erskine proposed to Madison, in the name of the British government, repeal of the Orders in Council and resumption of American commercial intercourse with Great Britain. Madison accepted this with alacrity and issued a proclamation that on June 10, 1809—the day on which the Orders in Council were supposedly to be withdrawn—nonintercourse with Great Britain would cease. On that day, 600 ships left American ports laden with raw materials and headed for British ports. Then came sad disillusionment. Erskine had concealed a part of his instructions, which stated that America must accept the rule of 1756 and also allow the British navy to capture American ships that continued to trade with France; the American government had of course accepted no such conditions. When news of what had happened reached London, the British Foreign Minister, George Canning, promptly rejected the agreement and recalled Erskine. There was nothing for Madison to do but proclaim a renewal of nonintercourse with Great Britain, and joy in American ports was again replaced by sullen commercial inactivity.

Relations with England now reached a new low. Erskine was replaced by Francis James Jackson, a most unpleasant individual imbued with a contempt for all things American. An ardent sportsman, Jackson took delight in flushing partridges within 300 yards of the Capitol. He sneered at Madison and the incompetent Secretary of State, Robert Smith, and declared that Dolley Madison was "fat and forty but not fair."

Jackson's relations with Madison rapidly deteriorated. In a series of notes, the British minister made the rash statement that Madison must have known Erskine's instructions and added certain blustering statements about defending England's honor. Madison thereupon refused to hold further communication with him, and Jackson left for New England and its sympathetic Federalist atmosphere. He declared that the President was "stubborn as a mule," and Mrs. Jackson wrote home that her husband's lack of success was due to his being accustomed to treat with civilized courts and governments, not with "savage democrats." Jackson was shortly recalled to London.

As Madison's first year in the Presidency wore to an end, there had been no improvement in the commercial situation. Anglo-American relations had gone from bad to worse, and Napoleon, using the Non-Intercourse Act as an excuse, was now confiscating American ships in French harbors on the ground that, since their presence there was contrary to American law, they must be English ships in disguise. Unrest and dissatisfaction with the existing situation was increasing throughout the United States, and Congress was looking for a plan of action that would allay domestic discontent and at the same time exert pressure on England and France to mend their ways.

The result was a measure sponsored by Nathaniel Macon of North Carolina and known as Macon's Bill #2, so called because Macon's Bill #1 had failed of passage. It freed American commerce from all restrictions, while still forbidding American waters to the armed ships of Britain and France. It also provided that, if either of the belligerents revoked its Orders in Council or its Decrees and the other failed to do so within three months, nonintercourse would be reinstituted against the obdurate party. On May 1, 1810, this bill became law.

The most notable consequence of Macon's Bill #2 was the opportunity it gave Napoleon to dupe the President of the United States. In August, 1810,

Napoleon's government informed the American Minister in Paris that the French Decrees were revoked. The language of this "Minute" was ambiguous, and it contained a reference to America's causing its rights to be respected by Great Britain. It was not an actual revocation, and, as a matter of fact, French seizure of American ships continued. But Madison precipitately leaped to the conclusion that the French Decrees were definitely revoked and issued a proclamation renewing nonintercourse with Great Britain. This was confirmed by act of Congress, March 1, 1811. England, seeing Napoleon's action as sheer duplicity, refused to repeal its Orders in Council and the drift toward a second war between Great Britain and the United States began in earnest.

The War Hawks

When the Twelfth Congress of the United States met in extra session on November 4, 1811, it had in its ranks some new and determined men. Henry Clay of Kentucky, John Caldwell Calhoun of South Carolina, Felix Grundy of Tennessee, and Peter B. Porter of New York, together with half a dozen others, promptly assumed leading roles. They were chiefly from frontier areas of the country. Patriotic, scorning vacillation and delay, imbued with the frontier's prejudices against the Indians and with the frontier's love of large designs, they were in a mood for action. Expansionists, they looked toward Canada and the Floridas, not so much out of land hunger as with a view to ending the Indian menace and opening up greater opportunities for trade by the conquest of those areas. The trans-Allegheny members of this group represented a section that had suffered hard times since 1806, that had staunchly upheld the policy of economic coercion, but that was now ready to fight in order to end trade restrictions and uphold the country's honor. John Randolph, satirical as always, gave this band of valiant spirits a name— the "War Hawks."

Circumstances fed the zeal of the War Hawks. The Federalists in Congress were a feeble minority, and the conservative Republicans lacked both unity and leadership. James Monroe, who became Secretary of State in April, 1811, believed in vigorous and decisive action. Madison had already shown his sympathy with expansionism by seizing West Florida at the behest of American frontiersmen in 1810, and he was maintaining an eager interest in East Florida as well. Furthermore, just as Congress met, the war whoop was ringing on the western frontier.

The great Shawnee chief, Tecumseh, had organized a confederacy of western Indian tribes to prevent land cessions. He looked to Britain for aid and, while the British government discouraged war, English supplies in considerable quantities found their way into Indian hands. In 1811, while Tecumseh was in the south seeking to organize the Indian tribes there against the whites, his brother, the Prophet, decided that the time for war had come and opened an assault upon the frontier settlements. American forces under William Henry Harrison, governor of Indiana Territory, met and defeated the red warriors at Tippecanoe Creek near the head of the Wabash River. The Indians had moved despite the efforts of British officials in Canada to keep them at peace, but the red men left on the field had British arms in their possession, and Tecumseh and hundreds of his warriors crossed over into Canada and safety. The frontier's zeal for war with England now markedly increased.

When Congress began its sessions, Henry Clay—"Harry of the West"— was elected Speaker of the House and promptly put War Hawks on all the the principal committees. Madison's annual message viewed with alarm the state of relations with Great Britain. As resolutions for war poured in from state legislatures, Congress passed measures for raising 25,000 regular troops and 50,000 volunteers, and authorized a 6 per cent loan of $11,000,000.

Madison accepted these measures; though he did not actually want war, he regarded it as inevitable unless Great Britain changed its policy toward neutrals. At the same time, he refrained from appointing a new minister to Great Britain to replace William Pinkney, who had come home in a huff some months before. An experienced diplomat in London would have been useful at this juncture, but Secretary of State Monroe told the new British Minister, Augustus Foster, that any nomination to London could scarcely be confirmed while Britain was pillaging American commerce. Foster effected a satisfactory settlement of the *Chesapeake* affair, with the return of the two remaining seamen to America and a monetary settlement for the families of those killed, but this did little good. Early in April, 1812, the government at Washington—obviously preparing for extreme steps—placed a ninety-day embargo on American shipping.

Why War Came

While Congress and the administration moved steadily toward war, the British government was preparing to moderate its policy toward the neutral nations. Britain was feeling the economic strain of the long duel with Napoleon. British manufactures were in the doldrums, and merchants and manufacturers alike viewed with alarm the way in which American industries were pouring out goods to take the place of English supplies. The 1811 harvest in England had been poor, and farmers and artisans were in dire straits. The prospect of an additional war increased the general discontent, and Parliament bent before the growing storm. On June 16, 1812, the government decided to repeal the Orders in Council.

No indication of this shift in policy had reached the American capital. On the contrary, toward the end of May, Foster communicated to Madison and Monroe a message from the British Foreign Office which still insisted upon maintenance of the hated Orders. Madison then made the final decision that there was no further hope in negotiation and drafted a war message which was sent to Congress on June 1. It denounced Britain for impressment, the harassment of American commerce, and the inflexible maintenance of the Orders in Council. A bill declaring that hostilities had begun passed the House by a vote of seventy-nine to forty-nine and the Senate by nineteen to thirteen. On June 19, 1812, Madison issued a proclamation of war.

The War of 1812 was the result of a complex of factors. British policy had deeply affronted the American sense of national honor. Spokesmen for the South and West were convinced that only war could bring respect for neutral rights and a revitalization of American trade and prosperity. Frontiersmen were confident that Canada and Florida would be easy conquests. Expansion was a particularly tempting prospect for the West because of that section's relative immunity from attack by the British fleet, and because of the Indian threat, which frontiersmen believed was constantly being fortified by the British in Canada. The War Hawks bore down opposition and provided dynamic leadership in bringing on the struggle, and Madison was carried along on the tide, more and more convinced as the months went by that war must come. "I flung forward the flag of the country," he said in later years, "sure that the people would press onward and defend it." He also stated, again in retrospect, that an earlier repeal of the Orders in Council would have prevented the declaration of war and opened the way for continued negotiation on "the other great cause" of the struggle, impressment. A switch of four votes in the Senate would, in fact, have defeated the war declaration, but whether an Atlantic cable in 1812 would have prevented war will always remain a mystery.

War with Great Britain was a hazardous venture for the United States in 1812, one for which there was little real justification. It might equally well have been waged against France, from the point of view of injustice suffered. That country had treated the United States with contempt and, under Napoleon's domination, offered no better prospect of peaceful future relationships. But the military problem of attacking France was practically insuperable, and so America plunged into the conflict with Britain. It was a war fought largely in defense of "free trade and seamen's rights," but maritime New England was opposed to it from the outset. The country entered the struggle divided in spirit and, what was even worse, woefully unprepared.

A Sad State of Preparedness

An objective view of the country's situation in 1812 was enough to chill the hearts of all save the most ardent War Hawks. Army generals were either old and incompetent or young and inexperienced. The regular army, at the outset of the struggle, consisted of only 6,700 men. The country had to rely upon state militia or volunteers, the consequence being that efficiency in the military arm became apparent only toward the close of the war. The navy had only a dozen ships, the largest a forty-four-gun frigate. There were some excellent naval officers, trained in the Barbary wars, and American sailors were superb seamen, but these advantages were scarcely a counterbalance to England's mammoth navy of 800 ships.

The country was as badly prepared financially as it was in a military sense. The Treasury was practically empty, for the revenues (which came chiefly from imports) had gone into eclipse with the Embargo and Non-Intercourse Acts. The national bank had come up for recharter in 1811, only to be destroyed in a burst of Republican fanaticism as a Federalist device. Congressional orators thundered against an institution the major part of whose shares were owned abroad, chiefly in England at that, with the remainder in the hands of wealthy Federalists. Strict constructionists joined with state banking interests in opposition to recharter, and it was voted down. The country therefore entered the War of 1812 without this useful financial agent, and with the state banks freed from the salutary control it had exercised over their note issues. The state banks mushroomed, their currencies of varying and often uncertain values. In August, 1814, when the fortunes of war were at a low ebb, all of the banks save those in New England suspended specie payment, and their currencies promptly declined in value. It was not surprising, in view of the banking situation and the uncertain fortunes of the struggle, that the government's war loans soon fell below par. In order to carry on financially, Madison's administration had to use that hated Federalist device, the excise, together with other internal revenue taxes. The general financial situation was such that from government loans of over $80 million between 1812 and 1816, the treasury raised only $34 million in specie value.

It was difficult enough to fight a war with uncertain financial resources and inadequate military preparation, but there was also sectional division over the conflict. Most of New England was apathetic toward and many of its citizens were hostile to the struggle. The final stronghold of Federalism held that the conflict was being waged, as Timothy Pickering put it, against "the world's last hope, Britain's fast-anchored isle." New Englanders resented a "Virginia-dominated" policy that had first hurt their commerce by embargoes and nonintercourse and was now ruining by war their commercial ties with England. It was true that New England merchants had suffered from English seizures of their ships and goods, but the profits of successful voyages were so enormous that these confiscations were endurable. During the war, much of New England was in a state of incipient treason. Men like Pickering openly yearned for a New England republic. The orators of the Essex Junto shouted for states' rights, and young Daniel Webster in the House of Representatives waxed eloquent against the war as an unconstitutional struggle, the result of the "folly" and "wickedness" of the government. New England's subscription to the government loans only amounted to some $3 million as against $35 million from the Middle Atlantic states. Both Massachusetts and Connecticut withdrew their militia from the national government's service in the fall of 1814, and Massachusetts and Rhode Island exchanged notes in the manner of European Powers, guaranteeing one another protection in case of invasion.

The climax of New England's disaffection came with the Hartford Convention of December, 1814. Massachusetts, Connecticut, and Rhode Island sent delegates to Hartford, with New Hampshire and Vermont appointing unofficial representatives. Federalist hotheads rejoiced at this gathering of disgruntled men—one Massachusetts paper asserted that the convention was raising three pillars of a new federal edifice—but the proceedings were in the hands of the more cautious spirits. The sessions ended with a series of resolutions which aired the grievances of New England, declaring that the states had a right to protect themselves and demanding a series of amendments to the Constitution. These would eliminate the counting of slaves in establishing Congressional representation; require a two-thirds vote of Congress for admitting new states, imposing nonintercourse, or declaring war in any case save actual invasion; prohibit naturalized citizens (like Gallatin) from holding office in the federal government; make all presidents ineligible for more than one term; and provide that no successive elections to the presidency should be from the same state. The convention ended with the threat of another assembly, clothed with "necessary powers," if the war continued.

THE HARTFORD CONVENTION, OR "LEAP OR NO LEAP"

Massachusetts, Connecticut, and Rhode Island are shown shrinking from a final breakup of the Union. Britain is tempting them with promises of honors and trade advantages. Timothy Pickering, now a member of Congress from Massachusetts, prays that the leap will be made.

The Hartford Convention amendments showed clearly the fear and jealousy of the South and West that rankled in New England. Had the war continued, a dangerous secessionist movement would probably have resulted. As it was, a committee was sent to Washington to lay the Convention's resolutions before Congress. By the time the commissioners reached the capital, however, the war was over, their mission had lost its point, and nothing was left for them to do but return home covered with Republican ridicule.

The election of 1812, held during the early days of the war, indicated not only the attitude that was to characterize New England during the conflict, but also the existence in the middle states of a considerable amount of dissatisfaction with Madison's leadership. "Jemmy," as his friends and sometimes his foes termed him, was renominated by the Republicans, but dissatisfied party members in New York arranged a deal with Federalists there and in other states for a fusion ticket with DeWitt Clinton at its head. Madison won the election, receiving 128 electoral votes, but Clinton carried all of New England save Vermont, as well as New York, New Jersey, Delaware, and five votes in Maryland, for a total of eighty-nine votes in the electoral college. Had Clinton carried Pennsylvania, he would have been elected President, and Madison would have been turned out of office in the midst of the war.

Sectionalism, an empty treasury, and a woeful state of unpreparedness gave mournful presage of what the war was to be like. In fact, the struggle furnished few glorious moments in American history, and they were mainly the result of events that took place on the high seas.

The War on the High Seas

The war on the ocean saw a number of duels between warships in which the Americans bested their opponents. The *Constitution* and the *Guerriere*, the *Constitution* and the *Java*, the *United States* and the *Macedonian*, the *Wasp* and the *Frolic*, and a number of other encounters resulted in each case in American victory, occasioning great popular rejoicing. In most of these naval encounters, the American ship carried heavier metal and a larger crew than its opponent. The American people also heard with pleasure about the havoc spread among British whalers in the Pacific by the frigate *Essex* in the winter of 1812–1813, before it was overwhelmed by two opponents in Valparaiso harbor, and of how the eighteen-gun sloop *Argus* for a month terrorized British shipping in the English Channel and the Irish Sea, destroying twenty merchant ships and $2 million worth of cargoes. Indeed, the more than 1,000 captures of English merchant ships made during the war drove British insurance rates skyward and exerted a depressing effect upon the British spirit.

Effective as these American exploits were, however, their impact on the British navy and the war was negligible. By October, 1813, British fleets were tightly blockading the American coast, and the American navy was either bottled up in harbor or, like the *Essex*, maintaining a precarious existence in distant waters. Privateers slipped out from time to time and harassed British commerce, especially the large, slow-moving ships that serviced the West Indies, but of the 526 American privateers sent out only sixty remained afloat and under American registry by the end of the war. The most that can be said of the American effort on the ocean is that it made as good a record as could be expected, in view of the enormous disparity of forces. On Lake Erie and Lake Champlain, as we shall see, American sailors had some highly significant achievements to their credit.

Futile Attempts to Invade Canada, 1812

On land and on the lakes of the Canadian-American border, the war was a strange mixture of bravery, heroic exploits, humiliating failures, and sometimes sheer farce. The first year of the struggle saw four American attempts to invade Canada. The first was led by sixty-one-year-old General William Hull, who was supposed to move from Detroit into Upper Canada. Plagued by poor communications with his sources of supply and by an overcautious disposition, Hull moved from Detroit into Canada in July, 1812, and laid siege to Fort Malden. General Isaac Brock, Governor of Upper Canada, raised a force of militia and came to the relief of Malden. The British commander saw to it that stories of an enormous body of British and Indians reached the American camp, and Hull, alarmed, raised the siege of the fort and went back to Detroit, where he was in turn besieged by a very modest force of Canadians and Indians. Fearful of the Indians, despairing of adequate supplies, and more and more a prey to indecision, on August 16 he surrendered Detroit and an army of 2,500 men to the British. Not only had this attempt to conquer Canada failed, but now all of Michigan territory lay defenseless before the enemy. Hull was court-martialed for cowardice and condemned to be shot, but Madison pardoned him because he had had a fine record in the Revolution.

The second attempt to invade Canada in 1812 was made against Queenston Heights, opposite Lewiston on the Niagara frontier by United States regulars and New York state militia under Lieutenant Colonel Winfield Scott and Major General Stephen Van Rensselaer. On October 13, some 900 men landed on the Canadian shore. At first the lightly held British line was driven back, and as General Brock strove to rally them he was killed. Then British reinforcements arrived, including a band of hideously painted Indians uttering savage war cries. The invaders were now badly outnumbered, and Van Rensselaer went back to the American side of the river for help, but the militia there refused to move. Scott was forced to surrender his little band, most of whom had hidden in the caves by the river and had seen no fighting at all.

General Alexander Smyth, a regular, now succeeded General Van Rensselaer in command on the Niagara frontier. He gathered a force at Buffalo and in November tried to move across the river. The attempt was an utter fiasco, devoid of management and discipline. In the end, despite bombastic proclamations by Smyth, there was no invasion, and the camp of 4,500 men dissolved into bedlam, with muskets being discharged right and left and a considerable number of bullets whistling close to Smyth's headquarters. Peter B. Porter, who had left Congress to fight on the Niagara front, accused Smyth of cowardice, and a bloodless duel was fought at twelve paces. If current reports were true, the seconds had removed the bullets from the pistols.

The fourth attempted invasion of Canada was under General Henry Dearborn, who was succumbing to the aches and pains of age and was so stout that he had to travel in a specially constructed carriage. He marched the militia under his command at Plattsburg out in the general direction of Montreal, but at the border his band of heroes refused to set foot on foreign soil and there was nothing to do but return to his base.

The complete failure of the invasion attempts in 1812 was humiliating to American pride. It was also a sad commentary on western boasts made before the war that a few companies of Kentucky and Tennessee riflemen would be sufficient to conquer Canada.

The West in 1813

The military situation in the West improved during 1813. William Henry Harrison, the hero of Tippecanoe, succeeded Hull in command. His presence in the field lent spirit to the force of some 6,500 militia and volunteers that gathered for the fray, but commissary and transportation problems remained formidable and there was a lengthy frontier to defend. The general situation improved, however, in part because of the incompetence of the British commander, Colonel Henry Proctor, but even more because of a brilliant American victory on Lake Erie. As a result of great exertions, Oliver Hazard Perry put together a fleet that, September 10, 1813, decisively defeated its British counterpart under Captain Robert H. Barclay. At the close of the battle, Perry scrawled in pencil on the back of an old letter his famous message to General Harrison: "We have met the enemy and they are ours; two ships, two brigs, one schooner and one sloop. Yours with great esteem and respect. O. H. Perry."

Perry's success put the vital line of communication on Lake Erie in the hands of the Americans, compelled the British to abandon Detroit and Fort Malden, and opened the way to a second invasion of Upper Canada. In October, 1813, Harrison ferried his army across Lake Erie from Sandusky and won the battle of the Thames at which Tecumseh was killed. The American West was now secure, but transportation problems remained, and there was much politiking and divided counsel at Washington. Harrison re-

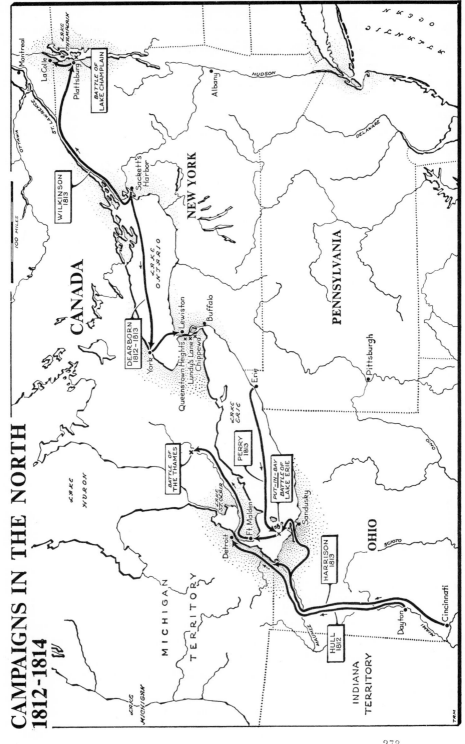

CAMPAIGNS IN THE NORTH
1812-1814

signed his command and the American force that had been under his orders was content to hold Detroit.

The East in 1813

In the East during 1813, that tarnished hero, General James Wilkinson, and General Wade Hampton of South Carolina, who despised and distrusted Wilkinson, were the principals in charge of military operations. More invasion fiascoes were the result. An attempt to take Montreal was a miserable failure, and the only success, if success it can be called, was a hit-and-run military and naval attack on York (later to be called Toronto). This assault was under Commodore Isaac Chauncey, who commanded a small squadron on Lake Ontario, and General Zebulon Pike, who led the ground forces in place of the ailing General Dearborn. The expedition resulted in the death of General Pike and the burning of the public buildings in York, an act which was not the result of American orders but for which the British took signal revenge in the following year.

The victory of Lake Erie had been glorious and the battle of the Thames was an American triumph, but otherwise American operations against Canada in 1813 had been a complete failure. This was all the more disheartening because the American army, taken as a whole, far outnumbered the British forces committed to the defense of Canada.

Offense and Defense in 1814

The year 1814 saw two offensives mounted by the United States: one at Niagara against Canada, the other against the Creek confederacy in Alabama and Mississippi. The Creeks, who had been stirred up by Tecumseh, were plundering and marauding frontier settlements, and American efforts to punish them had so far been unavailing. In March, 1814, however, a forty-seven-year-old planter and turfman named Andrew Jackson, a man of iron will and with a passion for military glory, led a force of 2,000 men against the Creek stronghold at Horseshoe Bend on the Tallapoosa River. There he destroyed the main body of Creek warriors, 1,000 strong, and crushed the power of the Creek nation.

A few weeks after the Creek confederacy was destroyed, a last attempt was made to invade Canada. General Jacob Brown with 3,500 men crossed the Niagara River just north of Buffalo. The Americans beat 4,000 British regulars near Chippawa, but without a supporting fleet (Commodore Chauncey was bottled up at Sackett's Harbor by Sir James Yeo) Brown could go no further. The British under Brigadier General Riall were reinforced, and on July 25 attacked the Americans at Lundy's Lane. Both sides claimed victory in this bloody battle, but the British held the field and had only 84 men killed as against 171 Americans. One of the American brigadiers, however, had displayed real qualities of leadership. He was a young giant of twenty-eight, six feet five inches in height and weighing well over 200 pounds, who had been captured by the British at Queenston Heights and then paroled. The troops he drilled proved the equals of the British regulars and his battle dispositions, both at Chippawa and Lundy's Lane were masterly in character. In the latter encounter he had two horses shot under him and was carried, seriously wounded, from the field. Overnight, Winfield Scott had become a national hero.

Despite the valor displayed by Scott and his men at Lundy's Lane, the invasion of Canada petered out in the face of determined British resistance. By November, 1814, the troops under Brown's command had left Canadian soil, and at the end of the war no considerable post in Canada remained in American hands.

Jackson in Alabama and Brown at Chippawa had been on the offensive, but the other American military operations of 1814 were defensive in character. Britain was in a stronger position than had been the case at any previous period of the struggle, for Napoleon had been defeated and exiled to Elba. With the Napoleonic threat apparently at an end, British veterans of the war in Spain were shifted across the Atlantic, and Major General Robert Ross was ordered to execute a diversionary movement on the Atlantic coast in order to relieve American pressure on Canada. Early in August, Ross's force joined the fleet of Vice Admiral Sir Alexander Cochrane, which for a year and a half had controlled Chesapeake Bay, and Cochrane and Ross decided to strike at the American capital.

Washington had no fortifications, and the general in command of its defense, William H. Winder, owed his appointment as much to political considerations as to his military prowess. Ross with 4,500 men landed unopposed at Patuxent Creek. As he moved toward the capital, General Winder with a motley force of some 6,000 to 7,000 infantry regulars, dragoons, naval militia, secretaries, and clerks moved out to bar the British advance. The two armies met, if meeting it could be called, at Bladensburg, five miles north of Washington. The President and the Secretary of State were on the field, the former equipped with a pair of duelling pistols that were stolen from him during the course of the day. As the engagement was about to begin, Madison said to Monroe, "It would now be proper for us to retire in the rear, leaving the military movements to military men." It was well they did so, for, after a light initial resistance, there was a precipitate retreat, covered only in part by the 400 sailors under Commodore Joshua Barney.

Ross's troops moved into the now defenseless capital on August 24. In revenge for the burning of the buildings in York, the British fired the capitol, the President's mansion, and other public buildings. The Americans themselves burned the navy yard and the ships there, including a new ship of

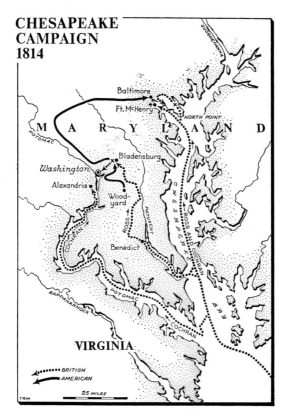

CHESAPEAKE CAMPAIGN 1814

Baltimore
Ft. McHenry
NORTH POINT
M   A   R   Y   L   A   N   D
POTOMAC
Bladensburg
Washington
Alexandria
Wood-
yard
ROSS
PATUXENT
CHESAPEAKE
ROSS AND COCHRAN
Benedict
COCHRAN
POTOMAC
RAPPAHANNOCK
COCHRAN
VIRGINIA
BRITISH
AMERICAN
25 MILES
TRM

the line. Then the invaders left, the President and other government officials who had wandered off into the Virginia woods returned, and Congress came back to begin conducting a resolution of inquiry into the state of the defenses of the city of Washington.

Ross and Cochrane next moved against Baltimore, but there adequate defensive preparations had been made for their reception. Forts and a line of sunken ships barred the approach to the city by water, and 10,000 soldiers manned the land fortifications. The land attack failed, and Ross was killed. The assault by water was equally unsuccessful, although it did provide inspiration for an eyewitness, Francis Scott Key, to write the *Star Spangled Banner*.

While the British were being repulsed at Baltimore, another British squadron occupied without difficulty some 100 miles of the Maine coast in the general vicinity of Penobscot Bay. The inhabitants of the region took the oath of allegiance to Great Britain without any apparent reluctance, moved it may be by the sack of Washington, or perhaps by the hearty willingness with which New York and Vermont farmers sold supplies to the British, and Boston bankers helped finance the armies of the king.

On still another northern front, the British did not fare so well as they did on the Maine coast. During the summer of 1814, an army of British veterans, some 11,000 strong, under Sir George Prevost, started an invasion of New York by Burgoyne's old route down Lake Champlain. Prevost was supported by a naval force under the command of Captain George Downie, consisting of twelve gunboats, two sloops, the sixteen-gun brig *Linnet,* and a thirty-eight-gun frigate, the *Confiance.* The American government summoned against the invaders some 4,700 regulars, militia, and volunteers under Colonel Alexander Macomb, and a fleet commanded by a veteran of the Barbary wars, Captain Thomas Macdonough, consisting of ten gunboats, a seven-gun sloop, the seventeen-gun schooner *Ticonderoga,* the brig *Eagle,* twenty-six guns, and the frigate *Saratoga,* also twenty-six guns. The two naval forces were very evenly matched.

On September 11, 1814, Prevost ordered a general attack by land and water. The engagement on the lake, where Macdonough's fleet lay anchored at the mouth of Plattsburg Bay, was decisive. Both sides fought bravely, but the fact that Macdonough had anchored with spring cables that enabled him to warp his ships about and bring fresh batteries to bear on the enemy turned the tide in favor of the Americans. After two hours and twenty minutes of fighting, the British fleet surrendered. The land attack of the British was making some progress when news came of the surrender of the fleet. Prevost thereupon halted the assault, and under cover of night his army began a retreat that did not stop until he had crossed the border into Canada. The British commander was court-martialed for this hasty withdrawal, but died before his trial.

A Peacetime Military Victory, 1815

The British now made one last effort to turn the tide of the war. The War Office in London determined to send an expedition to capture New Orleans and close the mouth of the Mississippi. It ordered the expedition that had failed at Baltimore to rendezvous at Jamaica, where it was joined by veterans of the Peninsular campaign and one Scottish regiment sent from the Cape of Good Hope. Some 10,000 men and fifty ships gathered under the command of Major General Sir Edward Pakenham, brother-in-law of the Duke of Wellington.

JOHN BULL making a new BATCH of SHIPS to send to the LAKES

COURTESY OF THE NEW-YORK HISTORICAL SOCIETY, NEW YORK CITY

A New Batch of Ships for the Great Lakes

England is shown trying desperately to make up for the losses it has suffered on the Great Lakes, especially in the defeat on Lake Champlain by Commodore "Mac Do-enough." It is John Bull who wears the crown, rather than the King of England; George III had become permanently insane in 1811.

While this formidable British force was preparing for the assault, Andrew Jackson, the conqueror of the Creeks, was appointed Commander of the Seventh Military District. He reached his headquarters at Mobile on August 15, 1814, convinced that the enemy would attempt to reduce that town before attacking New Orleans. With his usual stubbornness, he held to this conviction until almost the last minute, and with nearly fatal consequences.

Shortly after Jackson reached Mobile, a few hundred British marines landed at Pensacola. There the Spaniards welcomed them and began spreading reports that Mobile was their next objective. Jackson now decided to attack Pensacola, despite pleas from the citizens of New Orleans for protection and a letter from President Madison (which may never have been delivered) warning him against becoming embroiled with Spain. With 3,000 men, Jackson stormed Pensacola, while the British hastily decamped. Then

"Old Hickory," as his soldiers called him because of his remarkable powers of endurance, hurried back to Mobile, which he reached on November 11, 1814.

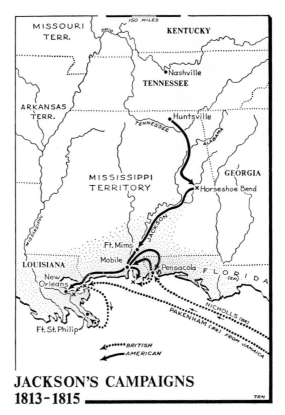

**JACKSON'S CAMPAIGNS
1813-1815**

Another appeal from the Louisianans for aid awaited Jackson at his headquarters. He was now willing to go to New Orleans, but he still thought Mobile was the primary British objective and so divided his forces, leaving several thousand men to defend the Alabama town. Jackson found much anxiety but little preparation for attack at New Orleans. He was suffering badly from dysentery, but with his accustomed energy he declared martial law, had Governor Claiborne call out the militia, and began studying the lay of the land and raising fortifications.

Just as Jackson was beginning to prepare New Orleans for defense, the British armada set sail from Jamaica. On December 9, they were at the gates of New Orleans, and Jackson began calling frantically for reinforcements from Mobile and from Kentucky and Tennessee. He also accepted the aid of Jean Lafitte and his Baratarian pirates, a group previously described by Old Hickory as "hellish banditti."

Pakenham anchored off Lake Borgne to the east of the city. Informers pointed out to him Bayou Bienvenue, by which small boats could go a good part of the way to the Mississippi and easily reach a point some nine miles south of New Orleans. On December 23, Pakenham landed 1,800 men at the head of the bayou, which, despite Jackson's orders, had been left unguarded. Jackson moved at once to meet the foe, and during the next two weeks a series of heavy engagements took place, both sides being continually reinforced. In the final encounter (January 8, 1815), over 5,000 British veterans assaulted a line held by 3,200 Americans behind breastworks, many of them armed with the Kentucky rifle, a weapon of such remarkable accuracy that a good marksman could easily kill a squirrel at 100 yards. The result of the attack was a massacre. Pakenham was killed and the British lost in killed, wounded, and captured 2,600 men, while the Americans lost eight killed and thirteen wounded.

The battle of New Orleans was far and away the most decisive land victory of the war. It did much to take away the sting of the failures on the Canadian frontier and the easy surrender of Washington. It also made Jackson a hero. His errors of judgment in the campaign were forgotten, and a Jackson myth began to develop. Audiences in western theatres roared with applause as actors garbed in buckskin, moccasins, and fur caps sang of how:

> Jackson he was wide awake and wasn't scar'd of trifles,
> For well he knew what aim we take with our Kentucky rifles.

Years later, Vachel Lindsay evoked the spirit that flamed through the country on the news of Jackson's victory:*

> He licked the British at Noo Orleans;
> Beat them out of their elegant jeans,
> He piled the cotton bales twenty feet high,
> And he snorted "freedom," and it flashed from his eye.

> And the American Eagle swooped through the air,
> And cheered when he heard Jackson swear:—
> "By the Eternal, let them come.
> Sound Yankee Doodle. Let the bullets hum."

> And his wild men straight from the woods fought on
> Till the British fops were dead and gone.

In the midst of all the pleasurable excitement over the New Orleans triumph, people quite forgot that the battle had been fought two weeks after peace had been signed.

---

* From COLLECTED POEMS by Vachel Lindsay, Copyright 1920 by The Macmillan Company, renewed 1948 by Elizabeth C. Lindsay. Used by permission of The Macmillan Company.

THE BATTLE OF NEW ORLEANS—ENGRAVED BY D. L. DEBUCOURT

This engagement made General Jackson a national hero, even though it was fought after the peace treaty had been signed. The solid ranks of British veterans were easy targets for the American riflemen sheltered behind breastworks.

Peace Overtures

One of the remarkable features of the War of 1812 was that almost as soon as it began, both sides began making overtures for peace. Madison's offer of an armistice was refused by the British government because it was coupled with the abandonment of impressment, and Britain's offer was refused by the United States because it contained no concessions on the same subject. Russia offered mediation in 1813, and Madison at once accepted, appointing John Quincy Adams, then Minister to Russia, United States Senator James A. Bayard of Delaware, and Albert Gallatin to represent the United States. Bayard was a Federalist, and Adams, always an independent spirit, had broken with the Federalists in 1807 over the embargo and was still a political independent.

The American "team" gathered in St. Petersburg, only to learn that Great Britain had refused the Tsar's offer. They were saved from a humiliating return home by England's proposal of direct negotiations, which was at once accepted by Madison. Two more Republicans, Jonathan Russell of Massachusetts and Henry Clay, were added to the three commissioners already in Europe. Despite the inevitable clash of personality between the ebullient Clay and the puritanical Adams, it was an able delegation, especially when compared to the three mediocrities—Lord Gambier, Henry Goulburn, and William Adams—who acted as messenger boys for Lord Castlereagh, the British Foreign Secretary and leader of the House of Commons.

Much time was spent in deciding on the place of negotiation and in travel, but all the commissioners finally gathered in Ghent at the beginning of August. There followed four and one-half months of proposals and counterproposals that tried the patience of the Americans.

The Treaty of Ghent, 1814

The tortuous ways of diplomatic negotiation are well illustrated by the proceedings at Ghent. Each side began with demands that the other could not possibly meet. The Americans requested damages for property destroyed, the end of impressment, and the cession of Canada. The British asked that a large part of the Old Northwest be set up as an Indian buffer state, that the United States cede part of Maine, and that there be other rectifications of the Canadian-American frontier. When finally signed (December 24, 1814), the treaty mentioned scarcely any of the propositions that had been discussed, left each side in possession of the territory it had held at the beginning of the war, and provided commissions to settle boundary lines that had been left vague or undetermined at the close of the Revolution.

The tame conclusion of the peace negotiations was due to a number of factors. The British government's attitude softened with Prevost's failure at Plattsburg and disquieting rumors that Napoleon was planning a return from Elba, and Wellington advised peace in America. Both sides recognized that impressment and the seizure of American shipping were closely linked to war in Europe, and with peace in that part of the world these causes of war between Great Britain and the United States would no longer be operative. Finally, in view of the outcome of American attempts north of the border, there was little enthusiasm in the United States for continuing a war of conquest.

The Impact of the War

As wars went a century and a half ago, the War of 1812 was not costly from the American point of view. Total losses, sea and land, including killed, wounded, prisoners, and those who died in hospitals, were not over 30,000—about 2 per cent of the military population. The financial cost, including pensions to veterans and their dependents, was about $200 million. The national debt at the close of the war was approximately $15 per capita, compared to the $20 per capita it had been in 1791.

But the modest amount of blood and treasure poured out by the country was productive of important consequences for the United States. The burning of Washington and the victories of the war (few and far between though they were) had fired national patriotism and overwhelmed with unpopularity the Federalist states' righters of New England. The war gave a great stimulus to western expansion, for, the strength of the Indian power in the South and West having been broken during the struggle, all the areas east of the Mississippi now lay open to American frontiersmen. Wartime needs and the blockade had stimulated the drift of capital, already begun, from seagoing activities into manufacturing, and by 1815 textile, iron, wood, glassware, leather, and pottery production was firmly established and able to supply all or a large part of the American market.

Last but not least, the period from 1809 to 1815 had seen a further modification of the strict Jeffersonian principles of the 1790s. The Republicans, it is true, had destroyed the Bank of the United States in 1811, but in a number of other respects they had moved toward or accepted Federalist principles and practices. They had declared and fought a war despite protests on the grounds of states' rights; in so doing, they had raised an army. They had advocated and stimulated the development of domestic manufactures and had reinstituted a program of internal taxation which included excise taxes. Perhaps most significant of all, they had accepted as necessary the formulation of national policies in response to national needs with a consequent expansion of the powers and prerogatives of the central government. Madison's message to Congress in December, 1815, emphasized the importance of adequate national defense, of a national system of roads and canals, of protection for manufacturing, of a national university and, cautiously, of reinstituting a national bank. It was becoming more and more difficult, as the years went by, to distinguish Republicans from Federalists, on the basis of either platforms or principles. In one sense, this was a tribute to the stability of a political system built around a middle-class norm, but in another sense it showed that both parties were under the influence of social pressures in which nationalism and capitalism were playing increasingly important roles.

Suggested Reading

The causes of the War of 1812 have been the subject of considerable controversy among historians. Julius W. Pratt, *The Expansionists of 1812* (new ed., 1949) emphasizes the importance of frontier expansionism in bringing on the war, while A. L. Burt, *The United States, Great Britain, and British North America* (1940), stresses free trade and seamen's rights as the principal causes of the war. Bradford Perkins, *Prologue to War; England and the United States, 1805–1812* (1961) is an important study. The student should also consult C. B. Coleman, "The Ohio Valley in the Preliminaries of the War of 1812," *Mississippi Valley Historical Review,* VII (June, 1920), 39–50. J. F. Zimmerman, *Impressment of American Seamen* (1925) is also useful.

Francis F. Beirne, *The War of 1812* (1949) gives an excellent account of the war itself. Charles P. Lucas, *The Canadian War of 1812* (1906) presents the story of the war from the Canadian point of view. George Dangerfield, *The Era of Good Feelings* (1952) has some suggestive observations on the war period. A. T. Mahan, *Sea Power in its Relations to the War of 1812* (2 vols., 1919) is the most authoritative account of the naval aspects of the war.

Henry Adams, *History of the United States,* already cited, is indispensable; vols. VII and VIII are excellent on the war itself and on the Hartford Convention. S. E. Morison, *The Life and Letters of Harrison Gray Otis* (2 vols., 1913) is also useful for the Hartford Convention. See also George Dangerfield, *The Era of Good Feelings* (1952).

Wartime diplomacy and the peace negotiations are admirably covered in S. F. Bemis, *Secretaries of State,* already cited, and *John Quincy Adams and the Foundations of American Foreign Policy* (1949). On the peace, see also G. G. Van Deusen, *The Life of Henry Clay* (1937). Bradford Perkins, *Castlereagh and Adams* (1964) is important, as are certain chapters in S. E. Morison, *The Maritime History of Massachusetts* (1921); Reginald Horsman, *The Causes of the War of 1812* (1962), and R. H. Brown, *The Republic in Peril: 1812* (1963).

GROWTH

[1815-1860]

AND CHANGE

13 ˒ The Growth of a National Spirit

DURING THE FIRST PART of the nineteenth century, and especially in the years immediately following the War of 1812, there developed in the American people a consciousness of America's potential in wealth and power and a deep sense of pride in the nation and its future. The establishment of a strong and stable national government and the acquisition of a splendid western domain had fostered this

The Era of Good Feelings frame of mind. Then, too, the humiliations suffered at the hands of the British and the French, whether on the high seas or in the capture and devastation of Washington, had excited in many citizens a sense of national injury and a determination to uphold the national honor. Conversely, the shattering defeat of the British at New Orleans also did much to stimulate national pride. Once the war was over, the attention of Americans could concentrate upon the homeland; and the possibilities for western expansion and development, together with the opportunities for material gain that could accompany the development of a national economy, excited the popular imagination. Americans thought of the United States not only as an evangel of political and social democracy, but also as a land with immense potentialities for growth in size and wealth and power. The story is told of an Alabama congressman of those days who, when overwhelmed by the grandeur of the American future, would run down the aisle of the House of Representatives and turn a somersault over his desk, exclaiming as he did so, "This is a wonderful country!" This nationalistic mood took concrete form in a variety of political, cultural, diplomatic, and judicial activities that had profound effects upon the life of the nation.

The trend of the country toward national unity was manifested, in a political sense, by the elections of 1816 and 1820. James Monroe, the heir apparent of Madison's administration and the last of the so-called Virginia Dynasty, was the Republican candidate for the presidency in 1816, and against him the Federalist remnant pitted Rufus King of New York. The result was a smashing Republican victory. Monroe had 183 votes in the electoral college to thirty-four for King, who carried only Massachusetts, Connecticut, and Delaware. Even New York went for Monroe, and the Federalists had only feeble representation in both houses of Congress. When, shortly after his inauguration, Monroe went on a kind of sentimental journey to Boston, he was everywhere received with enthusiasm—and nowhere more than in that erstwhile Federalist stronghold. In the presidential election of 1820 there was no contest, as the Federalists did not even put up a candidate. Monroe was re-elected with only one dissenting vote in the electoral college—that of William Plumer of New Hampshire, who felt that this was a good time and place to put John Quincy Adams before the public as a presidential possibility in 1824.

During Monroe's administrations the Federalist party disappeared as an organization of national significance. It never recovered from the stigma of disloyalty that it had incurred by its opposition to the War of 1812, and politically ambitious men now began designating themselves as Jeffersonian Republicans, regardless of their previous political affiliations. Such erstwhile Federalists as James Buchanan of Pennsylvania and Roger Brooke Taney of Maryland moved into the party founded by Jefferson, and an intimate friend of Daniel Webster told President Monroe that "Black Dan" could easily be tempted into the Cabinet as Attorney General. The so-called Era of Good Feelings was in full swing.

Development of Cultural Nationalism

The emphasis on national unity in a political sense was accompanied by a growth of cultural nationalism, for educators, writers, and orators, alike sang the praises of America. Of these, none were more zealous in their efforts than those who prided themselves on being educational reformers. Confident in the perfectibility of mankind, especially of American mankind, and convinced that a people who govern themselves must be armed with the power of knowledge, men like Noah Webster (1758–1843) and Caleb Bingham (1757–1817) undertook the establishment of a system of education that would end cultural subservience to Europe and would create a characteristically American social consciousness and patriotic spirit. Noah Webster especially, in the speller, the grammar, and the dictionary that he compiled, tried specifically to establish a uniformity in spelling and word usage that would be stamped as peculiar to the United States. He also tried, through the use of selected readings in his grammar, to inculcate a spirit of national patriotism.

Like the educators, men of letters sought to depict outstanding characteristics of the American cultural tradition, as well as the peculiar charm of the American scene. Washington Irving's *Diedrich Knickerbocker's History of New York* (1809) was a humorous treatment of the Dutch forebears, and his *Sketchbook* (1819) paid tribute to the Hudson Valley's romantic charm. James Fenimore Cooper's *Leatherstocking Tales,* beginning in the 1820s, contained some excellent descriptions of nature, as well as a romantic picture of the Indians and the American frontiersman. George Bancroft gave an oration at Springfield, Massachusetts, on July 4, 1826, which demonstrated the devotion to democracy and to American nationalism which characterized his subsequent historical writings, especially his *History of the United States,* the first volume of which appeared in 1834. Here, as in the nine subsequent volumes, he told the American people with enthusiastic conviction what they themselves believed—that America was the promised land of opportunity and progress.

Patriots used other media than schoolbooks and literary masterpieces in stimulating a spirit of nationalism. By 1815, "Yankee Doodle" was being sung everywhere and with an infinite variety of verses, and "Uncle Sam" had become a national symbol. Fourth of July orators, writers for the literary periodicals, and other molders of the popular taste, thundered against provincialism and its slavish imitation of things foreign, especially English. They preached the value of an independent spirit and outlook and repeatedly declared that America was a specially favored land with a population of extraordinary virtue, and that the great American experiment in democracy placed the United States at the head of the world's march toward that great day when all men should be free.

National Defense and Economic Development

The development of cultural nationalism was accompanied by a surge of interest in national defense and in the utilization of the nation's economic potential. Taught by the lessons of the War of 1812, the Republicans now felt it necessary to provide a respectable military establishment. While he was still Secretary of War, Monroe recommended a standing army of 20,000 men at a cost of $5 million a year. This was too much for Congress, but a bill was passed and became law providing for a 10,000 man army. During the war, Congress had provided for building sixteen additional warships, including six frigates and four seventy-fours; shortly after the war was over, an appropriation of $4.4 million was made for the maintenance of this naval force. And even while these measures for defense were being formulated, a drive for strengthening the nation's economy gathered momentum.

The years between 1806 and 1815 had seen a vigorous growth in American manufacturing, but no sooner had peace been declared than British manufacturers began dumping their goods on the American market. United States imports, which had totaled only $13 million in 1813, shot up to $147 million in 1816. Many of the country's infant industries were now hard hit, and textile firms were ruined right and left. Petitions for relief poured into Congress from the New England and Middle Atlantic areas. Elder statesmen such as Jefferson and Madison, and rising young national leaders like Clay and Calhoun felt that something must be done to promote national self-sufficiency, especially with a view to establishing the kind of balanced economy that would sustain the country in the event of another war with a great naval power. The result was the tariff of 1816.

This tariff measure was intended to be protective legislation. Its duties ranged from 7.5 to 30 per cent ad valorem, and it gave special protection to cottons, woolens, iron, and other manufactured commodities the production of which had markedly increased during the war. There was considerable southern opposition to its cotton schedules, and Daniel Webster, who then represented New England's commercial interests, opposed its passage. Nevertheless, it is significant that it received votes from every state save North Carolina and that no prominent southerner ranged himself in opposition to the measure. Nationalist sentiment predominated in Congress in 1816, and many southerners expected to see manufacturing develop in their own section of the country. Furthermore, it was not extreme protection, its highest permanent rate of duty being 20 per cent. The success of the manufacturing interest in getting still higher tariffs during the 1820s was to bring a swift and violent reaction from a disillusioned South.

While Congress was establishing a tariff for the protection of the national industries, it passed another measure designed to strengthen the country's economy. At the end of the war, the nation's currency was in a chaotic condition, and the state banks were obstinately refusing to return to specie payments. President Madison, concerned "that the benefits of an uniform national currency should be restored to the community," had suggested the desirability of chartering another national bank. A. J. Dallas, Madison's Secretary of the Treasury, favored a national bank, and the Republican leaders in Congress who had destroyed the first bank now led the movement for another such institution. Clay asserted that, had he foreseen in 1811 the results of their action at that time, he would have voted for a recharter, and Calhoun now declared that a bank was in the national interest. The Republican leadership united behind a bank bill sponsored by Calhoun. It became law in 1816, providing for a bank with $35 million capital, one-fifth of which was subscribed by the government. Five of the twenty-five directors were appointed by the national administration, and the bank was obligated to maintain specie payment and to serve as a depository for government funds. It was designed to bring order out of chaos in American banking by furnishing a sound currency and by exerting pressure on the local banks to establish and maintain their own currencies on a specie payment basis.

The Bank of the United States now chartered had great potential power. This was in part due to its practice of presenting state bank notes to those institutions for redemption in specie, and in part to the fact that it could and did make loans and discounts in the millions of dollars. As a result of its establishment, state bank notes decreased 40 per cent, the state banks—not without grumbling—resumed specie payment, and the general condition of the currency markedly improved.

As the tariff and bank bills were being passed, a demand for improved means of travel was heard in all sections of the country. The lessons of wartime, especially those furnished in the Northwest, as to the importance of rapid and easy transit for men and supplies were still vivid in men's minds. They were reinforced by the demands of emigrants to the frontier, by the patriotic arguments of expansionists like Clay and Calhoun, and by the interest of businessmen and farmers in lowering the expense of transportation. When the cost of shipping a ton of goods from Baltimore to Cincinnati was $150, and from Buffalo to New York $100, and when corn and tobacco could not be raised for market more than fifty miles from a navigable river, the transport situation was indeed a formidable obstacle to progress. For nationalistic thinkers, these arguments for internal improvements were given further point by a growing tendency on the part of western New York and the Old Northwest to use the relatively cheap transport facilities furnished by Lake Ontario and the St. Lawrence River. A freight charge of $30.00 a ton from Buffalo to Montreal tended to obscure the advantages of the Union from the viewpoint of western New York and the northern parts of

Ohio, Indiana, and Illinois. It was as a nationalist, rather than as a southerner, that Calhoun spoke when he said in 1817, "Let us bind the republic together with a perfect system of roads and canals. Let us conquer space." In this same speech the South Carolinian declared himself no foe of broad construction of the Constitution. That document, he said, should be construed with common sense, and roads and canals would certainly aid the nation's defense and promote the general welfare.

A bill providing funds to be used by Congress in the construction of internal improvements passed both houses early in 1817, only to be vetoed by President Madison on strict constructionist grounds, and similar scruples on the part of President Monroe prevented the enactment of a similar measure a few years later. Eastern jealousy of the West, New England's fear of the depletion of its factory labor supply by westward emigration, and the reluctance of New England and the South to be taxed for the internal improvements of other sections prevented the passage of these bills over the presidential veto. The result was a dearth of federal funds, save for post roads and for the Cumberland Road which by 1818 was completed from tidewater to the Ohio River. The national need for internal improvements had to be met in other ways, and in consequence the states shouldered the burden.

State construction of internal improvements was at first largely confined to chartering private companies which then proceeded to build toll roads and bridges. The same was true of canals, which were costly to construct and about the engineering of which little was known. In 1816, there were only 100 miles of canals in the United States and only three of these were as much as two miles long. Then came the Erie canal. Due primarily to the energy and drive of Governor DeWitt Clinton of New York, this engineering marvel of the age, thirty feet wide and four feet deep, was started in 1817 and finished in 1825. Scoffers had dubbed it "Clinton's Folly" and "Clinton's Ditch" and had proclaimed that its cost of $7 million would never be liquidated, but when the cost of transporting freight from Buffalo to New York sank from $100.00 to $8.00 a ton, and nine years of tolls paid the entire cost of constructing this artificial waterway from Buffalo to Albany, scepticism was replaced by a great wave of enthusiasm for canal building. By 1840, there were 3,326 miles of canals in the United States, largely in the North and West, that had been built at a cost of $25 million. One way or another—by spontaneous community effort, by state authorization of private companies or the direct effort of the states themselves, and even by limited national activity—the various parts of the nation were being linked by means of transportation.

The Indians—And Florida

As roads and canals were being built to meet the demand of the nation's farmers and business men, pressure by the white citizens of the country upon the Indians increased. The battle of Tippecanoe had opened the way for an extinguishing of Indian titles in the Old Northwest, and there large sections of Indiana, Illinois, Ohio, and Michigan were ceded by the tribes, often under duress. In the South, the Creeks gave little trouble after the chastisement administered to them by General Jackson, but the Seminoles in Florida, especially those whose Georgia lands had been seized by the whites, constituted a formidable problem. Indignant at the treatment to which they had been subjected, they were easily persuaded to raid across the border into American territory. They were encouraged to do this by one Colonel Nichols, who had been British commander in Florida during the War of 1812 and who had remained there for some months after the signing of the treaty of Ghent. Spain failed to quiet the Indians after Nichols' departure, and President Monroe ordered Jackson to move into Spanish territory and punish the raiders. He was told to "adopt the necessary measures" to end the conflict and at once replied in his famous "Rhea letter" that if he were told through any channel that the possession of the Floridas was desirable, he would see that it was done within sixty days.

Jackson later claimed that through "Mr. J. Rhea," a Tennessee Congressman, he received the President's approval of the course he was to pursue in the Floridas. This Monroe denied, and the question of responsibility for Old Hickory's subsequent actions has never been satisfactorily settled. What is indisputable is that Jackson stormed into the Spanish territories, scattered the Indians right and left, took possession of Pensacola, and seized and hung two British subjects, Alexander Arbuthnot and Robert Ambrister, for having incited the Indians to commit outrages against citizens of the United States. He then retired across the Florida border, very much a hero in the eyes of most Americans. His action was highhanded and involved the danger of war with both Spain and England, but the Indians had been severely chastised and the way opened for the acquisition of East as well as West Florida.

Spain's protest against Jackson's invasion of East Florida was sternly rebuffed by the United States. Secretary of State John Quincy Adams defended Jackson's conduct and warned Spain that it must either establish and maintain order in Florida or cede it to the United States. Spain, too weak to pursue the first alternative, perforce entered into negotiations for cession.

The Transcontinental Treaty

On February 22, 1819, a date fixed at the suggestion of Secretary Adams, Spain ceded both the Floridas to the United States. The latter country assumed up to $5 million of the claims of its citizens against Spain, thus adding 37,931,520 acres to the national territory, at a cost of $.171 an acre.

The Florida treaty recognized Spain's possession of Texas and fixed a transcontinental boundary line between all Spanish and American claims west of the Mississippi. The Sabine River was made the boundary between Texas and the Louisiana Purchase, and, primarily because of Adams' insistence, a line was drawn north and west from the Sabine to the Pacific by which Spain acknowledged the title of the United States to the Oregon country.

The Treaty of 1819 was, in truth, a transcontinental treaty, one that opened the path of the United States to the Pacific. Its only unfortunate aspect was the fixing of the Sabine River as the westward boundary of Louisiana, for the evidence indicates that Adams and Monroe, had they pushed hard enough, could have obtained title to all or most of Texas from weak and faltering Spain. But at the time, the Floridas and the transcontinental boundary seemed big enough prizes to the American statesmen.

Careful Negotiation with a Great Power

While the Florida treaty was being prepared, Adams pressed vigorously for the settlement of two questions that were provocative of discord with Great Britain. The first of these concerned certain boundaries between the United States and Canada, and the second involved fishing rights in northern Atlantic waters. In both cases, Adams' efforts were attended by considerable success. The Rush-Bagot agreement of 1817 virtually demilitarized the Great Lakes and set a precedent in international relations for reciprocal naval disarmament. Conventions signed in 1818 recognized American fishing rights along the coasts of Newfoundland and Labrador, established the forty-ninth parallel as the boundary between Canada and the United States from the Lake of the Woods to the "Stony" Mountains, and set up joint occupation of Oregon for ten years (an agreement continued until 1846). By these temperate and judicious measures, a far cry from the brusque

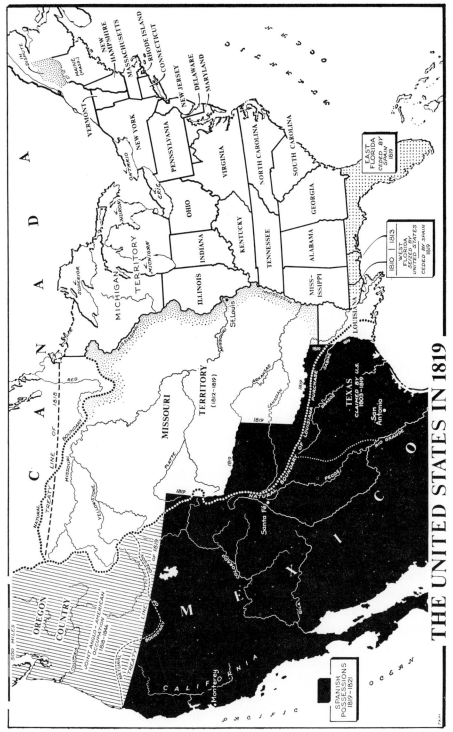

THE UNITED STATES IN 1819

299

methods employed against weak Spain, Monroe and his Secretary of State went far toward defining America's rights along the border and protecting those rights by suitable arrangements.

Background of the Monroe Doctrine

That Monroe's administration, in its desire to establish and protect American rights, took the whole western hemisphere to be its province was manifested by the deep interest of American statesmen in the fate of Latin America, and by the President's pronouncement in 1823 regarding Spanish American affairs. These developments were the result of stirring events that had taken place in South America. There a series of revolts against Spanish authority, headed by such Latin American patriots as Simon Bolivar (1783–1830), José de San Martin (1778–1850), and Bernardo O'Higgins (1776–1842), had by 1822 freed the continent from Spanish and Portuguese control. The United States had watched these revolutions with great interest, but had at first maintained a policy of strict nonintervention. Some American statesmen had as early as 1816 urged recognition of the South American states that gained their freedom; Henry Clay in particular envisioned a hemispheric system of American republics guided and directed by the United States. Other American leaders, however, especially Secretary of State John Quincy Adams, counseled delay. Adams felt that the new republics were turbulent and unstable; that precipitate recognition might serve as an excuse for European intervention in South America on behalf of Spain; and, most particularly, that nothing should be done to offend Spain while the United States was negotiating with that country over Florida.

At first the views of Adams prevailed, so far as American policy was concerned. Sentiment in favor of the struggling young republics increased, however, and in 1822, after Florida was safely in the possession of the United States, the American government formally recognized the independence of the new Latin American states.

While these developments were occurring in the New World, events were taking place in Europe that had direct impact upon American foreign policy. Europe was in a restless and troubled state at the end of the Napoleonic wars. Napoleon had played havoc with the power and authority of the dynastic rulers, and the democratic and equalitarian ideas unleashed by the French Revolution kept advocates of the old order in a state of continual alarm. The basic aim of the dynasts—the Hohenzollerns, the Hapsburgs, the Romanoffs, and their ministers—was to prevent any new revolutionary outbreaks and, as far as possible, to restore the old monarchs to the positions of authority that they had occupied before 1789. To this end, a Quadruple Alliance of Austria, Prussia, Russia, and England was formed in 1815 to keep France and "French ideas" in check. The nations of this Alliance met in congresses, at which it speedily became apparent that the Continental courts were becoming more and more conservative in their point of view. They became intent upon upholding monarchical authority everywhere, and upon crushing out all manifestations of democracy and democratic nationalism. In 1821, the Continental powers crushed revolutions in Italy. The following year, the conservative French Bourbon King Louis XVIII, acting with the approval of the Continental courts, put down a rebellion against the reactionary Ferdinand VII of Spain, and rumors began flying about that the monarchs on the European continent were planning to restore Spanish authority in Latin America.

As the policies of the Continental courts became more and more repressive in character, the English government became increasingly discontented with the trend of events. Britain was building a thriving trade with South America and did not wish to see this disturbed by any return of Spanish monopolies. The British government looked with disfavor on any increase of French prestige in Spain or in the New World. George Canning—who, by 1820, was once more influential in shaping the British government's foreign policy, and who took over the Foreign Office in 1822—was sceptical of international conferences in general and those of the Quadruple Alliance in particular. The net result was that, from 1820 on, Britain was critical of intervention in the affairs of other states and adopted a benevolent attitude toward movements that were national and liberal in character. In 1822, England refused to join the Continental courts in repressing the Spanish revolution, and in 1823 Canning turned to the United States and urged a joint Anglo-American declaration against any European interference in the affairs of Spanish America.

While these events were transpiring in Europe, Russia was manifesting an interest in trade on the western coast of North America. A Russian-American trading company had been chartered by the Russian government in 1799, and in 1812 Russians established a trading settlement in California within fifty miles of the Golden Gate. In 1821, the Tsar's government issued a ukase claiming a monopoly of trading rights north of the fifty-first parallel and warning the ships of other nations to keep 100 miles off the coast.

President Monroe and Secretary of State Adams were alarmed at the Russian move, fearing that it meant further trade limitations and that it foreshadowed actual territorial settlement. They also suspected that the Continental courts were scheming to restore Spanish America to Spain. Such a move would not only conflict with the American policy of recognizing the Latin American Republics, but would also check the growth of liberty and democracy in the western hemisphere and throughout the world. In the face of this situation, Monroe and Adams began consultations as to the proper method of procedure.

Jefferson, Madison, Calhoun, and even Monroe himself were at first favorable to joint action with England as a counter to the designs of the Continental courts. Adams, however—secure in the knowledge that a stand in opposition to European intervention in the New World would be backed by Great Britain—opposed such a course. He preferred to see the United States act in such a way that it would be left free of commitment to England, rather than, as he put it, bobbing about "like a cock boat in the wake of a British man-o'war."

Adams' viewpoint prevailed with President Monroe. Instructions to Richard Rush, American Minister to England, left the door open for joint action in the future, but on December 2, 1823, in his message to Congress, the President laid down the policy that has since come to be known as the Monroe Doctrine.

Monroe's "Doctrine"—Diplomatic Nationalism

The American continents, said Monroe, were free and independent, and no longer subject to colonization by any of the European states. The United States had not interfered and would not interfere with "the existing colonies or dependencies of any European power," but interference by Europe with the newly formed Spanish American republics would be regarded "as the manifestation of an unfriendly disposition toward the United States." It was America's policy to keep hands off Europe's internal concerns, but the United States could not look with indifference upon an effort to extend Europe's political system to America.

Monroe's pronouncement did not have any great immediate significance. No European country had plans for any major interference in the affairs of Spanish America, and Russia was not contemplating a colonization effort on the west coast. The Continental courts did not like the American statement—Metternich condemned it as "blustering" and "arrogant"—but they made no formal protest. Canning was displeased by the noncolonization principle, but he professed satisfaction at this blow to the prestige of the Continental powers and later grandiloquently declared, "I called the New World into existence to redress the balance of the Old." As for the Latin

American countries, they were moderately pleased by Monroe's stand, but were more inclined, if trouble came, to look for aid to Great Britain rather than to the United States.

But, though the famous statement had no great initial impact, it had great historical significance. A manifestation of American nationalism, it served notice on Europe that the American continents were not proper objectives for their expansionist and imperialist designs, and that it was the purpose of the United States to thwart any aggressive designs which they might have in the New World. It also symbolized the repugnance to despotism and arbitrary controls, the regard for the freedom of peoples and the dignity of the individual citizen, that has always lain at the basis of American democracy. Even though in recent years the Monroe Doctrine has been transformed from a unilateral to a multilateral policy, its principles of action remain cardinal aspects of American foreign policy.

Judicial Nationalism

The executive and legislative departments were not the only branches of the national government that fostered the development of a national spirit. Significant developments in this direction took place in the Supreme Court under Chief Justice John Marshall (1755–1835). Marshall was a Virginian who had served in the Revolution, in the Virginia legislature, and on the commission sent to France in 1798, before he was made Secretary of State under John Adams in May, 1800. Adams appointed him Chief Justice of the Supreme Court, and he assumed this office February 4, 1801, at the same time retaining his position in the State Department. He is the only man in American history who has held both of these posts at the same time, but for him there was no conflict of duties, so far as the two offices were concerned. The Court had no cases before it in its February, 1801, term, and Marshall's first duty as Chief Justice was to administer the oath at Thomas Jefferson's inauguration on March 4, 1801.

Prior to Marshall's appointment, the Supreme Court had played a decidedly minor role. From 1789 to 1801, only 100 cases had come before it, and of these only six had been of constitutional importance. John Jay, the first Chief Justice, had felt promoted when he became Governor of New York in 1795, and declined reappointment because he felt the Court was doomed to a subordinate role. John Rutledge declined the Chief Justiceship in favor of a similar post on the South Carolina Supreme Court. It was Marshall's destiny to change the relatively insignificant status of the Court to one of great importance.

Marshall made a profound contribution to American life during his thirty-five years on the Court. His personality was engaging and his mental equipment little short of superb. Careless of dress, fond of quoits and convivial companionship, amiable but resolute, he was a born debater and a natural leader of men, one equipped with uncommon powers of logical analysis. His forceful personality impressed itself upon the members of the Supreme Court as it had upon the Virginia Federalists. There was rarely a dissenting opinion when he was on the bench, and Justice Joseph Story, a Massachusetts Republican, who entered the court in 1811 when he was thirty-two years old, came to write decisions which, in their argument and philosophy, were scarcely to be distinguished from those of the Chief Justice. Jefferson was right when he told Madison that "it will be difficult to find a character with firmness enough to preserve his independence on the same bench with Marshall."

Nationalism and individualism were the guiding lights of Marshall's philosophy. In *Fletcher v. Peck* (1810), the case involving the Yazoo land frauds, Marshall's decision held void an act of a Georgia legislature rescinding a previous legislature's sale of land to the Yazoo companies. This decision made no reference to the fraud and corruption in the Yazoo land sales, thus avoiding what might have proved a precedent for a dangerous extension of the Court's power over state legislatures, but was based simply upon the fact that under the national Constitution no state could enact any law impairing the obligation of contract. However corrupt the original sale, it had resulted in some legal land sale contracts that could not be lawfully revoked. This was the first case in which the Court had held a state law unconstitutional, and the resentment of states' rights political leaders was intense, for the establishment of this power of the federal judiciary was a great victory for nationalism over localism.

Even more significant than the decision in *Fletcher v. Peck* was that in *McCulloch v. Maryland* (1819). The establishment of a second Bank of the United States had met with opposition in a number of states, and they were threatening the newly chartered bank with destructive taxation. In 1818, Maryland had passed a law imposing a tax of $15,000 a year on the branch of the Bank of the United States located in that state. When the branch refused to pay, it was sued in the name of its Baltimore cashier, J. W. McCulloch. The Bank lost the case in the state courts and appealed to the federal courts.

As *McCulloch v. Maryland* was argued, the constitutional issue was uppermost. If the Bank lost, not only could the individual states put it out of business (Ohio had imposed a tax of $50,000 on each of the two branches in that state), but the federal government would be unable to charter corporations or move in other directions beyond a strict interpretation of the Constitution.

Marshall's decision in *McCulloch v. Maryland* was subscribed to by all the associate justices. It had transcendent importance, for it went far beyond the legality of the Bank itself. It declared that federal institutions were not subject to state regulation; that "the power to tax is the power to destroy, and may defeat and render useless the power to create," and that the Constitution permits the Congress to make "all laws necessary and proper" for carrying into execution any powers of the national government.

> Let the end be legitimate [said Marshall], let it be within the scope of the constitution, and all means which are appropriate, which are plainly adapted to that end, which are not prohibited, but consist with the letter and spirit of the constitution, are constitutional. . . .

The *McCulloch v. Maryland* decision gave great support to nationalists as well as to partisans of the Bank. It angered the exponents of states' rights and the defenders of local banks. John Taylor of Caroline attacked it bitterly, and Jefferson characterized the national judiciary as "the subtle corps of sappers and miners constantly working underground to undermine the foundations of our confederated fabric. . . ." But, despite such laments, it gave flexibility and vitality to the "necessary and proper" clause in the Constitution, imbuing that clause with a scope that has enabled the federal government to act vigorously and effectively in times of crisis in the nation's history.

In two other cases, *Cohens v. Virginia* (1821) and *Gibbons v. Ogden* (1824), Marshall's decisions had great significance for the Union. In *Cohens v. Virginia*, the point at issue was the superiority of the federal courts to the state courts, where an interpretation of the federal Constitution was involved. Against the strenuous opposition of Virginia, the Supreme Court ruled that such cases could be transferred from state to federal courts. This decision, taken in conjunction with that in *Martin v. Hunter's Lessee* (1816), laid down the great principle that under the Judiciary Act of 1789 the Supreme Court had appellate jurisdiction over the state courts. Marshall's opinion in *Cohens v. Virginia* included a ringing assertion of the necessity of "a close and firm Union," if the liberty and happiness of the American people were to be preserved. It came at a time when southern threats of secession were being hurled in the controversy over the admission of Missouri to the Union as a slave state, and the advocates of slavery and of states' rights denounced the decision as evidence of the way in which the Court was expanding the power of the federal union at the expense of the states. Demands were heard that the Supreme Court be abolished or, at the very least, that the section of the Judiciary Act of 1789 that gave appellate jurisdiction to the Supreme Court in cases involving an interpretation of the Constitution be repealed.

If *Cohens v. Virginia* asserted the paramount authority of the judicial arm of the federal government where cases involving an interpretation of the Constitution were involved, *Gibbons v. Ogden* established the predominance of the national government in the regulation of interstate commerce. After the state of New York had granted a monopoly of steam navigation in its waters to Robert Fulton and Robert R. Livingston they obtained similar rights in Louisiana, and other persons had obtained the same privileges in still other states. The granting of such monopolistic rights was defended in New York by no less an authority than Chancellor James Kent as a legitimate exercise of state power, but in *Gibbons v. Ogden* the Supreme Court declared the New York monopoly unconstitutional as being in conflict with the right of Congress to regulate interstate commerce. Marshall, in rendering the decision, re-emphasized his stand in *McCulloch v. Maryland* on the loose construction of the Constitution. "Commerce," he asserted, meant not only the exchange of commodities but the means of their transportation as well. The regulation of commerce between the states or with foreign nations was clearly and indisputably lodged by the Constitution in the national government, and this power could be exercised "within the limits of every state" when the navigation involved was in any manner connected with interstate or foreign trade.

Gibbons v. Ogden is important as the first great Court decision against monopoly in the United States. It is of even greater importance because it was vital to the existence of a strong and unified American nation. Coming at a time when the proponents of slavery and the opponents of high tariffs and of internal improvements at national expense were strenuously supporting strict construction of the Constitution and the doctrine of states' rights as bulwarks for their positions, the decision was a ringing affirmation of the superiority of national needs over local interests. Its interpretation of the commerce clause was essential to the development of that great national market which has been so fundamental to the economic growth of the United States. Had state monopolies in transportation become the order of the day, welding the American people into a nation would have been a most difficult task.

Marshall was a staunch defender of individualism as well as of nationalism. In such cases as *Fletcher v. Peck,* and especially in the *Dartmouth College Case* (1819), in which the Court ruled that a corporation charter was a contract that could not be impaired by subsequent action of a state legislature, Marshall and his fellow judges went to great lengths in upholding property rights against state regulation. Unfortunately, this fostered shoddy practice and outright wrongdoing through the immunity it gave chartered corporations from legislative interference, an immunity only gradually weakened in the nineteenth century by the development of the police powers of the state and by the later decision under Chief Justice Taney in the *Charles River Bridge v. Warren Bridge* case (1837). On the other hand, this emphasis upon the sanctity of contracts checked a growing legislative practice of passing contract-breaking laws, and by placing contractual obligations, business or otherwise, under the protection of the courts, it definitely fostered the development of a national economy.

Marshall's decisions, taken as a whole, were of great importance in building the United States into a strong and powerful nation. As such, they aroused the bitter dislike of those who believed in strict construction of the Constitution and a Union in which the states would remain powerful agencies of government. "All wrong," groaned John Randolph of Roanoke, "but no man in the United States can tell why or wherein." Jefferson, too, denounced what he described as the judicial tendency "which, working like gravity without any intermission, is to press us at last into one consolidated mass." But, despite these laments, the decisions were framed with such telling logic and fitted so well the needs of a growing nation that the Old Republican champions of states' rights could find neither ways nor means of matching the arguments of the Chief Justice or of nullifying the impact of his rulings upon the national life.

The eight or ten years immediately following the War of 1812 may be regarded as a period of national affirmation. During these years, the United States laid the basis of a military establishment, pushed the Indians back toward the Mississippi, defined and expanded the national borders, and protected and fostered the business of the country by tariff and financial legislation. Judicial pronouncements strengthened the national government and greatly promoted the development of a national economy. A distinctively American cultural nationalism became a part of American life. President Monroe declared the American continents no longer subject to colonization by European powers and warned Europe not to interfere with the affairs of Spanish America. But, even while the United States was asserting and developing its national strength and its right to a place among the more important nations of the world, the restless push of settlers into the West, the growth of sectional interests and aspirations, and the political rivalries of ambitious men were producing problems that would eventually test the wisdom of statesmen and the strength of the ties that bound the Union together.

Suggested Reading

Aside from the standard works and the biographies of contemporaries mentioned in the previous chapter bibliographies, the following books furnish useful material on the subject of this chapter.

There is a good discussion of cultural nationalism in John A. Krout and Dixon Ryan Fox, *The Completion of Independence, 1790–1830* (1944). See also Harry Warfel, *Noah Webster: Schoolmaster to America* (1936), and E. C. Shoemaker, *Noah Webster* (1936); and George Dangerfield, *The Awakening of American Nationalism* (1965). The reader interested in this subject should also consult Hans Kohn, *American Nationalism* (1957); Ralph Gabriel, *The Course of American Democratic Thought* (1940); and Merle Curti, *The Growth of American Thought* (1951).

On the political parties in the period, see the lively and perceptive Wilfred E. Binkley, *American Political Parties* (1956); George Dangerfield, *The Era of Good Feelings* (1952); and Charles S. Sydnor, "The One-Party Period of American History," *American Historical Review,* LI (April, 1946), 439–451.

On the re-establishment of the Bank of the United States, Ralph C. H. Catterall, *The Second Bank of the United States* (1903) is still decidedly useful, and Bray Hammond, *Banks and Politics in America* (1957) is indispensable.

On diplomatic aspects of the period, see the article by Dexter Perkins, "John Quincy Adams," in Bemis, ed., *The American Secretaries of State and Their Diplomacy,* previously cited, vol. IV (1928), 86–103; Dexter Perkins, *The Monroe Doctrine* (1927); and Bradford Perkins, *Castlereagh and Adams* (1964).

On the judicial aspects of nationalism, see Albert J. Beveridge, *The Life of John Marshall* (4 vols., 1919); E. S. Corwin, *John Marshall and the Constitution* (1919); Charles Warren, *The Supreme Court in United States History* (2 vols., 1937, 1947); and Carl Brent Swisher, *American Constitutional Development* (1954). The great Supreme Court decisions of this period are to be found in J. A. Garraty, ed., *Quarrels That Have Shaped the Constitution* (1964).

14 ⟩ Westward Expansion and the
Growth of Sectionalism,
1790-1830

D URING THE PERIOD from 1790 to 1830, the American population
manifested that propensity for restless movement that has become
one of its marked characteristics. If today half a million Americans
live in trailers, they are only carrying on a tradition that began in colonial
times as the population expanded from the seaboard to the foothills of the
Appalachians, and that was strikingly exemplified
by the westward migration during the first forty
years under the Constitution.

Character and Causes of the Westward Migration

The trek into the trans-Appalachian region that
took place during the early nineteenth century had
been foreshadowed a quarter of a century before. As
early as 1775, pioneers had pushed into Kentucky and Tennessee. It was in
the spring of that year that a few settlers around a stockaded fort in the
Blue Grass region of Kentucky, heard the news of the fighting that had
begun on certain New England commons and determined, in honor of the
event, to name their own town Lexington. But from 1775 to the close of the
century, migration into the trans-Allegheny West was at best a slow affair.
The Revolution itself, the Indian menace, Spanish intrigue and design in

the Mississippi Basin, and the problem of establishing a workable system of government in frontier regions, were all major deterrents to a western movement of any great magnitude. As late as 1790, 94 per cent of the nation's population of four million still lived in the original thirteen states, while only some 240,000 people were located in the West.

The prospects for migration to the West improved somewhat during the latter 1790s. The Jay and Pinckney Treaties minimized the danger of foreign interference with western settlement. Wayne's victory over the Indians at Fallen Timbers and the ensuing treaty of Greenville (1795) opened the way to settlement in the Ohio region. By 1800, pioneer families were pushing into central and western New York, there were 300,000 people in Kentucky and Tennessee, and thousands were moving yearly into the fertile lands of the Ohio region. The first great wave of migration to the West had begun.

The westward movement gathered impetus during the first ten years of the nineteenth century, and by 1810 the population of the trans-Appalachian region was over one million. The War of 1812 put a damper on this movement toward the Mississippi, but not for long. The 1820 census showed a population of nearly two and a quarter million and that of 1830 some 3,700,-000 western citizens. Between 1810 and 1830, the West took over two million people out of the seaboard states, and the movement westward was continuing with unabated vigor.

The migratory waves that flooded into the interior of the continent may be compared to the waves that the tide brings in on an ocean beach—a resistless forward movement, irregular in its outline of advance, seeking always the easiest path into the mainland. And, just as the sea waves contain many different forms of life, the sporadic, ever-changing, ever-shifting waves of migration contained a wide diversity of human elements. Fur traders and trappers, missionaries anxious to convert the heathen, speculators or their agents, and ne'er-do-well backwoodsmen who loved solitude and would move further on when their neighbor's axe was heard in a neighboring clearing, were apt to be the major element in the first wave. Then came an irregular procession of boatmen, drivers, farmers, lawyers, journeymen printers, millers, merchants, blacksmiths, artisans, card sharps, and desperadoes. Some of these were single men, many were young husbands with or without their wives, and there was always a considerable number of hardy, middle-aged family heads who had pulled up stakes and were ready for a new venture in living. At first, these migrants were chiefly Americans but, as the Middle Period wore on, an equally variegated horde of hundreds of thousands of foreigners, chiefly from western Europe, flung themselves into the business of populating western America.

The basic causes of the American westward movement were many and various. It is possible to regard it as a response to drives so deeply imbedded in man's nature that they are beyond analysis. "It were," says Dr. Guglielmo Ferrero, the Italian historian, "as if the whole American nation unconsciously or almost unconsciously was being driven forward by a superior, not to say mystic force, to reach in pain and travail the goal of its destiny." There are, however, other factors, some idealistic and some realistic in character, that explain this great modern exodus more simply.

The direct relationship between westward migration on the one hand and the waning of Indian power and the weakening of foreign influence in the Mississippi Valley on the other has already been noted. But other influences were also at work. Such considerations as the lure of adventure, the belief that more beautiful lands lie beyond the horizon, the attraction that the unknown holds for venturesome and imaginative souls, and that strain of Utopian idealism in mankind which rises to the challenge of building a new social order that will be better than the old, undoubtedly influenced some of the migrants to break loose from their moorings in the East. More important still was the economic urge. Dissatisfaction with the taxation levied for the benefit of the established Congregational church in Massachusetts sent some New Englanders westward, and men of all religious faiths—or of none at all —found it hard to continue tilling the rocky New England hillsides when reports kept coming in about rich and easily cultivated lands that were abundant in western New York and Pennsylvania and Ohio. The New England or Middle Atlantic farmer who tried to buy fertile lands in the East found it selling at up to $50.00 an acre, with the prospect of high taxes to boot. But on the rolling hills and in the valleys of the Appalachian plateau and further west, he could buy plenty of good tax-free land at from $2.00 to $5.00 an acre. Moreover, the planters and farmers in the South Atlantic states were face to face with the specter of soil exhaustion. Erosion (that ever-present menace in the South), the constant cropping by such heavy feeders as corn and tobacco, and, after 1793 and the invention of Eli Whitney's cotton gin, the phenomenal increase in cotton culture had greatly depleted the lands of the Southeast; and the small farmer in that area, as his yields of cotton went down and his profits became marginal, faced damaging competition from the planters who were pushing into the Piedmont and the Great Valley of the Appalachians that stretches between the Blue Ridge and the Appalachian Front. The planter, working on a larger scale than the small farmer, could get along with a much smaller amount of profit per hogshead of tobacco or bale of cotton, and under such circumstances his humbler rival had no choice but to pull up stakes and move on into the richer and more sparsely populated lands of the West.

Finally, as an explanation of the westward movement, it is important to note that travel into the trans-Appalachian region, if still difficult and fraught with danger, was becoming an easier undertaking in the early nineteenth century. Beginning in the 1790s, states and local communities made extensive efforts to improve their roads. The old trails leading to the West were replaced by highways ten to thirty feet wide. These were cleared of underbrush, and, while the largest trees were left standing in the highway, the others were cut off at the level of about eighteen inches from the ground. Primitive though such roads seem to the twentieth century, they were passable for the pioneers. Along such routes went the householder and his family, driving such livestock as they had before them, and with their household goods packed on their backs, slung across a horse or mule, or carried in the rough, cumbersome, but sturdy carts and wagons of the period. When the Ohio was reached, the weary pioneer could load his belongings on a barge, flatboat, or keelboat and float down its broad waters toward his destination.

The Routes of Travel

The voyagers to the West traveled chiefly by four great main routes laid out along river courses and through mountain valleys. The southern route led from the Carolinas through central Georgia and into southern Alabama and Mississippi. Another highway, much used by Virginians and North Carolinians, led to the Cumberland Gap and then into Tennessee and upper Alabama and Mississippi, or by the Wilderness Road into Kentucky. A third avenue of travel, the Ohio River route, took the travelers either by the National (Cumberland) Road to Wheeling on the Ohio, or directly to Pittsburgh and then down the Ohio. Still another path of the pioneers was a route through New York state. Migrants from eastern New York and from New England would gather in Albany, the wagon trains organizing atop the Albany hill, for a westward journey that took them along the Mohawk or the Catskill turnpikes.

Toiling singly, in families, or sometimes in church congregations from New England along the rude highways, the pioneers willingly endured the hardships of the trek for the sake of the future that lay beyond the western horizon. The American ethnologist Henry Rowe Schoolcraft described such a band of travelers on their way to the West not long after the War of 1812:

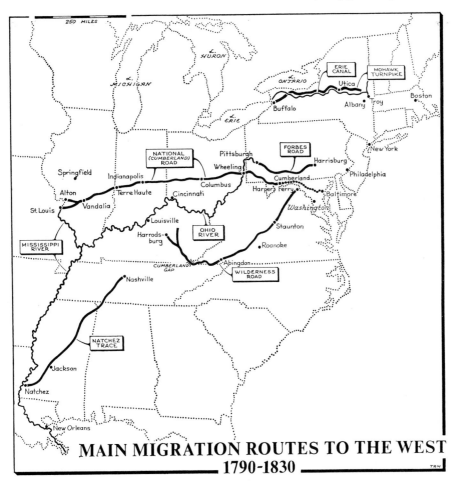

MAIN MIGRATION ROUTES TO THE WEST
1790-1830

The children of Israel could scarcely have presented a more motley array of men and women, with their "kneading troughs" on their backs and their "little ones," than were there assembled, on their way to the land of promise. To judge by the tone of general conversation, they meant, in their generation to plough the Mississippi valley from its head to its foot. There was not an idea short of it. What a wealth of golden dreams was there.

Retreat of the Indians

The relentless surge of these waves of pioneers was made easier by a number of momentous developments. The Indians were pushed further and further into the West. Land speculators acquired vast tracts which they sought to make attractive to settlers by various "hothouse" methods of improve-

COURTESY OF THE MARYLAND HISTORICAL SOCIETY

SCENE ON THE CUMBERLAND ROAD (1817)

Coaches, carriages, covered wagons, and herds of livestock made travel difficult on this artery of western travel. The livestock in the picture are being driven to eastern markets. The covered wagons—whose drivers and passengers have stopped at the Fairview Inn, near Baltimore, for refreshment—are chiefly westward bound.

ment, and federal legislation eased the acquisition of a farm in the public domain. As the West grew in population and in representation in Congress, it battled more and more effectively for other laws that brightened the future for the pioneer.

It was inevitable that the red man should go on yielding before the white. The powerful Iroquois Confederacy that had blocked the path to white settlement in central and western New York was broken up by the punishment it received during the Revolution and the subsequent Indian exodus to Canada. The remnants of the tribes in the Confederation gave up their New York State lands and were settled on small reservations. Many thousands of acres of fertile land were in this way opened to the pioneers. As the tide of white settlement moved into the Old Northwest, the Lake Plains Indians were bought out, and cozened and cajoled on to reservations or pushed beyond the Mississippi. The United States government built an extensive system of garrisoned forts from Detroit to Prairie du Chien in Wisconsin, a display of might which helped to overawe the red man. Indiana, Illinois, and Michigan were almost completely in the hands of the whites by 1822, and still the relentless rolling back of the tribes continued. When the Indians did not give up to the inevitable, as in the case of the Sauks of Wisconsin and Illinois under their leader Black Hawk, the hopelessness of resistance was speedily demonstrated. The Bad Axe massacre (1832) of some 850 men, women, and children in Black Hawk's band showed the Indians of the further regions of the Old Northwest what was likely to happen where there was even a show of resistance. Between 1832 and 1837, some 200 million additional acres of land were secured from the Indians at a cost of approximately $70 million and Iowa and Wisconsin lay open to white settlement.

The Role of the Speculators

As the Indians moved out of New York, Pennsylvania, and the Old Northwest, the speculators moved in. During the 1780s and 1790s, the conflicting claims of New York and Massachusetts to lands in the western part of the former state were settled by mutual agreement, a pre-emption line was surveyed from Sodus on Lake Ontario to the Pennsylvania border between the holdings of the two states, and both sold huge tracts to speculative interests. Two wealthy and influential American speculators and land jobbers named Oliver Phelps and Nathaniel Gorham, a syndicate of English capitalists headed by Sir William Pulteney, and a group of Dutch bankers organized as the Holland Land Company obtained title to a large part of western New York and to fifteen million acres of land in western Pennsylvania. The agents of the speculators laid out town sites and set up gristmills and sawmills. They also advertised extensively and flamboyantly the merits of the region they had to sell, and a considerable migration to those parts, especially from New England, was the result. By 1812, there were 200,000 settlers in western New York, where small but thriving towns such as Geneva, Canandaigua, and Rochester had been established.

Once again, as during the colonial period, speculators were playing both a good and a bad role. In some cases, they were responsible for improvements that made the lot of the pioneer considerably easier and facilitated the settlement of the area. At the same time, their primary objective was to profit by retailing the land to settlers. The prices they charged, ranging from $1.50 to $5.00 an acre were often exorbitant, especially when they had paid from $.07 to $.10 for the same land. They also were wont to hold the best locations for themselves or their favorites, in this way limiting the opportunities and hampering the efforts of those who did the actual work of settling and developing the frontier.

Government Policy and the National Domain

Speculators were active on the national domain, as well as in the lands owned by the individual states. Those hundreds of millions of acres of fertile land that became the property of the national government between 1780 and 1802, and the other millions that came in the Louisiana Purchase, offered glittering possibilities of profit and of gracious livelihood, and presented the federal government with the difficult problem of developing a land policy that would be of maximum benefit to individuals, to the states, and to the nation as a whole.

In establishing a method of disposal for the public lands, Congress had to grapple with several questions. Should the land be regarded primarily as a source of revenue or as an area to be settled as rapidly as possible? The decision here would directly affect the price at which the land would be sold and, consequently, the speed with which it would contribute to the strength of the national economy. Secondly, should the land be sold in large or in small tracts? The latter would facilitate purchase by the average settler, but it would also increase the cost of survey, tend to scatter the settlers and thereby lay them open to Indian depredations, and make it highly probable that the good land would be sold and the government find itself holding vast areas of unproductive domain. Thirdly, should actual occupation be required? To do so would discourage speculators and favor the small buyer, but would be apt to retard purchase and thereby depress the price and lower the nation's revenue. Finally, for how much should the land be sold, and should it be sold for cash or for credit? A low price and a liberal allowance for credit would favor the pioneer, while a high price and cash sales might mean more money for the government but would favor the speculator.

The best liberal thought of the early nineteenth century favored low land prices, or even free land, on the ground that a landowning population was one of the soundest bases for a democracy. Thomas Jefferson, and later Thomas Hart Benton, represented this point of view. The best conservative thought of the period regarded the public domain as a source of revenue to be used by the government for promoting the well-being, the happiness, and the education of all the people. Henry Clay and John Quincy Adams took this point of view. The latter, particularly, wanted the government to maintain a firm control over the public lands so that it could curb speculation, promote orderly settlement, obtain the maximum amount of revenue from its natural resources, and preserve those resources for the benefit of the whole nation. Adams wished to use the land revenues for a comprehensive system of internal improvements, and a modern economic historian has said that his plan "contained the germ of future conservation and land planning."

The government's policy regarding land sales varied widely over the years. The Ordinance of 1785 provided for sale by auction, half in townships and half in sections of 640 acres each, at a minimum price $1.00 an acre. The results in amount of sales were meagre. Auctions were held in New York City, where only a few speculators and no settlers were present. The pioneers who went west simply squatted on unsold land, hoping that time and the government would eventually validate their claims. It was during this period, as a result of strenuous lobbying in Congress, that the Ohio and Scioto Companies were granted millions of acres at actual prices ranging from $.08 to $.66 an acre.

In 1796, Congress passed an act raising the price of public lands to $2.00 an acre, but allowing a year's credit on one-half the cost. The minimum amount that might be purchased was still a section, so that a settler had to pay $1,280 for his farm if he purchased directly from the government—$640 down and the remainder within twelve months. There were many farmers who could not raise this amount, even when they had a year in which to pay half the total sum. The West was dissatisfied, sales languished, and "squatting" flourished.

The first real break for the actual settler came in 1800, when Congress passed a bill sponsored by William Henry Harrison, the first congressional delegate from Ohio Territory. This bill considerably modified the law of 1796 and, in the main, represented western ideas of a good land law. It retained the minimum price of $2.00 an acre, but it lowered the minimum amount of land that could be purchased from 640 to 320 acres, and allowed the buyer to pay down only one-quarter of the purchase price, the rest being paid over a period of four years. The measure also established land offices in the West, at Cincinnati, Chillicothe, Marietta, and Steubenville. Any individual afflicted with land hunger could now purchase a farm for $160.00 down payment, and, just as important, he could make the purchase in the West, rather than at an auction in New York.

The sale of public lands picked up prodigiously after the passage of the Land Act of 1800. "Doing a land office business" became part of the American vocabulary, and Congress was so impressed by the increase in revenue that, in 1804, the minimum amount purchasable was reduced from 320 to 160 acres. Between 1800 and 1811, more than three and a quarter million acres of land were sold in the Northwest.

The operation of the Land Acts of 1800 and 1804 gave a great impetus to the settlement of the West, but by 1820 clamor had once more risen for changes in the national land policy. Both speculators and actual settlers used the credit system to buy more land than they could utilize, and between 1789 and 1819 the government had sold $44 million worth of land but received only one-half of this amount in cash payment. Overextended purchasers of land were continually besieging the government for relief legislation. To their clamors were added those of the increasing numbers of squatters, who had settled on unsurveyed and unsold tracts and who demanded preemption legislation that would give them the first right of purchase for the lands they had improved. Also, after the War of 1812, a situation developed that was full of ominous possibilities. In a great wave of speculative land buying, aided and abetted by the easy money and credit policies of the state banks, thousands of eager purchasers became heavily involved in debt, and many banks were overloaded with mortgages resting on gross overappraisals of land values. The stage was set for an explosion that would add greatly to the woes of the West.

The boom times that followed the War of 1812 lasted only three years. The exuberant land buying of that period was coupled with extravagant purchases of European goods, and European dumping in American markets. The second Bank of the United States, far from checking the speculative mania, actually increased it by its blundering policies. Then, in 1818, the Bank of the United States decided upon a policy of contraction. This brought pressure in turn upon the state banks, and foreclosures of land mortgages became the order of the day. In this same year, cotton glutted the foreign markets, and upland cotton prices declined from $.295 in 1816 to $.24 per pound in 1819 and to $.17 per pound in 1820. The net result of all this was a wave of bankruptcies and unemployment, a collapse of prices, and a general distress that lasted from 1819 to 1822.

Nowhere were the hard times felt more than in the West. There were foreclosures in the country and in the western cities. The Bank of the United States, which came to own a large part of Cincinnati by the foreclosure route—to say nothing of 50,000 acres of fertile farm land in Ohio and Kentucky—became known in the South and West as "The Monster." Benton roared in the Senate that "all the flourishing cities of the West are mortgaged to this money power. . . . They are in the jaws of the monster! A lump of butter in the mouth of a dog! one gulp, one swallow, and all is gone!" Federal as well as state revenues fell off alarmingly, state relief laws became general, and it was only natural that the federal government should respond to the clamor for more money in its own tills and for assistance to the debtors. The result was the Land Acts of 1820 and 1821.

The Land Act of 1820 was a compromise between the demands of western farmers for relief and of those eastern elements which wished to impede the exodus to the West and, in consequence, desired a more conservative land policy. The bill lowered the minimum price of land to $1.25 an acre, and reduced the minimum amount that could be purchased from 160 acres to 80 acres. At the same time, it abandoned the credit feature of previous land legislation, and required complete payment in cash. A settler could buy an eighty-acre farm for $100.00, but he had to be ready to pay down the specified amount. Though the lowering of land prices fostered sales, the elimination of credit terms gave a great advantage to the speculator, the only man who was likely to have any considerable amount of cash in his pocket; nor did it help the settler who faced eviction because of foreclosure. The result was continued dissatisfaction in the West and the passage of the Land Act of 1821.

The Act of 1821 was clearly a relief act. It allowed previous purchasers of land to cancel the purchases for which they had not paid, and to apply payments already made to the purchase of the remainder of their claims. Any interest that might be overdue was remitted.

The legislation of 1820 and 1821 eased but by no means solved the western land situation, and there was a steadily growing demand for a further democratization of land policy. Many men were unable to purchase a farm, even of eighty acres, and much public land remained unsold. State governments complained that their revenues lagged, in part because of unsold and therefore nontaxable public lands, and in part because nonpopulated areas were also nonproductive. It was not long before Senator Benton, the great spokesman of the West, began urging the graduation of land prices, the land to be given to settlers after it had been offered without takers at $.50 an acre. A clamor also arose for a general preemption law that would safeguard the rights of all squatters. Gradually the western point of view was moving toward the idea of converting the public domain into free land for actual settlers.

The West and the Growth of Sectionalism

Despite the defects of the land policy during the period from 1796 to 1821, the West grew by leaps and bounds and began to speak with a more and more authoritative voice in the political and economic affairs of the nation. Of the six new states (Indiana, Illinois, Mississippi, Alabama, Maine, and Missouri) that were admitted to the Union between 1816 and 1821, all save Maine were carved out of the public lands. The population of the western states rapidly increased. That of Ohio doubled between 1810 and 1820, the West, counting Kentucky, Tennessee, and Missouri, but excluding nessee had a total of some one million inhabitants, the population of Indiana numbered 147,000, that of Illinois 55,000, and that of Missouri 66,000. In 1820, the West, counting Kenutcky, Tennessee, and Missouri, but excluding the cotton belt states of the Southwest, contained 19 per cent of the nation's population, and in the Eighteenth Congress, elected in 1822, it had twelve United States Senators and forty members of the House of Representatives. By 1840, the West had 29 per cent of the total population of the country, and in the Twenty-seventh Congress of 1841 it had sixteen Senators and fifty members of the House. Obviously, the West was a section whose aims and aspirations had to be taken into account by the political leaders of the nation. Even by the middle 1820s, its appearance had complicated the problem of maintaining an harmonious national union.

The westerners—whether the wheat farmers of Ohio and northern Indiana and Illinois, or the corn and livestock and tobacco producers of southern Illinois and Indiana, Kentucky, and Tennessee—had well-defined views on certain great economic problems. They wanted cheap public lands, which could be carved into farms for the landless or added at minimal expense to their own acreages. A major part of the western population also felt that the problem of marketing crop surpluses could best be met by a protective tariff that would develop markets in the industrial East. And westerners, lacking reserves of capital and fearful of high taxes, were overwhelmingly in favor of the building of roads and canals at federal expense.

The cotton South, stretching from South Carolina and Georgia across Alabama and Mississippi to Louisiana, looked at national economic policy from its own agrarian point of view. The cotton producers marketed the major part of their product abroad, and purchased in Europe or in the North the manufactured goods that they consumed. They wanted low tariffs on the manufactured articles that they bought, so that their cost could be kept at a minimum. But the possibility of maintaining the tariff at a low level became less and less likely as the South saw itself being steadily outstripped in numbers in Congress. It therefore looked askance at the use of implied powers in the passage of tariff legislation, for sanctioning the use of implied powers meant increasing the authority of the central government. As to public lands, southerners wished to keep their price high, fearing that low land prices would mean decreased national revenues and thereby stimulate the demand for higher tariffs. They also opposed internal improvements at national expense, partly because they had no pressing need for them, partly because such improvements again required loose construction of the Constitution and strengthening of the national government's power, and partly because the improvements would consume so much of the public funds that high tariff duties would be needed to increase the revenues of the federal government.

In the New England and Middle Atlantic states, a powerful industrial interest was stridently demanding protection against the importation of foreign manufactured goods. More and more, too, the northeastern section of the country leaned toward internal improvements at national expense. To be sure, the shipping and commercial classes of New England had little use for such improvements, but eastern industrialists were beginning to favor them, believing that such expenditures would consume the nation's funds and thus make necessary the raising of revenue by higher tariffs. They were also beginning to see internal improvements as a means of developing home markets for their manufactured goods. Finally, the commercialists and industrialists of the East opposed cheap land prices; they feared that cheap land, coupled with internal improvements, would result in an undue drainage of their labor supply.

Sectional interests showed some similarity and some divergence. The East and the West were inclined to favor high tariffs and internal improvements, but differed on the price of public lands. The East and the South favored high priced public lands, but differed on the tariff and internal improvements. The South and the West were generally opposed on all three issues. The result was an increasing conflict of interest between the sections, with ambitious leaders rising to champion each area and to propose a variety of plans and schemes that would combine sectional votes and carry some of the major interests of two sections through the halls of Congress.

One leader who thought he had a plan of procedure that would unite the interests of two sections without unduly arousing the hostility of the third was Henry Clay of Kentucky. Clay developed what he himself called the "American System," defined as being directly opposed to the "foreign" system of free trade. It was built on a protective tariff for industry, so that industry would flourish, stimulating the growth of an urban population capable of consuming the nation's agricultural output. The Kentuckian wished to keep public land prices high enough so that, together with customs revenue, the government would have ample funds for a liberal program of internal improvements. Clay thought of the national government as an agency to be used in promoting the public welfare. He believed that his stand on public land prices, plus the fact that he was a Kentucky slaveholder, would blunt southern dissatisfaction with his program. He did always command considerable support in the South, and he had a great following in New England, the Middle Atlantic states, and the West, but the appeal of his American System was weakened by hosts of conflicting local interests and ambitions, and by southern suspicion of his nationalistic program.

The Struggle over Missouri

The growth of sectionalism during this period was well illustrated by two developments—the struggle over the admission of Missouri to the Union, and the increasing conflict over the tariff. The Missouri crisis was the first to center the attention of the nation.

The rapid march westward of the pioneers had sent thousands of southerners into Missouri, and as early as 1817 they were demanding admission to the Union as a state. An enabling act was presented to the House early in 1819, whereupon Congressman James Tallmadge of New York proposed an amendment forbidding further introduction of slaves in Missouri and freeing all children born of slave parents in that state as soon as they reached the age of twenty-five. This produced a furious contention in Congress, and the Missourians made no progress toward admission as a state during the rest of that year. In December, 1819, a bill was introduced admitting Maine as a free state. The Senate tied this bill to unconditional admission of Missouri, and once again debate between North and South waxed hot and heavy. On February 3, 1820, Senator Jesse B. Thomas of Illinois, a moderate pro-slavery man, proposed admitting Missouri as a slave state, with the provision that the rest of the Louisiana Purchase north of 36° 30′ should be forever free. Maine would be admitted at the same time. This proposal had the support of Henry Clay, at that time Speaker of the House. It was adopted by a narrow margin, and with its adoption the crisis over Missouri appeared to be at an end.

It then developed, however, that the Missouri state constitution prohibited free Negroes and mulattoes from entering the state. When this document was submitted to Congress for approval, the antislavery members refused to recognize Missouri's statehood. The electoral vote for President was counted on February 14, 1821, both with and without the vote of Missouri (at the suggestion of Clay), but only amid scenes of the wildest excitement. Finally a resolution was drawn up declaring that the state must never use its constitution or any of its laws to deprive any citizen of any state of his rights and privileges under the federal Constitution. Largely through Clay's influence, this resolution passed the House by a vote of eighty-seven to eighty-one, and the Senate accepted it, twenty-eight to fourteen. Four months later, the

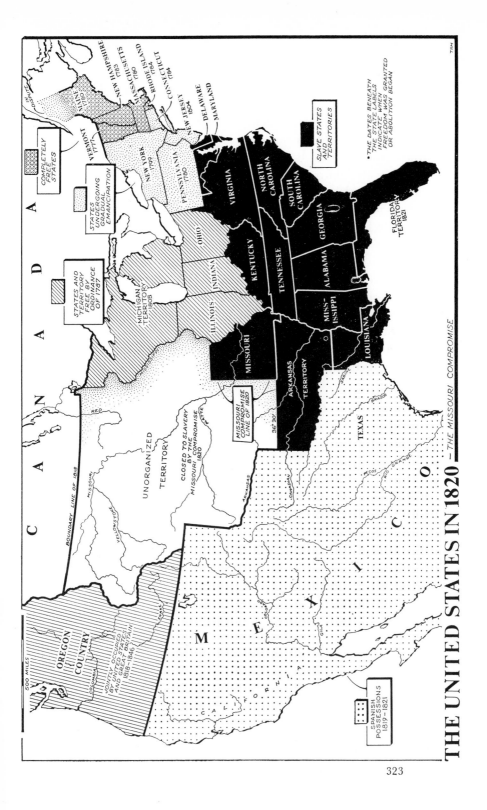

THE UNITED STATES IN 1820 — THE MISSOURI COMPROMISE

- COMPLETELY FREE STATES
- STATES UNDERGOING GRADUAL EMANCIPATION
- STATES AND TERRITORY FREE BY ORDINANCE OF 1787
- SLAVE STATES AND TERRITORIES
- SPANISH POSSESSIONS 1819–1821

*THE DATES BENEATH THE STATE LABELS INDICATE WHEN GRANTED OR FREEDOM WAS ABOLITION BEGAN OR GRADUAL

CANADA

MAINE 1783 (IN DISPUTE)
NEW HAMPSHIRE 1783
MASSACHUSETTS 1780
RHODE ISLAND 1780
CONNECTICUT 1784
NEW JERSEY
DELAWARE
MARYLAND

VERMONT 1777
NEW YORK 1799
PENNSYLVANIA 1780

MICHIGAN TERRITORY 1805
OHIO
INDIANA
ILLINOIS

VIRGINIA
NORTH CAROLINA
SOUTH CAROLINA
GEORGIA
KENTUCKY
TENNESSEE
ALABAMA
MISSISSIPPI
LOUISIANA

FLORIDA TERRITORY 1821

MISSOURI
ARKANSAS TERRITORY

MISSOURI COMPROMISE LINE OF 1820

CLOSED TO SLAVERY BY THE MISSOURI COMPROMISE 1820

UNORGANIZED TERRITORY

BOUNDARY LINE OF 1818

36 30

TEXAS

M E X I C O

OREGON COUNTRY

COUNTRY JOINTLY OCCUPIED BY UNITED STATES AND GREAT BRITAIN 1818–1846

500 MILES

CALIFORNIA

323

Missouri legislature made the required promise, adding that it had no power to bind the state, and in August, 1821, Missouri was admitted to the Union by presidential proclamation.

The struggle over the admission of Missouri was significant for several reasons. With North and South arrayed against each other on the subject of slavery extension, the debates that raged in Congress covered a wide ground. They brought out the moral objections of the North to slavery and the southern moral justification of its "peculiar institution." They revealed northern dislike and southern defense of the three-fifths rule for determining representation in the House of Representatives, a rule counting five slaves as three white men and thereby increasing southern membership in Congress beyond the ratio of the South's white population. They made clear the South's anxiety to maintain its right to expand slavery into new territories, and in that way bolster its membership in Congress. Behind the arguments and attitudes on both sides lay considerations of economic and political advantage for the section involved, and a growing realization that the agrarian, slaveholding South and the free North with its diversified economy had strikingly divergent interests.

The Tariff Becomes a Sectional Issue

The conflict between North and South over slavery extension was bad enough, but the tariff provided another source of sectional discord. When the depression of 1819 spread over the country, it brought, as we have seen, not only popular distress but also a depleted and shrinking national revenue. This latter fact, plus the distress of the manufacturers, produced a movement for a tariff increase. The protectionists argued that raising the general level of the tariff would help develop a home market for wheat and corn as well as cotton and tobacco surpluses, would guard American manufacturers from foreign dumping, and would give more revenue, particularly through such duties as those on sugar, coffee, and salt.

The tariff bill of 1820, framed in response to protectionist ideas, found strong opposition in the South. Lowndes of South Carolina, who had supported the tariff of 1816, was now one of the principal opponents of protection. He denied that the home-market argument had any validity whatsoever, and his words were echoed by other southern Congressmen. The bill passed the House, but failed in the Senate by one vote. The House vote showed New England split, the commercial interests being in opposition and the manufacturing centers favoring the measure. The Middle Atlantic states and the Ohio Valley strongly supported the bill, while the South and Southwest were just as strongly opposed.

After the tariff of 1820 failed of passage, no formidable effort was made until 1824 to revive the movement for increased protection. In that year, with Henry Clay as Speaker of the House, the protectionists made a successful attempt to raise the tariff level. The debate brought from "Harry of the West" one of his best speeches, in which he explained and defended his American System of protection, and argued compellingly for bolstering the national revenue. The bill, as it was finally passed, replaced the 20 to 25 per cent ad valorem level of duties then existing by a 30 to 36 per cent level and raised the tariff on both wool and woolen goods and on lead, glass, and iron. The duties on raw wool and on woolen goods tended to offset one another. It imposed a 25 per cent duty on imported hemp, which was of a better quality than that grown in the United States and was suitable for making cordage and cables, but the only important effect of this duty was to injure the shipbuilding interest.

New England commercial interests, and commercialists everywhere else, opposed the tariff of 1824. The wool growers of Ohio and the Middle Atlantic states, the iron interests of Pennsylvania, the Kentucky hemp growers, and the great majority of manufacturers supported the bill. Once again, the strongest opposition came from the South, which felt that it was being exploited for the advantage of northern manufacturing interests. Only narrow majorities in both houses of Congress could be mustered for the bill. It passed the House by 107 to 102 and the Senate by twenty-five to twenty-one. An analysis of the vote shows an alliance of the Ohio Valley and Middle Atlantic states against the South and Southwest. The vote distribution was very much like that on the question of Missouri's admission. A northern section was forming, one that would become more and more clear-cut as industrialism developed in New England, and the South became finally convinced that its interests were endangered by the northern majority in the House of Representatives.

The Influence of the Frontier on American Life

The westward expansion of the United States did more than complicate the pattern of sectional interests and divisions. It made the frontier a vastly important part of American life. The impact of the frontier on American civilization became more and more apparent as the nineteenth century drew to its close, and in 1893 Frederick Jackson Turner advanced what has been called a "new hypothesis" about the relationship of the frontier to American history.

The frontier itself has been variously defined—sometimes as the advanced line of settlement, sometimes as that area, or areas, where the population was approximately two to the square mile. Turner himself regarded it not as a place but as a continuous process of exploration and settlement pushing across the continent. He believed that the frontier, so conceived, was a great source of nationalism and democracy in the United States. It promoted nationalism because it was the place, par excellence, where a mixing of nationalities readily occurred. It fostered democracy because it was an area where there were neither very rich nor very poor; where the way was open to talent and industry, regardless of birth; and where the strata of society never became widely separated.

Turner found still other virtues in the frontier. As a region which lacked binding traditions and organized restraints, it gave free rein to versatility, ingenuity, and self-reliance. As such, it had had a mighty influence in developing that independent individualism so characteristic of the American people. The needs of the frontier, too, had played an important part in shaping such fundamental policies of government as tariffs, internal improvements, and land legislation. Turner also suggested that the frontier had acted as an outlet for the eastern masses, who were oppressed by lack of opportunity to rise in the crowded urban centers. It had, therefore, been a "safety valve" for social discontents. Thus Turner explained why radical social theories, especially Marxian concepts, had never taken deep root in America.

Turner's hypothesis was taken up by an enthusiastic band of disciples. They overdeveloped certain aspects of it, the "safety valve" theory in particular, and took extreme positions that have been refuted by later scholarly research. Indeed, the frontier hypothesis in general has been subjected to a barrage of criticism.

The critics of Turner's theory have pointed out that he never made clear his conception of either the frontier or democracy, and that in consequence his work suffered from lack of a definition of terms. He never explained why the southern frontier, where slavery flourished, should be described as either democratic or a process making for democracy. He tended to underestimate or ignore European influences on American character and American thought; eighteenth-century European rationalism and nineteenth-century European romanticism, for example, certainly contributed to the development of American nationalism and to American ideas about the democratic process. European economic thought—the writings of Adam Smith, the Physiocrats, and the nineteenth-century classical economists—also had considerable impact upon American economic concepts, but Turner neglected these factors, and they were minimized or ignored by his more extreme disciples.

Turner's critics have also questioned the thesis that the frontiersman was more individualistic than the eastern entrepreneur or reformer. They point out the likelihood that the existence in America of a rapidly expanding economy, rather than the frontier, was the real reason for the development of American individualism. Certainly the concept of the frontier as the great source of individualism is somewhat belied by the eagerness with which frontiersmen looked to Washington for help in getting cheap land, internal improvements, protective tariffs, and aid in sweeping back the Indians. And the "safety valve" idea has been to a large extent discredited by the fact that urban dwellers, especially when times were hard, had neither the funds nor the propensity for pulling up stakes and moving into the West and a life with whose techniques they were completely unfamiliar. In fact, between 1860 and 1900 despite periods of urban depression and unemployment, the population movement in America was from the country to the city, rather than in the opposite direction.

The thesis has recently been developed that urban proletarian forces have had great significance in the development of American life; that the working classes of eastern cities were influential in the development of the democratic process; and that western cities, such as Pittsburgh, Cincinnati, Lexington, and Louisville, as early as 1815–1820 exerted considerable influence upon American life. These cities were centers of commerce, finance, and budding industry, and therefore had considerable economic power. They, as well as the rural frontier, had a significant role to play in the social and cultural development of the West, and they exerted not a little influence upon local and national politics.

Finally, Turner's propensity to idealize the frontiersman has been subjected to sharp attack. It has been justly pointed out that by no means all dwellers on the frontier were highminded men and women; that living conditions in the West fostered crudity and brutality; and that many frontiersmen were rough, reckless, careless people, whose morals were decidedly easy and who were wasteful of soil, timber, game, domestic animals, and even of human life.

But though much legitimate criticism has been leveled at the frontier hypothesis, a considerable part of it has survived attack. No one today would question that the frontier movement had an important part to play in the expansion of American territory. The evidence is overwhelming that the frontier was both a democratic and a nationalistic force, which operated with little thought of or dependence upon Europe. The frontiersmen were bold and imaginative. There was a high proportion of young couples in the frontier regions, and these young men and women, with their zest for living and dreams of a better future, provided a valuable dynamic for American society. The frontier West at least rivaled the East in furnishing a great impetus to education through the formulation of a definite ideal of statewide, democratic schooling that extended from the common school up to the state university. And if the frontier was not the safety valve for American labor pictured by Turner's disciples, it may at least be regarded as having had some indirect effect upon the labor force. It gave the laboring man a psychological outlet ("If I had the gumption, I, too, could go West") and, by attracting eastern farmers and European farmer-immigrants, it prevented concentrations of population in eastern urban centers that would have been provocative of radical thought and action.

For better or for worse, the rapidly growing, rough, rude, and ebullient West was helping to shape American life and character. Painfully, with much woe and much achievement, it was becoming a granary for the nation and for Europe, a potential center for an industrial development which would rival that of the East, and a voice in the nation's councils. There could be no question of its high political significance, for the presidential election of 1824 was largely a struggle among the candidates for western support.

Suggested Reading

The causes and character of the westward migration are dealt with in Robert Riegel, *America Moves West* (1956); Roy M. Robbins, *Our Landed Heritage* (1942); and Thomas D. Clark, *Frontier America, The Story of the Westward Movement* (1959), an excellent account.

The routes of travel are fully described in Archer B. Hulbert, *Historic Highways of America* (16 vols., 1902–1905) and Charles H. Ambler, *A History of Transportation in the Ohio Valley* (1932). The Erie Canal, completed in October, 1825, promptly became an important waterway between East and West. The story of this canal is told in Ronald Shaw, *Erie Water West: A History of the Erie Canal, 1792–1854* (1966), an indispensable study.

The Indian retreat is portrayed in Annie H. Abel, "Indian Consolidation," American Historical Association, *Annual Report, 1906* (1908), 235–454, and Henry P. Beers, *The Western Military Frontier* (1935).

The role of the speculator is graphically described in Billington, *Westward Ex-*

pansion (rev. ed., 1960) and the volumes by Clark and Riegel listed above. For one of the outstanding speculative developments, see Paul D. Evans, *The Holland Land Company* (1924).

Government policy and the national domain is well developed in Benjamin H. Hibbard, *A History of the Public Land Policies* (1924) and Payson J. Treat, *The National Land System, 1785–1820* (1910).

Much information on the West as a new section and on sectional aims is to be found in Roscoe C. Buley, *The Old Northwest, Pioneer Period, 1815–1840* (2 vols., 1950); John E. Wright and Doris S. Corbett, *Pioneer Life . . . in Western Pennsylvania* (1940); James M. Miller, *The Genesis of Western Culture* (1938); Frederick J. Turner, *The Significance of Sections in American History* (1932) and *The Rise of the New West* (new ed., 1958); and Charles S. Sydnor, *The Development of Southern Sectionalism, 1819–1848* (1948). See also Glyndon G. Van Deusen, *The Life of Henry Clay* (1937); Thomas P. Abernethy, *From Frontier to Plantation in Tennessee* (1932); Everett Dick, *The Dixie Frontier* (1948); Richard C. Wade, *The Urban Frontier* (1959); and P. W. Gates, *The Farmer's Age* (1960).

The Missouri Compromise is treated in Van Deusen's *Clay*, Sydnor's *Development of Southern Sectionalism*, and Frank H. Hodder's "Sidelights on the Missouri Compromise," American Historical Association, *Annual Report, 1909* (1911), 151–161. The best full treatment of the subject is Glover Moore, *The Missouri Compromise* (1953).

For the tariff issue in the early 1820s, see Frederick J. Turner, *Rise of the New West* (new ed., 1959) and Frank W. Taussig, *The Tariff History of the United States* (1923).

The literature on the Turner hypothesis is voluminous. Basic are Frederick J. Turner, *The Frontier in American History* (new ed., 1948) and *Rise of the New West*. Different points of view and conflicts of opinion regarding the hypothesis are well indicated in George R. Taylor, ed., *The Turner Thesis Concerning the Role of the Frontier in American History* (1956).

15 ⸱ The Era of Bad Feelings, 1822-1828

DURING THE SECOND TERM of the presidency of James Monroe, the "Era of Good Feelings" came to an end. These four years also marked the last stage of the Jeffersonian Republican party, as it had come to be by the early 1820s. We have seen, beginning with President Jefferson's first term and continuing to 1815, how that party took on many of the aspects of Federalism. The same trend con-

End of the Old Republican Party

tinued after the War of 1812. Madison willingly signed the Republican bill re-establishing a national bank. Monroe himself was an avowed "amalgamation man," a fusionist who sought to bring moderate Federalists and Republicans together into harmonious support of his administration. He was careful to express a decent regard for states' rights, and he vetoed an internal improvements bill in 1822 on constitutional grounds. But he also urged increased protection for domestic manufactures, signed the protective tariff of 1824, recognized the West's demand for internal improvements by signing a General Survey bill (April 30, 1824) for the development of national communications, and accepted a measure authorizing Congress to subscribe $300,000 to the Chesapeake and Delaware Canal Company (March 3, 1825). The right kind of government, as Monroe visualized it, was an amalgam of respect for the rights of the states with such expansion of the powers of the central government as was clearly necessary for the public good.

The other Republican leaders in the 1820s, and the Republican rank and file, differed as to the wisdom of this amalgamation. Such Federalized Republicans as Clay and Calhoun approved it, but Madison and Jefferson, the elder statesmen of the party, looked upon it askance, as, in part, did Monroe's Secretary of the Treasury—a big, burly Georgian named William Harris Crawford, who professed a deep regard for states' rights, though in other respects he was a fusionist. Still another politician, a New Yorker, was seeking, or professed to seek, a return to the Republican first principles of 1798. Suave and self-possessed, this man had established a name for himself as a skillful manipulator of political adjustments, and in 1821 became a United States senator. He was Martin Van Buren of Kinderhook. All of these men, save Madison and Jefferson, were intensely ambitious of political preferment.

It is sometimes stated that the breakup of the "Era of Good Feelings" into one of intense and bitter political rivalry had its origins deep in the social and economic developments of the time. The people, it is alleged, were beginning to feel that the noble experiment, begun in the Revolution against Great Britain and rescued from the Federalists in 1800, was in danger of being abandoned like a waif on a doorstep. For Federalized Republicanism now supported the very industrial and moneyed interests against which it had fought in the 1790s. Its leaders had reinstituted that money power, the Bank of the United States, and were pampering the manufacturers behind a wall of protection. The party, as a national entity, was doing nothing for the western debtors, hard hit by the depression of 1819–1822, nor was it catering to the urban proletarians in the rapidly growing eastern cities, or to the southern planters and farmers. The Republican leadership—so runs this thesis—was no longer interested in agrarian democracy as the one sound basis for the nation's life. It had lost touch with the democratic idealism of the Republicans of 1798.

It is true enough that the Republican party in the early 1820s bore many resemblances to the Federalism of old, but concrete evidence is lacking that this fact produced any popular revolt against it during Monroe's second term, or any demand for a new party organized for the redress of grievances. There was no question, during the period from 1820 to 1824, of developing any new political organization, though there was deep popular discontent with existing social, economic and, to a limited extent, political conditions.

Western debtors and eastern proletarians, businessmen, and southern planters as well, were looking for relief, and for constructive leadership in meeting the problems of the day. There were omens of a rising democratic storm. Most of the states recently admitted to the Union had come with complete manhood suffrage, the older states were ending their voting restrictions, and the common man was beginning to take more interest in the democratic process. Local parties were springing up to deal with local problems. A dislike of the legislative caucus as a method of nominating political candidates was making itself felt. Sectional aims and interests were growing sharper and more clear-cut. Change was in the air.

Monroe was not the man to guide the Republican party in the face of these developments. Ineffectual as a leader, suffering from the fact that the third-term tradition was now in full force, and unable to control factional struggles in the Congress, his influence upon the course of immediate political events deteriorated from the moment of his re-election. Far from his being able to name his successor, it was obvious that the road to the presidency was open to any man who could command a large enough national following, and four outstanding candidates soon appeared, anxious to reach the highest office in the land.

Presidential Aspirants in 1824

John Quincy Adams was the favorite candidate of New England. He had a distinguished name and great experience in public affairs. He had served for over five years as United States Senator from Massachusetts, for eight years as Secretary of State, had been a member of the peace commission at Ghent, and at various times had been United States Minister to the Netherlands, Prussia, Russia, and England. Adams could temporize when the need was great, but on the whole was a man of high principle and great integrity. He had undoubted competence for holding office, and a deserved reputation as an ardent nationalist. His political and social philosophy was fundamentally conservative.

The South had two candidates for the White House. William Harris Crawford was a popular Georgian, Secretary of the Treasury under Monroe, an old Jeffersonian in his attitude toward states' rights, but a moderate fusionist in his stand on tariffs, internal improvements, and the Bank of the United States. He had wanted to supplant Monroe in 1820, and since that time his relations with the President had become anything but cordial. In one stormy interview he called Monroe "you damned, infernal old scoundrel"; in reply, the President grabbed a pair of fire tongs and threatened to have the servants throw his visitor out of the White House.

The other southern candidate was John C. Calhoun, Secretary of War.

He was still a nationalist, an advocate of the Bank, moderate tariffs, and internal improvements, one who disliked Crawford's trumpeting of states' rights and hated the Georgian for his vicious attacks upon the management of the War Department. If there was anything Calhoun wanted more than the presidency, it was to keep Crawford from gaining that coveted prize.

The West also had two candidates for the presidency in the election of 1824. Henry Clay came back to Congress in 1823, where he was promptly and overwhelmingly elected Speaker of the House. He longed for the White House with a mighty longing, his key to its door being his American System. That System, as one observer has acutely remarked, was not a clarion call to the political wars, for it appealed to the reason more than to the emotions of men. In the eyes of the South, moreover, it was a vicious proposal that would beggar the planter to enrich the northern industrialist. But "Harry of the West" had been a War Hawk and a member of the Ghent peace commission, was both charming and masterful as a congressional leader, and had thousands of devoted followers in Kentucky, along the Ohio, and in the New England and Middle Atlantic states.

The other western candidate was Andrew Jackson. Born March 15, 1767, probably in South, rather than North Carolina, he came of sturdy, Scotch-Irish farm parentage. As a boy in the Revolution he was captured by the British, and he carried to his grave on hand and head the scars of wounds inflicted by an officer's sabre when he refused to black that gentleman's boots. He was successively a saddler's apprentice, a school teacher, and, at twenty, a lawyer before the North Carolina bar. A year or so later he migrated to Tennessee, with, according to tradition, two horses, a pair of fox hounds, and a Negro slave girl. In Tennessee, he quickly rose among the frontier aristocrats, a group always ready with argument and pistol and with an eye to the main chance. He was a judge in the Tennessee courts, a sound-money man who distrusted the masses, opposed relief laws, and generally sided with the haves against the have-nots. Like his fellow aristocrats of the frontier, he distrusted the business aristocrats of the East.

One success followed another in Jackson's career. He was a United States attorney at twenty-three, a congressman at twenty-nine, a United States Senator at thirty, and a Justice of the Supreme Court of Tennessee at thirty-one. He was an Indian fighter of renown and had whipped the British at New Orleans. His main interests were in land speculations, frontier business ventures, and military glory. His Revolutionary experiences had bred in him a fierce patriotism which never left him, for he was an obstinate, opinionated man who seldom lost a conviction, once formed. He had great personal courage and could be grave, courteous, and gentle in demeanor. He had great loyalty, and demanded loyalty in return. Not an intellectual, his views were formed by his austere code of honor, his simplicity of perception, and the advice of those he trusted, rather than as the result of profound thought and meditation.

Old Hickory did not have many convictions on the issues of the day. He was a moderate protectionist who wanted a tariff high enough to safeguard the home market and to make the United States economically independent in time of war. He probably regarded both the Bank of the United States and internal improvements as unconstitutional. Such theories of government as he held were close to those of 1798. He did believe that the United States was and should remain a land of opportunity for all, but he had no real understanding of the fundamental trends in the national economy. His lack of a clearly thought-out philosophy of government did him no harm politically. Far more important, from the point of view of his political availability, was the fact that he was a military hero and a terror to the Indians.

Jackson had shown no early aspirations for the presidency. In 1821, he declared that he was not fit to be President, but by the summer of 1822 he was a candidate for the White House. His Tennessee friends put him forward with shrewdness and enthusiasm, not as an economically successful westerner, but as a man of the people who had served his country brilliantly on the field of battle, who hated caucus nominations, and was a devotee of popular rule. The Tennessee legislature endorsed him for the presidency in July, 1822, and elected him to the United States Senate in 1823, and a Jackson boom began to grow in other states.

The Struggle for the Succession

The presidential campaign was in full swing by 1822. Everywhere candidates were being nominated by state legislatures and by mass meetings of the people, and the city of Washington was full of political intrigues. Crawford and Calhoun were sparring with one another in and out of the Cabinet, and in the South as well. Clay in the House of Representatives and Jackson in the Senate were hard at work marshaling friends and supporters, while they pretended friendship for one another. Secretary of State Adams would not intrigue, but his principles allowed him to offer foreign posts to all of his rivals, offers that were politely but firmly refused.

The list of candidates had narrowed somewhat by 1824. Calhoun, the nationalist, had no special basis for appeal to narrow sectional ambitions and prejudices even in the South. His hopes were blasted by failure to obtain the endorsement of such crucial states as Pennsylvania and New York, and he withdrew from the race, content to accept a vice-presidential nomination for which there was no other powerful contender. Crawford remained in the running for the presidency, but his hopes were dimmed when, in the fall of 1823, he suffered a paralytic stroke that left him helpless and nearly blind for weeks. He recovered somewhat during the following winter. Virginia stood by him, as did New York, where Martin Van Buren kept his banner aloft, but his physical and mental condition played into the hands of the remaining aspirants.

THE FOOT-RACE (1824)

On the left, John Quincy Adams, Crawford, and Jackson are shown running a close race for the White House. John Adams cheers on "our son Jack," while a supporter of the General shouts "hurra for our Jackson." Clay, on the right of the picture, has given up the race.

By 1824, the race for the White House was reaching its final stages, and the supporters of all the candidates were descending to personal vituperation. Clay was portrayed as immoral, reckless, and without principle. The followers of Calhoun denounced Crawford and saw their candidate denounced in turn. Anti-Jackson orators declared that he was a tyrant, a man of violent and uncontrollable impulses. Adams was assailed by accusations that varied from the charge of being an aristocrat to the allegation that he went to church barefoot. At the same time, all sorts of combination tickets for President and Vice President, such as Clay and Adams and Adams and Jackson, were tried. In many places in the South a favorite ticket was:

> John Quincy Adams
> Who can write
> And Andrew Jackson
> Who can fight.

Adams himself favored putting Jackson in the vice presidency. As Adams told a friend, it was "a station in which the General could hang no one, and in which he would need to quarrel with no one." But such tickets were either daydreams or local and transient.

But, despite the effort to whip up interest in the election by name-calling and the use of combination tickets, the voters remained apathetic. The national average of voter participation in the 1824 contest was only 26.5 per cent. This was probably due to the collapse of a clear-cut two-party system, the large number of avowed candidates, and, in most states, the elimination of any real contest because of the great popularity of one or another of the contestants.

Crawford's chances, dimmed as they were by his illness, had a further setback when he was nominated by a rump congressional caucus on February 14, 1824. Only sixty-six out of 216 congressional Republicans attended this caucus. Its principal significance was its demonstration of the growing unpopularity of this means of choosing candidates. But, though the Georgian slipped further and further behind, he was still very much in the running.

A curious mischance now took Clay out of the race. The choice of presidential electors by the New York state legislature was at hand. The Adams and Clay supporters in the legislature were prevailed upon by Thurlow Weed, a rising young politician from Rochester, to accept a split ticket which would give "Harry of the West" seven of the state's electoral votes. That number, it was calculated, would be enough, added to those he would receive from other parts of the country, to insure his name going into the congressional election. This ticket won in the New York state legislature and, had it remained intact, Clay would have tied Crawford for third place in the election. But when the New York electors met in December, 1824, three of the supposed Clay men defected. As a result, the vote in the electoral college stood Jackson ninety-nine, Adams eighty-four, Crawford forty-one, and Clay thirty-seven. Since no man had a clear majority, according to the twelfth

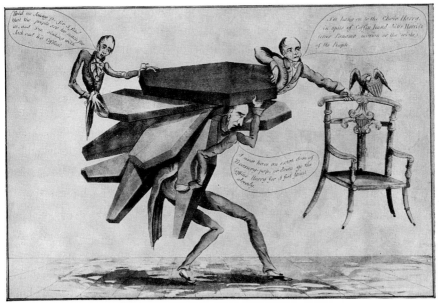

THE PEDLAR AND HIS PACK

This pro-Jackson cartoon of the election of 1828 shows Adams, Clay, and editor John Binns, who circulated the "coffin hand-bills" representing the coffins of soldiers shot by order of General Jackson. They were supposed to symbolize Jackson's tyrannical nature. Quite correctly, the cartoon shows the hand-bills as a burden to Adams' Administration; they created sympathy for Old Hickory.

amendment the names of the first three in number of votes would go before the House of Representatives, where one of them would be chosen President of the United States. But Henry Clay was not one of the first three.

Was It Bargain and Sale?

Congress convened early in December, 1824, amid scenes of wild political excitement. It was generally recognized that Clay's influence would be decisive in choosing the next President, and the supporters of all three candidates assiduously courted him. Actually, he had made up his mind to vote for Adams before he left Kentucky for Washington, and by December had so informed a number of friends and acquaintances. Lafayette, then visiting in the United States, was one of those Clay took into his confidence. The Kentuckian felt that health alone was enough to rule out Crawford. As for Jackson, there could be small reason to vote for a western rival whose chief claim to fame, in Clay's opinion, lay in "killing 2,500 Englishmen at New Orleans." On the other hand, Adams was from New England, where Clay wished to build up his own strength, and the two men had generally similar views on both domestic and foreign policy. Decided though he was, however, Clay had not made any public pronouncement, nor had he spoken directly to Adams about his course of action; but this conversation was not long delayed.

On January 9, 1825, Henry Clay called on John Quincy Adams and was closeted with him for three hours while they exchanged views on the great public questions of the day. Clay stated that he would come out for Adams when it seemed to him the proper moment had arrived. If when the two men parted, a bargain had been struck, it was in the most general terms. It is more likely that the meeting had resulted in a general understanding, an entente cordiale, from which a closer relationship might easily flow, for, as both men recognized, the situation was a delicate one. Some two weeks before, Adams had written in his diary, "incedo super ignes," and the two men certainly walked over fires that January night. Shortly thereafter, Clay wrote to a close friend and kinsman that no offer of position had been made to him, but he also made clear his conviction that he could have any post in the Cabinet that he chose to fill.

Adams' stock rose, following his conversation with Clay. Ohio's congressional delegation, among whom Clay's influence was strong, decided to go for Adams. On January 24, both Ohio and Kentucky announced that they would vote for Adams, and Crawford and Jackson newspapers began attacking Clay for having sold the West and himself for the succession. Clay was supporting Adams, they declared, in return for being made Secretary of State. The shape of things to come was already apparent.

The House balloted on February 9. It voted by states, the majority of each delegation determining the vote of the state, and thirteen were necessary for election. Adams had surely twelve states, but the New York state delegation stood seventeen for Adams, sixteen opposed, and one—General Stephen Van Rensselaer—doubtful. The General was an Old Federalist and inclined to Crawford, but Adams had assured him that he would not proscribe Federalists, if elected, and Clay and Webster had harrowed his feelings by picturing the terrible consequences, if there were no election. As the ballot box neared his desk, Van Rensselaer dropped his head in prayer. Opening his eyes, he saw lying on the floor a ticket bearing the name of one of the candidates. It looked like the answer to prayer, and he picked it up and dropped it in the box. This gave New York State and the presidency to John Quincy Adams.

John Quincy Adams

A brilliant conservative, Adams was not a great President. His high place in history is due to his diplomatic skill, the part he played in forging the Transcontinental Treaty and the Monroe Doctrine, and his distinguished service in Congress after he left the White House.

"King John the Second"

The sixth President of the United States was five feet seven inches tall, and stout, for he weighed close to 180 pounds. He was fifty-seven years old, bald, with a round face and black eyes. Adams was fond of good living. A connoisseur of Madeira wines, at a dinner party he once identified eleven out of the fourteen vintages that his host brought to the table. But he was also a slave to duty and, though under pressure he could temporize, in the long run a slave to conscience as well. An ambitious and prodigious worker, he found time to keep a voluminous diary, to read widely in history, philosophy, and poetry, and to take a deep interest in science, painting, and sculpture. He was one of the finest diplomats that the United States has produced. He was also self-righteous, censorious of all men, including himself, introverted, humorless, and, as events were to prove, woefully inept as a political leader.

On the evening of the day of his election, February 9, Adams went to a reception already scheduled at the White House. Jackson was there, and the two men greeted one another calmly, almost cordially. For a few days quiet reigned, but it was like the calm preceding an electrical storm.

Adams offered the State Department to Clay on February 12, and eight days later Clay accepted the office. When he heard this news, Jackson's wrath boiled over. The General had stood high in the popular vote, 153,544 againt 108,740 for Adams and a total for Old Hickory's three opponents of 202,494. Six states (Vermont, New York, Delaware, South Carolina, Georgia, and Louisiana) chose their presidential electors in their legislatures, and therefore between a quarter and a third of the qualified voters in the country had been unable to express a preference among the candidates. This, together with the fact that only about one in four of those privileged to vote had gone to the polls, made it difficult to determine the popularity of any one candidate among the rank and file, but Jackson was convinced that he was the choice of the people. Now, however, Adams had been chosen President through Clay's influence in the House of Representatives, and Clay had been made Secretary of State. It was clear to Old Hickory that this could only be the result of an infamous bargain, a deliberate thwarting of the popular will. "The Judas of the West," he wrote to a friend, "has closed the contract and will receive the thirty pieces of silver." He vowed hostility to both Adams and Clay, and his partisans began a drumfire of accusation about "bargain and sale" that was used at appropriate times throughout Clay's lifetime. In becoming Secretary of State, Clay had made one of the greatest blunders of his long political career.

Adams' Program and Its Reception

Adams was a minority President, but he sought to be the leader, not of any party or group of interests, but of the whole people. "Like George Washington," says his latest and best biographer, "he did not believe in parties or in sections, the essential realities of American politics . . . and they did not believe in him." Adams, nevertheless, had some very definite ideas about his role as President. His great objective was to promote the strength and continental power of the American nation. He also felt that personal liberty in the United States was more secure than property. To safeguard the latter, he wanted a stout and equitable bankruptcy law, the continuation of the Bank of the United States, and a strong national government willing and able to use its authority in promoting the national welfare. Sectionalism should be curbed by the development of a great national program of internal improvements and the use of the public lands for the benefit of the whole people. The government should provide a tariff high enough to guard manufacturers against excessive foreign competition and to provide national self-sufficiency in time of war. The government should have a department of the interior which would be of assistance in promoting such ends as the development of general public education, the establishment of a national university, geographical discoveries, and the advancement of scientific knowledge. He spoke feelingly of the fact that, while Europe had 130 astronomical observatories, the United States had not a single one of "these lighthouses of the skies."

Adams' general program, as outlined in his first message to Congress in 1825, struck a sour note in many quarters. The South was aghast at the spectacle conjured up by the President of a vigorous national government steadily expanding its influence and control over the country, and westerners disliked the President's support of the Bank of the United States. The phrase "lighthouses of the skies" was made the subject of ribald comment.

The defeated presidential candidates and their coteries promptly seized upon these and other points as a basis for criticizing the Chief Executive and his Secretary of State. Vice President Calhoun intrigued tirelessly against Adams, and the Crawford, Calhoun, and Jackson factions began to draw together. Gradually they formed a new political party, supposedly devoted to returning to the first principles of the Republican party—those of 1798. Martin Van Buren had an active hand in these proceedings, the movement was skillfully organized, and it prospered. At first it was simply called the Opposition, but after it had gained control of the House of Representatives in the 1826 elections it was known as the Democratic-Republican party, or simply as the Democratic party. Its leaders dedicated it to retrenchment and reform in the national government and to the overthrow of the Adams-Clay party, whose members called themselves National Republicans; this party was composed of the supporters of the Administration, but was poorly organized and weak.

One of the great difficulties facing the Adams Administration was that it was theoretically the head of a party that was actually breaking in two. Adams inherited, not a compact and well-organized political machine, but one that was falling into pieces that ambitious politicians were eager to pick up and put together for their own advantage. Of his rivals in 1824, only Clay remained loyal to him, and Congress was full of dissident and rebellious elements which he could not control. He also declined to go about the arduous business of building up a corps of loyal party leaders who could be depended upon to keep in line the rank and file. He stood doggedly by the merit system, refusing, unlike Clay, to remove officials who were clearly working in the interest of his enemies. The consequence was that the National Republican organization never gained strength, complaints from his supporters swelled in volume, and many of the complainants deserted to the Opposition.

From that Opposition, Adams met a mounting barrage of criticism and factious assault. Southerners denounced his nationalism with increasing violence; they felt, as John Randolph plainly said, that, if Congress had the power to do what Adams wanted done, it could easily emancipate the slaves and might even do so if the northern majorities grew large enough. Crawfordites, Calhounites, and Jacksonites jibed and jeered at the proposal for a national bankruptcy law, the proposed department of the interior, the national university, and the "lighthouses in the skies." They proposed constitutional amendments, such as one limiting the appointment of congressmen to federal office, that were designed to keep alive the charge of bargain and sale. They industriously circulated reports that the President was wasting the people's money. When Adams bought with his own funds a set of chessmen costing $23.50 and a billiard table with balls and cues costing $61.00, his critics declared that these had been paid for out of the public treasury, and that they showed the President's propensity for gambling. Adams at a Baltimore banquet gave a toast in which General Ross's "coat of arms" and the militia which had faced him were characterized as "Ebony and Topaz" (the spirit of Evil as opposed to the spirit of Good); the allusion was so involved and obscure that it gave opportunity for derisive comment, and thereafter a nickname for the President was "Old Ebony."

With admirable impartiality, the Opposition devoted itself to attacks upon Clay as well as upon Adams. No sooner were the plans of the Secretary of State for foreign policy announced than they ran into a storm of congressional criticism, and the attacks upon Clay's character were unceasing, with "bargain and sale" the continual cry. In vain Clay published a lengthy vindication of his conduct, for it was made the basis for fresh sneers and innuendoes. In vain Harvard gave him a LL.D. in 1825, in recognition of his character and achievements. The blasts against "Bargain, Management, and Intrigue" continued, and in March, 1826, John Randolph brought matters to a temporary climax.

Randolph rose in the Senate and, in his shrill voice, denounced both Adams and Clay for corruption. He accused them of crucifying "this miserable Constitution of ours" and of making an unholy alliance. "I was defeated, horse, foot, and dragoons," cried the Virginian, "cut up . . . and clean broke down . . . by the coalition of Blifil and Black George . . . by the combination, unheard of till then, of the Puritan with the black-leg." The allusion to characters in Fielding's *Tom Jones* made this attack the more biting, and Clay challenged Randolph to a duel. It took place on April 8,

1826, just across the Potomac from Georgetown and at ten paces. Each man fired twice, and Clay's bullets pierced Randolph's voluminous dressing gown but did not wound him. Randolph fired his second shot in the air. Then the men shook hands. "Honor" was satisfied, but the attacks on Clay continued from other quarters.

General Collapse of the Administration's Program

As the troubled years of his Administration slipped away, John Quincy Adams saw his program for action disappear in the sloughs of political factionalism. Congress paid no attention to his plea for setting up a national system of internal improvements. It did appropriate some $2 million for repairing the Cumberland road and for various canal and harbor projects, but in a piecemeal and haphazard fashion. Intriguing, logrolling, jamming, hesitating, invoking the specter of states' rights, it produced nothing that remotely resembled Adams' project for a great network of roads and canals built at national expense. Vexed and helpless, the President saw one of his most cherished dreams vanishing into thin air.

The Administration's record in foreign affairs was equally disappointing. Clay could get no satisfaction from the French regarding damages to American commerce arising from the French Revolutionary and Napoleonic wars, and dilatory action by the United States in making concessions to British commerce resulted in the closing of British West Indian commerce to American shipping. Clay was unable to obtain a reversal of London's policy, and this furnished political capital for the congressional Opposition. But worst of all was the hullabaloo raised over sending American representatives to the Congress of Panama.

The Panama Congress

Clay and Adams were anxious to extend America's influence in the southern hemisphere, not only for the purpose of developing democratic institutions in Latin America, but also for purposes of trade. Simon Bolivar, the Spanish American patriot and liberator, had long cherished the idea of bringing the South American states together in a federation for the insurance of liberty and peace, and in December, 1824, an invitation had gone out to the principal Latin American states for a meeting at Panama. Great Britain had been invited to this gathering, and in the spring of 1825 Mexico and Colombia inquired as to whether the United States would come to Panama.

Clay was enthusiastically in favor of attending the Panama Congress. Adams was more cautious, but finally accepted the invitation. Congress was so informed in December, 1825, and the names of Richard C. Anderson and John Sergeant as delegates were sent to the Senate for its approval.

Politics now took a hand in the game. Southerners argued that the Panama meeting would be inimical to slavery, isolationists quoted Washington's Farewell Address warning against foreign entanglements, and states' rights advocates declared that participation meant increasing the power of the national government. Van Buren, among others, asserted that such a meeting menaced the sovereignty of the United States. Approval of the delegates, and the necessary appropriations for their expenses, were delayed for months. As a result, neither Anderson nor Sergeant reached the conference. The former died en route, and the latter, learning that the conference had adjourned, never made the trip to Panama.

The debates and the voting in Congress on American participation in the Congress of Panama showed that a new political party was being formed, with Calhoun and Van Buren among its chief architects. The latter was busy forging that alliance of southern planters with the "plain republicans of the North" that was to be the core of the Democratic organization in its first years.

Public Lands Policy

Adams' desire to use the public lands as a source of revenue for internal improvements ran counter to western hopes for "cheap and easy" disposal of the public domain, but no great struggle over land policy developed between the President and such stalwarts of the budding Democracy as Senator Thomas Hart Benton of Missouri. The President made his views known but left the formulation of land policy to Congress. He also signed a number of bills giving relief to westerners and others who were in debt because of land purchases. Adams knew the West's desire for free land. He wished to be reelected and was aware that western support was important for realization of his hopes. Political considerations rather than his own preferences shaped his policy regarding the public lands.

Indians and States' Rights

Indians and their land claims, however, brought the President into sharp conflict with the state of Georgia and gave the Opposition further opportunity for harassing the Administration. Monroe had been averse to coercing the Indians into removal to the West, and Adams determined to follow this same policy. When he discovered that the Treaty of Indian Spring, exchanging all the Creek lands in Georgia for an equal area west of the Mississippi, had been made with only a few of the Creek tribes, he told the protesting red men that they should have justice. This brought him into conflict with fiery Governor Troup of Georgia, who insisted upon enforcing the treaty. Adams' Administration saw to it that a new Treaty of Washington was negotiated, ceding all Creek lands in Georgia except those lying west of the Chattahoochee River, the United States guaranteeing to the Indians all lands not ceded. This was supposed to abrogate and supersede the Treaty of Indian Spring, but Governor Troup refused to honor the new treaty. He declared that the Treaty of Indian Spring was not annulled, and began surveying lands claimed by the Indians. Undecided as to what further action to take, Adams put the matter up to Congress. Two committees reported on the subject, one upholding Georgia and the other the Treaty of Washington. Both advised purchasing the remaining Indian lands in Georgia, which was what the President was already attempting to do. Before the end of his term of office, the rest of the Creek lands had been ceded and Georgia had taken possession of them. The Creek problem in Georgia had been settled, but Adams' effort to deal fairly with the Indians had driven that state into the political ranks forming behind that hater and fighter of the Indians, Andrew Jackson.

The Tariff of Abominations

Adams was more cautious in dealing with the tariff than he was in his handling of Indian affairs, but nevertheless his Administration was clearly marked as protectionist. Manufacturing interests in New England and the Middle Atlantic states were clamoring for tariffs higher than those in the bill of 1824. Their efforts were aided by the energetic support of Richard Rush, Secretary of the Treasury, and by Henry Clay. The latter, who wished to identify the National Republican party with his American System, especially those aspects of it which involved protection and internal improvements at national expense, heartily approved a bill raising the duty rates on both raw wool and woolen goods; this measure passed the House in 1826 but failed in the Senate by the casting vote of the Vice President, John C. Calhoun. Clay also supported the Harrisburg Convention of sheep raisers and manufacturers which met in 1827 to frame a new bill boosting tariff rates. "Harry of the West" wished to make protection a leading issue in the campaign of 1828. So did the Opposition, but for entirely different reasons.

Jackson men controlled the House of Representatives after the congressional elections of 1826, and it was a Jacksonian committee on manufactures that drew up the tariff of 1828. It was a bill, as John Randolph remarked, that "referred to manufactures of no sort or kind except the manufacture of a President of the United States." Furthermore, this President's name would not be John Quincy Adams. The measure was protective, but with clever distinctions that were Machiavellian in character. The duty it placed on woolen goods was not as high as that demanded by the manufacturers, and, at the same time, the rates on raw wool, sail cloth, high grade hemp, and molasses —all heavily used by New England manufacturers—were graded steeply upward. It was believed by the sponsors of this bill that these features would rally a goodly number of New England votes against it, which would enable Jackson men in northern areas where protectionist sentiment was strong to vote for the measure and yet have it fail. The South, of course, would vote solidly against it, the northern Jacksonians could then claim credit for being in favor of protection, and the Administration could be charged with its defeat wherever such allegations would be politically useful. It was a plan worthy of Van Buren at his best, but it miscarried. When the woolen manufacturers prevailed upon the Senate to raise somewhat the duties on medium-priced woolens, the New Englanders swallowed their resentment, and the bill passed and became law.

The tariff of 1828 was known in the South as the "Tariff of Abominations." Duties paid under it in the year 1830 constituted 61.69 per cent of the value of all dutiable goods imported, and 57.32 per cent of the value of all goods imported. The value of dutiable goods in 1830 was $46 million, and the value of free goods $3.5 million. The country now had really high protection.

The tariff of 1828 had other significant aspects besides the fact that it represented the establishment of high protection. Webster voted for it, an indication of the growth of the manufacturing interest in his New England constituency. The South's bitterness against the bill far surpassed that evoked by the measure of 1824. Calhoun, who had supported the tariff four years earlier, was now convinced that protection was viciously sectional. He had countenanced the scheme by which the tariff of 1828 had been concocted as the best way of breaking down protection, but he regarded the passage of the measure as a breach of faith. In response to its becoming law, and to the explosion of rage and resentment in the South, he wrote one of the most famous papers in American history.

Calhoun's Exposition and Protest

The South Carolina Exposition and Protest declared that the Constitution gave the United States government the taxing power solely for the purpose

JOHN C. CALHOUN
(1782–1850)

This fine portrait by Charles Bird King was painted in the South Carolinian's earlier days, when he was an ardent nationalist.

of raising revenue. Since, therefore, the protection involved in a tariff law must be purely incidental, the tariff of 1828 was plainly unconstitutional, as was the whole system of protection, which levied enormous taxes on the South for the benefit of a monied northern aristocracy. The North was able to do this because it outnumbered the South two to one in population and could command a majority in Congress, but for this inequitable situation there was a remedy—the right of "interposition" by a state against "unconstitutional" acts of the federal government. In other words, a state had a right to nullify acts of the federal government that the state held to be clearly unconstitutional, for the federal government had been formed by the states, and their power, in the last analysis, was paramount. This was the doctrine of 1798 all over again, but this time it was presented not as a political talking point, but as a proposal for direct action.

The Slanderous Campaign of 1828

While the South was fulminating against the "Tariff of Abominations" and Calhoun was marshaling the arguments for his *Exposition and Protest,* the presidential campaign of 1828 was in full swing. Jackson and Adams did not go on any barnstorming trips during that canvass, for it was not then customary for presidential candidates to appeal directly to the voters. Jackson made three speeches at a New Orleans festival commemorating his victory there in the War of 1812—speeches for which he was carefully coached —but the Hero wished to avoid any appearance of electioneering and stayed close to the Hermitage during most of 1828. Adams remained at the White House; only a Fourth of July speech on internal improvements could possibly be regarded as campaigning on his part. But if the principals preserved the traditional custom of silence, their supporters more than made up for it by their vociferous and slanderous outbursts.

It seemed as though the partisans of each man strove to outdo one another in blackening the reputations of the candidates. The Jackson orators and newspaper organs rang the changes on the supposed corruption that had disgraced the last election. Clay, they declared, had sold his vote and his influence because he needed the salary he would receive as Secretary of State. He was said to be an unprincipled gambler, who had cheated two carpenters out of their wages and had once kidnapped a free Negro. Adams, they said, was seeking, by the use of power and money to "retain the throne and continue the succession." His mania for office had supposedly brought him government money equal to $16.00 a day for his entire life. Called a hypocrite by nature, one corrupted by long residence in royal courts, this Sabbath-breaker was said to have once acted as "pimp" for Tsar Alexander I, prostituting to his Majesty a beautiful American girl. The people were told that Adams had wasted their money by extravagant expenditures in the White House, and was the fit representative of a party that contained all the Old Federalists and that despised democracy. The time had come for "Retrenchment and Reform."

To this stream of abuse and vilification, Adams' supporters replied in kind. They accused Jackson of every crime in the decalogue: he had participated in land frauds; he was a gambler, cock-fighter, horse-racer, and bloody duellist; and he was a military butcher. Coffin handbills were printed representing the execution of six militiamen at Jackson's orders:

> Oh! Did you hear the plaintive cry
> Born on the southern breeze?
> Saw you John Harris earnest pray
> For mercy, on his knees?

When his detractors asserted that Jackson was an adulterer, they disregarded the fact that he and Rachel Robards had married believing that Lewis Robards had obtained a divorce. Jackson and Rachel, they clamored, had lived in sin, and, moreover, Jackson's mother had been a prostitute who married a Negro, and his brother was a Carolina slave. In person or by heritage, the

General apparently had not a single redeeming feature, and yet this was the man the Opposition had put forward for the chief office in the land.

The election of 1828 was fought over personalities, not issues. In the background were the conflicting interests of western agrarians and eastern businessmen and southern planters in such matters as land policy, internal improvements, and the tariff. The shouting and the tumult cloaked the growing restlessness of urban labor, and concealed, if poorly, the unquenchable ambitions of local and national political leaders. Still further back—so far back that it did not appear in any of the mass meetings—was the specter of slavery. But neither party took a clear-cut stand on any issue over which the sections were divided. The politicians relied heavily upon falsehood and vilification to win the day. It was also highly important that the candidate of the National Republicans had no personal appeal, while the Democratic candidate was a popular Indian fighter and military hero.

Beginning of the Antimasonic Movement

As the campaign neared its close, the situation of the National Republicans became desperate. In only one quarter was there a ray of hope. New York and Pennsylvania were key states. Pennsylvania was lost, but New York had possibilities.

In 1826, William Morgan of Batavia, New York, an obstreperous brick and stone cutter with literary tastes, had undertaken to disclose the secrets of the Blue Lodge of the Masonic Order. These were supposed to be closely guarded, and the other Masons of the area determined to prevent their disclosure at all costs. Morgan was put in jail for debt. On his release he was abducted and taken to Niagara Falls, where all trace of him vanished.

When it became apparent that Morgan had disappeared, there was wild excitement in the western part of New York State. Inquiries were set on foot, and as it became evident that prominent Masons were obstructing these investigations, a popular clamor arose against that "horrid, oath-binding system," the Masonic Order. The tumult began to flow in political channels.

Thurlow Weed, a budding genius in the school of politics and the publisher of a newspaper in Rochester, New York, joined the hue and cry about Morgan. His efforts, and those of others, resulted in the organization of the Antimasonic party in New York State. Weed was also instrumental in aligning this party with the National Republicans in the campaign of 1828. Jackson was a Mason, Adams not. If the Antimasonic Movement spread fast enough and was managed shrewdly enough, there was a possibility that it might carry the state for Adams. Actually, Antimasonry did help divide the electoral vote in New York State. Adams had sixteen out of the state's thirty-six votes, and most of his support came from the Antimasonic western districts.

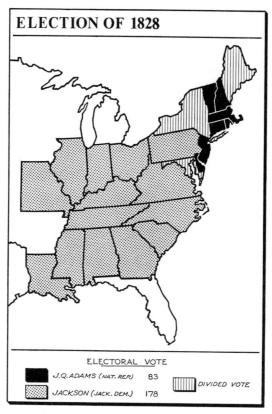

ELECTION OF 1828

ELECTORAL VOTE

J.Q.ADAMS (NAT. REP.) 83

JACKSON (JACK. DEM.) 178

DIVIDED VOTE

The Election of 1828

The election of 1828 did not bring out a great new tide of "common men" rushing to the polls to vote for Jackson. There were only a few states in which the turnout of voters equalled or exceeded maximum levels of voting in state-wide elections held during previous years. Nevertheless, this election was a smashing victory for Jackson and the Democratic party. Old Hickory carried New York and Pennsylvania, all the western states and all the South save for Delaware and Maryland. In the electoral college he had 178 votes to eighty-three for Adams, while the popular vote (with only the electors in South Carolina and Delaware chosen by the legislatures) was 647,286 to

508,064. The Democrats also had both houses of Congress. In the Senate there were twenty-six Democrats and twenty-two National Republicans, a loss of two seats for the Democracy but still a safe majority. In the House the parties stood 139 to seventy-four, a Democratic gain since 1826 of twenty seats. National Republicanism had gone down to defeat and a new party, led by an indomitable chieftain and calling itself the party of Retrenchment and Reform, had come into power.

Suggested Reading

For a survey of the period, brilliantly written but abounding in intuitive judgments, see George Dangerfield, *The Era of Good Feelings* (1952). Arthur M. Schlesinger, Jr., *The Age of Jackson* (1945) deals with the social and economic background of the era in provocative fashion. The policies of the leading statesmen of the period are well developed in John S. Bassett, *The Life of Andrew Jackson* (2 vols. in one, 1928). Wiltse's *Calhoun,* Bemis' *John Quincy Adams,* and Van Deusen's *Henry Clay,* all previously cited, should also be consulted. Marquis James, *The Life of Andrew Jackson* (1938), is brilliant but biased in favor of Old Hickory. There is a first-rate analysis of Jackson in Richard Hofstadter, *The American Political Tradition* (1948). See also K. H. Porter, *A History of the Suffrage in the United States* (1918); A. B. Darling, *Political Changes in Massachusetts, 1824–1848* (1925), and D. R. Fox, *The Decline of Aristocracy in the Politics of New York* (1919).

For the Indian troubles of Adams' Administration, see Annie H. Abel, "The History of Events Resulting in Indian Consolidation West of the Mississippi," American Historical Association, *Reports,* vol. I (1908).

On the beginnings of Antimasonry, see Charles McCarthy, "The Antimasonic Party," American Historical Association, *Reports,* vol. I (1902) and Glyndon G. Van Deusen, *Thurlow Weed, Wizard of the Lobby* (1947). Wilfred E. Binkley, *American Political Parties* (rev. ed., 1956), is useful for Antimasonry and other party aspects.

The best secondary account of the campaign of 1828 is Florence Weston, *The Presidential Election of 1828* (1938). Richard P. McCormick, "New Perspectives on Jacksonian Politics," *The American Historical Review,* LXV (Jan., 1960), 288–301, has a significant voter analysis of the 1828 election. Richard P. McCormick, *The Second American Party System: Party Formation in the Jacksonian Era* (1966) is first rate on party organization in this period.

16 ⋎ Jacksonian Democracy
Triumphant

I N ORDER TO UNDERSTAND the Jacksonian era, it is necessary to have a
clear conception of the great economic developments that had appeared
by the time Old Hickory took office. Transportation, urbanization, a
booming business development, and a rising proletariat were beginning to
transform the whole American scene and to affect directly the politics of
the period.

Economic
Background
of the
Jacksonian Era

By 1830, the transportation revolution was under way. The steamboat had arrived on the lakes
and western waters. Thousands of miles of canals
were projected in the North and West, and Charles
Carroll of Carrollton, a signer of the Declaration
of Independence, had laid the first stone of the
Baltimore and Ohio railroad track in 1828. Within one generation, the cost
of transporting bulky products by land was to fall by nearly 95 per cent,
freight rates on the Mississippi and Ohio were to decrease some 75 per cent
for downstream and 90 per cent for upstream traffic, and canal freightage
between Buffalo and New York fell from $100.00 to less than $8.00 a ton.
At the same time, the general speed of freight transportation quintupled, and
that of passenger traffic was notably advanced.

Paralleling the swift development of transport was the spread of urbanization. Cities were growing rapidly in both the East and the West. New York jumped from 123,706 in 1820 to 202,589 in 1830, and to 312,710 ten years later. Philadelphia's population of 63,802 in 1820 increased to 80,462

NEW YORK IN THE EARLY 1820s

The magnificent harbor of New York had already made it a center of commercial activity. Its strategic location and the completion of the Erie Canal in 1825 were to bring on an era of phenomenal growth.

in 1830, and to 93,665 in 1840. Pittsburgh, a town of 7,248 souls in 1820, had 15,639 by 1830 and by 1840 some 31,204 inhabitants. Cincinnati leaped from 9,642 in 1820 to 24,831 in 1830 and then to 46,338 in 1840. The urban population, in fact, was increasing faster than the rural population. In 1800, the ratio between the two was 15.4 to 1; in 1820, it was 12.9 to 1. In 1830, the spread had narrowed to 10.4 to 1, and ten years later it was 8.2 to 1. America was still predominantly agrarian, but that large numbers of its people were beginning to congregate in the cities was a factor of prime significance for the future of the nation.

The growth of the urban population meant, for one thing, an increase in the diversification of economic activity. By 1830, the merchandizing and transporting business had assumed large proportions throughout the interior of the country, and inland markets of great importance had appeared. Cincinnati was the "Porkopolis" of the West, and also had a flourishing steam engine manufacture. Louisville, Kentucky, was the center of the tobacco trade, and St. Louis, Missouri, the center of the traffic in lead and furs. Foreign commerce, which in 1830 had scarcely recovered from the blows inflicted upon it by the embargo and the War of 1812, was on the verge of a substantial development. In 1830, the United States exported over $70 million worth of merchandise and imported over $62 million worth of goods. Seven years later, exports had increased to over $110 million and imports amounted to approximately $130.5 million in value. Even more remarkable was the growth of manufacturing.

During the 1820s, manufactures had increased by leaps and bounds, the value of the woolens output tripling and that of pig iron increasing eight times over. By the early 1830s, the country was teeming with firms producing textiles, boots and shoes, iron works of all kinds, leather goods, glass, and a host of other products. The vast majority of these were small businesses, ranging from a few hundred to a few thousand dollars capital, but there were also a considerable number of manufacturers producing from $20,000 to $100,000 worth of goods yearly, while some textile firms, such as the Boston Manufacturing Company and the Appleton Company, were million-dollar corporations.

The corporation as a form of business organization was just entering into its own. It had become popular after the War of 1812 as a means of accumulating the necessary capital for business ventures and of assuring the smooth continuity of business from one generation to another. By the later 1820s, corporations, especially in New England, were replacing family, partnership, and joint-stock ownerships as the favored means of banking and industrial organization, and they continued their rapid spread during Jackson's term of office.

The business community of the Jacksonian period was made up of two main groups. The first was composed of powerful businessmen and bankers, successful operators who made large profits and wielded much influence in the business and banking communities of the nation. The second group consisted of bankers, insurance men, merchants, and manufacturers doing business on a smaller scale, striving to make profits and to grow. This portion of the business world was pushing, eager, and jealous of those who had already arrived at positions of wealth and power. Such, for example, was the situation of the majority of the 329 banking organizations that existed in 1829, and of the new members of that fraternity who swelled the number of banks to 788 by 1837.

The American business community was not only growing with great rapidity; it was also of a highly competitive and often speculative nature. The Jacksonian era was fertile with opportunities for industrial development and the accumulation of wealth. It was the heyday of captains, and would-be captains of industry. John Jacob Astor (1763–1848) accumulated a fortune of between $20 million and $30 million out of the fur trade and investments in real estate on Manhattan Island. Glue-making and iron manufacturing made Peter Cooper (1791–1883) a wealthy man. Shrewd and able merchants and textile manufacturers such as Nathan Appleton (1779–1861) and Abbott Lawrence (1792–1855) accumulated fortunes. But this was also an era when business was beset by hosts of dangers and difficulties. The great majority of these early businessmen were pioneers who had to contend with poor communications, uncertainty in the day-to-day supply of raw materials, currency confusion, and stiff foreign competition. The records of the time present a picture of a business class that could make large profits, but that was afflicted from 1815 on by an almost constant succession of crises and depressions, with the mad inflation of the middle 1830s adding chaos to confusion.

As urban concentration and business development moved at an ever-increasing tempo, the urban proletariat assumed a position of increasing importance on the national scene. This was all the more true because by 1830 suffrage qualifications had been lowered to the point where thousands of laborers in such manufacturing states as Massachusetts, New York, and Pennsylvania could vote. And the laborers had many grievances. "Sun to sun" hours of labor in the factories were still the rule throughout the country, as were imprisonment for debt and compulsory militia systems that fined the rich for nonattendance but sent the poor to prison. The courts persecuted labor unions as illegal conspiracies. The monetary system enabled unscrupulous employers to pay wages in depreciated bank notes. The workers resented these inequities in a land where justice and equality of opportunity were supposed to prevail. They were also well aware of the absence of such legislation as mechanics lien laws for the protection of wages, and of child-labor laws, and they were bitter over the lack of good free schools for their children.

As a result of the situation of the laboring class, workers became ardent champions of reform. There was a rapid spread of trade unionism, with its inevitable demand for better hours, wages, and working conditions. By 1834, there were 25,000 trade unionists in New York, Boston, Philadelphia, and Baltimore, organized in city centrals, and there was even a movement toward a national trades union as a means of meeting growing employer opposition. There was also a proliferation of workingmen's political parties in the more industrial states, with platforms calling for the abolition of imprisonment for debt and the compulsory militia system, the establishment of free public schools, and other improvements. These working class political movements mushroomed and died away, some through lack of money and skillful leadership, others because the major parties stole parts of their programs. But they were symptomatic of labor's discontent, and they were closely watched as storm signals by the leaders of the National Republicans and the Democrats.

When the Democracy took over the reins of office, the country's economic situation was dynamic, full of movement and growth, aspiration and discontent. Most of the political turmoil of the 1830s stemmed directly from the ambitions of individuals and economic groups, and from the conflicts of interest between farmers and businessmen, capitalists and laborers, during these hectic years.

Composition of the Parties

The Democratic party which came into power in 1828 was an unstable combination of a wide variety of elements. Since it not only numbered many workingmen, small farmers, and debtors of all classes in its ranks, but also contained large numbers of planters, bankers, merchants, and other devotees of business enterprise, it had a right and a left wing. The former was composed in part of southern middle-class farmers and aristocratic planters fearful of internal improvements at national expense and looking to the party in power for relief from the "Tariff of Abominations." Small businessmen in the towns and cities felt that the "upper crust" of the business world (the larger textile operators, the rich Boston, New York, and Philadelphia merchants, and the like) had too much power and privilege, and that one way in which such power could be curbed would be by abolishing the general practice of granting individual state charters to business corporations. Such men gravitated into the conservative side of the Democratic party. There, too, were to be found state bankers, jealous of the Bank of the United States, who saw that its control over note issues and other forms of credit often curbed their opportunity for profit, and looked to the Democracy to see to it that the "Monster" was destroyed.

The leaders of the left wing of the Democracy relied mainly upon the support of the farmers and city laborers of the North and West. This radical wing felt that American democracy was in danger of being corrupted and destroyed by the greed of the business community, especially by the bankers and the industrialists of the era. They made little or no distinction between the élite and the common run of the business class, but were critical of them all. The Democratic left believed that the national government, and the state governments also, had fallen under the influence of the "haves"; that the politicians had forgotten, or were neglecting, the rights and aspirations of the common man; and that the affairs of the nation must be restored to popular control. This radical wing later came to be known, for reasons that will become apparent, as the Loco Foco Democracy.

Both wings of the Democratic party united in believing that the national government should be limited to the specific powers granted it in the Constitution. State governments—which were easily amenable to popular control—might assist aspiring entrepreneurs and farmers and laborers in such matters as improving education, or in building roads and canals; but since the federal government was, for the most part, far away, the men in Washington, under pressure to think in national terms and open to lobbyists from any and all quarters, were not so apt to legislate in the local interest. The federal government's principal function, then, was a negative one. It should see to it that wealth and power did not limit freedom of enterprise; that freedom of speech, press, and opinion was not invaded; that, to the fullest possible extent, free speech should be preserved, together with a maximum freedom of opportunity to acquire land. Frank Blair's Washington *Globe*, soon to become the great national organ of the Democracy, adopted as its motto "The world is governed too much." This symbolized the Democracy's dislike of a strong central government. Its leaders were prone to voice the reverence the party professed for the old Jeffersonian states' rights point of view and to manifest it by a due and proper regard for strict construction of the federal Constitution.

The National Republican party—if so poorly organized an entity could be called a party—was not devoid of adherents in the West and South but had its chief centers of strength in New England and the Middle Atlantic states. Like its opponent, it was a mélange of farmers, businessmen, and industrialists, together with laborers and mechanics who saw in high tariffs and internal improvements a form of security for their own employment. Those who believed in using the central government as an agency for promoting the national welfare, those who believed that the Bank of the United States was essential for the maintenance of a sound currency, and those whose instinct it was to fear the mob and trust to an élite for leadership were apt to be National Republicans. As a whole, National Republicanism was optimistic about the future of the country, was respectful of the business class, and put more emphasis on national development than on rights and privileges of the states.

The Democratic victory in 1828 had made the National Republicans helpless to direct the course of events. Their chief hope was that the Jacksonian leadership would make mistakes offering opportunity for destructive attack, and that the Democracy's unstable equilibrium might be upset and destroyed by assault from without and dissension within.

Jackson's inaugural, delivered before a crowd of 15,000–20,000 people, was a composite of his views and those of his advisers at home and in Washington. The white-haired chieftain, dressed in mourning for his wife, who had died the previous December, spoke in a low voice as he pledged the government to respect for the rights of the states, economy, and the payment of the national debt. The tariff, he declared, should "equally favor" industry, commerce, and agriculture, and at the same time should encourage the production of articles necessary for "national independence." He labeled internal improvements "of high importance." The new President promised that there would be reform, and invoked the assistance of Almighty God in the performance of his duties. His utterances skirted controversial subjects and offered little opportunity for criticism. The opposition, therefore, was glad to turn its attention to the spectacle at the White House that followed the inauguration.

No preparation had been made for policing the reception which had been prepared at the Mansion, and a motley crowd of all colors, ages, and ranks in life poured into the house and grounds. Chaos reigned, ladies fainted, gentlemen's noses were bloodied, and thousands of dollars worth of china and glassware were smashed. The General, saved from being trampled by a cordon of his friends, escaped by a back door to Gadsby's Tavern. Tubs of punch taken out on the lawn then drew the crowd out of doors and saved the White House from further damage. Justice Joseph Story, an eyewitness, termed it "the reign of King 'Mob'," and the fastidious recoiled in horror from this manifestation of popular sovereignty.

Organizing the New Government

Jackson—who, like Lincoln at a later date, grew in the presidency—seemed at first only a tired, sick, old man of sixty-two, who lacked political experience and was face to face with problems that were new to him. Relying on the advice of friends, he appointed a Cabinet that he regarded as exceptionally able, but that was mediocre save for Van Buren as Secretary of State. Those officeseekers who were rebuffed in their search for Cabinet and other posts were quick to voice their bitter disappointment, and others, alarmed by the White House reception, feared that the new rulers of the nation would be socially crude. The Administration was ushered in amid a tumult of criticism, but the old chieftain had in Van Buren a master of tact and diplomacy who possessed the confidence of the politicians, and the President himself had that hard common sense and capacity for decision in times of crisis that are the marks of a statesman.

Closer to the President than his official family was a shifting, changing group of men who came to be known as the Kitchen Cabinet. Van Buren was the most influential member of this group. Others were Amos Kendall, a skillful writer and ardent partisan whom Jackson made Fourth Auditor of the Treasury; Isaac ("Ike") Hill, a New Hampshire newspaper man; Francis Preston Blair, a newspaper editor from Kentucky; and Major William B. Lewis, a long-time friend and supporter from Tennessee. Jackson looked to these men, and others who were brought into the circle from time to time, for advice, and much of the administrative policy of the Administration undoubtedly derived from them. But the composition of this "Cabinet" was constantly altering, and it was far from being a body which dictated policies or procedures to Old Hickory.

Making Good on Retrenchment and Reform

Much ado had been made during the campaign about retrenchment and reform, and one of the first steps of the Administration was an attempt to make good these promises. A real effort was made to cut government expenses, and the budget was temporarily reduced something like $2 million a year. These retrenchments, however, were spotty and temporary, and the post office, under "General" William T. Barry of Kentucky, was wastefully managed from the start. By 1833, Treasury expenditures had risen from some $15 million in 1829 to approximately $23 million a year.

"Reform," the other part of the campaign slogan, turned out to be an overhauling of the federal bureaucracy and the establishment of the principle of rotation in office. This was not simply a case of applying the rule so bluntly put by Democrat William L. Marcy of New York, "to the victor belong the spoils." Jackson believed that rotation in office was highly commendable procedure, since it was based on the belief that the citizens were competent to run their own government and, moreover, gave the people a sense of direct participation in the conduct of public affairs. It is also only fair to point out that removals were not at all as sweeping as the National Republicans charged. During Old Hickory's two terms of office, somewhere between one-tenth and one-fifth of the federal officeholders were dismissed. Many of these dismissals were thoroughly justifiable, the outstanding example being that of the embezzler Tobias Watkins, friend of Adams and Clay, who fled but was caught, convicted, and sentenced. Others, however, were purely partisan, and not a few of the replacements were unfit. Conspicuous among these was Samuel Swartwout, whom Jackson appointed collector of the port of New York and who later defaulted for $1.25 million. Despite the honesty of Jackson's purpose, he fostered the development of a spoils system in the national government that, in the long run, made for inefficiency and lowered the tone of the public service. "Retrenchment and reform," the glittering campaign slogan, had produced little in the way of concrete results.

The "Eaton Malaria"

Rotation in office raised a great hubbub, especially among the National Republicans, but most politicians regarded it as a realistic practice, in keeping with the equalitarian spirit of the times. It strengthened the Democratic party's organization by holding out the possibility of reward for faithful service. But another development that came within the first months of Jackson's presidency bade fair to have more serious consequences for the stability of the Administration. This was what Van Buren referred to as the "Eaton malaria."

Even before the election of 1828, tongues had wagged in Washington circles about Jackson's friend, thirty-eight-year-old John H. Eaton, a well-to-do widower, and Margaret (Peggy) O'Neale Timberlake, the widow of a navy purser. Peggy, who was now thirty-two years old but still very attractive to men, was the daughter of the keeper of a Washington tavern where Eaton had stayed at various times, and gossip had linked his name with that of the vivacious beauty even before her husband's death. Then the rumor spread that Timberlake had cut his throat because of this affair, and the gossip grew to scandalous proportions. When Eaton consulted with Jackson, who liked Peggy, Old Hickory advised marriage as the best means of quieting the gossip-mongers, and on January 1, 1829, the marriage took place. Then Eaton was made Secretary of War, and people began to wonder how his wife would be received in the social circles of the Administration. They had not long to wait. Led by Floride Calhoun, the gracious, popular, and high-spirited wife of the Vice President, the Cabinet ladies ignored Mrs. Eaton.

Jackson was furious over this snub to his friend's wife, the more so because he felt that the slurs cast upon Peggy were partly meant to stir up the embers of the old scandal about himself and Rachel. He declared that Mrs. Eaton was "chaste as a virgin," and his defense of her began to take on the dimensions of an Administration policy. The husbands of the puritanical Cabinet ladies found themselves embarrassed.

THE CELESTE-AL CABINET

Celeste was a popular Parisian actress and dancer who came to the United States on several occasions. Here she symbolizes Peggy Eaton, supposedly brought before the judgment bar of the Cabinet. Jackson is represented as looking aghast (actually, he was one of Peggy's strong defenders). Van Buren, at the right, peers at the lady through a lorgnette.

The snubbing of Mrs. Eaton was Van Buren's opportunity. This exquisite dandy, who affected snuff-colored coats and yellow gloves to set off his blond complexion, had already won great credit with his chief for the diplomatic way in which he handled importunate officeseekers. "The Red Fox" was a widower, and so free from control by a prudish wife. He called on the ostracized lady, and arranged dinner parties to which she and her husband were invited, all very much to Jackson's delight. The latter, prone to find political implications in the affair, at first thought Clay was to blame for the tempest stirred up over Peggy, but his suspicions finally centered upon the Calhouns. And, as a result of this social squabble, a gulf began to appear between the President and the Vice President.

WEBSTER'S REPLY TO HAYNE

Perhaps the most famous speech in American history. G. P. A. Healy's painting shows Webster speaking in the little Senate chamber. Vice President Calhoun stands at the far left, while Benton leans against a pillar at the rear. Hayne is in the left center of the picture, next to a Senator with long gray curls.

Tariff and Public Lands—the West-South Alliance

When Congress met in December, 1829, it concerned itself with more prosaic matters than the Eaton affair. Southerners were disappointed by Jackson's cautious handling of the tariff in his message. The President told the representatives of the people that some of the provisions in the tariff of 1828 required modification, but that revision was a delicate and difficult operation which should be approached with the "utmost caution" and that local feelings and prejudices must be subordinated to the best interests of the nation. This was cold comfort to the South Carolinians, and the nullification advocated in Calhoun's *Exposition* began to grow in favor. The South also began looking for more conservative ways of forcing tariff reform, and a movement began in Congress which was designed to place South and West in close cooperation for their mutual benefit.

The South's determination to have a lower tariff was paralleled by the West's eagerness for cheap land. The latter section was alarmed because Jackson, in his message, had advocated distributing the surplus revenue among the states as soon as the national debt was extinguished and also said that he believed that the debt would be paid off within "a very short time." But distribution of the surplus revenue would almost certainly anchor the price of public lands at around $2.00 an acre, and westerners were determined to prevent a stabilization of public land prices at current levels. The result was that, under the guidance of Senators Thomas Hart Benton of Missouri and Robert Y. Hayne of South Carolina, the two sections began drawing together in an alliance that would promote both tariff reduction and a lowering of the price of lands put up for sale by the national government.

The Webster-Hayne Debates

This West-South alignment was brought out into the open when (December 29, 1829) Senator Samuel A. Foote of Connecticut offered a resolution of inquiry into the expediency of limiting the sale of public lands. No sooner was Foote's proposal made, than Benton rose to the attack, denouncing it as an effort to retard western settlement so that the East could have a cheap supply of labor for its factories. Hayne supported Benton, emphasizing the justice of a cheap land policy and declaring that the national government had dealt hardly with the West. The idea of using the public lands as a source of national revenue filled him with horror, for he believed it was bound to be a source of corruption and, even worse, would enhance the strength and power of the national government. Contending that government derived from the states, and that they had authorized the Constitution, he argued that the government at Washington was answerable to them when it overstepped the bounds of its authority.

Webster rose to answer Benton and Hayne. The Senator from Massachusetts was a man of extravagant tastes, altogether too fond of alcohol, and a faithful servant of the business interests in his constituency, but he was also an authority in matters of finance, a nationalist, and a superb orator. In his deep voice, he denounced both the extreme advocates of states' rights and the attacks leveled against the East: "Consolidation! that perpetual cry, both of terror and delusion—consolidation!—The East! the obnoxious, the rebuked, the always reproached East!" He denied that the East's policy toward the West was either illiberal or hostile, declaring that the public lands should be sold at a low but reasonable price. He deplored sectional cleavage and viewed the power of the national government, not with alarm, but as a means for developing the wealth and the resources of the entire nation.

Hayne's response to Webster assailed the latter's nationalistic point of view. It came with poor grace, said the South Carolinian, from a New England that had been anything but loyal during the War of 1812. New England had then applauded interposition by a state when the federal government acted in an unconstitutional manner. This was the same position now being defended by Hayne.

Webster's second reply to Hayne pointed out that, whatever New England had done in the past, that section was now seeking the best interests of the whole nation. The federal government, said Webster, was the product, not of the states, but of the people of the whole nation, and the national interest was paramount over that of any state or section. The peroration of this address, in which Webster warned against the states' rights theory as leading to discord and civil war, and exalted the glory of the Union, has become part of America's national literature.

The Jefferson Day Dinner, 1830

The Webster-Hayne debate had set the issue clearly between states' rights and nationalism. A few weeks later, Jackson had an opportunity to show where he would take his stand. South Carolina was the center of resistance to the tariff of 1828 and of the nullification threat, and after the clash between the giants in the Senate, the South Carolinians were determined to bring the President out on their side. Duff Green's United States *Telegraph*, which reflected Calhoun's views and was supposed to be the Administration's organ, heaped praise upon Hayne and declared that Webster had joined Clay in a crusade against Old Hickory and his policy. Then on April 13, 1830, the anniversary of the birth of Thomas Jefferson came a subscription dinner organized by the South Carolinians and their friends. A series of toasts and speeches were arranged glorifying states' rights and the Virginia resolutions of 1798 and, by clear implication, approving South Carolina's resistance to the tariff. The President was invited to attend, and it was understood that he would offer the first toast after the formal program was over.

Though all Washingon was agog over whether Jackson stood with Hayne or Webster, no inkling of the old chieftain's position had come to light. Considerations of personal friendship would have inclined him to side with Hayne, but after Webster's second speech Van Buren became convinced that South Carolina's attitude, and even the Jefferson Day dinner itself, could easily "menace the stability of the Union," and the President shared this point of view. He came to the dinner, Van Buren later recalled, with emotions suitable to "the field of battle instead of the festive board."

ANDREW JACKSON, PRESIDENT

Coming out of the West, Jackson a Tennessee aristocrat was very different from the Virginia and Massachusetts aristocrats who had preceded him in the presidency. The straight line of the mouth and the direct gaze from behind the steel-rimmed spectacles denote the force and energy of the man.

When it was Jackson's turn to give his toast, he raised his glass, a sign that the toast should be drunk standing. Van Buren, short of stature, climbed on his chair to get the full effect. Jackson fixed his glance on Calhoun—"Our Union, it must be preserved." Complete silence fell on the assemblage. Isaac Hill saw Calhoun stand with his hand shaking so that a little of the yellow wine spilled over the side of the glass. "A proclamation of martial law in South Carolina, and an order to arrest Calhoun where he sat," Hill later remarked, "could not have come with more blinding, staggering force." The South Carolinian was resourceful. His answering toast—"The Union, next to our liberty, most dear"—was intended to recover lost ground, but Old Hickory had spoken. The President left the celebration shortly thereafter and within five minutes two-thirds of the diners had followed him out of the hall. The plans of the gentlemen from South Carolina had gone all awry.

The Jackson-Calhoun Breach and the Triumph of Van Buren

The Jefferson Day dinner made evident the growing breach between Jackson and Calhoun. Van Buren was delighted with this situation, for he and the South Carolinian were rivals for the succession. The friends of the "Red Fox" now brought to Jackson's attention the fact that, in 1818, Secretary of War Calhoun had urged Monroe to censure Old Hickory for his conduct in Florida. Calhoun had had good grounds for urging such a censure, for Jackson's activities in Florida had been of a highly questionable character, but the President never liked criticism of himself or his policies. He now asked for Calhoun's account of what had happened in Monroe's Cabinet, to which Calhoun replied with a fifty-two-page résumé of the events of 1818, showing clearly that there had been no treachery to Jackson and that bringing up the matter at this time was a political maneuver designed to destroy Calhoun's political career. He was told that this was absolutely unsatisfactory, that it did not explain why, in his letters to the General, Calhoun had always professed to be his friend and to have approved his conduct in the Seminole campaign. Jackson now declared among his confidants that Calhoun was his enemy, a man who had attempted to "shoot me in the dark." Furthermore, he was now convinced that Calhoun's course in the Eaton affair had been an undercover assault on Rachel Jackson. The South Carolinian's chances for the succession had gone glimmering.

Van Buren's friends now hastened to complete the destruction of Calhoun's presidential hopes. They brought Francis Preston Blair from Kentucky in December, 1830. This exceedingly able scarecrow of a man, who stood five feet ten but weighed just over 100 pounds, was to set up a newspaper in Washington that would replace Duff Green's United States *Telegraph* as the organ of the Administration. Blair established the Washington *Globe,* and political pressure on federal officeholders, among others, shifted many of the *Telegraph's* subscribers to the new sheet. Steadily, too, the Van Burenites chipped away at the Vice President's control over patronage. Finally, in the spring of 1831, Van Buren prevailed upon Jackson to reorganize the Cabinet. After the "Red Fox" and Eaton had resigned, Jackson asked the pro-Calhoun members to follow suit. The outcome was a new official family, free of the Calhoun taint, with Van Buren appointed Minister to England.

It was clear that the "Red Fox" and his supporters were now riding the crest of the wave, but the course of events had produced discord and dissension within the Democratic party. Calhoun proclaimed the severance of all relations with Jackson, and declared that he would be a candidate for the presidency in 1832. The followers of the South Carolinian began stirring up dissension in such key states as Virginia and Pennsylvania, and even in Jackson's home state of Tennessee. The Democracy was having its troubles, but its leader was a resolute and determined man who was idolized by the people, and who every day was becoming more experienced in the arts of political leadership.

Suggested Reading

For the economic background of the Jacksonian era, the student should consult George R. Taylor, *The Transportation Revolution, 1815–1860* (1951), a very valuable work; John R. Commons *et al., History of Labour in the United States* (4 vols., 1918–1935), which is indispensable; and Victor S. Clark, *History of Manufactures in the United States, 1607–1928* (3 vols., 1929), a standard treatment. Walter B. Smith and Walter H. Cole, *Fluctuations in American Business, 1790–1860* (1938) and Kenneth W. Rowe, *Matthew Carey, A Study in American Economic Development* (1933), are useful works. Bray Hammond, *Banks and Politics in America* (1957) is a study of first-rate importance.

For an analysis of the composition of the Democratic and National Republican parties, see John Spencer Bassett, *Andrew Jackson* (2 vols. in one, 1928), Binkley, *Political Parties;* and Glyndon G. Van Deusen, *The Jacksonian Era, 1828–1848* (1959).

For the inauguration of Jackson, see Margaret Smith, *The First Forty Years of Washington Society* (ed. by Gaillard Hunt, 1906) and William W. Story, ed., *Life and Letters of Joseph Story* (2 vols., 1851). On the administrative side, see G. G. Van Deusen, *Jacksonian Era* and Richard P. Longaker, "Was Jackson's Kitchen Cabinet a Cabinet?" *Mississippi Valley Historical Review*, XLIV (June, 1957), 94–108. Also see Leonard D. White, *The Jacksonians* (1954), Arthur Schlesinger, Jr., *The Age of Jackson* and Carl R. Fish, *The Civil Service and the Patronage* (1905). The Eaton scandal is fully portrayed in Marquis James, *The Life of Andrew Jackson* (2 vols. in one, 1938). The curious may also consult Queena Pollack, *Peggy Eaton, Democracy's Mistress* (1931) and Benjamin Perley Poore, *Reminiscences* (2 vols., 1886). The story of the growing breach between Jackson and Calhoun is well developed in Bassett's *Jackson* and Wiltse's *Calhoun*. For the West-South alliance regarding tariff and public lands, see Raynor G. Wellington, *The Political and Sectional Influence of the Public Lands, 1828–1842* (1914).

Other important works dealing with Jacksonian Democracy are J. W. Ward, *Andrew Jackson: Symbol for an Age* (1955); T. P. Abernethy, *From Frontier to Plantation in Tennessee* (1932); C. G. Sellers, Jr., *James K. Polk: Jacksonian, 1795–1843* (1957); W. N. Chambers, *Old Bullion Benton: Senator from the West* (1956). Indispensable is Alexis de Tocqueville, *Democracy in America,* which is published in a number of modern editions. See also Marvin Meyers, *The Jacksonian Persuasion* (1957), and Harold C. Syrett, *Andrew Jackson: His Contribution to the American Tradition* (1953). Lee Benson, *The Concept of Jacksonian Democracy: New York As a Test Case* (1961) is an able and convincing analysis of New York politics in the Jacksonian era. The student should also consult Walter Hugins, *Jacksonian Democracy and the Working Class* (1960).

17 ′ Jacksonian Democracy in Action

DESPITE THE INTERNAL FEUDS and bickerings engendered by rivalry for office, the Peggy Eaton affair, and the struggle for power between Van Buren and Calhoun, the Democratic party's hold on the electorate remained strong and undiminished at the end of two years. Democrats were still in a majority in both houses of Congress after the election of 1830.

Continued Popularity of the Jacksonians

Antimasonry, to be sure, was a political movement that showed increased strength in that contest, emerging with two United States senators and fourteen congressmen to its credit. The Antimasonic movement had spread out of western New York and into New England, Pennsylvania, and Ohio, but it tended to draw recruits from disaffected National Republicans, rather than the Democratic party. Although many Democrats, including Andrew Jackson himself, were Masons, the rich and powerful "aristocrats" of this secret order were apt to be National Republicans. The honest plebeians in the National Republican party, therefore, tended to defect from its ranks. Since the Democratic party prided itself on being the party of the common man, not so many of its members felt the appeal of Antimasonry.

Much of the undiminished popularity of the Democratic party was due to the skillful way in which its leaders handled political issues during Old Hickory's first term of office. Foremost among such issues was that of internal improvements.

Internal Improvements— The Maysville Veto

As a westerner, Jackson was bound to favor internal improvements, and during his term of office expenditures for roads and canals almost doubled those that had been made under his predecessor. But transportation development was also a fundamental part of Clay's American System, and the Democrats were determined to present Clay's grand plan to the public as a wasteful and extravagant scheme. Their opportunity came in 1830, when Congress passed a bill providing federal aid for a road from Lexington to Maysville, Kentucky.

The Maysville road was only some sixty miles long, and was wholly within the borders of the state. Jackson signed bills in 1830 giving aid to projects that were intrastate in character, but he vetoed the Maysville road bill and several other local improvement bills. His stated reasons in the Maysville case were that it was intrastate and therefore unconstitutional, and that such local improvements tended to waste the government's resources and to interfere with the extinction of the national debt.

The Maysville veto was a clever political move. Since the road was short, only a small number of voters were directly affected. It showed the Administration's regard for strict construction of the Constitution and for a national government that would be limited in its powers and economical in its disposition, rather than one that would welcome a logrolling flood of local projects. It was sure to be well regarded in such key states as New York and Pennsylvania, which took care of their own internal improvements and had no desire to be taxed for the support of western development. Moreover, the South would welcome the veto, for the powerful plantation owners in the river bottoms and along the coast were not interested in the building of roads and canals.

The National Republicans, with Clay at their head, raised a great outcry over the Maysville veto, and drew up resolutions of protest over such callous disregard of the best interests of the country. But, since there was no prospect of overriding the President's will, the Democrats were left in much the same position they had enjoyed after the passage of the tariff of 1828. In those areas where internal improvements at federal expense were unpopular, they could point to the Maysville veto; where internal improvements were popular, great emphasis could be laid upon the road and canal bills which Old Hickory had signed—bills which totaled about $1 million a year in value. At the same time, Democratic leaders were left free to denounce Clay's American System as an extravagant program which was bound to impoverish the nation and corrupt its citizenry.

A Diplomatic Triumph

The Maysville veto was an asset to the Jacksonians on the domestic front. They scored another success in the field of diplomacy. Clay, as Secretary of State, had been unable to obtain concessions from the British in regard to West Indian trade, largely because the United States had been stubborn about relaxing its own trade regulations. Van Buren now succeeded where "Harry of the West" had failed, telling England that the Adams Administration had adopted an unwise course which had been rejected by the people in 1828, and that the government under Jackson would no longer maintain the claims made by its predecessor. On receipt of this information, coupled as it was with other evidences of American moderation, Britain opened the West Indies trade to American shipping in the autumn of 1830.

The Democrats hailed the English government's action as a triumph of American diplomacy. The National Republicans were critical, on the ground that Van Buren's withdrawal of the former American demands should have been made as a concession, rather than on the ground that the previous Administration had acted in an unwise manner. The matter thus was tossed into the maelstrom of politics, but, regardless of charge and countercharge, the fact remained that Jackson and Van Buren had succeeded where Adams and Clay had failed.

The Plot Against Van Buren

In the spring of 1831, Jackson appointed Van Buren Minister to England. The appointment was made in June, too late for the Senate to act upon it, and the "Red Fox" simply went to England, where he conducted himself in admirable fashion as the representative of the United States. When the Senate convened the following December, however, Clay, Webster, and Calhoun joined in a plot which was meant to destroy Van Buren's political career. They marshaled their followers and, in secret session, by the deciding vote of Calhoun as presiding officer, the Senate rejected Van Buren's nomination. The plotters supposed that this rejection would cover Van Buren with ignominy and destroy the likelihood not only of his being elected Vice

President in 1832, but also of his succeeding Jackson in 1836. As Calhoun remarked after the deed was done, "It will kill him, sir, kill him dead. He will never kick, sir, never kick."

As a matter of fact, the plot against Van Buren boomeranged, for when news of the Senate's action reached Jackson, it roused the General's fighting spirit—"By the Eternal! I'll smash them!" The President threw himself forcefully into the business of avenging his trusted supporter. The Administration organs portrayed Van Buren as a martyred public servant. Far from hurting him, the Senate's rebuff was an asset in his march toward the presidency.

Clay's Land Bill

The opposition to Jackson was continually probing for grounds on which to attack the Administration. One of the great controversies that arose between the parties concerned both the tariff and public land policy. The West-South alliance continued to work for a lower tariff and cheaper land prices and, in the latter part of Jackson's first term, Democratic leaders in Congress showed themselves more and more favorable to both of these demands. They also concocted a plan which was designed to put Clay, as the natural leader of the National Republicans, on the horns of a dilemma.

In the Senate, the committee on manufactures, which was wrestling with the tariff, was ordered to report on the propriety of reducing the price of public lands. Since Clay had been elected to the Senate in 1830 by the Kentucky legislature, and had been made a member of the commitee on manufactures, the report on the price of public lands was assigned to him. His opponents hoped that he, a known advocate of high protection and of the maintenance of existing land prices, would offend either the industrialists or the western advocates of cheap land by any report which he might write. But the Kentuckian came up with a proposal that demonstrated his poltical ingenuity and saved him from serious political damage.

Clay's Land Bill, as it was called, remained for years a basic part of National Republican and Whig platforms. It was critical of proposals for reducing land prices, and opposed an Administration scheme for selling the public domain to the states in which it lay. The essence of Clay's proposal was the use of land revenue for internal improvements. After 10 per cent of the government's income from the sale of the public domain had been given to the states in which the land lay, the rest should be divided among all the states in proportion to their congressional representation, with the understanding that it would be applied to such objects as education, the building

COURTESY OF THE AMERICAN ANTIQUARIAN SOCIETY

BRAG IN POLITICS

Brag was an early form of poker. This cartoon, published by H. R. Robin-son, probably in 1831, portrays four prominent political leaders in Jackson's first term. Jackson calls Clay, who spreads the cards on which he hopes to win the election of 1832, while Wirt, the Antimasonic candidate, bolts. Calhoun bides his time, holding his nullification cards below the table.

of roads and canals, and the reduction of state debts. This disposition of the government's income would make it feasible to keep the price of the public lands at existing levels, and this, in turn, would protect other land values and would keep the urban East's labor supply from being depleted by the lure of cheap land in the West. Distribution, too, would keep the tariff high, since the government must have revenue to meet its expenses. Clay's Land Bill was meant to serve as one of the chief pillars of the American System.

The Administration's answer to Clay's plan was to refer it to the committee on public lands, which reported in favor of lowering and graduating land prices, so that the longer lands remained unsold, the cheaper they would become, and proposed in addition a 15 per cent distribution of land revenues to the new states only. Neither bill passed Congress, but the issue between the Democracy and the National Republicans had been made plain. Clay's plan was national in scope and sought to satisfy industrial as well as agrarian interests, while the Democracy's cheap land policy favored the landed interests and offered a sop to the laboring class whose leaders were beginning to manifest an interest in free land as an economic escape for the city worker.

The Tariff of 1832

Behind Clay's desire to please all sections by his land policy lay his determination to maintain high protection as a sine qua non. To do that, he declared, he "would defy the South, the President, and the Devil." But Clay's former chief, John Quincy Adams, had been elected to the House of Representatives, and the Speaker of the House made him chairman of the committee on manufactures in the Twenty-Second Congress, a position of power in relation to the tariff. Since Adams believed with the Administration that there should be a considerable lowering of duties, the result was the tariff of 1832.

The Adams bill of 1832 swept away some of the worst abuses of the tariff of 1828. Cheap wool was admitted duty-free, a sop to the southern planters who used the coarser grades of woolen cloth in the garments of their slaves. The minimum valuation system on woolens, which kept the duty up on low-grade stuffs, was replaced by an ad valorem duty. Other reductions came mostly in noncompetitive articles. The protection of higher-grade textiles and of iron goods was still high, but the over-all tariff on dutiable articles ranged between 30 and 36 per cent, about where it had been in the tariff of 1824. Jackson signed the new bill on July 14, 1832, believing that it would end or at least blunt the edge of southern discontent. Clay and Webster disliked the bill because it subjected the woolen manufacturers to considerable foreign competition, but the protectionists in general were well satisfied with the measure.

The struggles in the Twenty-First and Twenty-Second Congress over the tariff, internal improvements, and public lands showed the importance of balancing sectional interests in the passage of national legislation. In the voting on the tariff of 1832, the parties split repeatedly along sectional lines, but when the final vote came, a majority of the southern members of the House voted for it because it was an improvement over the "Tariff of Abominations." Regarding the public lands, however, the South did not give the West the help necessary to effect a real reduction of land prices, the West was dissatisfied, and the uneasy West-South coalition came to an end. With the disappearance of western support on the tariff, Calhoun and his friends, deeply resentful of the protective policy still in effect with the tariff of 1832, were unable to count on the support from other sections that would be necessary to force a further reduction of duties. Their protests over the situation appeared less and less likely to have any real effect.

The Administration had reason to congratulate itself, or so it appeared, on its strong position. It had evinced a sympathy for lower land prices that the West might reasonably feel would soon be translated into action. It had demonstrated an interest in internal improvements that pleased the West, without going so far in that direction as to alienate other sections, and it had passed a tariff bill that removed the worst features of the protective system and at the same time left the great majority of industrialists well pleased. There was very little here that could afford aid and comfort to the National Republicans.

Indian Removal

Another Administration policy that produced a clash with the leaders of the National Republicans, and also demonstrated the strength of will of Old Hickory, emerged during Jackson's first term. This involved the Indian tribes and their lands, and particularly concerned the Cherokees of Georgia.

We have already seen how relentlessly the Indian tribes of the Old Northwest were pushed out of their hunting grounds and across the Mississippi; how Black Hawk and his little band of Sauks were treated in 1832; and how, during the Administration of John Quincy Adams, the Creeks in Georgia were forced to cede their lands. It was obvious that the Cherokees and other tribes in the South would have to follow the same path, but the Cherokees were among the most progressive of all the tribes east of the Mississippi. They had mastered many of the white man's arts, and possessed some five million acres of the most fertile lands in Georgia. Treaties with the United States government recognized them as a nation that could make peace and war, that owned land, and that possessed various and sundry lawmaking powers.

The Cherokees might reasonably feel that they were safe from molestation, since Georgia was bound by the Constitution to observe treaties concluded by the United States government, but such was not the case. The Georgia whites refused to recognize the Cherokees as possessing any rights as a nation, and demanded that they give up their control over the lands which they claimed as their national property. Georgia, Alabama, and the other southern states were determined to gain possession of the Indian lands by hook or by crook, and to force the removal of the tribes to areas west of the Mississippi. In this the southern states had the full sympathy and support of Jackson's Administration.

The Georgia Cherokees went to law, and in two cases that came before the Supreme Court their rights as a nation were upheld. Georgia refused to recognize, much less abide by, these decisions, and the pressure on the Indians continued.

Jackson upheld Georgia in its defiance of the Supreme Court. He is reported to have said, "John Marshall has made his decision. Now let him enforce it." This was at least a fair representation of his attitude toward the Cherokees and the other tribes, which were left at the mercy of the southern states. Old Hickory had asked Congress to set aside an area in the trans-Mississippi West as a new home for these Indians, and by a strict party vote this was done. There ensued a wholesale forced migration of the southern tribes that lasted throughout the 1830s.

The story of the removal of the southern Indians from their homes forms a tragic chapter in American history. The President had declared that the Indians should be treated fairly and with humanity, but the whites cared little about the hardships that removal meant to the red man. He was defrauded right and left by the state governments and by agents from Washington. Lands assigned to the Indians in the West were often far inferior to those taken from them. To make matters worse, many of the Indians were forced to move before preparations for their departure were complete, and they looked in vain to the Great White Father in Washington for justice. Creeks in Alabama who refused to migrate were marched out of the state in chains, and the Seminoles of Florida were tricked into an agreement to migrate. The Choctaws of Mississippi, trekking out into the Red River country in the winter of 1831–1832, suffered terribly from cold and privation. The removal of the tribes to the West was the most logical solution of the problem of relationship between the Indian and the white, but it was the responsibility of the government at Washington, as well as the state governments, to see that this removal was accomplished in the easiest and most equitable fashion. Neither nationally nor locally did those in power live up to their responsibilities.

The Indians generally bowed to the inevitable, even though with bitterness of spirit, but there were instances of rebellion. Some individuals became outlaws, and many of the Florida Seminoles who refused to leave for the West fought for three years (1835–1838), under a young chief named Osceola, against the troops sent by the United States government. This Seminole War cost approximately $14 million before the Indians were subdued. Their chief died a prisoner in Fort Moultrie.

Both political and religious leaders noted the sufferings of the Indians and were loud in their condemnation of the proceedings. Clay declared that

Jackson's attitude toward the Indians was disgraceful, and tried to stir up popular feeling against the Administration. Methodists and Quakers, who were particularly interested in missionary work among the red men, vigorously denounced the government. These criticisms had some slight effect. Van Buren estimated that the Indian policy cost the Democrats eight thousand votes in western New York alone. Jackson, however, paid no attention to his critics, and he lost little face among his admirers. The people as a whole, perhaps with some secret misgivings, accepted the Indian policy as inevitable.

The controversy over Indian removal raised a point of constitutional law that was of considerable importance. The President defended his ignoring the Supreme Court decisions in the Georgia Cherokee cases by the argument that, since the executive department was coordinate with the judiciary, he was not bound always to follow the Supreme Court's interpretation of the Constitution. The opposition seized upon this as evidence that Jackson felt completely free to interpret the Constitution in any way that he saw fit, which was hardly the case. But the carping of his critics, in this as in other matters, had little effect upon Old Hickory's popularity.

Jackson and the Bank of the United States

The Administration's policies in regard to land disposal, the tariff, internal improvements, and Indian removal manifested an earnest endeavour to move in accordance with the will of the people. The same may be said of its attitude toward the United States Bank, although here the government encountered powerful opposition and Jackson had to feel his way with caution.

The second Bank of the United States had had a checkered career since its charter in 1816. Its first president, William Jones, had badly managed and almost wrecked this supposed pillar of the nation's finance. Under Jones' successor, Langdon Cheves (pronounced Chivis), who was president during the depression years from 1819 to 1823, the Bank became very unpopular because of its vigorous efforts to force state banks on to a specie-paying basis and because of its drastic foreclosures on mortgaged property. Then, in 1823, Nicholas Biddle was made president, and the Bank's affairs took a turn for the better. By 1828 it was a well-run, conservatively managed institution.

Nicholas Biddle was forty-three years old when Jackson entered the White House. Handsome and aristocratic in bearing, he came of a wealthy and distinguished Philadelphia family. Refused a degree at the University of Pennsylvania on account of his youth (he was then thirteen years old), he went on to Princeton, where he graduated at the age of fifteen. He traveled widely, became interested in Greece and in Hellenic culture, and served for a time in 1806 as secretary to United States Minister James Monroe in London. Biddle was a Republican in politics, and Jefferson held the young man in high regard. Sometime after writing the history of the Lewis and Clark expedition, he became interested in banking; President Monroe made him one of the five directors of the Bank of the United States in 1819, and at the age of thirty-seven he became its president. Witty and urbane, a man of culture and intelligence, Biddle was essentially honest and straightforward by nature, but on occasion he could also be domineering and arrogant. He was naturally an optimist, prone to be unsuspecting of his fellow men and more than a trifle naive.

The Bank of the United States, when Jackson became President, was in many respects a valuable institution. The Treasury Department found the Bank useful in funding operations, using it repeatedly as a market for government bonds. Its swift and cheap exchanges helped to move crops and facilitate commercial activities in all parts of the country. It was a valuable agent in international finance, for it acted as a balance wheel of the currency. Its own notes were always receivable at par, and it helped maintain the quality of state bank notes by its practice of systematically presenting them to the banks of issue for redemption in specie. Its stock was a good investment for government money, and for that of the public as well. Indeed, so useful had the Bank become that in the 1820s the government repeatedly urged it to expand its operations.

But if the Bank had many points in its favor, it also had some decidedly vulnerable aspects. Its organization permitted a concentration of power in the hands of one man, its president. Biddle knew much more about banking than did his board of directors, and this knowledge, coupled with a personality that was strong-willed and impatient of opposition, almost reduced his board to ciphers in the formulation of the Bank's policies. The Bank's charter did not subject it to anything like strict regulation on the part of the government. Its power of arbitrary discount and of currency control was great, and, furthermore, it could and did use its lending power in doing favors for influential people. It extended a long-overdue loan to Postmaster General Barry, and lent money to Amos Kendall. It permitted Asbury Dickins, chief clerk of the Treasury under Jackson, to settle a loan for $.50 on the dollar. It was very useful to William Henry Seward in settling the affairs of the Holland Land Company, and Daniel Webster borrowed thousands of dollars from it, serving with satisfactory fees as its legal counsel; in 1833, at the height of the Bank war, Webster suggested to Biddle that, if he was to continue as legal adviser to the Bank, his retainer should be "renewed, or *refreshed* as usual." The Bank lent money to leading newspaper editors on both sides of the political fence. There could be no question of its great power. Up to 1833, this was not misused, and it was exercised with a real degree of political impartiality, but this did not alter the fact that the power did exist.

The Bank had many enemies. Hard-money men who believed that all paper currency should be rigidly restricted, working men suspicious of all banks, western speculators who wanted money that was cheap and easy, politicians who saw votes in anti-Bankism, men who honestly believed that the Bank was inimical to a democratic way of life, all these were ready and willing to attack the institution. So, too, was the President of the United States.

Jackson, by his own account, had always disliked banks in general. His attitude toward the Bank of the United States, when he took office in 1829, was one of suspicion deeply tinged with resentment. Stories were afloat that the Bank had played politics in the election of 1828, and these aroused his ire. He regarded the institution as a "monopoly." In his first annual message, he said that consideration of the Bank's recharter could not too soon be presented for "deliberate consideration" by Congress and the people; that the constitutionality and the expediency of the law creating the Bank were "well questioned"; and that all must admit that it had failed in establishing a sound and uniform currency. His hostility was not so marked in later messages, but by 1832 it was nevertheless plain that the charter, which was to expire four years later, would not be renewed if the President could help it.

Biddle had tried to win the President's favor. He had appointed Democrats as directors of various branches of the Bank and had presented Jackson with a plan for hastening the payment of the national debt. He became convinced, however, of the President's hostile intent, and it only remained to determine when application to Congress for a recharter would have the best prospect of forcing from Jackson an unwilling assent, or perhaps of overriding a presidential veto.

Clay, Webster, and Biddle's own agent, Thomas Cadwalader, advised application for a recharter early in the election year 1832. They believed that Congress would pass such a bill, and that it would put Old Hickory in a most embarrassing position. The President would be up for re-election. A veto would kill him in Pennsylvania, a key state where the Bank was very popular, but signing the bill would expose him to criticism in view of his known attitude toward the institution. Biddle decided to follow their advice.

A bill for the recharter of the Bank came before the Senate in March, 1832. A number of its provisions were designed to meet criticism of the Bank, but they still left it a powerful institution. After lengthy debate and investigation, the bill passed the Senate on May 20 by a vote of twenty-eight to twenty, and it passed the House on July 3 by 107 to eighty-five. One-third of the Democrats in the lower house favored its passage, formidable opposition to the Bank there as well as in the Senate coming only from the South and New York State.

Jackson vetoed the bill on July 10, 1832. The veto message was drawn up with the assistance of Amos Kendall (who wrote much of the first draft), Levi Woodbury, the Secretary of the Navy, and Roger B. Taney, the Attorney General. It declared that the amendments to the charter were of little worth, for the Bank was altogether too big and too powerful. The Bank was called a monopoly and not a "purely American" institution, since much of its stock was held abroad. It was held to be unconstitutional, for by invading the rights and powers of the states by its very existence, it violated the principle that the "true strength" of the national government "consists in leaving individuals and states as much as possible to themselves. . . ." The veto message closed with a denunciation of the bill as one permitting the rich and powerful to bind the government to their selfish purposes and it pledged a firm stand "against any prostitution of our Government to the advancement of the few at the expense of the many. . . ."

Authorities differ as to the validity of the reasoning in this famous veto message. Some applaud it for the bold and challenging way in which it stated the President's belief in the rights of the common man, while others denounce it as contemptible in reasoning and demagogic in character. It did betray an ignorance of economic reality, and its definition of the Bank as a monopoly was incorrect. But, though the veto failed to recognize the valuable services performed by the Bank, it did make clear the Administration's belief in equality of economic opportunity as the true basis of social and political democracy.

The National Republicans and Biddle were delighted with the veto. The Bank's president declared that it had "all the fury of a chained panther biting the bars of his cage"; that it was a "manifesto of anarchy." Clay and Webster denounced it in the Senate, and the National Republicans printed thousands of copies of the veto and scattered them throughout the country. The Democrats were also delighted, for entirely different reasons, and they, too, helped to spread the message of the veto abroad.

The Campaign of 1832

The campaign of 1832 had opened before Jackson sent the Bank bill back to Congress. The Antimasons held a national nominating convention at Baltimore, September 26, 1831, at which Thurlow Weed and his young, red-haired, beak-nosed little lawyer friend, William Henry Seward, were leading spirits. The convention would not support Clay, who was a Mason; instead, it nominated a scholarly Virginia lawyer named William Wirt, who was not an Antimason and who cared little about the Antimasonic crusade, but who accepted in the hope that the National Republicans would also choose him as their standard bearer. Wirt's hopes of a second nomination did not materialize, and he then wished to withdraw from the race. But he could not do this without deserting his Antimasonic friends, and the party had an unwilling candidate, something decidedly unusual in American politics. More significant than the fact of Wirt's nomination was the fact that the party's use of a national convention established a method of nominating presidential candidates that was regarded as definitely more democratic than the old congressional caucus, and that has been the mode ever since.

There was only one possible candidate for the National Republicans—Henry Clay. When he came back to the Senate in December, 1831, he was already the nominee of state legislatures and popular mass meetings in various parts of the country. A National Republican nominating convention at Baltimore (December 12–16, 1831) chose him by acclamation and issued an address to the voters criticizing Jackson's Administration for its "hostility" to internal improvements, its stand on the tariff and the Bank, its surrender to Georgia on the Cherokee question, and, generally, for partisanship, corruption, and abuse of power. The nomination was ratified in May, 1832, at a young men's National Republican convention in Washington. This issued the first platform adopted by a national nominating convention, advocating internal improvements and "adequate protection to American industry," and generally supporting the address issued by the Baltimore gathering.

Jackson and the leaders of his Administration had decided in 1831 that he should be renominated, a decision supported by the rank and file of the party in hundreds of mass meetings and conventions throughout the country. When the Democratic national convention assembled at Baltimore (May 21, 1832), it was really for the purpose of choosing a vice-presidential candidate. There were several contenders for this honor, but Martin Van Buren was Jackson's choice. The New Yorker was definitely unpopular in the South, especially among the admirers of Calhoun, but he had an overwhelming majority of the votes in the convention. On the second day, the convention adopted a rule that nomination had to be by a two-thirds vote. No other candidate could possibly hope to acquire that number of supporters, and on the first ballot Van Buren was chosen as Jackson's running mate. This was the beginning of the famous "two-thirds rule" that became traditional Democratic practice in nominating presidential and vice-presidential candidates.

The campaign of 1832 was bitterly contested. The National Republicans reiterated the charges made in their convention against the Democrats, denouncing Jackson as a tyrant and Van Buren as a lackey who had knelt in homage before the King of England and been given an opportunity to kiss the royal hand. The Democrats retorted that Clay was a tool of the Bank and of the money power, and declared that Jackson was the nation's great bulwark against oligarchy and eventual monarchy. Both parties used cartoons, which were becoming very popular, in caricaturing the opposition. The National Republicans relied heavily upon pamphlets, as well as printed speeches and addresses which the business class read but few of the common people saw. The Democrats made great use of speeches before crowds of people and other direct personal appeals.

Jackson and the Bank were the great issues of the campaign of 1832, and the result was never really in doubt, for the masses loved the one and loathed the other. Moreover, the opposition was split between Clay and Wirt. "Workingmen's" parties, organized during the preceding two years, often by National Republicans seeking to weaken the appeal of the Democracy to the common man, had little effect upon the outcome of the presidential campaign. Old Hickory rode to triumph in whirlwind fashion.

When the polls closed throughout the nation, it became apparent that Clay had carried only Massachusetts, Rhode Island, Connecticut, Maryland, Delaware and Kentucky. Wirt had the electoral vote of Vermont. South Carolina, bitter about the tariff, voted for a candidate of its own, John Floyd of Virginia. Jackson swept the rest of the country; he had 219 electoral votes to forty-nine for Clay, and, out of a total of 1,250,799 ballots cast, a popular majority of 124,205. It was a great personal triumph.

The congressional elections showed that Jackson ran well ahead of his party. While bona fide Democrats increased from 141 to 147 in the House, the new Antimasonic party gained no less than thirty-nine seats. And in both houses of Congress the appearance of states' rights Democrats and Nullifiers dissatisfied with the Administration's attitude toward the tariff created a troublesome situation. When need and opportunity arose, these dissident

Democrats would combine with the National Republicans and wrest control of legislation out of the hands of the Democratic leadership.

The National Republicans were despondent over the election. Their champion had been badly defeated, and they had lost one seat in the Senate and

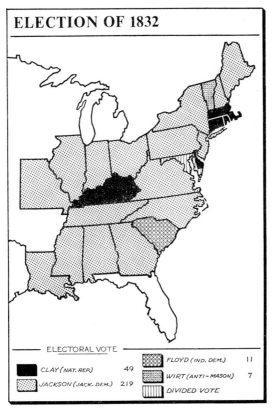

ELECTION OF 1832

ELECTORAL VOTE

CLAY (NAT. REP.)   49

JACKSON (JACK. DEM.)   219

FLOYD (IND. DEM.)   11

WIRT (ANTI-MASON)   7

DIVIDED VOTE

fifteen in the House, this last being largely due to the rise of Antimasonry. The leading National Republican organs were full of dire prophecies about the impending destruction of the tariff and the collapse of internal improvements. The Democrats, on the other hand, were jubilant and twitted their opponents about the poor showing they had made. William Cullen Bryant's *Evening Post* wondered editorially how such a weak thing as National Republicanism could have made so much noise during the presidential campaign.

The Democratic party was now clearly under the dominance of Jackson and Van Buren. It had emerged from the election victorious, but during the past four years it had lost a considerable number of adherents. Many southern states' righters and opponents of the tariff, religious elements disgusted by the treatment of the Indians, strong Democratic advocates of internal improvements angered by the Maysville veto, and Bank Democrats alienated by the veto of the Bank's recharter had left, or were soon to leave, the ranks of the faithful. The logic of events was now to produce new political combinations among those who disliked Old Hickory and the Democratic party policies.

The election of 1832 was the prelude to a series of dramatic events. The President, elated by his triumph, pressed forward to complete the destruction of the "Monster." The nullifiers of South Carolina, their anger mounting as they viewed the government's continued devotion to a protective policy, undertook a program of direct action against the tariff that in turn brought vigorous response from the determined Hero in the White House.

Suggested Reading

For the furious party battles of this period, Claude G. Bowers, *Party Battles of the Jackson Period* (1928) gives tone and color, though it is decidedly biased in favor of the Jacksonians. Wellington, cited in the previous chapter, is best for the controversy over public lands. On Indian removal, see Angie Debo, *The Road to Disappearance: A History of the Creek Indians* (1941); Annie H. Abel, already cited, and Grant Foreman, *Indian Removal* (1932). The important Supreme Court decisions are *Cherokee Nation v. State of Georgia,* 5 Peters 17, and *Worcester v. Georgia,* 6 Peters 521–579.

Charles McCarthy, "The Antimasonic Party," American Historical Association, *Reports,* vol. I (1902), is still standard, but see also G. G. Van Deusen, *Thurlow Weed* (1947). On the tariff, see Bemis, *John Quincy Adams and the Union* (1956), F. W. Taussig, *Tariff History* (rev. ed., 1931), Edward Stanwood, *Tariff Controversies in the Nineteenth Century* (2 vols., 1903); and G. G. Van Deusen, *Henry Clay* (1937).

There is much secondary literature on the second Bank of the United States. Bray Hammond, *Banks and Politics in America* (1957); Walter B. Smith, *Economic Aspects of the Second Bank of the United States* (1953); and Ralph C. H. Catterall, *The Second Bank of the United States* (1903) are all scholarly and favorable to the Bank. The same may be said of T. P. Govan, *Nicholas Biddle: Nationalist and Public Banker* (1959). Schlesinger's *The Age of Jackson,* presents the arguments against the Bank. Sister M. Grace Madeleine, *Monetary and Banking Theories of Jacksonian Democracy* (1943) is an honest and careful study. Samuel R. Gammon, Jr., "The Presidential Campaign of 1832," *The Johns Hopkins Studies in Historical and Political Science* XL (1932), 11–162, is the standard work for this election.

18 ⸱ The Full Flower of Jacksonianism

A
FTER THE SOUND AND TUMULT of the election of 1832 had died away, it was almost immediately replaced by the fury of another struggle that threatened the very existence of the Union. South Carolina found the tariff of 1832 completely unacceptable, and the discontent of the South Carolinians with the national government steadily mounted. The state threw away its vote in the presidential contest and chose a legislature that was ready for drastic action. The legislature summoned a state convention, which, on November 24, passed an ordinance declaring null and void as of February 1, 1833, the tariffs of 1828 and 1832. The convention further declared that the federal government must not collect duties in South Carolina under those tariff acts after February 1, 1833; that appeal of the validity of nullification to the Supreme Court would not be allowed; and that federal coercion would result in South Carolina's going out of the Union. The "Nullies," as they were coming to be known, were in control of the state and were openly threatening secession. The legislature provided funds for the purchase of arms and ammunition, and gave the governor authority to enlist volunteers. There was a minority of Unionists in the state, one of their leaders being Joel Poinsett, but they were helpless to stem the tide.

Crisis over Nullification

385

THE MENACE OF NULLIFICATION

This anonymous cartoon, drawn in 1833, shows Calhoun mounting the steps that lead from nullification to despotism. Two prominent South Carolinians, James Harvey Hammond on his left and Robert Y. Hayne on his right, urge him to grasp the glittering crown. Jackson, with a firm grip on Hayne's coattails, warns them of the consequences of their course.

Jackson's policy in answer to these developments in South Carolina was a mixture of warning and conciliation. His message to Congress (December 4, 1832) stated that the rapid approach of the end of the national debt would make possible substantial further reductions in the tariff, and he viewed with regret the state of excitement existing in South Carolina. In letters to Poinsett, who was keeping him abreast of events, Jackson declared that South Carolina's attitude verged on treason, and that he would take all the steps necessary to meet this deluded attempt to destroy the Union. This, of course, was meant to be disseminated at Charleston. And then, on December 10, Old Hickory issued his "Proclamation to the People of South Carolina."

In firm and unmistakable language, the President told the South Carolinians that their action meant the destruction of the nation. No state had any right whatsoever to annul a federal law, or to secede from the Union, either peaceably or by the use of violence. "Disunion by armed force is *treason*," he told them. "Are you really ready to incur its guilt?" He backed the Proclamation by troop orders, and when he requested Congress for additional powers in the collection of duties, it complied with "An Act further to provide the Collection of Duties on Imports." This was known as the Force Bill, and Jackson signed it March 2, 1833.

While preparations were being made to subdue the nullifiers by force of arms, the government made an effort to resolve the crisis by a substantial lowering of the tariff. The Verplanck bill, an Administration measure reported on the floor of the House on January 8, 1833, proposed reductions in duties that would lower the tariff 50 per cent within little more than a year.

The Compromise Tariff of 1833

Clay, leader of the National Republicans in the Senate, supported the Force Bill but viewed the Administration's drastic tariff cut with the utmost disfavor. As an ardent nationalist, he was disturbed by the threat to the Union implicit in South Carolina's action. As a politician the Kentuckian was also aware of the fact that, with Jackson breathing fire and slaughter against Calhoun and his sympathizers, anyone who rescued them from their predicament would be popular in the South. This was an area where he, as sponsor of the American System, was decidedly weak, and his popularity would be the more enhanced if it were achieved through a lowering of protective duties. After consulting with Senator John Tyler of Virginia, a states' rights Democrat who cast the only vote recorded in the Senate against the Force Bill, and with several other leading political figures, including Calhoun (who had resigned the vice presidency to come into the Senate), on February 12 Clay brought into the upper house the compromise tariff of 1833.

Clay's compromise provided for gradual reductions, at two-year intervals, of all schedules over 20 per cent in the existing tariff. Between 1840 and

1842, there were to be two sharp reductions of such duties. By July 1, 1842, there would be no duty rate above 20 per cent ad valorem.

This tariff of 1833 was not a very good bill. It was supposed to apply to all types of duties, but provided no ad valorem scales of reduction in specific duties. The reductions proposed were irregular in amount and in time, and the 20 per cent level set up an arbitrary standard with no discrimination among the various protected articles. Many protectionists, including Webster and Senator George M. Dallas of Pennsylvania, strongly opposed the bill. It did, however, offer a way out of a dangerous situation.

The voting on Clay's bill showed that the tariff was a local rather than a party issue. Southern congressmen were almost a unit in its support, and a large majority of New Englanders and of representatives from the Middle Atlantic states voted against the bill. Though eight of the eleven Democratic congressmen from the north central states of Ohio, Indiana, and Illinois voted for the measure, while only one out of the five National Republicans from that area supported the bill, the almost even split in the vote of these states indicated discontent with the failure of the South to support western land policy, on the one hand, and a desire for compromise, on the other, rather than any divergence on the ground of party doctrine. In the great majority of cases, the economic interest of their constituents dictated the votes of the men on Capitol Hill.

Jackson signed the compromise tariff as well as the Force Bill on March 2, 1833. South Carolina promptly nullified the latter but accepted the former, and with this acceptance the danger of civil strife was, for the time, averted.

The compromise tariff of 1833 was significant for a number of reasons other than the fact that it removed the danger of having to use armed force against a rebellious state. To some extent, it weakened the National Republicans as a party, for Webster and other strong protectionists were bitter about its passage. Adding to Clay's fame and popularity as a "Great Pacificator," it gave him considerable prestige among such exponents of states' rights as Virginia's John Tyler. It also marked the beginning of an understanding between Clay and Calhoun that was to be embarrassing to Jackson for the remainder of his second term. Most important of all, it was a gloomy portent of the future, for it was now obvious that the diversity of aims and objectives that existed between North and South was full of peril for the Union. Secession had been openly threatened by South Carolina, and, while the other southern states had shown no disposition to spring to the support of their beleaguered sister, a philosophy of action had been set up that would have greater and greater appeal throughout the South if the sections continued to diverge in their interests and aims.

Withdrawal of the Deposits

While Jackson was grappling with the Nullifiers, he was also moving against the Bank of the United States. Advisers such as Taney and Amos Kendall reinforced his own opinion that that institution was unconstitutional and corrupt, and that it was still plotting to force a renewal of its charter. The charter had four more years to run, and the President decided that the Bank's power must be immediately curtailed. He made up his mind to remove the government's money from the Bank by putting all the new government deposits in specially selected state banks, at the same time running off the government funds already in the Bank of the United States by using them for current federal expenditures. This would result in a drastic reduction of the Bank's deposits, and the institution would be forced to reduce its assets and its influence by calling in loans and refusing new ones.

A majority of the Congress opposed removal of the deposits, and so did Louis McLane, the Secretary of the Treasury. McLane was then shifted to the State Department and William J. Duane of Philadelphia was put in the Treasury. But Duane, who disliked all banks, could see no good reason for the transfer of government money to state banks that would be apt to use it for currency inflation and speculation in general. He refused to do the President's bidding, whereupon he also was removed, and Roger B. Taney was shifted from the office of Attorney General to that of Secretary of the Treasury. At last Jackson had found his man.

The government now began putting its money in selected state institutions that speedily became known as "Pet Banks," or "The Pets." As anticipated, this produced a marked diminution in the deposits of the Bank of the United States. These deposits shrank from $19,593,000 in 1832 to $9,496,000 in 1834.

Biddle took the removal of the deposits as an act of war, and began in turn contracting the Bank's obligations. This was inevitable, since the Bank's funds were rapidly diminishing, and he had to gird himself for possible further assaults. He pushed this curtailment further than was necessary, however, since he hoped by drastic reduction of loans and discounts to produce economic distress and a demand for a recharter. Biddle's policy of contraction was at its height during the winter of 1833–1834. It delighted the National Republicans, and Clay pushed through the Senate resolutions censuring the President for removing Duane from office and the deposits from the Bank. The Senate also rejected Taney's appointment as Secretary of the Treasury, and, some months later, it prevented his appointment as an Associate Justice of the Supreme Court.

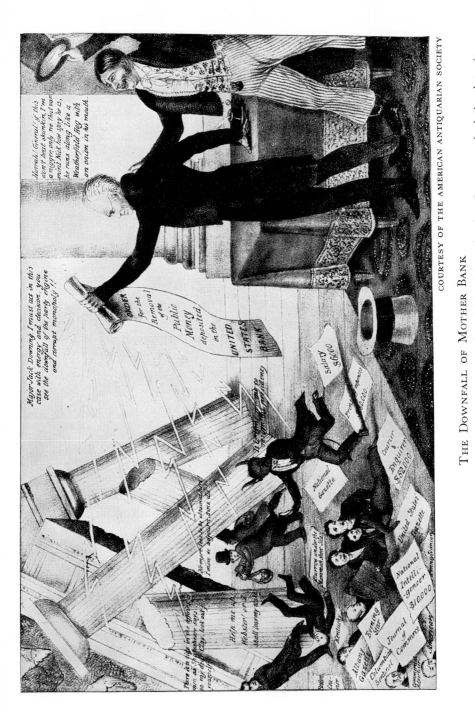

The Downfall of Mother Bank

Published by H. R. Robinson, this cartoon shows Jackson flourishing his order for the removal of the deposits. Jack Downing, a symbol of the people, applauds Jackson's course. As the pillars of the institution crumble, Bid- dle, equipped with horns and various Whig editors and politicians seek to escape from the ruins.

Biddle's scheme for forcing a recharter boomeranged. It probably increased a credit stringency that was being produced by other factors, but its effect upon the economy was exaggerated for their own purposes by both the friends and the enemies of the Bank. Jackson and Congress were besieged by petitions for relief through a restoration of the deposits, but Old Hickory was adamant. He told the supplicants to "go to the Monster, go to Nicholas Biddle," and declared that he would never recharter the Bank of the United States, or sign a charter for any other bank. As for stock jobbers and brokers, he wished that they could all be swept out of the land. Since popular opinion supported the President, the Bank's defenders began dropping away, and all prospect of a recharter vanished.

Last Days of the Bank

The Bank of the United States, as such, went out of existence at the expiration of its charter in 1836. It then received a new charter from the state of Pennsylvania, but it soon became involved in heavy foreign borrowings and in a disastrous attempt to support falling prices for United States cotton, and went into bankruptcy in 1841. Although Biddle had resigned as its president in 1839, he had remained in close association with the Bank and was involved in the cotton venture. The stockholders sued him for damages, and he was arrested on charges of criminal conspiracy, of which he was exonerated. Other charges were then preferred, but he died in 1844 at the age of fifty-eight.

The war on the Bank of the United States had many tragic aspects. The Bank was a valuable institution, but the power that it enjoyed made it an object of suspicion in an era that prided itself upon its democratic simplicity. The President, who had only a superficial understanding of the services it performed, disliked and distrusted the Bank, and when it became involved in the political struggles between him and his opponents, he crushed it. The Bank's destruction symbolized the intent of the Jacksonians to preserve freedom of economic opportunity in the United States, but its elimination opened the way to money and credit inflation by the "Pets," and was a blow to sound banking practice. Politically, the war on the Bank was profitable, for it helped identify the Democratic party in the public mind as the champion of the common man against undue privilege and power.

The Democratic Party in the 1830s

During Jackson's second term, there were changes of great importance in the American political scene. Two national political parties disappeared, and a new party came into existence. The Democracy itself continued in being, but there were some significant modifications in its composition and orientation.

During the 1830s, the Democratic party became more and more clearly identified as representing the interests of the common people. The great planters and conservative states' righters of the South left its ranks, repelled by Jackson's nationalism, but a majority of the South's small farmers remained loyal Jacksonians. In New England and the Middle Atlantic states, it was the natural home of a majority of the small farmers and fishermen and of a considerable portion of urban labor. The foreign-born, especially the Irish, became Democrats, attracted by Jackson's war on privilege and the friendly helpfulness of such Democratic organizations as New York City's Tammany Hall. In the West, the farmers and frontiersmen responded to the party's sympathy for a more liberal land policy, and to its championship in the states of free, tax-supported public schools. But the Democracy was in no sense a class party; its leaders stressed equality of opportunity for business men and bankers as well as for farmers. Despite its emphasis on the rights of the "common man," it was essentially middle class in composition and in aims.

Since the Democratic party was oriented around a middle-class norm, its vitality was due largely to its "crusade" for equality of opportunity. In its search for this goal, the party moved slowly and cautiously left of center. This was evidenced in the Supreme Court, where eight appointments made by Old Hickory resulted in a bench much less respectful of the sanctity of contracts than it had been during the palmy days of John Marshall's dominance. Roger Brooke Taney, appointed Chief Justice in 1836 despite Whig opposition, distrusted corporations, although he recognized them as necessary social instruments. In his famous *Charles River Bridge v. Warren Bridge* decision (1837), he proclaimed the paramount rights of the community over those of the holders of private property. This reversed the attitude of the Court in the *Dartmouth College Case* (1819) and was much disliked by the holders of vested interests, although it was socially useful in clearing the path of the mushrooming canal, steamboat, and railroad companies. The party also espoused the free incorporation of business and banking firms, an effort to escape from the lobbying and corruption that had come to characterize the granting of charters by legislative acts of incorporation but that opened the door wide to the corporate form of business enterprise. These developments indicated the persistence of a mildly reforming spirit in the party, and more radical tendencies in the ranks of the Democracy were made evident in the middle 1830s by the emergence of Loco Focoism.

Thomas Hart Benton
(1782–1858)

This splendid photograph was taken sometime between 1845 and 1850. It reveals the rugged quality and the forcefulness of one of Jackson's staunch supporters.

COURTESY OF THE CHICAGO HISTORICAL SOCIETY

The Loco Foco movement arose in New York City as a protest of the Democratic rank and file against the control of the city and state Democratic party organizations by bankers and commercialists. It took its name from the use of "loco foco" matches to light candles at a meeting where conservative Democrats, being in a minority, strove to put an end to the proceedings by shutting off the gaslights. The Loco Focos looked with hearty disfavor upon monopolies and corporations. Detesting bank notes and banks, they advocated a specie—that is, a hard-money—currency. They were free traders, hostile to imprisonment for debt, and to inequity and privilege in any form. Although not abolitionists, they were opposed to slavery. Radical spirits such as Frances Wright, Robert Dale Owen, and William Cullen Bryant sympathized with them, although they did not actually become identified with the movement.

New York's Loco Focoism was paralleled to a considerable extent in Massachusetts and Pennsylvania. In the former state, men like Seth Luther, Samuel Allen, Theodore Sedgwick, and the historian George Bancroft were spokesmen for the grievances of mill laborers and poverty-stricken farmers. They denounced paper money, corporations, and the financial aristocracy of the Bay State, and helped rally the workingmen in Massachusetts back of hard money and Andrew Jackson. In Pennsylvania, a similar movement split the Democratic party into progressive and conservative wings.

Character and Composition of the Whig Party

The Democracy's great political opponent in the middle 1830s and for twenty years thereafter was the Whig party. It was a coalition of National Republicans (whose organization virtually dissolved after the 1832 election), the Antimasons—who were led into the fold by Weed, Seward, and their allies—and a considerable number of conservative Democrats thoroughly disgusted with Old Hickory and his policies. Viewed from one point of view, Whiggism was simply a coalition of anti-Jacksonians, to which James Watson Webb, editor of the New York *Courier and Enquirer,* gave a name. "Whig" appeared on a New York City ballot in 1834, and the term spread rapidly to other parts of the country. It was designed to show the sound, middle-class nature of the party, and to indicate that the followers of "King Andrew," as the Whigs termed the President, were really Tories at heart.

The economic structure of Whiggery was much the same as that of National Republicanism. It attracted eastern commercialists and industrialists, western entrepreneurs and farmers, southern planters, commercialists, and bankers, and those financially dependent upon them. Members of the laboring class who felt that their jobs were tied to their employers' prosperity joined the Whig party. It caught the imaginations of men like Lincoln, Seward, and Greeley, who were attracted by the grand scope of Clay's American System, and who saw little of a constructive nature in the Democratic concentration upon preserving a society of equals.

Though the Whig party was predominantly one of the economic "haves," it had other characteristics as well. It harbored a states' rights element which was alienated from the Democracy by Jackson, and which joined the Whigs chiefly because it had no place else to go. Whigs, in general, were social conservatives. They distrusted the masses but refused to recognize any class structure in society, preferring to regard mechanics, farmers, businessmen, and bankers as all bound together in a mutual harmony of interest. They accepted universal male white suffrage, but without any real enthusiasm. They felt, as their organ, the *American Review,* said, that the ignorant and the vicious had the right to vote simply because there was no remedy that was not worse than the disease. Finally, the Whig party was basically national in its point of view. By 1841, even the southern Whigs were supporters of Clay's nationalist policies. The party members could generally be relied upon to have some concept of the nation's potential for economic development, and their views on banking, currency, internal improvements, and government spending were considerably ahead of their time.

The Trend Toward Hard Money

The congressional election of 1834, held while the Whig party was gathering its disparate elements into shaky formation, saw the Democrats increase their majority in the House but emerge with an often unmanageable majority of two in the Senate, where Clay and Calhoun were trying to work together. The party that had triumphed in its war on the Bank now manifested a tendency to leave the battle against privilege to its state organizations. But the sympathy of Jackson's Administration with the struggles that were being carried on in the states remained plain for all to see. The President's messages to Congress repeatedly criticized monopoly, legislation for special interests, and Clay's American System, and they urged cheap land policy. Jackson proposed suppressing all bank notes below $20.00, thus favoring a trend which, by 1836, saw thirteen states prohibit bills of less than $5.00 face value.

The Whigs, generally speaking, opposed this hard-money trend. They wanted a sound circulating medium that would be a judicious mixture of specie and specie-backed paper, the latter controlled by some government agency such as the Bank of the United States. They viewed the Administration's attitude with deep suspicion, for they believed that there was not enough specie in the country to permit its widespread use as a circulating medium, and that the movement away from bank notes and toward a hard-money currency would handicap economic expansion.

The Administration's antipathy for bank notes was made manifest by more than presidential recommendations. The Coinage Act of 1834, changing the ratio of silver and gold in the coinage from fifteen to one to sixteen to one, overvalued gold at the mint. The effect of this Act was to drive silver out of circulation and to demoralize the fractional coinage. It was a partisan move, designed to stimulate gold mining in the southern states and to bring more foreign gold into the country. This, it was believed, would increase the supply of gold coins to such an extent that the notes of the Bank of the

United States could be more easily driven out of existence and the nation brought closer to a hard-money standard. Two years later another move, this time in connection with land policy, also emphasized the government's interest in hard money as well as its desire to check the inflation that was now part of the national scene.

Land Speculation and the Specie Circular

During 1835–1836, a great mania for speculation swept over the land. In this period, adventurous spirits looking for quick profits concentrated on land rather than stocks. Real estate values moved upward at a dizzying pace, and the sales of public lands tripled and quadrupled in amount; in 1836, no less than 20,074,871 acres of the public domain passed into the hands of private purchasers.

The Administration at first regarded this great increase in the sale of the public lands as evidence of the prosperous condition of the country, but it soon became convinced that the situation was an unhealthy one. As the speculation in land rose to fever pitch, so did the demand for currency with which to pay off the obligations involved in the purchases. Banks expanded their loans, often on dubious security, and their expanded currency issues were frequently of very doubtful character. The restraining influence of the Bank of the United States on the issues of the state banks was felt no longer, and the money that the government received as revenue from land sales rapidly deteriorated in quality. Alarmed, the Administration began to take steps. In April, 1835, the Treasury ordered the land offices to accept only bills of $5.00 or more in face value, and on July 11, 1836, President Jackson issued the Specie Circular, which prohibited payment for the public lands in anything except specie.

The Specie Circular was designed to check speculation in land, and to serve as a warning to the country that inflation had reached dangerous heights. Indirectly, it demonstrated the evil inherent in a paper currency, and thus fitted in well with the hard-money doctrine preached by the Democratic radicals. But it also drained specie from the East into the West, and put the small land purchaser, who had little hard money, at the mercy of the wealthy speculator who had specie reserves. It was an unpopular measure. The Whigs denounced it, and a majority in both houses of Congress wished to see it modified, if not repealed. Jackson was adamant, however, and the Circular remained in effect until it was repealed by a joint resolution of Congress in 1838.

Distribution of the Surplus

The Bank, hard money, and the Specie Circular were not the only issues that produced political controversy during Jackson's second term. Whigs and Democrats both sought political capital out of the surplus that appeared in the Treasury; the moral issue of slavery began moving into the arena of politics; and a long-standing controversy with France became an issue between the contending forces in Congress.

By the middle of the 1830s, the United States government was out of debt, and money began to pile up in the Treasury—or, rather, in the Treasury's depositaries, the "Pet" banks. In January, 1836, the surplus exceeded $30 million. The states wanted this money, and both parties recognized the importance of handling out largesse in a presidential year. The Whigs proposed an outright distribution among the states, a move that Jackson now opposed in a reversal of his previous attitude, but the Democrats were not disposed to let the Whigs make any political capital out of the surplus. The result was a curious bill which "deposited" the surplus over $5 million with the states, in proportion to their representation in Congress and subject to to recall by the Treasury. This was actually a distribution of funds, and the Whigs loudly proclaimed that no one really expected the money to be paid back. Both sides claimed credit for the measure during the campaign, although the Democrats became critical of it after the election was over, when, unfortunately, it stimulated an already dangerous inflation.

Growth of Antislavery Agitation

As the national election drew near, it became apparent that the issue of slavery was entering the political picture. Antislavery agitation was growing in the North, fostered by such men as the New Jersey Quaker Benjamin Lundy, the fiery William Lloyd Garrison, and Theodore Dwight Weld, the great evangelist of abolitionism. Antislavery petitions began pouring into Congress, and congressional representatives of areas where moral opposition to slaveholding was increasing were eager to present these documents in the House and the Senate. The petitions denounced slavery as a blot upon American civilization, many of them urging that, as a beginning, slavery be abolished in the District of Columbia.

The South reacted vigorously to these petitions, and to antislavery activity in general. In 1831, a slave uprising in Virginia, known as Nat Turner's Rebellion, had resulted in the massacre of over fifty whites. Southerners believed, with some reason, that the agitation against slavery, whether in Congress or in pamphlet literature mailed to the South, increased the danger of slave insurrections, and they demanded that Congress refuse to entertain the antislavery petitions. Gag resolutions passed both houses of Congress under southern pressure. In the Senate the petitions were received, and then either tabled or rejected, and in the House they were received and tabled, but neither the Senate nor the House allowed discussion of or debate on the offending documents. In addition to these gag rules, Amos Kendall, now Postmaster General, ruled that abolition literature might be mailed in the North, but need not be delivered by southern postmasters.

The reaction of the national government to southern pressure gave the abolitionists ground for declaring that freedom of the press, freedom of speech, and freedom of petition were being denied in Washington—good missionary propaganda for their cause. It was also becoming apparent that, in such northern states as New York, Massachusetts, and Ohio, the party which took a sympathetic attitude toward the antislavery forces would be likely to gain a considerable number of votes. Slavery was threatening to become a political question, and both Whig and Democratic leaders saw danger in any such development.

Texas Becomes a Problem

Along with slavery, another problem that had political implications was looming on the southwestern border of the country. By 1836, some 30,000 Americans, chiefly from the South, had settled in the Mexican province of Texas. They had brought their slaves with them, for cotton land was one of the chief attractions of this area west of the Sabine River. The Mexicans, who had at first welcomed immigration from the United States, were now becoming alarmed by this influx of "gringoes." They tried, belatedly, to enforce Mexican laws against slavery, and General Antonio Lopez de Santa Anna, the Mexican dictator, undertook to establish a firm control over the area north of the Rio Grande. The alarmed Texans proclaimed their independence on March 2, 1836. Santa Anna moved at the head of the Mexican army into Texas, massacred the garrison of the Alamo, at San Antonio, and at Goliad executed some 350 prisoners.

On April 21, Sam Houston, a colorful Texan leader known as "The Raven," struck back. Santa Anna's army was routed, and he himself was taken prisoner and forced to sign treaties by which he agreed to evacuate Texas and use his influence to free from Mexican control the territory claimed by the Texans. Mexican forces were indeed withdrawn south of the

Rio Grande, but Mexico obstinately refused to recognize the independence of Texas.

The United States had been interested for some time in the acquisition of Texas. President John Quincy Adams had tried to buy that territory, advancing to the Mexicans an ingenious argument that the cession would put Mexico City, their capital, much more nearly in the center of the Mexican state. Old Hickory had vainly offered Mexico $5 million for Texas, and Sam Houston was a close friend of the American President. Jackson moved cautiously, however, for antislavery people were beginning to raise a hue and cry about a southern conspiracy for the acquisition of more slave territory, and there was no point in weakening Democratic strength in the North during a presidential election year. This reasoning was all the more cogent because such prominent Whigs as Daniel Webster and John Quincy Adams were openly opposed to recognition and Clay was urging delay. It was only after the campaign was over that Jackson, on March 3, 1837, acted by nominating a chargé d'affaires to the Republic of Texas.

The Spoliation Claims Against France

Texas was politically troublesome, but relations with France assumed a positively menacing tone during Jackson's second term. Ever since the French Revolution and the Napoleonic wars, the United States had been presenting damage claims for losses to American shippers during that time of troubles. American claimants declared that they should receive $7,775,000. France did not deny the existence of just claims, but kept putting off any settlement. The French government was glad to spend $200 million indemnifying royalist émigrés who had come back home, but it had little interest in paying damages, however justified they might be, to Americans. Clay, as Secretary of State, had proposed that Congress be asked to issue letters of marque and reprisal against France as a means of obtaining satisfaction, but Adams had rejected this as likely to endanger peaceful relations.

Jackson inherited the French controversy, and, as a result of the July Revolution in 1830, Louis Philippe became King of France. Lafayette, America's old friend, was a power behind the throne, and the new French monarch had himself spent some time in the United States and liked Americans. In 1831, a treaty was signed between France and the United States by which France was to appropriate $5 million for the satisfaction of American claims, and the latter country agreed to pay $300,000 for the release of French counterclaims. The United States Senate ratified the treaty, as did

Louis Philippe. France was to pay in six annual installments, from each of which a proportionate amount of the American payment was to be deducted. But when the time came for payment of the first installment, and the Secretary of the Treasury sent to the Bank of the United States for collection a draft on the French Treasury for the scheduled amount, the French Treasury refused payment, for the French government had not even requested the Legislative Chambers to make the necessary appropriation. As was customary under such circumstances, Biddle presented the United States government with a claim for interest and 15 per cent damages. The claim amounted to $170,041.18, and the American government refused to pay it. This incident increased Old Hickory's dislike of the Bank as well as his mounting irritation over French delay in meeting a just obligation.

The President had, in fact, been unusually patient in his handling of the debt question, but his forebearance was now nearing an end. He reviewed the case in his message to Congress on December 1, 1834, pointing out that twenty-five years had elapsed since the claims had first been presented, and that another quarter of a century ought not to be wasted in futile negotiation. He asked Congress to pass a provisional law authorizing the seizure of French property to the required amount if the next session of the Chambers failed to pass the appropriation bill. France, greatly affronted, recalled its Minister from Washington, and eventually the American Minister to France also returned home.

The Whig Senators wanted to make political capital out of this French imbroglio. Clay reported from the Senate Committee on Foreign Relations a resolution that it was inexpedient at this time to authorize reprisals, asserting that it would probably be regarded by France as an act of war. The Senate agreed to the Kentuckian's temperate report without a dissenting vote, but the House Democratic majority wanted a firmer stand, and was backed in this by John Quincy Adams. The House, therefore, while expressing no opinion on Jackson's proposal, approved a fortifications bill amendment appropriating $3 million for the defense of the country. This was voted down on party lines in the Senate, and a compromise conference between House and Senate agreed on an appropriation of $300,000 for fortifications and $500,000 for the navy. But this agreement came at the close of the session, and when, at 2 A.M. on March 4, 1835, the report of the conference committee reached the House, there was no quorum in that body. The fortifications bill, and with it the appropriation for defense, had failed of passage, and the Democrats thereupon loudly proclaimed that the Whigs were responsible for leaving the country naked to the foe.

While Congress was out of session during the summer of 1835, the French

Chambers passed the necessary appropriation to satisfy the terms of the treaty, but with the proviso that it would not be paid until there was some satisfactory explanation of the language the President had used in regard to France. Though Jackson was inclined to be obdurate, his advisers prevailed upon him to include in his annual message of December, 1835, a statement which denied any intention of menacing or insulting the French government. This, the President made clear, was not an apology. France was at this time facing a delicate international situation, particularly in regard to Russia and the Eastern Question, and the Chambers were glad enough to accept Jackson's statement as an apology, whether or not Old Hickory had the same point of view. British good offices had a further ameliorating effect on both sides. France began payment of the treaty installments, and diplomatic relations between the two countries were resumed in 1836, thus eliminating what some Whigs had hoped would be an effective campaign issue in the election of that year.

The 1836 Presidential Campaign

Jackson's choice as his successor was Vice President Van Buren, and the old Hero's word in this regard was law. The Democratic national convention met at Baltimore May 20, 1835. The South was cool to the "Red Fox," both the Alabama and Tennessee legislatures having already rejected him as the party's nominee. The full force of the executive patronage was exerted on his behalf, however, and he was made the unanimous choice of the convention. There was no platform. The party stood on its record.

The Whigs, full of conflicting views as to candidates and any possible platform, refused to hold a national convention and issued no statement of principles. They put up a number of candidates in various parts of the country where these men were regarded as strong, hoping in this way to throw the election into the House of Representatives. Webster, for example, was nominated in Massachusetts, and Hugh Lawson White, a recreant Democrat, received the accolade in Tennessee. As it developed, the strongest Whig candidate was the sixty-three-year-old William Henry Harrison, whom the Pennsylvania Whigs put in nomination; his chief claim to fame was his record in the War of 1812, and he was popular in both the West and in the Middle Atlantic states.

There was no issue of any great importance in the campaign of 1836. The Democrats tried hard to identify the Whigs with the Bank of the United States, and the Whigs sought with equal vigor to avoid such an identification. The Whigs lacked unity and a popular issue on which to make a stand.

The Democrats were riddled with factionalism in a number of states, and Van Buren, who hailed from a state where antislavery sentiment was strong and growing, was distrusted in the South. White carried Georgia and Tennessee. South Carolina, as it had done four years previously, voted for its own particular candidate, United States Senator Willie P. Mangum of North Carolina, who had opposed the Force Bill and had also voted for the censure of President Jackson.

The outcome of the election was another Democratic victory, though by no means a decisive one. Van Buren had 170 electoral votes, to 124 for his combined opponents. No vice-presidential candidate received a majority and, for the first and only time in American history, that election went to the Senate, which chose Richard M. Johnson of Kentucky, Van Buren's running mate. The Democracy had a narrow majority of 27,027 votes out of a total of 1,498,329. It had a working majority in the Senate, but the situation in the House, where "radical" Whigs and conservative Democrats held the balance of power, was anomalous.

The chief significance of the election was its indication that the country now had two major political parties that were relatively evenly balanced in power. The election also showed that the Democratic reform movement was losing something of its potency as a political battle cry. The Bank was gone, and no other "Monster" which could be tied to the Whigs had taken its place.

Andrew Jackson was delighted with Van Buren's success. Ill, pain-wracked, but indomitable, the old chieftain, now nearing his seventieth birthday, attended the presidential inauguration on March 4, 1837. There he saw Van Buren sworn into office by Chief Justice Roger B. Taney, which gave him great satisfaction. Both men were Old Hickory's close friends, and both were men whose careers the Whigs had attempted to ruin.

Suggested Reading

On nullification, see David F. Houston, *A Critical Study of Nullification in South Carolina* (1896); Chauncey S. Boucher, *The Nullification Controversy in South Carolina* (1916); C. S. Sydnor, *The Development of Southern Sectionalism, 1819–1848* (1948), and Frederic Bancroft, *Calhoun and the South Carolina Nullification Movement* (1928).

The Compromise Tariff of 1833 is examined in Van Deusen's *The Life of Henry Clay*, Charles Wiltse's *Calhoun*, and Frederick L. Nussbaum's "The Compromise Tariff of 1833—A Study in Practical Politics," *South Atlantic Quarterly*, XI (Oct., 1912), 337–349.

The removal of the deposits is treated in the works already cited by Catterall, Walter B. Smith, and Bray Hammond. See also Carl Brent Swisher, *Roger B. Taney* (1935).

For the Democratic party in the 1830s, see the works by Schlesinger and Binkley and Van Deusen's *The Jacksonian Era,* all previously cited. The rise of the Whig party is studied in E. Malcolm Carroll, *Origins of the Whig Party* (1925); Arthur C. Cole, *The Whig Party in the South* (1913); Henry R. Mueller, *The Whig Party in Pennsylvania* (1922); Paul Murray, *The Whig Party in Georgia* (1948); Charles M. Thompson, *The Illinois Whigs Before 1848* (1915). See also G. G. Van Deusen, "Some Aspects of Whig Thought and Theory in the Jacksonian Period," *American Historical Review,* LXIII (Jan., 1958), 305–322.

The standard work on the distribution of the surplus is Edward G. Bourne, *The History of the Surplus Revenue* (1885).

Important books on the antislavery controversy in the middle 1830s are Russell B. Nye, *Fettered Freedom* (1949); Gilbert H. Barnes, *The Antislavery Impulse, 1830–1844* (1933); Dwight L. Dumond, *Antislavery Origins of the Civil War in the United States* (1939).

On the election of 1836, W. Dean Burnham, *Presidential Ballots, 1836–1892* (1955) is especially useful; it includes valuable statistics. See also Edward M. Shepard, *Martin Van Buren* (1899); Dorothy B. Goebel, *William Henry Harrison* (1926); and the works previously cited by Carroll and Cole.

19 ʼ Van Buren's Time of Troubles

MARTIN VAN BUREN came of middle-class parentage; his father was a tavern keeper and truck farmer at Kinderhook, New York, near Albany. Young Martin had the usual village schooling, read law, and was admitted to the bar. Clever, clear-headed, an ardent Republican from an early age, the yellow-haired youth rose rapidly in his profession and

Van Buren and His Program

in politics. His five-foot-six-inch frame was always immaculately garbed, and his cheerful demeanor indicated a friendly disposition that kept him on good terms with his political opponents. Powerful in debate and anxious to get ahead, by 1820 he had become one of the leading Jeffersonian Republicans of New York State. As chief of the Albany Regency, a remarkable group of New York Republicans who guided the state party in the 1820s and 1830s, he demonstrated that he was amiable, tactful, cautious and shrewd. John Randolph once remarked of him, with justice, that he had a propensity for "rowing to his object with muffled oars," but he was honest and courageous, and a tincture of idealism in his makeup kept him from being merely a political opportunist. Now, at the age of fifty-five, balding but benignant, his hair and sideburns shot with gray, he would have need of all his sagacity. As Jackson's heir, it was his responsibility to carry on the Jacksonian enlightenment in the face of powerful Whig opposition and despite the fact that he himself lacked that great personal appeal which had been such an asset for Old Hickory.

Van Buren's Cabinet and his inaugural address both indicated the line that he proposed to follow. With one exception, Secretary of War Joel Poinsett, his official family remained as it had been at the close of Jackson's second term. At his inauguration, he promised to follow in Jackson's footsteps, to uphold the Jacksonian tradition. Emphasis was put on maintaining that national unity which had so triumphantly weathered all storms. Slavery was perhaps the greatest remaining source of discord and disaster, but the new President pledged himself to resist all attempts to abolish it in the District of Columbia, or to interfere with it in the states where it already existed. It was clear that he meant to base his Administration on principles satisfactory to both planters and plain Republicans.

The Panic of 1837

Van Buren declared in his inaugural that "in all the attributes of a great, happy, and flourishing people we stand without a parallel in the world." The optimistic exuberance of this statement was scarcely justified, for already there were ominous signs of economic disaster. Scarcely a month after he took office, the panic of 1837 burst upon the land.

"Overbanking and overtrading," to use a Democratic expression, had grown to dangerous proportions by 1837. The mania for land speculation, in boom years that few thought would ever end, had produced an excess of loans and note issues by the unregulated state banks. Fortunes were made overnight in western and southern land speculations, and the selling price of real estate in eastern urban areas rose to spectacular heights, the value of real estate in New York City increasing 50 per cent in five years. The states had embarked upon ambitious internal improvement programs, often borrowing from state banks that had been specially created to furnish the necessary loans, and one state after another had gone heavily into debt. An influx of foreign capital had augmented what appeared to be endless supplies of credit. By 1836, over $90 million, most of it from England, had been invested in northern canals and railways, and foreigners had also purchased large amounts of southern state bank securities that carried interest rates as high as 9 and 10 per cent. But still the future had seemed rosy. When New York was devastated by a great fire in 1835, the rapidity with which the city was rebuilt excited the wonder of natives and foreigners alike, and seemed to prove that American prosperity was based upon solid foundations. Then came the deluge.

A variety of factors contributed to the depression of 1837. The Specie Circular drew gold and silver into the West, made money tight in the East, forced western banks to curtail discounts, and spread doubt as to the soundness of banks in general. Rumors that all was not well with the nation's economic situation began to circulate as early as April, 1836, and multiplied as the year went on. A depression in England lessened the demand for American cotton and started a drain of specie abroad as foreign investors began to sell their holdings in American canal and bank stocks. Doubts now began to change into alarm. The situation was grave when Van Buren delivered his inaugural address, and within a month it was clear that the economy was in a most serious depression.

The Times

A representation of the panic of 1837. Note the workmen without shoes, the crowd of depositors before the bank that has stopped specie payments, the line before the pawnbroker's shop, and the Loco Focos who are drowning their sorrows with a bottle of gin.

The character of the collapse soon became distressingly apparent. A run on the New York City banks took $1 million in gold and silver from their vaults. On May 10, 1837, they suspended specie payment, an example speedily followed by banks throughout the country. In New York City alone, hundreds of business concerns failed, and Philip Hone, prosperous New York merchant, found himself plunged into debt from which he emerged only after two-thirds of his fortune had disappeared. Benjamin Rathbun, leading Buffalo promoter and philanthropist, saw his speculative enterprises collapse in a welter of fraudulent endorsements, and he himself landed in jail. Bankruptcies became everyday occurrences throughout the country, as land values collapsed everywhere, and southern plantations sold for a song. As late as 1842, a federal Bankruptcy Act which was in force only four months wiped out $450 million in debts that affected one million creditors.

Labor suffered with business, for wages dropped and unemployment was widespread. In New York, flour stores were sacked by a hungry mob, and a city journal told of 500 men answering an advertisement for twenty spade laborers to work in the country for $4.00 a month and board. Young Horace Greeley, prowling the poorer streets of the metropolis, saw filth and disease rampant, thousands living in quarters "unfit for cleanly brutes," and able-bodied and ambitious men pleading in vain for employment. The nation had entered a depression from which it was not to recover fully for at least seven years.

Political Implications of the Depression

From its beginning, the depression had profound political implications. The Whigs promptly declared that it was due to Jackson's financial policies. Everywhere they denounced the Specie Circular. The Democracy's hard money policy came under heavy indictment, as specie was hoarded and the lack of bank notes in the lower denominations resulted in a fantastic emission of paper notes known as "shinplasters" which were issued by business concerns, stores, and even barber shops.

The voters responded to the Whig onslaught. As early as the fall of 1837, the Democracy lost heavily in local and state elections. In that year, the New York State assembly changed from thirty-four Whigs and ninety-four Democrats to 101 Whigs and twenty-seven Democrats, and there were similar Whig gains in other states. The Democratic party itself was riven by division of opinion over the merits of hard money and of banks. Factional fights split the Democratic state organizations in New York, Virginia, Pennsylvania, New Jersey, and North Carolina. In New York State, the Democratic Conservatives, led by United States Senator Nathaniel P. Tallmadge, broke with Van Buren's leadership and worked with the Whigs in state elections; their example was followed in other parts of the Union.

Whig scorn for Jacksonian finance and Whig appeals to Democrats to transfer their political allegiance found the Democratic leadership very much

on the defensive. Loyal Democrats insisted that speculation and bad banking practice were the true causes of the depression. Insisting that the people
were still loyal to the party of Andrew Jackson, and explaining Whig victories by charges of fraud and corruption, they repeatedly warned the country to beware of a Whig plot to bring back the Bank of the United States.
Meanwhile, the Administration in Washington faced the hard task of establishing an economic policy that would rally the wavering and hold them
firm to the party's main objective of maintaining social justice and equality
of opportunity for every citizen. As Van Buren wrote to Jackson, now in retirement at the Hermitage, the task was one of great difficulty and delicacy.

Proposed Repeal of the Specie Circular

The immediate problem that confronted the national Administration was
a mounting demand for the repeal of the Specie Circular, which arose from

THE MODERN BALAAM AND HIS ASS (1837)

*Jackson cudgels his Ass, "Specie Currency," with the President's veto of
a bill repealing the Specie Circular, but the ghost of the bankrupts of
1837 blocks the path. The newly elected President Van Buren tags along
behind Jackson, promising to follow in his footsteps.*

COURTESY OF THE NEW-YORK HISTORICAL SOCIETY, NEW YORK CITY

THE MODERN BALAAM AND HIS ASS.

Democratic as well as Whig quarters. The argument was that the Circular had a bad deflationary effect, and that its repeal would not only help restore confidence, but also increase the revenues of the government. Van Buren considered the problem carefully and finally decided to keep the Circular in effect. His action was couragous, for he knew that it would displease business circles and raise a chorus of Whig and Democratic criticism. He was determined to brave his critics, however, for he still believed that the best remedy the federal government could provide for monetary ills was its policy of encouraging a currency consisting largely of specie.

The Extra Session of Congress and Van Buren's Proposals

Maintenance of the Specie Circular did not solve the embarrassments which the depression brought upon the national government, the chief among these being a drastic decline in revenue. Van Buren summoned an extra session of Congress for September 4, 1837, to deal with this and kindred matters.

The President told Congress, in his message to the special session, that it had been called for the primary purpose of ameliorating the difficulties of the government. He advocated postponement of the distribution of the Treasury surplus, so that it might be used to cover the deficit already accumulating in 1837; the issuance of Treasury notes to meet immediate governmental needs; and passage of a law that would enable the government to keep its receipts in its own Treasury vaults, in this way separating its fiscal operations completely from the country's banks. The only measure that he proposed for the direct aid of business was postponement of the payment of bonds furnished for duties by the politically powerful importing merchants of New York and other ports. He also suggested a law providing bankruptcy procedures against banks that suspended specie payment.

Van Buren hoped that the measures he advocated would be of some use to the country as a whole, but he cautioned citizens against looking to Washington for relief. Government aid for any portion of the citizenry would be using the property of some to benefit others, and any laws designed to relieve "mercantile embarrassments" would not only be unconstitutional but would also fail to promote "the welfare of those they might be designed to aid." His argument for completely separating the Treasury from the banks, which took up a large part of his message, also showed that he held a very limited view of the government's responsibility for coping with the depression. Controlling domestic and foreign exchange was not a governmental responsibility, he said, for private interests ought not to be mixed up with the public business. He wished to avoid any new national debt, and to limit the expenses of the government to its wants, and its revenues to its expenses. He believed in strict construction of the national government's powers over commerce and currency, and there was not the slightest attempt to invoke the general welfare clause of the Constitution.

This limited concept of the national government's powers and responsibilities was a fair enough representation of the Democracy's concept of the role of the national Administration. It was not characteristic of the party's attitude in the states, where Democrats had rivaled the Whigs in granting corporation charters and aiding in the construction of roads, canals, and railroads.

The President's proposals were at once taken up in Congress. The Democrats had been able to organize the House as well as the Senate, and, save for the bankruptcy law, which was unfavorably reported by the Judiciary Committee of the House, a number of measures were speedily put in the legislative mill. Despite Whig opposition, the distribution of the surplus was indefinitely postponed (never to be resumed); $10 million in Treasury notes were authorized; and a delay of six months was provided in the payment of duty bonds. But separation of the government from all banks became a source of political conflict that lasted until 1840.

The Independent Treasury Bill

On September 14, 1837, Van Buren's close supporters introduced simultaneously in both House and Senate the Independent Treasury, or Subtreasury, bill. It ordered customs officers, postmasters, and other receivers of the public money to hold their receipts until ordered to pay out or transfer them. Government funds would be withdrawn from the "Pet Banks" as soon as possible, and placed in the various subtreasuries.

At Calhoun's suggestion, a provision was incorporated providing that, after January 1, 1838, the notes of specie-paying banks received by the government would be gradually reduced in amount until, by January 1, 1841, only notes, bills, or paper issued by the United States would be accepted. Furthermore, after the latter date, federal disbursements would be only in specie, or in such notes and paper as were authorized by law. The South Carolina leader in this way announced his support of the bill and signalized the fact that, after some four years of flirtation with the Whigs, he was returning to the Democratic fold.

The Independent Treasury bill was significant for a number of reasons. It demonstrated the Administration's continued acceptance of the belief that paper money should be restricted and specie should become a larger and larger element in the currency, for without government deposits the ability of the state banks to expand their note issues would be markedly reduced. It manifested sympathy with labor, which wished to see state bank notes curtailed in volume. It enabled the Democrats to deny the charge that their monetary policy was controlled by state banking interests, a charge that was being used by the Whigs with considerable effect. The Democracy could also assert that it had a due and proper regard for the safety of government funds and that, outside of the coinage, responsibility for the regulation of the currency lay with the states rather than with the national government, a point of view vigorously denounced by the Whigs. The Democracy's attitude toward the Independent Treasury was a means of identifying that party as one still opposed to fostering privilege and still imbued with due regard for strict interpretation of the Constitution.

The introduction of the Independent Treasury bill precipitated long-drawn-out debates in Congress. The Whigs declared that the bill was a withdrawal of the government from its obligation to provide a sound national currency, asserting that provision for such a currency would have a most salutary effect in countering the depression; their hope, it was clear, was the reinstitution of a United States Bank. The Conservatives also attacked the bill, but they had a different alternative from that of the Whigs. They regarded the Independent Treasury as merely a national bank in disguise, and, being opposed to such an institution as an unjustified extension of the national government's authority, they wished to have the national funds kept in carefully selected and controlled state banks. The Administration Democrats denounced any restoration of a United States Bank, and had no interest in continuing the use of the state banks as depositories for government funds. They declared that the country's banking system was in a sad condition, but that its renovation was the province of the states. An independent treasury would free the government from the trammels of the money power, for the revenues of the government would be free from harm and no longer available for exploitation by unscrupulous moneychangers. Keeping the government's money in its own vaults would act as a check on any renewal of speculative tendencies, and the specie clause would limit unhealthy bank-note expansion and improve the general condition of the currency. Such remedial effects emanating from Washington were permissible, from the Democratic viewpoint, since they did not involve any loose construction of the Constitution or any expansion of the power of the central government.

The struggle over the Independent Treasury showed the parties very evenly balanced in Congress. Whigs and Conservatives defeated the bill in the House during the special session by a vote of 120 to 106. When the bill was again introduced in the regular session that followed, it could only be passed in the Senate by the elimination of the specie clause, and again it failed in the House. During the Twenty-sixth Congress (1839–1841) however, the depression came to the aid of the administration. As economic conditions had improved somewhat in 1838, the banks had resumed specie payment, but when the country's situation grew worse in 1839, the banks again suspended; there could have been no better demonstration of their unfitness to serve as government depositories. The increasing difficulties of the United States Bank of Pennsylvania also served the Democrats well, enabling them to point with horror to any steps leading to a resurrection of the "Monster." Once again the Independent Treasury bill, still shorn of its specie clause, was introduced. It passed both houses of Congress by narrow majorities, and Van Buren signed it July 4, 1840. The Democratic leadership regarded this as an eminently fitting date, for they held that the national government was now freed from the trammels of the money power.

The Independent Treasury did indeed put the government's revenue in safer hands than those of the state banks. "Pet Banks" were no longer able to use government funds as a basis for overextension of loans and credits. Whig fears that the act would draw specie out of circulation were unfounded, since government expenditures and income tended to balance in the ensuing years. The act was an abdication of governmental responsibility for establishing a regulated national currency, a step quite in keeping with the Jacksonians' narrow concept of the role of the government at Washington.

The National Domain Problem

While Congress struggled with the Independent Treasury, it also attempted to deal with the ever-present problem of the national domain. This involved both political and economic interests. Though most of the Whigs, and a number of the eastern Democrats, still preferred distribution of land sales to the states, westerners of both parties were cool to this proposal. The West continued to want a cheap and easy land policy: restriction of land sales to actual settlers; the graduation of land prices so that they would steadily decrease for those lands that remained unsold; and a pre-emption law which would give the squatter priority in purchase rights for the land on which he had settled.

Van Buren sought to steer a careful way through this conflict of desire concerning the disposal of the public lands, but the force of circumstance pushed him toward satisfaction of western aspirations. Hoping to curry support in the West for the Independent Treasury, he came out in 1837 for both graduation and pre-emption. The Whig leaders denounced these proposals, and in this they were joined by Calhoun. The Whigs still wished to use the public land revenue for a comprehensive scheme of internal improvements that would promote the development of the nation's economy. Calhoun, totally averse to any such program, proposed instead the outright cession of the public lands to the states in which they lay, together with some compensation to the older states. His influence, together with that of Whigs like Clay and Adams, helped to crystallize eastern opposition to the land legislation sought by the Democratic Administration. A pre-emption bill was passed in 1838, and a similar measure two years later extended the act of 1838 to 1842. Permanent pre-emption was blocked, however, and graduation was twice defeated in the House.

In 1840, there was a Whig movement to couple distribution with the assumption of state debts. A number of states, especially those in the West and Southwest, found themselves in serious financial difficulties because of the hard times and overambitious schemes of internal improvements. Nine states stopped paying interest on their obligations, and three (Michigan, Mississippi, and Florida) openly declared that they would never pay their debts. The Whig scheme proposed distribution of land sale proceeds to the states as a means of assuming their debts. Investors in state bonds relished this plan, as did those who wished to stimulate the revolution in transportation. The West, however, feared that the Whig proposal would endanger both pre-emption and graduation, and the South was sure that such use of land revenues would generate a new demand for higher tariffs. Benton and Calhoun attacked this project, Whig resolutions favoring it were defeated in the Senate early in 1840, and the Whigs avoided making it an issue during the presidential campaign of that year.

Rising Contention over Slavery

While the Administration, caught in the grip of the depression, fought for the Independent Treasury and for a land policy pleasing to the West, it also found itself confronted by continued antislavery agitation. The political leaders of both parties were loath to see this development, for they well knew the strain that sectional division over slavery, once it became a political question, would inflict upon national party organizations already strained by conflicting views on such problems as the tariff and land policy. They were helpless, however, to stem the course of events. As abolitionists increased their agitation and antislavery societies spread in the North, the clamor against slavery steadily arose, until during 1837–1838 no less than 412,000 antislavery petitions were presented to the House of Representatives by the American Antislavery Society. The excitement about slavery was further increased by the slaveholding Republic of Texas, which indicated that it was disposed to favor annexation to the United States.

Toward the close of 1837, Calhoun introduced in the Senate a series of resolutions concerning slavery. These declared that the Union had been formed by independent and sovereign states; that the states had absolute control over their domestic institutions, where such control had not been expressly delegated to the national government, and that attempts originating in other states to interfere with this local control menaced the Union itself; that it was the duty of the national government to safeguard the states in the management of their domestic institutions; that slavery was a significant part of those institutions; that attempts to abolish slavery in the District of Columbia or in the territories were attacks upon the institutions of the slave states; and that refusing, on antislavery grounds, "to extend to the Southern and Western States any advantage which would tend to strengthen, or render them more secure, or increase their limits or population by the annexation of new territory or States" would be contrary to their equality of rights and advantages under the Constitution and would, in effect, be a disfranchisement of the slaveholding states.

Calhoun's resolutions stated the extreme southern position in regard to slavery. Opposition to them promptly developed, and the statements referring to annexation and the obligation of the national government to safeguard existing institutions were stricken out. The Senate then passed the remaining resolutions by large majorities, and also tabled a resolution offered by Senator Allen of Ohio to the effect that nothing in the Calhoun resolutions should be regarded as abridging freedom of speech and press, or the right of petition; the vote on the Allen resolution, twenty-three to twenty-one, represented an almost complete division between Senators from the slave and the free states.

The fate of the Allen resolution and the continuance of the gag in both houses of the national legislature showed that the South still had a whip hand over Congress where slavery was concerned. In the House, beginning in 1840, antislavery petitions were not even received, but as the fight for freedom of speech continued, John Quincy Adams made himself the great champion of the right of petition. Dauntless in the face of southern taunts and threats of censure, he led the fight against the gag resolutions until the mounting pressure of northern public opinion, together with increasing representation in Congress from the free states, brought a change. It was Adams' particular triumph that, on December 3, 1844, the House finally rescinded its gag rules. In the Senate, which had never been a center of abolitionist attentions, the flood of petitions ebbed, and they ceased to be a matter of controversy.

The right of petition was not secured in Congress until almost four years after Van Buren left the White House. During his term, southern influence concerning slavery remained dominant in the legislative halls. Stung by Adams' campaign, the floods of antislavery propaganda, and the refusal by the governors of Maine and New York to cooperate with Georgia and Virginia in extraditing individuals charged with slave stealing, southerners looked to the federal government for support of their "peculiar institution," and did not look in vain. This was illustrated not only by the continuance of the gag rules in Congress, but also in a number of other situations.

When the *Enterprise,* an American coastal slaver, entered a Bermuda port, the Bermudian authorities freed the slaves on board the ship. The United States demanded and Great Britain refused an indemnity, and Calhoun thereupon introduced in the Senate resolutions declaring that Britain had acted unjustly and had violated international law. His case was decidedly weak, for the slaves had been freed by habeas corpus proceedings in a country where slavery was unlawful, and there was no international law which recognized slaves as property. The Senate, however, was respectful of the South Carolinian's argument, and, by a vote of thirty-three to nothing, though with eleven abstentions, it adopted his resolutions.

The shipment of African slaves to the North American continent was a flourishing traffic. Though it had been unlawful since 1808 so far as the United States was concerned, Congress did nothing to stop it, and Van Buren's Administration manifested such violent opposition to the visit and search of American vessels that the British government was unable to take effective measures for ending the horrors of the trade. In June, 1838, came the *L'Amistad* case, which further illustrated the Administration's determination to cooperate with its southern supporters.

L'Amistad, a Spanish ship, had on board fifty-three African Negroes who had been illegally brought from Africa to Cuba, where they had been given slave status. While sailing from one Spanish Caribbean port to another, the Negroes seized the ship and tried to force the crew to sail toward Africa. *L'Amistad* finally came to anchor off the coast of Connecticut, however, and a federal revenue cutter picked up the "slaves." Van Buren was anxious to surrender them to their "owners," who sued for their return in a Connecticut federal court. The President ordered that if the court found against the

Negroes, they were to be hurried off to Cuba without opportunity for an appeal. Despite his instructions, however, the case was carried to the Supreme Court, which freed the Negroes.

The Canadian Rebellion and American Policy

Slavery was not the only problem that involved Van Buren's Administration in international difficulties. Of more immediately serious consequence were developments along the Canadian border. These strained relations between the United States and Great Britain.

In 1837, a series of difficulties involving religious conflict and other troubles between French and English Canadians, together with dissatisfaction over the strict governmental control exercised from London, brought on a movement for Canadian independence. William Lyon Mackenzie in Upper Canada and Louis Joseph Papineau in Lower Canada raised the standard of rebellion. These outbreaks were quickly repressed, and the leaders, together with numbers of their adherents, fled into the United States.

Many Americans living near the Canadian border sympathized with the rebels. Talk of annexing Canada had never quite died out since the War of 1812, and not a few United States citizens thought it was America's duty to extend the area of freedom by helping the downtrodden Canadians. Such sympathizers, together with the exiles, organized societies known as "The Patriots" and "The Hunters," which recruited men and collected supplies at Rochester, Buffalo, and a dozen other places along the frontier. The insurgents also had a base on Navy Island in the Niagara River above the falls.

The Canadian government was irked by the harboring of these exiles in the United States, and by the suspicion that Americans were intent upon acquiring control of Canada. Relations between the two countries were further strained by a succession of incidents that occurred along the frontier. The insurgents had rented a small American steamer named the *Caroline* that carried supplies from the United States to the rebel base on Navy Island, and, on December 29, 1837, a little band of Canadian volunteers crossed over the river and seized the *Caroline*. In the fight that followed, a United States citizen was killed on American soil, and the ship was towed out into the river, where it was set on fire and sank a short distance above the falls. This act aroused much resentment on the American side of the border. Insurgent recruitments flourished, raids into Canada increased, and a British steamer, the *Sir Robert Peel,* was seized and burned in retaliation for the *Caroline.*

President Van Buren warned American citizens not to give aid and encouragement to the insurgents, and declared that those who participated in the invasion of a friendly country would be left to their fate. He sent General Winfield Scott to the Canadian frontier, and the general, with considerable effect, exhorted the citizens to maintain a neutral attitude. The snuffing out of the rebellion by the Canadian authorities led to further improvement of the situation, but the British government refused an American demand for reparations for the *Caroline*. Then, in November, 1840, a new crisis was precipitated.

A variety of none too creditable individuals stated that Alexander McLeod, a Canadian deputy sheriff, had boasted that it was he who had killed the American in the *Caroline* affair. When McLeod's duties brought him across the border, the New York authorities arrested and jailed him for murder. Great Britain promptly protested to Washington, only to be told that the federal government could not interfere with New York State legal procedures. Relations between Britain and the United States were thus brought to a new low as Van Buren's term of office neared its close.

The Northeast Boundary Dispute

The strain on good relations between the American and British governments was not due solely to events connected with the Canadian rebellion. Boundary disputes on the northeastern frontier—various parts of which had been either loosely or inaccurately defined—gave additional cause for alarm. The treaty of 1783 stated that the line between Maine and the Canadian provinces of Nova Scotia and New Brunswick should run along the highlands dividing the rivers that emptied into the St. Lawrence from those that had their outlet in the Atlantic Ocean. The British contended that the highlands near the upper waters of the St. John River, which actually empties into the Bay of Fundy on the Atlantic, lay south of that river, while the American government held that all the region south of it belonged to the United States; some 12,000 square miles of territory were in dispute, including rich timber lands and fertile soil. Great Britain was the more anxious to possess this area because it made possible a military road to a warm water port on the Atlantic, an important consideration in view of the fact that the St. Lawrence was blocked by ice in the winter. Another area in dispute involved 100,000 acres at the northwestern head of the Connecticut River, and still another centered around the outlet to Lake Champlain, where the United States had built a fort at Rouses Point.

In 1826, the United States and Great Britain had agreed that the King of the Netherlands should arbitrate these boundary differences. His Majesty heard the arguments of both sides and declared that the relevant provisions in the treaty of 1783 were "inexplicable and impractical." He suggested that the boundary between the Connecticut River and the St. Lawrence be re-surveyed, and proposed that a new line be established along the Maine frontier giving 4,119 square miles of the disputed territory to Canada and 7,908 square miles to the United States. Maine refused to accept this (a refusal that eventually cost the United States 900 square miles of territory), and the proposed settlement collapsed.

While the governments of Great Britain and the United States were wrestling futilely with these boundary problems, popular feeling in Maine and in Nova Scotia and New Brunswick became more and more inflamed. When Canadians moved into the disputed area and began cutting timber along the Aroostook River, the Maine legislature voted $800,000 for defense, and Governor Fairfield called out the state militia. The belligerent Maineites set up forts on the land to which they laid claim and tried to eject the Canadian settlers, and, when Nova Scotia and New Brunswick also began military preparations, what was known as the "Aroostook War" of 1838 had begun. Congress, rallying to the support of Maine, voted $10 million for defense and authorized Van Buren to call out 50,000 volunteers.

The situation along the northeast boundary was tense, but Van Buren preserved his equanimity. He asserted that he wanted only an honorable peace, and his actions bore out his words. Once again, Winfield Scott was despatched to the northern frontier, where he persuaded Governor Fairfield to withdraw his troops from the area in contention. The Canadians agreed not to attempt taking military possession, and diplomatic negotiations between London and Washington were resumed.

Van Buren's attitude in this trying situation was unpopular along the northern border and undoubtedly contributed to the election of William Henry Seward as governor of New York in 1838. It did avoid an open conflict, however, even though final settlement was delayed until after the Administration of the "Red Fox" had come to an end.

The Campaign of 1840

Before Van Buren's term was half over, the parties began preparations for the campaign of 1840. Clay, who was very popular in the North and West, hoped to be the Whig presidential nominee, and he tried to bolster his support in the South by indicating that he regarded the tariff as settled by the compromise of 1833. He also declared that internal improvements had been largely taken care of by the states, and that reinstitution of a national bank should await a clear manifestation of popular approval. Clay was no longer ready to defy the South, the President, and the devil for his American System, and southern Whigs were willing to accept him as their candidate.

But, though Clay was busily seeking the nomination, strong forces in the Whig party were opposed to making him their standard bearer. Many Whigs in both the South and the North felt that he could not carry the states below the Mason and Dixon line. Webster and his New England following were cool to Clay's candidacy, for Webster himself had presidential ambitions. And in New York, a key state, the Whig organization led by Thurlow Weed was convinced that the opposition of the antislavery men and the old Antimasons, together with Clay's close identification with the Bank of the United States, made it most unwise to nominate him. Recognizing the situation in New York, Clay made a trip through that state in the summer of 1839. He was well received by the Whig rank and file, but both Weed and Governor Seward vainly urged him to withdraw from the race.

The Whig national convention met at Harrisburg, Pennsylvania, early in December, 1839. Clay had a plurality of the delegates, but the convention adopted a system of balloting by states that reduced the importance of the Kentuckian's support. There was strong support for William Henry Harrison, who had demonstrated his popularity in the 1836 campaign, and another promising aspirant was Winfield Scott, the Virginia-born hero of Lundy's Lane, whose diplomatic conduct in connection with the troubles on the Canadian frontier had brought him prominently into the public eye. The supporters of the two generals were quick to point out that much of Clay's strength at the convention came from areas which the Whigs were unlikely to carry. Despite the preference of the New York State leadership for Scott, the convention turned to Harrison, who was aided by the support of Webster and an enthusiastic Pennsylvania delegation. Clay's strength melted away, and on the second day of the balloting New York, Michigan, and Vermont swung from Scott to Harrison, who then received the nomination.

Clay was deeply disappointed by his defeat, and many of his followers were bitter in their complaints. To placate the malcontents, and to achieve a balanced ticket, the convention nominated for Vice President John Tyler of Virginia, an advocate of states' rights and a strict constructionist who had supported the Kentuckian's candidacy and who was popular with the southern Whigs. No weight was attached to the fact that Harrison was almost sixty-seven years old, and that Tyler might possibly find himself installed in the White House. Since the Whigs held disparate views on questions of national importance, it was deemed best to adjourn without adopting a platform.

On April 1, 1840, a new party put in its appearance. Antislavery delegates from six states met in Albany, New York, and nominated as their standard bearer James G. Birney, a Kentuckian and former slaveholder. The sponsors of this move, a group of New York abolitionists, felt that the major parties had failed to safeguard America's heritage of freedom. They emphasized the current interference with the right of petition and the circulation of anti-slavery literature in the South, and pointed to the murder of abolitionist Elijah Lovejoy in 1837 at Alton, Illinois, as evidence that the time had come to organize a northern party dedicated to the weakening of the South's influence at Washington and to the destruction of slavery. The convention adopted no platform and gave the movement no name, but it quickly became known as the Liberty party.

The Democratic national convention met at Baltimore, on May 5, 1840, with the delegates in a somber mood. There was no opposition to the renomination of Van Buren, for he had conducted himself as President with tact and diplomacy and to reject him would have been tantamount to rejecting the party's Jacksonian principles. But there was widespread opposition to the renomination for Vice President of Richard M. Johnson. Jackson, who had forced Johnson's nomination in 1836, now opposed him, and rumors of his living in adultery with a Negress in Kentucky made him a political liability. He was discarded, and the choice of a running mate for Van Buren was left to the state organizations. The convention adopted a platform endorsing the Independent Treasury and opposing internal improvements at national expense, a national bank, high protection for manufacturers, and interference with slavery where it already existed. The Whigs jeered at the Democrats for their inability to nominate a vice presidential candidate, to which the Democrats retorted that, if they were not united on men, they were at least united on principles.

The campaign of 1840 was fought in part over serious issues. The Democrats made much of the Independent Treasury and tried to identify the Whigs as the National Bank party. Van Buren established a ten-hour day for government employees in March, 1840, and this was used as evidence that the Democracy had the interests of the laboring man at heart. The Whigs refused to be identified as Bank men, devoting a good deal of talk in the appropriate quarters to the advantages of protection for industry, the government's responsibility for a sound currency, and the importance of freedom of speech and of the press. The major part of the campaign, however, was devoted to personalities and to ballyhoo.

The Democrats asserted that "Granny" Harrison was an illiterate "Old Lady," and a defaulter to boot. Senator Benton declared that "availability" was the only ability sought by the Whigs, and this contemptuous reference to the Whig candidate was echoed by the rank and file of the Democracy. One of the Democratic papers gleefully published the supposed comment of a Clay supporter that, given a pension of $2,000 and a barrel of hard cider, Harrison would be glad to spend the rest of his days in a log cabin by a sea coal fire, studying moral philosophy.

The Whigs had at last come to realize that they must follow the example of the Democrats and convince the voters that Whiggery was the best hope of the common man. They seized upon Harrison's alleged penchant for a log cabin and hard cider, using those symbols of country life to identify their candidate as a simple, honest, son of the soil. Harrison really lived in a comfortable farmhouse, but the voters were told that the latchstring of his log cabin was always out for visitors and that a barrel of cider (prohibitionists were assured that it was sweet cider) was ready for their reception. If he were elected, the laboring man could expect "two dollars a day and roast beef." Van Buren, on the other hand, was ridiculed up and down the land; identified as "Martin Van Ruin," or "Sweet Sandy Whiskers," the Whigs portrayed him as one who would give the common man "fifty cents a day and French soup," while he indulged his own extravagant tastes. When Whig Congressman Charles Ogle of Pennsylvania gave an oration on "The Royal Splendor of the President's Palace," according to which the Chief Executive wasted the people's money on gold plate, costly carpets, and huge mirrors with golden frames, the Whigs spread this nonsense broadcast. Meanwhile, Webster publicly regretted that he had not been born in a log cabin, but fondly told of his own humble origin, and other Whig orators spoke in similar vein. The Whigs organized parades, with huge victory balls rolled for miles along the highways, flags waving, bands playing, and the stalwarts shouting themselves hoarse in rendering such songs as:

> Ye jolly young lads of Ohio
> And all ye sick Vanocrats too,
> Come out from amongst the foul party,
> And vote for old Tippecanoe.

Another favorite Whig song was:

> What has caused the great commotion, motion, motion,
> Our country through?
> It is the ball arolling on, on
> For Tippecanoe and Tyler too—Tippecanoe and Tyler too,
> And with them we'll beat little Van, Van, Van,
> Van is a used up man,
> And with them we'll beat little Van.

The Whig tactics, coupled with the depression, were effective. Harrison carried nineteen of the twenty-six states, including seven states in the South and all the North save New Hampshire and Illinois. His plurality was only 138,845 out of 2,411,187 votes, but he had 53 per cent of the vote cast by the two major parties and the Whigs won control of both houses of Congress. The Liberty party made a sorry showing, polling only 7,069 votes, half of them in New York State, and failing to carry a single county in any state.

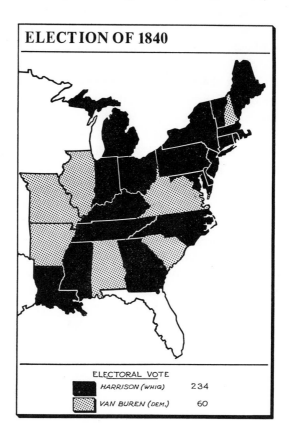

ELECTION OF 1840

ELECTORAL VOTE
HARRISON (WHIG)   234
VAN BUREN (DEM.)   60

Significance of the 1840 Election

The election of 1840 showed that the two major parties were still fairly evenly balanced in their appeal to the voters, although the balance had now swung in favor of the Whigs. It indicated that, under the influence of hard times and the assertion that the Whigs had the interest of the common man at heart, the electorate was becoming indifferent to the claim that the Democracy was the ordinary citizen's best safeguard against the machinations of the rich and the powerful. From this time on, the Democratic party was to begin looking for other issues, and hereafter the slaveholding South was to exert an increasing control over the party's policies. Finally, despite the sorry showing of the Liberty party, the election of 1840 marked the emergence of politically organized opposition to slavery—which was indeed an omen of troublous times to come.

Suggested Reading

On Van Buren and his Administration, see Edward M. Shepard, *Martin Van Buren* (1889), still the best of the Van Buren biographies. Holmes Alexander, *The American Talleyrand* (1935) is very critical of Van Buren. Denis T. Lynch, *An Epoch and a Man, Martin Van Buren and His Times* (1929) is a popular treatment favorable to Van Buren. R. V. Remini, *Martin Van Buren and the Making of the Democratic Party* (1959) deals with the earlier years.

The panic of 1837 and the depression that followed are studied in Reginald C. McGrane, *The Panic of 1837* (1924) and Samuel Reznick, "The Social History of an American Depression, 1837–1843," *American Historical Review,* XL (Oct., 1934), 662–687.

The role of the parties at this time is examined in Louis Hartz, *Economic Policy and Democratic Thought: Pennsylvania, 1776–1860* (1948) and *The Liberal Tradition in America* (1955); Oscar Handlin, *Commonwealth; A Study of the Role of Government in the American Economy, Massachusetts, 1774–1861* (1947); and Van Deusen's *The Jacksonian Era* and the same author's "Some Aspects of Whig Thought and Theory in the Jacksonian Period," *American Historical Review,* LXIII (Jan., 1958), 305–322.

Useful for a study of the Independent Treasury are David Kinley, *The Independent Treasury of the United States and Its Relations to the Banks of the Country* (1910) and "The Influence on Business of the Independent Treasury," *Annals of the American Academy of Political and Social Science,* III (Sept., 1892), 52–82. See also Esther R. Taus, *Central Banking Functions of the United States Treasury, 1789–1941* (1943).

For the continuing battle over land policy, see the works by Wellington, Chambers and Wiltse already cited.

The rising slavery controversy is treated in Julian P. Bretz, "The Economic Background of the Liberty Party," *American Historical Review,* XXXIV (Jan., 1929), 250–264; Theodore C. Smith, *The Liberty and Free Soil Parties in the Northwest* (1897); W. E. Burghardt DuBois, *The Suppression of the African Slave Trade* (1904), and Hugh G. Soulsby, "The Right of Search and the Slave Trade in Anglo-American Relations, 1814–1862," *The Johns Hopkins University Studies in History and Political Science,* series LI, No. 2. Also see Van Deusen's *The Jacksonian Era,* and Russell Nye's *Fettered Freedom.*

Canadian-American relations during the Van Buren period are dealt with in Albert B. Corey, *The Crisis of 1830–1842 in Canadian-American Relations* (1941) and in Henry S. Burrage, *Maine in the Northeast Boundary Controversy* (1919). Valuable articles on the subject are Thomas Le Duc, "The Maine Frontier and the Northeastern Boundary Controversy," *American Historical Review,* LIII (Oct., 1947), 30–41; Orrin E. Tiffany, "Relations of the United States to the Canadian Rebellion of 1837–1838," Buffalo Historical Society *Publications,* VIII (1905), 7–147; Wilson P. Shortridge, "The Canadian-American Frontier During the Rebellion of 1837–1838," *Canadian Historical Review,* VII (Mar., 1926), 13–26; and Alastair Watt, "The Case of Alexander McLeod," *Canadian Historical Review,* XII (June, 1931), 145–167.

For the election of 1840, see Goebel, *Harrison,* Lynch, *Van Buren,* the volumes by G. G. Van Deusen on *Clay, Weed,* and *The Jacksonian Era,* and R. G. Gunderson, *The Log Cabin Campaign* (1957).

20 ⠋ The Booming Northern Economy, 1830-1860

URING THE YEARS 1830 to 1860, the population of the northern part of the United States grew by leaps and bounds, and occupied vast new areas of land on the frontier. New England and the Middle Atlantic states, which had 5,542,381 inhabitants in 1830, reached 10,594,-268 by 1860. An even more startling development occurred in the region west of New York and Pennsylvania. The Old

Population Growth

Northwest had a population of 1,610,473 at the beginning of this period; thirty years later, 9,096,716 people inhabited the northern regions that lay west of the Alleghenies. The North's population had almost tripled.

While these swelling numbers were due in part to natural increase, for large families were still common in the country as a whole, it was also the result of a steady flow of immigrants from the Old World. In the years 1830 to 1845, inclusive, an average of some 65,000 foreigners, chiefly western Europeans, flocked into the country. In the period 1846–1860, when hard times were prevalent in Ireland and war and revolutionary disturbances vexed western and central Europe, an average of better than 250,000 foreigners came every year to seek their fortunes on American soil. The great majority of these immigrants settled in the northern part of the United States.

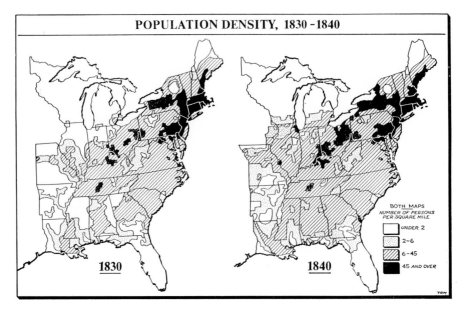

POPULATION DENSITY, 1830-1840

1830

1840

BOTH MAPS
NUMBER OF PERSONS
PER SQUARE MILE

UNDER 2
2-6
6-45
45 AND OVER

The Expansion of Northern Agriculture

A major result of this growth in population was a great increase in the number of northern farms and in agricultural production. The frontier moved westward at bewildering speed. As early as 1840, much of the forest-covered region from the Appalachians to a line running from the westward end of Lake Erie to the mouth of the Ohio River had been converted into tillable acreage. Settlers had by then reached the eastern edge of the prairies. During the next ten years they occupied all of the prairie lands east of the Mississippi that were not in the hands of speculators, and began a trans-Mississippi expansion that, by 1860, resulted in the occupation of Iowa, Wisconsin, and large parts of Minnesota.

As these western lands were taken up, agricultural production in the North increased with great rapidity. In 1840, the wheat crop was 85,000,000 bushels; twenty years later, it was 173,000,000 bushels. Corn rose from 85,000,000 bushels in 1839 to over double that amount in 1860. There were similar increases in oats, hay, potatoes, and dairy products.

This increase in production, especially in the frontier areas, was as wasteful of soil fertility as it was remarkable in amount. The vast quantities of land, together with the scarcity of capital and labor, tempted the American farmer into extensive rather than intensive farming. The western farmer

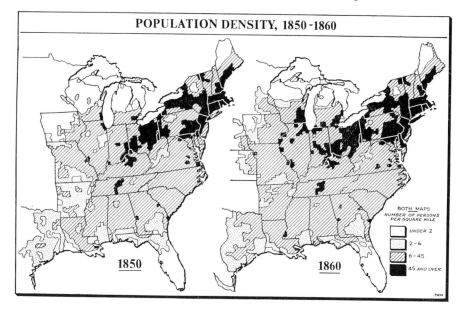

valued quantity of acres more than he did quantity per acre. His great objective was to clear, plough, and plant as much land with as few hands as possible, with little thought of maintaining the fertility of the soil. This attitude led to soil exhaustion, an evil result which was widespread in the East as well as in the West.

Progressive Aspects of Northern Farming

But, though waste abounded, signs of change were at hand. A number of progressive stimuli appeared, each exerting some influence upon the more

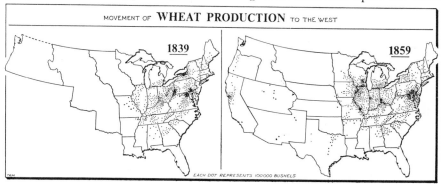

intelligent members of the farming population. The growth of urban centers provided an ever-increasing market for farm produce, while the cheapening cost of transportation that came with the development of the steamboat, canals, and railroads made these markets accessible and increased the profits of agriculture. Better markets and higher profits called for improved farming methods that would increase production, and information about such methods became available through the formation of farm societies and by means of printed publications.

Societies for the spread of information about scientific agriculture had appeared shortly after the close of the Revolution, but those chiefly interested had been town folk such as lawyers, merchants, ministers, and doctors. After 1811, however, when Elkanah Watson organized the Berkshire Agricultural Society in Pittsfield, Massachusetts, these societies began to include more and more farmers. These organizations spread into the West and by the 1850s were exerting a valuable influence. They offered prizes for fine quality produce, held ploughing matches, and organized county fairs where farmers could exhibit prize stock and vegetables, listen to talks on scientific farming methods, and enjoy some relaxation by renewing old acquaintances and viewing the wonders of the midways' collections of freaks and monstrosities.

The growth of agricultural literature rivaled the spread of agricultural societies and the county fair. Farm papers appeared: the *American Farmer* (1819), the *American Agriculturist* (1842), the *Country Gentleman* (1853), and others. Their information on crop statistics and scientific farming was supplemented by such books as Jesse Buel's *The Farming Companion* (1839) which emphasized the importance of drainage, deep plowing, cultivation, and crop rotation, and the great German chemist Justus Liebig's *Chemistry in its Application to Agriculture and Physiology* (1841), which taught the farmer much about the scientific fertilization of crops and incidentally inspired a host of fake soil "chemists" and "professors" who sold their wares to the gullible.

Government also became interested in aiding the farmer. Federal agencies in 1839 began collecting and disbursing agricultural statistics and free seeds; the initial appropriation of $1,000 passed by Congress for such aid had risen to $105,000 by 1856. States began establishing boards and departments of agriculture, and in 1857 Michigan opened the first agricultural college in the United States. In 1862, Congress established the United States Department of Agriculture, the modest beginning of what was to become a mammoth government agency in later years.

The mid-nineteenth-century farmer had the benefit not only of a considerable amount of scientific information about agriculture but also of new and improved tools. Horse-drawn hay rakes appeared that could do the work of from six to ten men with the old-fashioned hand rake, and horse-drawn cultivators came into common use. The lumber wagon replaced the two-wheeled ox cart. The tough prairie sods demanded better plows than the cumbersome wood and iron implements that had long been in use, and in 1837 John Deere, an Illinois blacksmith, turned out his first steel plow, an instrument light in weight and with a moldboard which would "scour" the heavy soil of the prairie. Deere established a plow factory at Moline, Illinois, in 1847, and by 1858 he was turning out 13,000 steel plows a year.

One of the most spectacular developments in farm machinery came in the harvesting of grain. At the beginning of the century, wheat, oats, and barley were cut with sickles, bound by hand, and threshed out by tramping or with flails; in rapid succession, cradles replaced sickles and threshing machines replaced the threshing floor. But the most significant advance came with the invention of a mechanical grain harvester.

Cyrus Hall McCormick (1809–1884), a big, hard-headed, tight-fisted Virginia farmer of Scotch-Irish parentage, invented the first practical reaper in 1831. He patented the machine in 1834. For nine years he did not sell a single machine, and he lost the family farm during the panic and depression of 1837, but his spirit was indomitable. With the 1840s, the reaper began to sell in the West. Transportation difficulties developed, and in 1847 McCormick moved his business to Chicago. Constantly involved in litigation with Obed Hussey (1792–1860), who had taken out patents for a similar reaper in 1833, and involved in law suits with other inventors as well, McCormick's driving energy and superior selling methods triumphed over every obstacle. His harvester demonstrated its superiority over all others at the London Exposition of 1851, won the gold medal at a Paris exposition four years later, and by the time of the Civil War was selling widely in Europe as well as in the United States.

The reaper, as developed by McCormick, Hussey, Deering, and others, was a giant step in mechanizing and revolutionizing wheat production. It released thousands of farm boys to fight on the Union side during the Civil War and was a great factor in the exportation of over 200 million bushels of wheat to Europe during that struggle. When McCormick died in 1884, 500,000 of his machines were in operation, doing work that would have required five million men to do by manual labor, and the United States was then producing ten bushels of wheat per capita, as against four bushels per capita in 1847.

As tools improved and scientific information spread, northern agriculture entered upon an era of experimentation and specialization. More and more farmers began utilizing chemical fertilizers, barnyard manure, and scientific stock-breeding. New varieties of seed improved the yields of wheat and corn, and, with lighter tools, especially plows, horses replaced oxen as draft animals. The focus of production in crops and in animals shifted, and the centers of wheat and corn crops moved into the Middle West, while Ohio displaced New York for sheep and wool. Cattle raising, which had earlier been a chief source of revenue for New York and Pennsylvania, moved to Texas, Missouri, and Iowa for grazing and Indiana, Illinois, and Ohio for fattening. As hog raising went west, the half-wild porkers of two generations before— known as "Alligators," "Razorbacks," "Seven Mile," and "Hazelnut Splitters"—were crossed with better breeds, and pork production soared. By 1860, Cincinnati was slaughtering 400,000 and Chicago 230,000 hogs yearly.

As western agricultural production increased, the emphasis in eastern agriculture shifted. The wool growers and cattle raisers of New England were forced out of business. Eastern farmers resorted to small-scale, general purpose farming, or devoted themselves to truck and market gardening and dairying in order to supply the rising urban centers.

The Hardships of Farm Life

The expansion of northern agriculture bore witness to the lure of nature, and to the deep-seated desire for land ownership that lies in the hearts of many men. It was also a testimony to the fact that many of the immigrants came from foreign agricultural stock. But, despite the satisfactions that derived from land ownership, the lot of the farmer was not an easy one. Agricultural leadership, like farm labor, was in scant supply, as the ablest and most progressive farm talent in community after community disappeared, drained off by the lure of better opportunities further west, and by city life, the Mexican War adventure, and the California gold rush. The youth on the western farms had little opportunity for a good secondary education, or for training in the business aspects of agriculture; most farmers had only the rudiments of common schooling, and few kept accounts. Marketing facilities were poor, for buyers usually paid one price for all qualities of farm products and often circulated false rumors to depress the price paid. The keep of four to six middlemen between producer and consumer often left the farmer with little profit for long hours of grinding toil. Working capital and bank credit were chronically in short supply, and all too many farmers were forced to operate on storekeeper credit, at 25 to 30 per cent above cash prices, and had to sell their crops at harvest time when a glut of produce meant a minimum return. Statistics for this period are inadequate, but the evidence indicates that in the 1850s about one-third of the eastern farms were mortgaged, that many western farmers were under the same handicap, and that tenantry, which always tends to deplete farm fertility, was widespread. When one also considers the lot of the farm women of that day, with wood-burning stoves, no sanitary conveniences in the home, running water a rarity, and little or no social life, it is evident that there was something of the heroic about the men and women who, in search of a better life for themselves and their children, pushed the frontier rapidly westward.

The Transportation Revolution— Canals

The great expansion of northern agriculture in the decades before the Civil War would have been impossible without the revolution in transportation that came between 1830 and 1860. In a previous chapter, we have noted the drastic reduction in freight rates and the increase in the speed of freight transportation during this period—changes which were due to improvements in water and land communication.

Canals in the northern states were significant in the development of water transportation. Spurred on by the success of the Erie Canal, other eastern states, especially Massachusetts and Pennsylvania, began constructing inland waterways. New York itself built feeders to the Erie. The West was also interested, and between 1825 and 1840, Ohio, Indiana, and Michigan poured millions of dollars into canal construction. By 1840, there were 3,326 miles of canals in the country, mainly in the North and West, built at a cost of $125 million and financed by local and state government aid, together with some private subscription to canal-company stocks. Many of these canals were wastefully financed and proved to be economic white elephants. Others, however, were of great value, for they helped to double the price of wheat for the farmers of Ohio and Indiana and to halve the cost of the goods they had to purchase.

After the depression that began in 1837 was over, there was a steady development of canal building in the western states, and by the 1850s these western waterways were a major factor in deflecting the trade of the West from the South to the East. Such canals as the Wabash and Erie in Ohio, the Illinois and Michigan in Illinois, and the Sault-Ste. Marie, or "Soo," (which was completed in 1855) connecting Lake Superior with Lake Huron, were of great value in moving the West's agricultural products to the roaring markets of the Atlantic seaboard.

The canals facilitated trade and travel, but the life of a canal-boat traveler had its drawbacks. The boats were seventy to eighty feet long, eleven feet wide, and the height from keel to roof was seldom more than eight feet. They moved at a majestic pace, drawn by horses that were often cruelly abused. More than 100 people would sometimes be crowded into the single cabin; Harriet Beecher Stowe declared that the berths were only a foot wide, and Philip Hone, in his *Diary* in 1847, asserted that the sleepers were "packed away on narrow shelves fastened to the side of the boat, like dead pigs in a Cincinnati pork warehouse." But travel was cheap—$.015 a mile on the smaller boats—and in good weather this leisurely progress toward the land of opportunity had its charms, especially if there was an organ or a fiddler on board and the nights were moonlit and balmy.

Early Travel on the Rivers

During the first three decades of the nineteenth century, a motley collection of flatboats, rafts, arks, keelboats, and barges were the principal means of river transportation. Useful for carrying goods downstream, they were tedious and uneconomical means of upriver travel, for the river current had to be fought with oars or the "setting pole," one end of which was pushed into the river bottom while the other was walked from the front to the rear of the craft.

Slow as this means of trade and travel was, the crews of these early river boats played an important part in moving the frontier westward and in the economic development of the interior. For years they formed the main connecting link between the new homes of the West and the old homes of the East. They brought the peoples of the world together in the new territories, where they could join in the process of creating new states, enacting laws, and establishing a social order that made the West a part of the United States. Many of these early rivermen were rough and boisterous; Mike Fink, a man of phenomenal strength and skill, has become a legend symbolizing their prowess. But it is significant that national figures—Clay, Lincoln, and Grant among them—labored at the oar and the setting pole and could qualify as boatmen. In one way or another, river traffic touched the lives of all the citizens of the West.

The Steamboat Era

Many inventors contributed to the development of the steamboat, but Robert Fulton (1765–1815) was the most successful. In August, 1807, his

"Clermont" puffed its way up the Hudson from New York to Albany, and Fulton and his associates had plans for transportation on the Mississippi river system. They built the first successful steamboat on midwestern waters, the "New Orleans," which descended the Ohio and Mississippi in 1811. By 1816, steamboats began appearing on the Great Lakes.

The great days of steamboating in the West, however, did not come until the 1830s. There were architectural difficulties to surmount, the depression of 1819–1822 retarded capital investment in this new mode of travel, lateral feeders (roads, canals, and widened local rivers) had to be developed, and agricultural surpluses had to grow before steamboat commerce could be practical. But from 1830 to 1860, the steamboat was an important means of inland commerce. By 1850, there were approximately 1,000 such craft on western waters, rolling majestically along, night and day, on the Ohio, Missouri, and Mississippi. In that year, river boating was still carrying three times as much domestic commerce as the railroads and almost three times as much as the canals of the country.

Steamboating was a highly individualistic type of enterprise, with a large element of risk involved. The average boat of the 1850s cost $20,000 to $40,000 to build. Some of them made large profits, occasionally as much as $40,000 on a single voyage up and down river, but the rank and file steamboat operators worked on a marginal basis. They were engaged in a difficult and dangerous business, for snags, sand and gravel bars, drought, floods, and ice (John Randolph of Roanoke said that the Ohio was frozen over for half the year and dry the other half) made river travel hazardous. Then there was always the danger that overloaded boilers would burst, scattering death and destruction; in 1838, for example, three of the four boilers on the "Moselle," en route from Cincinnati to St. Louis, exploded, leaving eighty-one known dead and fifty-five missing, with bodies thrown on the Kentucky shore a quarter of a mile away. In March, 1854, the "John L. Avery" hit a submerged tree forty miles from Natchez and sank in deep water with a loss of ninety lives. Some steamboats saw long service, but the average life of a riverboat was about five years.

The steamboat was a great boon to the settlement of the West. The two-way transport on the great rivers which it made possible halved haulage time and reduced costs proportionally. It formed an economic link between West and South, carrying the fruit, flour, pork, yarn, bale-rope, and bagging of the West to southern markets, and bringing the westerners cotton, tobacco, sugar, indigo, and salt.

But with the 1850s, the great days of the steamboat drew to a close, for another means of transportation, steadier and more reliable, had appeared.

Desperately, but to no avail, the steamboat captains cut their rates for haulage. The railroad era had begun, and this, combined with the success of the canals in diverting traffic from the Ohio-Mississippi river system, spelled the doom of the floating palaces.

Dawn of the Railroad Age

Railroads—"dry canals" they were sometimes called—had been used in European mines and as canal feeders as early as the fifteenth century. Such roads, operated by wind, water, or horsepower, were not uncommon in early nineteenth-century England, and by the 1820s they had appeared in the eastern part of the United States. Meanwhile, stimulated by English inventors, especially James Watt (1736–1819), Americans had begun experimenting with steam power. John Stevens (1749–1838) in 1825 at Hoboken, New Jersey, built the first crude American locomotive, which was a harbinger of great things to come.

There is still controversy as to which was the first American railroad, but the first to lay any rails was the Baltimore and Ohio. Chartered in 1827 by the city of Baltimore, the first stone of its track was laid, July 4, 1828, by Charles Carroll of Carrollton, one of the signers of the Declaration of Independence. Then the "B&O" began pushing its long and toilsome way across the Alleghenies to the Ohio River.

By 1830, other roads were fanning out from other eastern cities, and in that same year the "Best Friend," an effective steam engine, appeared on the Charleston and Hamburg in South Carolina. In 1831, Peter Cooper's "Tom Thumb" began drawing cars on the Baltimore and Ohio. When that road then turned to steam power, the others followed suit.

These early railroads were crude affairs. Wooden rails capped with iron strips were soon abandoned, for the strips would loosen and one end turn up into a "snakehead," derailing trains or plunging through the flimsy floors of the stagecoach cars. One New England road experimented with granite rails which wore out the iron wheels of the trains. Some of the early coaches were open affairs, and the passengers had to beat out the clouds of flying sparks from the wood-burning locomotives. The roads themselves were short and of different track widths, making transport aggravatingly slow and costly. Then, too, canal advocates and turnpike and stagecoach lines would combine to oppose the granting of railroad charters, and farmers objected to their stock being terrified by screaming monsters that belched fire and steam. Popular bitterness because of frequent accidents combined with superstitious fears that travel at the prodigious speed of twenty miles an hour was showing contempt for God's will added to the difficulties of the early railroad companies.

But, despite all obstacles, more and more railroads were built. The eastern states led the way, the principal stimulus being trade competition between such growing municipal centers as Philadelphia and Baltimore. Western states, such as Indiana, Illinois, and Michigan, authorized the construction of state-owned railroads, but these were hampered by the hard times of 1837–1843, and private capital was left to do the work. Construction expanded in the later 1840s, especially in New England and the Middle Atlantic states. The Pennsylvania Railroad began pushing out from Philadelphia toward Pittsburgh, and the Hudson River Railroad, from New York to Albany, began competing for trade with the Hudson River steamboats. Eight short, separate lines, some of them built a dozen years before, stretched between Albany and Buffalo, and the Erie Railroad moved sluggishly across New York's southern tier of counties toward Lake Erie. A network of roads fanned out from Boston into New England, putting that city in position to compete with New York for the profits of western trade and commerce. By 1850, the country had 9,000 miles of railroad, most of them in New England and the Middle Atlantic States, though there was also increasing railroad building in the Old Northwest.

The decade of the 1850s saw a tremendous railroad boom. Sparked by increasing evidence of the utility of railroads as a steady, economical, and increasingly comfortable mode of transport, by federal grants of public lands, and by the rapid development of Wall Street investment houses' offerings of railroad securities, the iron bands of travel developed in both the East and the West. In 1853, Erastus Corning consolidated the roads between Albany and Buffalo into the New York Central. In that same year, the "B&O" reached the Ohio river, and Cleveland, Toledo, Indianapolis, and Chicago had rail transport to New York, Boston, Philadelphia, and Baltimore. When, in 1854, the Rock Island was completed from Chicago to St. Louis, passengers and freight could travel from the Atlantic to the Mississippi entirely by rail. By 1860, a network of lines covered New England and the Middle Atlantic states, and four great roads—the New York Central, the Erie, the Pennsylvania, and the Baltimore and Ohio—connected the East and the Middle West, where other railroad networks branched out from Cincinnati, Chicago, and St. Louis. Of the nation's 31,000 miles of railroad, 22,000 were in the North and West. The great day of the iron horse had arrived.

The rapid advance in railroad construction during the 1850s had its questionable aspects. There was frantic lobbying for public land grants. Railroad promoters like Erastus Corning saw nothing reprehensible in making fortunes out of selling iron and other goods manufactured by themselves to the rail-

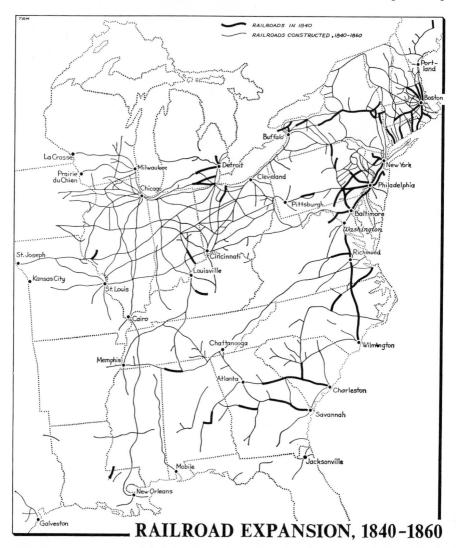

RAILROAD EXPANSION, 1840-1860

road companies they controlled. Harebrained promotion and wildcat railroad banking companies ruined investors.

But, despite such drawbacks, the railroads made a great contribution to the antebellum economy. By making possible the settlement and development of vast areas untouched by water highways, by releasing commerce from climatic limitations because of their year-round operations, and by providing speed and continuity of service that were more valuable to shippers than cut-rate water transport, they added enormously to the nation's productivity and wealth. Fully as significant was the way in which they strengthened the East-

COURTESY HARRY SHAW NEWMAN, THE OLD PRINT SHOP, NEW YORK

An Express Train in the 1850s

The express train, carrying both passengers and merchandise, was an indispensable part of the railroad systems that stretched from the Atlantic seaboard into the Middle West.

West economic bonds which the canals had earlier begun to establish. By the time of the Civil War, the railroads were carrying two-thirds of the nation's internal trade, the great bulk of it between the Middle Atlantic states and the Middle West, and plans were well advanced for roads that would span the continent.

The Overland Mail

As interest in the Far West increased, there rose a demand for transportation between the Atlantic and Pacific coasts which was better and cheaper than that around Cape Horn. In the later 1840s government subsidies led to the foundation of two mail steamship lines, the United States Company between New York and Panama and the Pacific Company operating between Panama and San Francisco. Commodore Vanderbilt, already growing rich from steamboat operations in the New York and Hudson River area, established an Accessory Transit Company that carried mail and passengers across Nicaragua, and in 1855 a railroad opened across the Isthmus of Panama.

Costs were high on these new routes; the traveler on the Panama railroad, for example, had to pay $25.00 for a journey of forty-seven miles. The majority of passengers and the great bulk of mail and freight still went by the Horn, but agitation for an overland service grew and bore fruit. In 1848, regular mail transport began between Independence, Missouri, and Salt Lake City, and a year later a mail route was established to Santa Fe. During the next nine years, efforts to set up a fast and continuous service to the coast finally brought into being the Butterfield Overland Stage Company, subsidized by the federal government at $600,000 a year and running the 2,795 miles between St. Louis and Memphis on the Mississippi and San Francisco. This opened in 1858, carrying both passengers and mail. During the three weeks of traveling day and night that it took to make the trip, food and water were scarce, bathing was impossible, and there was very little sleep for the passengers. Though dust, soaking rains, and desert sun drove them to the whiskey bottle and left them looking like scarecrows at the end of the journey, the trip was nevertheless shorter and less expensive than by the water routes.

By the close of the 1850s, rivals to the Butterfield Company had appeared, and one of these—Russell, Majors and Waddell—introduced the Pony Express. With relays of horses and riders, the Pony Express carried mail from St. Joseph, Missouri, to Placerville, California, in nine days. Its spectacular service received much publicity, but it went bankrupt after telegraph lines crossed the plains in 1861.

During and after the Civil War, the dominant figure in stagecoach transportation was Ben Holladay. At one time, he had control of over 3,000 miles of stage line. But the days of the overland stage were already numbered, for it could not compete with the transcontinental railroad. By 1870, the stagecoach was becoming a relic of the past, so rapid was the development of the American system of transportation.

Foreign Trade

The foreign commerce of the United States had been hard hit in the days of the Embargo and the War of 1812, and it was not until the 1830s that it regained the volume it had enjoyed in 1805. From then on, as the domestic economy expanded, and as wealth and the demand for foreign goods increased, there was a great expansion of foreign trade. In 1825, some $67 million worth of American products were shipped abroad, but by 1860 American exports had risen in value to over $300 million. Wheat, cotton, and tobacco constituted the bulk of these shipments, which went mainly to England and the European Continent. Meantime, American imports grew with even greater rapidity. Two-thirds of these imports consisted of manufactured goods, but coffee, sugar, tea, hides, and skins were also brought to the United States in considerable quantity.

Between 1815 and 1860, the total excess of merchandise imports over merchandise exports in value was $724 million. This unfavorable balance in foreign trade gave a great opportunity for protectionists to paint a doleful picture of the American future, and helped rally support for Clay's American System. But the superiority of British iron and steel products, the country's need for manufactured goods, and the South's opposition to protection bolstered the position of the exponents of a tariff primarily for revenue. They could also point out that the unfavorable balance of trade was more apparent than real. The profits earned by the United States merchant marine, the commissions of merchants in the re-export trade, the millions invested by Europeans in American securities, and, finally, the flood of gold that poured into the country from California after 1849 made the unfavorable balance of little consequence.

It is small wonder then, that during this period the tariff took a generally downward direction. The compromise tariff of 1833 held until 1842, and the tariff of that year restored duties almost to the level of 1832, but in 1846 the Walker tariff pushed the level downward once more. Still lower was the tariff of 1857. By 1861, duties collected had fallen to 18.18 per cent of the value of dutiable imports, as against 61.69 per cent in 1830, and to 14.21 per cent of the value of all imports, as against 57.32 per cent in 1830. The tariff was still protective in its general outlines, but the country was moving in the direction of free trade.

The Rise and Fall of the Merchant Marine

Like overseas trade, American shipbuilding suffered heavily between 1805 and 1815, but the commercial development of the Middle Period saw a great expansion of the American merchant marine. By 1846, there were 943,000 tons of American owned shipping carrying cargoes across the oceans of the world. Nine years later, our shipping tonnage nearly equalled that of Great Britain, and in 1861 better than 1.3 million tons were registered under the American flag.

The great triumph of American shipbuilders during this era was the clipper ship, which lent a dramatic aspect to the merchant marine during the two decades before the Civil War. Small but fast, these beautiful, three-masted, wooden-hulled vessels carried American and foreign goods to every port of the world, offering effective competition to the merchant marines of all other nations. The "Flying Cloud," designed by master builder Donald McKay, had a deck length of 229 feet and was forty feet eight inches broad, with a registered tonnage of 1,783. On her maiden voyage in 1851, she made a day's run of 374 miles, reaching San Francisco out of New York, via Cape Horn, in eighty-nine days.

The discovery of gold in California and the consequent booming trade with the Pacific coast gave impetus to the building of the clippers, but these lordly ships symbolized at once the glory and the doom of the old merchant marine. For Yankee ingenuity in shipbuilding failed to keep abreast of the times. Hampered by American inability to manufacture iron as cheaply as the British, American shipyards persisted in building wooden sailing ships to compete with British and French iron steamships. Even during the 1850s, Yankee shipowners found themselves handicapped by insurance and traffic rates higher than those of their rivals, with a consequent loss of premium trade in both passengers and freight. The China trade, once a lucrative source of revenue, declined as Americans came to prefer European to Chinese porcelain, and Brazilian coffee to Chinese tea, while changes in men's fashions lowered the demand for Oriental silk. The West Indies trade also fell off, and the railroad opened across the Isthmus of Panama in 1855 robbed the clippers of the California trade. American capitalists lost interest in a dubious marine investment that could not offer as attractive possibilities for profits as those afforded by domestic manufacturing and internal improvements. Finally, after the Civil War dealt a heavy blow to the prosperity of American shipping interests, the great days of the nineteenth-century American merchant marine had come to a close.

One of the most remarkable aspects of American foreign commerce during this period was the predominance acquired by the port of New York. In 1820, New York handled some 20 per cent of the nation's traffic with the outside world, and forty years later almost one-third of the nation's exports and imports passed through New York. Its share of the nation's total foreign trade was $248 million. Boston was next in line, with $41 million.

A variety of factors accounts for the busy lives of the New York merchants and commission agents. The city's excellent harbor and geographic location, its position as a terminus for goods shipped by the Erie Canal and by two great railway systems, the New York Central and the Erie, made it a natural entrepôt for western produce seeking export and for foreign imports coming into the American market. For a generation, it had had packets, such as the "Black Ball" line, with regular transatlantic service. These, together with an auction system for the centralized sale of European imports, were important factors in attracting commerce. Moreover, the city's merchants and bankers had been quick to take advantage of southern passivity in the handling of cotton shipments. New York had developed an artificial triangle trade in cotton: instead of going direct from Charleston, Savannah, Mobile, and New Orleans to England, cotton shipments were dragged 200 miles out of their way, and transshipped in New York, while the South's imports were brought back by the same roundabout route. The cotton filled the holds of outgoing vessels, many of them New York-owned. The merchants and bankers of the metropolis also profited hugely by this cotton traffic, for their enterprising agents established themselves in southern cities, lending money to southern planters and bankers, and acting as middlemen in marketing the cotton crop. Probably as much as 40 per cent of the value of the South's cotton exports went to swell the coffers of New York's businessmen, and to create among them a sympathetic interest in the aims and aspirations of "King Cotton."

Industrial Development

Agricultural expansion, the transportation revolution, and the growth of domestic and foreign commerce were clear indications of national growth. It was natural that they should be accompanied by great advances in the North's industrial activity. Urban development, noted in an earlier chapter, continued until, by 1860, one out of every seven Americans lived in cities of 8,000 population or more. Many of these had great pools of workers and were hives of industrial activity. New York and Brooklyn had a total population of 1,080,330 in 1860, and turned out each year nearly $200 million worth of manufactured products. Philadelphia, with 565,529 inhabitants in 1860, was, in value of products, the second manufacturing center of the country. Western cities had mushroomed. Cincinnati, Ohio, had a population of 160,000 in 1860; its packing business had given it the name of "the Porkopolis of the West," and it was also producing $18 million of manufactured goods each year. Pittsburgh, a center of iron foundries and the manufacture of iron products, was a bustling town of 50,000, Chicago had 100,-000, and St. Louis, center of the nation's trade in furs and lead, had 160,000 people within its corporate limits by the time of the Civil War. The North was dotted with centers of industry as well as of commerce, and the manufacture of textiles, boots and shoes, and a host of other products increased with each passing year. The nation's production of pig iron reached 900,000 tons in 1860, and its looms turned 423 million pounds of cotton into cloth. In that year, the nation had nearly $2 billion invested in manufacturing, 85 per cent of this located in the North.

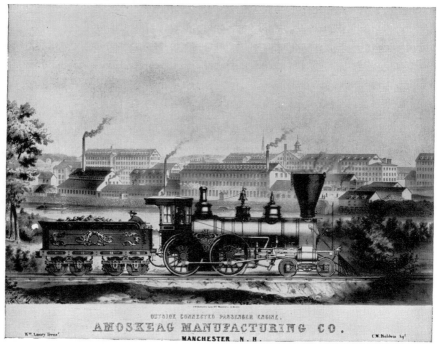

A BUSY TEXTILE MILL OF THE 1850s

The Amoskeag Company plant symbolizes the flourishing state of American manufacturing in the middle 1850s. The locomotive in the foreground was a type in common use for short runs and switching operations.

As northern industry grew, it developed marked characteristics. The size of manufacturing plants and the use of the corporate form of business organization increased. Household manufacturing, so important half a century before, disappeared from New England and the Middle Atlantic states and declined drastically in the West. As industrialism spread from East to West, it, like agriculture, developed areas of specialization. Two great manufacturing zones were clearly defined, the first a textile area in New England and the Middle Atlantic states and the second a belt that fanned westward from a line extending roughly from Utica, New York, to Harrisburg, Pennsylvania. In this second area river boats were built, flour and lumber were milled, cordage and distilled and brewed liquors were produced, and meat was packed.

Manufacturing also followed the path marked out by agriculture as it pushed westward. While before 1840 the Northeast led in the production of agricultural machinery, after 1840 this industry became concentrated in the trans-Allegheny region. The chief center of iron ore production shifted from Pennsylvania to Ohio. Distilling and brewing centered in Ohio by 1850, and flour milling showed signs of starting on the long trek that eventually would take it from western New York to eastern Minnesota.

The shifting pattern of industrial activity showed enterprise and ingenuity on the part of American businessmen. It was also a constant incentive to far-sightedness and progressive tendencies, for the movement of industry from one section of the country to another provided excellent opportunities for discarding old and adopting new and better machines and modes of production.

The Rise of Invention

A great and growing national market constantly stimulated industrial activity and also called for new and better methods of production. So, too, did the interest of Americans in increased physical comfort. The result was an upsurge in invention and in the improvement of a variety of technological processes. The number of inventions patented yearly rose from seventy-seven in 1810 to 544 in 1830 and 4,778 in 1860, and they affected every segment of the economy.

Europeans marveled at our elevators, furnaces, hot-and-cold-water systems, and railroad improvements that even included crude berths for the overnight traveler. John Goulding's carding machine, rated by authorities as the greatest nineteenth-century contribution to the world's card-wool industry, and a new power loom invented by Harvard graduate Francis Cabot Lowell and a mechanic named Paul Moody revolutionized the textile industry. After years of experimentation, Charles Goodyear in 1844 patented a process called "vulcanization" that brought a great development in the production of rubber goods. Only a little earlier, Samuel F. B. Morse had brought into being a new mode of communication; eventually, with money obtained from Congress, he built a telegraph line between Baltimore and Washington, which carried not only the inventor's message, "What hath God wrought?" but also the news of James K. Polk's nomination by the Democratic national convention of 1844 to members of Congress in the nation's capitol. By 1860, there were 50,000 miles of telegraph wire in the United States, and in response to this speeding up of news communication, which called for bigger and better newspapers, Richard Hoe's cylindrical press and other improved processes in the 1850s effected great changes in newspaper production.

By the middle of the nineteenth century, the United States was well on the way to the era of mass production and machine tools. Eli Whitney's achievement in producing a musket with interchangeable parts was duplicated in revolvers by Samuel Colt. Sewing machines (Elias Howe took out his first patent in 1846) were on the way to standardization, as were harvesters and other improved tools for farmers. Inventors developed mechanisms for turning out finished iron products—nails, tacks, bolts, files, spikes, chains—which had formerly been produced by hand. By the time of the Civil War, American machine tools were more numerous, more varied, and more efficient than those of Europe.

The Business Class

The lot of the businessman in the Middle Period was by no means an easy one. The vast majority of manufacturing businesses were small, few outside of the textile field producing over $100,000 worth of goods in a year. Transportation and supplies of raw materials for the manufacturer were often uncertain, due to the hazards of water routes, weather conditions, and difficulties of transshipment. Capital and credit were frequently scarce, especially in the West, where business ventures were of a more hazardous and speculative character than they were in the East. The paper-currency situation, after the destruction of the second Bank of the United States, was chaotic, and foreign competition was stiff. There were frequent recessions, periods of high inflation and speculation, a major depression (1837–1843), and a short but sharp financial panic (1857–1858). But these were handicaps, rather than insurmountable obstacles, to business enterprise. By and large, the era was full of exciting opportunities, and there were many businessmen who could justifiably be called "Captains of Industry."

In the American towns and cities of the eighteenth century, commerce had been the principal form of economic activity. Industrial production had been of much less significance and, save for shipbuilding, was on a small scale. With the development of a national market, however, the character of urban economic life perceptibly changed; while the distribution of agricultural staples remained an important and growing part of urban activity, industrial production and distribution rose sharply in amount and significance. In the business world of 1840, there were many more manufacturers than there had been a generation before. The merchants who handled industrial products were also much more numerous, and had larger establishments and greater means at their disposal than had been the case in earlier times. The business class was definitely changing in character and in outlook.

Better than two-thirds of this new business class were self-employed entrepreneurs who owned and managed their enterprises. They would usually have a number of irons in the fire—merchandising, moneylending, shipping, and manufacturing in a small way, in some or all of these combinations. There was also an élite business type, the energetic and creative owner and builder who, by a combination of skill, vision, and good luck, achieved outstanding financial success. There are many illustrations of this élite type: Cyrus Hall McCormick was one example and Peter Cooper (1791–1883) another.

By the time he was sixteen years old, Cooper was a veteran workman with experience in hatmaking, brewing, brickmaking, and storekeeping, all under the guidance of his father. In 1827, young Cooper purchased for $2,000 a glue factory at Fourth Avenue and 33rd Street, New York, now the site of the Metropolitan Life Insurance Office Building. There, by constant experimentation, he produced a glue that could compete with those of European make, and a fine grade of gelatine as well. He managed the business, was his own bookkeeper and salesman, and at the year's end drove around town settling his balances in gold. When railroading next attracted him, he became one of America's first builders of locomotives, and also established an iron foundry, while still continuing in the glue business. In 1833, he estimated his wealth at $123,459, and in 1846 at $385,500. Participation in the telegraph industry added to his fortune. Simple, kindly, shrewd, rugged, methodical, a radical in regard to the rights of labor and of the poor, he was one of the best of the early "Captains."

While Cooper was building his fortune in glue and iron, Nathan Appleton (1779–1861) and his associates in the textile business were demonstrating the possibilities of the corporate form of business enterprise. In 1813, they organized the Boston Manufacturing Company at Waltham, Massachusetts, financing it liberally with an investment, cash and reserves, of over $1 million. Building a cotton manufacturing plant that was integrated from the raw cotton to dyeing and printing, they established their own selling agencies for the finished products. They constantly introduced technological improvements, built company towns to house the factory girls, and established strict discipline in the mills. Despite the hard times that followed the War of 1812, their company was an immediate success. By 1822, better than 100 per cent in dividends had been paid to investors, and by 1835 the founders had opened nine new companies, each specializing in a particular textile product. They also founded insurance companies, banks, real estate companies, and water power companies, all with a view to aiding the development of the textile industry. In their hands, the corporate form became an instrument by which a few able men, owners of only a fraction of the stock in a business, could use their talents in many and varied enterprises.

Social Significance of the New Business Class

Of the successful businessmen of the period before the Civil War, almost 50 per cent came from the lower social and economic strata of society. This had a twofold significance. On the one hand, they signalized and furthered a movement toward the concentration of wealth and power in the hands of a relatively few individuals, thereby creating a business and manufacturing aristocracy that claimed at least parity with the old, family-conscious, Federalist commercial aristocracy. On the other hand, stemming as they did in considerable part from the ranks of the toilers, they represented a partial democratization of the aristocratic principle.

A prime political manifestation of this democratizing influence was the rise of the Seward-Weed group to power in the New York State Whig party, for the conservatism of this group was quite different from that of the Hamilton-Jay Federalist tradition. Sympathetic to and aligned with business interests, it also appreciated the political power of the masses, and understood the need for satisfying at least some of the aspirations of the common man. Liberal Whigs of this type did much to keep the classes in touch with the masses. This was significant, for it indicated the possibility of an American way of life that would permit the achievement of material success while undertaking to satisfy the aspirations of the common man. The way to this goal, as American experience was even then giving witness, was through an ever-rising level of productivity coupled with an increasing sense of social responsibility.

The Problems and Aspirations of Northern Labor

In a growing free economy such as that of the North, labor and its problems were bound to play an important role. During the colonial period, slaves, apprentices, and indentured servants had constituted the labor force. In such shops as did exist, where employers and employees worked side by side to satisfy the demands of local consumers, anything like a wage system simply did not exist.

The wage system took form toward the close of the eighteenth century. After the adoption of the Constitution, with the widening of both internal and external markets, there began an expansion of business activity. Since indenture and apprenticeship did not constitute a stable labor supply, they were not suited to such a development. Furthermore, most states held masters responsible for the debts of such laborers and for care of them during illness. The wage system rapidly gained ground and by 1820 was generally established in the Middle Atlantic states and New England, where industry required a sizeable labor force.

Coincidental with the rise of the wage system came the beginnings of labor unrest. Town and city laborers were required to work the long hours customary in agriculture, and the seventy- to eighty-hour work week was common practice. Owners of workshops paid little or no attention to sanitation or ventilation. Still more important was the depression in labor's wages that came with the advent of the merchant-capitalist.

The appearance of the merchant-capitalist was an inevitable consequence of business expansion. He understood how to gauge market possibilities and capacity for producing finished products, and he developed and organized markets on a large scale. He could enlist the confidence of bankers and other possessors of capital in growing business undertakings. Dealing in large quantities, he utilized various means of obtaining goods at the lowest possible price, such as buying from prisons or sweatshops, and in areas where labor was relatively abundant and cheap. He drove hard bargains with the small employer-producers, who, in turn, cut down the wages of their employees; these reductions were made easier by the general decline of the price level, for wages always tend to fall more rapidly than the price of commodities. Under these circumstances, the wage earners were driven to begin organization.

Until about 1822, labor organization was confined to the skilled and semi-skilled workers in shoemaking, tailoring, and printing. These early unions sought better wages and hours through strikes and picketing, but had little success. Employers were obdurate, and the courts ruled against unions and strikes as "criminal conspiracies." The hard times from 1819 to 1822 weakened labor organization.

The next fifteen years, however, were a period of growing labor agitation. A scarcity of skilled labor and the extension of the franchise gave the workers an increased sense of power, and urban labor concentrations prompted at least the beginning of a consciousness of labor solidarity. Trade unionism spread until by 1834 there were 25,000 trade unionists in New York, Boston, Philadelphia, and Baltimore, and "City Centrals," affiliations of unions in various trades in a given city, became popular. There was even a movement toward a national union that would comprise the various trades in Boston, New York, Brooklyn, Poughkeepsie, Newark, and Philadelphia.

Labor was now obviously on the offensive. Between 1822 and 1828, it concentrated chiefly on strikes intended to force a ten-hour day for sixty hours a week. Employer combinations, blacklists, and adverse court decisions rendered these tactics largely ineffective, and during the next four years the workers centered their attention on political action. Parties of the "Workies," as they were called, appeared in New York, Pennsylvania, and other states, demanding better wages and hours, more educational opportunity for the children of working-class families, the abolition of compulsory militia systems and of imprisonment for debt, and mechanics lien laws protecting the wages of workingmen whose employers went bankrupt. The abolition of monopolies, especially banking monopolies, was a favorite objective of the "Workies," for laborers often found that their wages were paid in depreciated bank notes.

These labor parties were of temporary duration. They were always short of funds, and their leaders had little political skill. Then, too, their principal demands were often taken over by the major parties. When, between 1832 and 1837, the workers again concentrated on union organization and strikes as means of bettering their condition, they won the ten-hour day in a number of machine-run industries. But in the textile industry labor organization was weak, and there the eleven- to thirteen-hour day remained the rule.

There are varying accounts of conditions in the New England textile mills. As Charles Dickens saw them at Lowell in 1842, conditions were almost ideal. The laborers, mostly women and girls from the New England farms who made $2.00 net a week, appeared happy and well dressed. The factories were neat, clean, and orderly, the boarding houses well chaperoned, and the food good. Most of the girls subscribed to circulating libraries and a magazine, *The Lowell Offering*, was made up chiefly of stories and articles by the workers. Dickens—rightly—thought this a labor paradise, compared with English factory conditions.

But there was another side to the picture. Even in Lowell, the boarding houses were overcrowded, the hours long, and the paternalistic control of the owners extremely strict. Workers were discharged for immodesty, profanity, or dancing, and all were expected to attend church. Boarding house doors closed at 10:00 P.M. In nearby Rhode Island, where whole families were induced to move into town and become permanent mill hands, the workers were mercilessly exploited. And as industrialism developed, conditions in textile factories everywhere deteriorated. In the late 1840s, women operatives worked a seventy-five-hour week and earned net pay of less than $1.50 for six days' labor; they tended four looms instead of two, as had been the case in the previous decade, and the boarding houses became more and more congested. Under these circumstances, the New England farm girls quit the mills, their places being taken by Irish, German, or French-Canadian immigrant girls who would work for whatever was paid. Massachusetts had no ten-hour law until after the Civil War, and in those states that did have such a law, "special contract" clauses usually made it ineffective. By 1850, a depressed and depressing condition of society existed in the New England manufacturing towns.

Conditions in other labor centers paralleled those in New England. As hundreds of unskilled immigrant laborers swarmed into the cities, terrible slums developed. In 1850, one out of every twenty inhabitants of New York City lived underground. The New York *Tribune* published a series of articles called "Dens of Death," based on police records, showing how mortality rates rose in the dark, overcrowded tenements and filthy lodging cellars. Sweatshops multiplied, and the needle trades were flooded with workers who labored fifteen to eighteen hours a day for from $.14 to $.25. As the influx of gold in the 1850s brought higher prices, real wages lagged, and shoemakers, hand-loom weavers, and hatters were hard pressed to make a living. New printing presses and steam power threw printers out of employment and weakened their unions. Much the same situation developed in the garment trade, where the invention of the sewing machine revolutionized the clothing industry. As the factory system spread, the numbers of those entirely dependent upon wages increased, and the rise of corporate industry helped to depersonalize the relationship between employer and employee.

Faced by such conditions, the labor movement went through two distinct phases between 1840 and 1860. At first, it assumed a defensive and Utopian character. While resisting the lowering of standards of employment, little effort was made to use strikes and boycotts for the improvement of labor conditions. Aggressive energies were principally directed toward obtaining better educational and cultural opportunities for society in general, and toward schemes that would put the instruments of production and distribution in the hands of the workers themselves. Much of labor's attention was centered on socialistic communities such as those of the Fourierites (see page 468), on efforts to establish cooperative societies for production and distribution, and on the hope of cheap land as a means of escape from intolerable urban working conditions. One of the reform ideas that found considerable favor in labor circles was that of George Henry Evans of New York, who proposed giving the public domain to the users thereof in small, unalienable holdings.

These idealistic efforts to better the lot of the workingman found favor and support from the reformers of the period, but they had serious weaknesses. Much of the support they received came from groups that were more interested in temperance and slavery than they were in labor conditions in the northern mills and factories. The socialistic communities faded out, as did the cooperative societies, which were undercut by capitalist rivals and lacked efficient management. The skilled workers, lacking mobilization for clear-cut and realizable goals, were further handicapped by the shifts and changes of rapid industrial development, and by the influx of masses of unskilled laborers willing to work at any price. There were no appreciable gains for industrial workers in hours of employment or real wages.

There were a few bright spots for labor in the 1840s. President Van Buren, in 1840, established the ten-hour day for federal employees, and the Massachusetts Supreme Court, in the case of *Commonwealth v. Hunt* (1842), ruled that workers had a legal right to unionize and adopt peaceful measures to achieve their ends. The way was thus paved for the legalization of unions in the other northern states, though, by and large, labor's cause was in the doldrums. There was need of more practical leadership.

The labor movement of the 1850s turned its back upon Utopianism, and union leaders devoted themselves to improving the situation of their followers, rather than undertaking radical transformations of society. Little attention was paid to cooperatives, general social reforms, or improvements of the condition of unskilled workers. City trade unions spread, and national craft unions appeared, such as the National Typographical Union, the National Molders Union, the Machinists and Blacksmiths National Union, and the National Protective Association for Railway Engineers. Craft unions used the strike vigorously in attempts to improve hours and wages.

This change of attitude on the part of labor cost it the support of Greeley and other reforming spirits. The unions were also hard hit by the depression of 1857–1858, and toward the close of the decade the labor movement was limited by division of opinion among the workers over slavery. New England textile workers were sympathetic with the abolitionists, but white labor in other areas, especially New York, was often anti-Negro, insisting that labor's chief concern was the improvement of the lot of the northern worker.

Norman Ware's assertion that the labor movement from 1840 to 1860 ended "as it had begun—practically in nothingness" would appear to be too harsh. There had been no tremendous strides forward, but the picture in 1860 was somewhat brighter than it had been twenty years before. Labor's right to unionize and to strike had won a real victory in *Commonwealth v. Hunt,* and some progress had been made toward acceptance of the ten-hour day. The working class had aided in the improvement of educational opportunity and the elimination of imprisonment for debt, and, through its interest in land reform, in paving the way for the Homestead Act of 1862. The experience that had been gained in labor organization—its mistakes and achievements—was to prove useful when, after the Civil War, labor resumed efforts to find its place in the sun.

Suggested Reading

On forces changing the economy, see D. C. North, *The Economic Growth of the United States* (1961), and Stuart Bruchey, *The Roots of American Economic Growth* (1965). Nevins, *Ordeal of the Union* has some excellent chapters on the economy at mid-century.

On immigration, the standard work is M. L. Hansen, *The Atlantic Migration* (1940); see also by the same author, *The Immigrant in American History* (1940). There are new insights in Oscar Handlin, *Uprooted: The Epic Story of the Migrations that Made the American People* (1951). See also Carl Wittke, *We Who Built America* (1939), and M. A. Jones, *American Immigration* (1960).

The standard work on northern farming is P. W. Bidwell and J. P. Falconer, *History of Agriculture in the Northern United States, 1620–1860* (1925). L. Rogin, *The Introduction of Farm Machinery in its Relation to the Productivity of Labor in the United States* (1931) is also useful, as are T. D. Clark, *Frontier America* (1959), and P. W. Gates, *The Farmer's Age* (1960).

There is much material on transportation in B. H. Heyer, ed., *History of Transportation in the United States before 1860* (1917). Indispensable is G. R. Taylor, *The Transportation Revolution, 1815–1860* (1951). A. P. Hulbert, *The Paths of Inland Commerce* (1920) is useful, and C. H. Ambler, *A History of Transportation in the Ohio Valley* (1932) is a sound and readable study. A. F. Harlow, *Old Towpaths* (1926) is a colorful account of canal travel. L. C. Hunter, *Steamboats on the Western Rivers* (1949) is scholarly and complete.

Literature on the early railroad era is voluminous. F. A. Cleveland and F. W. Powell, *Railroad Promotion and Capitalization in the United States* (1909) and L. H. Haney, *A Congressional History of Railways in the United States to 1850* (1908) are essential for the serious student. C. E. Carter, *When Railroads Were New* (1909) is a lively account. Useful and interesting are T. C. Cochran, *Railroad Leaders, 1845–1890* (1953) and A. D. Chandler, *Henry Varnum Poor* (1956). There are many studies of individual railroads. Among the most important are P. W. Gates, *The Illinois Central Railroad and its Colonization Work* (1934); G. H. Burgess and M. C. Kennedy, *The Pennsylvania Railroad Company, 1846–1946* (1949); and Edward Hungerford, *The Story of the Baltimore and Ohio Railroad, 1827–1927* (2 vols., 1928). The New England railroads are covered in E. C. Kirkland, *Men, Cities, and Transportation* (2 vols., 1948).

Commerce in general is adequately dealt with in E. R. Johnson, *et al., History of*

Domestic and Foreign Commerce in the United States (2 vols., 1915) and J. H. Frederick, *The Development of American Commerce* (1932). There is much material on foreign trade in S. E. Morison, *The Maritime History of Massachusetts, 1783–1860* (1921) and Robert G. Albion, *Square Riggers on Schedule* (1938) and *The Rise of New York Port* (1939). Those interested in the clipper ships should consult A. H. Clark, *The Clipper Ship Era, 1843–1869* (1910) and C. C. Cutler, *Greyhounds of the Sea* (1930).

For industry and invention, see V. S. Clark, *History of Manufactures in the United States* (3 vols., 1929), a standard work; M. Holland, *Industrial Explorers* (1929); J. W. Roe, *English and American Tool Builders* (1926); and J. A. Kouwenhoven, *Made in America* (1948). Allan Nevins, *Abram S. Hewitt, With Some Account of Peter Cooper* (1935) has much useful information, as does Waldemar Kaempffert, ed., *A Popular History of American Invention* (2 vols., 1924). See also H. J. Habbakuk, *American and British Technology in the Nineteenth Century* (1962), and J. W. Oliver, *History of American Technology* (1956).

On business and the business class, see W. B. Smith and A. H. Cole, *Fluctuations in American Business, 1790–1860* (1935); T. C. Cochran and W. Miller, *The Age of Enterprise: A Social History of Industrial America* (1942); and, for biographical studies, such works as W. T. Hutchinson's *Cyrus Hall McCormick* (2 vols., 1930–1935), Nevins' *Hewitt*, and K. W. Porter's *John Jacob Astor, Business Man* (2 vols., 1931). Also useful are L. H. Jenks, *The Migration of British Capital to 1875* (1927); F. X. Sutton *et al., The American Business Creed* (1956), and Roger Burlingame, *March of the Iron Men* (1938).

Labor history during this period is covered in J. R. Commons *et al., History of Labor in the United States* (4 vols., 1926) vol. I. Norman Ware, *The Industrial Worker, 1840–1860* (1924) is an important work, and Robert Ernst, *Immigrant Life in New York City, 1825–1863* (1949) is interesting and valuable.

21 ⸱ The Northern Social Order, 1830-1860

I T IS OBVIOUS from the preceding chapter that northern society centered
much of its attention upon material success and paid high regard to
those who achieved it. Textile manufacturers like Nathan Appleton,
rising industrialists like Peter Cooper, successful producers of farm implements like Cyrus Hall McCormick and John Deere, and tight-fisted John
Jacob Astor (1763–1848), busy amassing millions

Aims and Ideals

through the fur trade and real estate operations,
were highly respected members of the communities
in which they lived. Businessmen worked hard and
took few vacations. New York, the great trading center of the country, was
a city where strenuous competition was the order of the day; bankers, merchants, and manufacturers raced through their meals at Butter Cake Dick's
and also at Delmonico's, and even cabbies and omnibus drivers hurried.
Small wonder that in the North dyspepsia was a common complaint.

If Americans living in the North put high value upon economic achievement, they also had a genuine faith in the ideals that are basic to a democracy. Many neglected voting at election time, but there was a general belief
in the superiority of democratic government to all monarchical systems and
in democracy as an ideal way of life. Despite glaring contradictions in practice, it was an article of faith that legitimate government rested upon the

consent of the governed, that men were created equal, and that each individual had a right to life, liberty, and the pursuit of happiness.

Belief in these democratic dogmas was brought about by a number of factors. The Declaration of Independence had great prestige as the charter of American liberties, government of the people by their representatives had been proven a workable and satisfactory means of national organization, and the ideal of democratic equality was being constantly fortified by the equalitarian experiences of an ever-advancing and always present frontier. The people were proud of their nation and its accomplishments. They believed that Europe was effete; that the United States had the mission of carrying aloft the democratic torch that could light the way for the rest of the world; and that it could do this in triumphant fashion.

There were definite symbols of the popular faith in America. Religion and moral law were felt to be the foundations of the national existence. George Washington was regarded as an epitome of the American virtues, "first in war, first in peace, and first in the hearts of his countrymen." The Fourth of July was a holiday celebrated by great mass meetings at which orators read the Declaration and made patriotic speeches, while veterans of American wars sat upon the platform. When John Adams and Thomas Jefferson died on July 4, 1826, and the messengers carrying the sad news North and South met in Philadelphia, almost in the shadow of Independence Hall, many an American felt, as did young Horace Greeley, "that a Divine attestation had solemnly hallowed and sanctified the great anniversary by the impressive ministration of Death."

Belief in political democracy led to its extension in practice. As the new states entered the Union with universal white manhood suffrage, the older states followed their example and lowered or abolished their suffrage qualifications, for they had no desire to see their congressional delegations outnumbered as the population of the West swelled. From 1826 to 1850, save for Rhode Island (and there the suffrage was substantially broadened after the Dorr Rebellion of 1842), the northern electorate was approximately equal to the adult white male population. Even after that, despite local restrictions upon adult white aliens by means of residence requirements, there was universal suffrage in the North for white, adult citizens. Further, officeholders were increasingly chosen by the people instead of being appointed, and property qualifications for officeholding practically disappeared. In national politics, the old system of nominating presidential candidates in a caucus of the national legislature had disappeared by the middle 1830s; in 1812, the legislatures of eight of the seventeen states in the nation chose the presidential electors, but in 1832, every state save South Carolina chose them by popular vote.

Women and Negroes still could not vote, however. Secret ballots were not yet in vogue, and at the polling places on election day there was ample opportunity for fraud and intimidation. But, despite these limitations, political democracy was an ideal that was being extended in practice. Even conservatives, who doubted that the right to vote was a natural law accepted white suffrage as a necessary part of the American political order.

Penal Reforms

Northern society demonstrated the vitality of the democratic ideal in other ways than the growth of political democracy by producing a variety of social and moral reforms, including real improvement in the attitude toward crime and criminals. There was a growing agitation against imprisonment for debt, and this practice, so oppressive of the poor, had largely disappeared by 1850. There was a marked reduction in the number of death punishments for crime, and a strong agitation developed for abolishing the death penalty altogether. The practice of herding criminals together, regardless of age, sex, or the nature of the offense, began to give way to segregation according to sex and the nature of the misdeeds. The best prisons adopted the individual-cell system, and the utilization of prison labor, which often resulted in the prisoner's mastering a trade, made headway over the utter boredom of mere confinement. Here and there juvenile reform schools appeared.

Much remained to be done in the way of penal reform. Some of the improvements, such as the introduction of prison labor, were subject to grave abuse, and the advances had been centered chiefly in the New England and Middle Atlantic states. Local jails everywhere were still a blot upon American civilization. But the heroic efforts of such reformers as Francis Lieber, Dorothea Lynde Dix, and Samuel Gridley Howe had borne fruit, and America had a penal system advanced enough to prompt visits by Europeans interested in new methods of dealing with crime.

Help for the Handicapped

Prison reform was closely connected with changes in the treatment of the insane, for many of the latter were housed in jails and other penal institutions, where, as late as the 1830s, the demented were chained, flogged, and left without heat in winter, just as had been the case at the beginning of the century. The story of reform in their treatment is largely the story of Dorothea Lynde Dix (1802–1887). This New England schoolteacher had a frail physique but was blessed with enormous energy and a deeply compassionate spirit. Conditions that she observed in 1841 in an East Cambridge, Massachusetts, jail led her to make a systematic examination of the treatment of the insane in the jails, almshouses, and houses of correction throughout the state. The terrible conditions that she described in her report shocked the legislators, and her efforts, backed by those of Horace Mann and others, led to the provision of decent hospital accommodations for the demented. Successful in Massachusetts, Miss Dix extended her work throughout a major part of the Union, and her appeals to wealthy philanthropists and to state legislatures had effect; sixteen states founded hospitals for the insane. In 1848, she had introduced in Congress a bill providing land grants for national hospitals; this bill was finally passed in 1854, only to be vetoed by President Pierce.

While Miss Dix was carrying on her crusade for the insane, other reformers were quickening the public conscience about the condition of the nation's poor. There were numerous cases of the "sale" of indigent adults and the farming out of poor children by township authorities to those who exploited their labor. As a result of agitation, many of the destitute were removed from jails and placed in orphanages, houses of correction, and almshouses. At the same time, public-spirited citizens like Thomas Hopkins Gallaudet of Connecticut and Samuel Gridley Howe of Massachusetts had much to do with establishing throughout the country a number of schools for deaf-mutes and for the blind.

The Battle Against Demon Rum

One of the outstanding reform movements of this period was that directed against liquor. Drink was common and cheap during the first part of the nineteenth century; it was proverbial that "a man could get drunk twice in America on six-pence." Rum, cider, and whiskey, to say nothing of beer and wine, were consumed in great quantities by both men and women.

The effort to curb the liquor traffic came from a variety of sources. The pervasive spirit of humanitarianism, and the religious revivalism that saw in alcohol a menace to spiritual improvement, aided the campaign against strong drink. Those interested in political democracy argued logically that the ballot should be cast with wisdom, rather than by voters whose intelligence had been stupefied or destroyed by liquor. Another influential argument was that indulgence in liquor meant economic waste; the poor spent

SIGNING THE PLEDGE
PHOTOCOPY OF LITHOGRAPH
BY J. ROPES (1846)

This was one of the innumerable pictorial presentations by which the Washingtonians and other temperance crusaders strove to bring home at once the vicious effects of strong drink and the happiness that would result from sobriety.

COURTESY OF THE LIBRARY OF CONGRESS

their money for rum and whiskey as readily as they did for food, to the detriment of themselves and of society, for the drunken and debauched were always inefficient workmen. Finally, the foes of strong drink were quick to point out the close correlation between drunkenness and crime that appeared in statistics from various towns and cities.

The first major attacks upon drink and drinking came early in the century from such influential men as Dr. Benjamin Rush of Philadelphia and the Presbyterian cleric and revivalist Lyman Beecher, who thundered against intemperance from his pulpit in Litchfield, Connecticut. Numerous temperance societies developed during the second and third decades of the century. After about 1825 the emphasis of the reformers shifted from temperance to abstinence, and the movement began to gain force, supported by college presidents such as Eliphalet Nott of Union and Mark Hopkins of Williams, and by a number of other influential citizens. The American Society for the Promotion of Temperance, founded in 1826, had 5,000 local chapters and about one million members by 1834; it centered in New England, New York, and Pennsylvania, but also had much strength in the Old Northwest. Prominent abolitionists, among them the wealthy landowner Gerrit Smith and the New York merchant and publisher Arthur Tappan, were active in this society. But during the later 1830s it lost influence as a result of factional fights over abolitionism, quarrels between advocates of temperance and prohibition and, possibly, the hardships of the depression years.

The temperance movement revived in the 1840s, a major factor being the Washingtonian movement led by the self-styled "Six Reformed Drunkards of Baltimore." Converted to prohibition by a temperance lecturer in the spring of 1840, they formed an organization to save drunkards from their fate, using meetings arranged between alcoholics and former victims of the habit. Their general approach to the problem of alcoholism afforded some precedents for today's Alcoholics Anonymous.

The Washingtonian movement spread to thousands of cities and towns, and under its influence a considerable temperance literature developed. The poem "Father, Dear Father, Come Home with Me Now," the song "The Old Oaken Bucket," T. S. Arthur's *Ten Nights in a Bar Room,* and various contributions by Whittier, Oliver Wendell Holmes, and Horace Greeley, fostered the temperance crusade. One of the great temperance lecturers of this period was the English immigrant John B. Gough, who took the pledge of abstinence in 1842.

Steadily the temperance movement spread as other societies appeared, among them The Order of the Sons of Temperance. The movement had its international aspects, and world temperance conventions were held in London and New York.

During the 1840s the American foes of liquor began to center their efforts on local and state prohibition of intoxicants. The first state-wide prohibition law was that of Maine, passed in 1846. By 1855, thirteen northern states had practically abolished the sale of spirituous beverages; only three of these— Maine, New Hampshire, and Vermont—remained steadfast, however, for the movement generally declined as the country's attention turned more and more to the crisis over slavery. The crusade had raised the question of whether or not it is wise to use force to settle a moral issue, and had demonstrated that the tyranny of the majority feared by the Founding Fathers could become a reality in the United States, but it had also shown that American society possessed a passion for moral betterment that could be easily roused into action.

The Antislavery Movement

It was inevitable that the northern reformers of the early nineteenth century should concern themselves with slavery as a denial of human rights. In the North, however, it was also unprofitable, and it had been replaced by a free white labor system. Antislavery sentiment found a fertile seedbed among northern humanitarians uninhibited by economic considerations, or by the problem of what could be done with millions of slaves if they were freed.

During the period following the War of 1812, some northern moderates, Daniel Webster among them, thought that colonization in Africa might be at least a partial answer to the slavery problem, but this proposal soon lost what popularity it had above the Mason and Dixon line and was replaced by more radical propositions. Advocates of a general slave emancipation began agitation in the North and, to a limited extent, in the border slave states. Scores of societies devoted to emancipating the Negro appeared, centering more and more in the North. Antislavery newspapers sprang up; one of the most influential of these was the *Genius of Universal Emancipation,* with Benjamin Lundy, a mild and gentle man of Quaker descent, as its editor.

Lundy was a gradual emancipationist. Not so his assistant editor, William Lloyd Garrison, a Massachusetts firebrand who found Lundy's efforts too tame and established his own *Liberator* in Boston, January 1, 1831. The motto of this paper was "Our country is the world, our countrymen mankind"; it had as a pictorial head the capital at Washington flying a flag marked with the word "Liberty," and in front of the capital a slave auction and a Negro chained to the whipping post. In the first issue, Garrison said, "I am in earnest—I will not equivocate—I will not excuse—I will not retreat a single inch—AND I WILL BE HEARD."

The *Liberator* roused furious resentment in the South but, save for the free Negroes, carried little weight in the North. By nature an extremist, Garrison was more a discordant element than a constructive force, although he did found the New England Antislavery Society in 1831. More important in organizing the antislavery movement was the work of such men as the preacher-reformer Theodore Dwight Weld, the revivalist Charles Grandison Finney, and other opponents of slavery, whose efforts were centered in the Old Northwest. Under their guidance, and with the financial aid of philanthropists such as the brothers Arthur and Lewis Tappan, the American Antislavery Society (1833–1840) was organized. It spread until it had hundreds of chapters, and Garrison also joined it.

The nation's leading statesmen stood aloof from these societies, but the influence of the indefatigable spokesmen for abolitionism steadily increased. They spread thousands of tracts and pamphlets throughout the land and enlisted the aid of James G. Birney, a former Alabama slaveholder, the Quaker poet John Greenleaf Whittier, and other influential men of letters. Many revivalist preachers joined the movement, incorporating abolition in their exhortations and winning numerous converts to the cause.

In the later 1830s, dissension broke out in the American Antislavery Society, for many of its members disliked Garrison's refusal to use political action, his denunciation of the Constitution, and his intolerance of those who differed with him. When Garrison and his friends captured the Society by 1840, a considerable number seceded from its ranks. Those favoring political action formed the Liberty party, which ran James G. Birney for President in that same year.

A very considerable number of the abolitionists were descended from the

Old Federalists of Puritan New England. They themselves were Whigs, with little sympathy with the aims of urban industrialists and little understanding of the problems of urban labor. They were anxious, however, to influence the currents of American life and threw themselves energetically into the promotion of abolitionism and other moral reforms.

Abolitionism also had a lunatic fringe. Meetings were occasionally disrupted by the appearance of such individuals as "Father" Lamson, who dressed completely in white and wore a long white beard, or George Washington Mellen, who forced upon the assemblies his "Mellen-cholics"—disquisitions on the chemical cause of color. Sometimes Abigail Folsom, called by Emerson "the flea of conventions," would appear at an abolitionist gathering, her disheveled hair streaming to her waist; her wild, incoherent orations frequently ended with a yell of, "It's the capitalists!" and on one occasion she screamed as she was being bodily removed from a meeting, "Christ had one ass to carry him; I have two." Small wonder that Maria Chapman, a more sober antislavery spirit, remarked that "the good Lord uses instruments for His purpose I would not touch with a fifty foot pole."

The antislavery movement was hampered by fanatics, by controversies between the advocates of immediacy and gradualism in attacking slavery and by fear on the part of businessmen that it might lead to violence. White labor had no love for free black competition, and many western farmers disliked the prospect of free Negro farmers appearing as competitors for western land. Mobs often threw stones and rotten eggs at antislavery speakers and broke up their meetings, and in 1837, at Alton, Illinois, a mob murdered Elijah Lovejoy, clergyman-editor and advocate of gradual emancipation. But influential men—Ralph Waldo Emerson and William Ellery Channing among others—denounced such outrages, and popular sentiment rallied to the cause of free speech. Slowly but steadily, as the 1840s wore on, the antislavery movement in the North became a force that had to be taken into consideration by the politicians of both major parties.

Women's Rights

In addition to being wives and mothers, women have always played an important role in other aspects of American society. We have noted the responsible positions they frequently held in colonial days, and, as the frontier moved to the Mississippi and beyond, their participation in religious and educational activities was vital to the development of the West. Great as their contributions were, however, their legal and political status remained humiliating in the extreme. In the early part of the nineteenth century, a married woman could not control property or make a will. Her husband could collect and use her wages and select her food and clothing, could will their children to the care of other guardians, and in almost every state of the Union could beat his wife, provided it was "with a reasonable instrument." Few occupations were open to women, and the professions, save school teaching, were closed to them. It was considered unseemly for women to preach, or testify, or vote in church meetings. No college for men admitted women, until Oberlin broke precedent in 1833, for it was generally felt that Greek and higher mathematics, then the cornerstones of education, were too difficult for the feminine mentality. And the ballot was denied them as a matter of course.

But as the nineteenth century wore on, as women became deeply involved in the crusades for temperance, abolition, and other social reforms, they began to demand more rights and privileges. More and more women invaded the literary world: Margaret Fuller edited the *Dial,* a magazine dear to the hearts of the New England literati; Amelia Bloomer (1818–1894), famous for the reform in feminine attire that still bears her name, edited a temperance magazine, the *Lily;* and others became famous as writers of familiar essays. Men recognized the achievements of the opposite sex, and welcomed women's assistance in the temperance and abolition movements. Gradually, too, women were instrumental in establishing papers that championed their cause, and in organizing state and local societies that demanded equal rights with men. Women of strong character and marked intellectual ability, such as the New England Transcendentalist Margaret Fuller (1810–1850) and a sturdy teacher of Quaker parentage named Susan B. Anthony (1820–1906), began agitating for woman's right to practice law and medicine, for equality of status before the law, and even for the right to vote.

When, in 1840, a World Antislavery Convention was held in London, Lucretia Mott (1793–1880), a sprightly and energetic Quaker preacher, and several other prominent women went as delegates from the United States. Graciously permitted to sit in the gallery of the convention, but refused participation in the proceedings because they were women, they came home more resolved than ever to work for the equality of the sexes. Mrs. Mott, Elizabeth Cady Stanton (1815–1902), ardent leader in temperance and abolition movements, and a few others called the first Women's Rights Convention on July 19–20, 1848, at Seneca Falls, New York. There Mrs. Stanton read a Declaration of Sentiments modeled on the Declaration of Independence, with *Man* substituted for *King George* in the list of grievances. A similar meeting was held in Rochester, New York, a month later, and by 1850 annual women's rights conventions had become the order of the day.

The women's crusade for equality bore some fruit. Gradually the right of young women to study that indecent subject, physiology, was recognized, and, though not without difficulty, women invaded the ministry and the field of medicine. Here and there states began giving married women the right to hold property and make wills, and divorce laws were, to a limited extent, liberalized. But the concept of woman as a fragile flower, to be shielded and protected in the home from rude contact with the outer world, died hard. With the privilege of the franchise still a long way off, the most that could be said was that, slowly and painfully, progress was being made toward equality of rights for the "gentler sex."

The Peace Movement

Another manifestation of the reforming spirit that bloomed so vigorously in the North during this period was the peace crusade. Like most of the other reform movements, this, too, had its roots in the eighteenth century. William Penn, Benjamin Rush, Noah Webster, and others had published plans for abolishing war, and Franklin had said that "there never was a good war or a bad peace." The nineteenth century saw a considerable number of Americans devoting time and energy to propaganda for peace among the nations. The American Peace Society, organized by William Ladd in New York City in 1828, offered a prize every year for the best essay on "A Congress of Nations for the Prevention of War," and systematically distributed peace literature. Emerson, among other intellectuals of the time, denounced war and declared that world peace was inevitable.

The peace crusaders had their differences, however, and the American Peace Society split in 1837 over the thorny problem of whether or not defensive wars are ever justifiable. But, at the same time a vigorous nonresistance movement was inaugurated by William Lloyd Garrison and the Utopian John Humphrey Noyes, and the many peace advocates who were also abolitionists were therefore able to oppose the Mexican War on both grounds. These idealists made contact with pacifists in England and France, and in 1843 participated in an international peace congress held in London. In the 1840s, Elihu Burritt, of Connecticut—"the Learned Blacksmith," who hammered horseshoes, taught himself fifteen or twenty languages, and composed a Sanscrit grammar—became the most prominent champion of peace. Perhaps America's first genuine internationalist, in 1846 he founded the League of Universal Brotherhood that, by 1850 had 40,000 British and American signers of its pledge of complete abstinence from war. Burritt was also one of the founders of the Brussels Peace Congress of 1848, a meeting followed by five similar international congresses in succeeding years.

The peace movement was the weakest of all the reform efforts of this period. Its sponsors lacked realism and had little influence upon the course of events, either at home or abroad, but they were a facet of that aspiration for the improvement of man's lot which was such a prominent characteristic of northern society during this period.

The Religious Ferment

Religion was another field in which nineteenth-century northern society strove for perfection, sometimes in strange and bizarre ways. The Great Awakening of colonial times had been followed by quarrels between the Old and New Lights, and then by a development of deistic, rational thought that stemmed from the European rationalism of the eighteenth century. These deists—Franklin and Jefferson are good examples—rejected revealed religion, but retained belief in a First Cause, a Divine Being to whom man could pray, but who did not interfere supernaturally in the affairs of this world.

Deism was abhorrent to the orthodox of all faiths. Bitterly denounced, it slowly declined after the beginning of the nineteenth century, to be replaced in New England by another form of religious rationalism, the Unitarian church.

Unitarianism began in New England before 1800 and grew steadily during the early nineteenth century, numbering among its adherents former Presbyterians, Congregationalists, and some Episcopalians. A crucial point in its development came with the Baltimore sermon of William Ellery Channing, May 5, 1819, in which that great minister stated the Unitarian arguments against belief in the trinity, the atonement, and salvation through Christ's death. With the formation of the American Unitarian Association in 1825, a new church had clearly emerged in American life, one whose creed was, basically, belief in a loving God and in the fundamental nobility of man. The Unitarians had little interest in missionary work; the appeal of the movement was primarily to the intellectual and well-to-do elements of society, and its strength centered in New England.

While Unitarianism preached a rational concept of God and scorned proselytizing, the evangelical churches developed powerful missionary and revivalist crusades. Methodist, Baptist, and Presbyterian Bible and tract societies inundated the country with religious literature. Missionaries were sent out to the western frontier, to India, and to other foreign fields. Revivalism became a prominent characteristic of northern religious life, both in the more settled districts of the East and on the frontier. A second Great Awakening, known as the Great Revival of the West (1797–1805), produced much excitement as thousands were converted in the frontier regions, and the strength of the evangelical denominations greatly increased. Their success furnished inspiration for a host of similar movements, and revivalist meetings became a characteristic of northern life. The many revivals in western New York during the period between 1815 and 1850, joined to a variety of other religious excitements, gave that area the name of "the burned-over district."

Revivalism was by no means the only evidence of the strength of American religious interest. Faiths followed many different paths during that period in the search for ultimate truth. Their variety, and the ease with which they grew, gave evidence not only of the vitality of religion, but also of an optimistic confidence in man's ability, with God's help, to create, if not a new heaven, at least a new earth.

On the intellectual side, this search for truth expressed itself in the Transcendentalist movement. Strongly influenced by French revolutionary thought, Kantian idealism, and English Romantics such as Wordsworth and Coleridge, the Transcendentalists also owed much to their Puritan background and to the American faith in liberty and reform. Emerson, Amos Bronson Alcott (1799–1888), Theodore Parker (1810–1860), Margaret Fuller, and Henry David Thoreau (1817–1862) were some of the oustanding figures in the Transcendental Club, organized in 1836 in Boston. Its leading spirits wrote, lectured, held conversations, and for twenty years markedly influenced the intellectual tone of America; they published a literary review, the *Dial* (1840–1844). One group founded a Utopian community at Brook Farm, near Boston, and Bronson Alcott and others established Fruitlands, near Harvard, Massachusetts. Thoreau rebelled against the authority of the state, becoming a philosophical anarchist. Parker fought against slavery and for women's rights, and was sharply critical of capitalism, while the humane but strong-willed William Ellery Channing (1780–1842) was a protagonist of peace and a stern opponent of slavery.

The inner core of Transcendentalism was a belief in the natural goodness of man, his capacity for improvement, and the indwelling presence of God in the human individual. This immanence of the Eternal Spirit made the mind always open to the influx of light and power from the Great Beyond. The Transcendentalists also laid great stress upon reason and the power of critical intelligence. They utilized both spiritual fervor and Yankee shrewdness in their search for a better life here on earth.

Some of the expressions of religious zeal in the Middle Period took extreme and radical forms. The self-styled Prophet Matthias walked the streets of New York City brandishing a sword and a seven-foot ruler and proclaiming that he had come to redeem the world. In southern Ohio one Dylks, called "The Leatherwood God," proclaimed to groveling congregations his own divinity. The Fox sisters, in the little town of Hydesville in western New York, started a great spiritualist excitement in 1848. John Humphrey Noyes (1811–1886), the Perfectionist, announced in 1834 that he had attained a state of sinlessness, and, developing his social and theological views during the succeeding years, he founded in 1848 the Oneida Community on a triune base of Bible communism, free love, and the scientific propagation of the species.

One of the major religious extravagances of this period was Millerism. William Miller (1782–1849), a Vermont farmer and a converted deist, preached the doctrine of the imminent second coming of Christ with great effect in the rural districts of New England and New York. Careful study of the Bible had convinced him that the world would come to an end on March 22, 1844, and the approach of this date threw thousands into a state of wild excitement. Asylums and hospitals in New England and New York were crowded, but the appointed day brought no cataclysm, and the jibes of the scoffers ("What! Not gone up yet?") were hard to bear. Miller made another calculation and arrived at a date in October, 1844. Again there was great excitement, but the crowds of Millerites assembled in their white robes on house and hilltops were once more disappointed. This ended the great delusion, although here and there adventist sects continued to exist.

During the height of this adventist excitement, a Millerite approached Theodore Parker on a Boston street and asked if he realized that the world was rapidly spinning to its end; "It does not concern me," said Parker, "I live in Boston."

Still another religious movement, and one of longer range impact, was Mormonism. Joseph Smith, its founder, was born on December 23, 1805, in a humble and shiftless New England agricultural family which, in 1819, settled near Manchester in Wayne County, New York. There Joseph grew up as a farmhand, with a propensity for tall and loose talk and for living without work. When a religious revival gripped the neighborhood in 1820, the family became addicted to seeing visions, and Joseph declared that, in a "sylvan glade," God and the Savior had appeared to him and warned him against joining any of the existing sects. Three years later, the Angel Moroni appeared before Joseph and led him to certain golden plates buried in a neighboring hill; with the aid of two magic stones, Urim and Thummim,

Joseph translated the writing on these plates, and the Book of Mormon was thus launched upon the world. Mixed in with the supposed history of early America and of certain wandering Jewish tribes, it contained anachronistic references to steel and the mariner's compass, a quotation from Shakespeare, and chapters out of the Old and New Testaments. Though it was heavy reading (Mark Twain later called it "chloroform in print"), it referred with authority to the approaching millenium and gave a vague outline of an associative communism in which all good Mormons would hold their property at the will of the Mormon church.

On such questionable foundations, together with Smith's claim that he could perform miracles, the Mormon church was reared. When missionaries were sent out, converts swelled the ranks, and such able lieutenants as Orson Pratt, Brigham Young, and others appeared. They moved the "church" to Kirtland, Ohio, where no one knew of Smith's sordid past, and he himself developed real qualities of leadership. But as they became prosperous, the Mormons grew arrogant, and their religious ideas excited derision and suspicion among the gentiles. The Mormon colony in Ohio broke up, and when another group in Jackson county, Illinois, was driven out by its irate neighbors, its members wandered from place to place, their ranks now decimated by schism, now swelled by restless frontier spirits and by thousands of converts from England who were lured by the promise of salvation and of land. In 1839, the Mormons moved to Nauvoo, Illinois, where Smith authorized polygamy and where he was murdered in 1844. Three years later, under the masterful leadership of Brigham Young, bands of Mormons began making the arduous trek across the plains to Salt Lake in Utah, where they finally established their "Stake in Zion." Such were the foundations of a great church that today numbers its faithful in the tens of thousands and that every year, on Hill Cumorah in western New York, celebrates with a grand pageant the discovery of the golden plates and the founding of Mormonism.

The Utopians

Northern society in the early nineteenth century found room for many Utopian experiments, some religious and others secular in character. The religiously inclined derived inspiration from the simple, communal life of early Christians in the Roman Empire and sometimes turned to a communistic form of existence so that the few who had capital might support the many who were without worldly goods. Able leaders often dictated the form of social organization. The same influences operated in the secular Utopias, although these arose chiefly out of protest and rebellion against the suffering that accompanied the Industrial Revolution.

The religious Utopias were numerous. There were the Indianâ Rappites (in origin German peasants), the Separatists of Zoar in Ohio, The Amana Society (again of German origin), the Swedish colony of Bishop Janson in Illinois, and the Shaker communities in New England and eastern New York. These groups generally held their property in common, believed in miracles and the second coming of Christ, and led simple and devout lives.

Other Utopias had religious overtones, but their primary objective was the creation of a good society in an evil world. Such were the Hopedale Community (founded in Massachusetts about 1840 by the Reverend Adin Ballou), the Fruitlands project of Bronson Alcott, the Brook Farm experiment of the Transcendentalists, and the Oneida Community of John Humphrey Noyes. Finally, there were the Utopian Socialist experiments that owed their existence to the efforts and the teachings of Robert Owen and Charles Fourier.

Robert Owen (1771–1858) was, first and foremost, a humanitarian. Appalled by the brutality that accompanied rapid industrial change, he had established a model factory at New Lanark, Scotland, and had supported social legislation in Great Britain. He thought he saw an opportunity to establish a model society on the frontier of freedom-loving America, and in 1825 purchased from George Rapp 30,000 acres of land in Indiana, which he named New Harmony. There, with 900 settlers, he started his great experiment, but it did not prosper. A strange conglomeration of idealists, ne'er-do-wells, and sharpers flocked to New Harmony, and its affairs went from bad to worse; within one year it had seven constitutions, ranging from a democratic form of communal living to dictatorship by Owen himself. After some two years, it broke up.

Some half-dozen other short-lived efforts to establish ideal societies derived inspiration from Owen and his ideas, or were similar in outline. Of these, perhaps the most famous was that established by Frances Wright (1795–1852) at Nashoba, Tennessee, a community where Negroes were gradually to acquire freedom while living with whites in a state of cooperative bliss. It had a chaotic two-year span of life.

More spectacular and, for a time, giving promise of more vitality were the experiments in Association that derived from the doctrines of Charles Fourier (1772–1837). This French Utopian and mathematician, an eccentric and fanatical idealist, proposed to divide society into small units called "phalanxes," each containing 1,620 laborers, capitalists, and men of talent; soldiers, politicians, lawyers, philosophers, and political economists were told that they need not apply for membership. There would be a common dwelling, called a "phalanstery," with a common dining hall, seven meals a day, and free love. Each phalanx was to be organized on the joint-stock principle, and, after equal-subsistence portions were distributed, five-twelfths of the profits would go to labor, four-twelfths to capital, and three-twelfths to talent.

Fourier had his home in Paris, and there a western New York reformer named Albert Brisbane (1809–1890) came to sit at the feet of the master. Brisbane received twelve lessons at $1.00 a lesson and brought back the doctrine, minus free love, to the United States as the gospel of Association. He converted Horace Greeley, and the columns of the New York *Tribune* helped to spread the word throughout the United States. It influenced the thinking of many of the Transcendentalists, for it was highly idealistic, promised something to all classes of society, and came when the depression that began in 1837 was emphasizing the deficiencies of the existing social order. Between forty and fifty phalanxes were established, all in northern states; their average length of life was two years.

A final Utopian experiment begun in this period was that of the Frenchman Etienne Cabet. His "Icaria" was an attempt at socialistic communism, originally planned for location on the Red River in Texas in 1848, but settled in 1849 at Nauvoo, Illinois. After several years of more or less successful operation, it went down in ruin, partly because of Cabet's determination to exercise autocratic power and partly because of financial difficulties arising from the panic of 1857.

The Utopian movement of the early nineteenth century was a passing phase of American life. Many individuals found temporary happiness and contentment in one or another of these experiments, but all of them had fundamental weaknesses. Many of the participants were people incapable of adjusting to any social situation, and their presence was bound to be disruptive; the authoritarian aspects, where they existed, conflicted with the individualism that was even then deeply rooted in the United States; and the general tendency of the Utopians to organize small, self-sufficient communities ran counter to the industrial and nationalistic trends in world affairs that made for the establishment of large units of human society with national markets and international connections. Utopianism, in essence, was a futile protest by idealists against the world as it was. But its relatively free expression in the United States at least testified to the vitality of the libertarian ideal in northern society.

Antidemocratic Aspects

Not all developments in Northern society during the Middle Period were manifestations of a love of liberty. The persecutions suffered by the Mormons and the abolitionists demonstrated that the general spirit of tolerance had definite limitations, and the Antimasonic movement, in its attempt to destroy the Masonic Order, resorted to proscriptive policies that varied from social pressure to preventing Masons from serving on juries or sitting as judges in cases where non-Masons were suing members of the Order. More enduring and more dangerous to democratic liberty were the anti-Catholic and nativist movements that grew up and flourished in many northern states.

Popular sentiment directed against foreigners in general and Catholics in particular was already a part of the American tradition. The Quebec Act of 1774 had produced mob demonstrations in Puritan New England against the menace of so-called Popery. The Alien and Sedition Acts of 1798 had roots in antiforeign prejudice. At other times fervent believers in maintaining the sanctity of American republicanism voiced fears of the intrusion of foreigners and foreign ideas that might sully the democratic faith, on occasion even challenging the use of the common law of England in American courts.

As the immigrant tide mounted after 1830, and foreigners, many of them Catholics, offered competition in the labor market and made their influence felt in politics, traditional prejudices intensified. Alarm mounted as Catholic missionaries in the United States increased their activity. Many Protestants resented the writings of the German scholar Friedrich von Schlegel, who attacked American Protestantism as the nursery of revolutionary movements and implied that democracy in America should be destroyed by the establishment of Catholic missions. There was a widespread belief that Catholics owed allegiance to a foreign prince, the Pope, who claimed spiritual authority over them and who was himself a temporal ruler in Italy. Some thought that European monarchies were using the Catholic church to overthrow American democracy.

These doubts and fears about Catholics and foreigners became a subject of open debate. Such eminent Protestants as Lyman Beecher (1775–1863) and the inventor of the telegraph, Samuel F. B. Morse, warned the country in speeches, books, and pamphlets against the "Catholic menace." Catholic polemicists like Father John Hughes (1797–1864), later Bishop of New York, counterattacked with vigor. Protestant and Catholic journals engaged in wordy wars about liberty of thought and opinion, the reading of the Bible in public schools, and whether or not local government should give financial aid to parochial schools.

Public opinion was inflamed by these controversies, and outbreaks of violence occurred. In 1834, a mob destroyed the Ursuline convent in Charlestown, Massachusetts, under the delusion that a nun was being detained there against her will. Stories of immorality in convents multiplied with the publication in 1836 of the *Awful Disclosures* of Maria Monk, a depraved young woman who told elaborate lies about her life as a "prostitute" in the Hôtel Dieu Nunnery in Montreal. Impartial investigation showed that Maria was an impostor, but her *Disclosures* had a wide circulation and heightened the general excitement. Anti-Catholic and antiforeign riots burst out repeatedly in Boston, New York, and Philadelphia, and such attitudes began to find expression in politics.

Immigrants during this period tended to join the Democratic party, partly because of a belief that its patron saints, Jefferson and Jackson, had regard for the rights of the common man and partly because Democratic political organizations, such as Tammany Hall in New York, seized the opportunity to increase their power by showering favors on the newly arrived foreigners and by fraudulent registration of alien voters. Nativists responded by political activity, as independents, or in alliance with the Whigs. In 1835, Nativists organized a political party in New York City, and in 1837 they fused with the Whigs and carried the city election. Similar movements appeared in other states, North and South, and in 1845, Nativist delegates from thirteen states met in Philadelphia. Their attempt to form a national political party was stillborn, but in the 1850s the flood of foreign immigrants stimulated the growth of such secret anti-Catholic organizations as the Order of the Star Spangled Banner, the members of which, when questioned, always replied that they "knew nothing" about their secret society. Out of such movements came the Native American, or Know-Nothing party, which sought to exclude Catholics and foreigners from all public offices and to change the naturalization laws so that twenty-one-years residence would be necessary to become a citizen.

Suggested Reading

For ideological developments in this period, the reader should consult M. Curti, *The Growth of American Thought* (1943) and Ralph Gabriel, *The Course of Amer-*

ican Democratic Thought (1940). See also A. A. Ekirch, *The Idea of Progress in America, 1815–1860* (1944). Every student should become acquainted with Alexis de Tocqueville, *Democracy in America* (2 vols., 1835 and subsequent editions), a penetrating and suggestive analysis of American institutions.

The American social order is portrayed in Meade Minnigerode, *The Fabulous Forties, 1840–1850* (1924); E. D. Branch, *The Sentimental Years, 1836–1860* (1934); and R. E. Riegel, *Young America, 1830–1840* (1949). Interesting and illuminating is Carl Bode, *The Anatomy of American Popular Culture, 1840–1861* (1959).

The literature on refrom in this period is extensive. A. M. Schlesinger, *The American As Reformer* (1950) is a good introduction. A. F. Tyler, *Freedom's Ferment: Phases of American Social History to 1860* (1944) is an excellent general account. For political reforms, the reader should consult R. G. Gettell, *History of American Political Thought* (1928); C. R. Fish, *The Rise of the Common Man, 1830–1850* (1927); and E. C. Evans, *A History of the Australian Ballot System in the United States* (1917). Blake McKelvey, *American Prisons* (1936) gives a sketch of prison conditions in this period and furnishes bibliographical aid for further study. Help for the handicapped is dealt with in Albert Deutsch, *The Mentally Ill in America* (1949) and H. E. Marshall, *Dorothea Dix, Forgotten Samaritan* (1937). On prohibition, the standard work is J. A. Krout, *The Origins of Prohibition* (1935). Light is thrown on the antislavery movement by three significant books: G. H. Barnes, *The Antislavery Impulse, 1830–1844* (1933); D. L. Dumond, *Antislavery Origins of the Civil War in the United States* (1939); and R. B. Nye, *Fettered Freedom* (1949). In this connection, see also A. Whitridge, *No Compromise: The Story of the Fanatics Who Paved the Way to the Civil War* (1960); H. H. Simms, *Emotion at High Tide: Abolition as a Controversial Factor, 1830–1845* (1960), L. Filler, *The Crusade Against Slavery, 1830–1860* (1960), and L. Lader, *The Bold Brahmins* (1961). Concerning women's rights, see E. C. Stanton, S. B. Anthony, *et al.*, *History of Woman Suffrage* (6 vols., 1889–1922). The peace movement is covered admirably in M. Curti, *The American Peace Crusade, 1815–1860* (1929).

On religious developments, see W. W. Sweet, *The Story of Religions in America* (1930). C. E. Sears, *Days of Delusion* (1924) is a study of the Millerite movement. Fawn Brodie, *No Man Knows My History: the Life of Joseph Smith, the Mormon Prophet* (1945) is an excellent biography. W. R. Cross, *The Burned-over District* (1950) is a first-rate account of religious enthusiasms in western New York, 1800–1850. The Utopians are treated at some length in Alice Felt Tyler, *Freedom's Ferment*, and the Utopian Socialists are dealt with in D. D. Egbert and S. Persons, *Socialism and American Life* (2 vols., 1952). The nativist and anti-Catholic movements are effectively analyzed in R. Billington, *The Protestant Crusade, 1800–1860* (1938). Transcendentalism is dealt with in F. O. Matthiessen, *American Renaissance* (1941), and Van Wyck Brooks, *The Flowering of New England, 1815–1865* (1936). See also A. M. Schlesinger, Jr., *Orestes A. Brownson: A Pilgrim's Progress* (1939), H. S. Commager, *Theodore Parker: Yankee Crusader* (1936), J. W. Krutch, *Henry David Thoreau* (1948), and R. L. Lusk, *The Life of Ralph Waldo Emerson* (1949).

22 ′ Northern Culture, 1830-1860

EDUCATION AND RELIGION were closely connected in the life of early America. Such colleges as existed were primarily training schools for ministers, and the common schools showed marked evidence of religious influence in their courses of instruction. This gave a strong moral tone to the educational system, as even a glance at the textbooks of the period will testify. On the other hand, it tended to narrow the outlook of the student, for theological prejudice sometimes limited the pursuit of truth for truth's sake. Lack of means and the movement of the population into the frontier regions were more serious handicaps. Since the training of youth in a land which was only beginning to develop its natural resources, and where large areas were sparsely settled, was no easy matter, it is not to be wondered at that educational opportunity in the northern states, immediately following the War of 1812, left much to be desired.

Northern Interest in Education

There was a general belief that all boys at least ought to be taught to read, write, and cipher, but this was the practice only in scattered portions of New England and the Middle Atlantic states. The East's common schools, New England's among the rest, had fallen into a shocking state, being inadequately housed and manned by poorly paid and often grossly incompetent teachers. The West was almost illiterate, for there scarcity of funds and teachers, together with thinly spread settlements, had blocked any significant development in public education.

So far as secondary schools were concerned, New England had good private academies but few public high schools. The North had a fair share of the country's colleges and universities; New England, indeed, was the nation's center of higher education, opportunities for which again steadily decreased as the citizens moved toward the frontier. Trade and vocational schools were practically nonexistent, Rensselaer Polytechnic Institute at Troy, New York, founded in 1824, being a pioneer effort in the field of technical education.

The decades from 1820 to 1860 saw considerable advances at all levels in northern education. Many new colleges and universities were founded, chiefly in the new states and as denominational institutions. Of these Oberlin (1833), Congregational in origin, distinguished itself by being coeducational and coracial. This increase in numbers at least demonstrated a laudable zeal for higher education, and interest developed in technical education. The United States Naval Academy at Annapolis was founded in 1845, and Yale and Harvard established scientific schools. Interest in the ideas of the Swiss pedagogue, Pestalozzi, who argued that child-training should center on fitting the individual to play a constructive role in society, resulted in the establishment of several progressive schools in the New England area. Emma Willard's Female Seminary at Troy, and Mary Lyon's seminary for girls at South Hadley, Massachusetts (later Mount Holyoke College) were trail-blazing developments in female education.

More striking was the advance in the public school system of the North. There a great struggle developed over the issue of free, tax-supported public schools. The focal point was Pennsylvania, where in 1835–1836, the legislature established free public school education. This was largely due to the powerful drive of a young Vermonter who had made his home in Pennsylvania, whose name was Thaddeus Stevens. A few northern states had preceded, but the majority followed the example of the Keystone State.

As the free public schools became more numerous, their quality improved, men like Horace Mann (1796–1859) in Massachusetts and Henry Barnard (1811–1900) in Connecticut and Rhode Island being responsible for this. Mann was a tremendous worker who knew little about children but was a fanatical reformer. Disbelieving in the natural depravity of man, he held that human nature could be improved by education and that society ought to be taxed for the benefit of posterity. Many of his contemporaries differed with him on these points, also suspecting him because he was supported by such dangerous radicals as Dr. Channing and Theodore Parker. But, despite opposition, Mann accomplished great things. Under his leadership the Massachusetts school system was correlated and given central supervision. In 1837, a state board of education was established, and for the next eleven years Mann was its secretary and guide. In 1839, the first state-supported normal school in the country was established at Lexington, and by 1845 Massachusetts had a state association of teachers. Before Mann left office, financial support of the public schools doubled, numerous high schools had been established, and the quality of textbooks and teaching improved.

The example of Massachusetts was contagious. By 1860, city superintendents of schools were appearing in the North and West, and several states had appointed superintendents of education.

Educational improvement also reached the adult population, through an institution that originated in Massachusetts in 1826 and was nationally organized at New York in 1831 as the American Lyceum. It established lecture courses and sent lecturers out to thousands of state, county, and town organizations. It centered in the North and East, but was also popular in the West. Emerson, Greeley, Wendell Phillips, Henry Ward Beecher, and other prominent Americans went on the Lyceum lecture circuits. Lecturers were also in demand at state and county fairs, and Greeley has left a spirited account of the difficulties he experienced in making himself heard on the fair grounds in competition with squealing pigs, braying donkeys, bleating sheep, and neighing stallions.

Northern education and educational standards had scarcely reached a state of perfection before the Civil War. School faculties and teachers' salaries were pathetically inadequate. Compulsory education was still in the future. College teaching was dull and pedantic, and overburdened professors had little time for research. The denominational institutions were hampered by restrictions on freedom of teaching, and state universities were subject to attack as seedbeds of godlessness.

But, despite these limitations, real progress had been made in education. Public responsibility for elementary education was generally acknowledged in the North and West, and the conviction was growing that this responsibility should be extended to secondary schools, and even to colleges. As the new states came into the Union, their constitutions generally provided for state universities, the University of Indiana being set up in 1820 and the University of Michigan in 1841. These early establishments were often poorly supported by the states that created them, but they were at least harbingers of the great land-grant universities of a later day.

A Broadening Outlook in Science

The broadening of educational opportunity in the North was accompanied by an increased interest in science and scientific research. Pressure from reformers who wished to see the United States lead the world in all aspects of life, and sometimes from influential merchants and businessmen whose aims were strictly utilitarian, brought state and national contributions for the promotion of learned societies and scientific expeditions and surveys. In 1830, Massachusetts established a geological survey, and by 1844 twelve other northern states had followed her example. An increasing number of scientists interested in geology appeared in New England and the Middle Atlantic states. They took a leading part in forming the American Association of Geologists at Philadelphia in 1840, and in the establishment, eight years later, of a professional society, the American Association for the Advancement of Science.

Geological research stimulated interest in kindred scientific fields, and specialists made extensive mineral, botanical, and paleontological investigations in various parts of the country. Boston, perhaps the greatest center of scientific interest in the nation, became host to such distinguished foreign scientists as the eccentric botanist Constantine Samuel Rafinesque (1783–1840), John James Audubon (1785–1851), whose *Birds in America* became internationally famous, and Jean Louis Rodolphe Agassiz (1807–1873), celebrated for his great contributions as teacher and scholar in the field of natural history.

And while these developments were occurring, medical science and the study of public health began at last to show signs of advance, particularly in New England. It was already a tradition for American medical students to study in England, and American medicine was stimulated by French clinical and pathological research during the first half of the nineteenth century. In the period after 1800, American medical men who flocked to Paris came back enthusiastic over the critical investigation of disease through clinical research. They followed the same lines, beginning research into the nature of typhus, typhoid, and other diseases that won European recognition.

Striking evidence of the rise of interest in the clinical approach to medical problems came on the western frontier when William Beaumont (1785–1853), an army surgeon at Fort Mackinac in Michigan, in 1822 began studying gastric digestion by direct observation through a permanent fistula, a "window," in the stomach of a Canadian frontiersman, Alexis St. Martin.

Though the patient was reluctant to cooperate and ran away a number of times, Beaumont always captured him and in 1833 was able to demonstrate conclusively the nature of the digestive process in the stomach.

Other American physicians began systematic attempts to improve surgical procedures. They also undertook difficult surgical operations rarely attempted in Europe. In 1846, a dentist, W. T. G. Morton, gave a successful demonstration of ether as an anesthetic in the Massachusetts General Hospital, thus introducing its use into both American and European surgical practice.

While advances in pathology and medicine were heralding the dawn of modern medicine, its relationship to society in general was becoming a subject of serious study. The New Englanders Edward Jervis and Lemuel Shattuck were pioneers in the fields of public health and vital statistics. Their work helped to bring young men of talent to the study of medicine, and also brought to public attention the importance of dealing with slum conditions in the growing cities. Progress in this field was slow and halting, but it led finally to the establishment of city and state boards of public health.

Eventually the government at Washington began promoting scientific advance. Early Presidents, Jefferson and John Quincy Adams especially, had been interested in science, one of the reasons Jefferson had sent the Lewis and Clark expedition into the Far West being to discover something about the fauna and flora of that region. The national government, however, had been laggard, so far as the acquisition of scientific knowledge was concerned, and it was not until the late 1830s that it began to manifest a real interest in that field. Then the Wilkes expedition (1838–1842) was sent out to explore large areas of the Atlantic and Pacific oceans; it gathered a great amount of information in the fields of geology and natural history. In 1846, due to the gift of $500,000 by an eccentric Englishman, James Smithson, and to the efforts of John Quincy Adams and others, the Smithsonian Institution was organized at Washington for the promotion of science on a national scale.

The Play's the Thing

Science and education interested the people of the North, but they also had time for the theater. There were many plays and some outstanding actors. New York was the theatrical center of America, but by 1850 Philadelphia had three standard theaters, to say nothing of a circus, and there were five theaters in Boston. Actors of note went on tour, visiting St. Louis, Chicago, and San Francisco.

Edwin Forrest (1806–1872) made his New York debut in 1826 as Othello. The following year, the English-born Louise Lane, later Mrs. John Drew (1820–1897), made her first American stage appearance in Philadelphia as a child actress. William Charles Macready (1793–1873), the famous English tragedian, made several American tours, and Junius Brutus Booth (1796–1852), also English-born, competed with Edwin Forrest for the favor of audiences which preferred Shakespearian plays. In 1840, Fanny Elssler (1810–1884), a brilliant ballet dancer from Austria, drew capacity audiences at the Park Theater in New York. Edwin Booth (1833–1893) began his great career in New York in 1857 as Richard III. Miss Laura Keene (c. 1826–1873) opened in October, 1858, at Wallack's Theater in New York in *Our American Cousin,* which ran continuously for five months. This was the longest run in any first-class New York theater up to that time, though it was by no means as popular as *Uncle Tom's Cabin* which, during the 1850s, played to thousands of audiences throughout the North.

The theatrical world had its frivolous aspects. Phineas T. Barnum (1810–1891), showman extraordinary, began his career in New York during the 1840s, presenting variety acts and a collection of freaks, including the marvel of the age, Tom Thumb, a midget under two feet in height and weighing less than sixteen pounds; Tom first appeared at the age of five, but Barnum advertised him as eleven years old. During the 1830s Thomas D. Rich (1808–1860) began presenting Negro imitations and singing "Jump Jim Crow," and out of the immense popularity of his presentations emerged the minstrel show, which swept the country in the following decade and attained a vogue that endured for almost a century.

Theater audiences were usually well mannered, but this was not always the case. Edmund Kean (1787–1833) gave a performance of *Richard III* in dumb show at New York in 1825, assailed by taunts, jeers, eggs, and oranges as the result of his walking out on a previous audience and a scandal in which he had been involved in his native England. In 1849, Macready, the English rival of the American Edwin Forrest, attempted to play *Macbeth* at the Astor Place Theater in New York while Forrest was playing the same role at the Broadway; the result was the Astor Place riot, in which the militia was called out and finally fired on the crowd, killing and wounding fifty-eight people.

The traveling showmen, who wandered all over the country attempting Shakespeare and giving any number of highly romantic plays long since forgotten, sometimes found themselves confronted by unexpected situations. In a Kentucky town, during a play in which a gambler's family was depicted as starving, a member of the audience rose and declared that they should do something for the afflicted wife; throwing a bill on the stage, he told the heroine not to let her husband know about it or he would lose it at faro, and then sat down, saying, "Now go on with the play."

Music Hath Charms

The people of the North had a genuine interest in music as well as in the theater. Patriotic songs were especially popular. As we have seen, "Yankee Doodle" had become a national tune at the time of the Revolution, and it remained in favor during the whole period before the Civil War. "Hail Columbia," the music of which was written in 1789, was another popular favorite; its words were composed in 1798 by Joseph Hopkinson, later President of the Pennsylvania Academy of Fine Arts. As everyone knows, Francis Scott Key wrote the words of "The Star-Spangled Banner" on the deck of a British warship in 1814, during the bombardment of Fort McHenry at Baltimore; the music was that of an old English drinking song, "To Anacreon in Heaven." Hard as it was to sing, it caught on immediately and became to all intents and purposes the national anthem, but it was not until 1931 that it was recognized as such by act of Congress. The words of "My Country 'Tis of Thee" were set to the melody of the British national anthem, "God Save the King"; written by the Reverend Samuel F. Smith, it was sung for the first time in 1832, at a Fourth of July celebration in Boston, and, despite the origin of its music, it immediately became popular and has remained so ever since. "Dixie" was written by a northerner, Dan Emmett, and first sung in a minstrel show on Broadway, a couple of years before the Civil War. It struck the people's fancy and many northerners, including Kentucky-born Abraham Lincoln, were fond of the tune.

In addition to patriotic songs, the North produced religious and secular songs of genuine merit. Massachusetts-born Lowell Mason (1792–1872) wrote choir music and hymns. "Nearer My God to Thee" and "From Greenland's Icy Mountains" were among his compositions, which reflected the religious spirit of the times and were immensely popular. More than any other one man, Mason established the teaching of music in the public schools, beginning in 1836 in Boston. Thomas Hastings (1784–1872) wrote another popular hymn, "Rock of Ages."

New York, Boston, and Philadelphia had many composers of secular songs and societies devoted to the rendering of secular music. Many of the songs that achieved wide popularity—such as "The Grecian Daughter," by Joseph P. Knight, and "Woodman Spare That Tree," by Henry Russell—reflected the love of sentimental pathos that characterized the period. Stephen Collins

Foster (1826–1864) was born near Pittsburgh and never traveled in the South until 1852, but he composed songs dealing with love and death and escape from the realities of life that gave a romantic and often melancholy impression of the antebellum South; "My Old Kentucky Home," "Swanee River," "De Camptown Races," and other Foster songs have become a part of the American tradition.

Americans were partial to hymns and popular songs, but they also appreciated more serious music and welcomed enthusiastically foreign virtuosi who came to the United States. Jenny Lind, "the Swedish Nightingale," brought to America in 1850 by P. T. Barnum, charmed thousands with her magic voice. Despite lavish charities, she made $100,000 during her two-year tour of the country. Ole Bull, the brilliant Norwegian violinist, played to huge audiences. Devotees of the opera and of orchestral music organized concerts in the great cities. The Philharmonic Society of New York was established in 1842, a tribute to the discriminating taste of the music lovers in the metropolis.

Templed Hills and Marble Figures

The people of the North loved music, but they did not produce any great composers. They were also interested in architecture and sculpture, but here, too, their taste was not highly developed, and they made few significant contributions. Throughout the land, the Greek Revival continued to provide the dominant architectural theme. There were a number of reasons for its popularity. In part a more or less blind revulsion against English styles, it was sustained and nourished by sympathy for the Greeks in their struggle for independence. Impressive in appearance, for many Americans it typified elegance, and it was not expensive to construct. The United States in the 1820s and 1830s was covered with Grecian churches and public buildings, and houses that varied from pillared mansions to small but temple-fronted dwellings. The New York Custom House was an attempted reproduction of the Parthenon, and Girard College, commissioned in 1833, was a $2-million marble temple. There were often Attic details on the otherwise barren fronts of mills and factories, and practically all of the western communities bore witness to the prevalence of the Greek ideal. Only slowly, in the succeeding decades, was this architectural form challenged by a growing taste for Gothic and Italian designs.

The public taste in architecture was satisfied by importation of styles from abroad, for there were no distinguished or genuinely American architectural developments during this period. The same can be said for interior decoration, which mainly was an unimpressive melange of Greek frescoes, classical furniture, large gilded mirrors, gaudy carpets, and what have been called "Jacksonian" bookcases and bedsteads. There was, however, one outstanding name in the field of interior furnishings: Duncan Phyfe (1768–1854) produced tables, chairs, and bookcases of exquisite design. The styles of the Napoleonic Empire influenced his work during the latter part of his life, and his mahogany and rosewood pieces of that era were heavier and more ostentatious than the products of his earlier period.

While architecture and interior decoration bore witness to a popular taste that was largely unsophisticated and immature, sculpture, too, was in the doldrums. Horatio Greenough (1805–1852) went to Rome in 1826 to begin his serious study of the art. Sensitive, immensely industrious, and reverent of what he saw in the Imperial City, the style he developed was in the classical mode. His grandiose "Washington," commissioned in 1833 and shipped across the Atlantic on a sloop of war ten years later, weighed twenty tons and cost $21,000. The entrance to the Capitol had to be widened before the huge object could be admitted. The floor well-nigh gave way under the enormous weight, and "Washington" was soon removed to the eastern front of the Capitol. Greeted with jibes and witticisms, it was later placed in the Smithsonian, where the curious may view it today. Though Greenough helped to establish the Italian influence in American art, he was no innovator, and his work had only moderate merit.

"THE GREEK SLAVE," BY HIRAM POWERS

This celebrated piece of sculpture in white marble, finished in 1843, was purchased by the New York merchant A. T. Stewart. The statue was approved from a moral standpoint by a committee of Cincinnati clergymen, and miniatures of it soon decorated thousands of American homes. This is a photograph of the original statue in the Dusseldorf Gallery, New York City.

Hiram Powers (1805–1873), like Greenough, a New Englander by birth, had a considerable talent that was exercised during the early part of his life in Cincinnati and then in Washington. During this period, he made busts from life of Chief Justice Marshall, Webster, Calhoun, and other national figures. In 1837, he went to Florence, where he spent the rest of his life, although he continued to use American subjects. Powers's work was graceful in line and appealed to the popular taste; sometimes bold and virile, it was more often flat and insipid. His statues of Franklin, Jefferson, and Webster attracted favorable attention, but his most famous work was the "The Greek Slave," finished in 1843. The great acclaim received by this beautiful nude was perhaps enhanced by the flutterings of those who regarded themselves as the custodians of the nation's morals.

Thomas Crawford (1813–1857), a third sculptor of some importance, also lived and worked abroad, mainly in Rome. He executed portrait busts, bas-reliefs, and grouped figures usually mythological and allegorical in character. His industry was admirable, but he produced too much. His work often lacked finish, and he accepted commissions that were beyond his powers of artistic execution. The bronze doors and the marble pediment of the Senate wing of the Capitol at Washington are his, as well as a huge equestrian statue of the Father of his Country done for the city of Richmond.

Dozens of other aspiring sculptors went to Italy, and America was flooded with their efforts, most of which were commonplace pieces classical in form and inspiration, and produced for pecuniary return rather than as a result of the flowering of genius.

Painting for the People

American painting, like American sculpture, was prolific but without great distinction. There was a flood of historical paintings, often on large canvases. Characteristic of this school, though larger than many, was "Westward the Course of Empire Takes its Way" by Emmanuel Leutze, which covered 600 square feet on the wall of the Capitol. Oliver Larkin remarks that one critic's comment on this work, "Confusion reigns paramount," applied to most of the efforts to reproduce American history in paint.

There were hundreds of portrait painters, good and bad, among whom Thomas Sully (1783–1872) and Henry Inman (1801–1846) were useful and competent artists. Some good work was also done by the so-called Hudson River School of landscape painters. Thomas Doughty (1793–1856), Thomas Cole (1801–1848), Asher Durand (1796–1886), J. F. Kensett (1816–1872), and others painted scenes along the rivers and the lakes, and

"THE POWER OF MUSIC,"
BY WILLIAM S. MOUNT
(1848)

Mount painted for the many, and his pictures were representations of life among the common people. Mount had considerable talent, and—as Oliver Larkin says—he painted people, not stereotypes. This lithograph is by Goupil, Vibert & Co.

COURTESY OF THE LIBRARY OF CONGRESS

in the Rockies. Their canvases, often gigantic, showed considerable talent but no great genius.

Two interesting developments along artistic lines lay in the fields of genre painting and of photography. The former flourished in America before the Civil War. Its portrayal of life on the frontier, the ways of country folk, and urban living conditions was replete with warmth and gentle humor. William S. Mount's (1807–1868) "The Power of Music" and Richard C. Woodville's (1825–1856) "Politics in an Oyster House" are excellent examples of genre painting. It was also in this period that Matthew Brady (*c.* 1823–1896), pioneer photographer, established a portrait studio in New York City. A consummate artist, he won fame for his daguerreotypes in the 1840s and 1850s, the great monument to his talent being the 3,500 pictures he took during the Civil War, which graphically portray the experiences of the common soldier in that bloody conflict.

American art in the Middle Period was voluminous; some of it was of good quality, but most of it was imitative and mediocre. The development of individual talent came as a result of study abroad, and the absorption of European ideas and techniques. Still bound to classical and European traditions, the artists of the United States failed to create a distinctively American school in painting, sculpture, or architecture.

The Literary Renaissance

The best that the North could do in the field of cultural achievement came in the literary field. There were a number of reasons why American literature in the Middle Period should emerge into a vigorous life of its own.

"THE OXBOW," BY THOMAS COLE

This scene on the Connecticut River near Northampton is typical of the landscape school of American painting. The beauty and mystery of rivers, lakes, mountains, and forests appealed to the imaginations of Americans who took a patriotic pride in their country and were a part of this romantic period.

The improvement in education, the development of transportation, and the increasing prosperity of the country produced in turn a potentially large reading public. Increased pride in the United States as a land that ought to lead the world in all fields of endeavor stimulated American writers to chart their own course with vigor and independence, an attitude that was strengthened by the savage criticism of American culture indulged in by English travelers and literary critics. Emerson's Phi Beta Kappa oration at Harvard in 1837, *The American Scholar,* which was a declaration of American cultural independence from Europe, as well as an assertion of the scholar's duty to think and act with objectivity and wisdom, brought instant response from American intellectuals. The time had come for achievement in the literary field, and there were men of talent to meet the challenge.

It was to the credit of these men that they were not deterred by the popular taste in reading. The public still preferred the novels of Dickens and Scott to those of American authors; when the former's *The Old Curiosity Shop* was being published in a London magazine, crowds would gather on a New York wharf and shout to an incoming ship, "Is Little Nell dead?" In domestic literature, American readers centered their attention upon the Bible, religious tracts, manuals of behavior such as W. G. Eliot's *Lectures to Young Women* and *Lectures to Young Men,* the sentimental novels of Susan Warner and Mrs. E. D. E. N. Southworth, and the saccharine poetry of Felicia Hemans and Lydia Huntley Sigourney. This was, obviously, a deterrent to American writers of genius, but they faced the handicap with spirit and courage.

New York was one of the centers of literary activity. There Washington Irving was still a figure of importance. His *Sketchbook* (1819–1820) made Rip Van Winkle and Ichabod Crane household words in the United States; his *Tales of the Alhambra* (1828–1832) catered to the popular taste for foreign lands and foreign faces; and *A Tour of the Prairies* (1835) and other books based on his travels at home gave Americans a first-hand, if commonplace, picture of life on the frontier. Popular with all classes of the reading public, his sales in the 1850s alone were estimated at over 500,000 copies.

William Cullen Bryant (1794–1878)—lawyer, newspaper editor, and poet—published *Thanatopsis* in 1817, an elegy that at once established his reputation, and later poems demonstrated his love of nature and his power of description, all pervaded by a melancholy sense of the transitory character of human nature that suited the romantic taste of the period. Bryant turned editor, and for almost fifty years, beginning in 1829, guided the destinies of the New York *Evening Post*. A stalwart Jacksonian Democrat who became a Republican in the middle 1850s, when the slavery controversy was dividing the nation, his editorials showed his stern convictions and his sympathy for the common man, whatever might be the color of his skin. Not of the same stature in newspaperdom as his contemporaries (Greeley of the *Tribune* and Henry Jarvis Raymond of the *Times*), he nevertheless belonged with those great representatives of an era of personal journalism that has long since passed away.

Another New Yorker, one whose popularity rivaled that of Irving until savage criticism of American life brought an equally savage reaction, was James Fenimore Cooper (1789–1851). Sea stories such as *The Pilot* (1823) helped to establish his reputation, but his fame rests chiefly upon *The Leatherstocking Tales,* which were published between 1823 and 1841. Their hero, Natty Bumppo, was a creature of romantic fancy, as were such noble Indians as Chingachgook and Uncas, but his wilderness backgrounds were authentically American and the whole pleased American taste.

More significant than the New York writers were those of New England.

There the outstanding figure was Ralph Waldo Emerson, Transcendentalist spokesman for the God-in-Man idea and exponent of plain living and high thinking. An incorrigible optimist, he told his countrymen, with grace and humor, that man is capable of self-improvement, that he has a soul, that he must trust his instinct as well as his reason, and that, blessed as he is with intuitive power, each individual can traverse the whole range of human experience. Emerson was a firm believer in the potential for good of American democracy. His *Essays* (1841, 1844) and his *Poems* (1847) contained the distillation of his ideas and gave him a deserved reputation as the "Plato of Concord," although he was more essayist than he was poet or philosopher.

Henry David Thoreau (1817–1862) was another of the shining stars in the galaxy of New England's literary talent. His *Walden* (1854) marked him as an individualist and an egotist, a lone wolf but a trenchant critic of existing institutions, and one who wrote in quiet and delightful prose about the beauties of the simple life. He preached freedom of thought and action for every man, though he held the community responsible for providing intellectual opportunities for its citizens. His essay on "Civil Disobedience" was one of the chief bases for Mahatma Gandhi's doctrine of passive resistance.

Nathaniel Hawthorne (1804–1864), friend of Thoreau and of President Franklin Pierce, was not a popular writer, but his best work, like that of Thoreau and Emerson, has stood the test of time. Hawthorne emphasized the crises arising from conflict in the realm of ideas, and the tragic effects of egotism. Preoccupation with the darker forces in human nature runs like a somber thread through much of his work. "Rappaccini's Daughter" (written sometime between 1842 and 1846) is a striking short story in which poison is used as a symbol of evil. His greatest novel, *The Scarlet Letter* (1850), is a study of egotism under the stress and strain of life in seventeenth-century Puritan New England; the Reverend Arthur Dimmesdale and Hester Prynne are characters not easy to forget.

Henry Wadsworth Longfellow (1807–1882), cheerful, kindly, and modest, was the most popular American poet of his time. His poetry gave expression to the optimism then so characteristic of America, dwelling with emphasis upon the middle-class virtues which were generally accepted as the American guide to life. *Evangeline* (1847) and *The Courtship of Miles Standish* (1858) are romantic treatments, touched with human sympathy, of distinctly American themes. Poems such as "The Saga of King Olaf" and "The Golden Legend" (1851) were of real value in interpreting the Old World to the New.

It is a far cry from Longfellow to Herman Melville (1819–1891). This wild and stormy spirit, who voyaged for years in the South Seas, wrote romantic tales of Polynesian life, which sold far better than did his finest novel, *Moby Dick* (1851). This saga of the white whale and of its relentless and reckless pursuit by Captain Ahab, the "ungodly, god-like man," is a study of Homeric proportions, a searching analysis of the heights and depths of human nature. It remains one of the great classics of American literature.

A lighter touch than was to be found in *Moby Dick* and *The Scarlet Letter* abounded in the writings of the period that dealt with Down East humor. Seba Smith's Jack Downing, a fictitious character who claimed to be an intimate of Old Hickory and commented with wit and acerbity upon the political squabbles of the Jacksonian period, had a host of successors. Sam Slick, the Yankee peddler, a creature of Thomas C. Haliburton's fancy, was one of these, and another was Hosea, the chief character in the first series of James Russell Lowell's *Bigelow Papers* (1846–1848). The sayings of the Widow Bedott and of Mrs. Partington, comic figures created by Frances M. Whitaker and B. P. Shillaber, respectively, had a wide audience. The characters in all these writings depended for their appeal upon quaint dialect, and shrewd, pungent observations regarding contemporary individuals and events. Yankee humor, whether in poetry, monologue, or dialogue, delighted thousands of readers all over the country.

Historical writing shared the literary movement that Van Wyck Brooks has well called "The Flowering of New England." George Bancroft (1800–1891), in his *History of the United States,* which he began writing in 1834, reflected the patriotic fervor of his compatriots. The colonies were, to him, the nursery of liberty, and he declared that the organization of the Federal Union was "the most cheering act in the history of mankind." He portrayed the development of America to the conclusion of the Revolution as though the country had been under God's special guidance. William Hickling Prescott (1796–1859) wrote about Spain in Europe and of Spanish conquests in the New World; his *History of the Conquest of Mexico* (1843) and *History of the Conquest of Peru* (1847) give vivid pictures of exciting and dramatic events, but say little about social and economic conditions. John Lothrop Motley (1814–1877) wrote with dramatic power of the *Rise of the Dutch Republic* (1856), with special emphasis on the struggle for political and religious liberty. Jared Sparks (1789–1866), the first great collector of historical manuscripts, has over 100 volumes of historical works to his credit, among them such compilations as *The Writings of Washington* (1834–1837) and *The Works of Benjamin Franklin* (1836–1840); Sparks' arbitrary editorial prunings of the documents he published were designed to present the great figures of American history in the best possible light, but he did give Americans a vivid conception of their past, and of the value of historical study.

Richard Hildreth (1807–1865) wrote a six-volume *History of the United States of America* (1849–1852) that stressed economic factors in American development. Hildreth's critical spirit deepened into bias in his treatment of Jefferson and the Jeffersonian Republicans, but his writing showed a conception of the role of the common man that was unusual among the historians of the period.

Though the works of the best writers of history in the Middle Period were widely read in their day, they have few modern readers, save among professional historians. The tendency of Bancroft, Motley, and the rest to regard history as past politics, together with the advent of the modern critical spirit, which seeks to test all statements, to explore social, economic, and cultural aspects of society, and to emphasize new views of the past, has relegated their works to the shelf of superseded books. Their chief significance is the picture they give of the modes of thought that were prevalent a century ago in regard to the story of the past.

Suggested Reading

Valuable studies of educational developments are G. P. Schmidt, *The Liberal Arts College* (1957); S. L. Jackson, *America's Struggle for Free Schools* (1941); and M. Curti, *The Social Ideas of American Educators* (1935). L. H. Tharp, *Until Victory* (1953) is excellent on Horace Mann. Carl Bode, *The American Lyceum, Town Meeting of the Mind* (1956) tells the story of this important educational institution. P. Monroe, *Founding of the American Public School System* (1940) is useful. R. Hofstadter and C. De Witt Hardy, *The Development and Scope of Higher Education in the United States* (1952) and R. Hofstadter and W. P. Metzger, *The Development of Academic Freedom in the United States* (1955) are important contributions.

The scientific advance is treated in E. S. Dana *et al., A Century of Science in America* (1918); D. J. Struik, *Yankee Science in the Making* (1948); R. H. Shryock, *The Development of Modern Medicine* (1936) and *American Medical Research* (1947); and F. R. Packard, *History of Medicine in the United States* (2 vols., 1931).

Cultural aspects are dealt with in Carl Bode, *Anatomy of American Popular Culture* (1959); Constance Rourke, *American Humor* (1931); Walter Blair, *Native American Humor* (1937); and H. N. Smith, *Virgin Land* (1950). The story of the American stage is told in A. Hornblow, *A History of the Theater in America* (2 vols., 1919) and G. Hughes, *A History of the American Theater, 1700–1950* (1951). L. C. Elson is an authority on *The History of American Music* (1904), but see also J. T. Howard, *Our American Music* (1931).

For the fine arts, the student should consult Samuel Isham, *The History of American Painting* (rev. ed., 1936); William Dunlap, *A History of the Rise and Progress of the Arts of Design* (3 vols., 1918); O. A. Larkin, *Art and Life in America* (1949), which is both instructive and delightful reading; J. Burchard and A. Bush-Brown, *The Architecture of America* (1960); and A. T. Gardner, *Yankee Stone-cutters: The First American School of Sculpture, 1800–1850* (1945).

For the literature of the period, see Van Wyck Brooks, *The World of Washington Irving* (1944) and *The Flowering of New England* (rev. ed., 1937). The penetrating analyses in F. O. Matthiessen, *American Renaissance* (1941) should by no means be overlooked. The historians of this period are covered adequately in J. S. Bassett, *The Middle Group of American Historians* (1917). On Bancroft, Sparks, and Hildreth, see Harvey Wish, *The American Historian* (1960).

23 ⸴ The South

T HE SOUTH, THE SOUTH," murmured John C. Calhoun, as he lay
on his deathbed in the year 1850. "God knows what is to become
of her!" The words of the dying statesman were more ominous than
he could know. They symbolized the difficulties and problems of a section
that he had long loved and tried to serve.

Climate, Soil, and Crops

The antebellum South comprised some million
square miles of territory, stretching from Chesapeake Bay westward to San Antonio, Texas, and
from the Gulf of Mexico northward to the Ohio.
The region has hot summers, usually with a drought period, and a growing
season that varies from six months in northern Virginia and Kentucky to
nine months in the Deep South.

The soil of this area is chiefly sand and clay in varying proportions, with
little lime or humus, save at the top. It is usually hard-packed, partly because
of the lack of deep frosts, and also because of the pelting rains that come from
a considerable height. Hence floods are common, as well as the leaching of
the flat lands and the erosion of the hills. Mountainous and semi-mountain-
ous areas, the Piedmont regions, and the rich river bottoms erode with equal
ease. The rivers, clouded in dry weather, are brick red in times of flood.
Many years ago, a Georgia planter voiced a complaint that could be echoed
throughout the South. His land title, he declared, was defective, since it
could not hold his soil from being washed beyond recovery into the creeks
and rivers.

489

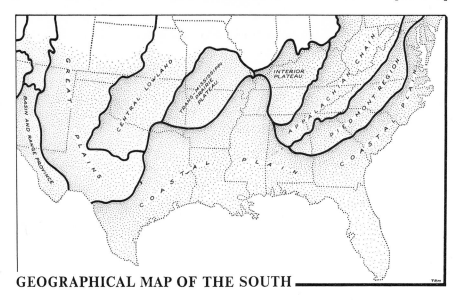

GEOGRAPHICAL MAP OF THE SOUTH

The South has six main geographical regions: the eastern and southern coastal plain, the Piedmont stretching from the heads of navigation in the eastern rivers to the foot of the mountains, the Appalachian chain itself, the great plateau stretching westward from those cliffs and ridges, the lower Mississippi valley with its tributary streams, and the prairie plateau west of the Mississippi. The fertility of these regions varies, from the long reaches of the sandy "pine barrens" in the Carolinas and the lean soil of the mountains to the fertile "Blue Grass" counties of central Kentucky and the rich alluvial valley bottoms and deltas of the main rivers. Very fertile, too, are the silt loams of the Alabama Black Belt, parts of north-central Louisiana, the "black-waxy" zone in Texas between Dallas and Austin, and the region between the Delaware and Chesapeake Bays.

From the beginning, these productive areas made for an agricultural economy, and the South of the period with which we are dealing produced bountiful and varied crops. Tobacco was the staple of its northern states, cotton that of the great belt stretching from east to west that is called the Deep South. Rice grew abundantly in South Carolina, Georgia, and south-central Louisiana, as did sugar cane on the plantations along the lower Mississippi. White corn was (and is) a favorite crop, for from it are made delectable spoon bread, corn pone, and hoe cake. In 1850, the South produced 87 per cent of the hemp raised in the United States, and 80 per cent of the nation's peas and beans. But heat, together with the tendency of water to run off the top of the soil, made the land unsuitable for such shallow-rooted crops as grain and hay, which meant, in turn, that the region did not raise a great deal of livestock and the lack of barnyard manures made it difficult to maintain the fertility of the soil.

The raising of tobacco in the upper South was practically a year-round job. The tiny seeds were planted as soon as the ground was ready in early spring. Thinning and hoeing in the summer were followed by stripping and drying in the fall, and, finally, by packing in great 1,000-pound hogsheads in the late fall and winter. One "hand" was necessary for every three or four acres of the crop, and by 1850 some 350,000 slaves were employed on the tobacco farms and plantations.

Since tobacco is a heavy feeder and exhausts the soil, in the early years of the nineteenth century it did not yield much profit. But Edmund Ruffin (1794–1865), James Hammond (1807–1864), and others taught the Virginia and Maryland planters to replenish their land with marl and fertilizers, and new varieties and new curing methods improved the quality of the leaf. Demand at home and abroad then expanded, and the crop took on a new lease of life. Between 1850 and 1860, the South's yield of tobacco increased 115 per cent. Maryland and the Old Dominion prospered.

If tobacco was the great crop of the upper South, cotton was that of the belt of states that stretch from the Carolinas and Georgia across to Texas. Like tobacco, it depleted soil fertility, but the world demand for it constantly increased and the cotton plantations moved steadily westward.

Long-staple cotton of fine quality and with relatively few seeds flourished on the Atlantic seaboard, but this type was sensitive to climatic conditions and could not be produced profitably inland. Whitney's cotton gin solved the problem of cleaning the short-staple variety, and it was this which became the great crop of the Deep South.

Like tobacco, cotton required labor throughout the year, one "hand" being necessary for every three to ten acres, depending upon the character of the land and the general efficiency of the operation. In March and April, the seeds were thickly sown in prepared soil. Thinned and cultivated through the spring and early summer, the young plants grew to a height of two to three feet, producing a heavy foliage and blossoms that swiftly changed from creamy white to purplish red; when the bolls, or pods, were about the size of an egg, cultivation stopped. The bolls changed in color from green to brown as they ripened, and then split into segments disclosing masses of lint and seeds. After picking and ginning, the crop, packed in bales, was ready for shipment to the factory.

Cotton production increased with great rapidity. In 1810, the South's output was 178,000 bales. (A bale might weigh anywhere from 383 to 500 pounds.) This leaped to 1,348,000 bales in 1840, then to 2,136,000 bales in 1850, and 3,841,000 bales in 1860. By the middle of the century, the South was producing seven-eighths of the world's supply, and the cotton fields employed 1,815,000 slave hands, over five times as many as labored on the tobacco farms and plantations. "Cotton was king," the principal crop of the South, and the great cotton growers with their plantations of 1,000 to 2,000 acres were important figures in the southern community.

The Southern People

The southern population, in the period just "before the war," consisted of some twelve million whites, blacks, and a few remaining Indians. At the top, socially speaking, were the "gentry," comprised chiefly of the planters and the professional classes; many of the gentry were cultured representatives of the nation's finest traditions, while others were nouveau riche, vulgar boors, ignorant, arrogant, and full of bullying insolence. Next in line came the great mass of generally respectable middle-class farmers and tradesmen. Below that group were the poor whites who lived in the pine barrens and other unproductive regions into which they had been forced by lack of capital and planter competition; these were generally listless, uncouth and illiterate, tipplers of "bust-head" (moonshine whiskey) and often victims of hookworm, a parasitic disease of the small intestine usually contracted through the soles of the feet and sometimes referred to as "southern laziness." A special group were the southern mountaineers, poor and often illiterate, but in mind and character definitely above the poor whites. At the bottom of the social ladder were the slaves.

Planters, poor whites, and slaves made up less than half of the South's total population. The great bulk of the remainder were independent yeomen farmers, who tilled their own fields with little or no help outside their families.

In the South of 1860 only 4.4 per cent of the population was of foreign birth, as against 18.7 per cent for the rest of the country. Immigrants preferred the North as a land of better opportunity for the city dweller, and one with a more familiar pattern of agriculture. The southern population was also more diffused than that of the North—13.65 per square mile, as against 20.59. New Orleans, with a population of 168,675 in 1860, was the only "big" city in the United States that was truly southern in character; Charleston had only 40,578, Savannah 22,292, and Mobile 29,258.

Southern society had certain marked characteristics, the necessity of preserving white domination at all costs being its basic concept. It was also more aristocratic in tone than that of the North, and essentially conservative in its outlook. Southerners regarded themselves as providing a stabilizing counterpart to the wildly radical notions that emanated from northern quarters.

Southerners were intensely loyal to their own social and political institutions. The state and the family were objects of great devotion. They passionately defended the southern way of life, and were quick to point with pride to the South as an area that had accomplished and was accomplishing great things. This sometimes led to a boastful and truculent attitude, exemplified by the remark of Robert Toombs of Georgia to Lord Elgin in 1854—"Yes, my lord, we are about to relume the torch of liberty upon the altar of slavery." The Union was revered in the South, but southerners were determined that it should not interfere with their own way of life.

Hot tempers and a tendency to violence were also southern characteristics. In the North, brawls and bloodshed were largely confined to the lower classes, but in the South the feuds of the mountaineers were notorious and, as Allan Nevins has observed, "hot words and hair-triggers were the mark of the gentleman." Duels were common occurrences, and the unwritten law was customarily invoked to save a man from the death penalty. The southern code of honor permitted a "gentleman" affronted by some member of the lower classes to kill the offender forthwith.

The Southern Economy

The twentieth century has demonstrated that the South is a region where industry can be profitably developed, but in the antebellum period its economy was overwhelmingly agricultural. The great bulk of the industrial products that it used, from textile goods to household utensils and farm implements, came from the North.

There were several reasons for the South's preoccupation with farming. The profits from cotton, sugar, and tobacco, together with the widespread belief that capital invested in land and slaves yielded more income than any other type of investment, did much to prevent the development of a diversified economy. Captains of industry were few and far between; when they appeared, they were apt to move north, as did Cyrus Hall McCormick, where there were greater opportunities for business profits. Some prejudice against manufacturing, which was thought to be dirty and sordid, existed; at one time, Charleston had ordinances against machinery operated by steam because it would create a smoke nuisance in the city. The transportation system was inadequate. Important, too, was the scarcity of free labor and, to some extent, the low efficiency of southern labor. The poor whites and the mountaineers, accustomed to independence, were apt to be undisciplined, careless and intractable. Indeed, the general tempo of labor activity in the South was lower than that in the North.

Perhaps the most significant opposition to industrial development was that of the immensely influential southern planters. In their opinion, it was a "foreign system" that would bring in immigrant free labor opposed to slave competition, and thus result in training slaves to be skilled workers and so make them dissatisfied with their status. An industrial class, the planters held, would be a threat to their own influence and interests. It would mean a contraction of agriculture through a diversion of its labor force, and would foster support in the South for a higher tariff. The manufacturers, it was alleged, would have to have liquid capital and therefore would not invest in slaves; they might well become advocates of freeing the Negroes. These arguments did much to influence popular opinion in the South.

Despite the resistance to manufacturing, many southerners were irked by their section's preoccupation with agriculture and its consequent dependence upon northern and European manufactured goods. During the 1840s, when the price of cotton was for several years less than $.10 a pound, earnest attempts were made by prominent figures such as William Gregg (1800–1867), James H. Taylor, and others, to promote industrial diversification. Nearly every year from 1850 to 1860, conventions were held in the South, seeking ways to correct the economic imbalance of the section.

These efforts produced some results. Manufacturing by steam and water power increased, and there was a rapid increase after 1845 in cotton textile production along the fall line from Virginia to Alabama. Columbus, Georgia, with 6,000 inhabitants, had twelve cotton factories by 1849. Between 1840 and 1860, capital invested in the manufacture of cotton in the South rose from $6 million to nearly $12 million and that invested in the manufacture of cotton, wool, and iron rose more rapidly than in the United States as a whole.

Despite these healthy developments, the South was nevertheless falling behind the North in over-all manufacturing. In 1840, 20 per cent of the total capital invested in manufacturing in the United States was in the South, but by 1860 southern manufacturing capital was less than 16 per cent of the national total. The South was continuing on its agricultural way.

Problems of Southern Agriculture

Like northern farming, southern agriculture was extensive and wasteful in character. Though the tobacco farmers of Virginia and Maryland adopted scientific methods of restoring the fertility of the soil, in the cotton states of the southeast the advice of men like Ruffin and Hammond was not generally followed, and the cotton yield per acre steadily declined. The planters benefited by an increase in the general price level during the 1850s that was due to California gold and the mounting world demand for cotton, but, ironically enough, a better price for cotton acted as a barrier to crop rotation and diversification. At the same time, lack of an urban population of any size prevented the planters and farmers from turning to market gardening and dairying as means of making a living.

Another problem of the cotton raiser was the tribute paid to northern middlemen and brokers. Between 1830 and 1860, 75 to 80 per cent of the cotton crop found its way to European markets, and the northern profits on this export trade reduced the profits of the planters to the vanishing point in years when cotton prices were low. (See the account in Chapter 20 of the rise of the port of New York.)

A third difficulty with which cotton growers had to deal was price fluctuation in both cotton and slaves. In 1818, the average price of upland cotton was $.29 a pound; the depression of 1819 cut this almost in half. By 1835, it had risen to $.175, but the panic and depression that began in 1837 produced a cotton crisis, and by 1845, when there was acute distress, cotton stood at $.055 a pound. Thereafter conditions improved, and between 1850 and 1860 the price averaged around $.11.

The price of slaves also had a wide range. The average price of a prime field hand, $1,000 in 1818, was $1,300 by 1837. It declined to $600 in 1844, but rose rapidly thereafter until, by 1860, it averaged from $1,500 to $1,800, with as much as $2,000 being paid for such a slave in central Georgia.

The speculative character of large investments in cotton lands and slaves was enhanced by mortality risks. A planter whose labor force was depleted by a yellow fever or smallpox epidemic might find himself reduced in a few weeks from affluence to a state bordering on poverty. These risks, however, did not result in any diminution of the South's devotion to the raising of its great staple.

The Impact of Slavery on Southern Agriculture

Was slavery a detriment to southern agriculture? The answer is not easily determined, for there is evidence on both sides of the question. In many ways, slavery was an asset. It provided a stable labor supply; there was no unemployment problem, and no lockouts, blacklists, or strikes. Slavery was competitively superior to a free labor system, since it made easy the appropriation of the slave's surplus labor value above the subsistence level. Slave labor made possible the plantation system and thereby gave a great impetus to the growing of southern staples. It must also be remembered that wasteful farming methods, rather than slave labor, were the chief cause of soil depletion. Slaves, properly handled, did good work, and wages for white and hired slave labor in the South did not differ to any significant degree.

A plantation efficiently managed, where the owner saw to it that his slaves were humanely treated, given garden plots of their own, and perhaps allowed to earn a little money by "outside" employment, was a money-making proposition. There is also evidence that the small planters with ten or less slaves and 500 or fewer acres, who owned perhaps 75 per cent of the landed wealth in the Black Belt, were making money during the decade before the Civil War.

The economic weakness of the slave labor system lay in its lack of incentive for the laborer. The field hand had no education, and only the most favored house servants had any kind of schooling. While on such a plantation as that of Jefferson Davis in Mississippi slaves were encouraged to earn money for themselves, the vast majority had no such opportunity; consequently, among nine-tenths of the South's landowners, the ignorance and inefficiency of slave labor was conspicuous, and progressive farmers and hustling business entrepreneurs simply could not emerge from the South's labor force.

The Negro in Southern Society

The South in 1860 contained some six million whites, four million slaves, and better than 200,000 free Negroes, the latter being the result of manumission and natural increase. The slaves were owned by some 385,000 masters, of whom less than 2,000 owned 100 slaves or more; two-thirds or more of the owners had title to less than ten slaves each. Nearly three-fourths of the South's white population had no direct interest in slave labor, but southerners as a whole accepted and defended slavery.

It is easy to understand why those with a capital investment in slaves upheld the system. Many of the others hoped to become planters, thereby moving into the upper circles of southern society. The social hierarchy was not a closed one, and if a man had enough cotton or tobacco, slaves, and reasonably good manners, he might well gain access to upper-class circles. Then, too, there was general acceptance of leadership by the gentry in the churches, county courts, and politics, and the gentry (with only a few exceptions) staunchly defended slavery. Yeomen and poor whites also upheld bondage, because they hated the idea of equality for the Negro that was implied in abolition. Finally, as Ulrich B. Phillips has pointed out, fear of the Negro made free hovered like a specter over the South.

The status of the free Negro in the South illustrates both the possibilities of freedom and the whites' determination to prevent the spread of liberty for those in bondage. The South's free Negroes in 1860 owned some $25 million worth of property. Some were slaveholders, with the rank of middle-class planters (one free Negro rented a pew in Charleston's most aristocratic church), and a goodly number ranked, in economic status, with the more prosperous yeomen farmers. But as a group the free Negroes were looked upon with fear and suspicion by a society that had no place for them, and that longed to see them transported to Africa or reduced to bondage. Outcasts, often degraded and degenerate, they were more and more put on a par with the slaves, so far as rights and privileges were concerned, by the laws of the southern states.

The general status of the slaves was a controversial question, especially from 1830 to 1860. The abolitionists pictured it as cruel and degrading. Citing whippings, brandings, and brutal and inhuman exploitation to prove their point; according to them, the slaves were groaning and tortured human beings. Southern protagonists of the "peculiar institution" minimized its hardships and declared that the slaves were generally contented, a laughing, joking, carefree, happy-go-lucky lot, who sang in the cotton and tobacco fields, had their own simple amusements, and were far better off than they would be in a state of freedom. There was an element of truth in the contentions on both sides of the controversy.

The condition of the slaves was certainly better than had been that of their African forebears, and the majority of them were well off as compared with the laborers in the sweatshops and depressed trades of the North. Many of them found satisfaction in singing and dancing to the strumming of the banjo, and derived great emotional and spiritual solace from religion, particularly of the Baptist and Methodist varieties. Save in unusual circumstances, they could count upon the master for their subsistence—food, clothes, rude cabins, firewood, and medical attention; these provisions, though coarse, were usually adequate, for a slave who fell sick or died at an early age was an economic loss. If the slave fell foul of the law, through stealing or more serious crimes, the master would take his part, if for no other reason than fear of the loss of his services. In many cases, house servants were well treated. The "mammy" nursemaids, the valued cooks, and the body servants of men like Clay and Jefferson Davis had very comfortable lives.

But slavery did have another side, one that was often dark and terrible.

RAFFLE

Mr. Joseph Jennings respectfully informs his friends and the public that, at the request of many acquaintances, he has been induced to purchase from Mr. Osborne, of Missouri, the celebrated

DARK BAY HORSE, "STAR,"

Aged five years, square trotter and warranted sound; with a new light Trotting Buggy and Harness also, the dark, stout

MULATTO GIRL, "SARAH,"

Aged about twenty years, general house servant, valued at *nine hundred dollars*, and guaranteed, and

Will be Raffled for

At 4 o'clock P. M., February first, at the selection hotel of the subscribers. The above is as represented and those persons who may wish to engage in the usual practice of raffling, will, I assure them, be perfectly satisfied with their destiny in this affair.

The whole is valued at its just worth, fifteen hundred dollars; fifteen hundred

CHANCES AT ONE DOLLAR EACH.

The Raffle will be conducted by gentlemen selected by the interested subscribers present. Five nights will be allowed to complete the Raffle. BOTH OF THE ABOVE DESCRIBED CAN BE SEEN AT MY STORE, No. 78 Common St., second door from Camp, at from 9 o'clock A. M. to 2 P. M.

Highest throw to take the first choice; the lowest throw the remaining prize, and the fortunate winners will pay twenty dollars each for the refreshments furnished on the occasion.

N. B. No chances recognized unless paid for previous to the commencement.

JOSEPH JENNINGS.

ADVERTISEMENT FOR A RAFFLE

The Negro was a commodity in the antebellum South. Here a girl and a horse are being put up in the same raffle, the only indication of the difference between the two being that "Sarah" is valued at $300 more than the horse.

498

Against a brutal master or overseer, the slave had only one recourse—to run away. While the laws of the southern states forbade masters to kill their slaves or punish them in a barbarous manner, the owner was guiltless if the slave was killed while resisting punishment. Furthermore, brutality was almost impossible to prove, for slave testimony against white men was excluded from the courts. Charges of slave breeding were magnified by the abolitionists, but there is no doubt that it did occur, especially during periods when prices were attractive, or when the planters were hard pressed to make a living and needed to sell some of their chattels. The large number of mulattoes in the South was witness to another evil practice—that of the white master forcing sexual relations upon attractive female slaves.

And not all the slaves were happy and contented. There were constant rumors and some actual cases of slave insurrections. Denmark Vesey (c. 1767–1822), a free mulatto, tried to organize an uprising in Charleston in 1822; the conspiracy collapsed, but 135 Negroes were brought to trial and thirty-five were hanged. When Nat Turner (1800–1831) of Virginia, a religious fanatic, persuaded himself and others that he was a Moses destined by God to lead the slaves to freedom, over fifty white men, women, and children were killed in August, 1831, before the revolt which he led was put down; Turner and sixteen of his followers were executed, and twelve were transported. This insurrection filled the South with fear and put an end to southern movements for freeing the slaves. After such uprisings, and after white women had been raped, innocent Negroes were whipped and hanged by mobs, and Negro religious meetings broken up by white patrols—the "pater-rollers," as the Negroes called them.

One of the worst aspects of slavery was the slave trade, which was chiefly from the upper southern states to the Deep South. This was at its height around 1836, when out of Virginia alone 120,000 slaves were sold to the Black Belt. As the economic situation in Virginia and Maryland improved, this exodus decreased, but slave trading and coffles of slaves moving from one part of the South to another were always part of the social order. The auction block, the coarseness of the auctioneer as he sold female slaves to the highest bidder, and the breakup of families, were sad and often heart-rending spectacles. When John Randolph of Roanoke was once asked who was the greatest orator he had ever heard, his answer came promptly: "A Negro slave, sir. She was a mother, and her rostrum was the auction block."

The South's Defense of Slavery

During the years before 1830, the South's attitude toward slavery had been defensive and apologetic, rather than militant. Washington, Jefferson,

Madison, and many other southerners believed in democracy and disliked slavery; they accepted the doctrine of natural rights, one of the great bases of the Declaration of Independence and of democratic thought. Among the societies in the South organized for the purpose of ridding the country of slavery, the American Colonization Society, founded at Washington in 1816 for the purpose of sending free Negroes to Africa and encouraging the manumission of slaves, enlisted the support of Henry Clay, Andrew Jackson, William Harris Crawford, and other prominent southerners hopeful that it would be a means of gradually ending human bondage in the United States. The Negroes, however, were not enthusiastic about transplantation to a new and difficult life in Liberia, financial support for colonization lagged, and by 1860 no more than 4,000 emancipated slaves and an equal number of free Negroes had been sent to Africa. Colonization was obviously not the answer to the slavery problem.

As the colonization project withered and the South's profits from slavery grew, and as the northern abolitionists began their crusade, southerners abandoned their apologetic attitude and began an aggressive support of human bondage. This new attitude was widespread in the southern press after 1830 and found its most powerful expression in the writings and speeches of prominent statesmen and other leaders of southern thought.

Calhoun was one of the most ardent defenders of slavery. He supported it vigorously, both in and out of the Senate. Thomas R. Dew (1802–1846) of Virginia, who taught political economy and other subjects at William and Mary and became president of that institution in 1836, was as outspoken as Calhoun; his *Pro-Slavery Argument*, first published in 1832, with later editions in the 1850s, was widely read. William Harper (1790–1847) of South Carolina, prominent lawyer and for many years chancellor of the state, was an exponent of nullification and a defender of slavery, whose *Memoir on Slavery* (1837) was a reasoned defense of the institution. George Fitzhugh (1806–1881), another Virginian, lawyer, sociologist and, ironically enough, a relative of the northern abolitionist Gerrit Smith, was a stout supporter of slavery. He published *Sociology for the South: or the Failure of Free Society* (1854), and *Cannibals All! or Slaves Without Masters* (1857), stirring indictments of the northern treatment of wage earners as compared with the South's labor system.

The arguments of these men, and others like them, were more and more generally accepted in the South. They ran along the following lines:

(1) There are no such things as natural rights. Men's rights are established only by their exercise; that is to say, they are prescriptive rights.

(2) Slaves do not have the same rights as white men, because they have not established those rights.

(3) Men are created unequal. The men of property are superior to others and hence should control society.

(4) Slaves are naturally the lowest members of society. They are like children, and must be guided, directed, cared for, and trained for the only life to which they are suited—one of toil. The chasm between them and the leaders of society is so great that slaves cannot cross it. They constitute the "mud sill" of society, that element which must of necessity perform the necessary sordid, servile, and laborious tasks, and in so doing free the whites for higher things.

(5) Slavery is recognized and implicitly justified in the Bible as a social institution. It is, said Dr. Benjamin Palmer of New Orleans, really God's plan for instructing the black man in the Gospel and securing for him salvation and eternal bliss.

Influenced by these arguments, stung by the taunts of the abolitionists, and fearful of the social consequences of Negro freedom, the South excluded the black man from the benefits of democracy. Southern society before the Civil War was dominated in thought and in practice by an aristocratic ideal.

Cultural Aspects of the Antebellum South—Religion

Deism and free thought were widespread in the South during the first years of the nineteenth century. Jefferson, Thomas Cooper, Horace Holley, and many other intellectual leaders were heterodox in their religious opinions. The college of William and Mary, and the universities of Transylvania, Virginia, North Carolina, and Georgia were centers of religious infidelity.

Free thought, however, was more a temporary reflection of eighteenth-century rationalism than a deep-seated conviction in the South. By 1830, it had practically disappeared. Orthodoxy was now the order of the day. The great planters were mainly Episcopalian—the gentleman's road to heaven. The lesser gentry and the masses favored the evangelical denominations, which were strengthened by the frequent Baptist, Methodist, and Presbyterian revivals that swept over the land.

The southern churches and churchmen were conservative as well as orthodox. They became increasingly intolerant of free thought and, indeed, of heterodoxy in any form, accepting and defending southern institutions, and denouncing their critics. In the two decades before the Civil War, the Methodist, Baptist, and Presbyterian churches split with their northern brethren over the slavery question and established their own separate church organizations. On the other hand, the southern churches were more tolerant of Catholics than were the northern Protestants. The Know-Nothing movement in the South was directed more against foreigners and the "isms" that they brought into the United States than it was against the members of the church of Rome.

Education and Interest in Science

Superficially at least, higher education flourished in the antebellum South. There were some half-dozen state universities and numerous private colleges. In 1850, the South had 120 colleges and universities, as compared with 111 in the North. Taking into account the considerable number of southern youths who went to such northern institutions of higher learning as Yale and Princeton, the South could point with pride to the number of its college-trained youth. But southern colleges were smaller and more meagerly supported than those of the North, and the educational standards were of a lower order. The University of Virginia, founded in 1825, was a center of classical learning and was free of sectarian controls, but most of the colleges and universities were controlled by one or another of the religious denominations.

The South had a considerable number of private academies for the sons of the well-to-do, and public high schools were increasing in number prior to 1860. There were state-supported common schools in some states, though only North Carolina and Kentucky had good public school systems. But reluctance to face taxation and a general feeling that it was the duty of the individual to see to the education of his own children were barriers to the development of public education. There were rural areas where the poorer classes had practically no educational opportunity. A large part of the white population of the South was illiterate, and a considerable number of the planters never learned to read and write. According to the census of 1850, the southern native white population had an illiteracy ratio of 20 to 30 per cent, as compared with 3 per cent in the Middle Atlantic states and .42 per cent in New England.

The colleges and universities of the South placed their main emphasis on the classics, but they also showed considerable interest in science. Constantine Samuel Rafinesque (1783–1840) at Transylvania University, Elisha Mitchell (1793–1857) at the University of North Carolina, Gerard Troost (1776–1850) at the University of Nashville, and others were distinguished scientists. The Virginia Military Institute, organized in 1839, had as its first superintendent General Francis H. Smith, a West Pointer and a mathematician of note. The South also had distinguished scientists outside the academic halls, such as the oceanographer Matthew Fontaine Maury (1806–1873),

Henry W. Ravenel (1814–1887), a plantation owner who became a leading authority in botany, and Edmund Ruffin, "the father of soil chemistry in America." Five southern states (Tennessee, Maryland, Virginia, South Carolina, and Alabama) established geological surveys in the 1830s and 1840s. There were few scientists of the first rank, no scientific foundations, and little efficient organization of scientific research, but for interest in the subject and for individual scientific achievement the South compared favorably with the North.

Freedom of Thought

Widespread interest among southern intellectuals in science and the classics could in no way be said to indicate an equal devotion to freedom of thought, for there was a striking lack of this precious commodity in the southern states. School and college textbooks were constantly scrutinized for passages that might be offensive to southern taste. Academic freedom did not include freedom for antislavery opinions or heterodox religious views, and offenders were apt to be given short shrift; some were dismissed from their posts, and others were forced to leave. Transylvania University, founded in 1780, was a progressive institution under Horace Holley (1781–1827), a Unitarian who was president of the institution from 1818 to 1827, when he was driven out by the Presbyterians, who had long been influential in the affairs of the University and who resented his liberal views; thereafter, Transylvania's educational standards steadily declined. In 1856, Professor Benjamin Sherwood Hedrick (1827–1886), professor of chemistry at the University of North Carolina, was dismissed because of his criticism of slavery. Berea College in Kentucky, a biracial institution founded in 1858, was forced to close by enraged proslavery Kentuckians.

Intolerance of liberal religious views increased throughout the period, largely because literal interpretation of the Bible could be used to defend slavery. It also became increasingly dangerous to hold antislavery opinions. Newspaper editors were intimidated and sometimes mobbed for their antislavery views, and the pressure of public opinion acted as a restraining influence upon those who were hostile to the "peculiar institution."

Southern intolerance was due to several factors. The lack of urban life, with its cultural opportunity and liberalizing influence was a handicap to the growth of toleration. The ignorance bred of illiteracy kept alive violent prejudices. There was a general feeling that slavery must be protected at all costs from abolitionist attacks, as well as widespread fear that antislavery propaganda would promote slave insurrections, and such fears and prejudices were often deliberately excited by clever and designing politicians as a means of ensuring their own rise to power.

The South and Reform

In view of the limitations on freedom of thought, it is not remarkable that the spirit of reform found only feeble nourishment in this period of the South's history. Such radical experiments as Fourierism, socialism, spiritualism, and free love aroused only aversion south of the Mason and Dixon line; regarded as northern middle-class aberrations, they were therefore suspect. The women's rights movement had no support in the South, where feminine education was generally neglected and woman's place was regarded as in the home. Foreign radicals, as the experience of Etienne Cabet proved, found the area inhospitable to their ideas.

The South's attitude toward reform, however, was not wholly negative. There was considerable interest in improving the treatment of the mentally deficient, and of the sixteen states that founded hospitals for the insane five were in the South. The temperance movement aroused a good deal of enthusiasm, with temperance societies in every southern state, for it was in harmony with the religious and quasi-Puritanical spirit which animated many southerners. But the number of ardent temperance advocates was small, and only some 15,000 took the total-abstinence pledge. A few people, notably the Grimké sisters of South Carolina, joined the peace crusade.

A number of factors serve to explain the southern lack of interest in reform. The southern churches looked askance at the radical reform movements, especially those of foreign origin. Southern prejudice was aroused by the close association of northern abolitionists with such crusades as those against liquor and for women's rights. The Lyceum movement, a useful vehicle in distributing reform ideas in the North, had only feeble support in the South. And the overwhelming predominance of a rural population undoubtedly reinforced the South's conservatism in matters of reform. The great majority of southerners were very well content with the South as it was.

The Fine Arts and Literature

The cultured southern gentleman took a genuine interest in the fine arts, but southern genius did not flower in this particular field. In music, Louis Moreau Gottschalk (1829–1869) was a composer for the piano and a fine pianist, the folk songs of the South and the Negro spirituals still enrich and beautify American life, and New Orleans was the first American city to establish a permanent opera company. But, in the main, southerners were content to enjoy the great compositions of foreign masters and to listen with pleasure to such foreign artists as Jenny Lind and Adelina Patti.

Much the same situation prevailed in other fields. The South continued to prefer the architectural beauty of the Greek Revival; the homes of the great planters featured columned porches and Corinthian capitals—reminiscent of the Greek way of life with its superstructure of gentry and its masses of helots or slaves. Though many wealthy southerners had their portraits painted, the region produced no first-rate artists. In sculpture, perhaps the most distinguished southern name was that of Clark Mills (1810–1883), who was born in New York but lived and worked in South Carolina. His equestrian statue of General Jackson, designed at the behest of a special committee, is spirited and realistic, but scarcely distinguished art; it still stands in Lafayette Square, opposite the White House.

EDGAR ALLAN POE
(1809–1849)

Despite the tragedy of his brief life, Poe achieved a high place in American literature. The photograph is by Brady.

COURTESY HARRY SHAW NEWMAN,
THE OLD PRINT SHOP, NEW YORK

Save in a few urban centers, southerners had little opportunity to patronize the theatre or to watch the performances of outstanding actors. The only great actor of whom the South could boast, Edwin Booth (1833–1893), though born in Maryland, spent his stage career chiefly in the North and West.

In the fine art of literature, the South could lay claim to a writer of genius—Edgar Allan Poe (1809–1849). Though Poe was born in Boston, both of his parents were actors who died when he was very young, and, having been brought up by foster parents in Richmond, he always considered himself a Virginian. His brief and tragic life, marred by violent quarrels with his foster father, John Allan (who finally disowned him), dissipation, dire poverty, tragic love affairs, and spells of insanity, ended at Baltimore in agony and delirium. In the midst of all this turmoil, he nevertheless secured for himself undying fame as a poet, critic, and writer of short stories. As editor of the *Southern Literary Messenger* and other publications, he set high standards of literary criticism, and his great lyrical talent produced such poems as "To Helen," "The Raven," and "El Dorado," which will always be included in American anthologies. In prose, *The Narrative of Arthur Gordon Pym* (1838) was a masterpiece of science fiction, and such tales as "The Gold Bug" and "The Murders in the Rue Morgue" entitle him to rank as one of the originators of the detective story. Many of his poems have a haunting beauty that lingers in the memory, and it is easy to believe that the gloom and terror in such tales as "A Cask Of Amontillado" and "The Fall of the House of Usher" reflect the dark tragedy of his own life.

Other than Poe, the South produced no outstanding man of genius in the field of belles-lettres. There were, however, some writers of merit. William Gilmore Simms (1806–1870), Henry Timrod (1828–1867), and Paul Hamilton Hayne (1830–1886) extolled southern virtues and the southern way of life in prose and poetry. A. B. Longstreet (1790–1870), in *Georgia Scenes,* and Joseph G. Baldwin (1815–1864), in *The Flush Times of Alabama and Mississippi,* portrayed with real humor the life of the yeomen, gamblers, "crackers," and riff-raff of the South. But Simms and Hayne did not receive the recognition in the South that they deserved, and southern literary publications and literary figures were only meagerly supported; around 1850 the South had only twenty-four of the 345 publishing houses in the United States. Sales of books by southern writers were small, and editions were limited.

The literary interest of the South tended to center in politics. Political journals such as the Richmond *Whig,* the New Orleans *Bee* and *Picayune,* and the Louisville *Daily Journal* were excellent newspapers, ably edited. The editorials were intelligent, often pungent, and the papers themselves furnished opportunity for publication to southern writers of prose and poetry. Two of the best editors were John H. Pleasants (1797–1846) of the Richmond *Whig,* and the witty George D. Prentice (1802–1870) of the Louisville

Daily Journal, whose excoriations of leading Democrats resulted in his fighting several duels.

Cultured southerners read their newspapers and often read widely in history and the English classics, with a marked preference for romantic tales. The works of the favorite southern author, Sir Walter Scott—full of lofty gentlefolk forever breaking lances on behalf of high morality and beautiful ladies—sold by the carload; enthusiasm for Scott went so far that tournaments like that described in *Ivanhoe* were features of public celebrations. The southerner's reading bolstered his concept of himself as a chivalric figure, always ready to defend the purity of southern womanhood and to repel attacks upon southern institutions.

The South as a Conscious Minority

At the time of the War of 1812, the best example of a conscious minority in the United States was the Federalists of New England. Long before 1850, Federalism had disappeared, and New England was linked by economic and ideological ties with the rest of the North. The one example of a conscious minority that existed in the United States in the decade before the Civil War was in the South; it embraced not merely one party, but the rank and file of all the people, who had developed an economy, a way of life, and a point of view that was peculiarly their own. Primarily agricultural, and with a relatively static population, the South watched with envy the growing power of an economically diversified North and the rapid swell of a northern population that would increase its majority in Congress and produce national legislation favorable to northern interests and designs. The people of the North were coming closer and closer together in their support of a protective tariff, internal improvements at national expense, and free land for western settlers, and in the North antislavery sentiment was steadily growing—developments that filled the South with alarm. Badgered by the attacks of the abolitionists, confronted by the realization that the South remained the one great bastion of slavery in the civilized world, and appalled by the social and economic problems that would be involved in the destruction of slavery, southerners were now making the bondage of the Negro a symbol of the southern way of life, an institution to which all southerners could and must rally.

It is no wonder that, in the 1840s and 1850s, efforts were made to develop a consciousness of southern unity. Some extremists, such as Robert Barnwell Rhett (1800–1876) of South Carolina and William Lowndes

Yancey (1814–1863) of Alabama advocated secession and the formation of a southern confederacy. Others—Langdon Cheves (1776–1857) and Calhoun, for example—were cooperationists, reluctant to take the giant step but urging southerners to unite in defense of their way of life and in the promotion of their common interests.

Calhoun was a symbol of this trend in southern thought. Originally an ardent exponent of national unity, he never lost his love for the Union, but his devotion to the South modified his original viewpoint. In defense of southern interests, he became an ardent advocate of interposition and nullification, and one of the staunchest defenders of slavery. He declared that the national government must safeguard control by the states of their own institutions. In his "Disquisition on Government" and "Discourse on the Constitution and Government of the United States," both published after his death, he demanded sweeping safeguards for the South, urging that there be set up a system of "concurrent majorities" by which a minority of the national population could compel the majority to compromise issues between them. He also advocated an amendment to the Constitution that would provide for two Presidents, one selected by the North and the other by the South, the assent of both being necessary before any act passed by Congress could become law. These proposals, had they become law, would have promoted sectional division rather than national unity.

Suggested Reading

The standard work on southern agriculture is L. C. Gray, *History of Agriculture in the Southern United States to 1860* (2 vols., 1933).

There are a number of one-volume general studies of the South in the pre-Civil War period. Clement Eaton, *A History of the Old South* (1949) covers the ground admirably. See also E. Q. Hawk, *Economic History of the South* (1934) and F. B. Simkins, *A History of the South* (1953). L. E. Atherton, *The Southern Country Store, 1800–1860* (1949) is informative, as are Everett Dick, *The Dixie Frontier* (1947) and R. W. Shugg, *Origins of Class Struggle in Louisiana, 1840–1875* (1939).

On slavery and its role in southern life, see Allan Nevins, *Ordeal of the Union* (2 vols., 1947) and *The Emergence of Lincoln* (2 vols., 1950). K. M. Stampp, *The Peculiar Institution* (1956) is excellent. See also J. H. Franklin, *From Slavery to Freedom: A History of American Negroes* (1947), and Stanley Elkins, *Slavery: A Problem in American Institutional and Intellectual Life* (1959). Also see U. B. Phillips, *American Negro Slavery* (1918) and *Life and Labor in the Old South* (1929). W. D. Postell,

The Health of Slaves on Southern Plantations (1951) is useful. Frederic Bancroft, *Slave-Trading in the Old South* (1931) is authoritative. A. H. Conrad and J. R. Meyer examine "The Economics of Slavery in the Ante Bellum South," *The Journal of Political Economy,* LXVI (Apr., 1958), 95–130. See also W. S. Jenkins, *Proslavery Thought in the Old South* (1935). W. E. Dodd, *The Cotton Kingdom* (1921) is a vigorous criticism of the South and slavery. For the free Negro, see L. P. Jackson, *Free Negro Labor and Property Holding in Virginia* (1942) and J. H. Franklin, *The Free Negro in North Carolina, 1790–1860* (1943). In 1953, A. M. Schlesinger edited F. L. Olmsted, *The Cotton Kingdom* (1861), which presents an observant traveler's description of the South in the 1850's. R. C. Wade, *Slavery in the Cities* (1964) is interesting and instructive.

Students of antebellum southern culture should consult W. J. Cash, *The Mind of the South* (1941), a brilliant study; Clement Eaton, *Freedom of Thought in the Old South* (1940); and T. C. Johnson, Jr., *Scientific Interests in the Old South* (1936). Ina W. Van Oppen, *The South, a Documentary History* (1958) is useful, as is Jay B. Hubbell, *The South in American Literature, 1607–1900* (1954).

The South's apartness is well brought out in Avery Craven, *The Growth of Southern Nationalism, 1848–1861* (1953); C. S. Sydnor, *The Development of Southern Sectionalism, 1819–1848* (1948); and J. T. Carpenter, *The South as a Conscious Minority* (1930). See also D. R. Fox, "Cultural Nationalism in the Old South," in *Ideas in Motion* (1935); R. G. Osterweis, *Romanticism and Nationalism in the Old South* (1949); and J. H. Franklin, *The Militant South, 1800–1861* (1956).

24 ⸴ The Far West

O
UR NARRATIVE up to this point has been chiefly concerned with the historical development of the eastern and central part of the United States, but west of Texas and of the noble domain acquired from France in 1803 lay a great territorial expanse stretching to the Pacific Ocean. Though we have shown how exploration and settlement extended across the Father of Waters into Missouri, Iowa, Wisconsin, Minnesota, and other parts of the Louisiana Purchase, we have paid little attention to expansionist movements west of that area, save for noting the exploratory expeditions sent into the Far West by President Jefferson and the immigration of thousands of Americans into Texas during the 1820s and 1830s. If we are to understand the great westward thrust of the American people during the 1840s and 1850s, we must know something of the general topography of the far western region, of the Indian tribes that first inhabited it, and of the reasons why the people of the United States were not content until they stood in proud possession on the shores of the Pacific.

The Land and the Native Inhabitants

Let us look first at the geographical aspects of the Far West and at the character of its native inhabitants. West of Missouri lies a vast plateau known as the Great Plains, a grasslands area 300 to 400 miles in breadth stretching westward from the Central Lowlands to an elevation of some 5,000 feet and extending northward up to and beyond the Platte River. In the middle of the nineteenth century, this relatively level area, unbroken

510

by high hills or mountains, was treeless and semiarid. It was the land of the coyote, the prairie dog and jack rabbit, the antelope, and, above all, the buffalo. It was also the home of many Indian tribes, from the Blackfeet, Crows and Gros-Ventres in the North to the Cheyenne, Arapahoe, Comanche and others in the more central and southern parts; on the eastern edges were to be found the Mandans and Pawnees, while the Nez Percé, Utes, and others lived to the westward in the foothills and valleys of the Rocky Mountains. The Indians of the Great Plains were chiefly nomadic. Grouped in bands, loosely organized as tribes, they spoke seven different languages within which were a variety of dialects, and their chief means of subsistence were the millions of buffalo that, in vast herds, roamed the plains.

West of the Great Plains rose the giant masses of the Rocky Mountain chain, stretching from Alaska to the central part of New Mexico. In the northern part, below the forty-ninth parallel, the mountain ranges stretching north and south enclosed a level, forest-covered lowland known as the Rocky Mountain Trench. There farming of a sort could be carried on by adventurous settlers raising food for miners and prospectors. South of the Trench lay the Wyoming Basin, a 250-mile-wide upland of hills and sagebrush across which the pioneers found a relatively easy way as they strove to pass the first great barrier that stretched between the Louisiana Purchase and the Pacific coast. Below the Wyoming Basin stretched the Southern Rockies, a wild and forbidding mass of snow-clad peaks, tumbling streams, and high valleys, which constituted a formidable barrier to westward travel, for passes were few and difficult.

Snow fell heavily throughout the Rockies during the long winter seasons, piling up huge drifts and making travel impossible. Though grizzly bears and mountain lions made the mountain trails perilous, beaver abounded in the streams, black bear pelts also commanded good prices in the fur markets of the East, and there was gold in the Colorado mountains and other mineral deposits further north. The Rockies early lured prospectors, trappers, and traders.

West of the Rockies lay the Intermontane Province. From the Columbia Plateau in the north to the Great Basin (which included Nevada and parts of what are now Utah and southern California) and the Colorado River Plateau in the south, this entire region was arid, rough and inhospitable. Through the upper and central portions ran rivers—the Snake, the Humboldt and the Carson—along whose banks trudged the pioneers en route to California and Oregon.

Numerous Indian tribes lived in the Intermontane Province—the Snakes,

Bannocks, and Utes in the northern and central parts, and the Hopi, Zuni, Pima and other pueblo and village dwellers in the more southern regions, as well as the Navahoes and Apaches of western Texas and eastern New Mexico. Some of these tribes—the Pueblos, for example—had rudiments

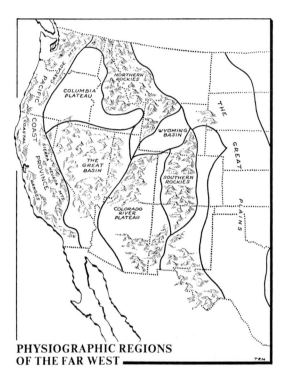

PHYSIOGRAPHIC REGIONS OF THE FAR WEST

of culture and were peaceful, but the Apaches, fierce and warlike, were a menace to red men and white alike. All lived hard, sedentary lives, and those in arid regions where grain was scanty were often on the brink of starvation.

Beyond the Intermontane region lay the Pacific Coast Province, with its Cascade Mountains in the north and below them the Sierra Nevadas stretching southward. West of the Cascades and Sierras still another range of coastal mountains extended along the shores of the Pacific, the Klamath Range of northern California connecting the Sierras with the coastal chain. Since these various mountain ranges had heavy rainfall, among them were four rich valleys that beckoned to prospective settlers—the Puget Sound Trough and the Willamette Valley to the north, the Sacramento and San Joaquin Valleys in California. About 150,000 Indians divided into numerous tribes (Hupas, Shastas, Yuroks and others)—some warlike, others peaceful; some utterly primitive and miserable, others in various low stages of civilization—were scattered through the Pacific Coast Province.

The Rise and Decline of Spanish Power
in the Far West

Long before the American frontiersmen pushed into the Far West other white men had appeared in that region. Lured by the hope of gold and silver, Spanish adventurers had pushed north from Mexico City, followed by miners, ranchers, and Catholic missionaries. By the close of the sixteenth century, the Spaniards had set up an outpost across the Rio Grande. They established Santa Fe as the capital of Mexico Province in 1609–1610, and by 1630 some 250 Spanish pioneers were struggling to maintain this remote bastion of the far-flung Spanish empire.

Gradually the Spaniards pushed still further north and west. During the eighteenth century, Jesuit and Franciscan missionaries moved into Texas and Arizona. French soldiers and traders from Louisiana sporadically threatened the Spanish control in Texas, and competed with the Spaniards for the fur trade along the Missouri River, but the French thrust did not generate enough power to displace the meagre number of Spaniards scattered over that vast territory hundreds of thousands of square miles in extent.

Still another threat to Spanish supremacy in the Mexican area appeared in the eighteenth century. After the discovery of Alaska by Vitus Bering in 1741, Russian fur traders pushed down the Pacific coast as far as Oregon, and British trading interest in this region also came to life. The ambitious José de Gálvez, *visitador-general* of New Spain, anxious to add to his glory by conquering a new province, used these movements by Spain's traditional enemy to urge the extension of the Spanish hold along the Pacific coast. In 1767, on the basis of a rather ambiguous approval from the court at Madrid and the viceroy of New Spain, he sent an expedition into California, which based at San Diego and established a post at Monterey Bay. In 1775, the Spaniards established an outpost on San Francisco Bay, and in 1781 still another at Los Angeles. The vast Spanish empire in the Southwest had now reached its limits, but in all its northern parts there were only a few weak and scattered settlements. It remained to be seen whether Spanish power could hold this great territory against all comers.

From 1780 through the next few decades, the Spanish empire in North America was subjected to increasing pressure. We have already seen how it fared in the central and eastern part of the continent, how it gained Louisiana in 1763 only to lose it forty years later, and how pressure by the frontiersmen and the government of the United States forced it out of the Floridas. In the west also, the omens were not auspicious for the continuance of Spanish control. By 1802, two British companies, the Hudson's Bay Company and the Northwest Company, stole the Indian trade from the Spaniards along the Missouri River. The expeditions headed by Lewis and Clark and by Zebulon Pike during Jefferson's Administrations were harbingers of American interest in the regions of the Far West, though they counted for nothing in establishing Indian trade relations with the young republic to the east. After the War of 1812 the United States government made a more serious move, by establishing military posts at Fort Snelling, where the Minnesota River joins the Mississippi, at Fort Atkinson, now Council Bluffs, Iowa, and at Fort Smith on the Arkansas River; these military expeditions accomplished little in the way of accurate surveys in the Great Plains area. but they were indicative of governmental interest in the Great Plains area. The forts were useful to the American fur traders who now swarmed into the region west of the Mississippi, financed and directed by a succession of companies, among them John Jacob Astor's American Fur Company. American traders were now beginning a move that was to carry them into all parts of the Far West.

The Fur Traders and Their Exploits

John Jacob Astor (1763–1848) played a major part in opening the Far West to American penetration. Born in Waldorf, Germany, he came to America by way of England in 1784, his only capital being seven flutes that he brought to sell in the United States. Establishing himself in New York, he quickly branched out from dealing in musical instruments into the fur trade. Success was at first difficult but then came with a rush. "My first ten thousand was the hardest," he said in later years, "After that the rest was easy." By 1806, he was reputed to be worth £200,000.

During Jefferson's Administrations, Astor organized the American Fur Company and moved into the far western trade. He planned a fur-trading monopoly that would reach to the Pacific. "It was his purpose," says his biographer, Kenneth W. Porter, "to concentrate the western fur trade in the hands of only such American citizens as had been born in Waldorf, Germany, in 1763, and had arrived in the United States from London in the spring of 1784. He had grave doubts whether more than one merchant could be found who would conform to these rather rigid qualifications."

In 1811, Astor established a short-lived trading post, Astoria, at the mouth of the Columbia River, but was forced to dispose of it during the War of 1812. Far more important were the activities of his American Fur Company in establishing a chain of trading posts from St. Louis up the

Missouri River, following the route of Lewis and Clark to the Pacific. His company made money, but his business ethics were questionable. He undercut and crushed out of existence individual traders and competing firms; like his rivals, he flooded the Indian country with intoxicants and was a major factor in demoralizing the Indian tribes, all of whom were peculiarly susceptible to the ravages of alcohol. From 1820 to 1834, when Astor retired to devote himself to real estate operations in New York City, the American Fur Company averaged in net profits $100,000 a year—gains made in part by debauching the Indians and by merciless exploitation of the traders and boatmen who gathered the furs in the Indian country. On the other hand, Astor's agents, like those of his rivals, performed a signal service for the frontiersmen who followed after them, for it was the fur traders who first discovered the passes through the mountains, who plotted the river courses, and who weakened the power and independence of the Indian tribes.

Subsequent to Astor's withdrawal from the fur trade on the Pacific coast, the trade in the Far Northwest passed almost completely into the hands of the Hudson's Bay Company. It was then that American traders, leaving that field temporarily in the hands of their British rivals, turned their attention to the central Rocky Mountain country, where the American Fur Company, the Rocky Mountain Fur Company, and others reaped a rich harvest in beaver skins. During this time, the "rendezvous system" of fur trading, developed by William Henry Ashley of the Rocky Mountain Company, produced a new type of frontiersmen, known as the "Mountain Men." Under this system of trading, the company sent out its own trappers each fall into the mountains, to make their catches and then in the spring to rendezvous by the hundreds at a given meeting place. These Mountain Men were bold and carefree individuals, lovers of solitude and of danger, ready to spend their winter's earnings in a few days of debauch in the spring. But they played a real part in opening up the far western frontier. Equipped only with a rifle, a few provisions, and a pack pony, they penetrated to all parts of the Rockies and, as Professor Billington has said, "blazed the trails that made possible the settlement of the Far West."

British and American trappers and traders in their search for gain on the west coast and in the central Rockies began encroaching upon the limits of the territories claimed by Spain. According to the Adams-Onis treaty of 1819, these extended north to the forty-second parallel and included California, the Great Basin, and the Colorado Plateau. This area, after Mexico achieved its independence in the early 1820s, passed into the possession of the Mexican Republic. Another group of adventurous

JIM BRIDGER, AS PORTRAYED BY FREDERIC REMINGTON

Bridger was a famous scout and frontier trader, supposedly the first man to visit Great Salt Lake (1824). He married three times during the course of his life, each bride being from a different Indian tribe. Completely illiterate, he was nevertheless very intelligent and had a commanding personality.

516

Americans pushed into what became in 1822 the Mexican territories in the Southwest. Fur traders moved up the Arkansas and Cimarron Rivers into forbidden territory, and others established commercial contacts between the cities of the Mississippi Valley and Santa Fe. The Americans brought cutlery, textiles and other goods to Santa Fe, exchanging them for furs and silver; by the 1830s, a regular trade had developed. The traveling merchants, well-provided with arms, made the 900-mile trip from Independence, Missouri, in heavy Conestoga wagons, each carrying two tons of goods and pulled by ten or twelve oxen. The citizens of Santa Fe welcomed their appearance, for the Americans brought supplies that otherwise would have had to come from Mexico City, 1,500 miles away.

The Santa Fe Trail occupies a place of some significance in the history of American expansion. The traders brought into the American economy thousands of dollars of useful specie. They perfected the wagon train technique of holding off Indian attacks, by forming a hollow square of wagons defended by rifle fire that the red men found impregnable, a technique that was used successfully by immigrants to the Far West. And, most important of all, they brought back word of the weak hold of Mexico on the Southwest, welcome news to the frontiersmen whose eyes always turned toward the setting sun.

Frontiersmen Move into California

California, in which more and more Americans became interested as the early decades of the nineteenth century wore on, played only a minor role in the revolution which brought independence to Mexico in 1822. When the news arrived there that the Mexican patriots under Iturbide had thrown off the Spanish yoke, the Californians willingly took allegiance to the new regime at Mexico City. In 1824, California ratified the Mexican Constitution and in so doing became a part of the Mexican federal republic.

During the next twenty years, California became restive under Mexican control. The Mexican governors were generally unpopular, and the weak hold exerted from Mexico City encouraged a growing interest on the part of both Anglo-American and Spanish Californians in the principles of constitutional and representative government. The dominant position of the ranching element in California was evidenced when, in the middle of the 1830s, the missions were secularized and some eight million acres of mission land were transferred into the hands of about 800 large ranch owners.

While the native Californians were moving toward the conviction that independence from Spain should be followed by at least some measure of independence from Mexico, American contacts with the region increased in number and in significance. Yankee ship captains regularly visited the coast, and the earlier trade in furs was replaced by a growing commerce in hides and tallow that was lucrative from the traders' point of view and brought needed foreign goods into the province. This trade development also served as a means of acquainting the citizens of the United States with the resources of California and the opportunities for settlement that existed in its fertile valleys. More and more Americans became interested in this land of the *vaquero,* where cattle and horses were so numerous that the latter had to be hunted down and shot to save pasture for the former, a country where grizzly bears were captured with lassoes, and where the inhabitants amused themselves with rodeos and with staged combats between bulls and bears.

American trade with California developed overland as well as by sea. In 1826, Jedediah Strong Smith, fur trader and explorer par excellence, took the first American overland expedition into the province, leading an eighteen-man party from Great Salt Lake across desert trails and mountain paths to San Gabriel on the California coast. His attempt then and in the two following years to establish trading contacts was frustrated by the California authorities, but he discovered two overland routes to that area, opened a trail from California to Oregon, and helped to stimulate American interest in the Far West.

Second only to Smith was Dr. James Ohio Pattie, trader, trapper, and explorer. Pattie discovered a route from Santa Fe to eastern California via the Gila Valley and also earned fame in California and in the United States by vaccinating 22,000 Californians when in 1828 a smallpox epidemic struck the province.

Other American traders followed the trails blazed by Smith and Pattie, exchanging blankets, woolen goods and silver for silks imported from China and for horses and mules, all of which commanded good prices in the United States. A considerable number of these traders established residence in California, among them Johann August Sutter, an Americanized Swiss who settled on the American Fork of the Sacramento River. There he ranched, traded, trapped, set up a mill, a tannery, and a distillery, and built a fort. This "hospitable, visionary, improvident land baron of the Sacramento" did everything possible to aid and encourage American immigrants, and the strength and location of his fort made it impossible for the weak Mexican authorities to exclude American migrants to the province. It was in Sutter's mill race that gold was discovered in 1848.

Americans gradually increased their influence in California, taking part in a revolution in 1836 which replaced a Mexican appointee, Nicolás Gutiérrez, with a native Californian, Juan Bautista Alvarado, as governor of the province. By 1840, there were some 380 American settlers in California, men who had learned Spanish, married California wives, and established almost complete control over the trade of the province.

During the early 1840s, American migration to California also increased, stimulated by such accounts of the region as Pattie's *Personal Narrative* and especially by Richard Henry Dana's *Two Years Before the Mast*, which appeared in the first year of that decade. Most of the new settlers came by the overland routes. In 1841, some sixty-nine men, women and children from the Mississippi Valley left a rendezvous in eastern Kansas for the West. At the beginning of the journey they followed the trail marked out by earlier migrants to the Far Northwest, a rough path across the Rockies into southern Idaho. There the party split, half of them going on to Oregon by way of a route already marked out by earlier pioneers, while the remainder crossed the desert to Great Salt Lake and then moved directly westward. Abandoning their wagons and much baggage, they struggled over the alkaline flats and across the Sierras (where winter mercifully set in late) and, with their provisions exhausted, arrived in the San Joaquin Valley at the end of October. Meanwhile another party of twenty-five came by way of the Santa Fe Trail and then by way of the Old Spanish Trail through southern Utah and Nevada, across the Mojave Desert and through Cajón Pass to Los Angeles. A handful of Oregon pioneers also moved down into California that same year.

No more California settlers came in 1842; indeed, some ten of the migrants of 1841 returned to the Mississippi Valley. But favorable publicity about the West continued, especially that resulting from an expedition to the Rockies made by explorer John Charles Frémont, a dashing adventurer whose exploits captured the public imagination. Glowing tales of life in the Sacramento and San Joaquin Valleys, together with hard times in the Middle West, brought larger migrations in 1843 and 1844 than had come earlier, and in 1845 no less than 250 pioneers braved the hardships of the trail to California.

The endurance of all the overland immigrants to California was tested by the perils of desert and mountain travel and the menace of Indian raids. The travelers also lacked experience in journeying hundreds of miles under necessarily strict discipline, and this sometimes bred disaster. Not infrequently bands would arrive at their destination bereft of members who had been killed by man or beast, or had died of exposure along the way. The

CROSSING THE SIERRA NEVADA

Pioneers made their way over hazardous roads through the mountains. Difficult enough in good weather, the perils of the journey were much greater in the winter season, as the fate of the Donner party bore witness.

worst experience befell the party of George and Jacob Donner, which started out from Independence, Missouri, in the spring of 1846. Bad information about the trail from Fort Bridger, Indian depredations, the mounting exhaustion of men and animals and the collapse of the morale of the group made the trip across the desert and into the mountains a succession of nightmarish tragedies, as individual acts of heroism relieved but could not conquer a situation that became more desperate each day. An early winter closed upon the party, and they were snowbound in the Sierra Nevadas, strung out in miserable encampments along the trail near what is now known as Donner Lake; of the seventy-nine men, women, and children who were snowed in, only forty-five survived, and some of these had been reduced to eating the flesh of their dead comrades.

By the close of 1846, despite the tragedy and privation of the trails, there were hundreds of seasoned American pioneers in California. Bold and self-reliant, they were increasingly irked by the inefficiency of the local authorities. Had the Mexican War not come in 1846, it is altogether likely that California would have become part of the United States by the same process that had earlier brought the Floridas and Texas into the Union.

The Great Basin Pioneers

While American traders, trappers, and settlers were pushing into California during the 1830s and 1840s, larger bands of pioneers moved into the newly established Republic of Texas, into the Great Basin between the Rockies and the Sierras, and into the Far Northwest. The rich Texan lands attracted the largest numbers of these migrants. In 1836 there were not more than 30,000 Anglo-Americans in the Lone Star State. Thereafter its population steadily increased, despite friction with Mexico, as a flood of Americans, Germans, and other nationalities pushed across its borders. In 1847, Texas harbored 100,000 whites and 35,000 slaves; three years later, its total population was over 200,000; and this number tripled during the next ten years.

The Great Basin frontier also became the Mecca of thousands of immigrants, the great majority of whom settled its inhospitable desert and alkaline soils primarily because of a desire for religious freedom. We have already examined the origins of Mormonism (Chapter 21) and shown how the members of the Church of Jesus Christ of Latter-Day Saints, driven from place to place because of their arrogance and their strange religious opinions, had settled during the early 1840s in Nauvoo, Illinois. There their leader and prophet, Joseph Smith, with the aid of Whig and Democratic politicians competing for Mormon votes, had established what amounted to a private commonwealth within the state. For a time they prospered, and Smith, emboldened by his success, announced his candidacy for President of the United States in 1844 on a platform containing an abolitionist plank and calling for the annexation of Canada and Mexico.

But, despite the high-flown aspirations of its leader, the beginning of the end was already in sight for the Nauvoo settlement: already Smith had issued a decree sanctioning polygamy, and already, for this and a variety of other reasons, powerful members of the Mormon community had begun to turn against him. Both of the major political parties in Illinois now abandoned him, and he and his brother Hyrum were thrown into prison at Carthage, Illinois, where, on June 27, 1844, a mob stormed the jail and killed both of them. It was impossible for the Saints to remain longer in Illinois.

Before his death Smith had been examining the possibility of a mass movement to Oregon or to Texas. Brigham Young, Smith's successor as head of the Mormon church, thought for a time of Oregon and California as places of refuge. He knew little about those regions, but did know that he wanted to find some place beyond the Rockies where the Mormons would be outside the reach of any existing government, either state or national. Influenced by Frémont's account of the Salt Lake district, Young finally decided on the Great Basin, since it was both remote and suitable for his purpose. With his remarkable capacity for organization, the move was carefully planned. In February, 1846, the exodus from Illinois started and it continued throughout that year. The Mormons gathered at Council Bluffs, Iowa, spent the winter there, and then in the spring of 1847, the great trek began. Slowly they moved across the Great Plains to Fort Laramie, then to Fort Bridger, where Bridger himself urged them to go to Oregon. Their leader's mind was made up, however, and they turned south over the mountains, struggling on until they reached Emigration Canyon and, in the shadow of the towering Wasatch Range, the broad plain south and east of Great Salt Lake.

By the autumn of 1847, some 4,000 Mormons had gathered in their Wilderness Zion. The land was dry and barren, there was much suffering during the first winter, but there was no thought of turning back. Under Young's remarkable guidance a quasi-communistic social order was established. The Mormon hierarchy allotted land for cultivation with the privilege of sale or exchange, but with the understanding that failure to cultivate would terminate possession. An elaborate irrigation system was developed, with rigid control over the use of water, and with similar controls over timber supplies and mill sites. Zealous missionary work brought in floods of converts, and gentiles also appeared, attracted by the growing prosperity of the region, until by the close of 1848 there were at least 8,500 settlers in the colony. In 1850, the provisional state of Deseret, with a population of over 11,000 people, became a territorial government under federal auspices, with Brigham Young as governor. Ten years later there were 40,273 inhabitants of what eventually became the state of Utah.

The Oregon Fever

If the establishment of the Great Basin frontier was primarily the result of religious discontent, that of Oregon was fostered by the same urge for trade and for land that sent the pioneers into Texas and California. Oregon Territory had been under joint occupation by Great Britain and the United

States since the treaty of 1818. This joint occupancy had been extended in 1827, with the understanding that either party might terminate it by giving a year's notice. Both countries had claims to the region. British explorers had paved the way for the Hudson's Bay Company, which established a fur-trading post on the Columbia River and encouraged over 1,000 British citizens to settle on the rich lands of the Puget Sound Valley. The American claim also originated with explorers, particularly with the Lewis and Clark expedition. Moreover, at first the Americans had controlled the fur trade along the Oregon coast, though by 1830 the Hudson's Bay Company dominated what was left of that enterprise. The British settlements in the Oregon country constituted a strong hold on the region.

American expansionists, however, were not discouraged by the achievements of the British. Men such as Dr. John Floyd, a Congressman from Virginia, and New Englanders with an interest in the Pacific trade began extolling the beauty and resources of the Far Northwest, arousing the interest of pioneering spirits. In 1828, Hall Jackson Kelley of Charlestown, Massachusetts, organized an emigration society for the purpose of encouraging settlement in Oregon. Since Kelley had no organizational ability, his society languished, but under his influence Nathaniel J. Wyeth, a well-

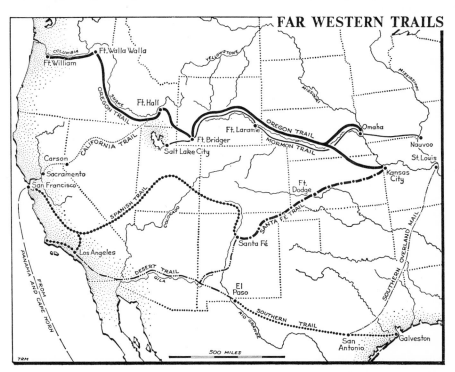

FAR WESTERN TRAILS

to-do businessman of Cambridge, established a company to trade in the Far Northwest. He sent a ship loaded with goods from Boston to the Columbia River, while at the same time he and a party of some twenty men started overland for the same destination. Guided by a mountain man, Milton G. Sublette, they reached the shores of the Pacific, only to learn that the ship had been lost at sea, and Wyeth and his party then retraced their steps across the continent. They were the first Americans to take the route that later came to be known as the Oregon Trail. A second Wyeth expedition in 1834 again reached the Columbia, but efforts to establish trading operations there were thwarted by the Hudson's Bay Company.

The activities of men like Floyd and Kelley and Wyeth aroused American interest in the Oregon country. Tales of the heathen Indians of the Far Northwest stimulated the interest of religious organizations, especially the Methodist church. In 1834, the Reverend Jason Lee and a small band of followers made the overland trip to Oregon and established missionary settlements in the fertile Willamette Valley. On his return to the East, Lee's tales of life along the Willamette started a pioneer movement, and settlers began making the long and toilsome journey across the northern Rockies and Sierras. The American Board of Commissioners for Foreign Missions now sent out more missionaries, among them a young enthusiast named Marcus Whitman.

The legend that Marcus Whitman "saved Oregon" is an exaggeration, but his exploits did help to arouse interest in emigration to that country. This vigorous, resourceful and optimistic man was born in Rushville, New York, in the year 1802. A practitioner of medicine, he offered his services to the American Board in 1834. During the next twenty-four months he made two trips to the West, on the second of which his wife and the wife of one of his associates were the first women to make the rough journey across the Great Divide. Whitman was also the first man to take a cart (legend glorified it into a covered wagon) across the high country between Fort Hall and Fort Boise. The publicity attendant upon these achievements, as well as statements made in Boston and Washington in 1843 when he came back east on behalf of the missionary work in Oregon, undoubtedly stimulated the movement of pioneers into the Oregon country.

The activities of Protestant missionaries in the West were paralleled, and in the matter of conversions far outdone, by the Catholic church, for the Indians were deeply impressed by the simple but vivid pageantry used by the Catholic missionaries. Their efforts—especially those of a Canadian, Father Blanchet, and the zealous American Jesuit, Father Pierre De Smet, who was given the title "Blackrobe" by the Indians—not only made many converts but also heightened the excitement about Oregon that existed in New England and the Middle West.

During the later 1830s and early 1840s, still other factors contributed to the mounting public interest in Oregon. In 1836, W. A. Slacum, a representative of President Jackson, made a survey of the Far Northwest and reported enthusiastically about grazing and farming possibilities in the Willamette Valley. Still more publicity attended a report by Lieutenant Charles Wilkes, who visited the Far Northwest in 1841. In the excited imaginations of Americans back home, Oregon took on the appearance of a Land of Promise like that which had beckoned the ancient Israelites.

When, in the year 1842, the Reverend Elijah White led a band of 120 pioneers over the mountains to Oregon, it was the van of a real migratory movement. The continuation of the depression of 1837 had provoked increasing discontent among the farmers of the Mississippi Valley, which, together with the spread of glowing reports about soil fertility and trading opportunities in the Columbia River region, had by now produced a regular "Oregon fever." In 1843, about 1,000 men, women, and children gathered at Independence, Missouri, for the journey along the Oregon Trail. They made their way to Fort Laramie and then to South Pass in the Rockies, where they crossed the continental divide. Fort Hall on the Snake River came next, and then they negotiated the rough passage to Fort Boise. Next came the arduous trip through the Blue Mountains, and then the wagon train moved down along the Umatilla River to the Columbia and on to Fort Vancouver. They had started from Independence on May 22, and they reached Fort Vancouver late in the month of November, after a journey of 2,020 miles. The expedition was a great success, and word of its achievement was quickly spread back home, the more so because Marcus Whitman had helped to guide this migration.

More pioneers came in 1844, and by the close of 1845 there were some 6,000 American settlers in Oregon, the great majority of them being located in the Willamette River Valley. Since, as early as 1843, the settlers had organized a provisional government for "Oregon Territory," to be operative until the United States extended its jurisdiction over them, all that remained was for the government at Washington to act.

By 1846, the expansive force of the American population was making itself felt throughout the Far West. Stimulated by hard times, lured by the prospect of adventure, trade, and fertile land, in some cases because of religious persecution and religious zeal, thousands of Americans had left their homes in the East and Middle West to seek their fortunes and a better life in the Southwest and beyond the Rockies and the Sierras. They were peopling Texas, the Great Basin, California, and Oregon Territory, and they were bringing ever closer the day when the government at Washington would have to decide whether the United States should remain within its existing limits or should attempt to extend those limits as far as the Pacific Ocean.

COURTESY OF THE LIBRARY OF CONGRESS

SHIPS OF THE PLAIN

The favorite vehicle of the frontiersmen was the Conestoga wagon, which first appeared about 1760. The settlers usually traveled in groups of ten or fifteen wagons, for protection against marauding bands of Indians.

The Credo of Expansionism

The excitement occasioned by reports of the resources of the Far West and the abundant opportunities for settlement there, coupled with demands that emanated from Texas and Oregon for incorporation into the republic, helped to create in the United States of the early 1840s a tide of expansionist sentiment. Thoreau felt it when he said that when he left his house for a walk he was always impelled to go westward. "The future lies that way to me. . . . I must walk toward Oregon and not toward Europe." Walt Whitman, in 1846, foresaw the United States annexing California and a large part of Mexico itself. The residents of Brook Farm, while deploring the American government's attitude toward Mexico, felt that expansion to the Pacific was the design of a Higher Power. A party of American traders on the road from Santa Fe to Independence, Missouri, saw, or thought they saw, the image of an eagle with its wings spread across the setting sun, and immediately to them it became the symbol of America spreading its protective pinions over the whole Southwest. Sam Houston believed that, if Texas was not made a part of the United States, it would become the nucleus of an empire stretching to the Pacific and up to 54° 40′, and including most of the southern slave states. There was talk in country stores and villages about Texas, and the Halls of Montezuma, and standing up to Johnny Bull. Both in and out of Congress arguments in favor of expansion grew and multiplied, providing a rationale for the movement; important among these was the thesis that augmenting American territory was a means of spreading democracy.

At the beginning of the nineteenth century, American thought had emphasized promoting the spread of democracy by example or, as Thomas Jefferson had suggested, by pioneer migrations that would carry the democratic ideal into the West and there set up sister republics. Thus the American way of life would expand in a manner that would not involve the creation of a mighty imperial domain, difficult to govern under republican principles and therefore dangerous to the liberties of the states and of individuals. But by the 1840s, fears of the evil influence of territorial expansion on the democratic way of life had been dispelled. Both the acquisition of Louisiana and the test of practical experience showed that American democracy continued to flourish when its control extended over a large continental area. The belief was now prevalent that expansion could be continued with perfect safety, so far as democratic principles and the rights of states and individuals were concerned.

Relieved of fear as to the danger attendant upon the extension of sovereignty, Americans began busily defending such a movement. As early as 1838, a writer in the *Democratic Review* prophesied that "the boundless future will be the era of American greatness." To many citizens of the United States in the 1840s, territorial expansion had become a natural destiny that would not only spread the nation's dominion over the North American continent, but would also advance everywhere the cause of democracy and freedom. This was all the more logical because of a growing belief that European intrigues and ambitions threatened fundamental American interests in the New World. Great Britain and France especially had designs that must be thwarted, as Jackson put it in 1843, by "extending the area of freedom"; it did not matter to Old Hickory and the other expansionists of the period that Europe's tendency to meddle in North American affairs was caused by anxiety over the obvious growth of the economic and political power and ambition of the United States.

Once it became clear that territorial expansion was not a menace but, indeed, a shield and bulwark for democracy and freedom, arguments multiplied in its justification. Pride in America and belief in its mission to spread democracy went hand in hand with contempt for Indians and Mexicans, and with the insatiable land hunger of the frontiersmen. National security meant the acquisition of such "natural frontiers" as the Rio Grande and the Pacific Ocean. It was argued that expansion was an inescapable aspect of national growth and vigor; that it was, indeed, God-directed, in the sense that the Almighty obviously intended the land and other resources of North America to be used to the best possible advantage. Expansion, its proponents contended, was only a logical development of the earlier movement that had added Louisiana and the Floridas to the United States; a further westward push, and one to the north and south as well, was natural and necessary, especially in view of the inevitable growth of the American population and its future need of elbow room. Since one enthusiast predicted that the United States would have a population of some 300 million by 1945, it is small wonder that another like-minded individual foresaw a future in which the Stars and Stripes would float "from Cape Horn to the Aurora Borealis."

To sum it all up, expansion was America's "Manifest Destiny," a term first used in 1845 by John L. O'Sullivan in an editorial on Texas in the *Democratic Review,* and one that very much caught the popular fancy. In the next two chapters, we shall see how this furor for the extension of American control in the western hemisphere helped to shape the foreign policy of the United States.

Suggested Reading

For general treatments of expansion into the Far West see, R. A. Billington, *Westward Expansion* (1949); R. E. Riegel, *America Moves West* (1956); and F. L. Paxson, *History of the American Frontier* (1924).

Physiographic features are studied in detail in N. M. Fenneman, *Physiography of*

Western United States (1931). See also A. L. Kroeber, *Cultural and Natural Areas of Native North America* (1939).

The literature on the Indians of this area is voluminous. Standard works are Clark Wissler, *The American Indian* (1938) and *North American Indians of the Plains* (1920). Accounts of the tribes in other localities are to be found in P. E. Goddard, *Indians of the Southwest* (1927) and *Indians of the Northwest Coast* (1924); A. L. Kroeber, *Handbook of the Indians of California* (1925); C. Kluckhohn and D. C. Leighton, *The Navaho* (1946); R. N. Richardson, *The Comanche, Barrier to South Plains Settlement* (1933); and G. E. Hyde, *Red Cloud's Folk: A History of the Oglala Sioux Indians* (1937).

For the rise and decline of Spanish power in the American West, see H. E. Bolton, *The Spanish Borderlands* (1921), *Texas in the Middle Eighteenth Century* (1915), *Outpost of Empire* (1931), and *Rim of Christendom* (1936). Other valuable accounts are R. N. Richardson and C. C. Rister, *The Greater Southwest* (1934); H. I. Priestley, *The Coming of the White Man* (1930); J. B. Brebner, *The Explorers of North America* (1933); G. P. Hammond, *Don Juan Oñate and the Founding of New Mexico* (1926); R. H. Richardson, *Texas, the Lone Star State* (1943); and G. J. Garraghan, *Chapters in Frontier History* (1934).

For the movement of American frontiersmen into California, see H. H. Bancroft, *History of California* (7 vols., 1884–1890); J. W. Caughey, *California* (1940); R. G. Cleland, *A History of California: the American Period* (1922); and K. Coman, *Economic Beginnings of the Far West* (2 vols., 1912). M. S. Sullivan, *The Life of Jedidiah Smith* (1937) is an interesting biography of this important figure.

On the Far Western fur trade, see H. M. Chittenden, *The American Fur Trade of the Far West* (3 vols., 1935); B. De Voto, *Across the Wide Missouri* (1947); K. W. Porter, *John Jacob Astor, Business Man* (2 vols., 1931); E. E. Rich, *Hudson's Bay Company, 1670–1870* (3 vols., 1961); and D. Mackay, *The Honourable Company* (1936). For the biography of a Mountain Man, see S. Vestal, *Kit Carson: the Happy Warrior of the Old West* (1928).

The Santa Fe Trail is well described in R. L. Duffus, *The Santa Fe Trail* (1930) and S. Vestal, *The Old Santa Fe Trail* (1939). See also G. Foreman, *Pioneer Days in the Old Southwest* (1926). The standard work on Texas colonization is E. C. Barker, *Life of Stephen F. Austin* (1925). The Donner tragedy is described in detail in B. De Voto, *The Year of Decision, 1846* (1943).

The frontier movement into the Great Basin is best studied in L. H. Creer, *Founding of an Empire* (1947); M. R. Werner, *Brigham Young* (1925); M. R. Hunter, *Brigham Young the Colonizer* (1943); A. I. Neff, *History of Utah, 1847–1869* (1940); and N. Anderson, *Desert Saints: the Mormon Frontier in Utah* (1942).

For the movement into Oregon, see J. Schafer, *History of the Pacific Northwest* (1918) and O. O. Winther, *The Great Northwest* (1947) and *The Old Oregon Country* (1951). See also C. J. Brosnan, *Jason Lee, Prophet of the New Oregon* (1932); W. J. Ghent, *The Road to Oregon* (1929); Jay Monaghan, *The Overland Trail* (1947); and J. C. Bell, *Opening a Highway to the Pacific, 1838–1846* (1921).

On the growth of a spirit of expansionism, see A. K. Weinberg, *Manifest Destiny* (reprint, 1958); N. H. Graebner, *Empire on the Pacific* (1955); and Bernard De Voto, *The Year of Decision, 1846*.

EXPANSION

[1840-1860]

GENERAL SCOTT LANDING AT VERA CRUZ

This picture was painted on the spot by Lieutenant Charles C. Barton, United States Navy. It marks the successful beginning of Scott's brilliant campaign against Mexico City.

AND DISCORD

25 ⟩ The Great Whig Experiment, 1841-1845

THE WHIGS were jubilant over their victory in the election of 1840, but more than jubilation was necessary for the tasks that lay ahead. For the first time, this conglomeration of nationalists and states' rights advocates, abolitionists and slaveholders, low- and high-tariff men had the responsibility for establishing a constructive legislative program.

Harrison's Brief Term Their adversaries pointed with scorn to the disparate nature of the party and predicted legislative chaos. And who, asked the Democrats, would be the leader in the attempt to bring order out of confusion? "Old Granny" Harrison, or Henry Clay?

There were at first no signs of discord and confusion among the Whigs. The President-elect visited Kentucky, where he publicly praised Clay and was royally entertained at the latter's Ashland home on the outskirts of Lexington. Harrison reluctantly agreed to Clay's demand for a special session of Congress and, with the Kentuckian's blessing, appointed Webster Secretary of State. Two Clayites, John J. Crittenden of Kentucky and Thomas Ewing of Ohio, were given Cabinet posts, the first as Attorney General and the other as Secretary of the Treasury.

Signs of rift appeared, however, when Harrison appointed Edward Curtis of New York, friend and ally of Seward and Weed, as Collector of the Port of New York, a patronage plum. Clay opposed this appointment so vigor-

DANIEL WEBSTER (1782–1852)

An able and eloquent exponent of nationalism, Webster had one of the best minds of his generation. He loved social life and was too fond of the bottle for his own good. This portrait by G. P. A. Healy brings out the forcefulness of Webster's personality.

COURTESY OF THE FRICK ART REFERENCE LIBRARY

ously that Harrison, already irked by the masterful manner of "Harry of the West," asked him to put further requests in writing and to stop calling at the White House. Clay bitterly resented this rebuff, and relations between the two men became very cool.

Harrison's general views on policy, insofar as he had any, were substantially those of Clay, and the two men might have been able to patch up their differences, once patronage disposal was out of the way. But the President's time was running short. Disturbed by the Kentuckian's domineering attitude, overwhelmed by floods of importunate Whig officeseekers, and harassed by complaints from the Democratic Conservatives that they were not being recognized in appointments, his health gave way. What looked like a common cold swiftly developed into pneumonia, and on April 4, 1841, Harrison passed away. Two days later, John Tyler, hastily summoned from Williamsburg, became President of the United States.

Omens of Discord

Tyler was fifty-one years old, the youngest President the nation had yet had. He was suave and genial, blessed with a naturally friendly disposition, and had a deserved reputation for honesty in thought and action. His political opponents declared that he lacked the power of decision, but his public career had been noticeable for its consistency. Always a rigid states' rights advocate and strict constructionist, he had abandoned the Jacksonians for the Whigs because he felt that Old Hickory had been false to those great principles. Though he was a personal friend of Clay, he had no sympathy for the latter's broad views of national policy.

Since Harrison was the first Chief Executive to die in office, a question promptly arose as to the status of his successor, but no sooner was Tyler installed in the White House than he showed his determination to be President in his own right. He asserted that he was not simply the Vice President executing the duties of the presidency, but was President in fact. He won his point, and in so doing established a lasting precedent.

Tyler might, indeed, be President, but Clay was sure that he himself was the leader of the Whig party. He saw his own position as being equivalent to that of a British Prime Minister, and, when Congress met in special session on May 31, 1841, "Harry of the West" and his friends controlled the most important committees in both House and Senate. The Kentuckian had prepared a legislative program, which he undertook without delay to put into law.

The program that Clay laid down was fundamentally that of his American System. He advocated the repeal of the Independent Treasury and the re-establishment of a national bank. Because of the need for additional revenue, he believed that the tariff should be raised, and he also argued in favor of a distribution of the proceeds of the public-land sales.

Though the states' rights Whigs were disturbed by Clay's proposals, they were powerless. The Kentuckian and his supporters repealed the Independent Treasury, and Tyler signed the bill. A select Senate committee on the currency was appointed, with Clay as its chairman, and the Senate passed a resolution sponsored by Clay directing Secretary of the Treasury Ewing to send down a plan for a national bank.

The Bank Issue—Clay vs. Tyler

Ewing's bill, which came to the Senate June 12, 1841, provided for a national bank, with powers of discount and deposit, and enabled the bank to establish branches, but only with the consent of the states. Tyler, influenced by Webster and other moderate Whigs, was reluctantly willing to accept this measure, and eastern businessmen favored it. But Clay would have none of the proposal, declaring that it would establish only a travesty of a bank; the Kentuckian was determined to establish his own leadership of the Whig party, even if he had to do so by driving Tyler to a veto.

Ewing's bill was referred to Clay's committee on the currency, and, on June 21, 1841, that committee reported out, not the Ewing plan, but a proposal by Clay himself that provided a bank of discount and deposit with unlimited branching power. A bitter fight ensued, with Conservative Democrats and states' rights Whigs joining the Democratic opposition. They forced an amendment providing that a state legislature could prohibit a branch of the bank within the borders of the state if it did so at the first session after the bill passed Congress. Even so, Clay's measure still gave Congress the power to establish a branch of the bank in a state where it had been prohibited if such a branch were deemed essential to the national welfare. In this form, Clay's bill went to the President, reaching his desk on August 7, 1841, and the Cabinet urged him to sign it.

Nine days later, on August 16, Tyler returned the bank bill to Congress with his veto. He specifically objected to the branching provision and to the power to discount notes. Tortured by indecision, his resolution had hardened under the influence of his Virginian states' rights friends. He felt, too, that he could count upon moderate Whig support, and might even be able to wrest the leadership of the party from Clay's hands. Visions of a presidential nomination in his own right danced before Tyler's eyes.

The Senate sustained the veto by a vote of twenty-five to twenty-four. The country now had neither an independent treasury system nor a national bank. But Whig opinion, always sensitive on the use of the veto power, began to crystallize in support of Clay, and a new bank bill was now framed, after congressional and Cabinet consultations—one which was supposed to have Tyler's approval. It would create a bank in the District of Columbia, which institution could establish branches without the consent of the states, though the branches would not have the power to discount notes or bills of exchange. Clay pushed this second bank bill through Congress, despite efforts at delay by moderate Whigs, and it went to the President. Tyler had at first approved this measure but then changed his mind. He had suggested a clause protecting the states against the establishment of agencies prohibited by their laws, but this was not included in the bill. Despite the agreement that he should see the measure before it was introduced in Congress, it had not been shown to him. He was also becoming more and more enamored of the idea of forming a new party, and to that end was planning a reorganization of his Cabinet. On September 9, 1841, Tyler returned the bill with another veto.

Two days later, all the Cabinet save Webster resigned, a move which delighted the President. Tyler would have dismissed Webster if a candidate had been available for the State Department. The new Cabinet contained not a single Clay Whig, being made up of former Jacksonians like the President himself.

The Whig party now rallied unmistakably to Clay, and the Whig press began terming the President "His Accidency." Tyler attempted to establish a new political organization made up of states' rights, antitariff, and anti-bank men from both the Whig and Democratic folds. The attempt failed, and then the President began to draw close to Calhoun and to seek the favor of southern Democrats by urging the annexation of Texas. Clay was left without a rival for the Whig nomination in 1844.

The Battle over Distribution and the Tariff

While Clay and his cohorts fought with the President over the bank, the Whigs began to move on the rest of their legislative program. Clay himself, Greeley, and other ardent Whigs held the distribution of the proceeds of land sales to be of vital importance; even Tyler was in agreement on this point. Distribution would relieve the states heavily burdened by debt as a result of the depression, and this outpouring of the public money would stimulate a return to national prosperity. Protectionists such as the "master of Ashland" believed that distribution would be useful in still another way: since the national government's great sources of revenue were the land sales and the tariff, if the land sale proceeds went to the states, the mounting expenses of the government at Washington could only be met by raising the tariff and thus increasing the revenue from that quarter, with "incidental" protection.

There were obstacles, however, in the path of distribution. It was a distinctively Whig measure, and the Whig majorities in both houses of Congress were small.* It was extremely difficult to keep northern, western, and southern Whigs in line for a party vote, for there were bound to be conflicts of economic interest between the sections. A considerable number of western Whigs, influenced by the mounting demands of squatters on the public domain, wished to give a general pre-emption law priority over distribution. They were the more inclined to this position because the Democrats, with Senator Benton in the lead, were thundering for permanent pre-emption

---

* In the twenty-seventh Congress there were in the Senate twenty-eight Whigs, two Tylerites, and twenty-two Democrats, and in the House 133 Whigs, six Tylerites, and 102 Democrats.

and attempting to stigmatize the Whig party as the protector of the "palaces" and the enemy of the "log cabins." Eastern Whigs, especially in New York and Massachusetts, were becoming strident for a bankruptcy law that would relieve business interests in their states which were threatened with ruin by the depression. Finally, southern Whigs, and the President himself, fearful that distribution would mean raising the tariff, had to be placated. The result was that, in forging ahead to distribution, the Whigs became involved in one of the greatest logrolling operations in the history of American politics.

To get distribution through both houses of Congress and then avoid the danger of a veto, Clay was compelled to take several complex steps. A distribution bill was first introduced and then coupled with another bill (the so-called Pre-Emption Act of 1841) that gave actual settlers pre-emption rights to 160 acres of public land not yet officially opened to settlement. When the land on which they squatted was officially designated as ready for settlement, these squatters would have a priority of right to purchase it at the minimum government price. Second, the bankruptcy bill so much desired in the East was introduced, and western support was enlisted for this measure in return for eastern votes for distribution and pre-emption. Finally, an amendment was tacked on to the distribution and pre-emption bill, providing that distribution would be suspended if the tariff went above the 20 per cent level established by the compromise of 1833. As a result of all this trafficking, the bankruptcy bill became law, and the Pre-Emption Act finally passed the Senate (August 26, 1841) by a party vote of twenty-eight to twenty-three. The House then accepted it by the close vote of 108 to ninety-four, and it became the law of the land.

The Whigs had now established distribution as a government policy, but at the cost of a compromise that would either make distribution unworkable or prevent them from raising the tariff. The political gymnastics required to pass the bill showed the unstable nature of the Whig party, and gave clear evidence of the mistake that had been made in choosing Tyler as Harrison's running mate in 1840.

Whig resentment against the President had now risen to fever pitch, and he could expect no cooperation from the party in Congress. In December, 1841, Tyler proposed a substitute for a national bank. His "Board of Exchequer" would have handled the public money and, through agencies established throughout the country, would have dealt in bills of exchange. The agencies would have issued certificates against specie deposits up to $15 million. As a constructive measure, a step toward a sound currency, some Whigs, including Webster, favored it, but, since it was Tyler's project, Clay scorned it, and it was defeated in the Senate.

Clay resigned from the Senate in March, 1842, with his legislative program an almost complete failure. The Independent Treasury had been repealed, but there was no national bank to take its place. The currency was still in a chaotic state. Distribution had been tied to a pre-emption measure that the Whigs had long opposed and for which they received no credit, and distribution itself, crippled by the tariff amendment, had an uncertain future. The government deficit of over $13 million was viewed with growing concern, for it was steadily increasing; duties were scheduled for a precipitate drop in 1842, but nothing had yet been done about the tariff. In bitterness of spirit, the congressional Whigs now turned to tariff revision, only to be plunged once more into a controversy with the President.

A tariff bill prepared by Secretary of the Treasury Walter Forward was introduced in the House by Millard Fillmore, chairman of the Committee on Ways and Means. It restored duties to the same general level as those of the tariff of 1832. Anticipating that its passage would take some little time, another bill, the so-called "Little Tariff," was introduced on June 7, 1842. This extended existing duty levels to August 1, 1842, its purpose being to prevent the duty reduction that, under the tariff of 1833, was scheduled to take place on the first of July.

The "Little Tariff" was a Whig, not an Administration, measure. It kept duties well above the 20 per cent level and contained a provision that nothing in the Act would prevent distribution of the proceeds from the sale of public lands. Tyler promptly vetoed it, and the Whigs were unable to pass it over his veto.

The Whigs then turned to the "Big Tariff" bill, incorporating in it a provision for the maintenance of distribution, despite the fact that it raised duty levels to between 30 and 36 per cent ad valorem. They passed it by a very narrow margin, but the veto which Tyler again used could not be overridden. At length the bill was passed, without provision for keeping up distribution, and Tyler signed it (August 30, 1842). Distribution was now lost and gone forever.

The tariff of 1842, as finally passed, was a sectional rather than a party measure. It passed because of votes from New England and the Middle Atlantic states, together with considerable support from the West. Since the South opposed it, northern and western Democratic votes were essential to its becoming law. It was frankly protective of textile and iron goods, and of a large number of the "infant industries" that were springing up in the North. Though this tariff had a favorable psychological effect (certainly, save for the cotton planters, prosperity returned to the country in 1843 and 1844), there is little evidence that the better times were the direct result of the tariff of 1842.

The Whigs had little cause for self-congratulation at the end of their first two years in power. They had raised the tariff, but in so doing had lost distribution. They had destroyed the Independent Treasury, but had not established any fiscal agency that would regulate the currency and promote national prosperity. They had passed a Bankruptcy Act, but it excited popular discontent and was soon repealed. Thanks principally to John Tyler, they had made but a sorry showing in the field of domestic legislation.

Settling Anglo-American Difficulties, 1841–1842

While Tyler quarreled with his party over domestic matters, his Administration grappled with the problem of relations with Great Britain, which had reached a critical state by the close of 1840. The *Caroline* incident had not been settled, and McLeod was still in a New York State jail; England was discontented over the failure of the United States to help in checking the international slave trade; and the two countries were still at loggerheads over the northeast boundary. British public opinion was bitter over losses suffered by the repudiation of American state debts. Americans smarted under savage criticism of their ways by British travelers, and watched with mounting alarm the reinforcement of British troops in Canada by the truculent Lord Palmerston, the British Minister for Foreign Affairs.

Relations between the two countries were indeed tense, but a conjunction of circumstances led to their improvement. Secretary of State Webster, a friend of England, was anxious to preserve peace. Palmerston was replaced in the British Foreign Office in 1841 by Lord Aberdeen, who also desired a resumption of good relations between the two countries. The latter sent as a special representative to the United States Alexander Baring, Lord Ashburton, who possessed a fund of good humor and an attractive American wife. Ashburton was authorized to settle all disputes between Great Britain and the United States, and was anxious to make his mission a success.

Negotiations were now resumed in a friendly atmosphere, and constructive results followed. Webster approached the McLeod affair with tact, for he had information from Governor Seward of New York that the Canadian was in no danger of punishment. Testimony proved that he had been five or six miles away from the scene of the raid when the *Caroline* was seized, and so could not have killed a New Yorker during the fracas. He was acquitted, and this troublesome dispute ended with Webster obtaining from

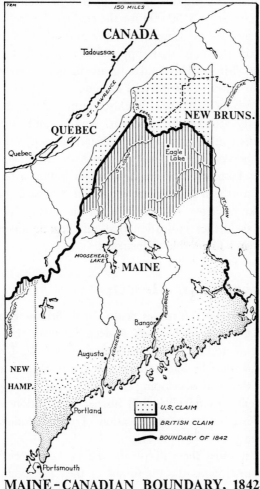

MAINE–CANADIAN BOUNDARY, 1842

Congress a law that provided for habeas corpus proceedings in federal courts when states arrested aliens for acts authorized by their own countries.

Ashburton, in his turn, expressed regret that Great Britain had not apologized for the sinking of the *Caroline*. It was agreed that the two nations should provide fleets in African waters for the suppression of the slave trade. Compromise settlements were reached in regard to the Vermont and New York Canadian boundaries, and on the boundary line stretching between Lake Superior and the Lake of the Woods.

The most important boundary dispute was over the line between Maine and Canada, and here, too, compromise ruled the outcome. Webster obtained consent to this by organizing propaganda in Maine and Massachusetts, by paying each state $150,000 for the relinquishment of claims in the disputed region, and by pointing out to the authorities of those states the existence of certain old maps that supposedly supported the boundary line demanded by the British. The final adjustment gave Maine 7,000 out of the 12,000 square miles of territory in dispute.

Though the Webster-Ashburton Treaty, comprised of all of these settlements, was bitterly attacked by Jackson, Benton, and Buchanan as dishonorable and disreputable, it was a substantial achievement. It ended the aggravating border disputes with fairness to all concerned and gave the United States fabulous iron ore deposits, including a large part of the Mesabi range in northern Minnesota, regarding the existence of which the British had no knowledge. The criticism of the treaty in England as a "capitulation" was further indication that this negotiation represented for both sides a fair and honorable adjustment.

A New Expansionist Movement

The settlement of the difficulties with Great Britain enabled Tyler to turn to a project in which he took a deep interest—the annexation of Texas. The idea of adding the Lone Star State to the Union had been much on his mind since he had entered the White House, and the expansionist sentiment that was developing throughout the country made such a move seem eminently practicable. Still further justification for pushing the annexation of Texas lay in a modification of the attitude and objectives of the Democratic party.

The Democrats, after their disastrous defeat in the election of 1840, still regarded themselves as the guardians of the "log cabins" against the "palaces," as the true defenders of the dignity of the individual and the right of every man to equality of opportunity. But many of them were disheartened by defeat and turned to a search for new issues that would enable them to regain power. Expansion excited their interest, and, in consequence, the Democracy of the 1840s became as closely identified with the conquest of additional territory as it was with the preservation of equalitarian principles. There were, as we shall see, far-reaching consequences of this shift in emphasis.

Tyler Moves to Annex Texas

Texas was a stimulus to the expansionist fever, for Texas was clamoring at the American gates. That independent state had proposed annexation in August, 1837, but Van Buren's Administration, and the Whigs as well, had recoiled, fearful of free state opposition and being without enthusiasm for a war with Mexico. Now, in March, 1842, another request for admission to the Union came from the Texas capital.

Tyler listened attentively to the Texas proposal. Alarmed, as were many Americans, over supposed British designs on Texas, he knew that there was considerable popular opinion in favor of its acquisition. Influential friends, such as Congressmen Henry A. Wise and Thomas W. Gilmer of Virginia and Senator Robert J. Walker of Mississippi, urged him on. Ambitious of fame and glory, hoping that annexation would be an issue enabling him to form a third party, or capture the Democratic nomination in 1844, he made up his mind to act.

One obstacle, a formidable one, lay in Tyler's path: Daniel Webster, his Secretary of State, opposed annexation. But after the Webster-Ashburton Treaty was signed, the Secretary of State, fearing that a longer stay in Tyler's Cabinet would prejudice the Whigs against him, resigned (May 8, 1843). In his place Tyler appointed Abel P. Upshur of Virginia, an ardent annexationist.

Upshur had a penchant for vigorous diplomacy, but he knew that the acquisition of Texas was a delicate matter and must be handled with care. There was some sentiment for it in the Northeast, considerably more in the West, and southern opinion heartily favored adding this great slaveholding state to the Union. Northern antislavery elements, however, were violently opposed, and it was doubtful that a two-thirds majority of the Senate could be mustered for ratification of a treaty of annexation.

Upshur and Tyler worked together to whip up sentiment for such a treaty, finally reaching the conclusion that they could get it through the Senate. It appeared that Texas would come into the Union without any great controversy until, on February 28, 1844, Upshur went with the President and others on a trip down the Potomac in the new man-of-war *Princeton*. The purpose of the run was to test a twelve-inch cannon named "The Peacemaker"; the gun exploded and Upshur was killed. A week later, John C. Calhoun became Secretary of State.

Calhoun, like Upshur, was anxious to annex Texas. He hoped to capitalize on the growing popular interest in that republic and in the Far Northwest, where American settlers were pushing across the Great Divide.

The South Carolinian dreamed of another West-South alliance, one that would not only bring Texas and Oregon wholly into the American orbit but also destroy the protectionist policy that southerners like himself hated and feared.

But where Upshur had been deft, Calhoun was heavy-handed; not for nothing was it rumored that he had once written a poem which began with the word "whereas." He now seized upon a statement by Lord Aberdeen of England's interest in extending freedom throughout the world. Calhoun used this as an excuse for issuing a vigorous defense of slavery as a positive good, and his words were widely circulated. At the same time, he brought the treaty of annexation before the Senate. These events occurred on the eve of the Whig national convention, which was gathering in Baltimore. Wittingly or unwittingly, the South Carolinian had closely coupled the acquisition of Texas with the slavery question, so that it looked as if the former was being undertaken not so much in the national interest as in support of the South's "peculiar institution." Calhoun's blunder, together with events occurring in connection with the presidential nominations of the two great parties, alienated enough northern support for the treaty so that, on June 8, 1844, it was defeated in the Senate.

The Presidential Nominations

The acquisition of Texas was now a political question that had momentous consequences for the presidential campaign of 1844. That campaign had really begun three years earlier, when the Clay-Tyler breach occurred. Whigs North and South rallied behind the Kentuckian, and months before the Baltimore convention met his nomination was a foregone conclusion. In the Democratic camp, Van Buren appeared to have no serious rival; Jackson was for him, and he had the support of a great majority of northern Democrats. Though southern and some western Democrats were cool to the man from Kinderhook, the malcontents could find no candidate upon whom they could unite.

In 1842, Van Buren had made a western tour that took him into Tennessee and Kentucky; he visited Jackson at the Hermitage and stayed for two days with Clay at Ashland. The supposition is that the two political rivals then and there agreed to take Texas out of the campaign of 1844. Be that as it may, on April 27, 1844, just before the Whig national convention, letters from both Clay and Van Buren were published in Washington. Both declared that the annexation of Texas at this time was inexpedient, because it would promote national discord and involve the danger of war with Mexico. Their obvious hope that this action would eliminate Texas as an issue in the impending national contest was sadly disappointed.

Clay's letter—called the "Raleigh letter," because it had been written in that "City of Oaks"—had no immediate effect upon his candidacy. The Whig convention met at Baltimore, May 1, 1844, amid scenes of great enthusiasm. The city was full of banners, triumphal arches, Clay hats, and the shouts of marching men—as well as numerous live raccoons, used as symbols of the Whig devotion to rural simplicity, and here and there a little fox, whose duty it was "to raise the old Harry." The confident Whigs nominated "Harry of the West" by acclamation. The convention passed a series of resolves favoring distribution, a tariff for revenue with incidental protection, a single term for the presidency, and resistance to "executive usurpation." It made no reference to Texas or to expansion.

The Democrats met at Baltimore on May 27. Ever since the publication of Van Buren's letter on Texas, a revolt had been brewing against him, spearheaded by southern politicians. He had never been popular south of the Mason and Dixon line, and southerners regarded him as a representative of the radical wing of the Democracy, a man who bore the stigma of defeat in 1840 and, most of all, an opponent of Texas annexation. Even his old friend Jackson now came out in opposition to his nomination. Van Buren's friends implored him to modify his stand on Texas, or at least to make a statement favoring the acquisition of Oregon, but he refused to identify himself as an expansionist.

A majority of the Democratic delegates at Baltimore favored Van Buren, but the convention again adopted the two-thirds rule for nomination. Though this had been used in the conventions of the 1830s to insure his nomination, now it was a weapon against him, for his friends could not muster a sufficient number of votes. Seven ballots showed the New Yorker's strength declining, but Lewis Cass of Michigan, James Buchanan of Pennsylvania, and a number of other would-be nominees could not develop sufficient strength to win the coveted prize. After much maneuvering behind the scenes in the deadlocked convention, votes began to be cast for a new man—a Jacksonian Democrat and expansionist from Tennessee named James K. Polk, who was known to have Old Hickory's support. The movement spread as New York gave in, though with bitterness of spirit, and on the ninth ballot Polk received the nomination.

The news that the Democratic convention had chosen Polk as its standard bearer, flashed over the newly set up telegraph line between Baltimore and Washington, was received with amazement by a crowd in the basement of the Capitol. For the first time in American history, a dark horse had been nominated for the presidency.

The Democrats nominated Silas Wright of New York for Vice President. Informed by telegraph, he promptly wired back that he could not run on a Texas ticket, and the Democrats then chose George M. Dallas of Pennsylvania as Polk's running mate. Resolutions were adopted favoring a revenue tariff, the independent treasury, and maintenance of the presidential veto. The convention went on record as opposing distribution, and it declared for "the reoccupation of Oregon and the reannexation of Texas at the earliest practicable period. . . ."

The Campaign of 1844

Four parties were in the field at the opening of the 1844 campaign. Tyler had been nominated, also at Baltimore, by an unofficial convention composed largely of officeholders. He withdrew during the summer, and his self-elimination was a definite aid to Polk's campaign. The Liberty party, once more in the running, again nominated James G. Birney. This anti-slavery movement became increasingly significant as election time drew near.

The Whigs entered the contest in a jubilant frame of mind. They regarded Polk as a nonentity, and the scornful cry "Who is James K. Polk?" echoed up and down the land. Clay was convinced that he could win on issues of domestic policy alone. Whig partisans, in speech and song, declared that the party stood for the common man just as it had in 1840, glorified those symbols of democracy, the log cabin and the coon, and extolled the virtues of "Harry of the West."

> High on a limb that "same old coon,"
> Was singing to himself a tune:—
> Get out of the way, you're all unlucky;
> Clear the track for Old Kentucky.

But the Whigs soon found that they had a hard fight on their hands. Jackson again raised the cry of "bargain and sale," and it was used repeatedly throughout the campaign. The Democrats accused Clay of dueling, gambling, profanity, and Sabbath-breaking, charges that the Liberty party men echoed while declaring that he was immoral and pro-slavery as well. Southern Democrats portrayed him as sacrificing Texas to the abolitionists and southern economic interests to those of the North.

The Whigs pronounced these accusations scurrilous, but they retorted in kind. According to them, Polk came of Tory stock. He was a free trader, and a servant of British interests, who stood for disunion. A vote for Birney, the Whigs declared, would be thrown away on an antislavery fanatic, and could only elect Polk and promote Texas annexation.

Both Democrats and Whigs paid some attention to domestic issues, but the crucial question was Texas. The Democrats charged that Clay was against annexation and asserted that Polk was unequivocally in its favor. Clay had been sure that his "Raleigh letter" could do him no harm in the South, but there the Democrats used it effectively against him. The gloomiest reports poured in, and, driven to explain his point of view, he tried to clarify and defend his stand on Texas in two "Alabama letters," written in July to a newspaper in that state. Slavery, he said, ought not to affect annexation one way or the other; he would be glad to see Texas annexed, but not at the cost of jeopardizing the Union. In another letter, published in the *National Intelligencer*, the Whig organ in Washington, on September 23, 1844, he defended himself against the charge of inconsistency and again declared that he did not favor immediate annexation.

In these letters, as in the "Raleigh letter," Clay strove to take middle ground between the proponents and opponents of annexation. On the whole, his statements helped him to stem the tide that had begun to run against him in the slavery states. He captured Maryland, North Carolina, Kentucky, and Tennessee, but his hedging on annexation hurt him in New York, where many Whig antislavery voters moved over into the Liberty party ranks. Clay was also handicapped in New York by the popularity of Silas Wright, who had been persuaded to run for governor on the Democratic ticket, and he lost possible support among the large numbers of foreign-born in New York City because of the close association there of Whigs and Nativists. The Whigs had high hopes that the tariff issue would give them Pennsylvania, but Polk's "Kane letter," so worded that the Democrats there could make him out a friend of protection, stultified Whig efforts and helped the Democrats capture the state.

Even if Clay had carried Pennsylvania, he would still have been defeated, for New York was the crucial state. Losing Pennsylvania, he would have been the next President of the United States, had he carried New York, but Birney had 15,812 votes there, and Clay trailed Polk by 5,106 ballots.

The presidential contest was close, in terms of the will of all the people. Out of a total of almost 2,750,000 votes cast, Polk had only 38,181 more than Clay. But the Democrats had also captured both houses of Congress, and Polk could look forward with reasonable certainty to cooperation from the other end of Pennsylvania Avenue.

The election of 1844 was highly significant for the nation's future. The

Democratic party had demonstrated its vitality by raising its portion of the two-party vote from the 47 per cent of 1840 to 50.7 per cent in 1844. It had carried New York and Pennsylvania, and had shown great strength in the West and South. But, at the same time, the rejection of Van Buren had embittered the powerful Democratic machine in New York State, and had sown seeds of doubt among northern Democratic radicals and anti-slavery men about the party's devotion to high principle—doubts that would grow with the passage of the years. The growth of the Liberty party vote from 7,069 in 1840 to 62,300 in 1844 showed that antislavery had potential for development as a political force in both major political parties.

An immediate and most important consequence of the election of 1844 was an invitation to Texas to join the Union. President Tyler declared that the result of the presidential contest signified a national demand for annexation, and urged prompt action by Congress. A joint resolution passed both houses, providing for admission of Texas either directly or through negotiation between Texas and the United States. Benton and a number of other Senators voted for this proposal on the understanding that a choice between these alternatives would be left to Polk, but Tyler would have no delay, and, on March 3, 1845, the national government issued an outright invitation to the Lone Star State to join the Union.

Suggested Reading

For the struggles over domestic politics in this period, the following biographies are useful: Glyndon G. Van Deusen, *The Life of Henry Clay* (1937), and *William Henry Seward* (1967); Dorothy B. Goebel, *William Henry Harrison* (1926); Lyon G. Tyler, *The Letters and Times of the Tylers* (3 vols., 1884–1896), an apologia; Oliver Chitwood, *John Tyler* (1939); William M. Meigs, *The Life of John Caldwell Calhoun* (2 vols., 1917); and Charles M. Wiltse, *John C. Calhoun* (3 vols., 1944–1951). Claude M. Fuess, *Daniel Webster* (2 vols., 1930) is adequate, and George T. Curtis, *Life of Daniel Webster* (2 vols., 1870) is still a useful study. Charles G. Sellers, *James K. Polk, Jacksonian, 1795–1843* (1957) is excellent. Robert Seager, *And Tyler Too!* (1963) is good on that President's private life.

George R. Poage, *Henry Clay and the Whig Party* (1936) is a careful monograph covering the decade from 1840 to 1850. James C. N. Paul, *Rift in the Democracy* (1951) is a perceptive analysis. The struggle over pre-emption is examined in Raynor G. Wellington's study of the public lands, already cited. For the tariff, see the works of Stanwood and Taussig previously cited, and Walter B. Smith and Arthur H. Cole,

Fluctuations in American Business, 1790–1860 (1935). The Bankruptcy Act is dealt with in Charles Warren, *Bankruptcy in United States History* (1935). The Harrison and Tyler Administrations are analyzed in Glyndon .G. Van Deusen, *The Jacksonian Era, 1828–1848* (1959).

The diplomacy of the Tyler Administration is examined in the biographies mentioned above and in Jesse S. Reeves, *American Diplomacy Under Tyler and Polk* (1907). See also Richard N. Current, "Webster's Propaganda and the Ashburton Treaty," *Mississippi Valley Historical Review,* XXXIV (Oct., 1947), 187–200. Albert B. Corey, *The Crisis of 1830–1842 in Canadian-American Relations* (1941) is excellent. Justin H. Smith, *The Annexation of Texas* (1941) uses source materials and is very well written. It should be used in conjunction with G. L. Rives, *The United States and Mexico, 1821–1848* (2 vols., 1913); Ephraim D. Adams, *British Interests and Activities in Texas, 1838–1846* (1910); Stanley Siegel, *A Political History of the Texas Republic, 1836–1845* (1956); Richard R. Stenberg, "Intrigue for Annexation," *Southwest Review,* XXV (Oct., 1939), 58–69; and Eugene C. Barker, "The Annexation of Texas," *Southwestern Historical Quarterly,* L (July, 1946), 49–74. See also Barker's *Life of Stephen F. Austin* (1925), and *Mexico and Texas* (1928).

For the campaign of 1844, see the abovementioned biographies of outstanding figures and Eugene I. McCormac, *James K. Polk* (1922). C. Sellers, *James K. Polk, Continentalist, 1843–1846* (1966) is the second volume in a definitive, three-volume study of the man.

26 ⸱ Manifest Destiny in Action, 1845-1848

WHEN THE ELECTION of 1844 was over, Andrew Jackson at the Hermitage scribbled on a piece of paper, " 'Who is J. K. Polk' will no longer be asked by the coons." This was true enough, but the President-elect was not at all the unknown that Whig sarcasm had depicted. Born November 2, 1795, of Scotch-Irish parentage, Polk was not yet fifty years old when he entered the White

Polk Charts His Course House, and he had been in politics for almost a quarter of a century. Elected to the Tennessee legislature in 1823, he was later governor of the state and member of Congress from 1825 to 1839; as Speaker of the House for four years, he had had plenty of opportunity to demonstrate his opposition to Clay's American System and his devotion to Democratic policies. Indeed, Polk's support of Jackson had earned him the nickname of "Young Hickory."

The new President was a firm-minded man and a tireless worker, possessing a keen sense of duty, tact, and good judgment. He was a devout Christian, inclining to Methodism for doctrine, and was always strict in his observance of the Sabbath. He was a good party man, to whom even the best of Whigs was more than a little suspect. But he was also cold and narrow by nature and, as a party leader, unimaginative and inept.

548

Polk's inaugural outlined the course he was to follow. He made clear his aversion to a national bank and a protective tariff, his dislike of abolitionists, and his love for the Union. Expansion received his unequivocal blessing. He made his aims even more specific a few days later when, in a conversation with his Secretary of the Navy, George Bancroft, he declared that his Administration had four great objectives: the tariff had to be reduced, the Independent Treasury re-established, the Oregon boundary settled, and California added to the Union. All of these goals were achieved before he left office—three of them in 1846 and the fourth, which involved war with Mexico, in 1848.

Domestic Policies of the Administration

With the reins of power firmly in their hands, Polk and the congressional Democrats turned at once to domestic problems. Since the repeal in 1842 of the Independent Treasury Act, the national government had again been keeping its money in the state banks. Polk's message of December, 1845, called for another independent treasury bill, and in March, 1846, the measure appeared in the House. The Whigs opposed it vigorously but fruitlessly; they prophesied that under it vast sums usable in trade and industry would remain idle in the government depositories, where their presence would excite greed and dishonesty among the government officials entrusted with their care. The Democrats minimized these dangers, declaring that the measure would serve to check the issue of bank notes of doubtful value, and would restrict the power of banking corporations, particularly those in which the government money was now deposited. The bill—a party measure—passed the House by a vote of 122 to sixty-six, and the Senate by twenty-eight to twenty-five, and Polk signed it on August 8, 1846.

The Independent Treasury remained in operation, although with some limitations, until replaced by the Federal Reserve Act of 1913. Though it produced none of the evil effects foreseen by the Whigs, neither did it exert the immensely salutary influence foretold by the Democrats. The most that can be said positively is that it probably had some effect as a brake on inflationary tendencies during the Mexican War. From a negative point of view, it ended the possibility of re-establishing a national bank, and it is probable, but not certain, that it delayed for several generations the development of a centralized banking system in the United States.

At the same time that the Independent Treasury was being re-established, the Democrats undertook to lower the tariff. The President asked Congress for a revenue measure that would afford only incidental protection, and only if equally applied to agriculture, commerce, manufacturing, and labor. His request was given force by an able report from the Secretary of the Treasury, Robert J. Walker of Mississippi, urging a substantial lowering of duties from those of 1842. One of Walker's main arguments was that such a bill would give labor a better opportunity to achieve a higher standard of living.

The Walker tariff of 1846, framed in accordance with the Secretary's suggestions, came before the House in April of that year. Its schedule of duties, established on a strictly ad valorem basis, put some items, such as tea and coffee, on the free list and taxed luxuries as much as 100 per cent. Articles around which the tariff controversy had raged most severely— for example, iron products, woolen goods, and glass—were charged a duty of 30 per cent. The average duty rate was 25 per cent, a considerable but not a drastic reduction of the previous duty level.

Northern Whigs and a number of Democrats from Pennsylvania and New York opposed this lowering of duties, but it was strongly supported in the South. It passed the House 114 to ninety-five, and the Senate by a vote of twenty-eight to twenty-seven. The bill became law on July 31, 1846.

The opponents of the Walker tariff prophesied economic disaster as a result of its passage. It did hurt the production of fine woolen goods in the United States, and possibly retarded the manufacture of iron. On the other hand, it had no effect upon the manufacture of cotton goods and the lower-priced woolens. The retardation of iron manufacturing was counterbalanced by the increase of iron imports sorely needed for railroad construction, and by the stimulus given to more efficient production methods on the part of domestic producers of iron goods. The bill aligned the United States with the European movement toward lower tariffs and facilitated the disposal abroad of America's surpluses of cotton and wheat.

Democratic interest in lowering the tariff and restoring the Independent Treasury was not paralleled by enthusiasm for internal improvements at federal expense. Clamor was rising in the North for aid in the construction of roads, canals, and railroads. In 1847, a Rivers and Harbors convention that met in Chicago and was attended by over 5,000 delegates passed resolutions favoring federal aid for such means of transportation and showed marked enthusiasm for a railroad to the Pacific. Reflecting this climate of opinion, a number of rivers and harbors bills passed Congress. Though they were strongly supported by the Whigs, President Polk vetoed them, and they could not be passed over his veto.

Foreign Policy—The Oregon Treaty of 1846

As became a President who was an ardent advocate of expanding American territory, Polk's Administration manifested great interest in foreign policy. It showed concern over relations between the South American states and France and England where such relations indicated an extension of European influence in the New World. By the treaty of 1846 with New Granada, it guaranteed the neutrality of the Isthmus of Panama. A number of reciprocity treaties were concluded with Latin American and European states, and plans were made for promoting commercial arrangements with China and Japan. Polk and his counselors eyed Cuba with longing and fruitlessly offered Spain $100 million for the island. All of these activities, however, were peripheral to the central objectives of the Administration in foreign affairs: the establishment of unilateral American authority in Oregon, and an adjustment of relations with Mexico that, it was hoped, would bring California into the Union. Both projects were pursued simultaneously.

The Webster-Ashburton Treaty had much improved relations between Great Britain and the United States, but when Polk entered the White House the situation in Oregon threatened a new crisis. As we have shown (Chapter 24), that territory had been under joint occupation by the two countries since the treaty of 1818, which had been extended in 1827 with the understanding that either party might terminate it by giving a year's notice. With both countries having claims to the region in question, 1,000 British citizens had settled on the rich lands of the Puget Sound Valley, and the Hudson's Bay Company had established a fur-trading post on the Columbia River, while a little further south, in the Willamette Valley, 6,000 American citizens were clamoring for the protection of the American government.

Earlier in the century, American statesmen and politicians had shown considerable interest in Oregon, but the great majority had thought it a land so far away that it would, in all probability, become an independent state. Now all was changed, for the rising tide of expansionism, the reports from settlers and missionaries, and the knowledge that thousands of their fellow citizens had already pushed across the Great Divide roused a clamor for the entire region. "Fifty-four forty or fight," a slogan that appealed to some Americans, asserted the claim of the United States to the whole of the

Far Northwest up to the southern border of the Alaska Panhandle. The most vocal sentiment in support of this claim came from the people and politicians of such states as Ohio, Indiana, and Illinois.

The Oregon fever in the Old Northwest was sufficiently strong for the Democrats to include in their 1844 platform a demand for the "reoccupation" of that territory, which had figured prominently in the Democratic campaign. In his inaugural, President Polk made a statement that roused British anger, declaring that the title of the United States to "the country of the Oregon" was beyond question, and that the people of the United States were "preparing to perfect that title by occupying it with their wives and children." As if to prove this statement, the population of the Willamette Valley doubled during 1845.

American statesmen had never seriously intended to claim all of the Oregon country. Beginning in 1818 with James Monroe, every administration had offered the forty-ninth parallel as a dividing line. Polk himself, despite his bold words, was favorable to compromise, and, in July, 1845, the American government renewed the offer made so many times before. Pakenham, the British envoy at Washington, refused it, and it was withdrawn. Pakenham's action was disavowed in London, but Polk now began claiming the whole territory. In his message of December, 1845, he declared that the rights of the United States in Oregon could not be abandoned "without a sacrifice of both national honor and interest . . .," and urged that Congress give the year's notice necessary to end joint occupation. A short time later, he told a member of Congress that "the only way to treat John Bull was to look him straight in the eye."

The notice requested by Polk passed Congress (April 23, 1846), but only after a bitter fight. The controversy was due, in considerable part, to the aspirations of ambitious men for the Democratic presidential nomination in 1848. Polk had stated that he would not be a candidate to succeed himself, and politicians like Senator William Allen of Ohio and Senator Edward A. Hannegan of Indiana were busy enhancing their own popularity in the Old Northwest by assuming leadership in the demand for an uncompromising statement on Oregon. On the other hand, Calhoun and the southern Democrats joined the Whig commercial and financial interests in pushing through Congress a notice that joint occupation must come to an end, but coupling with it a promise of cooperation with Great Britain in effecting a reasonable adjustment.

Polk would have preferred an unqualified notice, for he wanted a strong bargaining base. Circumstances were pushing him toward the compromise that, at heart, he desired. The Democracy was threatening to split apart on the issue of "fifty-four forty"; Great Britain, uncertain of the President's intentions, was strengthening its military and naval forces in the Canadian area; and the President, confronted by a threatening situation on the Mexican border, had no desire to become involved at the same time in a crisis with England. Public opinion, alarmed by the threats and general bellicosity of Allen and Hannegan, was manifesting in unmistakable fashion its desire for a peaceful settlement with Great Britain. The President sent the notice to Great Britain without comment, but the American government informed London that the forty-ninth parallel would be acceptable to the United States.

Britain was agreeable to compromise. The only territory over which there was any real contention lay between the forty-ninth parallel and the Columbia River. Great Britain's chief reason for insisting on the latter as a boundary had been that the Hudson's Bay Company had a trading post on that stream, but by 1846 this post had been moved to Vancouver Island; furthermore, the Columbia was not an outlet for western Canada, and therefore was not important to the Canadian populace for commercial purposes. Once more the forty-ninth parallel was proposed, this time by Great Britain, and on June 10, 1846, Polk sent this proposal to the Senate. By now the Mexican War had begun, and, with the only serious opposition to the treaty coming from the die-hard Senators from the Old Northwest, on June 18, 1846, the Senate approved the Oregon Treaty by a vote of forty-one to fourteen.

The Oregon Treaty of 1846 established the forty-ninth parallel as the boundary between the United States and Canada from the Rocky Mountains to the Straits of Vancouver. The line in the Straits was to be settled later by arbitration (as was done in 1872). The treaty gave the Hudson's Bay Company free navigation of the Columbia, and guaranteed property rights of British settlers in the territory now recognized as belonging to the United States. It was a fair settlement, and it eliminated the possibility of tense relations with England while the United States was engaged in war with its southern neighbor.

Relations with Mexico, 1845

The likelihood of war with Mexico had been increasing since early in 1845, when the joint resolution inviting Texas to become a part of the United States had passed Congress. After some hesitation, an act of admission passed Congress (December 29, 1845), and Texas accepted the offer. In February, 1846, equipped with a new constitution and a state government, the Lone Star State had formally entered the Union. The Mexican government, which had never recognized the independence of Texas, was greatly displeased by this sequence of events; on news of the passage of the joint resolution, it broke off diplomatic relations with the United States, and the Mexican press began demanding war. Washington heard reports of Mexican troop movements on the Rio Grande. Mexico was weak, and its government was unstable (United States citizens alone had claims of over $8 million against its nationals), but the Mexican leaders had an unfounded confidence in their arms and were unduly hopeful of foreign aid in case war should come with the "gringoes" of the North. They also supposed that the power of the United States was greatly weakened by internal dissension.

Polk was not at all disturbed by the Mexican attitude. He held that the annexation of Texas was a fait accompli, no longer subject to negotiation, and, in response to Mexican troop movements, ordered General Zachary Taylor to move from Louisiana to such points on the Rio Grande as would enable him to repel any invasion of Texas. Upon receiving his instructions from Washington, Taylor stationed himself at Corpus Christi, just south of the Nueces River, where, by November, 1845, he had 4,000 men under his command.

Polk's order to Taylor indicated that the American government thought of the Rio Grande as the boundary between Mexico and Texas, and this was clearly the Texan point of view. Mexico, still claiming possession of Texas, maintained that the southeastern boundary of that "province" was the Nueces River. At best, the Texan claim to the territory between the two rivers was doubtful, and the Mexicans regarded Taylor's move into this region as provocative. Polk, on the contrary, held it a logical step taken in defense of American territory. He was determined to uphold the Texan claim to the Rio Grande as the true boundary line between the two countries.

The President maintained that he did not want war with Mexico, and this was probably true. It seems clear, however, that, by taking a firm stand on the boundary, by keeping up pressure for payment of claims, and by offering millions of dollars for the cession of additional territory, he hoped to achieve a peaceful settlement that would establish the United States on the Rio Grande and would also bring California into the Union.

During the 1840s, as we have shown, American expansionists had become interested in California as well as in Texas and Oregon. Something less than 1,000 American pioneers had settled in California, where they were outnumbered ten to one by those claiming Mexican citizenship.

American public opinion looked upon this Pacific coast territory as an area important for settlement, as a natural terminus for a transcontinental railroad, and as a valuable center from which to develop trade with the Orient. Americans were also suspicious that England and France might seek to acquire a foothold in California; though there was no substantial ground for such concern, it nevertheless existed.

Polk Re-enunciates the Monroe Doctrine

Polk shared the views of the other expansionists. Determined to forestall possible British designs on California and wishing to counter a recent declaration by Premier François Guizot of France that the preservation of a balance of power in the New World was a matter of interest to the French government, the President held it important to restate with emphasis the principles of the Monroe Doctrine. On December 2, 1845, he told Congress that the government of the United States had not interfered with the relations existing between other governments, and that it could not be indifferent to the "attempts of European powers to interfere with the independent action of the nations on this continent." The peoples of the North American continent alone had the right to decide their own destiny, said Polk, and the concept of a balance of power could "not be permitted to have any application on the North American continent, and especially to the United States." With equal emphasis, he warned against any new colonization project in North America, the inference being that expansion on this continent was an American, not a European, prerogative.

The Slidell Mission—War

Polk undertook the re-establishment of diplomatic relations with Mexico, to which the Mexicans reluctantly agreed. On November 10, 1845, after consultation with his Cabinet, he appointed John Slidell of Louisiana as envoy extraordinary and minister plenipotentiary to Mexico. The American government ordered Slidell to obtain a settlement of the claims of American citizens against Mexico, and to purchase as much territory as possible. His instructions asserted that the land between the Nueces and the Rio Grande belonged to Texas, but that the United States was prepared to assume the claims of its citizens in exchange for a boundary running along the Rio Grande to its source and then north to the forty-second parallel. For the rest of New Mexico, Slidell could give $5 million, and, if possible, he was to purchase California, offering $20 million for the portion extending as far south as San Francisco, $25 million if Mexico ceded the land as far south as Monterey.

In his message to Congress on December 2, 1845, Polk in effect warned Mexico to meet Slidell halfway. He indicated that he would forbear recommending measures of redress for the wrongs and injuries the United States had suffered at the hands of the Mexican government until the results of Slidell's mission became apparent.

COURTESY OF THE NEW-YORK HISTORICAL SOCIETY, NEW YORK CITY

UNCLE SAM'S TAYLORIFICS

This cartoon by Edward W. Clay shows Uncle Sam cutting Mexico in two with a pair of shears, the blades of which represent the regular American army and the volunteers. John Bull, fishing for Oregon, thinks he has a bite but remarks that his catch does not seem to diminish the Union. The expansionist mood prevalent in the United States is well represented here.

Word of the Slidell mission and its objectives created much excitement in Mexico, and when the American representative reached Mexico City in December, 1845, the government there would not receive him. News of this was sent to Washington, whereupon Polk ordered Taylor to move his troops to the Rio Grande.

When Taylor had reached the Rio Grande, opposite the Mexican town of Matamoras, in the latter part of March, 1846, Mexico ordered him back to the Nueces, but he built a fort and proceeded to blockade the river in order to prevent supplies moving into Matamoras. Meanwhile, Slidell had returned to Washington and was urging forceful action upon a willing President. Polk and his Cabinet agreed that he should prepare a war message, a course made all the easier by momentous news which now came from the border.

After Taylor had camped opposite Matamoras, a Mexican force of 1,600 men crossed the Rio Grande, where it encountered some sixty-three American dragoons, killed a number of them, and captured the rest. News of this skirmish reached Washington on Saturday, May 9, and on Monday Polk sent his war message to Congress.

The message declared that, "after reiterated menaces," Mexico had precipitated war by invading American territory and shedding "American blood upon the American soil." It asked that Congress recognize the existence of war and promptly furnish means for its execution. The House immediately passed a bill, 174 to fourteen, authorizing a grant of $10 million for war purposes, and a call for 50,000 volunteers. This measure passed the Senate by a vote of forty to two. Polk signed it on May 13, 1846, and immediately issued a proclamation of war. Now that the issue was joined, he told Secretary of State Buchanan, the United States would take California and such other Mexican territory as would be necessary to settle American claims and pay the costs of the conflict.

The Mexican War was a direct outcome of American expansionist zeal, and a majority of Americans approved the course taken by President Polk in throwing down the gage of battle to the Mexicans. There was, however, some criticism. Many of the Whigs disliked the war, and the Democratic followers of Van Buren looked upon it with gloomy foreboding. Prominent leaders in Congress—John Quincy Adams, John C. Calhoun, and Thomas Hart Benton among them—regarded it as a war of aggression.

The Conduct of the Mexican War

At the very outset of the Mexican War, the Southwest and California fell into American hands. Brigadier General Stephen Kearny and his Army of the West, which was stationed at Fort Leavenworth in the Louisiana Purchase, marched out on the Santa Fe Trail in the spring of 1846. They reached Santa Fe on August 18, and a few weeks later set out for California. There John Charles Frémont (in the Far West on an exploring expedition),

CAMPAIGNS
OF
THE MEXICAN WAR
1846-1848

Commodore John D. Sloat, and the American settlers had already begun taking over the province. San Francisco fell into American hands (July 9, 1846), and Los Angeles was captured six months later.

Meanwhile, operations had been proceeding smoothly in the Rio Grande area. Despite the fact that his troops were far inferior in numbers, Taylor beat the Mexicans decisively at Palo Alto and Resaca de la Palma (May 6, 7, 1846). These victories raised Taylor's rating with the Administration at Washington, which had intended to replace him with General Winfield Scott. The latter, however, had begun quarreling with Secretary of War Marcy over his supposed preference for Democratic generals. When Scott grumbled about what he described as "a fire in his rear," Polk became convinced that he was too violent a Whig partisan to be trusted. Taylor, "Old Rough and Ready," as his soldiers called him, was therefore left in command on the Rio Grande.

While these political aspects of war-making were being dealt with, Taylor made ready to cross over into Mexico proper. He did so in July, 1846, and began an advance into the interior. An engagement in the latter part of September enabled him to capture Monterrey, but he allowed the Mexicans to leave the city armed, and without parole.

The success of the campaign against Monterrey put practically one-third of Mexico in the hands of the United States army. Taylor was the hero of the hour, and, though he had never voted, Thurlow Weed and other Whig leaders began thinking of him as a presidential candidate for 1848. Polk, however, became more and more cool to "Old Zack," partly because he was slow in moving his troops and, it was felt, had been too generous to the enemy at Monterrey, and partly because of his rising political stature.

The President had also decided, quite rightly, that the war could be better won by an army landed at Vera Cruz for a direct campaign against the Mexican capital. Polk reluctantly decided that the leader of the Vera Cruz campaign would have to be General Scott; though he would have much preferred a general who was a Democrat, there was no one in that category who was both able and available.

While the President was turning from Taylor and northern Mexico to Scott and Vera Cruz, he was also seeking peace in nonmilitary ways. Under a flag of truce, a letter was forwarded to President Paredes of Mexico suggesting negotiations, but with no results. Polk also aided Santa Anna, the former Mexican dictator who was now in exile, to return to his native land, the understanding being that after Santa Anna was back in power he would negotiate a generous peace settlement. The wily Mexican landed at Vera Cruz on August 16, 1846. Finding the Paredes regime in dissolution, he promptly took over the reins of government, but he showed small disposition to make peace.

While Santa Anna was on his way to Mexico, Polk took a step that produced significant but unforeseen consequences. Believing that the Mexican government would need a sum of money sufficient to pay off its army before it could ratify a treaty calling for a sale of land to the United States, he asked Congress for an appropriation of $2 million to be used in diplomatic negotiations. The House passed the bill, but to it was attached an amendment offered by Democrat David Wilmot of Pennsylvania. This Wilmot Proviso, as it became known, prohibited slavery in any territory that the United States might acquire from Mexico. The bill failed to pass the Senate, but the Proviso was destined to become a rallying cry for the antislavery forces of the North.

As the political consequences of territorial acquisitions from Mexico were making their appearance in the halls of Congress, Scott began gathering his forces for the Vera Cruz campaign. A good many of the regulars in Taylor's army were diverted to Scott's command, much to "Old Zack's" disgust. A more serious consequence was that the Mexicans received information of this weakening of Taylor's command. Thereupon Santa Anna, who had been building a force at San Luis Potosí in the central part of Mexico, broke camp on January 28, 1847, and headed north, with an army of 18,000 men, intent upon dealing Taylor's army a fatal blow.

Taylor lay camped at Buena Vista, south of Monterrey, with between 4,000 and 5,000 men. Santa Anna attacked him there, on February 22, 1847, and a two-day battle ensued. In what amounted to a drawn engagement, the Mexicans suffered heavy casualties. They then withdrew to the south.

The Buena Vista campaign had been a great disappointment to the Mexican leader, but it gave Taylor little credit with Polk's Administration. Polk criticized "Old Zack" for having advanced too far into Mexico, and when Taylor, already furious because his army had been depleted for Scott's benefit, became convinced that he was the victim of blind political partisanship, he applied for leave. It was granted, and in December, 1847, he reached New Orleans, where the populace lionized him. By this time he was more presidential candidate than general.

While Taylor was repelling the Mexicans at Buena Vista, Scott gathered approximately 10,000 men for the Vera Cruz expedition. He was an excellent organizer, and the campaign soon had auspicious results. He captured Vera Cruz on March 29, 1847, and then promptly moved into the interior. When Puebla fell before the Americans on May 15, Scott was within seventy miles of the Mexican capital.

Scott waited at Puebla until he was reinforced. Then, on August 7, with 14,000 men, he abandoned his communications with the coast and moved on Mexico City, where Santa Anna, with 30,000 men, awaited his approach. Though there was considerable hazard in this move, it was a brilliant success, for the battles of Contreras and Churubusco (August 20) opened the way to the capital. Despite Santa Anna's desperate resistance, the Americans occupied Mexico City on September 14, and a few weeks later all organized resistance had come to an end.

The Peace of Guadalupe Hidalgo

Previous to the Scott expedition, Polk had continued his attempts to open peace negotiations with Mexico, but the Mexican government had been in no mood for such discussions. After Buena Vista and Scott's capture of Vera Cruz, the President felt that the time was ripe for still another peace effort and appointed Nicholas P. Trist, a Virginia Democrat who was chief clerk of the State Department, as a commissioner with plenipotentiary powers. Trist was to accompany Scott's army and avail himself of any feasible opportunity for making peace overtures to the Mexican government.

Polk and Buchanan gave Trist a set of instructions for use in negotiation. He was to acquire territory for the United States, assuming all claims of American citizens against Mexico in the process. For New Mexico and Upper California, he could pay as much as $20 million, and if he also obtained the right of transit across the Isthmus of Tehuantepec, he might add another $5 million; if the Mexicans also ceded Lower California, Trist might pay them as much as $30 million.

Trist reached Vera Cruz on May 6, 1847. Initial difficulties with Scott, who had wanted to have charge of any peace negotiations, were smoothed over, and the two men became good friends. Negotiations were opened through the British legation while Scott was still on the way to Mexico City. Some progress was made until the fall of the Mexican capital opened vistas of greater gains in Washington, and the government decided that Trist's instructions must be revised. Secretary of State Buchanan ordered him to break off with the Mexicans and return home; if he had already concluded a treaty, he was to bring it back with him.

The orders from Washington put Trist in a quandary. On the one hand, he was under explicit instructions to return to the United States, and, on the other, he felt that to break off negotiations might mean a prolongation of the war and the disappearance of anything that could be called a Mexican government. He could foresee an indefinite period of guerilla warfare, with the United States involved in a lengthy and expensive policing process, and Scott and the British chargé, Edward Thornton, encouraged this point of view.

Trist finally decided to disobey the order to return to Washington, and wrote Buchanan that he was continuing his efforts to make peace. He also warned the Mexicans that, if they did not negotiate on the basis of his original instructions, much stiffer demands would come from the American government.

The Mexicans agreed to direct negotiations. These were opened at Guadalupe Hidalgo, just outside Mexico City, on December 28, 1847, and, after a month of argument and discussion, a treaty was drawn up for consideration by the two governments.

The Treaty of Guadalupe Hidalgo, signed on February 2, 1848, recognized the Rio Grande as the boundary between Mexico and the United States. Mexico ceded New Mexico and Upper California, receiving in return $15 million, and the American government assumed claims of its citizens against Mexico to the amount of $3.25 million. The Treaty was promptly forwarded to Washington, where it was very coolly received.

Polk's Cabinet divided over whether or not the treaty should be accepted. All the Cabinet, and the President as well, were angry with Trist for not breaking off negotiations, and Buchanan and Walker advised against sending the Treaty to the Senate. Polk hesitated; he wanted to demand more territory than New Mexico and California, but there were powerful reasons for bringing the war to a speedy conclusion. The Whigs, who had adopted a policy of decrying the war but voting supplies for it, had become more critical both of its origins and its continuance. This was especially true after the election of 1846, in which they gained control of the House of Representatives. Some Democrats, too, had become refractory. The followers of Van Buren were hostile to Polk, there was factional strife within the party in Pennsylvania, and the situation was further complicated by contention among such would-be leaders of the Democracy as Benton, Cass, and Calhoun. Polk found it increasingly difficult to rally solid Democratic support for his war measures.

Still another problem was the Wilmot Proviso. Polk considered it a mischievous measure, but it appeared in every session of Congress and, though blocked in the Senate, commanded the support of a considerable number of northern Democrats. To complicate matters further, a move to acquire all of Mexico gained considerable momentum during the last months of the war. It had its strongest support among eastern business interests who were looking for industrial and commercial advantages and among western expansionists, and its most vocal supporters came from northern Democratic circles. The Whigs generally, and the southern Democrats who followed Calhoun's leadership, opposed it. If it gained headway, it would undoubtedly prolong the war, which, in turn, would mean enhanced criticism from the Whigs, from such religious groups as the Quakers and Congregationalists, who had always been critical of the conflict, and from disaffected Democrats. The result might well be such a state of affairs in Congress that it would be impossible to obtain the grants needed for a war of outright conquest.

In view of all these considerations, Polk decided to submit the Treaty to the Senate, where it was ratified, thirty-eight to fourteen, with most of the Whigs and the Calhoun Democrats voting for it. The Mexican Congress signified its acceptance, and President Polk proclaimed the Treaty on July 4, 1848.

Peace had been made, but its chief American negotiator was in disgrace. Buchanan deprived him of his spot in the State Department because he had disobeyed orders. Polk regarded him as a "scoundrel," and withheld pay for his services as a diplomatic agent. It was only a quarter of a century later, just before his death, that Congress awarded to Trist $14,599.20 for negotiating the peace treaty with Mexico.

Significance of the War with Mexico

The Mexican War brought the United States 529,000 square miles of territory, outlets for trade in the Pacific and with the Orient and the rich gold mines of California, news of which began to spread as the Treaty was in process of ratification. The monetary cost of the war was just under $100 million, and, though some 13,000 Americans had lost their lives in the struggle, the great majority through disease rather than in battle, the immense economic gains had been achieved at relatively small cost. But the war also had long-range consequences. The acquisition of new territory stimulated controversy over the extension of slavery, which, in turn, produced bitterness and strife between the North and the South. The struggle with Mexico ushered in an era of conflict that was to culminate in civil war.

Suggested Reading

For the character and personality of Polk, see Milo M. Quaife, ed., *The Diary of James K. Polk* (4 vols., 1910) and the biographies by Sellers and McCormac already cited.

The Independent Treasury and its significance are examined in the monograph by Kinley, already cited, and Esther R. Taus, *Central Banking Functions of the United*

States Treasury, 1789–1941 (1943); H. P. Willis, *The Theory and Practice of Central Banking* (1936); and William G. Sumner, *A History of American Currency* (1874).

For the tariff of 1846, see the works by Stanwood, Taussig, and Dewey already cited.

As an introduction to the expansionism of the Polk period, see Bernard De Voto, *The Year of Decision, 1846* (1943).

There is much material on the Oregon treaty in Polk's *Diary* and in Sellers' *Polk*. Jesse S. Reeves, *American Diplomacy Under Tyler and Polk* (1907) is old but still very useful. Indispensable in this connection are the following articles: Frederick Merk, "The British Corn Crisis of 1845–46 and the Oregon Treaty," *Agricultural History*, VIII (July, 1934), and also "The Oregon Pioneers and the Boundary," "British Party Politics and the Oregon Treaty," "British Government Propaganda and the Oregon Treaty," to be found, respectively, in *American Historical Review*, XXIX (July, 1924), XXXVII (July, 1932), and XL (Oct., 1934); J. W. Pratt, "James K. Polk and John Bull," *Canadian Historical Review*, XXIV (Dec., 1943); H. S. Commager, "England and Oregon Treaty of 1846," *Oregon Historical Quarterly*, XXVII (Mar., 1927); R. L. Schuyler, "Polk and the Oregon Compromise of 1846," *Political Science Quarterly*, XXVI (Sept., 1911).

On the background and character of the Mexican War, see the volume by Reeves just cited, but Justin H. Smith, *The War With Mexico* (2 vols., 1919) is the standard work. Students should also consult G. L. Rives, *The United States and Mexico, 1821–1848* (2 vols., 1913) and E. D. Adams, *British Interests and Activities in Texas,* previously cited. Alfred H. Bill, *Rehearsal for Conflict* (1947) is a well-written account of the war. For the various campaigns, see Holman Hamilton, *Zachary Taylor, Soldier of the Republic* (1941), an excellent biography, and Brainard Dyer, *Zachary Taylor* (1946); also Charles W. Eliot, *Winfield Scott* (1937) and Arthur D. H. Smith, *Old Fuss and Feathers* (1937). Walter P. Webb, *The Texas Rangers* (1935) is enlightening as to the conduct of the war. See also Rupert N. Richardson, *Texas, the Lone Star State* (1943). For Frémont's part in the war, see Allan Nevins *Frémont, Pathmarker of the West* (1955).

On the origins of the Wilmot Proviso, see Charles B. Going, *David Wilmot, Free-Soiler* (1924) and Richard R. Stenberg, "The Motivation of the Wilmot Proviso," *Mississippi Valley Historical Review*, XVIII (Mar., 1932), 535–541. The movement for the acquisition of all Mexico is treated in John D. P. Fuller, "The Movement for the Acquisition of All Mexico, 1846–1848," *Johns Hopkins University Studies in Historical and Political Science,* series 54, No. 1 (1936).

27 ' Dissension and Compromise

URING THE MEXICAN WAR, patriotic necessity had imposed some restraint upon party feuds and sectional strife. With the end of the war, this restraint ended and discord and division increased among both Whigs and Democrats.

The Democratic party was in a weak and disrupted condition, both at Washington and in the states. Polk was no party leader, and the Van Buren and Calhoun wings of the Democracy in Congress drifted further and further apart during his term of office. In New York State, there was bitter strife between the followers of Van Buren, known as the "Barnburners" because of their supposed willingness to burn down the political barn in order to get rid of the rats, and a rival wing of the state Democracy known as the "Hunkers," so called because they were charged with "hunkering" for office. The Barnburners opposed canal enlargement and increasing the state debt and were hostile to any expansion of slavery. The Hunkers, less conservative in facing the state's economic problems, were sympathetic with the South's desire to keep the territories of the Union open for slaveholders. Since early in the 1840s, these rival groups had feuded, and by 1848 the New York Democratic party was in a chaotic condition. A similar situation existed in Pennsylvania, where radical free-soilers and supporters of the Wilmot Proviso fought bitterly with Buchanan and those loyal to the Administration at Washington for

The Deterioration of Parties

control of the state government. In Ohio, antislavery Democrats at times controlled the party, one of their outstanding leaders being Salmon P. Chase, a forty-year-old New England-born lawyer, who had been first a Whig, then a Liberty party man, then a free-soiler, and was now a moving force in the Democracy. In the New England Democracy there was open warfare between conservative Democrats and such rising men of anti-slavery views as Charles Sumner of Massachusetts and the fiery insurgent John P. Hale of New Hampshire.

The Whig party also was beset by difficulties. In one northern state after another, liberals and conservatives (known as "Conscience Whigs" and "Cotton Whigs") fought for control of the state machines. The struggle was particularly severe in New York State, where conservatives like Millard Fillmore, James Watson Webb, and Daniel D. Barnard attacked the liberal Weed-Seward-Greeley wing as tyrants and levelers who were tainted with abolitionism. But the greatest weakness of the Whigs was that they no longer had either a national program or national leaders around whom they could rally: Clay's American System, repeatedly rejected at the polls, had sunk into obscurity; "The Sage of Ashland" himself had been three times defeated for the presidency; and Daniel Webster, ablest of the party's prominent men, had little popularity outside of New England. Whiggery was sadly in need of new issues and new statesmen, possessed of breadth of vision and personal magnetism, around whom the party could rally.

The Campaign of 1848

Such were the situations of Whigs and Democrats as they faced the oncoming election of 1848. When the Democratic national convention met on May 27 of that year, in Baltimore, there were a number of aspirants for the nomination. James Buchanan was anxious for the honor, but he was closely associated with the Polk Administration, which was unpopular in Pennsylvania because of the Walker tariff. Van Buren, the choice of the New York Barnburners, was the best Democratic representative of the rising northern sentiment against the extension of slavery, but southern opposition to him precluded the possibility of his being the standard bearer. Levi Woodbury, now associate justice of the Supreme Court, opposed the Wilmot Proviso, and his name was put forward, but he came from a small state, New Hampshire, and had no great popular following.

The outstanding candidate for the Democratic nomination was Lewis Cass of Michigan. Sixty-five years old and well-to-do, he had served with distinction in the War of 1812, had an excellent record as governor of

Michigan Territory, and was now United States Senator from that state. He was an expansionist, one who had demanded all of Oregon and had no fear of the United States extending its power as far south as Yucatan. He was an opponent of the Wilmot Proviso, but a genuine moderate on the question of slavery extension who, in 1847, had taken the position that the question of slavery should be left to the people of each territory to settle for themselves. Popular in the South and West, from the politicians' point of view he was an admirable choice, perhaps the more so because he had lost much of the dynamic of his earlier career and could be counted on to be a safe and sane President.

Cass received the Democratic nomination on the fourth ballot. The vice-presidential candidate was General William O. Butler, who had gained military laurels in the War of 1812 and the Mexican War and was a Kentucky slaveholder to boot. The platform opposed the American System, but took no clear-cut stand on slavery extension. Antislavery Democrats were disappointed in both the candidates and the platform, and left Baltimore in anything but a happy frame of mind.

A week after the Democrats adjourned, the Whig national convention gathered in Chinese Hall in Philadelphia. The Taylor boom had been steadily growing, but there were other possibilities for the Whig nomination: Thomas Corwin, United States Senator from Ohio, was a candidate; there was some sentiment for associate justice of the Supreme Court, John McLean; and Henry Clay was an avowed candidate. In a political speech made in 1847, Clay had criticized introducing slavery into any of the territories acquired from Mexico. He thought of himself as "a western man with northern principles," and there was considerable sentiment for him in the North and West. Though past seventy, his health was still good, and he was as anxious as ever to become the master of the White House. He viewed Taylor's candidacy with growing concern and on one occasion was heard to say that he wished he, too, could kill a Mexican.

Taylor was something of an enigma. He declared that he was a Whig, but he thought of himself as the people's candidate and was ready and willing to accept nominations from any and all quarters. He had had no time, he said, to investigate the tariff, or internal improvements, or the banking situation, and so had no fixed views on such subjects. This made for some doubt as to his fitness for high office, but his admirers pointed out that he was a military hero, and an honest man without a stain on his record. A Louisiana slaveholder, he commanded the enthusiastic support of the southern Whigs, as well as that of conservative northern Whigs who believed that, under his administration, there would be an excellent opportunity for settling the problem of slavery in the territories in a fashion acceptable to popular opinion in both sections. Thurlow Weed, the powerful Whig boss of New York State, was for Taylor, and a group of "Young Indians" in Congress—Robert A. Toombs and Alexander H. Stephens of Georgia, Abraham Lincoln of Illinois, and others—helped to drum up sentiment for this distinctly available candidate.

Availability was indeed the keynote of the Philadelphia convention. The best evidence the politicians could muster indicated that Taylor would run much better than Clay in areas normally Democratic, and that Clay would have only a slight chance of election. The support of John J. Crittenden, United States Senator from Clay's own state of Kentucky, for Taylor was a body blow to Clay's hopes, and "Old Zack" received the nomination on the fourth ballot. The convention then chose Millard Fillmore of New York, a Clay supporter, for Vice President. There was no platform.

The Whig convention left much bitterness in its wake. Greeley was scornful of it as a "slaughter-house of Whig principles," and Webster and Seward were disgruntled and alarmed. Clay, resentful over his rejection and perturbed by the abandonment of his American System (a move which left a political vacuum into which the slavery issue could rush), retired to Ashland in gloomy silence. Antislavery Whigs in general had little enthusiasm for this Louisiana slaveholder who had become the party's nominee. Under such circumstances, a Whig victory at the polls was by no means certain.

A new political party appeared in 1848. Arising, like its predecessor, the Liberty party, out of the growing antislavery sentiment in the North and West, it was made up in part of dissatisfied Conscience Whigs. John Quincy Adams died in February, 1848, but his son, Charles Francis Adams, bolted from the Whigs, as did Henry Wilson, "the Natick Cobbler," another influential Massachusetts leader. Prominent antislavery Democrats, Barnburners from New York State, Gideon Welles of Connecticut, and David Wilmot from Pennsylvania organized a split from the Democracy. Late in June, 1848, the Barnburners nominated Martin Van Buren for the presidency and sent out a call for a national antislavery convention to be held in Buffalo, New York. The Whig bolters listened to this summons, as did a group of western free-soilers holding a Peoples' Convention at Columbus, Ohio. The old Liberty party had already nominated for President John P. Hale, a New Hampshire Democrat, but such former Liberty party leaders as Salmon P. Chase of Ohio and Edwin M. Stanton, recently of Ohio but now a Pennsylvanian, decided to go to the Buffalo meeting.

Some 10,000 antislaveryites, disgruntled politicians, and reformers of all shades gathered at Buffalo on August 9, 1848. Most of them milled around the streets and in hotel lobbies, while the business of the convention was conducted by a body of 465 delegates from various parts of the North and West—Barnburners and Liberty men, Conscience and Clay Whigs. They nominated Van Buren for President and Charles Francis Adams for Vice President. Their platform, which supported internal improvements, a homestead law, and a tariff for revenue, had as its cardinal plank a ringing proclamation of a crusade for "free soil, free speech, free labor, and free men." The Liberty party merged in this new Free-Soil party, which planned an active campaign.

The campaign of 1848 was a spirited one, despite the few issues between the Whigs and the Democrats. All of the candidates were subjected to personal attacks, Cass as a "Doughface" on the subject of slavery, Taylor as a slaveholder who bought and sold human flesh, and Van Buren as a traitor to the Democracy. During the campaign, Oregon was organized as a free territory; this angered the South and increased the vote for Taylor in that region.

For the first time in American history, the whole nation voted on the same day, November 7, 1848. As might have been expected, in view of the lack of issues between the two major parties, the voters split almost evenly between the Whig and Democratic candidates. Eight slave states and seven free states (including New York, Pennsylvania, and Massachusetts) went for Taylor, and seven slave states and eight free states were in the Cass column. Many voters stayed away from the polls. Since Taylor had 163 electoral votes to 127 for Cass, had either New York or Pennsylvania gone for the Democratic candidate, he would have been elected. As it was, the Democrats carried the Senate by a safe margin and emerged with 112 seats in the House to 109 for the Whigs, while in the House nine Free-Soilers held the balance of power.

The election of 1848 was significant for a number of reasons. It showed the even balance of the two parties in voting strength, Cass polling only 139,555 fewer votes than Taylor out of 2,580,643 ballots. It demonstrated the part played by the military tradition, exemplified by Washington, Jackson, and Harrison, in determining the choice of presidential candidates, for both parties had chosen as leaders men with martial records. Important, too, for the future, was the growth of antislavery sentiment. Van Buren as the Free-Soil candidate had received 10 per cent of the total presidential vote; almost half of the Democratic voters in New York State had defected to him, as well as a large number of northern Pennsylvania Democrats, and he had drawn heavily on theretofore Whig strength in the Old Northwest. The free-soil sentiment of the North was becoming a political force with which both major parties would have to reckon.

The election also indicated the weakening hold of the major parties on the loyalty of voters. This was shown by the Free-Soil strength in the North, and in the South the marked resurgence of the Whigs (Taylor lost only Virginia, Alabama, and Mississippi, all by very narrow margins) indicated a high degree of political fluidity.

There was good cause for this weakening of party ties, for the distinction between Whigs and Democrats by 1848 had become merely nominal. The national bank and distribution of land sales had disappeared as issues. Protectionists and foes of protection could be found in the ranks of both organizations, and, in consequence, the tariff was an issue that tended to subdivide rather than sharply to differentiate the parties. Prominent politicians in both camps believed that new party alignments were imminent.

The time for the reorganization of parties had not come in 1848. Compromise on the issue of slavery extension, if compromise should come, might hold the national parties together for a few more years. Nevertheless, the Free-Soil movement of 1848 was an ominous sectional development, a portent of trouble in the future of the nation.

The Crisis over the Territories

The Thirtieth Congress (1847–1849) moved toward its close in the midst of contention between North and South over whether or not slavery should be given an opportunity to move into the nation's new territories. The territorial organization of Oregon in 1848 had been stubbornly opposed by the South because it expressly prohibited slavery in that area. President Polk had urged the establishment of territorial governments in California and New Mexico, together with an extension of the Missouri Compromise line of 36° 30′ to the Pacific, but nothing had been done. There was controversy in and out of Congress over the Wilmot Proviso, slavery in the District of Columbia, and the rendition of fugitive slaves who had escaped into the free states of the North. Turmoil marked the closing sessions of the national legislature, with violent speeches extolling or denouncing slavery, fist fights in both Houses, and the passage of a needed appropriation bill so late that Polk had to sign it after his term of office had expired.

A situation already critical became worse during 1849. Over 80,000 Argonauts rushed by land and sea into the gold fields near Sacramento, and the Californians began to clamor for admission to the Union as a free state. A quarrel between the inhabitants of New Mexico and the state of Texas over their boundary line threatened to erupt into violence. Southern spokesmen became increasingly bitter over the continued growth of northern antislavery sentiment and the violent attacks of the abolitionists; hotheads in the South began to talk openly of secession, and at a dinner given to Senator Andrew P. Butler of South Carolina in April, 1849, the toast "a Southern Confederacy" was hailed with cheers. The Virginia legislature declared that if the Wilmot Proviso became the law of the land, the "sovereign people of Virginia" would "resist at all hazards and to the last extremity." Meanwhile, in the North, the abolitionists redoubled their propaganda against slavery, state legislatures and popular conventions passed scores of resolutions favoring the Proviso, and a stream of antislavery petitions poured into Washington. Partly out of moral aversion to slavery, partly because of a desire for protection of industry against an influx of foreign goods, partly for power in Congress to obtain the internal improvements that the South opposed, and partly because of the aversion of free farmers to slave labor competition, the North was determined that no more slave states should be carved out of the federal territories.

Old Rough and Ready

When Zachary Taylor took over the helm of state on March 4, 1849, he was sixty-four years old. Taylor was a simple, kindly man, by nature industrious, morally and physically brave, with a deserved reputation for integrity and good common sense. He was also a political amateur, ignorant of domestic and foreign affairs, and without experience in civil administration. As he and Polk were driving to the Capitol on inauguration day, the latter understood Taylor to remark that Oregon and California were too far distant to become members of the Union and had better form independent governments for themselves; Polk thought him ignorant of public affairs and concluded that his Administration would be run by others, with the Cabinet controlling the government.

Though Taylor had no intention of being a mere catspaw, his honesty and political naivete made it natural for him to seek counsel and guidance. Clay was more than willing to be the President's alter ego, but it soon became apparent that the Louisiana slaveholder had other ideas. To the surprise of nearly everyone, and to the disgust of the southerners, he chose William H. Seward of New York as his mentor. This was to some extent the result of gratitude to Seward's friend Weed, one of the earliest supporters of Taylor for President, but it was more particularly because Seward tactfully established close associations with such Cabinet members as John M. Clayton, Secretary of State, and Reverdy Johnson, Attorney General, sedulously cultivated a friendship with the President's brother, Colonel J. P. Taylor, and gave repeated proofs of his concern for the President's success in the White House. The President became convinced of Seward's sincerity and ability. "Old Zack" had at first been inclined to look upon Vice President Fillmore as a guide, but the Senator from New York became the right-hand man of the Administration and assumed great control over the patronage in the North, especially in New York State.

A Crisis Develops

In part because of Seward's influence, but more because the most influential members of his Cabinet were opposed to slavery extension, Taylor became committed to a speedy organization of both California and New Mexico as free states. News of this excited the bitterest resentment in the South; secessionist threats became bolder and more frequent, and southern Whigs in droves deserted the Administration at Washington. At the same time, a marked tendency developed in a number of northern states for coalitions of Democrats and Free-Soilers, both of the old parties manifesting a tendency to break up and reform along sectional lines.

The critical situation that existed throughout the country was mirrored in the Thirty-First Congress. When that body met in December, 1849, the air at the capital was tense. The House quarreled for a week over the election of a doorkeeper favorable or unfavorable to slavery, and the contest over the election of a Speaker consumed three weeks of balloting, while charges and countercharges were hurled by the supporters and critics of the South's "peculiar institution." At one time the lie was given and only the sergeant-at-arms prevented a fist fight on the floor of the House, but Howell Cobb of Georgia was finally elected Speaker by a plurality vote. Discussion of the underground railroad, the slave trade in the District of Columbia, and slavery in the territories and in the South was still a daily occurrence amid stormy scenes in both House and Senate. When on one occasion Toombs threatened secession in a speech in the House, he was cheered to the echo by the southern members.

The Compromise of 1850

Henry Clay came back to Washington at the close of 1849, after a seven-year absence. Once again he appeared at his old desk in the Senate,

THE NATION'S CAPITOL IN 1850

Compare this fine panoramic view with the picture of the Capitol in 1800. Here is one measure of the growth of national power.

and there in the stuffy little chamber, with its purple curtains and red carpet, he found companions of former days—Benton, Cass, Webster, Calhoun—and a galaxy of younger men—Seward, Chase, Stephen A. Douglas of Illinois, Jefferson Davis of Mississippi—all ready to take part in what they knew would be a fateful session. Like his fellows, the veteran Senator from Kentucky was perturbed by the tense situation of the country. Before the end of January, he saw bills and resolutions introduced for the organization of New Mexico as free territory, for the admission of California and New Mexico to statehood, for adjustment of the Texas-New Mexico boundary, for a stringent fugitive slave law, and for resistance to the extension of slavery and its exclusion from the District of Columbia. Washington was agog with rumors of a southern convention that planned to meet

CLAY ADDRESSING THE UNITED STATES SENATE (1850)

Engraved from a painting by Peter F. Rothermel. This was the beginning of the great debate over the Compromise of 1850. Fillmore is in the chair, with Calhoun just to his left. Webster, his head resting on his hand, sits in the second row behind Clay.

in Nashville the following June, and there were fears that it might set secession in motion—fears which were strengthened, on Clay's part, by the commotion in the House of Representatives.

What he saw and heard convinced the veteran statesman from Kentucky that the only salvation of the country would be compromise between the conflicting viewpoints, and Webster promised support in principle. On January 29, 1850, Clay rose in the Senate to begin his last and greatest effort for the Union, proposing a series of resolutions covering the principal subjects of controversy between the North and the South. He asked: (1) that California be admitted as a free state; (2) that the other territories acquired from Mexico be organized without any reference to slavery; (3) that a boundary line be drawn between Texas and New Mexico giving the latter nearly all of its claims in the disputed region; (4) that the United States assume the public debt owed by Texas at the time of annexation, some $3 million; and (5) that the traffic in slaves brought into the District of Columbia for sale or transportation be stopped; but (6) that slavery be not abolished in the District of Columbia without the consent of the people of Maryland and of the District and without compensation; (7) that Congress declare it had no power over the interstate slave trade; and (8) that the federal government pass a law rendering more effective the rendition of fugitive slaves.

A week later, Clay spoke at length on behalf of his proposals. California, he said, had a right to come in as a free state. There was no need to prohibit slavery in New Mexico, for Nature herself had made that area inhospitable to slavery, and the boundary settlement he proposed between Texas and New Mexico would, in effect, prevent the extension of slavery in the new territories above the Rio Grande. Prohibition of the slave trade in the District of Columbia would be pleasing to the North. An effective fugitive slave law would remove one of the South's main grievances against the North, and acknowledgment that Congress had no right to interfere with the interstate slave trade would placate passions aroused in the South by the onslaughts of the abolitionists. Clay asked both sides to compromise for the sake of the Union. Realizing that his proposals gave more to the South than to the North, he appealed to the latter section for magnanimity and closed with a graphic picture of the terrible consequences of secession —a move which, he asserted, no state or combination of states had the right to make.

The immediate popular reaction to Clay's proposals was favorable. Large nonpartisan meetings in both sections supported compromise and cheered Clay's name. Conservative northern Whig newspapers were enthusiastic, as was the Washington *Union,* edited by Thomas Ritchie of Virginia; and other Democratic organs, North and South, added their approval. But there was also criticism: Beverly Tucker of Virginia denounced Clay's "sneaking compromises," calling him a "prince of humbugs," and such northern antislavery leaders as Salmon P. Chase and Joshua Giddings of Ohio and Garrison and Wendell Phillips of Massachusetts thought it worse than useless. More ominous still for its chances of success, President Taylor, jealous of Clay and devoted to his own proposal to organize both California and New Mexico as free states, was hostile to the plan.

For two months, from the middle of February to the middle of April, 1850, the Senate debated Clay's proposals. The attack was opened by Jefferson Davis. A hero of the Mexican War and influential in the South, Davis dismissed Clay's plan as useless and argued for the unlimited right of the South to take its slaves into the territories. Even the Missouri Compromise, he said, was valid not because Congress had passed it, but because the states had accepted it. He suggested the practicality of peaceful secession; if the sections separated amicably, they might come together at some future time.

Calhoun was to speak on March 4. Though the great South Carolinian had prepared his remarks with care, he was in the last stages of consumption and was half-led, half-carried, into the Senate, where, swathed in flannels and with his eyes partly closed beneath their shaggy brows, he listened while his speech was read for him by Senator Mason of Virginia. Like Davis, he was against the Compromise, believing it could not save the Union, for the balance between the two sections had been destroyed by the tariff, by exclusion of the South from the territories of the Union, and by the growth of the power of the national government. The bonds holding the nation together were loosening, he argued, and the only way to keep this federal republic together was to give the South free access to the new territory, return fugitive slaves, stop antislavery agitation, and put through a constitutional amendment restoring equality of rights between the two sections. If these things could not be done, it would be best for the Union to come to an end by peaceful agreement, for, faced by the alternatives of submission or resistance, the South would know how to act.

Compelled by logic and conviction, Calhoun defended slavery even while it was being discarded in the western world, and upheld states' rights and the aspirations of an agrarian economy in an era when industrial development and business enterprise in the United States were becoming more and more national in scope. As Professor Craven has aptly put it, "he was forced to be a voice out of the past while he yet lived."

If Calhoun's point of view pleased southern fire-eaters but alienated moderate southerners who thought it extreme, Webster's "Seventh of March Speech" (the only one in American history that is known by its date) had exactly the opposite effect upon northern public opinion. Eloquently, he spoke of the impossibility of peaceful secession, and supported the main parts of Clay's proposal. Nature, said Webster, had forbidden slavery in the new territories, and the South was right, the North wrong, about the necessity of a more rigorous fugitive slave law. Both sides had legitimate grievances, but civil war would be criminal folly.

As in his replies to Hayne in 1830, Webster spoke for the Union, and conservative Whigs, moderate Democrats, and northern businessmen in general applauded him. But the Free-Soilers were critical, and the abolitionists covered him with abuse. Walt Whitman, just at the dawn of his greatness, in a poem called "Blood Money," sneered at Webster—"And still Iscariot plies his trade." Theodore Parker compared the Senator from Massachusetts to Benedict Arnold, and John Greenleaf Whittier pilloried him in "Ichabod":

> So fallen! so lost! the light withdrawn
>   which once he wore!
> The glory from his gray hairs gone
>   Forevermore!
> Revile him not, the Tempter hath
>   A snare for all;
> And pitying tears, not scorn and wrath,
>   Befit his fall!
>
>   *   *   *
>
> Then pay the reverence of old days
>   To his dead fame;
> Walk backward, with averted gaze,
>   And hide the shame!

Rising young leaders in the Senate also opposed the Compromise. Chase and Hale denounced it, and Seward opposed all compromises with and concessions to slavery, saying that the antislavery crusade would go on, for it represented right and justice. Congress had no basic authority for admitting slavery to the territories, he argued, and the national domain was not simply a possession "to be enjoyed either in common or by partition by the citizens of the old states. . . . We hold . . . no arbitrary power over it. We hold no arbitrary authority over anything. . . . The Constitution regulates our stewardship. . . . But there is a higher law than the Constitution, which regulates our authority over the domain." We are, said Seward, the stewards of the Creator of the Universe, acting on behalf of mankind, "and must so discharge our trust as to secure in the highest attainable degree their happiness."

Seward's "higher law" doctrine attracted wide attention. It took lofty ground, just as Sam Adams had done before the American Revolution when he argued that the law of Nature and of Nature's God forbade taxation without representation. In both cases, the difficulty lay in defining the "law" to which appeal was made, and in the justification that such a stand gave for rash and radical action under the guise of high principle.

Controversy continued over the form legislation should take, with Senator Douglas giving powerful aid to the compromisers. On April 18, the Senate agreed to the appointment of a committee of thirteen, with Clay as chairman, and this committee produced three bills. The first, known as the "Omnibus bill," would have admitted California as a free state, organized the territories of New Mexico and Utah without reference to slavery, and adjusted the Texas boundary and given that state compensation for relinquishing its territorial claims in the New Mexico region. The second bill provided a more effective fugitive slave law. The third prohibited importation of slaves into the District of Columbia for sale or transportation.

Clay fought hard for these bills, particularly for the Omnibus, but extremists on both sides continued hostile and Taylor clung doggedly to his own proposals. The debate dragged on through June with no progress in the Senate, but outside circumstances began to favor the compromisers: there was growing alarm because of threatened hostilities between Texas and New Mexico over their boundary line; the Nashville' convention met and, though largely controlled by moderates, denounced the Compromise and made arrangements for a subsequent meeting; and public opinion in favor of the Compromise, influenced by these events and by the debates in Congress, gained strength as time went on. Death itself intervened in the struggle, for President Taylor died unexpectedly on July 9 of cholera morbus and typhoid fever, and Millard Fillmore, friend of Clay and compromise, became President.

The more favorable prospect for the proposed adjustment was dimmed when the Omnibus was defeated by a parliamentary maneuver, and Clay, weary and worn out, went off to Newport for a rest. But under the energetic leadership of Douglas all the bills, save that concerning slavery in the

District of Columbia, were passed one at a time. After the Kentuckian had come back to push the remaining measure through the Senate, all the bills passed the House, and Fillmore signed them; by the middle of September, 1850, the Compromise had become the law of the land.

News of the final passage of the Compromise was received with wild jubilation in Washington and with expressions of relief and approval throughout the country. Free-Soilers and abolitionists, to be sure, were disappointed; some Conscience Whigs and antislavery Democrats caviled at the fugitive slave law; but the great majority of Whigs and Democrats approved the settlement. People believed that the Compromise had settled, once for all, the question of slavery in the territories. Together with the Missouri Compromise and the admission of Texas as a slave and Oregon as a free state, it appeared to determine the limits of slavery west of the Mississippi. Disunion no longer seemed a danger.

The Compromise of 1850 had a larger significance than the immediate easing of a situation that had nearly plunged the country into a civil war. The admission of California as a free state broke the balance theretofore existing between the slave and free states in the Senate, thus highlighting the steadily increasing political and economic power of the North and, in all probability, also postponing secession for a decade. Had the South seceded in 1850, it might well have established its status as a separate nation, for it is possible that the North might then have acquiesced in the peaceful departure of the slave states from the Union. Since northern superiority in wealth, population, transportation, and general resources was considerably smaller in 1850 than it was to be in 1861, it is certain that if war had come in 1850, the struggle would have been much more even than it was to be eleven years later. Finally, the Compromise was significant for a reason that was not perceived at the time of its passage; by the organization of New Mexico and Utah without reference to slavery, it put into law a principle already advocated by General Cass, that of allowing the people of the territories to decide for themselves whether or not they should have slavery. We shall hear more of this principle and its attempted extension, four years later, to the lands north of 36° 30' in the Louisiana Purchase.

The Election of 1852 and the Political Situation

The election of 1852 was heavily influenced by the Compromise that had just been passed. The Whig nominee, General Winfield Scott, was

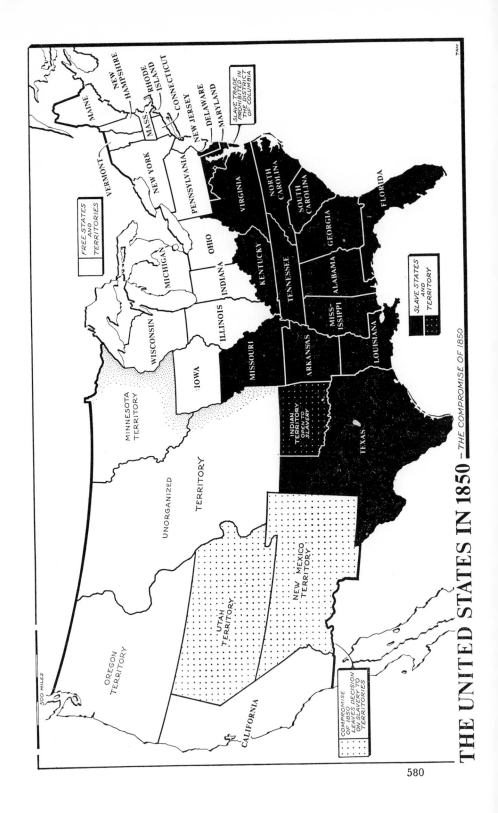

THE UNITED STATES IN 1850 — *THE COMPROMISE OF 1850*

FREE STATES
AND
TERRITORIES

SLAVE STATES
AND
TERRITORY

COMPROMISE
OF 1850
LEAVES DECISION
ON SLAVERY TO
TERRITORIES

SLAVE TRADE
PROHIBITED IN
THE DISTRICT
OF COLUMBIA

MAINE

NEW
HAMPSHIRE

MASS.

RHODE
ISLAND

CONNECTICUT

NEW JERSEY

DELAWARE

MARYLAND

VERMONT

NEW YORK

PENNSYLVANIA

VIRGINIA

NORTH
CAROLINA

SOUTH
CAROLINA

GEORGIA

FLORIDA

MICHIGAN

OHIO

INDIANA

KENTUCKY

TENNESSEE

ALABAMA

MISS-
ISSIPPI

WISCONSIN

ILLINOIS

IOWA

MISSOURI

ARKANSAS

LOUISIANA

INDIAN
TERRITORY
OPEN TO
SLAVERY

TEXAS

MINNESOTA
TERRITORY

UNORGANIZED

TERRITORY

NEW MEXICO
TERRITORY

UTAH
TERRITORY

OREGON
TERRITORY

CALIFORNIA

500 MILES

suspected of Free-Soil leanings. In consequence, though the Whig platform pledged support of the Compromise, many southern Whigs turned their backs on him. In the North, what was left of the Free-Soilers rejected him, nominating John P. Hale for President. Webster, too, deeply hurt at having been denied the nomination, advised his friends to vote for the Democratic candidate.

The Democrats, unable to decide among a host of active contenders for the nomination (Cass, Douglas, Buchanan, Marcy, and Sam Houston of Texas), on the forty-ninth ballot turned, as they had in 1844, to a dark horse, and Franklin K. Pierce of New Hampshire received the nomination. He and his party pledged support for the Compromise.

Pierce was elected by an overwhelming majority. The Whigs carried only Kentucky and Tennessee, Massachusetts and Vermont; the rest of the thirty-one states went for Pierce, who received 254 electoral votes to forty-two for Scott. The Free-Soil vote for John P. Hale, 156,000, was only a little more than half of the vote for Van Buren in 1848. An extremist Southern Rights party candidate, George M. Troup, polled only 3,500 votes in the entire South. And the Democrats had very comfortable majorities in both Houses of Congress.

The political situation that had developed by 1852 was significant in several ways. The virtual breakup of the Free-Soil party, many of its members going back into the old parties or staying at home, showed how the Compromise had blunted the appeal of the antislavery forces. The Whig party also emerged from the election in a greatly weakened condition; it lost, for the first time, every section of the country, its decline being greatest in the cotton states, where its popular vote fell from 170,000 in 1848 to 110,000 in 1852. Always a force for national unity, the Whig party was going to pieces on the issue of slavery; it never again entered a presidential contest with an independent nomination. Its decline pointed inexorably to an increase in sectionalism, but, even more than this, the Democratic triumph in the South indicated the likelihood of dominance by one party in that area of the country.

There was another disquieting factor in the general situation. The fugitive slave law was distinctly repugnant to many in the North. It did not permit jury trial, or even a hearing before a judge, for the fugitive. Title to the escaped slave was established by affidavit before a federal commission, and heavy fines and imprisonment could be imposed on citizens who aided black chattels fleeing before the law. The ardent opponents of slavery complained that this was a violation of the fifth amendment. Northern mass meetings and newspapers denounced the law. In 1851, a slave named Shadrach was rescued by a mob in Boston, and similar action a few months later in Syracuse, New York, freed the slave Jerry from the clutches of the federal marshals. There were only a few such instances of mob outbreak, but they acquired wide notoriety and nourished the resentment against the law that was especially keen in the northeastern part of the country. This resentment, however, was overshadowed by the general feeling of relief with which the country saw the establishment of the Compromise. National discord and division had lessened, and the outlook for the future seemed bright.

Suggested Reading

For the deterioration of parties in the period following the Mexican War, see Nevins, *The Ordeal of the Union*, vol. I, and Van Deusen, *The Jacksonian Era*, both previously cited, M. B. Duberman, *Charles Francis Adams 1807–1886* (1961), a first-rate biography, and Paul, *Rift in the Democracy*, heretofore cited.

The election of 1848 is covered in the works just mentioned, in Holman Hamilton, *Zachary Taylor, Soldier in the White House* (1951), and in biographies already cited of Cass, Van Buren, Calhoun, Clay, Webster, and Marcy. For a special study of the antislavery movement, see T. C. Smith, *The Liberty and Free Soil Parties in the*

The best recent study of the Compromise of 1850 is Holman Hamilton, *Prologue to Conflict* (1964). The biographies mentioned above are useful for the Compromise. See also R. H. Shryock, *Georgia and the Union in 1850* (1928); Ulrich B. Phillips, *The Life of Robert Toombs* (1913); P. M. Hamer, *The Secession Movement in South Carolina, 1847–1852* (1918); M. J. White, *The Secession Movement in the United States, 1847–1852* (1916); and G. F. Milton, *The Eve of Conflict: Stephen A. Douglas and the Needless War* (1934). There is an excellent and detailed account of the struggle over the Compromise in Nevins, *The Ordeal of the Union*, vol. I. See also A. O. Craven, *The Growth of Southern Nationalism* (1953).

For the election of 1852, see the works mentioned in the preceding paragraph, as well as the old but well-written, James Ford Rhodes, *History of the United States from the Compromise of 1850* (9 vols., 1893–1922), vol. I.

28 ⸳ The Fateful Administration of Franklin Pierce, 1853-1857

THE PERIOD FROM 1850 to 1856 was, from a social and economic point of view, one of rapid and prosperous growth. The excitement occasioned by the crisis over the new territories no longer vexed the country. The average output of the gold fields was $60 million a year; under the stimulus of this yellow flood, the retail price level rose and business circles became confident. Foreign trade expanded, money poured into transportation facilities, and manufacturing enterprises increased in number and in size. Railroad mileage in operation doubled from 9,000 to 18,000 miles; the production of pig iron jumped from around 560,000 tons in 1850 to one million tons in 1855; and the cotton mills of the country, which took 575,000 bales in 1850, consumed 706,000 bales five years later. Population steadily increased, pushed upward all the faster by the annual immigration of between 350,000 and 400,000 Europeans. To most Americans the future seemed bright.

Years of Growth and Plenty

There were, to be sure, areas of distress and signs of danger as the Administration of Franklin Pierce took over the reins of office. Native free labor was restive as wages lagged behind prices, and the labor supply was aug-

HARRIET BEECHER STOWE
(1811–1896)

Daguerreotype, probably taken in 1853. Mrs. Stowe's Uncle Tom's Cabin *did much to widen the breach between North and South.*

mented by tens of thousands of foreign workmen. Upland cotton prices, which had recovered sharply toward the close of the 1840s, dropped from $.12 a pound in 1850 to $.095 cents in 1852, and were not quite $.11 in 1854. A terrible yellow fever epidemic plagued the South in 1853, causing 8,000 deaths in New Orleans while other southern cities suffered only in less degree. And ominous, in a deeper sense, was the reception of a novel bearing the title *Uncle Tom's Cabin,* published in the winter of 1851–1852.

The author of this best seller was Harriet Beecher Stowe (1811–1896), wife of Calvin E. Stowe, a New England Presbyterian minister and professor of sacred literature. Mrs. Stowe, daughter of Lyman Beecher and sister of Henry Ward Beecher, was an absentminded, whimsical, but earnest individual, the devoted mother of a large family. She had the storyteller's gift and a profound moral hatred of slavery. *Uncle Tom's Cabin* is not great literature: its language is trite, its humor strained, and its style commonplace. Though neither an accurate nor an objective account of the "peculiar institution," it was the first American novel to take a black man for a hero, and it conveyed to the reader its author's passion over the wrong that was being done to a part of the human race. Its success was instantaneous; Mrs. Stowe almost literally woke up one morning to find herself famous. The book sold 3,000 copies the first day of publication, 10,000 copies in a week, and 300,000 copies in a year. It was translated into twenty different languages, and 1,500,000 copies in pirated editions were disposed of in the British Empire. The South with one voice condemned it and its author, but the antislavery people accepted it as gospel. The mothers of the North brought their sons up to read it, and many of those sons were of fighting age in 1861. After Fort Sumter, Lincoln is reported to have said, on meeting Mrs. Stowe, "Is this the little woman who made this big war?"

Franklin Pierce and the Democratic Party

There was no war scare when Franklin Pierce, then in his forty-eighth year, took the oath of office as President of the United States. A graduate of Bowdoin and a lawyer, he had risen rapidly in his home state, spending four years in the New Hampshire legislature while he was still in his twenties. The New Hampshire Democrats sent him to Congress at the age of twenty-nine, and when he was thirty-three elected him to the upper house of the national legislature, the youngest man in the Senate. He enlisted in the Mexican War as a private and came out as a brigadier-general, having served well under Scott.

Pierce was a handsome man with an engaging, almost boyishly friendly manner. He was graceful in bearing, attractive in personality, honest and religious in his approach to life. He was also essentially a weak mediocrity, with an intelligence that was quick but superficial, a facile desire to please all factions of his party, and an ambition for renomination that played into the hands of the leaders of the southern Democracy. Moreover, he had a distressing personal weakness in his fondness for liquor. The Whigs declared, all too truthfully, that he was indeed a hero, the hero of many a well-fought bottle.

Pierce's political principles were of the neo-Jacksonian variety. He was a nationalist and expansionist who believed in a vigorous foreign policy, respect for states' rights, and economy in government. He outlined his views in his inaugural, which he delivered without manuscript or notes. It began with a graceful allusion to his own deep grief and sorrow, for, scarcely a month before, his only surviving child, a boy of thirteen, had had his brains dashed out in a railroad accident before the eyes of his horrified father and mother. Pierce then went on to say that the Compromise of

1850 would be unhesitatingly enforced, and that he had "no timid fore-bodings of evil from expansion." The possession of slaves was an "admitted right" and the laws that upheld slavery must be respected and obeyed. References to "morbid enthusiasm" and "fanatical excitement" were clearly warnings to the abolitionists.

The President's Cabinet and his appointments abroad showed Pierce's southern leanings. There was not a strong antislavery man in the Cabinet; though William L. Marcy of New York disliked slavery, he could scarcely be described as an ardent free-soiler. On the other hand, the two strong men in the Cabinet, Jefferson Davis, Secretary of War, and Caleb Cushing of Massachusetts, Attorney General, were wholly pleasing to southern extremists. The southern Union Democrats had no representation in the President's official family. The same slant appeared in diplomatic appointments. No antislavery man was sent abroad; the fire-eater Pierre Soulé of Louisiana went to Madrid, Judge John Y. Mason of Virginia to Paris, and James Buchanan (from Pennsylvania but definitely pro-southern) to the Court of St. James.

Both Pierce's inaugural and his appointments showed that the fervor of idealism which, in the days of Jackson, had been one of the outstanding characteristics of the Democracy was no longer one of its guiding lights. That party was in a position of great power. It controlled the presidency and both houses of Congress, as well as the governors and legislatures of a great majority of the states. But in its national councils the great slaveholders of the South were rapidly becoming the most potent political force; it restricted its objectives to expansionism, fostering prosperity, and remaining in power; and it had as its leader a man who sought to please everybody and ended by pleasing none.

A Foreign Policy of Expansion

The Administration's foreign policy sought to assert and expand American interests abroad. By diplomatic negotiation, Pierce and Marcy tried unsuccessfully to obtain withdrawal by Great Britain from the footholds that country had obtained in Nicaragua and Honduras. On the other hand, no effort was made to check the filibustering activities of William Walker, "The Grey-eyed Man of Destiny," who in 1855 established a short-lived dictatorship in Nicaragua. In 1854, the United States negotiated a reciprocity treaty with Canada, which settled a dispute over the Newfoundland fisheries by giving the United States favorable fishing rights, while other provisions favorable to Canada granted free commerce in most of the natural products of the two countries. But most significant of all were the negotiations with Japan.

A naval expedition to Japan had been planned by the Fillmore Administration, but it was carried out under President Pierce. The extension of the United States to the Pacific, the magnificent harbors on the Pacific coast, the growing transit across the Isthmus of Panama, and plans for a transcontinental railroad aroused visions in the United States of an expanding Oriental trade. Japan, closed to western merchants, was a challenge. Besides, a coaling station there would be important for commercial activity in the Far Pacific. Commodore Matthew Calbraith Perry, commander of the expedition, was instructed to communicate directly with the Emperor and to obtain trading and coaling privileges for American ships and protection for American seamen shipwrecked or driven by weather to land in Japan.

Perry sailed into the Bay of Yedo in July, 1853, with a squadron of four ships. His firm and haughty demeanor, together with his two sloops of war, impressed the Japanese. Having made his demands, he informed his reluctant hosts that he would return for an answer in the spring. The Shogun and his advisers, who wielded the real power in the Japanese state, impressed by Perry's attitude and convinced that the United States would be easier to deal with than either England or Russia, decided to yield. Perry, fearful lest the European Powers anticipate him, came back earlier than he had planned, and Japan's first treaty with a western state was signed on March 31, 1854; American ships were given access to two Japanese ports (Shimoda and Hakodate), a United States consul could reside at Shimoda, and proper treatment was assured for shipwrecked American sailors. So began the opening of Japan to the West.

Protection and expansion of American rights went hand in hand with the extension of American controls. Through James Gadsden, a South Carolina railroad man who was Minister to Mexico, the United States gave $10 million for what came to be known as the Gadsden Purchase, some 45,000 square miles of land between the Rio Grande and the Colorado Rivers. This new territory contained the fertile Mesilla Valley and the lowest pass over the Southern Rockies, a route later to be used by the Southern Pacific Railroad. Negotiations were also begun but not completed for the acquisition of Hawaii and a naval base in Santo Domingo. The possibility of purchasing Alaska interested some members of the Pierce Administration.

In Secretary Cushing's view, Americans were the modern Romans who, like their ancient prototypes, were destined to follow a policy of conquest and annexation. Certainly the Pierce Administration was in an expansionist mood. This was never more clearly illustrated than in the case of Cuba and the Ostend Manifesto.

Cuba was badly governed by Spain, with landholders mercilessly exploiting their slaves. The island was tempting bait to southern expansionists, perturbed by fear of a slave insurrection there spreading to the mainland and anxious to add more slave territory to the Union. Between 1849 and 1851, Narciso Lopez, a Venezuelan-born adventurer formerly high in the Spanish service, led three expeditions from American ports against the "Pearl of the Antilles." The Spaniards captured and executed Lopez, but filibustering threats continued, and relations between Spain and the United States went from bad to worse. When, in February, 1854, the Spanish authorities at Havana seized the American steamer *Black Warrior* for a technical violation of customs regulations, southerners and southern sympathizers promptly called for a rupture of relations, if not for war with Spain. That country released the American ship and appealed to Britain and France for help in ending the filibustering expeditions. The crisis eased, but pressure for the annexation of Cuba increased.

Secretary Marcy was willing to get Cuba by peaceful means, but was by no means rabid on the subject of annexation. He informed minister Soulé that he might seek to "detach" Cuba from Spain, and might offer as much as $130 million for the island. Soulé had a penchant for swift and dramatic action; soon after his arrival at Madrid, he had become involved in a duel with the French Ambassador, and he now used threats in a blustering attempt to force Spain into selling Cuba but made no progress toward his objective.

Marcy was under continuing pressure from the southern expansionists. He believed that, in view of the Crimean War, which broke out early in 1854, Britain and France would take little interest in the Cuban situation, and he was thoroughly aware of the deplorable condition of the Spanish treasury. He now proposed that Soulé, Buchanan, and Mason leave the capitals to which they were accredited for a conference together at Ostend, where they should consult and adopt measures for a concert of action in aid of Soulé's efforts at Madrid.

The three envoys met at Ostend in October, 1854, and, under Soulé's leadership, drew up what became known as the Ostend Manifesto. It declared that the United States ought to purchase Cuba with the shortest possible delay, for a slave insurrection there would have evil consequences in the United States, and, furthermore, the island's geographical position was of immense significance. The United States, they asserted, would never be secure while Cuba was "the dependency of a distant power. . . . Indeed, the Union can never enjoy repose, nor possess reliable security, as long as Cuba is not embraced within its boundaries." They declared that it would be financially profitable for Spain to sell, especially since there was a real possibility of a Cuban revolution. But if Spain refused to part with Cuba, "we shall be justified in wresting it from Spain if we possess the power."

The Manifesto accomplished nothing concrete. Marcy repudiated the proposal that the United States seize Cuba, and rebuked Soulé; was Spain, the Secretary of State inquired, to be confronted with the alternatives of cession or seizure? Soulé resigned, the Spanish government declaring that parting with Cuba would be like parting with the national honor, and there the matter rested. The Manifesto remained, however, a monument to southern expansionist zeal and to the arrogance and blundering of incompetent diplomats, however much they might have logic on their side.

New Leaders of the Nation

The Thirty-Third Congress, which assembled in December, 1853, saw an emergence of new leaders, or would-be leaders. The giants of old—Clay, Webster, and Calhoun—had passed away, and public attention now began to focus on such new men as Douglas, Chase, Sumner, and Seward.

Senator Stephen A. Douglas (1813–1861), "The Little Giant," or "The Steam Engine in Britches," as his admirers called him, was the most spectacular of the men who now gathered in the Senate chamber. A son of New England, he had migrated to Illinois and there had been admitted to the bar before he was twenty-one years of age. His rise was rapid: he was in the Illinois legislature at twenty-three, on the state supreme court at twenty-eight, a representative in Congress at thirty, and a United States Senator at thirty-three; in the Senate, he was now chairman of the powerful committee on territories. Douglas was short and stocky with an enormous head, black hair, a strongly-marked face, and a great, sonorous voice. Though at first he lacked refinement of manner—speaking in the House, he would become excited and rant and rave, tearing off his cravat and unbuttoning his waistcoat as he stormed up and down the aisle—he acquired polish in Washington, and his second wife, the beautiful Adele Cutts, whom he married in 1856, was a reigning Washington belle. Douglas was no reader, but he was a shrewd judge of men, a brilliant and magnetic expansionist, a leader of the western Democracy, and a man whose gaze was fixed on the White House.

Salmon P. Chase (1808–1873) was born in New Hampshire but emigrated to Ohio at an early age. He graduated from Dartmouth, and then studied law and was admitted to the bar. Politically, he moved from one party to another, his guiding principle being opposition to slavery. He entered the United States Senate in 1849, elected by a combination of Democrats and Free-Soilers. As anxious to become President as Clay had ever been, Chase determined to play a prominent role in Washington. He was a handsome, almost a majestic figure, self-righteous, opinionated, and devoid of humor, but deeply religious, able, and strong of will.

Charles Sumner (1811–1874) of Massachusetts came to the Senate, like Chase, as the result of a Free-Soil–Democratic combination. Six feet, four inches in height, he was a massive figure, a man of learning and culture, an effective speaker, and a bitter opponent of slavery. His coupling of northern manufacturers and slaveholders—"The lords of the lash and the lords of the loom"—earned him the dislike of the powerful New England business element, but he had a devoted popular following. Intolerant, opinionated, with a pompous manner and what amounted almost to a genius for making personal enemies, he was also a hard worker and a man of undoubted integrity.

William H. Seward (1801–1872) had come to the Senate with a brilliant record as legislator and governor in New York State. "Little Bill" was red-headed and beak-nosed, with a weak voice and a penchant for taking a huge pinch of snuff at the conclusion of a speech. He was intellectually fastidious, a lover of history, philosophy, and poetry. Able, and possessing a liberal record, he was an outstanding leader of the antislavery forces in the Senate and in the country. Like the others, he was ambitious for political preferment. He had as his political mentor Thurlow Weed, one of the ablest politicians of the period, whose hold on the New York State Whig machine had helped put Seward in the Senate and, Seward hoped, would help him reach the White House.

All four men were to play leading roles in the calamitous events of the next six years.

The Kansas-Nebraska Bill

Even in its first year, the Pierce Administration got off to a bad start. As a horde of Democratic officeseekers descended upon Washington, the Whigs were turned out in droves, but for every Democrat satisfied with a position ten went away disappointed and bitter. Worse still, from the point of view of party harmony, was the way in which the President interfered in intraparty fights within the various states; in New York, Massachusetts, Missouri, Ohio, and Illinois, inept handling of the federal patronage fanned the flames of discord. It became evident also that Pierce had no program to offer Congress when that body met in December, 1853. Before his first year in office was over, thoughtful men were writing off the Administration of this miscalled "Young Hickory" as a failure. There were still more evil days to come.

There was at first scant prospect that the Thirty-Third Congress would enact legislation of serious consequence to the nation. Pierce called for a lowering of the tariff, since the government's receipts were exceeding its expenditures and also suggested, cautiously, a grant of public lands to railroad companies—a subject of some importance, since a Pacific railroad was being much talked about and surveys of possible routes were being made. It looked as though Congress would confine its attention to grants for internal improvements and some moderate tariff revision, when the introduction of a new piece of legislation changed the entire complexion of events.

Douglas had for some time wished to see the Louisiana Purchase north of 36° 30′ given territorial organization, since this move would foster settlement and brighten the possibility of a railroad being built by a central or northern route. On January 4, 1854, he introduced from the committee on territories a bill for the organization of a huge part of the Louisiana Purchase lying west of Missouri and Iowa, the so-called Nebraska Territory. The bill's only reference to slavery was an ambiguous statement that when the territory should be admitted as a state or states, it should be with or without slavery as the state constitution might prescribe.

Once the bill was on the floor of the Senate, Douglas found himself confronted by a rising tide of southern discontent. Many southerners who refused to believe that slavery had reached its natural limits in the United States contended that the Missouri Compromise was unconstitutional, and were anxious to have explicit freedom to take their slaves into any territory organized north of 36° 30′. Those primarily interested in a southern railroad route to the Pacific were reluctant to see Nebraska organized, all the more so if slavery were excluded from the territory. The South disliked the prospect of new free-soil states, and Missourians especially chafed at the thought of a neighboring free state that would be one more asylum for fugitive slaves. It became clear that in order to pass, the Nebraska bill would have to contain concessions to the southern point of view, and Douglas began to accept amendments.

The Kansas-Nebraska bill, as it was finally called, provided for the organization of the two territories named in its title and left the decision for or against slavery to the people of these territories, just as had been

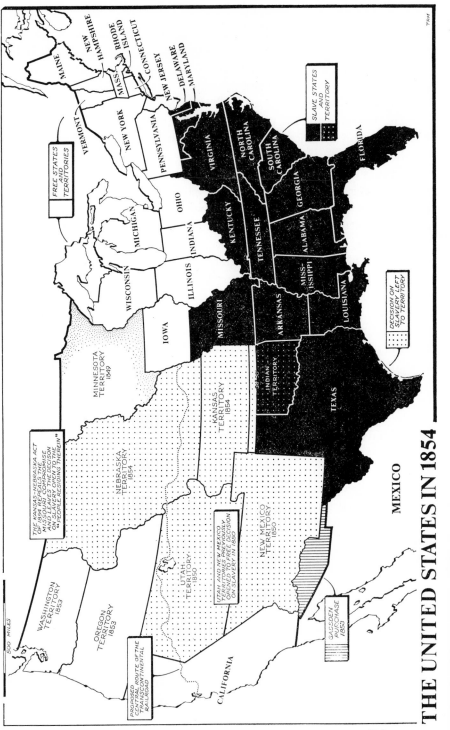

THE UNITED STATES IN 1854

Legend:
- FREE STATES AND TERRITORIES
- SLAVE STATES AND TERRITORY
- DECISION ON SLAVERY LEFT TO TERRITORY

Map labels:

MAINE
NEW HAMPSHIRE
RHODE ISLAND
MASS.
CONNECTICUT
NEW JERSEY
DELAWARE
MARYLAND
VERMONT
NEW YORK
PENNSYLVANIA
VIRGINIA
NORTH CAROLINA
SOUTH CAROLINA
GEORGIA
FLORIDA
OHIO
KENTUCKY
TENNESSEE
ALABAMA
INDIANA
ILLINOIS
MICHIGAN
WISCONSIN
MISSISSIPPI
LOUISIANA
IOWA
MISSOURI
ARKANSAS
INDIAN TERRITORY
TEXAS
MINNESOTA TERRITORY 1849
KANSAS TERRITORY 1854
NEBRASKA TERRITORY 1854
NEW MEXICO TERRITORY 1850
UTAH TERRITORY 1850
WASHINGTON TERRITORY 1853
OREGON TERRITORY 1853
CALIFORNIA
MEXICO

THE KANSAS-NEBRASKA ACT OF 1854 REPEALS THE MISSOURI COMPROMISE AND LEAVES THE DECISION ON SLAVERY OPEN TO THE "PEOPLE RESIDING THEREIN"

UTAH AND NEW MEXICO TERRITORIES PREVIOUSLY OPENED TO FREE DECISION ON SLAVERY IN 1850

PROPOSED CENTRAL ROUTE OF THE TRANSCONTINENTAL RAILROAD

GADSDEN PURCHASE 1853

500 MILES

done in organizing the territories of New Mexico and Utah. It declared that the Missouri Compromise provision excluding slavery from the Louisiana Purchase north of 36° 30′ was "inconsistent with the principle of non-intervention by Congress with slavery in the States and Territories," and was "inoperative and void." This last provision was agreed to by Douglas, despite his belief that it would "raise the hell of a storm." His prediction was justified, for by the time the bill in its final form reached the Senate (January 23, 1854), the North was full of sound and fury.

Various theories have been advanced as to why Douglas accepted these changes in his bill. He was influenced by his friend Senator Atchison of Missouri. He needed southern votes to get the territories organized so that Chicago could get a railroad to the Pacific, with benefit to his and his friends' real estate operations. Callous or indifferent to the moral wrong of slavery, he underestimated the intensity of northern antislavery sentiment, and he had convinced himself that Congress had no right to legislate on slavery in the territories and that therefore the Missouri Compromise was unconstitutional. He believed that the southern economic system had reached its natural confines and that popular sovereignty would not result in the establishment of slavery north of 36° 30′. He wanted, by a bold stroke, to distract the country's attention from the weakness and ineptitude of the Democratic national Administration. All of these factors may have played a part in Douglas's decision to make the Kansas-Nebraska bill what it was. But, having once made his decision, he threw all his splendid talents for political maneuver into getting the measure through Congress.

Those talents were needed, for the North was ablaze with wrath. The day after the bill in its final form reached the Senate, there appeared in the northern press the "Appeal of the Independent Democrats in Congress to the People of the United States." Written by Chase and signed by Sumner, Gerrit Smith, and others, six in all, it denounced the Kansas-Nebraska bill as a "gross violation of a sacred pledge." It was an act "worthy of an accomplished architect of ruin" who, with "meditated bad faith," was using it as a stepping stone to the presidency. The bill would result in a vast slaveholding belt of territory stretching from the Gulf of Mexico to Canada.

The Appeal, propaganda of a virulent kind, fanned an excitement in the North that mounted higher every day. The great majority of southerners accepted the Kansas-Nebraska bill as desirable, though many doubted its wisdom, but from northern pulpits and newspapers, from state legislatures and popular mass meetings, from merchants and laborers, came denunciation of this deliberate disruption of the calm which had been supposedly established for good and all by the "Finality" of 1850.

On January 30, 1854, Douglas opened a debate that was to run on for four months. Chase had asked for and been granted a week's postponement of discussion, and Douglas attacked him for requesting the postponement with the ulterior object of allowing the Appeal, with its slanderous misstatements, to carry out its deadly work throughout the country. The heart of Douglas's argument was that the principle of congressional non-interference with slavery in the territories had superseded the arbitrary principle of exclusion utilized in the Missouri Compromise.

On February 3, Chase answered Douglas, pleading the sacredness of the Missouri Compromise, the right of free labor not to be exposed to slave labor competition, and the wickedness of reopening the slavery agitation. Other Senators—Seward, Sumner, John Bell of Tennessee, and Sam Houston of Texas—supported Chase, while a number of Democratic Senators from both North and South came to the aid of Douglas. When, in the course of the debate, Senator Badger of North Carolina wanted to know why a southern gentleman should be prohibited from taking his old mammy, to whom he was bound by many ties of affection, into the territories, Wade of Ohio replied that to this there was no objection—"We only insist that he shall not be empowered to sell her after taking her there."

Douglas, alarmed by the growing opposition, enlisted the President's more than willing support and pushed the bill forward in the Senate. It passed that body by a vote of thirty-seven to fourteen in the early morning hours of March 4, 1854, after an all-night debate. As the weary Senators walked down the Capitol steps after adjournment, they heard the boom of cannon in the Navy Yard, fired in triumph by southern sympathizers; Chase turned to Sumner and said, "They celebrate a present victory, but the echoes they awake will never rest until slavery itself shall die."

For a time, the passage of the bill in the House was doubtful, for all the northern Whigs and half the northern Democrats opposed it. But Pierce used presidential patronage unsparingly, the prospect of a railroad as a result of speedy territorial organization was tempting bait for the Old Northwest, and the great majority of southerners, Whigs and Democrats, supported the bill. After stormily bitter scenes and threats of violence that seemed almost certain to provoke bloodshed, the measure passed the House on May 22 by a vote of 113 to 100. Pierce signed it eight days later, and it was then the law of the land.

The Kansas-Nebraska bill was one of the most fateful measures in American history. It revealed the weakness of Democratic leadership in both White House and Congress, a weakness that had made the bill progressively worse as Douglas moved from one amendment to another. It reopened

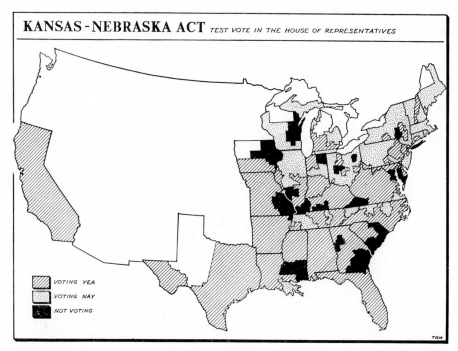

the whole slavery question: the rivalry for political power between slave states and free states and the issue of slave-economy and free-farm-economy competition in the territories, as well as the moral question of slavery. It roused a storm of angry emotion in the North so intense that Douglas said he could travel from Boston to Chicago in the light of his own burning effigies. It pushed forward the breakup of the Whig party as northern and southern Whigs split on the bill, and a widening cleavage showed within the ranks of the Democracy itself as northern anti-Nebraska Democrats deserted Douglas's leadership and voted against the measure. It ruined the Presidential hopes of Stephen A. Douglas, who lost a significant segment of his northern following without strengthening himself in the South. Last but not least, it played a significant part in the formation of one new political party and in the fortunes of another that had just come into being.

The Republican and Know-Nothing Parties

As the old parties disintegrated under the impact of the Kansas-Nebraska bill, a political combination of Old Whigs, anti-Nebraska Democrats, and Free-Soilers began to form. In states such as Ohio, where the

Whig party was weak, the Whigs dominated this fusionist movement. In New York, where the Whigs were in control of the political situation and Seward's re-election to the Senate had to be assured, the Whig organization remained intact until 1855, when it merged with the new, rapidly-developing organization. In a number of northern states, the Whig party simply ceased to exist, swallowed up in the new movement.

Quickly the new party took on a name proposed and adopted almost simultaneously in half a dozen places—Republican. Its leaders declared that the national interest had called it into being, but its appeal was purely sectional, its chief principle being opposition to the extension of slavery.

The Republican party at its inception was a general, spontaneous movement which did not crystallize around any one great leader. Chase, a former Democrat, was not popular with the Old Whigs; Seward, anathema to the Know-Nothings and suspect by the Old Democrats, was late in joining the movement; and Lincoln, whose star was just beginning to rise in Illinois, entered it late, being at first suspicious of the radical abolitionist element in the party. The party was sectional, heavily Yankee and rural, and strongly tinctured with reformism; abolitionists, prohibitionists, Fourierites, land reformers, evangelical revivalists, spiritualists, feminists and even nativists were to be found under its banner. It appealed strongly to exploited free labor, for many urban workers believed that the extension of slavery would slow down a hoped-for exodus to western farms that would lower rents and raise wages in the cities. It captured many of the northern men of letters, Whittier, Lowell, Emerson, Bryant, Longfellow, Holmes, and Motley among them. It had shrewd leaders in various parts of the North who emphasized the right issues for their respective sections. These leaders soft-pedaled radicalism of all kinds, for the radicals had nowhere else to go politically, and thus gave this party of reformers a conservative tinge and tendency that was distinctly appealing to the urban business class. And its rise was swift; in the congressional elections of 1854, fifteen Republicans were sent to the Senate and 108 to the House, while the Democratic membership in the latter body sank from 159 to eighty-three.

While the Republican party was beginning its spectacular rise, the Native American, or Know-Nothing, movement also gained great headway. Starting in the thirties and forties as a reaction, North and South, to the floods of immigrants (see Chapter 21), nativism had been given impetus by the acceleration of that flood in the early fifties. It was also stimulated at that time by the attacks upon Protestantism leveled by such prominent Catholic prelates as Archbishop Hughes of New York, and by excitement over the intervention of Rome in quarrels between the trustees of various Catholic churches and the Catholic hierarchy. Many well-meaning but deluded Americans who felt that the Catholic church was a menace to liberty joined what was known as the Order of the Star-Spangled Banner, a secret society with its own ritual, grip, and passwords; members recognized one another by the query "Have you seen Sam?" and when asked about the Order were to say "I know nothing." At the same time, American, or Know-Nothing, parties sprang up, devoted to resisting all foreign attacks upon American institutions and to electing only native-born Protestant citizens to public office.

The election of 1852 stimulated the growth of this mushrooming political movement. The Whigs generally ascribed Pierce's victory to the foreign-born vote, and as the Whig party weakened, many of its voters moved into the Know-Nothing ranks. Then came the Kansas-Nebraska bill, which split both the old parties asunder, and thousands of conservative Whigs and not a few conservative Democrats joined the American party. In the spring of 1854, it showed great strength in local elections, and the congressional contests of that fall saw five Know-Nothings elected to the United States Senate and no less than forty-three to seats in the House of Representatives; counting Republicans and anti-Nebraska Democrats who subscribed to the principles of the Order, there were approximately seventy-five Congressmen pledged to war against the Pope and the foreigner. The Know-Nothings had won triumphs in New England and the Middle Atlantic states, and had come close to victory in Virginia and the Gulf states. The party was weakest in the Old Northwest, with its large foreign population. But it had had a remarkable rise, southern Whigs were going over to it by the thousands, and its leaders looked forward to winning the presidential election of 1856.

The Crime Against Kansas

Before that election took place, however, other events that were direct consequences of the Kansas-Nebraska bill added dramatic elements to the political situation. Immigrants began moving into Kansas: a few of these were antislavery zealots sent out by the New England Emigrant Aid Society, which had been organized by Eli Thayer, Amos Lawrence, and other Massachusetts men; a few southerners also came, bringing their slaves with them; but the bulk of the settlers were men from the Middle West and the Middle Atlantic states, pioneer farmers, not much interested in slavery from the moral point of view, but determined that it should not compete with them in Kansas. Across the border in Missouri, the slave-holders were equally determined to make Kansas safe for slavery by fair means or foul, for they felt that the security of their own slave property was deeply involved.

When, on November 29, 1854, Kansas elected a territorial delegate to Congress, several hundred armed men crossed over from Missouri and voted, resulting in the election of a proslavery delegate. On March 30, 1855, at the order of Governor Reeder, a territorial legislature was elected, and this time some 5,000 Missourians ("border ruffians," Greeley called them), led by Senator Atchison and others, crossed the border and voted. The resultant overwhelmingly proslavery legislature set itself up, in defiance of the Governor, at Shawnee Mission, just across the line from Missouri, and passed laws providing dire punishment for all antislavery activity.

The free settlers viewed these proceedings with alarm and wrath. Under the leadership of a shrewd and able Forty-Niner, Dr. Charles Robinson, and an irresponsible orator and demagogue named Jim Lane, they proceeded to organize on their own account. They began setting up a framework of government, and at a convention in Topeka in the fall of 1855 drew up a constitution prohibiting slavery after July 4, 1857. This document was adopted by a free-soil vote of 1,731 to forty-six, an election was held in January, 1856, and Robinson was chosen governor. The free-soilers then submitted their constitution to Congress for approval.

By 1856, popular sovereignty in Kansas had resulted in making a farce of the democratic process. There were two rival governments there, and President Pierce pursued a wobbly course that favored the proslavery minority. He would have nothing to do with the Topeka constitution. Instead, on January 24, 1856, he proposed that the proslavery Shawnee legislature begin organizing Kansas as a state by setting up the election of a constitutional convention. This embittered the free-soil majority of the population, and violence and bloodshed ensued. Proslavery fanatics murdered six free-soil settlers, and, on May 21, 1856, a proslavery force destroyed two free-soil presses in the town of Lawrence, burned the hotel and Governor Robinson's house, and committed other depredations. In response, John Brown, an abolitionist fanatic with a streak of insanity in his make-up, organized a posse of four of his sons and two other men, set out along the Pottawatomie Creek, and on the night of May 24 dragged from their cabins and murdered in cold blood five men and boys of pro-slavery families.

Brown was an intensely religious man who read his Bible and believed firmly that without the shedding of blood there could be no remission of sins. But when in his cabin, to invoke the blessing of Almighty God, he had raised hands stained figuratively, if not literally, with the blood of these murders, he had become a symbol of the terror that now reigned in Kansas. The South sent aid to the proslavery settlers. From the North came boxes marked "books," but containing rifles, which were known as "Beecher's Bibles," for the eloquent minister, Henry Ward Beecher, advised arming the free-soil men in Kansas. Men on both sides went armed and neither property nor life was safe until, late in 1856, temporary order was restored by newly appointed Governor Geary.

While bloodshed and violence in Kansas focused the attention of the country upon that unhappy territory, an equally dramatic event occurred in the Capitol at Washington. On May 19 and 20, 1856, Senator Charles Sumner made a long speech on "The Crime Against Kansas," in which, with a wealth of classical allusions, he spoke in withering terms of "the rape of a virgin territory," and went on to denunciations of the Slave Power, of South Carolina and its Senator A. P. Butler, and of Senator Douglas as author of the Kansas-Nebraska bill. When he had finished, Douglas rose and answered him with sarcastic vituperation; was it Sumner's purpose, he asked, "to provoke some of us to kick him as we would a dog in the street, that he may get sympathy upon the just chastisement?" In response, Sumner told Douglas that he was "a common scold," and, declaring that Douglas switched "out from his tongue the perpetual stench of offensive personality," compared the Senator from Illinois to a skunk.

Sumner's attacks upon Butler and his state enraged Butler's nephew, Representative Preston Brooks, who also came from South Carolina. On May 22, as Sumner sat at his desk in the nearly empty Senate Chamber, Brooks approached him, holding in his hand a gutta-percha cane, an inch in diameter at the butt, three-quarters of an inch at the tip, and hollow for three-eighths of an inch, end to end—a light but strong instrument, distinctly serviceable for the purpose of its owner. Speaking quietly, he told Sumner that he had come to punish him and then struck him over the head and shoulders until he had shattered the cane. During this attack, Sumner struggled to rise, finally did so by wrenching his desk loose from its fastenings, and fell senseless and bleeding in the aisle. Badly injured, he was not able to resume his duties in the Senate until December, 1859.

Southerners praised Brooks for the whipping he had given Sumner and presented him with a number of canes to replace the one he had broken on Sumner's head. But wild indignation in the North intensified the feeling of outrage already felt in that section over the events in Kansas. To many Northerners, Sumner was a martyr in the cause of liberty.

The Election of 1856

Nine days after the caning of Sumner and in the midst of all the excitement occasioned by that event and the happenings in Kansas, the Democratic national convention met in Cincinnati. Pierce, Douglas and Buchanan were the leading contenders for the prize. The President courted renomination, but his ineptitude as a leader and his open involvement on the proslavery side in Kansas were fatal to his hopes. Douglas, the most popular and the ablest of the Democratic contenders, had also lost popularity in the North because of the Kansas-Nebraska bill. The principal criterion of the Democratic leaders was availability, and, since the South was sure, this pointed to the man who could command the most northern votes. Buchanan was a Pennsylvanian—and Pennsylvania was a key state—who had been in England when the Kansas-Nebraska bill became law, and hence had borne no responsibility for the Kansas troubles. Neither was he in any way connected with the attack on Sumner. He announced his willingness to abide by the new order marked out by Douglas's measure, asserted that he would see there was fair play for both sides in Kansas, and declared that he was anxious to add Cuba to the Union.

Buchanan was not immediately nominated. Douglas had many friends at the convention, and for a time there threatened to be a deadlock. Then, after seventeen ballots had been taken, the "Little Giant" withdrew his name for the sake of party harmony and the convention nominated Buchanan by acclamation. The platform pledged devotion to the Union and endorsed the Kansas-Nebraska bill as the true solution of the slavery problem.

Some two weeks later, the Republican national convention gathered amid scenes of great enthusiasm in the Musical Fund Hall in Philadelphia. It was almost purely sectional, for only four slave states (Delaware, Maryland, Virginia, and Kentucky) sent a handful of delegates. Though Seward might have had the nomination, and there is some evidence that he desired it, his political mentor, Weed, held that the chances of success for the newly formed party were slight, that it would be better to wait for 1860. To this counsel Seward yielded, and he was not a candidate.

One candidate for the Republican nomination was far ahead of all the rest, and the convention nominated him with great acclaim—the explorer John C. Frémont. Though he had had no experience in politics and was impulsive, egotistical, and sometimes erratic, he was young, like the party, and he was popular because of his exploring achievements and his romantic elopement with Senator Benton's daughter Jessie. While not radical in his general outlook, he believed that slavery should not be extended into the territories. The platform called for congressional prohibition in the territories of "those twin relics of barbarism, Polygamy and Slavery," and demanded admission of Kansas under the Topeka constitution. It urged the construction with government aid and by a central route of a railroad to the Pacific and denounced the Ostend Manifesto.

Months before the Democrats and Republicans met, the Know-Nothings, who had been so hopeful of success in 1856, had fallen upon evil days. Assembling in Philadelphia on February 22, 1856, their national convention found itself hopelessly at odds over the Kansas-Nebraska bill, with the southern delegates for it and the northern delegates resolutely opposed. At the insistence of the southerners, with the support of New York, Pennsylvania, and Delaware, the convention nominated Millard Fillmore for President on a platform vaguely endorsing popular sovereignty in the territories. Thereupon a split developed, and a large body of North Americans seceded and held a convention in Philadelphia at the same time the Republicans met there, finally endorsing the Republican presidential ticket.

Representatives of what was left of the Whig party, low in spirits, met in Baltimore in September and endorsed what was now known as the South American candidate. Fillmore's election, they declared, would be the best means of keeping the country safe from civil war.

The campaign of 1856 was not particularly colorful in the South. There Buchanan's success was assured, but in the North the contest fairly seethed with color and excitement. The Republicans were short of money, their organization was young and untried, but their enthusiasm was prodigious. Mass meetings, parades, transparencies, posters, and glee clubs kept their cohorts continually in motion, and everywhere appeared the slogan, "Free Speech, Free Press, Free Soil, Free Men, Frémont and Victory." The Republican orators declared that slavery must be restricted within its existing limits until some means could be found for its gradual extinction, and they extolled the homestead plank. They described Buchanan as "Old Obliquity," a time-serving, worn-out politician; they also termed him "Ten cent Jimmy," for years before he had made a speech suggesting that American wages should be adjusted to those of Europe in order to keep the tariff low.

The Democrats had a smoothly functioning organization, were able to draw liberally on monied men fearful of a Republican victory, and were

COURTESY OF THE UNIVERSITY OF ROCHESTER LIBRARY

THE GREAT PRESIDENTIAL RACE OF 1856

*In this Republican cartoon, drawn during the campaign of 1856, "Buck"
founders on the Democratic platform. Fillmore, seated "On the goose,"
runs behind Buchanan and prophesies disaster, while Frémont races to
victory.*

confident of success. They posed as the party of union, of reconciliation,
and portrayed Republicanism as a symbol of discord and division. Much
time was spent in personal attacks on Frémont, who was accused of being
a Catholic (which hurt him in the Northwest) and of having been involved in questionable financial transactions; the fact that he was of illegitimate birth was also stressed.

The Democrats made much of the threat of secession, if there were
a Republican victory. Democratic journals predicted, and men like Howell
Cobb and Senator Mason declared, that Frémont in the White House
would mean the end of the Union. Such threats and forecasts, though made
in the overheated atmosphere of a campaign, nevertheless showed that the
idea of secession was much in the air, and they were ominous for the future.

The Whigs and Americans campaigning for Fillmore fought a losing
battle from the start. Defections from the Whig ranks continued, and the
Americans themselves lost ground during the campaign. The great issue
was slavery extension, with Kansas in the foreground, and on this issue
Fillmore and his supporters could give only vague promises of a peaceful
adjustment.

The Democratic victories in the key states of Pennsylvania and Indiana, which held their state elections in October, indicated the trend. In the national election, Buchanan carried nineteen states with 174 electoral votes, while Frémont had eleven states with 114 electoral votes. Fillmore carried only Maryland with its eight votes. Buchanan had 45.3 per cent of the total vote. Frémont had 33.1 per cent, and Fillmore 21.6 per cent. The Democrats controlled both houses of Congress.

The Democracy, though battered and divided, had returned to power for four more years. The Americans, hopelessly split over slavery extension, had demonstrated, as Horace Greeley said, that they had about as much reason for permanence as an anticholera or an antipotato rot party would have. But the most significant thing about the election was the strength shown by the Republicans; a party new and untried, save in some state elections, with no voting strength south of the Mason and Dixon line, had captured a third of the popular vote, and had swept New England, New York, Ohio, Michigan, Wisconsin, and Iowa. The Republicans were tremendously encouraged. John Greenleaf Whittier expressed their exultation:

> If months have well-nigh won
>   the field
> What will not four years do?

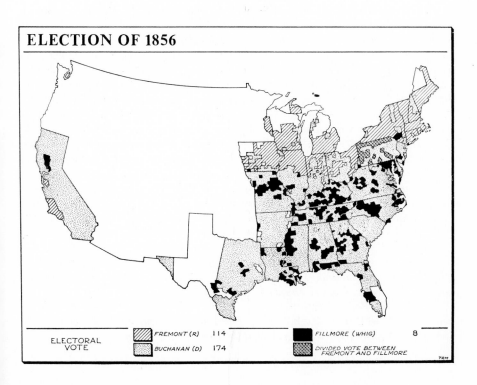

ELECTION OF 1856

ELECTORAL VOTE

FREMONT (R)   114

BUCHANAN (D)   174

FILLMORE (WHIG)   8

DIVIDED VOTE BETWEEN FREMONT AND FILLMORE

Suggested Reading

The best general account of this period is in the scholarly and interesting Nevins, *Ordeal of the Union,* vol. II. Rhodes, *History of the United States Since the Compromise of 1850,* vol. II, is old but still useful.

For social and economic conditions, see E. D. Branch, *The Sentimental Years* and A. C. Cole, *The Irrepressible Conflict, 1850–1865* (1934). R. F. Wilson, *Crusader in Crinoline: the Life of Harriet Beecher Stowe* (1941) is a good biography.

Pierce and the Democratic party in this period can be best studied in R. F. Nichols, *Franklin Pierce, Young Hickory of the Granite Hills* (1931), *The Democratic Machine, 1850–1854* (1923), and *The Disruption of American Democracy* (1948). See also by the same author, *The Stakes of Power, 1845–1877* (1961). The student should also consult the works by J. T. Carpenter, A. O. Craven, and R. R. Russell previously cited, and H. H. Simms, *A Decade of Sectional Controversy, 1851–1861* (1942).

Expansion is dealt with in the work by Nevins cited above, but Basil Rauch, *American Interest in Cuba, 1848–1855* (1948) should also be consulted. I. D. Spencer, *The Victor and the Spoils: A Life of William L. Marcy* (1959) has a thorough treatment of diplomacy under Pierce.

A brief biographical treatment of Stephen A. Douglas is G. M. Capers, *Stephen A. Douglas, Defender of the Union* (1959), but the student should also consult G. F. Milton, *The Eve of Conflict; Stephen A. Douglas and the Needless War* (1934). On Chase, see the old but still useful A. B. Hart, *Samuel Portland Chase* (1899) and T. G. and M. R. Belden, *So Fell the Angels* (1956). B. J. Hendrick, *Lincoln's War Cabinet* (1946) contains an interesting sketch of Chase. The standard biography of Sumner has been E. L. Pierce, *Memoir and Letters of Charles Sumner* (4 vols., 1877–1893). David Donald, *Charles Sumner and the Coming of the Civil War* (1960) is the first volume of what promises to be a definitive biography of Sumner. See also G. H. Haynes, *Charles Sumner* (1909), M. Storey, *Charles Sumner* (1900), and Carl Schurz, *Charles Sumner, an Essay,* edited by A. H. Hogue (1951). A biography of Seward based on his papers is G. G. Van Deusen, *William Henry Seward* (1967).

On Kansas and the Kansas-Nebraska bill, see J. C. Malin, *The Nebraska Question, 1852–1854* (1953) and *John Brown and the Legend of Fifty-Six* (1942). See also P. W. Gates, *Fifty Million Acres; Conflicts Over Kansas Land Policy, 1854–1890* (1954) and C. V. Woodward's essay on John Brown in D. Aaron, ed., *America in Crisis* (1952).

The rise of the Republican party is best studied in A. W. Crandall, *The Early History of the Republican Party, 1854–1856* (1930); G. G. Van Deusen, *Horace Greeley, Nineteenth Century Crusader* (1953); and J. A. Isely, *Horace Greeley and the Republican Party, 1853–1861* (1947). The Know-Nothing movement is competently dealt with in R. A. Billington, *The Protestant Crusade, 1800–1860* (1938) and in W. D. Overdyke, *The Know-Nothing Party in the South.*

For the campaign of 1856, see R. J. Bartlett, *John C. Frémont and the Republican Party* (1930) and G. T. Curtis, *Life of James Buchanan* (2 vols., 1883). Nevins, *Ordeal of the Union,* vol. 2, has an excellent analysis of this campaign.

29 , The March Toward War

WHEN JAMES BUCHANAN took the oath as President of the United States on March 4, 1857, he had behind him a long and varied experience in public life. Nearly sixty-six years old, this lawyer-politician who had turned from Federalist into a thorough-paced Jacksonian Democrat had been a public servant for over forty years. He had been at various times a member of the Pennsylvania state legislature and of both branches of Congress, Secretary of State under Polk, Minister to Russia and, recently, Minister to England.

*Buchanan
Takes Office*

A bachelor who had made money as a lawyer, Buchanan was worth perhaps $300,000. He was also a self-seeking politician who, by hard work and skillful pliancy had gained high place. By nature timid and irresolute, his tendency to avoid hard decisions had earned him his nickname of "Old Obliquity," but he had a horror of abolition, held slavery to be an ineradicable evil, and throughout his career had shown a marked partiality for the South. Though he believed in the Union, he held that continuance of abolitionist agitation would justify the South in seceding, and he had asserted that Frémont's election would make secession inevitable. Under the leadership of this weak, pro-Southern leader, the country was to move down the road toward war.

606

Buchanan's Cabinet, in which the aged Cass was Secretary of State, was mediocre in ability. Four of its seven members were southerners, and of these Howell Cobb of Georgia, Secretary of the Treasury, and Jacob Thompson of Mississippi in the Department of the Interior, together with John Slidell, the Democratic leader in the Senate, had enormous influence over the vacillating President.

The Dred Scott Decision

In his inaugural, Buchanan declared that he would only serve one term, a statement that promptly began eroding his influence with Congress. Aside from this unfortunate avowal, the address contained only one other item of importance—an allusion to the Dred Scott case, then pending before the Supreme Court. The case, Buchanan said, involved the question as to when the people of a territory could decide for slavery or freedom; to that decision he would "cheerfully submit," as would all "good citizens." In his opinion, the proper time was when the territory was about to become a state. The President did not disclose the fact that he had advance information as to what the decision would be.

Dred Scott was a Negro slave who had been taken by his master (an army surgeon, Dr. Emerson) from Missouri into Illinois, then into Wisconsin Territory, which was part of the Louisiana Purchase, and finally back to Missouri. In 1846, several years after his return to Missouri, Scott sued for his freedom in the Missouri courts, on the ground that his residence in a free state and in territory made free by the Missouri Compromise had made him a free man. There was precedent for his action, for the Missouri courts had so ruled in previous cases. A lower court freed Scott, but when the case was appealed to the Missouri supreme court, it reversed the previous ruling, holding that Scott was a slave under Missouri law, regardless of what his status might have been in a free state or a free territory.

While the case was dragging through the state courts, Scott had passed to a succession of owners. Dr. Emerson had died, and Scott became part of an estate owned jointly by his widow and her brother, John F. A. Sanford of New York. Mrs. Emerson moved to Massachusetts, where she married Dr. C. C. Chaffee of Springfield, a member of Congress and a staunch abolitionist. By Emerson's will and Missouri law, Mrs. Chaffee's second marriage deprived her of any control over Dr. Emerson's estate, and Scott passed into the hands of Sanford as trustee. Now the Negro, claiming to be a citizen of Missouri, sued Sanford, a citizen of New York, in the federal courts, again demanding his freedom. After the federal circuit court of Missouri upheld the decision of the Missouri supreme court that Scott was still a slave, the case was appealed to the Supreme Court of the United States.

Three fundamental questions confronted the Supreme Court: (1) Was Scott a citizen of Missouri? (If he was not, the case had no status in the federal courts.) (2) Had Scott's residence in free territory made him free? (3) Was the Missouri Compromise constitutional? There were marked differences of opinion throughout the Union over whether or not Negroes could be citizens, and over the constitutionality of the Missouri Compromise, and interest in the court's decision was keen indeed.

The Supreme Court consisted of nine men, five of whom were southerners and four northerners. Seven were Democrats, one a Republican, and one a Whig. The Chief Justice was Roger B. Taney of Maryland, then nearing his eightieth birthday. The prestige of the Court was high, and its decision would have great importance.

A majority of the Court, seven in all, held that Scott was not a citizen of the state of Missouri and therefore had no right to sue in the federal courts. Strictly speaking, this was all that was necessary for the Court to do, and rumors began to spread that the majority did not intend to deal, in their opinions, with the broader aspects of the case. Greeley's *Tribune* sneered that "the black gowns have become artful dodgers." It became apparent, however, that the two dissenting justices intended to defend congressional regulation of slavery in the territories. Perhaps because of this, though the evidence is far from conclusive, the majority reconsidered its position and decided to deal with the broader issues involved. All of the judges gave separate opinions, but those of Taney and the two dissenters commanded by far the greatest popular attention.

Could a Negro whose ancestors had been slaves be a citizen of the United States? Taney and two other judges declared that he could not be a citizen, two declared just as emphatically that he could be, and the others gave no clear-cut opinion. Had his residence in free territory made him free? Six judges, including Taney, asserted that he was under Missouri law, and hence was a slave. Was the Missouri Compromise constitutional? Taney argued that the clause in the Constitution giving Congress power to make all rules and regulations respecting the territory of the United States did not apply to territories obtained *after* 1789: such territories were acquired "for the common use and equal benefit of all," and slaves were property; since the fifth amendment forbade the national government to deprive a citizen of property without due process of law, depriving a citizen of his slaves just because he moved into a territory was scarcely due process of law. Five judges agreed with Taney in his conclusion that the Missouri Compromise was unconstitutional.

Two justices, Benjamin R. Curtis of Massachusetts (Whig) and John McLean of Ohio (Republican), differed with Taney on all three points. Their dissents argued that Dred Scott was a citizen; that his status, free or slave, was not controlled by Missouri law, since he had acquired freedom by living in free territory; and that Congress had a constitutional right to prohibit slavery in any territory of the Union.

It is probable that all the justices on the Supreme Court rendered opinions that, in their judgment, were honest, objective, and in accordance with law and precedent. The result, however, was anything but a settlement of the questions that agitated the country. Taney hoped the decision would quiet the controversy over slavery, but the North received it with rage and resentment. Bryant denounced it in unequivocal language; it made the Constitution, he said, a slaveholders' Constitution, and transformed slavery from a "peculiar" to a federal institution. Greeley declared that the Court's verdict was "entitled to just so much moral weight as would be the judgment of a majority of those congregated in any Washington bar room." Many northerners feared with Greeley that the striking down of freedom in the northern states was only a step away; that, as the fiery editor put it, if a single case drew from the Court an official judgment that slaves could be held and protected under national law, "we shall see men buying slaves for the New York market, while Mr. Toombs can call the roll of his chattels on the slope of Bunker Hill." The pulpits of the North resounded with indignation, and throughout that section there was widespread acceptance of the Curtis and McLean opinions as representing the true law of the land. On the other hand, Taney's opinion was received with great satisfaction in the South, where press and pulpit declared that it recognized historical fact and gave that section its just rights in the territories.

Southern joy over the decision was well justified, for now the federal government seemed definitely aligned with the South in the great controversy of the day. Congress, aided and abetted by President Pierce, had yielded to slavery in repealing the Missouri Compromise. Pierce had shown his southern sympathies in his attitude toward the struggle in Kansas, Buchanan was notoriously prosouthern in his point of view, and now the Supreme Court had established the constitutionality of slavery in all the territories of the Union.

The Dred Scott decision had intensified the struggle between the sections over slavery. It had also lowered the confidence of the people of the North in the Supreme Court, a loss of prestige which was to have significant results in the Civil War and Reconstruction era, when the Court would be forced to deal with highhanded action on the part of the executive and legislative branches of the government.

The one person who seemed irrevocably bound by the Court's decision was Scott himself. This was not for long, however, for trustee Sanford died, and abolitionist Chaffee, not wishing to serve as executor of an estate containing slaves, transferred title to Scott and his family to one Peter Blow, who freed them on May 26, 1857. Scott spent the rest of his life as a porter in a St. Louis hotel. He died of tuberculosis in 1858.

Kansas and the Lecompton Constitution

While the Dred Scott Decision added new fuel to the sectional controversy over slavery, the situation in Kansas remained unsettled and full of ominous possibilities. Governor Geary had attempted to maintain order and see that there was fair play for both sides. The proslavery legislature meeting in Lecompton was determined that, by hook or crook, Kansas should become a slave state. It passed a law providing for a constitutional convention so chosen that it would surely be proslavery. The constitution to be drawn up by this body would not be submitted to the voters for their approval, but would be forwarded to Congress with a petition that Kansas be admitted under it as a state. When Geary vetoed this bill, the legislature passed it over his veto, and, overworked and threatened with assassination, on March 4, 1857, Geary resigned.

Buchanan's course was clear: he had to appoint an impartial governor who would see that there was a fair election to a constitutional convention in Kansas, with an honest popular referendum on any constitution that might be drafted. The President made a good start along this line by appointing Robert J. Walker of Mississippi to replace Geary, and Walker accepted his commission with the clear understanding that it was his responsibility to see that a state constitution would be drawn up and adopted in a fair and democratic manner.

Walker found the free-state men and their "legislature" in Kansas aloof and sceptical, willing enough to accept such federal authority as he exercised, but determined not to bow down to the Lecompton legislature or to participate in any rigged election of a constitutional convention. The new governor declared that he would recognize the enactments of the proslavery legislature, which had been accepted by the Administration in

Washington as bona fide, but he also said that Congress would not admit Kansas as a state without a fair vote on any constitution that might be adopted. The proslavery leaders then served notice to the governor that the constitution would never be submitted to a popular referendum. All this while, thousands of settlers were pouring into the territory. With anything like democratic procedure, the proslavery cause was growing more and more hopeless.

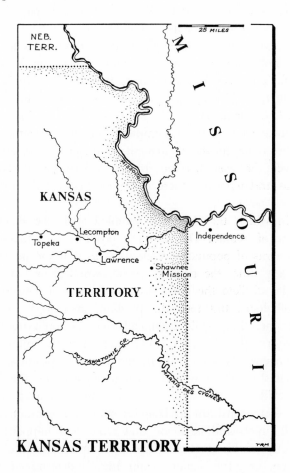

KANSAS TERRITORY

On June 15, 1857, came the election of the constitutional convention. Boycotted by the free-soilers, this produced a body of delegates who overwhelmingly advocated slavery. The result of their meeting at Lecompton in the fall of 1857 was a constitution drawn up with a special clause guaranteeing slavery. This document was presented to the voters in a peculiar way: they could not vote for or against the constitution as a whole, but only for it with or without this article; if they voted for it without the special clause, they were still voting for a document that guaranteed to their owners the some 200 slaves already in Kansas. Another article in the constitution forbade any amendment until 1864.

The free-soil settlers refused to vote in the referendum that followed. The Lecompton constitution was therefore accepted by a small minority of the Kansans, and forwarded to Washington with a plea for the admission of Kansas as a state under its provisions.

While these events were taking place, Walker returned to Washington. He hoped to hold Buchanan to his promise regarding Kansas, but the hope was vain. The President, influenced by violent southern criticism of Walker's conduct, terrified by mounting threats of secession, and dominated by the prosouthern members of his Cabinet, became convinced that Kansas should be admitted under the Lecompton constitution. Since he reasoned that if this were done, all the excitement would pass away and the Union would be saved, he was therefore ready to abandon the man he had sent to Kansas and who was there doing his best to preserve democratic procedure.

The way in which the President fumbled with the Kansas situation aroused the ire of Senator Douglas. His position, and that of the other northern exponents of popular sovereignty, was that the people in a territory had, at any time, the right to decide whether or not they wanted slavery. Douglas disliked the Dred Scott decision which opened the territories to slaveholders, but took the position, later to be known as the Freeport Doctrine, that, while technically settlers could not keep slavery out of a territory, they actually could exclude it by unfavorable police regulations. This was a far cry from the southern position, and that of Buchanan, that the territories were open to slavery and that it could not be excluded until the time had come for admission as a state and the drafting of a state constitution. Douglas stood for genuine popular sovereignty at all times, and he knew that what had happened in Kansas made a travesty of his doctrine. The Lecompton constitution was the crowning touch, and the Senator from Illinois determined to oppose it with all his strength.

On December 3, 1857, Douglas called at the White House and urged the President not to recommend acceptance of Lecompton, but rather to champion a new and fair election to a constitutional convention in Kansas. Buchanan, whose mind was already made up, said he would stand back of Lecompton, and he threatened Douglas if the latter persisted in his course. No Democrat, said the President, had ever differed from an Administration of his own choice without being crushed. Douglas should "Beware the fate of Tallmadge and Rives." Quickly came the reply—"Mr. President, I wish you to remember that General Jackson is dead."

Buchanan asked Congress to admit Kansas under the Lecompton constitution, and Douglas took the floor of the Senate in opposition. Knowing that the southern Senators and the power of the presidential patronage combined could force Lecompton through the upper house, he played for time so that the North would be aroused when the bill reached the House of Representatives. He also offered a temporary alliance to the Republicans, who, though mistrustful of him, came to his aid in the struggle. Their combined forces could not stop the progress of the measure in the Senate, where it passed, thirty-three to twenty-five. They did better in the House, thanks in considerable part to the pressure of northern public opinion. There, after the wildest kind of lobbying by both sides and a fist fight which involved thirty members of that august body, the bill appeared to be headed straight for defeat.

As it became apparent that Lecompton could not pass the House, the Administration made a last ditch effort to save the day by introducing the English bill. This provided for submitting the whole Lecompton constitution to the Kansas voters, with the provision that, if accepted, Kansas would at once get the usual gift of public lands. Rejection would mean delay in statehood and in the land grant for perhaps two years—that is, until the rise in population entitled Kansas to a representative in Congress. This deceptively fair resolution, though it was opposed by Douglas and many prominent Republicans, passed both houses. The Lecompton constitution was then submitted to the Kansas voters, who rejected it, 11,812 to 1,926. This demonstrated conclusively that the free-soil men were in control of Kansas Territory, which remained in that status until admitted as a free state (January 21, 1861).

The strife over Kansas drove a deep wedge between the northern and southern wings of the Democracy and produced a serious division in the northern Democracy itself. The South, where the Democratic party was now practically supreme, was wildly indignant over the outcome, and was bitter against Douglas as its betrayer. A majority of the northern Democrats supported "the Little Giant" in his stand on Kansas and in his rift with Buchanan's Administration. The Republicans watched these Democratic quarrels with joy and with increasing confidence in their own future.

The Panic of 1857

In the fall of 1857, while the conflict over Kansas was still on, the country was shaken by a sharp depression. The good times of the 1850s had produced an inflationary boom; the golden millions pouring out of California, a deluge of European investments in American securities, and a generally rising price level had, by the middle fifties, produced a great wave of overexpansion and wild speculation. Public land sales jumped wildly from one million acres in 1853 to seven million in 1854, and to 15,729,525 in 1855, a figure greater than anything that had gone before, save in the year preceding the panic of 1837; the price of real estate, whether on actual sites or in paper towns, shot up as if by magic. There was gambling in stocks, in commodities, and in railroad construction. Over-banking as well as overtrading was the order of the day, with bank funds loaned on the most dubious securities, and borrowers in the West and Southwest paying 10 to 20 per cent interest. Then, the Crimean War (1854–1856) with its accompanying rising interest rates in Europe suddenly checked the flow of European money into American ventures and prompted con-siderable European selling of American securities. The American economy was primed for a collapse.

In October, 1857, the Ohio Life Insurance and Trust Company of Cincinnati failed for $7 million. Money grew tight and stocks promptly fell in value. That fall all the New York City banks save one suspended specie payment, an example speedily followed in other parts of the country. The Illinois Central went into bankruptcy, and other railroads followed suit. Land values fell, and business failures mounted. Railroad construction stopped, textile and iron mills became idle, and there were hundreds of thousands of unemployed workmen. In the North and West, the winter of 1857–1858 was one of suffering and gloom.

The depression, if sharp, was also short. The continued gold output helped to restore confidence, as did the revenues in 1858 from a bumper cotton crop of three and three-quarter million bales, which sold at better than $.12 a pound and 60 per cent of which was exported. There was a strong European demand for American foodstuffs, especially wheat, of which there was a record crop of 180 million bushels. These were sure signs of a returning prosperity, and by the close of 1858 the panic was over and recovery on the way.

Brief though the panic was, it had important consequences. It accentu-ated the cleavage between North and South, for many northerners, especially in the industrial sections, blamed their troubles on the tariff which, under southern influence, had been lowered in 1857 from the levels established by the Walker tariff of 1846. On the other hand, the South had escaped the worst effects of the depression, and southern confidence in the stability of that section was greatly enhanced. "Cotton is King," cried Senator Hammond of South Carolina in a speech that was applauded throughout the South, and *De Bow's Review* voiced general southern opinion when it asserted that the South's economic system was permanent and real, while that of the North was "fugitive and fictitious."

To some extent, the panic and the accompanying distress played a part in the state and congressional elections of 1858, but more important was the North's reaction to the Administration's handling of the Kansas troubles. The outcome was a stunning defeat for Buchanan and his supporters. State after state in the North went over to the Republicans or returned Anti-Lecompton Democrats. New England went Republican, and so did New York and Indiana. His own state handed the President such a staggering blow that he wrote ruefully to a friend, "We have met the enemy in Pennsylvania and we are theirs." The Thirty-Sixth Congress saw the Democratic side of the House reduced from 129 to ninety-nine, seven of whom were Anti-Lecompton, while the Republicans swelled their numbers from ninety-two to 114. The North, plainly, was sick of Buchanan and of his Administration.

The Lincoln-Douglas Debates

One of the outstanding features of the election of 1858 was the series of debates that took place in Illinois between Douglas and a Republican, whose star was just beginning its rise in the national political firmament. Born in Hardin County, Kentucky, forty-nine years before, Abraham Lincoln had received a haphazard education as his father moved about from Kentucky into Indiana and then Illinois. Abraham read law, was admitted to the Illinois bar, and then went into politics. A Clay Whig, he served four years in the Illinois legislature (1837–1841), then practiced law in Springfield until elected to Congress (1847–1849), where he was the only Whig from Illinois. His congressional record was not distinguished, and there was no possibility of his re-election. He returned to Illinois, became one of its leading lawyers, and slowly widened the circle of his influence in politics. In 1855, he ran for the United States Senate but was defeated. Turning Republican, he campaigned for Frémont in 1856, and now was again seeking election to the Senate.

Eastern Republicans, Greeley among them, wanted Douglas supported for re-election, but the Illinois Republicans would have none of it. They gave Lincoln the nomination, and in accepting before the party's Illinois state convention, on June 16, 1858, he said:

> A house divided against itself cannot stand. I believe this government cannot endure permanently, half slave and half free. I do not expect the Union to be dissolved—I do not expect the house to fall—but I do expect it will cease to be divided. It will become all one thing, or all the other.

Since Lincoln had previously denounced the Kansas-Nebraska bill, the Dred Scott decision, and Lecompton, his position was clear.

Douglas and Lincoln were campaigning for the election of a Democrat or Republican legislature, which, in turn, would elect one of them to the Senate. They barnstormed through Illinois, and met in a series of joint debates, seven in all.

The contest was spirited. Buchanan and his followers, enraged with Douglas, were doing their best to defeat him. This delighted Lincoln, who said that his own attitude reminded him of the frontier woman, cruelly abused by her husband, who saw him one day in mortal combat with a bear; as one or the other would gain an advantage, the woman would exclaim, "Go it, husband!" and then "Go it, bear!" Douglas knew that his political life was at stake, and he exerted all his powers as a debater. Well-dressed, round-faced, radiating an air of confidence, and traveling in a private car, he presented a startling contrast to his tall, ungainly opponent with his lean, sorrowful face, battered stovepipe hat, coarse coat, baggy trousers, and bulging cotton umbrella. Lincoln traveled by day coach.

From the outset Douglas stood squarely on popular sovereignty, and made everything possible out of the "House divided" speech, which, he said, meant war. The Republican party, he declared, was abolitionist and sectional. Denying these charges, Lincoln pointed out that he was not for unconditional repeal of the fugitive slave law, or for the abolition of slavery in the District of Columbia, or for prohibition of the interstate slave trade. He did think it the right and duty of Congress to prohibit slavery in the territories, and he wanted slavery put in a position that would lead to its ultimate extinction.

At Freeport, Illinois, Lincoln asked Douglas if the people of a territory could lawfully exclude slavery from their limits. The Dred Scott decision answered this loaded question one way, the doctrine of popular sovereignty another, and Douglas had supported both. "The Little Giant" replied that, despite the Court's pronouncement on the "abstract question," the people of a territory could prevent slavery coming in by "unfriendly legislation." Douglas had stated this before, as had Cass, Alexander Stephens, and others. But Lincoln thought it worthwhile to make his opponent emphasize the power of police regulations over slavery in the territories, for by so doing he emphasized the difference between the Douglas point of view and that of the Buchanan Administration.

The Republicans lost the election by a narrow margin, and Douglas went back to the Senate for another term. His triumph, in the face of the general Democratic debacle in the North, was a brilliant vindication of his leadership in the party. But, as events were to prove, his Freeport Doctrine, which was repugnant to the South, was destined to have an important bearing on the next presidential election. Lincoln, the loser, came out of the struggle with an enhanced reputation, for, having crossed swords with perhaps the most formidable debater in the country, he had acquitted himself with great credit; from now on, his name would be familiar to a host of Republicans.

Increasing Tension

During 1858 and 1859, tension between North and South steadily grew as the viewpoints of the sections regarding slavery became further and further opposed. The Republican press and party leaders kept up their attack on the "Slave Power," and the abolitionists maintained their furious tirades against the slaveholders and their "peculiar institution." The northern attitude toward the Fugitive Slave Act made that measure practically impossible to enforce. New England, Pennsylvania, the states in the Old Northwest and Wisconsin now had personal-liberty laws that effectively blocked all attempts at the rendition of escaped slaves, and that carried the doctrine of states' rights almost to the point of nullification.

The South, for its part, became more and more defiant of northern opinion. Southern threats of secession were frequent, and southern extremists were now demanding that Congress protect slavery in the territories by the positive action of establishing slave codes. Thousands of slaves from Africa and Cuba were landed in southern ports in defiance of the law against slave importation, and there was increasing agitation for legally reopening the slave trade. The South became rebelliously defensive as it faced not only the attacks of the antislavery zealots but also the prospect of new free states—Oregon, Minnesota, Kansas, Nebraska—coming into the Union. These states would swell the power of the free-soil area, and with it the demand for a homestead act, the allocation of funds for internal improvements, and perhaps even a higher tariff, all projects that were anathema to the southern voters.

Two events occurring in 1858 further embittered southern feeling. When, in September of that year, Senator Seward spoke at Rochester, New York, of the "irrepressible conflict" between the free and slave systems of labor, and coupled this with a vigorous attack upon slavery as unjust and inhuman, many southerners took this as evidence that the Republican party was dedicated to the destruction of the southern way of life. The South was also exasperated by the ready sale of Hinton R. Helper's *Impending Crisis,* first published in 1857, and by the plan of Frank P. Blair, Jr., Cassius M. Clay, and others to reissue Helper's book as a compendium in a cheap edition—a plan backed by Weed, Bryant, Greeley and other leading Republicans. The *Impending Crisis* was an incisive attack upon slavery as detrimental to the nonslaveholding whites of the South. The abolition of slavery was essential to the improvement of this class, said Helper, who also argued that, even in agriculture, the South had fallen behind the free North. The book was hateful to the southern leaders both because of its arguments against slavery, bolstered by facts and figures, and its attempt to arouse discontent among the great body of nonslaveholders south of the Mason and Dixon line. After its publication, Helper did not dare return to his native state of North Carolina.

The growing tension between the sections found ready expression in the nation's capital. Buchanan, sympathetic with the southern expansionists, recommended to Congress that the United States take over northern Mexico to restore order there and, further, asked that $30 million be appropriated for the purchase of Cuba. Southerners applauded, but northern opposition brought these plans to nought. A homestead bill favored by the North passed the House but was killed by southern opposition in the Senate, and efforts emanating from northern industrial centers to increase the tariff on woolen and iron products ran into a stone wall of opposition from the southern bloc. The sections were fast approaching a condition of enmity out of which no constructive legislative program could emerge.

John Brown

Then, as though with the design of fostering further division, came John Brown's raid on Harper's Ferry. After the Pottawatomie Creek murders of 1856, Brown had raised money and arms among the New England abolitionists, and, thus equipped, had gone back to Kansas and organized a slave-stealing raid in Missouri, taking the eleven Negroes so obtained to

John Brown (1800–1859)

A paranoiac whose activities in Kansas and at Harper's Ferry hastened the march toward war, he was also an inspiration for an epic poem written in the twentieth century, Stephen Vincent Benét's John Brown's Body.

COURTESY OF CULVER PICTURES, INC.

Canada. Then he again came east, and abolitionists like Gerrit Smith and Theodore Parker helped him to gather money, rifles, pikes and other supplies for an operation in the South. This paranoiac planned to seize Harper's Ferry, a little town situated in Virginia on the Potomac, and there make himself master of the federal arsenal. He would then rally the neighboring slaves to his standard and move south, liberating as he went. He had convinced himself that this would inaugurate a collapse of the whole slavery system.

On the night of October 16, 1859, Brown, with three of his sons and a few others—twenty-eight in all—seized the arsenal. Slaves did not flock to his standard, but the white countryside promptly rose in alarm. Local militia gathered around Harper's Ferry on October 17, and on the following day came a company of marines under the command of two cavalry officers whose names were destined to become famous in the annals of the

Confederacy—Colonel Robert E. Lee and Lieutenant J. E. B. Stuart. The marines carried the arsenal by assault. Ten of Brown's little band, including two of his sons, were killed, and Brown himself fought bravely but was wounded and captured. The great uprising that was to liberate all the slaves was over.

The fanatic who had engineered this fiasco was indicted for treason to the Commonwealth of Virginia. In a fair trial, he was found guilty, and on December 2, 1859, he rode out to the gallows on his own coffin and was hanged. He died bravely, convinced that he was a martyr in the cause of liberty.

Governor Wise of Virginia could have commuted Brown's death sentence on the ground of insanity, but he chose not to do so. In the month that elapsed between his sentence and his execution, Brown, in interviews and in writing, had told of his noble aims, and his story had been given wide publicity in the North. Now he became a martyr. Greeley's *Tribune* declared that he had done more than lay down his life for a friend—he had offered himself up as a sacrifice "to deliver from bitter bondage and degradation those whom he had never seen." Emerson called him a saint. Thoreau said that the historian would record his deed and the poet sing of it. Some northern spokesmen, Seward and Lincoln among them, condemned Brown's action, but the South was both horrified and terrified by what had happened. Southerners believed that it was the forerunner of similar raids by abolitionist forces, and that it had been engineered by leaders of the Republican party. Brown's slave insurrection had ended in failure, but he had widened the chasm between the sections.

The national legislature met on December 9, 1859, and the first act of business in the Senate was a resolution of inquiry into the affair at Harper's Ferry. Events were proving, as John Bigelow said, that it had been easier to get John Brown on a scaffold than it was to get him down again. Such tension reigned in both houses of the legislature that a great majority of the House of Representatives, on both sides of the aisle, came to the sessions armed. The House spent two months in a bitter wrangle over the choice of a Speaker before William Pennington of New Jersey, the final Republican choice for the post, was elected. Repeatedly there were scenes of disorder. Shouts and insults were exchanged, and bloodshed was narrowly averted. Again and again, southern spokesmen asserted that the election of a Republican President would mean war.

More and more, sectional division made a mockery of the operations of government. The House passed but the South defeated in the Senate a bill calling for some small upward revisions of the tariff. Southern opposition was potent in the emasculation of a homestead bill and in sustaining Buchanan's veto of the measure. When the southern bloc could not prevail in Congress, it relied with confidence upon the action of the executive branch; in addition to the homestead act, Buchanan vetoed an internal improvements bill much desired by the Old Northwest. As government approached a stalemate, the country viewed the situation apprehensively. When the Covode Committee in the House disclosed shocking instances of weakness and malfeasance on the part of Buchanan, and after another investigation had pinned charges of weakness and corruption on Secretary of War Floyd, disgust for the reigning Administration was added to fear for the stability of the nation.

The 1860 Presidential Conventions

While the sections drifted apart and disclosure of administrative weakness and incompetence rocked the nation, the political pot was vigorously boiling as candidates for the presidency worked hard for position. Douglas was busy mending his fences in the North, hopeful of the Democratic nomination despite southern discontent with his attitude toward slavery extension. Seward made a speech in the Senate toward the close of February, 1860, that emphasized the moderation of Republicanism, denied that it was a sectional party, and pleaded for harmony and peace between the sections. Lincoln, before a distinguished audience at Cooper Union in New York, emphasized the repugnance to slavery that was felt by the Founding Fathers and then dwelt upon the conservatism of the Republican party; though it had had nothing to do with Harper's Ferry, was not revolutionary, and would concede everything possible to the South, it was committed to the proposition that slavery should not spread into the national territories, nor "overrun us here in these free states." Seward's speech strengthened him with the northern business class. Lincoln's address, generally praised, and his subsequent trip through New England, raised his stature in the Northeast, an important point in view of the approaching contest for the nomination.

The Democratic national convention met in Charleston, South Carolina, on April 23, 1860. There Douglas, with a majority of the delegates at his command, was in a powerful position; no one he opposed could be nominated. The great bulk of the southern delegates, however, despised and distrusted him, and they and Buchanan's followers controlled the platform committee. The majority report of that committee asserted that it was the right and duty of the national government to protect the rights and property of persons in the territories—an endorsement of the extreme southern position on slavery—while the minority report supported popular sovereignty. A furious controversy ensued on the floor of the convention, which was willing to have a platform that did not mention popular sovereignty but refused to support one that endorsed protection of slavery in the territories by the national government. When this became clear, the cotton states withdrew from the convention hall, and the Douglasites were then unable to obtain a two-thirds majority of all elected delegates. A deadlock ensued, and what was left of the Charleston convention disbanded in bitterness of spirit; with it disappeared, for the time being, the one great party that had been left to bridge the gap between the sections.

Two weeks after the Democratic convention broke up, the remnants of the Whigs and Know-Nothings met in Baltimore. Designating themselves as the Constitutional Union party, they decided that their best course was to play the part of conciliator in the raging sectional quarrel. They nominated John Bell of Tennessee and Edward Everett of Massachusetts as their presidential ticket. Their platform pledged devotion to "The Constitution of the Country, the Union of the States, and the Enforcement of the Laws." Both the ticket and the platform had special appeal for the voters in the border states, but the party organizations that supported them were decrepit.

The Republicans gathered in Chicago on May 16 at the Wigwam, a wooden structure erected specially for the occasion at the corner of Lake and Market streets, with the 466 delegates in a mood of great enthusiasm. Seward was the outstanding candidate for the nomination, but Greeley had thrown his support to Edward Bates of Missouri, a former Whig who seemed likely to command considerable support in the border slave states, and Lincoln's star had risen since his Cooper Union speech.

Lincoln had worked hard and effectively to further his chances of the nomination. In 1859, he had bought secretly an Illinois German newspaper, the *Staats-Anzeiger,* so that it would serve as a counterweight among the German residents of the state to the Chicago *Staats-Zeitung,* which had come out for Seward. Lincoln and his friends had operated so effectively in Illinois that the state's delegation to Chicago was solidly behind the man from Springfield.

The platform adopted by the Republicans at Chicago was conservative in tone. It denounced armed invasion of any state or territory—a slap at both the Missouri Border Ruffians and John Brown—and asserted the right of each state "to order and control its domestic institutions." In a weak and colorless statement, it denied "the authority of Congress, of a territorial legislature, or of any individuals to give legal existence to slavery in any territory of the United States." Only because Joshua Giddings threatened to bolt was a reaffirmation of the inalienable rights of man to life, liberty, and the pursuit of happiness included. The platform did, however, denounce disunion, popular sovereignty, Lecompton, and the African slave trade, and it also demanded a homestead act, a protective tariff, internal improvements, and a railroad to the Pacific.

With the platform adopted, the convention turned to the business of nominating a presidential candidate. It would be pleasant to record that prescience impelled the delegates irresistibly toward Lincoln, but such was

"THE IMPENDING CRISIS"

Webb of the Courier and Enquirer *accuses Greeley of pushing Seward off the dock. Raymond of the* Times *collars the culprit, who protests his innocence. Seward clutches in one hand the letter written to him by Greeley in 1854 dissolving the partnership of Weed, Seward, and Greeley. Note Greeley's trouser leg, a hit at his habitual carelessness in dress. This Currier and Ives cartoon was a commentary on Seward's defeat for the Republican presidential nomination in 1860.*

COURTESY OF THE UNIVERSITY OF ROCHESTER LIBRARY

THE IRREPRESSIBLE CONFLICT, OR "THE REPUBLICAN BARGE IN DANGER"

This Currier and Ives publication shows Lincoln at the helm of the Republican barge, while Greeley and Francis P. Blair throw Seward overboard. Brother Jonathan, looking on, suggests that the Republicans would do better to get rid of their Negro passenger.

not the case. There were three main causes responsible for his nomination —availability, bargains, and crowd psychology.

Distinguished as Seward's public career had been, there were weaknesses in his position as a candidate. His "higher law" and "irrepressible conflict" speeches had given him a reputation for radicalism that offended the sober-minded. Greeley was opposed to him, and Greeley and the *Tribune* had influence. Seward's attitude toward the foreign-born in New York State was abhorrent to the Know-Nothings, and they were strong in Pennsylvania, a crucial state. The New Yorker's intimacy with Weed told against him, for Weed had a reputation, not altogether undeserved, as an unscrupulous politician. There was doubt as to whether Seward could carry Pennsylvania, New Jersey, Indiana, and Illinois.

Lincoln profited by the doubts about Seward, for he had none of Seward's weaknesses. His astute managers, led by the rich, corpulent, and unscrupulous Judge David Davis of Chicago, "worked" the convention for him. They promised, or held out the hope of, Cabinet posts and other offices to prominent men in key delegations, Simon Cameron of Pennsylvania, Caleb B. Smith of Indiana, Gideon Welles of Connecticut, and Frank and Montgomery Blair of Maryland. Though Lincoln had told his managers to make no bargains in his name, with the nomination at stake they ignored this command, and he later honored their promises. The Lincoln leaders, moreover, packed the Wigwam with Lincoln rooters by printing 1,000 counterfeit tickets and distributing them to cohorts who were led by a certain Dr. Ames, reputed to be able to shout clear across Lake Michigan on a clear day, and another leather-lunged individual nearly his equal. The noise made by the Lincoln supporters at appropriate times during the proceedings was prodigious and, according to observers, had its effect. In addition, great play was made of Lincoln's humble origin, and of his ability to split rails. Two rails, supposedly the handiwork of "Honest Abe, the Railsplitter," were carried into the convention hall amid scenes of great enthusiasm. In this way, the "log cabin argument" of 1840 was used with effect.

On the first ballot, Seward received 173½ votes and Lincoln 102, the rest being scattered among favorite sons. On the second ballot, Seward had 184½, Lincoln 181, and Bates of Missouri thirty-five. The swing to Lincoln was on. When the third ballot gave him 231½ to Seward's 180, just one and one-half votes short of victory, four votes in the Ohio delegation were switched from Chase to Lincoln, and the battle was over. Unwittingly, the Republicans had nominated a great man.

The Democratic national convention reassembled at Baltimore on June 18, but it was hopelessly split into northern and southern factions. As it became evident that the popular-sovereignty men had control of the meeting, the great bulk of the southern and a scattering of the northern delegates withdrew. The Northern Democracy then nominated Douglas and endorsed the Democratic platform of 1856. The bolters gathered in a convention of their own and nominated John C. Breckinridge of Kentucky on a platform demanding protection by the federal government of slavery in the territories, and the earliest possible acquisition of Cuba. The Democracy had broken into two wings, and Republican chances of success were bright indeed.

Suggested Reading

Nevins, *The Emergence of Lincoln,* vols. I and II, is indispensable for a study of the events dealt with in this chapter. Also useful are Roy Nichols, *The Disruption of American Democracy* (1948); G. F. Milton, *The Eve of Conflict* (1934); and the works by Carpenter, Craven and Russell previously cited.

G. T. Curtis, *Life of James Buchanan* (2 vols., 1883) is old but still useful. P. G. Auchampaugh, *James Buchanan and His Cabinet on the Eve of Secession* (1926) is a favorable interpretation of Buchanan's role, as is P. S. Klein, *President James Buchanan* (1962).

The Dred Scott case is discussed in C. B. Swisher, *American Constitutional Development* (rev. ed., 1954), in his life of Taney previously cited, and in C. G. Haines and F. H. Sherwood, *The Role of the Supreme Court in American Government and Politics, 1853–1864* (1957). The student should also consult Nevins' analysis, Vincent Hopkins' *Dred Scott's Case* (1951), and the very readable account in A. J. Beveridge's *Abraham Lincoln, 1809–1858* (2 vols., 1928).

The story of developments in Kansas and the national reaction to them is dealt with in Nevins and the other general accounts of the period mentioned above and in the previous chapter.

For the panic of 1857 see G. W. Van Vleck, *The Panic of 1857; An Analytical Study* (1943).

On Stephen A. Douglas, see G. F. Milton, *The Eve of Conflict* (1934) and G. M. Capers, *Stephen A. Douglas* (1959). A life of Douglas is in preparation by Robert W. Johannsen.

The Lincoln-Douglas debates are examined in detail in Carl Sandburg, *Abraham Lincoln, the Prairie Years* (abridged one-vol. ed., 1929) and more briefly in Beveridge's *Lincoln.* See also William Baringer, *Lincoln's Rise to Power* (1937), readable and authoritative. D. E. Fehrenbacher, *Prelude to Greatness* (1962) is excellent.

The increasing tension of these years, and Brown's raid on Harper's Ferry are dealt with in the works by Nevins and Nichols cited above, in Craven's *The Growth of Southern Nationalism,* and in A. C. Cole's *The Era of the Civil War* (1919). The best life of Brown is O. G. Villard, *John Brown* (1910). The student should also consult C. V. Woodward's essay on John Brown, previously cited.

For the national conventions of 1860, in addition to the above general works, see E. D. Fite, *The Presidential Campaign of 1860* (1911), also the essays by Nichols and Van Deusen in G. H. Knoles, ed., *The Crisis of the Union* (1965).

DIVISION

ROBERT E. LEE (1807–1870)
Lee, like Grant, was a great general.
He was also a man whose wisdom and calm
judgment inspired confidence in all who
knew him. There is no more appealing
figure in the annals
of the Confederacy.

⟦1860-1876⟧

AND REUNION

30 ⸴ Secession

THE POLITICAL CONTEST that followed the presidential nominations of 1860 was quiet and well ordered. Previous campaigns in the nation's history had seen a general belaboring of political leaders. There were now, of course, contemptuous references to Lincoln in the South, but it was only the Douglasites and the Buchananites who spent much time denouncing "Old Buck" or "the Little Giant." It was primarily a campaign of education, each party striving to convince the voters that its victory would be for their best interests.

The Campaign of 1860

The Constitutional Unionist speakers praised slavery in the South and denied sympathy for or connection with it in the North. They argued that, though the Republican party might preach moderation, its real objective was the destruction of slavery and it would never be content until it reached its goal. The South, they asserted, knew this, and therefore Lincoln's election would make secession certain. The party labored under the handicap of an unimpressive ticket. Bell had been both for and against slavery in his career, and had never demonstrated outstanding qualities of leadership. Everett had in the past made violent antislavery statements, which the followers of Breckinridge made certain were circulated in the South. The party's platform was ambiguous, and its emphasis on preservation of the Union that, in stronger hands, might have had a potent influence, had but a limited appeal. The greatest impact made by the Constitutional Unionists

629

was in the border states, and in northern financial centers where business-men felt that the success of this ticket would be the best guarantee against war.

Breckinridge could count on the support of that great body of southerners who felt that Douglas had been false to southern interests, that of those con-genital Democrats who felt that their only genuine party ticket was that headed by the man from Kentucky, and that of the national administration; Buchanan himself, Cushing, Cass, Pierce and a number of prominent northern Democratic senators were in the Breckinridge camp, their principal interest being the ruination of Douglas as a political figure. Breckinridge did not openly advocate secession in the very few speeches that he made during the campaign, but the Southern Democracy with its rabid secessionist wing was for the Union only in lukewarm fashion. William Lowndes Yancey of South Carolina, a power in the party, refused to commit himself, saying only that he would go with his state when it made its decision after the election; but he organized a lodge of the "League of United South-erners," whose motto was "A Southern Republic is our only safety." There was no evidence that Breckinridge could carry a single free state, and the general tone of his supporters gave ominous indication that they would go for secession if Lincoln were elected.

The Northern Democracy was hampered not only by the opposition of Buchanan and his followers, but also by financial difficulties, for the busi-ness class saw little reason to support a candidate who was heartily disliked in the South and who was certain of defeat. Nevertheless, Douglas and his followers made a spirited campaign, with their marching clubs, such as the "Ever Readys" and the "Little Giants," putting on a brave show. Douglas assailed the Republicans as advocates of racial equality, wooed northern support by pointing to his voting record on homestead bills, and, most of all, stood for the Union, challenging his Democratic opponent on that ground.

As was his wont in a political fight, Douglas manifested great energy. During the earlier part of the campaign, he spoke in the Middle West, in New England, and in Maryland, Virginia, and North Carolina. After the October elections in Pennsylvania and Indiana had gone Republican and threats of secession multiplied, he said, "I will go South," and moved into Tennessee, Georgia, and Alabama, where he preached the doctrine of the Union, warning of the dangers and folly of secession. Repeatedly he chal-lenged Breckinridge to state whether, if Lincoln were elected, the South would be justified in seceding, and whether, if secession took place before the commission of an overt act against the constitutional rights of the states, he would advise or vindicate the use of force against the seceding states. His own stand on these points was clearly stated, but Breckinridge refused to answer the questions. Large and often enthusiastic southern audiences listened to "the Little Giant," but he had no appreciable effect on southern opinion.

Lincoln made no speeches during the campaign, on the ground that his views were already known and that anything he said was bound to be misrepresented. He saw many callers at Springfield but left direction of the contest to the Republican National Committee headed by Governor Edwin D. Morgan of New York. Campaign biographies of "The Rail-splitter" and selections from the Lincoln-Douglas debates, the Cooper Union address, and other speeches were printed and widely circulated. Seward, Chase, Carl Schurz, Frank P. Blair, Jr., and many others carried the burden of Republican electioneering, some speaking every day for two or three months.

There were 10,000 speeches for Lincoln in New York State alone, and 50,000 throughout the Union. They emphasized the party's stern opposition to the extension of slavery into the territories and to all schemes for acquiring more slave territory. They delivered a drumfire attack on the weakness and corruption of the Buchanan Administration and, where it would do the most good, stressed Republican interest in protection, internal improvements, a Pacific railroad, and a homestead law. The homestead plank in the platform was an asset, and the tariff plank helped in Pennsylvania and parts of the Old Northwest. The foreign-born were assured that under a Republican regime they need have no fear of restricted rights or of any form of persecution. These tactics helped to rally farmers and laborers to the Republican cause. Another aid was the selection of strong Republican tickets in such states as New York, Pennsylvania, Indiana, and Illinois.

Some Republican orators—Sumner and Carl Schurz are examples—made violent attacks on slavery, which were regarded in the South as representing the true spirit of Republicanism, but the general tone of the party orators and newspapers was moderate, the aim being to attract the great body of cautious-minded citizens rather than appeal to the extremist few. An important feature of the Republican campaign was the impressive display of enthusiasm—the rallies, mass meetings, and the Wide Awakes and other clubs with their brass bands, torchlight processions, smart uniforms and thousands of marching men.

The Republicans would not treat secession threats as serious. Lincoln thought they were largely bluff, and other leaders took the same attitude, partly out of conviction and partly to prevent fostering the impression that a Republican victory would mean war. But the Republicans were quick to denounce efforts at fusion between the two wings of the Democracy and the Constitutional Unionists that were made as the campaign progressed in New York, Pennsylvania, and two or three other states. What lay behind these efforts was the hope that the election could be thrown into the House of Representatives and a fusion candidate be put in the White House. In general, they were none too successful, for they involved abandonment of principles. The Republicans held up the specter of violence and strife in the House if the election were held there in a campaign with such momentous issues, and Douglas himself openly repudiated fusion.

Jefferson Davis tried to get Breckinridge, Bell, and Douglas to agree to withdraw in favor of a candidate who might unite their forces. The two former agreed to do so if Douglas would cooperate. He refused, on the ground that such a move would send thousands of northern Democrats into the Lincoln camp, and, in turn, argued that the one possibility of beating Lincoln would be for Breckinridge to withdraw and throw his support to Douglas, a move that the Kentuckian refused to make.

As the campaign wore to its close, it became clear that Lincoln would carry most of the northern states, that Breckinridge would win in the Deep South, and that Douglas's bid for the presidency was headed for certain defeat. Equally certain was the bitter feeling of the Cotton South, aflame with stories of northern plots, more John Brown uprisings, and Republican plans for enforcing social equality between Negro and white. Many southerners believed that a Republican victory would mean economic ruin and social chaos. The more intelligent among them discounted the lurid pictures of the future conjured up by the Rhetts and the Yanceys, but even moderates like Alexander H. Stephens of Georgia were convinced that Lincoln's election would make secession inevitable. The governors of the Cotton States even began taking counsel with one another as to how secession might be accomplished if the Republicans took over the national government.

Lincoln emerged the victor over his three competitors. He had an electoral vote of 180, as compared with twelve for Douglas (who carried only New Jersey and Missouri), thirty-nine for Bell, and seventy-two for Breckinridge. Lincoln's popular vote was 1,866,452; there were 1,375,157 votes for Douglas, 847,953 for Breckinridge and 590,631 for Bell. The next occupant of the White House would be a man whom southerners described as the agent of the diabolical Republican party, and antislavery fanatics like Wendell Phillips could call "the slave-hound of Illinois."

The election had significant and ominous overtones from the point of

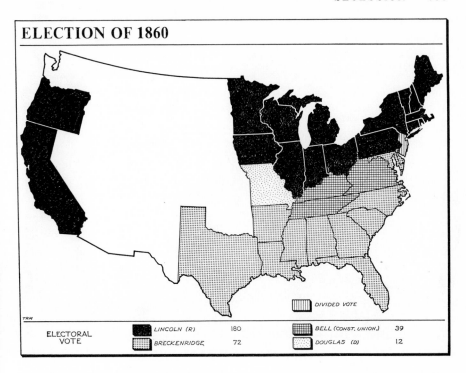

ELECTION OF 1860

DIVIDED VOTE

ELECTORAL VOTE					
	LINCOLN (R)	180		BELL (CONST. UNION.)	39
	BRECKENRIDGE	72		DOUGLAS (D)	12

view of national unity. It was almost as though two countries had voted each with a two-party system. In the North, neither Breckinridge nor Bell had won a single electoral vote, with only 78,063 ballots having been cast for Bell. Discounting fusion voting, there were probably not over 100,000 bona fide Breckinridge ballots north of the Mason and Dixon line. In the South, Lincoln received a total of 26,300 votes, 17,000 of these being in Missouri, where he carried St. Louis; not a ballot was cast for him in the Deep South. Douglas had some 160,000 votes in the South, but 70 per cent of these came from Virginia, Tennessee, Kentucky, and Missouri. The only real contest in the South had been between Breckinridge and Bell. The latter had carried Virginia, Kentucky, and Tennessee, and the other eleven slave states had gone for Breckinridge.

Another disquieting factor was the anomalous position of what the southerners called the "Black Republican" party. It did not have a majority in either the House or the Senate, and its chief, the President-elect, had received only 39.9 per cent of the popular vote. But, paradoxically enough, the incoming Republican Administration would be in a position of great power. All of the executive authority and patronage was at its disposal. It might even take command of the national legislature, for there was no assurance that northern Democrats would join with their southern brethren

THE NATIONAL GAME—THREE "OUTS" AND ONE "RUN"

Baseball was a popular American sport by 1860, although the rules were quite unlike those of today. This Currier and Ives publication shows Lincoln the victor in the presidential game of 1860, to the discomfiture of Bell, Douglas, and Breckinridge. The Railsplitter has skunked them.

in protecting slavery interests. The Democratic split greatly enhanced the prospect of government by a national minority, one that only partially represented the northern point of view.

There was a third feature of the election of 1860 that was fraught with uncertainty and peril for the nation. The hold on the national government, the direction of its leadership, that had been exercised by the South during the 1850s through its control of a united Democratic party was now at an end. That section could now have only a subordinate role in the framing of policies at Washington.

The Movement Out of the Union

Once Lincoln had been elected, the fundamental question facing the country was whether or not the Union would be preserved. There were still many moderates in the South to whom secession was utterly repugnant, but predominant southern opinion favored separation. Inflamed by the John Brown raid and by repeated rumors of impending slave revolts, believing that Republicanism meant enforced social equality between Negroes and whites, the populace paid little attention to the arguments by Unionists that the Supreme Court would protect the South and that the Republican minority in Congress would never be able to pass extreme measures. What seemed all too apparent was that northern hostility to slavery had developed to ominous proportions. There was little discrimination in the southern mind between shades of northern antislavery opinion, but, rather, the growing conviction that Republicanism represented them all, and that it would inevitably take drastic steps to destroy the southern way of life.

When Governor Gist of South Carolina had first asked the governors of the cotton states what action they contemplated if Lincoln were elected, the replies had indicated a general unwillingness to take the lead in a secession movement. After the election was over, however, commissioners from Mississippi and Alabama assured Gist that their states would follow the lead of South Carolina in seceding from the Union. Thereupon the South Carolina legislature, which had remained in session after casting the vote of the state for Breckinridge, issued a call for the election of a special convention; this met on December 17, and was overwhelmingly secessionist. On December 20, it passed by unanimous vote an ordinance of secession and, four days later, issued a *Declaration of Causes of Secession*. These causes included abolitionism, aid to fugitive slaves, and the election of Lincoln, who had declared that the nation could not live half-slave and half-free. Republicanism was described as an organized, powerful, and vicious attack on property and states' rights.

When the news of the convention's action was released, Charleston assumed an air of festival. The Stars and Stripes came down, and palmetto flags broke out all over the city. Liberty poles and banners inscribed "God is with us" were everywhere. Men on the streets clasped hands and spoke with tears in their eyes of the dawn of a glorious new day.

South Carolina had taken the lead, but the rest of the Deep South still hesitated to follow her example. Alexander H. Stephens, Justice Wayne of the Supreme Court, James L. Petigru the distinguished Charleston jurist, and some merchants, professional men, and nonslaveholding farmers counseled delay. There was still much Union sentiment in the cotton states, but it was not effectively marshaled to meet the secessionist drive, and was handicapped by the same cautious conservatism that made those loyal to the Union dread secession. In addition, the extremists used social pressure to effect their ends, aided by the widespread southern belief in states' rights and the right of secession, the hatred of northern free-soilism, and the belief that the southern way of life could be successfully preserved only in a separate southern confederacy.

In state after state, radical conventions took control of the proceedings, and during the month of January, 1861, Mississippi, Florida, Alabama, Georgia, Louisiana, and Texas passed ordinances of secession. The Deep South had gone out of the Union. In February, a Confederate government meeting in Montgomery, Alabama, drafted a provisional constitution closely resembling that which had been drafted at Philadelphia three-quarters of a century before, the chief differences being that it emphasized states' rights and specifically guaranteed slavery.

Fumbling at Washington

While the Deep South moved toward rebellion, the government at Washington was unable to formulate a clear-cut policy of action. Buchanan was determined to preserve peace as long as possible, hoping that delay would bring reflection on all sides and produce a saving compromise. However, he was the victim of his own vacillation, and of divisions in his Cabinet over the right of secession and the advisability of reinforcing the nine federal forts at Charleston, Mobile, and other southern ports. Prompt reorganization of his official family, with the elimination of secessionists Cobb, Floyd, and Thompson (Secretaries of the Treasury, War and Interior) would probably have bolstered the Unionist sentiment that still existed in the South, but for the time being the Cabinet remained intact.

Buchanan wanted to call a convention of all the states for the purpose of devising a compromise that would save the Union, but, after the Cabinet divided on the advisability of this idea, it was dropped. When Congress assembled on December 4, 1860, it received a long, labored, and inconclusive message from the President. In sum, this document declared that secession was unconstitutional, but that neither the Chief Executive nor Congress had the authority to coerce seceding states. Its one positive suggestion was an "explanatory amendment" to the Constitution which would recognize: (1) the right of property in slaves, (2) the duty of protecting this right in all the territories until they were admitted as states, and (3) the validity of the fugitive slave law and the unconstitutionality of all personal liberty laws passed by the states; that such an amendment could pass Congress by a two-thirds majority and be ratified by three-fourths of the states was highly improbable.

"LITTLE BO-PEEP AND HER FOOLISH SHEEP"

This cartoon, published by T. W. Strong, is directed against both secession and Buchanan. The foolish sheep are wandering into danger from the wolves with crowns on their heads. Dame Columbia, the shepherdess, wishes that "Old Hickory" were alive; she exhorts "Old Buck" to bring back the strays, but he is manifestly terrified at the prospect. "Virginia" represents southern desire for compromise as a means of ending the crisis.

The composition of the Cabinet changed considerably during the weeks following the convening of Congress. Cobb, Floyd, and Thompson resigned, and the President invited strong Union men, Edwin M. Stanton and Jeremiah Black, into his official circle. These changes came just in time to avert disaster.

On December 26, Major Anderson, in command of Fort Moultrie in Charleston harbor, transferred his little garrison of sixty men to the more defensible Fort Sumter. The South Carolinians and prominent southerners in Washington demanded that Anderson be sent back to Fort Moultrie. Buchanan wavered, but Cobb and Floyd were now gone from the Cabinet, and the Union members literally forced the President to support Anderson's move. Troops, stores, and ammunition were even despatched to his aid in a steamer, the *Star of the West,* but it was fired upon and driven away by Carolinian shore batteries.

The Attempts at Compromise

While one southern state after another was leaving the Union, Congress concerned itself with efforts at compromise. Adjustment of difficulties had become traditional in the United States, beginning with the compromise on slave representation in the constitutional convention of 1787. It was inevitable that such efforts would now be made, but it was most unfortunate that they had to take place in an atmosphere of mutual distrust and suspicion.

In the House, Speaker Pennington appointed a Committee of Thirty-Three to consider the state of the country, and this committee began an animated but inconclusive discussion of suggestions for compromise. It was the Senate that produced the first major plan of adjustment, when, on December 18, the Senate voted to establish a Committee of Thirteen, and at the same time Senator John J. Crittenden of Kentucky introduced in the Senate a series of resolutions and proposed amendments to the Constitution that, he hoped, would do for the nation what Clay had done in the Compromise of 1850. The amendments provided that: (1) the Missouri Compromise line should be extended to the Pacific, so far as existing territories were concerned; (2) Congress should have no power to abolish slavery in places under its jurisdiction in the slave states; (3) Congress could not abolish slavery in the District of Columbia, so long as it continued to exist in Virginia and Maryland, and not then without the consent and indemnification of slave owners; (4) Congress should have no power to interfere with the interstate slave trade; (5) Congress should indemnify owners prevented from recovering their fugitive slaves; and (6) no future constitutional amendment should affect the foregoing amendments. The resolutions called for statutory corrections of the fugitive slave law, and for the repeal or amendment of the states' personal liberty laws. They also reaffirmed the validity of the fugitive slave act and of the laws for the suppression of the African slave trade.

Crittenden presented his proposals to the Committee of Thirteen, of which he was a leading member. His compromise had wide support throughout the country, but it was doomed to defeat. Few of the great radical leaders, North or South, desired it, and Lincoln opposed it. He believed, as did many Republicans, that it would mean surrendering the key Republican position—opposition to the spread of slavery—since the extension of the Missouri Compromise line would only result in a renewed southern expansionist movement in the direction of Cuba or Central America, and a new series of crises would then be precipitated. Following the lead of the President-elect, the Republicans defeated the proposal in the Committee of Thirteen.

With the Crittenden compromise discarded, Seward made a series of proposals that, while conceding nothing on slavery extension, would have protected slavery where it already existed and would have provided for two Pacific railroads, one northern and one southern, to be built with government aid. The Senator from New York was listened to with respect, but that was all.

Meanwhile, the Committee of Thirty-Three came up with the proposal to extend the line of 36° 30′, only to have it defeated by the Republicans in the House. The sole suggestion of this committee that passed both the House and the Senate was a constitutional amendment to prevent the alteration of the Constitution in any way that would interfere with or abolish the domestic institutions of the states. This amendment was stillborn in the onrush of events, however.

The final compromise effort was a peace conference, called at Washington in February, 1861, on the initiative of Virginia. South Carolina, Arkansas, and the states of the Deep South refused to attend, as did five northern states. The conference was a welter of conflicting views, and its recommendation of the extension of the Missouri Compromise line, with the right of states to come in slave or free below or above that line as the case might be, was adopted by a majority of only one vote. Submitted to Congress, it received only seven votes in the Senate and the House refused to consider it.

But, even as one compromise after another failed, hope remained strong that peace would continue to prevail between the sections. The majority of people, North and South, believed that there would be no war. Northerners felt that the popular vote for Lincoln, Douglas, and Bell showed that a great part of the nation wanted a peaceful solution of difficulties; and that the vote in the seceding states had shown the existence there of a large minority opposed to secession, perhaps even a majority in Louisiana, Alabama, and Georgia. With time for reflection, this minority would grow in size. There was a widespread feeling in the North that the secession movement was only temporary, a flash in the pan. Greeley, Seward, and many others believed that if the erring sisters were allowed to depart in peace, they would be back in ninety days.

The South, too, believed that there would be peace, but for different reasons. Many there thought that the North, ridden by faction and interested primarily in moneymaking, would never fight. They were sure that the border states—Maryland, Virginia and Kentucky—would be a barrier to any coercive move on the part of the North and were also certain that England and France, dependent upon the South for cotton, would rally to their support at the first suggestion of a blockade of southern ports. Confident that the North would not dare to throw down the gage of battle, the leaders of secession seized federal military supplies in the South, took over one federal fort after another, pressed the recruitment of a southern army, and even dreamed of expansion via not only the border states but also Cuba, Mexico, and Central America.

Lincoln Goes to Washington

On February 11, 1861, Lincoln left Springfield for Washington. He spoke briefly at various places along the route. His speeches were commonplace, and his attempts at wit ill-timed. With seven states out of the Union, it seemed strange to hear the President-elect say that nothing was going wrong and that "there is no crisis but an artificial one." A change of route by which he avoided Baltimore, because of reports of an assassination plot there, also roused criticism. But in his speeches he made it clear that he did not intend to interfere with southern institutions, and that the government would not use force unless force was used against it.

Shortly after the election, Lincoln had begun selecting his Cabinet— an arduous task. The presence in the party of mutually suspicious Old Whigs and Old Democrats, the conflict of opinion between those who wanted to conciliate the South and those who believed in a no-compromise policy, and the intraparty feuds in such states as New York and Pennsylvania resulted in his being subjected to almost unbearable pressure from a variety of sides. Through it all he kept his equanimity, determined to have a strong Cabinet that would represent the main elements in the party.

Seward became Secretary of State, and Salmon P. Chase received the Treasury post. The Chicago pledges were honored by making Simon Cameron Secretary of War and putting Caleb B. Smith of Indiana in the Interior Department. Gideon Welles of Connecticut was made Secretary of the Navy, Montgomery Blair of Maryland became Postmaster General, and Edward Bates of Missouri was selected for Attorney General. Cameron was unfit for his post and Blair was a political appointment, but on the whole it was a good Cabinet, one in which Old Whigs and Old Democrats as well as radical and conservative opinion were represented. Lincoln's ability to stand up against pressures and get the kind of Cabinet he wanted augured well for the future.

The fourth of March, 1861, was a sunny day in Washington. Lincoln was inaugurated on a platform at the east portico of the Capitol. There is a story, possibly apocryphal, that as he looked around for a place to put his stovepipe hat, Douglas, sitting near him, took it and placed it on his own knees, a significant gesture of support. The inaugural was persuasive, conciliatory and yet firm. Though Lincoln denied the right of any state to leave the Union, and asserted that he would hold the federal posts in the South and collect the federal duties and imposts, he also pledged noninterference with slavery in the slave states and enforcement of the fugitive slave law. He told the southerners that in their hands was the issue of civil war. Then, in a conclusion the ideas and some of the phraseology of which were suggested by Seward, came one of the great passages in American political literature:

> I am loath to close. We are not enemies but friends. We must not be enemies. Though passion may have strained, it must not break, our bonds of affection. The mystic chords of memory, stretching from every battle-field and patriot grave to every living heart and hearthstone all over this broad land, will yet swell the chorus of the Union when again touched, as surely they will be, by the better angels of our nature.

In the North and in the border slave states, the inaugural had a mixed reception; as might be expected, Republicans generally praised and Democrats criticized it. In the Deep South, it was regarded as a declaration of war.

Presidential Policy and the Crisis

Lincoln's policy toward the South during his first six weeks in office was one of forbearance. He believed there was a powerful Union sentiment in the South that, given time for expression, would overwhelm the secessionists and bring about a restoration of the Union. He intended, therefore, to wait passively, retaining Sumter and Fort Pickens at Pensacola (all that the Union now had left of the federal property in the seceded states) as symbols of the Union. But almost as soon as he had entered the White House, word came from Major Anderson at Fort Sumter that the situation there was becoming serious and that, within a few weeks, the fort must be provisioned or surrendered.

A majority of the Cabinet favored evacuating Sumter. Seward, representing conciliation, was particularly anxious to do so, feeling that the retention of Fort Pickens, where the situation was not menacing, was all that was necessary. But Lincoln hesitated; as he weighed his course of action, he was also aware that agents of the Confederacy were in Washington, pressing for recognition of the government at Montgomery.

Seward, in his anxiety to prevent war, gave assurances to Supreme Court Justice Campbell of Alabama that Sumter would be evacuated within a few days. Campbell thereupon urged the Confederate commissioners not to keep urging recognition in view of the impending surrender of the fort, and gave solemn assurances to the government of President Davis that Sumter would soon be in Confederate hands. These events occurred shortly after the inauguration, and there ensued three tense and anxious weeks.

During this time, Seward, certain that Union sentiment in the South not only existed but would increase as time went on, and convinced that Lincoln was not the man to deal with the situation, believed that he himself should assume control of governmental policy. On April 1, he sent to the President an extraordinary document entitled "Some Thoughts for the President's Consideration." Beginning with the suggestion that, unfortunately, the Administration had no policy, he advised abandoning Sumter and reinforcing Fort Pickens. He also urged, as a means to reuniting the country, that war should be declared on France and Spain because of their ambitious designs in Mexico and Santo Domingo. Seward ended by remarking that whatever course was adopted must be vigorously pursued and, as for himself, "I neither seek to evade nor to assume responsibility."

Calmly, Lincoln set his Secretary of State right as to who was head of the government, scarcely mentioning Seward's argument for a foreign war. After this skillfully and tactfully carried out move, Seward was one of the most loyal members of the Cabinet.

For some time, the President hoped to reinforce Fort Pickens at Pensacola so that he could evacuate Sumter and end the menacing situation at Charleston. But the Pensacola plan miscarried. Thereupon (April 6), Lincoln notified Governor Pickens of South Carolina that Sumter would be provisioned, by force if necessary, and the Governor promptly informed the government at Montgomery of Lincoln's intent.

The Confederate government hesitated, for it much preferred peaceful secession. Fearing that South Carolina would act alone and precipitately, however, it sent instructions to General P. G. T. Beauregard, Confederate commander at Charleston. He was told to demand Anderson's surrender and, if Anderson refused, to reduce the fort.

Major Anderson refused to surrender but indicated that lack of provisions would compel him to evacuate the fort in a few days. This was reported to Montgomery, and the government there agreed to withhold bombardment if Anderson would guarantee not to fire unless attacked, and would state the time at which he would leave the fort. The young staff officers carrying this message to the fort were given the responsibility of determining whether or not Anderson's reply was satisfactory. He told them that he would be forced to surrender by April 15 unless he received supplies or countervailing orders from Washington. The staff officers told him that this was unsatisfactory, and that the Confederate batteries would open in one hour.

FROM THE COLLECTION OF THE UNION LEAGUE OF PHILADELPHIA

"BOMBARDMENT OF FORT SUMTER"
PAINTING BY ALBERT BIERSTADT

The scene is peaceful, save for the smoke drifting up from the Confederate mortars on the beach at Charleston harbor. Peace and war are here tragically intertwined.

At 4:30 A.M., on the stormy morning of April 12, 1861, a red ball rose from a mortar in the battery of Fort Johnson and broke over Sumter. The bombardment had begun. For over thirty hours Anderson fought back, and then, with most of his cannon silenced and his provisions nearly gone, he surrendered. On Sunday, April 14, he marched out with the honors of war, and he and his weary command were permitted to take ship for

New York. The next day, Lincoln called on the states for 75,000 militia to be enlisted for three months. Soon thereafter, Virginia, North Carolina, Tennessee, and Arkansas passed ordinances of secession. The Civil War had begun.

Why Did the War Come?

There have been numerous theories advanced regarding the coming of the Civil War. These generally center around two questions. What were its fundamental causes? Was it a repressible or an irrepressible conflict?

One school of thought holds that the causes of the war were almost exclusively economic; that it was one phase of the profound and irrepressible conflict between the capitalists, laborers, and free farmers of the North and West and the planting aristocracy of the South. From this point of view, the war was the result of a struggle between two economies which had divergent interests, a struggle which resulted in fierce political contention, but which, in its fundamental nature, was essentially economic.

A variant of this economic deterministic school adds a distinctly Marxian emphasis. Putting stress on the ideological aspects of the clash between the sections, it regards the war as a necessary phase in the long-range struggle between capitalists and proletarians. Just as the War for Independence had freed the American bourgeoisie from the clutches of British imperialism, so the Civil War was a bourgeois revolution that eliminated the power of the "counterrevolutionary" southern planters. It was an essential clearing of the way for the struggle between the capitalists and the working class.

A number of historians, while recognizing the importance of economic factors, treat the conflict from a broader point of view. They regard it as one between two cultures or civilizations, each with its own political, social, and economic customs and ideals. Some of those in this general category emphasize the emergence of two conflicting nationalisms, and marshal evidence showing the development of a southern nationalism. They are inclined to look upon the struggle as a "War for Southern Independence."

Some historians incline to the "blundering generation" point of view. War, they say, is abnormal and irrational; artificial factors, not fundamental motives, caused this needless struggle. In this view, the differences between the northern and southern civilizations, economic and otherwise, were by no means so important as to be the inevitable causes of war. Slavery itself being a dying institution, the argument runs, it was chiefly politicians, bigots, and extremists who magnified the differences between the sections out of all proportion and excited and deluded the people; the hostility and hatred thus stirred up were basically responsible for a bewildered generation allowing itself to be led into fratricidal strife.

Closely aligned with the "blundering generation" school of thought is one that puts emphasis on the political situation, pointing out that by the last half of the 1850s the two major parties, Democrats and Republicans, were more or less inchoate reflections of a conglomeration of state and local views and interests. Each had its own state organizations, many of them powerful machines that, in the measure of their power, influenced national party policy and even, on occasion, controlled it for longer or shorter periods of time; neither had great national leaders. Under these circumstances, it is argued, unified and harmonious national party policies simply did not develop, and the nation, politically rudderless, drifted helplessly toward war.

Still another approach emphasizes moral aspects. While it recognizes the importance of all the fundamental differences that had developed between the sections, it holds that the ideological and moral conflict was of supreme importance. Scholars who hold this view deny that slavery was a dying institution, and assert that it was essentially moral disgust with an outmoded and barbarous system arbitrarily maintained by the South that sent the North into battle.

Out of this welter of conflicting opinion, certain generalizations emerge. The Civil War had many underlying causes: economic jealousies and conflicts, opposing attitudes toward slavery, inept political leadership, blind partisanship and hatred, the plans and projects of ambitious and deluded men, ignorance and lack of understanding on the part of the masses, and sheer hysteria—all these played a role in driving the sections apart.

The immediate cause of the war, however, was the quarrel over slavery extension. This began assuming its final form in the controversy over the Wilmot Proviso, and with the Kansas-Nebraska bill emerged clearly as a struggle over the expansion of slavery into any of the territories of the Union. It was the principal issue in the election of Lincoln, and it was chiefly the refusal of Lincoln and his friends to permit slavery in any new areas south of the Missouri Compromise line that defeated the efforts at compromise in the winter of 1860–1861. Why men were willing to fight over this issue is subject to a variety of interpretations, but the fact remains that it was slavery in some form which always brought North and South nearest to open conflict, and that more and more it was the right of the slave system to expand into new ground which became the center of strife. The result was ghastly fratricidal bloodshed. The Civil War generation, as it endured the agony of battle, might well have echoed the plaint of the Swedish Chancellor Oxenstierna, 200 years before—"With how little wisdom the world is governed!"

Suggested Reading

Nevins, *Emergence of Lincoln,* vol. II, is very useful for a study of the various events covered in this chapter. A. Craven, *The Growth of Southern Nationalism, 1848–1861* (1953) has important insights, as do R. F. Nichols, *The Disruption of American Democracy* (1948) and J. G. Randall, *The Civil War and Reconstruction* (rev. ed., 1953).

E. D. Fite, *The Presidential Campaign of 1860* (1911) is a good study of that important election.

For Buchanan's policy during this crucial period, see Auchampaugh, *James Buchanan and His Cabinet,* previously cited, as well as the balanced treatment in the Nevins' volume referred to above, and the biography by Klein. The account of Lincoln in Carl Sandburg, *The Prairie Years,* is colorful. Benjamin P. Thomas, *Abraham Lincoln* (1954) is an authoritative and readable biography which has a good account of the period 1860–1861. See also the works by Barringer and Fehrenbacher, previously cited. Lincoln's formation of his Cabinet and his patronage problems are carefully dealt with in H. J. Carman and R. L. Luthin, *Lincoln and the Patronage* (1943).

Three valuable studies of secession are U. B. Phillips, *The Course of the South to Secession* (1939), edited by E. M. Coulter; D. L. Dumond, *The Secession Movement, 1860–1861* (1931); and D. M. Potter, *Lincoln and His Party in the Secession Crisis* (1942). See also K. M. Stampp, *And the War Came: The North and the Secession Crisis, 1860–1861* (1950), and R. N. Current, Lincoln and the First Shot (1963). The attitude of New York businessmen toward the secession movement is well described in P. S. Foner, *The New York Merchants and the Irrepressible Conflict* (1941).

T. J. Pressly, *Americans Interpret Their Civil War* (1954) is an excellent analysis of the various historical interpretations of the origins of the conflict.

31 ⸱ The Civil War—Military and Naval Aspects

THE TWO SECTIONS which locked in battle in 1861 were by no means evenly matched. The North had a population of over twenty million whites and not quite 500,000 Negroes; it had, moreover, the advantage of unrestricted European immigration. Against this array of manpower the South could muster only about five and one-half million whites and three and one-half million Ne-

The Balance of Resources groes and mulattoes. In potential soldiers, the North outnumbered the South by more than three to one.

In resources and supplies, the North enjoyed a greater advantage than it had in manpower, possessing 110,000 manufacturing establishments, as against 18,000 for the South. The North produced fifteen times as much iron, thirty-eight times as much coal, fifteen times as much cotton goods, and twenty-seven times as much in woolen goods as did the South, as well as four times the wheat, five times the oats, and ten times the hay raised in the Confederacy. After 1861, the northern armies were at times oversupplied with food and clothing, and the southerners picked up and used the clothing that the northern soldiers threw away, though they complained about the poor quality of northern shoddy provided by unscrupulous contractors.

In several other important respects, the North could claim superiority over the Confederacy. It possessed 31,000 miles of railroad, to 9,000 in the South, and the northern roads were definitely superior in their ability to move men and supplies from one part of the Union to another—an important factor in solving the logistical problems of the military. The North also had 4,600,000 draft animals, to 2,566,000 for the Confederacy, a great advantage in that day of horse and mule power. The great majority of the nation's powder factories were within the northern lines. It was also significant that the navy remained faithful to the Union, with only a few naval officers from the higher ranks resigning their federal commissions.

But the South, too, had its points of superiority in this great struggle. At first it had the best of the nation's military talent on its side. The North in 1861 had no match for Robert E. Lee, Thomas J. (Stonewall) Jackson, Joseph E. Johnston, or even Pierre Gustave Toutaint Beauregard. In contrast, Winfield Scott was infirm and Irwin McDowell, commander of the volunteer army assembled around Washington, was far from being a genius. George Brinton McClellan, who had left an army career for railroading, was only just back in service, and Grant's talents were as yet untested. The North had to develop able commanders by a long and painful process of selection.

The South also had an asset, during the early part of the war, in a slave population that remained at work in the fields, thus releasing the more war-inclined whites for military service. A strategical and tactical point in favor of the South lay in the conduct of military operations on interior lines and in familiar country.

Finally, though states' rights fanatics like Governor Joseph E. Brown of Georgia and Governor Zebulon B. Vance of North Carolina gave the Confederate government plenty of trouble, the opposition to the war and its conduct was less dangerous in the South than in the North. It is significant that, in an era when the press had great influence, there were seventy-three newspapers in the North in 1861 that were harsh critics of Administration measures and either wished to let the South go in peace or wanted the Union restored as it was. The South, on the other hand, had only twenty-three papers of Union sympathies, all in the border states, and almost all of them were under the protection of the national government. Defeatism and the "copperheadism" that deliberately sought to lend aid and comfort to the South, rancorous political opposition, and virulent criticism of Administration policies were handicaps of no mean proportions to the northern conduct of the war. They were particularly hard to bear in 1863 and 1864.

So far as preparation for the grim struggle was concerned, the sides were fairly well balanced in 1861. Unified training for more than a brigade or a division was conspicuous by its absence, and no supply of uniforms was available for either government. Weapons varied from the Springfield and Enfield rifles, just being introduced, to shotguns. Army discipline was something volunteers knew nothing about; privates on both sides brought cumbersome luggage into the camps, and sometimes a southern recruit would arrive with a couple of trunks filled with food and clothing, and a body servant to minister to his personal wants.

Significant Characteristics of the War

There was very little about the Civil War that corresponded to the romantic tales that later graced the stories of Joel Chandler Harris and Thomas Nelson Page. The average northerner, officer or private, handsome or homely, met no beauteous plantation belle who reciprocated his affection and promised to wait for him until the battle flags were furled. No authentic incident has been recorded of two soldiers, one in blue and one in gray, found dead on the field of battle, their hands clasped in the grip of Delta Psi Theta. The war was a grim, desperate struggle, much as it was described by Stephen Crane (who never saw it) in *The Red Badge of Courage*. Many brave men fought heroically on both sides, but there were also many who, having seen what it was like, wanted no part of it; there were in all, some 380,000 deserters, North and South.

To swell the ranks depleted by battle, disease, and desertion, both sides resorted to conscription. The South in 1862 conscripted able-bodied men between the ages of eighteen and thirty-five, though there were large exemptions and a man could furnish a substitute. The age limit was later extended to forty-five years, and finally to all men between seventeen and fifty, and toward the end some attempt was made to recruit slaves. The North, in 1863, began drafting men between the ages of twenty and forty-five, but release could be obtained by providing a substitute or paying the government $300.00. This inequitable law went far toward justifying the aspersion that it was "a rich man's war and a poor man's fight." It also led to the practice of local communities paying bounties for volunteers who could be counted against the draft quota of the area, and paying bounties led in turn to bounty-jumping, with repeated re-enlistments for pay. The draft produced much discontent in various parts of the North, and in New York City during July, 1863, there were bloody draft riots, with from 500 to 1,200 dead and more than $1 million worth of property destroyed.

The draft succeeded in producing a marked increase in enlistments,

COURTESY OF THE NEW-YORK HISTORICAL SOCIETY, NEW YORK CITY

BREAKING THAT "BACKBONE"—BY BENJAMIN DAY

This poses succinctly the problem of subduing the Confederacy. If military skill and strategy will not suffice, there still remain the draft and emancipation.

which were essential, for the loss of life was heavy on both sides. Of 160,000 engaged at Gettysburg, 50,000 were killed, wounded, or missing. During the campaign of May and June, 1864, that began in the Wilderness, Grant lost 54,929 men by death, wounds, disease and desertion—a 40 per cent loss, which almost equaled the number of Lee's whole army at the beginning of the campaign—and Lee lost 30,000—a 46 per cent loss that could be only partially replaced. Even with such heavy battle casualties, more died of disease behind the lines and in the prison camps than were killed at the front. The Union casualty rate, in proportion to its population, was over six times that in World War II.

As the losses indicate, this was primarily an infantry war, in which artillery and cavalry played important but secondary roles, though there were some brilliant cavalry exploits by Union General Philip Sheridan and Confederate General J. E. B. Stuart. There were also acts of ruthlessness on both sides: Sheridan devastated the Shenandoah Valley so thoroughly that it was said a crow flying its length would have to carry his provisions with him; Sherman left a swath of destruction in his march from Atlanta to the sea that was calculated, in his own words, "to make Georgia howl"; and at Fort Pillow, Arkansas, in 1864, hundreds of Negro troops serving in the Union army were needlessly killed by enraged Confederates.

Brutal though it may have been, the Civil War was the first "modern" war. The rifle replaced the old smoothbore musket, thus spelling the doom of the massed infantry attack, although generals on both sides stubbornly continued to use it. Total war it nearly was also, for as the Union armies moved south, they struck at resources as well as at troops. The war also saw the first use of the ironclad, the mine, the torpedo, and the submarine.

In its grand strategy, the war went according to the "Anaconda Plan" outlined for it by General Scott at its beginning—a naval blockade with military pressures narrowing the ring around the South. This explains the early Union attempt to get control of the Mississippi, and the strenuous efforts to seal off the harbors of the South. The Union government proclaimed a blockade of southern ports in April, 1861, and by the autumn of that year—due to the great energy displayed in building, equipping, and manning ships—it was largely effective. The South might have shipped out considerable quantities of cotton while the blockade was being established, but held it, hoping to produce a cotton famine that would force English interposition. The hope was vain, for there were large cotton reserves in British hands. By 1862, blockade running was encountering great difficulties, and these increased to the end of the war; the blockade runner was, at best, a minor factor in furnishing supplies for the Confederacy.

The fall of Vicksburg in 1863 sealed off another avenue of foreign supply for the Confederacy—the trickle of imports that had been coming in from Mexico by way of Texas. But there was one source of outside aid that remained available to the Confederacy almost to the end of the war—the North itself. There was always traffic across the lines of the Union and Confederate armies, southern cotton and tobacco being exchanged for northern drugs and other needed supplies. Grant estimated that, where such trade was carried on, it neutralized military effort by some 33 per cent, but it was not until 1865 that the northern government made serious efforts to stop it.

The South's most formidable answer to the blockade was the commerce raider. There were nineteen of these in all, four of them built or purchased in England. The most famous one was the *Alabama,* which inflicted a loss of $6,547,609 on American shipping before she was sunk outside Cherbourg by the *Kearsarge.* The Confederate raiders captured 270 ships and caused over 700 more to change to foreign registry. They were a major factor in the decline of the American merchant marine, but they were no counterweight to the blockade.

The Campaign of 1861

The raw condition of the opposing armies was manifested at the first major engagement between them—the battle of Bull Run, or First Manassas. A Union army, mainly volunteers, assembled around Washington during the early summer of 1861. Pressure for a movement "Forward to Richmond," sparked by the New York *Tribune* and other molders of public opinion, grew every day. Beauregard had 20,000 men at Manassas, a railroad center guarding the highway to Richmond which, in May, had been made the Confederate capital. McDowell reluctantly ordered an offensive operation, and the troops straggled out of Washington, accompanied by congressmen and other sightseers, and on occasion dropped out of ranks to pick blackberries. They met the enemy at Manassas on Sunday, July 20. At first the Confederates gave way in disorder, but then, reinforced, they counterattacked, and the Union army's retreat developed into a full-scale rout, not to be stopped until officers and men were back in Washington.

While the South was exultant and waxed contemptuous of its antagonist, the North was awakened by this disaster to the gravity of the conflict. A new army of 75,000 men, enlisted for three years or the duration, was promptly raised, and plans were made to bring 500,000 men to the colors. Lincoln replaced McDowell with George Brinton McClellan, a veteran of the Mexican War, who had just swept the Confederates out of northwestern Virginia; on November 1, McClellan also replaced Scott as commander-in-chief of all the Union armies.

During the fall and early winter of 1861, McClellan busied himself organizing and drilling his Army of the Potomac. By the middle of October, when he had 100,000 men ready for active campaigning, he might have moved against Joseph E. Johnston, who lay with 40,000 men at Manassas; such a move would probably have forced Johnston back to the Rappahannock and ended the blockade by southern batteries of the lower Potomac. However, McClellan was already beginning to display his inveterate tendency to overestimate the enemy and underestimate his own potential for offensive action, and he undertook only a small movement at Ball's Bluff, some forty miles from Washington, on October 21, 1861, where the Federals were rudely repulsed. As the weeks of inactivity went by, northern congressmen and newspapers became increasingly restive, but the general-in-chief was waiting until, with overwhelming force, he could move on the Confederate capital.

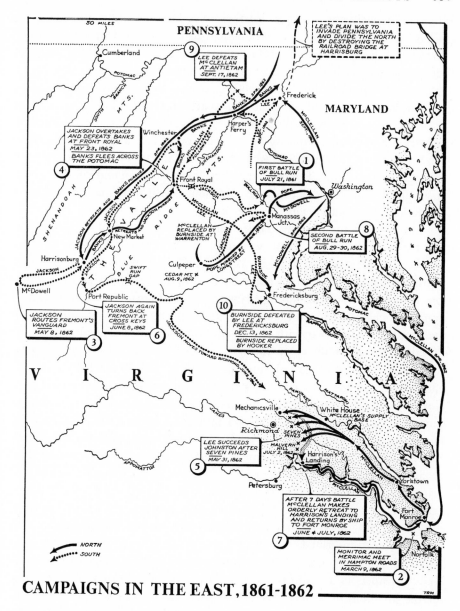

CAMPAIGNS IN THE EAST, 1861-1862

While McClellan organized his army for a decisive push in 1862, the West was the scene of bloody but indecisive movements. Local civil wars raged in Kentucky, Tennessee, and Missouri. Lincoln sent Frémont to clear Missouri of Confederate troops and then move down the Mississippi to Memphis, but, handicapped by green troops, lack of supplies, and the factious opposition of the powerful Blair family, the General made no progress in pacifying Missouri. Furthermore, his precipitate order emancipating the slaves of rebel Missourians had to be rescinded by Lincoln. The President relieved Frémont of his command in October, 1861, but not before the general had made an important appointment.

Ulysses Simpson Grant (1822–1885), a West Pointer and Mexican War veteran, had left the army some ten years previously, partly because of his drinking propensities. With the beginning of the war, he returned to military life. He had a capacity for bringing order out of chaos, and soldiers liked and respected him. He went from captain to colonel and then to brigadier-general, and Frémont then put him in command of the troops in southern Illinois and southeastern Missouri, with headquarters at Cairo. Before long he would begin to move South.

Grant's talent for winning battles was yet to be demonstrated, however, and the outlook for the North was dark in December, 1861. So far there had been no real progress in the West. McClellan, bemused by stories of enormous Confederate forces about to leap upon Baltimore and Washington, could think only of getting strength, rather than of using it. Congressional radicals, critical of Lincoln's leadership, organized a Committee on the Conduct of the War with Ben Wade as chairman, designed to spur the President and the military onward.

Ominous, too, was the ugly tone of relations with Great Britain, which had recognized the Confederate states as belligerents in May, 1861. On November 8, the Federal warship *San Jacinto*, Captain Charles Wilkes commanding, took James M. Mason and John Slidell, Confederate commissioners to England, off the deck of the British mail steamer *Trent*. There was no justification in international law for this act, and Britain began gathering ships and troops. Fortunately, Lord Palmerston and the British Cabinet, to say nothing of Queen Victoria and the Prince Consort, wanted war no more than did Lincoln and Seward. At Christmas time, the government at Washington decided to release the commissioners, and London was so informed.

But if relations with Great Britain eased, other problems remained. Radical leaders in and out of Congress were pushing to make the war one for the abolition of slavery. Secretary of War Cameron was daily demonstrating an incompetence that made his dismissal an absolute necessity. The fortunes of the Union appeared to be at a low ebb as 1862 dawned. In January, Edwin M. Stanton, a War Democrat and a driving force, replaced Cameron, and a short time later Lincoln told McClellan that he had to move against the Confederate lines.

The War on the Water, 1861–1862

Federal naval operations from the beginning to the end of the war were devoted to choking off Confederate privateering and tightening the blockade of the South. In April, Secretary Welles called in the forty-two ships scattered all over the globe that represented the entire commissioned strength of the Federal navy, and began posting them outside southern ports. New warships were promptly ordered, the so-called ninety-day gunboats, and plans were rushed for more formidable fighting craft.

In August, 1861, a joint military and naval expedition set out to take key positions on the Atlantic coast. It captured Forts Clark and Hatteras on the North Carolina shore, and by February, 1862, had control of Albemarle Sound, a haven for blockade runners. On March 12, Jacksonville, Florida, was occupied, and two days later the capture of New Berne, North Carolina, gave the Federals a base from which to threaten Richmond.

Five days before New Berne fell, came the battle of the ironclads. The Confederates had converted a former United States frigate, the *Merrimac,* into an ironclad with four-inch armor plate, renamed it the *Virginia,* and on March 8 sent it out from Norfolk against the blockading fleet in Hampton Roads. The *Virginia* sank the *Cumberland,* nearly destroyed the *Congress,* and drove the *Minnesota* aground, while the shots from these wooden frigates rattled harmlessly off her iron hull. When the news reached Washington, the government was distraught. But on the night following this catastrophe, a new fighting ship, the *Monitor,* designed by a Swedish immigrant-inventor, Captain Ericsson, arrived in Hampton Roads. The *Virginia* looked something like the roof of a barn, the *Monitor,* as a contemporary remarked, like a cheesebox on a raft. Its deck was almost level with the water and its revolving turret carried only two Dahlgren guns; it could scarcely be described as seaworthy, and had nearly sunk off Sandy Hook on its way to the Roads. On March 9, when the *Virginia* came out to complete the destruction of the Federal fleet, the two ironclads battled one another for three hours. Then the *Virginia,* her plates loosened and leaking at the waterline, went back to Norfolk. There was no further engagement between them and the blockade, so direly threatened by the *Virginia,* held. Two months later, when the Confederates abandoned Norfolk, her crew burned the ship to prevent capture. In December, the *Monitor* went down in a storm off Cape Hatteras. Despite the inglorious end of the two ships, they had ushered in a new era in naval warfare.

Some five weeks after the historic encounter in Hampton Roads, a Federal force of twenty-seven ships and 15,000 troops, commanded by flag-officer David G. Farragut and General Benjamin F. Butler, ran the Confederate forts below New Orleans. Only weak preparations had been made to stem such an attack. Troops landed, the fleet bombarded the city, and on May 1 it fell; the Mississippi was not yet open to the Union, but its mouth was closed to the Confederacy.

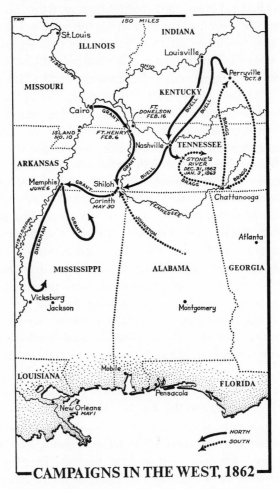

CAMPAIGNS IN THE WEST, 1862

Meanwhile, further up the river, great events had taken place. General H. W. Halleck ("Old Brains" the soldiers called him) had replaced Frémont in the West. Under Halleck's command, in February, 1862, Grant moved against two Confederate strongholds, Fort Henry on the Tennessee

River and Fort Donelson on the Cumberland. Grant took both these keys to the Confederate position on the Upper Mississippi, and with Fort Donelson captured 17,000 men, a victory which smashed the Confederate grip on northern Tennessee; and General Albert Sidney Johnston abandoned Nashville and fell back on the Memphis-Chattanooga line.

While Johnston prepared a counterstroke, Grant, with 30,000 men, moved South along the Tennessee River to Pittsburg Landing, near the town of Shiloh. At the same time, Commander Foote, with the Union gunboats, pushed down the Mississippi, capturing a key point, Island No. 10, and with it 7,000 Confederates. When, on April 6, General Johnston, with 50,000 men stormed across the Union picket lines at Pittsburg Landing, a fierce two-day battle ensued. At first the Union troops narrowly escaped being pushed into the river, but they rallied, were quickly reinforced, and finally drove back the Confederates.

Johnston lost his life at Shiloh, and Beauregard took command of the southern troops. Each army had lost over 10,000 men, killed, wounded, and missing, but Grant relentlessly pushed on. The weakened Confederates evacuated Corinth on May 30 and a week later surrendered Memphis. The Union now held the Mississippi as far south as Vicksburg in a firm grip.

The Confederacy was loath to accept the situation in the West. That fall, Confederate General Braxton Bragg attempted to advance against Louisville, Kentucky, but was checked on October 8 at Perryville by General Don Carlos Buell. Bragg then turned on Nashville, but was beaten at Stone's River in a four-day battle (December 31, 1862–January 3, 1863) by General William S. Rosecrans. Slowly but surely, the snakelike operation envisioned by General Scott was extending its length along the Mississippi and reaching out toward the heart of the Confederacy.

The Campaign in the East, 1862

While the Federal cause prospered in the West, it faltered in the East. McClellan finally decided that his advance on Richmond should go by water to the mouth of the James River, and then up the Peninsula between the James and the York. Estimating that General Joseph E. Johnston and his second in command, Robert E. Lee, had 120,000 men with which to protect Richmond, McClellan felt that if he left one army corps, under Banks, to guard the Shenandoah Valley approach to Washington, he could still have 150,000 men for the Peninsular campaign; but Lincoln, fearful that Washington was being left defenseless, kept an additional 30,000 men under McDowell to watch the approaches to the capital.

McClellan had, as usual, grossly overestimated the Confederate forces and underestimated his own. He took to the Peninsula what he thought were less than 100,000 men, but were probably at least 120,000 in number. There he settled down to a siege of Yorktown, which was so lightly defended that he could easily have taken it by assault. As he was finally about to attack on May 5, the Confederates fell back up the Peninsula, and the Union army followed them to Seven Pines, five miles outside Richmond.

While McClellan was making his slow way up the Peninsula, pleading all the while for reinforcements, Stonewall Jackson was conducting a brilliant campaign in the Shenandoah Valley, defeating one Union detachment after another and drawing into the Valley troops that would otherwise have been sent to McClellan's aid. This objective accomplished, Jackson and his 20,000 men slipped away and joined Lee, who was now in command of the Confederate forces at Richmond. Lee, with perhaps 100,000 men at his disposal, attacked in force and, in a series of bloody engagements, drove the Federals back down the Peninsula; so ended the campaign that was to have captured the Confederate capital.

Lincoln now appointed General Halleck commander-in-chief of the Union armies, and the Army of the Potomac, with a much disgruntled McClellan still in command, was withdrawn from the Peninsula. By the time McClellan and his troops were back up the Potomac, Lee was ready with a fall offensive that carried him into Maryland.

On August 9, 1862, Lee's advanced detachments under Jackson caught and defeated Union troops under Banks at Cedar Mountain. Three weeks later, Jackson drubbed Pope at the Second Battle of Bull Run. Lincoln now put McClellan in command of all the forces around Washington. On September 4, Lee crossed the Potomac and invaded Maryland.

Union and Confederate forces met at Antietam on September 17. McClellan had the advantage of knowing, by means of an intercepted dispatch, that Lee had sent Jackson to seize Harper's Ferry and so maintain his supply line south. The Union general moved so slowly, however, that Lee was able to reunite his forces before the battle was finally joined; the result was a hard-fought but indecisive engagement. Lee then fell back into Virginia, but McClellan, cautious as usual, did not cross the Potomac in pursuit until October 26.

This delay was too much for Lincoln who, on November 5, replaced McClellan with General Ambrose E. Burnside, who had done well in operations in North Carolina and was known as a fighting general. Burnside pushed into Virginia after Lee, but was badly defeated on December 13 at Fredericksburg, where, by sending his troops in waves against defenses impossible to storm, he lost 12,000 men. Six weeks of painful delay now ensued, and then Lincoln relieved Burnside of his command, appointing in his stead "Fighting Joe" Hooker. Lincoln was still looking for the right general in the East.

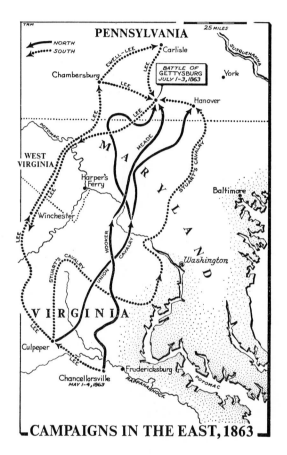

CAMPAIGNS IN THE EAST, 1863

The Campaigns of 1863

Hooker believed that he could force Lee to retreat to Richmond. The Union army crossed the Rappahannock, but instead of retreating Lee attacked. After four days of indecisive fighting (May 1–4) at Chancellorsville, Hooker retreated across the Rappahannock. It was a total Union defeat, except that when Stonewall Jackson, reconnoitering his front lines, was shot by his own men, the South lost one of its ablest commanders.

Hooker's officers distrusted him, and their complaints, together with his apparent inability to cope with Lee's menacing movements, convinced Lincoln that "Fighting Joe" in his turn must be removed. On June 28, George Gordon Meade became commander of the army—just in time, for Lee had pushed 80,000 men up the Shenandoah Valley and into southern Pennsylvania on his last and greatest invasion of the North.

Lee took Chambersburg, Carlisle and York, in Pennsylvania, and menaced Baltimore and Washington. When Meade moved westward, north of the Potomac, threatening to cut the Confederate line of communications, Lee concentrated his army at Gettysburg. The two armies met there, July 1–3, 1863, in the biggest and bloodiest battle ever fought in the United States.

In the battle of Gettysburg, the Union army was essentially on the defensive. The first day was one of probing operations by both sides. On the second day, the Confederates tried to seize two hills, Round Top and Little Round Top, on the Union left, the object being to roll up Meade's left flank, but this maneuver failed. On July 3 came Pickett's charge against the Union center; preceded by a furious cannonade from 160 Confederate guns, 15,000 men in gray swept across the broad valley that lay between the Confederate line and the Union forces posted on Cemetery Ridge. This was a superb demonstration of bravery, but the troops were so decimated by the Federal artillery and rifle fire that they had no force with which to meet the Union countercharge that came as they broke across the Bloody Angle. Lee had tried the old system of attack against the new weapons, and it had failed. The next day he took his battered army back to the Potomac and Virginia. This was the turning point of the war, for from then on the Confederacy, with waning resources, was on the defensive.

As Lee made his last great bid for victory in the East, a great Union triumph was shaping in the West, where Vicksburg and Port Hudson were the two remaining bastions of Confederate control on the Mississippi. Grant moved on Vicksburg, running the gunboats past the batteries to a point below the city, marching his troops down the west side of the river, and crossing (April 30) under naval protection some fifty miles below the Confederate stronghold. In a brilliant series of marches, he moved east; took the town of Jackson and Joe Johnston's army of 12,000 men there; doubled back; destroyed one-third of Pemberton's force of 42,000 men, with a loss of only 2,000 Union soldiers; and then settled down to besiege Pemberton in Vicksburg. On July 4, starved out, the town surrendered. When, four days later, Port Hudson fell to Banks, Texas, Arkansas, and Louisiana had been cut off from the Confederacy, and, as Lincoln said, "The Father of Waters once more flows unvexed to the sea."

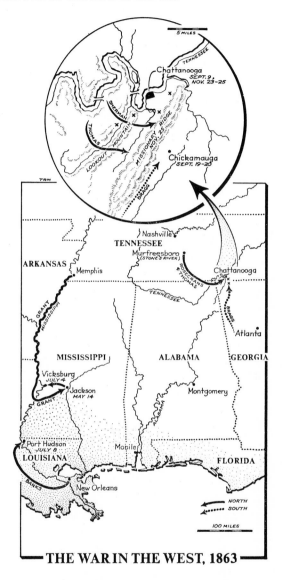

THE WAR IN THE WEST, 1863

There remained Braxton Bragg in central Tennessee, facing a superior Union force under General Rosecrans. Maneuvering beautifully in barren and desolate country, Rosecrans forced Bragg out of Chattanooga on September 9 and pursued him into the northwestern part of Georgia. There

Bragg, reinforced, turned on his tormentor and, on September 19–20, in the battle of Chickamauga, in which each army lost one-third of its effectives, Rosecrans was badly mauled. He fell back to Chattanooga, only saved from destruction by Bragg's slowness in following up his victory.

Lincoln now put Grant at the head of all the armies and departments in the West, with instructions to take charge of the Chattanooga situation. Grant relieved Rosecrans, appointing in his stead General George Thomas, who had behaved gallantly at Chickamauga. Then, reinforced by troops from Vicksburg under General William T. Sherman and from the Potomac under Hooker, Grant raised the siege of Chattanooga in three days of fighting; on the second day, November 24, Hooker stormed Lookout Mountain, and on November 25 Sherman's and Sheridan's men took Missionary Ridge in a wild charge against a weakly held line. The Confederates were now driven out of Tennessee, and the road to Georgia was open. President Davis replaced Bragg, who had lost the confidence and even the respect of his soldiers, with Joseph E. Johnston.

The Closing Phases of the War
1864–1865

As the spring of 1864 came on, Lincoln, more and more dissatisfied with Meade's dilatory tactics in campaigning against Lee, decided on a change in the top Union army command. On March 9 Grant was made a lieutenant-general and put in command of all the armies. Sherman took his place in the West, and Grant himself assumed direct control in the eastern theatre of war.

Grant's great objective was to attack and destroy Lee's army, the capture of Richmond being a secondary consideration. On May 3, the Union general crossed the Rapidan, swept by Chancellorsville, and began in the Wilderness a costly two-months campaign that in some quarters earned him the title of "Grant the Butcher." The Union forces outnumbered the Confederates two to one; they were well-equipped, and, though the carnage in their ranks was terrible, replacements were always at hand. Nevertheless, Lee, with his ragged, half-starved troops, conducted a brilliant defensive, while Grant vainly tried to outflank the Confederate leader. There was hard fighting around Spottsylvania Court House and on the North Anna River during May, and on the first three days of June at Cold Harbor. Giving up his attempt to defeat Lee in the field, Grant crossed the James and tried to capture Petersburg, a vital railroad and communications center with the rest of the South, twenty-three miles below Richmond. When

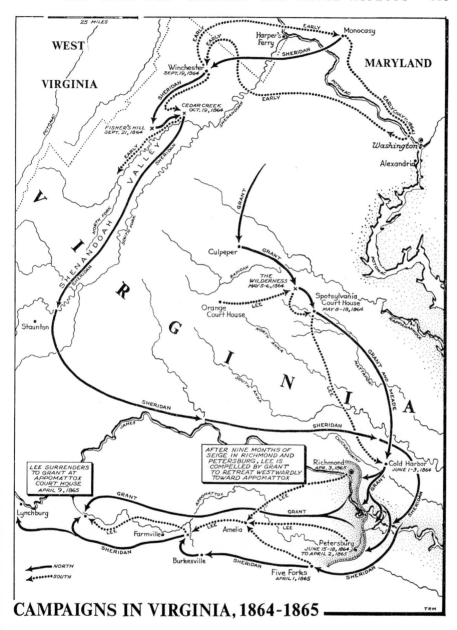

CAMPAIGNS IN VIRGINIA, 1864-1865

direct assault failed, Grant settled down to a siege that was to last for nine months.

To ease the pressure on Petersburg, Lee now sent General Jubal A. Early to threaten Washington. "Old Jube," an aggressive fighter and reputed able to outcurse any man in the Confederate army, led 8,000 ragged soldiers, almost half of them barefooted, into the Shenandoah Valley, where he was reinforced until he had 20,000 men. His cavalry raided into Maryland and Pennsylvania, and at one time came within sight of the new dome of the Capitol at Washington.

Grant sent Sheridan, his ablest cavalry leader, against Early. Sheridan, with 50,000 well-equipped troops, defeated Early at Winchester and Fisher's Hill in September. A third engagement at Cedar Creek, on October 19, pushed the Confederate forces out of the Valley, which Sheridan then laid waste before rejoining Grant at Petersburg.

While Grant was battering his way toward Richmond, the main theater of operation in the West shifted to the Deep South. Sherman started from Chattanooga on May 5, 1864, with 100,000 men, bound for the railroad center of Atlanta, Georgia. Joseph E. Johnston, with some 65,000 men, kept retreating to avoid the Union commander's flanking movements, but these Fabian tactics alarmed President Davis, who replaced Johnston with General John B. Hood on July 17, as the Federals neared Atlanta. Hood offered battle at Atlanta on July 22, but was defeated. He held the town until a flanking movement that threatened to cut his supply line with Macon forced him to evacuate. On September 2, he moved out and headed north, planning to reach the Tennessee River and cut Sherman's line of communication. Sherman followed him but, unable to force a battle, came back to Atlanta and decided to do without communications. He started for Savannah with 60,000 men living off the country—the famous, or infamous, march through Georgia. The rest of Sherman's force was sent north to join Thomas at Nashville, which Hood, with 25,000 men, undertook to besiege, but Thomas, with 60,000 men, on December 15 and 16, 1864, moved out and decisively defeated the Confederate general.

While Confederate strength collapsed in Georgia and Tennessee, Sherman moved to the coast, tearing up railroad lines and "foraging liberally" on the Georgia farms and plantations. The Union army reached Savannah in superb condition (December 20) and then turned north into South Carolina. There was considerable pillaging, some fine plantation homes being destroyed in the birthplace of the Confederacy, but there was no murder or rape. Columbia, the capital of the state, fell on February 17, 1865; it was burned as Sherman marched into the town, either accidentally by retreating Confederate cavalry or by drunken Union troops. Sherman next moved into North Carolina, still 60,000 strong. There Confederate remnants under Joe Johnston, outnumbered four to one, put up a desperate and hopeless resistance. They finally surrendered (April 26) at Durham.

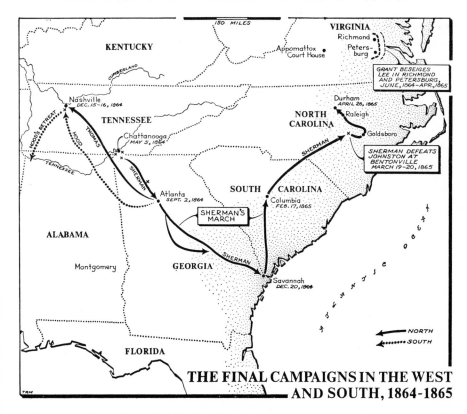

THE FINAL CAMPAIGNS IN THE WEST
AND SOUTH, 1864-1865

By the early spring of 1865, Lee's position was also desperate, for, caught between Grant and Sherman, he had no food supply. Sheridan, at Five Forks on April 1, beat Pickett and seized the South Side Railroad, which forced Lee to evacuate Petersburg and abandon the defense of the Confederate capital. Lee marched out toward Lynchburg, hoping to join Johnston, and the Confederate government precipitately left Richmond. Lee's army of 28,000 men, ragged and half-starved, began to disintegrate, while Grant captured Ewell's corps (April 6) and surrounded what was left of the forlorn Confederate forces. On April 9, 1865, at Appomattox Court House, Lee surrendered his 13,000 troops, all that remained of the once proud Army of Northern Virginia. The terms of capitulation were honorable: officers and men were paroled; the officers retained their side arms; and both officers and men kept their horses—to help, as Grant said, with the spring ploughing.

The war was now, to all intents and purposes, over. On May 10, Jefferson Davis, who had fled to Georgia, was captured and put in prison. The last Confederate army, under Kirby Smith, surrendered at Shreveport, Louisiana, on May 26.

The War and the Common Soldier

For the common soldier on either side during the Civil War, when there was efficient command, there was perpetual drill. Men on both sides could also count on crowded tent life, periods of boredom in camp waiting for the next move, some hard marching, and occasionally some very hard fighting—the last, more frequently than not, against an unseen enemy who was hidden in ditches, trenches or in the woods. Most of the men on either side, at one time or another, were afraid; some were heroic. In the armies of both North and South, there was much gambling with dice and cards, and a great deal of profanity and hard drinking.

Many of the northern soldiers disliked the climate of the South and were critical of its inhabitants, especially of tobacco-chewing and snuff-dipping females. On the other hand, several hundred Yankee soldiers found brides south of the Mason and Dixon line.

There was much sickness and suffering in the camps of both sides, despite the heroic efforts of Clara Barton in ministering to the afflicted in the northern camps and hospitals. Though medical care in the northern armies improved somewhat as the war went on, even there the inefficiency in the hospitals was shocking, and there was a hideous death rate. In the northern armies, four persons died of illness and wounds for every one killed in battle, and the ratio was probably three to one in the armies of the South. Measles, yellow fever, diarrhea, dysentery, and malaria took a deadly toll; soldiers also suffered from venereal infections. Fornication was a common practice, more so in the northern than in the southern armies, because the former had better pay, bigger bounties, and more access to commercialized prostitution in large cities.

The soldiers who wore the gray were, in general, more religious, showed more of a sense of humor in their correspondence, and felt a somewhat more personal commitment to the struggle than did their counterparts in blue. The Union soldiers were, on the whole, more literate, did more reading in camp, and took more interest in politics than did those of the Confederacy; this was in large part due to superior northern educational facilities, and partly also to the greater difficulties under which southerners fought, especially in the waning days of the Confederacy.

One of the saddest and most tragic aspects of the Civil War was the lot of the prisoners on either side. Some of the northern prisons were badly located from a sanitary point of view, in others there was congestion, and southern prisoners found the northern winter climate hard to bear. The southern prisons were also badly located, and in them, as the war went on, there was a sad lack of clothing, food, and medical supplies. Overcrowding became an evil of the first magnitude. At Andersonville, Georgia, conditions were at their worst, with by August, 1864, over 30,000 prisoners living under indescribable conditions of filth and misery. An awful stench hung over the camp, and disease was rampant. Of those confined there, 23.3 per cent died in seven months time, 12,000 federal prisoners being buried at Andersonville.

Stories of the hardships of prison life circulated in both sections, and northerners and southerners came to believe that friends and relatives were being deliberately tortured and murdered. The North accused the South of fiendish inhumanity. The South returned the charge, and denounced the North for refusing to permit a general exchange of prisoners. This refusal was by order of General Grant, who believed, with some reason, that the North, with its superior man power, would profit by refusal to exchange. Grant's order held good from April, 1863, to February, 1865, but, unfortunately, augmented the sufferings of northern prisoners.

The charges and countercharges about the treatment of prisoners left their legacy of hatred after the war. Captain Henry Wirz, one of the high officials at Andersonville, was tried for cruelty and murder before a military commission; in a trial that was not fair, he was found guilty, and the North applauded when he was hanged. The psychotic hatred generated by the treatment or supposed treatment of prisoners was to prove one of the real obstacles in the road to reunion.

No account of the Civil War would be complete without reference to the role played by the Negro. As has been previously noted, the slaves kept at work in the fields during the early part of the struggle. In some parts of the South there were fears of slave revolts, but only in isolated instances did such uprisings occur. From 1863 on, a considerable number of slaves were impressed by the Confederate government and used as laborers on such military projects as fortifications and railroad repair.

As the war went on, however, the usefulness of slavery to the South markedly decreased. When the Federal armies moved into a southern area, the great majority of field slaves became disloyal to their masters, and there is accurate evidence that, after the Emancipation Proclamation, a majority of them realized that their freedom was at stake in the struggle. So many of them flocked into Sherman's camp that he ordered them to keep away. Before the war was over, many former slaves had enlisted in the northern armies.

Some 175,000 Negroes had served in the Union armies by the end of the war, the great majority entering the service during the last two years of combat. They were used mainly for garrison duty and manual labor, but Negro regiments officered by white men participated in perhaps a dozen battles. The Negro in the northern army was discriminated against in equipment, and not until 1864 did the Negro soldier get the same pay as the white. But, despite such discrimination, they established an admirable service record, and the testimony regarding their spirit of initiative and their bravery under fire is impressive. The Negro veteran had a right to be proud of the part he played in the Civil War.

Suggested Reading

The first two volumes of Allan Nevins, *The War for the Union* (1959–1960), carry the story of the conflict through 1863. They have a number of fresh and suggestive insights.

Fletcher Pratt, *Ordeal by Fire* (1935) is a vigorous and lively study of the struggle. For short, general accounts the student should consult the works by Thomas, Randall, Cole, and Eaton previously cited, as well as William B. Hesseltine's *A History of the South, 1607–1936* (1936).

For an excellent depiction of the Civil War era, the student can consult the works by Bruce Catton, *War Lords of Washington* (1948), *Mr. Lincoln's Army* (1950), *Glory Road* (1952), *A Stillness at Appomattox* (1953), *U. S. Grant and the American Military Tradition* (1954), *Banners at Shenandoah* (1955), *This Hallowed Ground* (1956), *America Goes to War* (1958), and *Grant Moves South* (1960). The student should also consult T. Harvey Williams, *Lincoln and His Generals* (1952), E. D. Adams, *Great Britain and the American Civil War* (2 vols., 1925), M. B. Duberman, *Charles Francis Adams* (1961), and G. G. Van Deusen, *William Henry Seward* (1967).

Of particular importance are Carl Sandburg, *Abraham Lincoln, the War Years* (4 vols., 1939); Kenneth Williams, *Lincoln Finds a General: A Military Study of the Civil War* (4 vols., 1949–1956); and F. A. Shannon, *The Organization and Administration of the Union Army, 1861–1865* (2 vols., 1928). Favorable treatments of McClellan are W. W. Hassler, *General George B. McClellan* (1957) and H. J. Eckenrode and B. Conrad, *George B. McClellan* (1941).

On the Confederacy, see Clement Eaton, *A History of the Southern Confederacy* (1934), F. L. Owsley, *State Rights in the Confederacy* (1925). Confederate foreign relations are admirably covered in F. L. Owsley, *King Cotton Diplomacy* (rev. ed., 1959). The standard work on the Confederate Navy is J. Thomas Scharf, *History of the Confederate Navy* (1894). On the military side, D. S. Freeman, *R. E. Lee, a Biography* (4 vols., 1934–1935) and *Lee's Lieutenants* (3 vols., 1942–1944) are excellent. Ella Lonn, *Desertion During the Civil War* (1928) is authoritative. The life of the common soldier is portrayed in Bell I. Wiley, *The Life of Johnny Reb* (1943) and *The Life of Billy Yank* (1951, 1952). William B. Hesseltine, *Civil War Prisons* (1930) is the standard account. The story of the Negro in wartime is admirably told in Dudley T. Cornish, *The Sable Arm* (1956) and Bell I. Wiley, *Southern Negroes, 1861–1865* (1938).

32 ، Government and People in Wartime

JUDGED BY TWENTIETH-CENTURY standards, Lincoln had a number of deficiencies as a political leader. One was a lack of interest in what we call public relations. It was the smart thing, as James G. Randall observes, for intellectuals in general and writers in particular to hold the President up to ridicule, thereby proving that they themselves were sophisticates. They called him "timid and ignorant," "a man of no education." "You cannot ... fill his ... empty skull with brains," said Count Adam Gurowski, an acidulous commentator on the Washington scene. When his opponents shouted that he was nothing but poor white trash, afraid to move against slavery and against the South, Lincoln and his staff made practically no attempt to counter this outcry, or to build up the President as a great human figure.

Lincoln as a Political Leader

Lincoln made few speeches, those he did make were not highly regarded at the time, and his staff made no attempt to impress upon the public the outstanding character of the Gettysburg Address and the Second Inaugural. Neither was there a consistent effort to build up a good press for the Administration. Lincoln never held press conferences, and, though he made some efforts, especially with Greeley and James Gordon Bennett, to align powerful newspapers in support of his plans, most of the outstanding newspapers at the beginning of his term of office were opposed to him and remained so throughout the war. Indeed, many mercilessly berated him, calling him such names as "a half-witted usurper," "a simple Susan," a "baboon," a "gorilla," and "the head ghoul at Washington."

Lincoln never succeeded in rallying a majority of his party leaders behind him, or in immobilizing those that could not be brought to his active support. He had repeated rows with Republican leaders in Congress, and there was much backbiting and intriguing against him in the Cabinet. In 1864, practically every outstanding Republican figure either doubted the advisability of a second term, or actively tried to prevent his renomination.

Lincoln had other handicaps as a political leader that were especially in evidence during his first months in office. He yielded to pressure and sent an unready army out to defeat at Bull Run. He made little effort to establish an organized and smoothly functioning Cabinet, leaving each member to run his own department, and consumed much of the time in Cabinet meetings with droll stories and random observations. War Democrats and Republicans of all shades of opinion kept asking him what his policy was as to the conduct of the war, the administration of finances, and the freeing of the slaves; to these inquiries the President repeatedly returned the baffling and irritating reply, "My policy is to have no policy."

But, despite these limitations, Lincoln had great qualities of leadership, qualities that became more and more apparent during his four years in the White House. An adept at the game of politics, he handled the patronage in masterful fashion as a means of holding his party together and keeping within bounds factional fights in such important states as New York, Pennsylvania, Ohio, and Indiana. The Cabinet was so skillfully composed that neither Old Whigs nor Old Democrats could claim ascendancy there, and the suspicions of one another entertained by the Cabinet members prevented any formidable combinations in the official family against the head of the government. While the President himself remained silent as to his desire for renomination in 1864, his agents used the patronage so skillfully that one state delegation after another was gathered into the fold and the nomination assured. During the campaign of 1864, in order to conciliate the radical element in the party, he removed the conservative Montgomery Blair as Postmaster General, but he also accepted the resignation of the radical Salmon P. Chase as Secretary of the Treasury, a move that pleased the conservatives. In American history, Lincoln has had few equals and no superiors in the art of political adjustment.

Lincoln was not only a shrewd politician, but also a very canny judge of men, who knew how to work with those who held divergent views. He

ABRAHAM LINCOLN
(1809–1865)

This superb Brady photograph was taken in 1863.

converted Seward from a disappointed and sceptical lieutenant into a loyal and devoted follower. Despite the bitter criticism heaped upon him by men like Thaddeus Stevens, Charles Sumner, Ben Wade, and Henry Winter Davis, the President managed to keep up reasonably good relations with this radical wing of his party. Though Salmon P. Chase, an Old Democrat and a radical, and William Henry Seward, an Old Whig and a conservative, had no love for one another, Lincoln kept Chase in the Treasury until the summer of 1864, and Seward remained in the State Department throughout Lincoln's presidency and that of Andrew Johnson as well.

The best evidence of the quality of Lincoln's leadership is to be seen in his gradual approach to the solution of great problems, an approach in which his superb sense of timing had full play. He would not use force unless force was used against the government, and at Sumter the South was maneuvered into striking the first blow. We shall see later on how skillfully he parried and played for time in dealing with emancipation, in developing a policy of reconstruction, and in formulating an attitude toward the Negro.

In two other respects, Lincoln possessed qualities that are extremely important in a democracy: he had both humility and a kindly spirit. He visited the soldiers in the hospitals. He was always ready to receive those who came to Washington seeking his aid for relatives and friends who had run afoul of army regulations, and he made generous use of the power of pardon, on occasion in defiance of Secretary of War Stanton. Only a genuinely humble man could say quite simply and sincerely, after discourteous treatment by McClellan, that he would willingly hold the General's horse for him if he would only win victories for the Union.

Emancipation and the War

When the war began, it was waged by the northern government simply as a war for the Union. Lincoln's proclamations in April and May, 1861, as well as his message to the special session of Congress which met in July, ignored slavery and centered on the necessity of dealing with the insurrectionary movements that had broken out in the southern states. When Frémont, on August 30, 1861, issued a proclamation in Missouri freeing the Negroes of those who actively aided the enemies of the United States, Lincoln rescinded the order; he took the same stand in May, 1862, when General David Hunter issued an order freeing the slaves in Georgia, Florida, and South Carolina. The President also faithfully enforced the fugitive slave law.

Lincoln knew that emancipation would ensure the support of radical antislavery leaders in Congress. He knew also that it would find favor among European liberals and lessen the possibility of European intervention on the side of the South. He himself disliked slavery and wanted to see it abolished, but he refrained from making emancipation an immediate war objective for two reasons: he and his party had pledged themselves not to interfere with slavery in the states where it existed, and he had a lively conception of the importance to the Union of the border areas. The states of Kentucky, Missouri, Maryland, and Delaware, together with the western portion of Virginia and southern Ohio, Indiana, and Illinois had a population of over five million, immense resources in grain, hemp, and livestock, and flourishing manufacturing establishments. It was imperative to retain the loyalty of this border region. The predominant sentiment there was Unionist, but to make the war a struggle for emancipation at this early stage would have alienated many northern Democrats and undermined, if not destroyed, the allegiance of the border state loyalists.

Lincoln hoped that he could end slavery by a system of compensated emancipation. In March, 1862, he recommended to Congress a joint resolution offering financial assistance to any state that would undertake a gradual freeing of its slaves with compensation to the owners. The resolution passed Congress, and the President tried to interest the border states in such a program, but they remained cold to the idea.

The radicals in Congress had no enthusiasm for compensated emancipation, and they were outraged by Lincoln's treatment of Frémont and Hunter. They wanted drastic action, and in 1861 and 1862 Congress passed a number of acts which showed that the legislative branch was ready to move faster than the President against slavery. In August, 1861, a confiscation act declared that the services of slaves engaged in military effort against the United States were forfeited by their owners. A second confiscation act in July, 1862, although vague as to enforcement procedures, "freed" the slaves of anyone committing treason or supporting the rebellion. Other laws prohibited the rendition of fugitive slaves to rebel owners and abolished slavery with compensation in the District of Columbia and without compensation in the territories. Furthermore, the Senate ratified a treaty with England providing for the effective suppression of the foreign slave trade.

Lincoln accepted these measures, but still delayed putting the full seal of his approval upon emancipation. Three times he tried to interest the border states in compensated emancipation, only to be rebuffed. In August, 1862, when Horace Greeley's "Prayer of Twenty Millions" appeared in the *Tribune,* imploring the President to take a decided stand on slavery, Lincoln replied mildly that his paramount object was neither to destroy nor safeguard slavery, but to save the Union. He also hinted that a new executive policy was in the offing.

By the summer of 1862, the President had decided to issue an emancipation proclamation when military affairs were auspicious. On July 22 of that year, at a Cabinet meeting, he read a proclamation that he had prepared, freeing all slaves in the rebellious states. Seward advised delay until a favorable military situation developed, and all felt that this advice was sound. The battle of Antietam (September 17) gave the President his opportunity, and five days later he issued his "preliminary proclamation." On January 1, 1863, the final proclamation appeared; it declared free the slaves in those areas that were in rebellion against the Union.

The Emancipation Proclamation did not actually free more slaves than had already been freed by Congress. Like the congressional acts, it ended human bondage where no power of enforcement existed and left slavery untouched in the loyal areas. Its reception was mixed. Proslavery northern Democrats denounced it as an extremist measure, while abolitionists complained that it did not go far enough. There was some unfavorable reaction to it in the border states, but since they were untouched by it and it was clearly identified as "a fit and necessary war measure," the border state opposition was not serious. Though it did not produce slave insurrections (that, of course, was not its intent) it did have two important consequences: it stimulated desertion of Negroes to the Union camps as the invading armies moved south, and in this way weakened the Confederacy's economic power; and it also had a decisive influence upon popular opinion in Europe, especially in England, where it was now believed that the cause of the North was truly the cause of freedom.

Constitutional Problems in Wartime

Slavery and military combat were by no means the only problems that Lincoln and his government had to face during the Civil War. The cleavage of the Union produced constitutional problems of importance. There is an ancient Roman maxim that "in the midst of arms the laws are silent," and it is worthwhile to examine the extent to which the Constitution of the United States and the protection it affords the citizen were violated during this internecine conflict.

One of the first problems confronting the national government was whether or not to regard the secessionists as traitors—in other words, what was the character of this movement that had divided the Union into two warring camps? Lincoln's Administration took the attitude that the Confederacy was not a new government or an independent nation, but simply a rebellion by individuals against the duly constituted authorities of the nation. The government at Washington never recognized the government at Richmond as one with which negotiations could be conducted. Paradoxically, however, Confederate ships, soldiers and civilians, when captured, were treated not as traitors, but as though they were the subjects of a foreign power with which the United States was at war. The Supreme Court held that the United States in its relations with the Confederacy had the "double character" of belligerent and sovereign, together with the rights of both.

Another problem, it soon became apparent, concerned the executive authority in wartime. Lincoln took a broad view of his powers as the head of the nation, proclaiming a state of insurrection on April 15, 1861. At the same time, he called Congress to meet in special session on July 4, but that body did not get around to recognizing the state of insurrection until July 13. Despite the fact that under the Constitution the power to declare war is vested in Congress, during the period from the middle of April to the middle of July the Administration established blockades, seized ships, and altogether proceeded on the assumption that a state of war existed. Chief Justice Taney held the President's action unconstitutional, but the Supreme Court eventually upheld Lincoln on the ground that a domestic war could start without any formal declaration.

Lincoln's attitude during the early months of the war was symptomatic of a tendency on his part to act independently of Congress. Instead of regarding himself as a leader who would push through legislation implementing his policies, the President preferred to act as much as possible on his own. He seldom asked for specific legislation, interpreted the powers of the Executive broadly, and not infrequently moved in such a way as to stretch those powers to their limits. It became clear during the war that the President's modest and unassuming demeanor cloaked a firm purpose and an iron will.

Lincoln believed existing laws were inadequate to restrain the treasonable and quasi-treasonable activities of northern opponents of the war and of Administration policies. He therefore repeatedly suspended the privilege of the writ of habeas corpus—at first in a given area, then to all military prisoners, and finally, in 1863, throughout the Union whenever state courts interfered with the draft law. In September, 1862, a presidential proclamation made all persons who discouraged enlistment or were guilty of disloyal practices subject to martial law; none of the thousands who were arrested had the protection of the writ of habeas corpus.

The suspension of civil liberties involved in Lincoln's attitude produced an early reaction from a distinguished member of the Supreme Court. In the case of *Ex Parte Merryman,* Chief Justice Taney authorized a writ of habeas corpus which was refused by the commanding officer, General Cadwalader, at Fort McHenry, where the offender, one John Merryman, was imprisoned. Taney cited Cadwalader for contempt, but the general refused to receive the writ. The old judge then filed an opinion declaring that only Congress could suspend the writ of habeas corpus, and charging that Lincoln had violated the Constitution. Lincoln denied that the Constitution specified Congress as the only agency of government with the authority to suspend the writ of habeas corpus and justified his act on the ground of national security.

Another case that involved both the Supreme Court and the famous writ was that of Clement L. Vallandigham. This Ohio Democrat publicly accused the Administration of needlessly prolonging the war and making it one for the freeing of the slaves and the enslaving of the whites. He also bitterly denounced the draft—and in 1863, a crucial war year.

General Burnside, in command of the Military Department of the Ohio, had issued Order No. 38, threatening arrest and trial by court-martial of those who expressed sympathy for the enemy. When Vallandigham announced his contempt for this order, and further declared that free men who would submit to the draft deserved to lose their freedom, Burnside arrested him, and he was tried by a court-martial and sentenced to confinement for the duration of the war. The privilege of habeas corpus had been denied.

Vallandigham promptly began issuing statements from his "military bastile" and, to prevent his becoming a martyr in the eyes of southern sympathizers and Peace Democrats, Lincoln commuted his sentence to banishment beyond the Confederate lines. His imprisonment was brought before the Supreme Court on a motion to review the sentence of the court-martial, but the Court ruled that review of the proceedings of a military commission was beyond its jurisdiction.

Suppression of free speech was not confined to agitators such as Merryman and Vallandigham. At various times during the course of the war the Chicago *Times,* the New York *World,* the Baltimore *Gazette,* and other newspapers were suspended by government officials. The Administration policy in these cases was to act only where the press was doing "palpable damage" to the military effort. No effort was made to establish a general censorship, punitive action being left to the discretion of the military commanders in the various districts.

COURTESY OF THE NEW-YORK HISTORICAL SOCIETY, NEW YORK CITY

THE BURIAL OF THE CONSTITUTION

This bitter attack on Lincoln's Administration portrays the President and his supporters as burying the Constitution, the Union, Free Press and Free Speech, and Habeas Corpus. Published in 1864, it illustrates the spirit of criticism and the war weariness that abounded in that election year.

Lincoln defended his action in arresting agitators, invoking martial law and suspending the writ of habeas corpus on the ground that the emergency was great, and that the regular courts were inadequate to deal with a situation dangerous to the country. He did, on occasion, act in arbitrary fashion, especially in curbing the right of free speech. But it is clear that he meant his activities to maintain rather than to undermine the principle of freedom. He had much sympathy for the conscientious objector and was generous in releasing political prisoners, refusing to treat them as war criminals. Free speech in the United States was subjected to fewer curbs during the Civil War than it was to experience during World War I.

In 1863, Congress passed an act indemnifying the President, his Cabinet, and all those who with the authority of the government had made arrests during the rebellion; it was perhaps well that this was done, in view of

Secretary Stanton's comment that if all the prosecutions against him for illegal arrest held, he would be in prison for at least 1,000 years.

Congress and the President

After the southern states left the Union, the Thirty-Seventh Congress of the United States was predominantly Republican—which did not mean, however, that Lincoln's war policies encountered little opposition. After the initial surge of patriotic sentiment that came with the firing on Fort Sumter, partisanship again appeared. While many Democrats supported the war and the government's war policies, others were quick to criticize what they regarded as incompetency, violations of the Constitution, and failure to take proper steps toward restoring the Union.

There was also plenty of criticism and even outright opposition directed toward the Administration from within the President's own party. The Republican ranks, it is true, contained many moderates and conservatives who approved Lincoln's cautious approach to slavery because they had some conception of the enormous problems involved in destroying it. On the other hand, the Republican radicals (Lincoln's secretary, John Hay, called them "the Jacobins") were from the start ardent emancipationists and were critical of Lincoln for moving as slowly as he did toward freeing the slaves.

The radicals, in general, had no real unity of purpose so far as a social and economic program was concerned, nor were they at one in their attitude toward Lincoln. Some, like Ben Wade of Ohio and Zachariah Chandler of Michigan, were bitterly hostile to the President. On the other hand, a radical member of the House, Owen Lovejoy, supported the President consistently, and between a thorough-paced radical like Charles Sumner and Lincoln there was a cordial working relationship. Though the radicals by no means constituted a solid block in the party during the war, they all hated slavery and its exponents, urged punishment of the South for starting the war, and believed in making the struggle one which would be at least as much for freedom as it would be for the Union. It was radicals who organized the Committee on the Conduct of the War and dominated its investigations, which became more and more critical of Lincoln, until by 1864 the Committee was an anti-Administration organization.

Most of the radicals were critical of Lincoln not only for his caution in approaching emancipation, but also for his ideas on Reconstruction. The President wished to begin rebuilding the Union at the earliest possible moment. During the first six months of 1862, he established military governments in Louisiana, Arkansas, and Tennessee, so that, with order reinstituted, loyal state governments could be restored. In December, 1863, he issued a proclamation promising full pardon, with only a few exceptions, to those implicated in the rebellion if they would take an oath pledging loyalty to the Constitution and support to acts of Congress and presidential proclamations referring to slaves; when in any of these states a number of qualified voters equal to one-tenth of those voting in 1860 took this oath, they could re-establish a democratic state government.

Lincoln wanted these southern states to reconstruct themselves. He opposed accepting southerners in Congress before resistance ended and there were assurances of loyalty, but he also opposed having northern men go south so that they could be sent as "carpetbagger" congressmen to Washington. He felt that if the southern people saw only carpetbaggism, the continuance of military occupation, and the prospect of indefinite repression, progress toward reunion would be sadly delayed, and military victory would lose much of its value.

At first, radical Republican leaders—Sumner, and even Wade and Chandler—professed admiration for Lincoln's plan of amnesty, but most of them disliked it as being too lenient. They wished to impose harsh conditions on the conquered South—including Negro suffrage, which, they believed, would be good insurance for the continuation of Republican rule. Two of the radicals, Ben Wade in the Senate and Henry Winter Davis in the House, sponsored a bill providing a much harsher plan of Reconstruction than the President had devised.

The Wade-Davis bill of 1864 required a pledge of loyalty from the majority of a state's voting population before a state government could be formed. It excluded all who had willingly served the Confederacy from voting for delegates to state constitutional conventions, and from serving as delegates to these conventions. Under this plan, not only would slavery be prohibited and the "rebel" debt repudiated, but also no official of any Confederate government, state or national, could serve as a legislator or as a governor of one of the newly formed states.

This bill by no means represented the position of the extreme radicals, but by signing it Lincoln would have recognized congressional control over Reconstruction; to the rage of its sponsors, the President pocket-vetoed the measure. The authors of the bill thereupon issued a Manifesto, published on August 5, 1864, in the New York *Tribune*. This bitter statement, coming from two members of his own party, accused Lincoln of dishonesty and of "dictatorial usurpation" in pursuing his plan of Reconstruction. The Manifesto declared that the authority of Congress in the political reorganization of the South was paramount.

The storm aroused by the veto of the Wade-Davis bill illustrated the divergence of viewpoint over Reconstruction between the President and some of the radical leaders that developed during Lincoln's last year in office. Lincoln was not sure that his own plan of Reconstruction was the only one that should be adopted. He was willing to keep the situation fluid as long as possible, hoping that finally the best possible solution of the problem would emerge. Though he did not like the Wade-Davis bill, he announced his willingness to have any southern state that wished to do so adopt that particular plan, but there were no takers. Tennessee, Arkansas, Louisiana, and Virginia set up state governments under Lincoln's plan. In no state, however, was that plan completely put into effect, for radical opposition prevented the states so constructed from ever being fully represented in Congress.

Intimately bound up with the Reconstruction of the South was the future of the freed slaves, and over this Lincoln and the congressional radicals were also at odds. Lincoln was a friend of the Negro, as he was of all the downtrodden, though he did resent the idea of intermarriage between Negroes and whites and was cautious about the possibility of establishing political and social equality between the two races. He saw the problem of racial relationship for what it was, full of dangers and difficulties, but by 1864 he had come to believe that it would be wise to have a limited Negro suffrage. In March of that year, he asked the governor of federally occupied Louisiana "whether some of the colored people may not be let in—as, for instance, the very intelligent, and especially those who have fought gallantly in our ranks. They would probably help, in some trying time to come, to keep the jewel of liberty within the family of freedom."

Lincoln favored the idea of equal rights for the Negro and the white as a high moral ideal, but he would move toward it only slowly and with caution. The radicals, however—and on this issue they were on their way to becoming a unified bloc during the last year of Lincoln's life—took a more extreme position than did the President. Like him, as events were to prove, they had considerable interest in the social and economic improvement of the Negro, but they went far beyond him on Negro suffrage. In their zeal for a reconstruction policy that would ensure Republican control of the country for many years, they were determined to force wholesale Negro suffrage upon the South.

Wartime Economic Measures

With eleven southern states out of the Union and Republicans dominating both the House and the Senate during the war, the way was cleared for some highly significant economic legislation. Even before Sumter fell in the spring of 1861, the so-called Morrill Tariff Act started an upward trend in rates that continued throughout the war years. The Morrill tariff itself was moderate, returning duties only to where they had been under the Walker tariff of 1846, and was primarily intended as a revenue-producing measure. The subsequent changes were particularly favorable to manufacturers, justified either on the ground of need for additional revenue or as safeguards for producers who found it difficult to meet foreign competition and pay the heavy internal taxes that were a part of the revenue-producing system. By 1865, the general duty rate was 47 per cent, about double what it had been under the tariff of 1857. The increased influence at Washington of the manufacturers became even more clearly evident when the end of the war brought repeal of the internal taxes but no lowering of the tariff.

The institution of a protective system was only one aspect of wartime economic policy. More immediately important was the financing of the war, in which Secretary of the Treasury Chase was a guiding spirit. At first, under the assumption that the struggle would be of short duration, the chief reliance of the Treasury was on the heightened tariff rates and on short-term loans. Chase, who favored hard money, tried to pay all government obligations in specie and kept issuing short-term Treasury notes payable in specie on demand. This policy, plus military reverses which led to hoarding, made money tight, and the repudiation of southern debts to northern creditors further complicated the situation. In December, 1861, both the banks and the government had to suspend specie payments. The latter then turned reluctantly to the printing press, and on February 25, 1862, came the first of a series of "greenback" issues which were made legal tender for everything except payment of the customs duties and the interest on government securities, and which amounted in all to $450 million during the war.

The country now had two kinds of money—paper and gold—which constantly changed in value relative to one another. Gold speculation became rampant, especially when the value of the greenbacks fluctuated with the fortunes of war. In 1864, an investor could change $400 in gold into $1,000 in greenbacks, which in turn would purchase a $1,000 gold bond bearing 6 per cent interest; he would then be receiving 15 per cent interest on his original investment. It has been estimated that the total effect of the greenback issue, with the consequent rise in prices, was an increase in the cost of the war between $528 million and $600 million.

The government's financial situation improved during the latter part of the war. Internal taxation was greatly increased, and more reliance was placed upon the issuance of long-term bonds, which lessened the need for constant refinancing of the government's obligations. Jay Cooke and Company, Philadelphia bankers, undertook a systematic bond-sales campaign that greatly aided the marketing of government securities. From a longer-range point of view, more important still was the National Banking Act of 1863, passed at the request of Secretary Chase.

Since the destruction of the second Bank of the United States, the country had had nothing remotely resembling a national banking system, but the act of 1863 provided one. It authorized national banks with a minimum capital of $50,000, which were placed under the supervision of the Treasury Department. Each bank would buy United States government bonds to the amount of one-third of its capital; these would be deposited with the United States Treasurer as security for bank notes that could be issued up to 90 per cent of the value of the bonds. The banks would benefit by drawing interest on the bonds, by profits from lending their bank notes, and by the stability afforded by the government's guarantee of the ultimate redemption of the bank notes. The people would gain by the emission of a currency much more stable than that of the 1562 banks, some good and some bad, that, without national control, were issuing currency in 1860. And the government would benefit by the establishment of a ready market for its bonds.

The state banks were reluctant to participate in the national banking system, fearing a diminution of their profits, but a 10 per cent annual tax on state bank notes, passed in 1865, brought them into line. By the end of that year, there were 11,582 national banks in the country, owning some $440 million worth of government bonds and circulating bank notes to the amount of $213 million. The National Banking Act marked a forward step in banking practice, even though there remained such grave defects as the immobility of bank reserves and the possibility of concentration of financial power in the hands of a few powerful bankers.

While the government grappled with wartime financial problems and placated manufacturing interests by raising the tariff, it also made good the promises of the Republican platform of 1860 by passing a homestead law. The Homestead Act of 1862 pleased everybody—farmers, the business class, and labor. All were interested in western development, particularly in the utilization of over one billion acres of undistributed lands—over one-half of the area of the United States. The law provided that heads of families and persons twenty-one years of age or over were entitled to 160 acres of the public domain, provided they established a five-year residence on the land, made certain improvements, and paid from $26.00 to $34.00 in registry and other fees. Under this act, by June 30, 1890, 48,225,736 acres of land had been homesteaded, and a greater amount was taken up in subsequent years.

The Homestead Act did not represent a complete and absolute change in federal land policy. The government continued to give public lands to the states, to sell lands containing mineral deposits, and to make large railroad, wagon company, and canal land grants. But the Act did indicate a decided shift in the direction of using the public lands as a means of fostering settlement rather than as a source of revenue and, with some modifications, this precedent has been followed ever since. The Homestead Act was the culmination of the western drive for free land.

Of the lands granted by Congress to the states, the most significant were those under the Morrill Land-Grant Act, or land-grant-college bill, which was also passed in 1862. Under this act, each state establishing a college of agriculture and the mechanic arts received 30,000 acres of the public domain for every Senator and Representative that the state had in Congress. At first confined to the loyal areas, it was later extended to all the states of the Union. It gave a great stimulus to education in those states that had state universities, and was one of the happiest and most successful pieces of wartime legislation. The "A. & M." colleges and universities of today bear witness to its lasting effect.

Another important piece of economic legislation during the war was the passage of laws aiding the construction of transcontinental railroad lines. Agitation for a railroad stretching from the Mississippi to the Pacific had been vigorous during the 1850s, but intense rivalry over the eastern terminus among cities such as New Orleans, Memphis, St. Louis, Chicago, Minneapolis, and Duluth had barred legislation. Now the southern influence was gone, and an added argument for such a road lay in the need for joining together the loyal parts of the Union.

In 1862, Congress passed an act creating the Union Pacific Railroad Company, which was to build a road west from Nebraska to California. In that state, a group of railroad promoters, among them Leland Stanford and Collis P. Huntington, organized the Central Pacific, which would build eastward from Sacramento (eventually they obtained a terminal in San Francisco). Congress granted enormous subsidies to both companies for construction purposes: $16,000 a mile in level country, $32,000 a mile in areas lying between mountain ranges, and $48,000 a mile across the mountains. In 1863, Congress gave another company, the Atchison, Topeka, and Santa Fe, 6,400 acres of land for every mile of railroad built, and in 1864 the Northern Pacific was subsidized with land grants that totaled an area greater than that of New England.

Though the economic measures passed during the Civil War were Republican in origin, it cannot be demonstrated that they represented any deep-laid plot on the part of the business community to build a nation that would be subservient to its merchants and industrialists. The various bills were passed by an alliance between the northeastern and northwestern parts of the country, by votes from the agrarian as well as from the industrialized states. Bankers opposed while other businessmen supported the National Banking Act of 1863. Despite the fact that more than one congressman voted without any real comprehension of the significance of the acts under discussion, in retrospect it is clear that this wartime legislation tended to identify the interests of the agrarian West and the industrial East with the Republican party, and that it furnished a basis for that predominance of the business community that was to be such a marked characteristic of the post-Civil War period.

Politics in Wartime

The Republican majorities in the Thirty-Seventh Congress together with Unionist representatives who resolutely supported the war but had not joined the Republican party left the Democrats with very small minorities in both the House and the Senate. By the fall of 1862, however, a variety of events had lowered Republican prestige and increased the popularity of the Democrats: the growing rift between Lincoln and some of the radical leaders (exemplified in mounting criticism of Seward and the furor over Frémont's dismissal), the military defeats and disappointments of 1862, arbitrary arrests and military trials, the offense to conservative sentiment given by the preliminary emancipation proclamation of September, 1862, and intraparty squabbles in various states, all played a part in reducing popular confidence in Republican rule. Radicals felt that Lincoln was not prosecuting the war vigorously enough, while conservatives thought he was exceeding his constitutional authority and taking steps dangerous for the future of the republic.

The election of 1862 was fought out between the regular Democratic organization and what in some states was called the Republican party but in most was designated as the Union party, and was really a coalition of Republicans, those who had termed themselves Unionists in 1860, and War Democrats. The regular Democratic organization held that victory and a restoration of the Union could never be achieved under the existing Administration. The Union party, with varying degrees of warmth, supported the

Administration and its measures, and it, also, was pledged to victory over the rebellious South.

When the elections of 1862 were over, the Administration supporters had won, but only by a narrow margin. New York, Pennsylvania, Ohio, Indiana, and Illinois, all of which had gone for Lincoln in 1860, now sent predominantly Democratic delegations to Congress. The Administration majority in the House of Representatives was reduced to eighteen votes; had it not been for returns from the border states, where Federal troops interfered with the electoral process, the Democrats might have organized the House.

The Administration's political woes increased during the next two years. Conscription was unpopular, resentment of arbitrary arrests continued, and increased taxation tried the tempers of many citizens, while others feared the centralization of authority in the national government. Democratic critics of the government and its policies, called "Copperheads" by Administration supporters because they wore as their badge the head of Liberty cut from the copper one-cent piece, became more and more vocal. Lincoln and the radicals were coming to an open break over the proper policy to be pursued in reconstructing the southern states. By the beginning of 1864, despite the victories of Gettysburg and Vicksburg, a spirit of gloom was widespread in the North, and it was deepened by the slaughter in the campaign against Richmond and the seeming invincibility of Lee's army. Defeatism spread, and a peace movement appeared in the North, with no less influential a person than Horace Greeley taking a leading part in abortive negotiations with Confederate agents who were in Canada for the purpose of sabotaging the northern war effort.

It was inevitable that, under such circumstances, efforts would be made to prevent Lincoln's renomination in 1864. Greeley came out against it in the *Tribune*. A boom for Salmon P. Chase, launched in February, 1864, by the so-called Pomeroy Circular, rose and then faded, largely because it was so obviously an attempt to undercut the President by a member of his official family. Frémont was next in line as a potential candidate, and a convention of 400 radicals met at Cleveland on May 31 and nominated him for the presidency.

But while these and other dissident movements had been stirring, Lincoln's agents had not been idle. Senator Pomeroy of Kansas, sponsor of the ill-fated Circular, found himself bereft of patronage. In state after state, office and the promise of office was used to round up delegates, and when the Union (Republican) convention met in Baltimore on June 7, it unanimously renominated the President. Giving emphasis to its "Union" character, it gave Andrew Johnson, a War Democrat from Tennessee, second place on the ticket. He may have been the President's choice, but, if so, Lincoln moved so skillfully that this has always remained in doubt.

RUNNING THE MACHINE

Stanton, after Bull Run, had accused Lincoln of "running the machine" into disaster. His words recoil on his own head in this 1864 cartoon published by Currier and Ives. It depicts Secretary of the Treasury Fessenden grinding greenbacks out of "Chase's Patent Greenback Mill" at the behest of contractors for army supplies. Welles is inefficient, Seward is a tyrant, Stanton is ineffectual, and it all reminds Lincoln of one of his jokes. The "machine" is obviously headed straight for disaster.

Despite the outcome of the Baltimore convention, Greeley, Chase, and other radicals remained dissatisfied and uneasy. Their discontent increased with the pocket-veto of the Wade-Davis bill, and what looked like a continued war stalemate. During the summer, another radical revolt began to take shape, when Ben Butler and Henry Winter Davis attempted to organize a bolt from Lincoln as the Union party nominee. At the end of

August, an inquiry went out to key Republican governors, asking their opinion on organizing a convention and substituting another candidate for Lincoln.

As the radicals developed their plans for abandoning Lincoln, the Democratic convention met, on August 29, at Chicago. Defeatist in mood, it nominated McClellan for the presidency on a platform which declared the war a failure and called for a cessation of hostilities so that peace and the federal Union could be restored at the earliest possible moment. What this meant, in essence, was an armistice that would have strengthened the position of the Confederacy, but that might possibly have resulted in the restoration of the Union as it had been before the war. McClellan, in his acceptance speech, declared that the re-establishment of the Union must be "the indispensable condition in any settlement."

The capture of Atlanta (September 2) and the consequent change in the complexion of the war strengthened Lincoln and the Republican position in general. The radical revolt collapsed, even Chase and Henry Winter Davis taking the stump for Lincoln. On September 22, Frémont withdrew from the race, and with military victory in sight, the Democratic charge that the war was a failure began to look silly. When the polls closed, Lincoln had 55 per cent of the popular vote and 212 votes in the electoral college, his party had overwhelming majorities in both houses of Congress, and there were Republican governments in every northern state except New Jersey. McClellan carried only Kentucky, Delaware, and New Jersey, with twenty-one votes in the electoral college.

The President's triumph, however, was not as decisive as these figures would seem to indicate. In New England and the Middle Atlantic states, the presidential vote was very close, and even in Illinois and Indiana Lincoln's majorities were not large. Indeed, had not thousands of soldiers been sent home from the army at Lincoln's directive to vote in state and national elections, the election might have been much closer. It was only in such frontier states as Kansas, Iowa, and Minnesota, into which homesteaders from the free states had moved, that the Republican party showed itself to be much stronger and the Democratic party much weaker than had been the case in 1860.

Social and Economic Conditions of Wartime

War and wartime conditions affected northern society in a variety of ways. Imponderable but ever-present were the strain and anguish caused by the casualty lists and the defeats and military disappointments that were

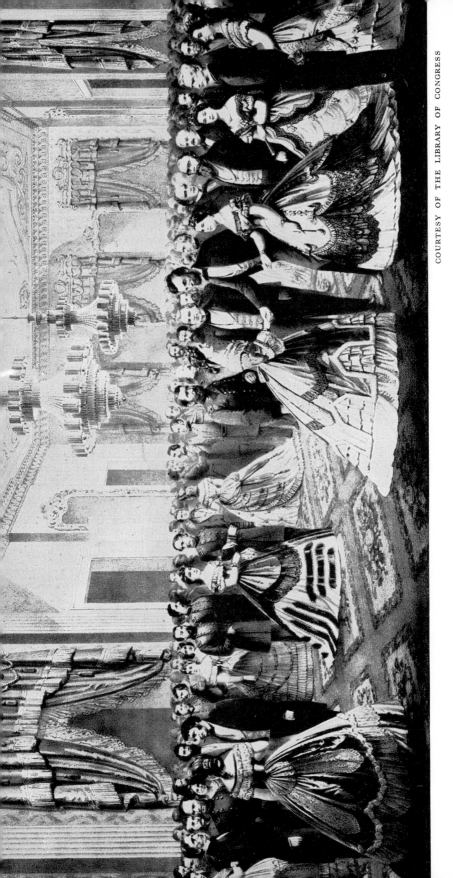

GRAND RECEPTION OF THE NOTABILITIES OF THE NATION (1865)

The northern nouveaux riches of wartime spent money on lavish social entertainments. The White House also entertained, though on a more modest scale. This reception in 1865, however, when the war was coming to a victorious close, was a joyous and brilliant affair.

especially numerous in the early part of the conflict. The psychotic hatred deriving from stories of life in the southern war prisons was strengthened by the appeals to hatred and revenge that emanated from such volunteer patriotic organizations as the Union League and the Loyal Publications Society of New York.

Other manifestations of war strain and of the social dislocations of wartime could be seen in the flagrant prostitution that flourished in the cities and the army camps, and in the gross corruption that appeared in various quarters. Whiskey distilleries produced far beyond demand as the excise tax gradually rose from $.25 to $2.00 a gallon, and by a congressional lobby of monstrous proportions escaped the increased tax on the whiskey in hand. Woolen manufacturers raised a cry of "patronize home industry" and then put out millions of pounds of shoddy cloth for military use and private wear. Rifles manufactured by the government armory at Springfield, Massachusetts, cost $9.00, while private contractors charged from $16.00 to $20.00 for the same guns. Hundreds of state banks overextended their note issues, and counterfeiting of bank notes flourished. There was much illicit trading of cotton across the lines. The nouveaux riches flocked to the theatres and spent lavishly on silks and jewelry, dancing parties, burlesque shows, and other forms of amusement.

Education both gained and suffered during the war. The Massachusetts Institute of Technology dedicated its first buildings before the conflict was over, and a dozen other colleges were founded in different parts of the North. College endowments increased, in some part as the result of wartime profits. On the other hand, college enrollments drastically declined, and the number of trained teachers in both colleges and secondary schools diminished through lessening of demand and the pressure of enlistments and the draft. War hysteria resulted in a considerable amount of witch-hunting and proscription that extended from the public-school teachers and principals to college presidents.

The war brought unqualified gains to some segments of society. Wartime prosperity made for generous contributions in the field of pure and applied science; with interest heightened in scientific devices for combat, in 1863 the National Academy of Science was founded so that the government might easily make use of American scientific contributions. The war furnished other incentives for inventive genius as industries rose or were expanded and as demands for production increased. More patents were issued in the North in 1864 than had been granted before in any year for the entire Union, and labor-saving devices from machine-made horseshoes to floating grain elevators were adopted or their use extended.

There was also a considerable development of interest in social welfare during the war. Ladies Aid Societies devoted themselves to the care of sick and wounded soldiers, and the United States Sanitary Commission, a private organization that was a forerunner of the Red Cross, established "sanitary fairs" at which large sums were raised for hospital and relief work. Public and private agencies raised and spent millions in care for the dependents of enlisted men and in support of displaced persons, whether southern loyalists or freed Negroes.

The economy of the North, like its social organization, felt the impact of the war. At first a panic of considerable proportions developed, starting as secession became an imminent probability and becoming worse with the outbreak of the struggle. When southerners repudiated debts to northern creditors in the amount of nearly $300 million, this, together with the military situation and fear of the future, led to a general curtailment of business and produced failures in 1861 and 1862 with liabilities of over $200 million.

The initial wartime depression was followed by increasing confidence and prosperity. With government spending and inflationary war financing resulting in a steady price rise, optimism replaced pessimism as war profits rolled in. Railroads, banks, and woolen manufacturers made enormous amounts of money, and the lucrative occupations of iron, coal, and gold mining were made more so by war needs. Wartime prosperity descended upon the farms, for European crops were short, especially in England, and there was a heavy demand for American wheat. Thanks to labor-saving machinery and to the hard work of those left on the farms, agricultural production was generally well sustained and in some instances markedly increased. The cry for more and more wool resulted in its production being doubled between 1860 and 1865.

It must not be thought, however, that the war produced only gain for the northern economy. The cotton industry was hard hit by the dwindling supply of raw cotton. The merchant marine, its fortunes already declining before the war, was badly damaged by the Confederate raiders and, through fear of loss, some 5,000 ships were transferred to foreign registry. One of the unfortunate results of the trend toward high protection during the war was the abrogation in 1864 of the Canadian reciprocity treaty concluded ten years earlier. It is also significant that the rate of development in iron production, railroad building, and, indeed, in most forms of manufacturing and in agriculture slowed during the war, as contrasted with the progress that had been made during the preceding decade. The economy in general did not regain its former rate of growth until some years after the war was over.

The war also meant hardship and loss for certain elements in the population. Teachers, ministers, and professional people in general went through the struggle on relatively fixed incomes. Labor, too, was hard hit, for, while prices more than doubled between 1860 and 1865, money wages rose only a little over 40 per cent. The government's deliberate stimulation of foreign immigration (especially the Contract Labor Law of 1864), the prevalence of sweatshop conditions in the clothing industries, and the development of employers' organizations which were quick to use lockouts and blacklists made the lot of the working class all the harder. Under these circumstances, it is not surprising that unionization efforts flourished and strikes increased during wartime. Trade assemblies developed in most of the cities, and a number of national unions, among them the Brotherhood of Locomotive Engineers, the Cigar Makers' National Union, and the Iron

JEFFERSON DAVIS
(1808–1889)

The President of the Confederacy had been for years a believer in southern nationalism. He was an egoist whose strong convictions and imperious temper, aggravated by ill-health, made difficult his role as the Confederate leader. But he was also a man of lofty spirit who strove manfully against overwhelming odds.

Molders' International Union had been organized by the end of the war. Over 100 strikes in 1864 testified to the discontent of the nation's laborers with their lot.

Life Behind the Lines in the Confederacy

Life was full of problems for the Confederate civilians, but those of a political nature were not immediately apparent. A governmental system was set up which took over, with adaptations, the laws as well as the Constitution of the United States: Jefferson Davis was made provisional President on February 18, 1861; the Confederate constitution was ratified by state conventions; in November, 1861, a general election chose the Congress and the presidential electors who, in turn, unanimously elected Davis as President of the Confederacy—there was no opposition to his election and the Confederate government was nonpartisan.

But, if the Confederate government was not plagued by partisan strife, it found itself involved in other political problems. The conditions of wartime made imperative a marked degree of centralization. This clashed with the tender regard for state sovereignty that was deeply rooted in the South. Governor Brown of Georgia and Governor Vance of North Carolina, who were determined to wage the war in independent fashion, raised their own troops, resisted taxation by the central government, and denounced conscription; they also opposed the suspension of the writ of habeas corpus, to which the central government resorted on occasion, beginning in February, 1862.

The traditional reluctance of the southern people to see governmental action that would in any way limit individual freedom also produced difficulties for the Confederate authorities. Since the maxim "that government governs best which governs least" was still of potent force in the South, both national and state authorities found it difficult to enforce laws curbing speculation and profiteering, drafting soldiers into the army, limiting cotton acreage, and the distillation of alcohol or whiskey in order to conserve the grain supply.

Another southern problem, one never satisfactorily solved, was that of obtaining foreign aid. England, indeed, early recognized the belligerency of the Confederacy, but the fundamental policy pursued by all the European nations was one of neutrality. The Confederacy sent its agents abroad seeking both financial aid and recognition of its status as an independent power. The English and French governments came closest to recognition in the summer and fall of 1862. France would probably have been glad to follow England's lead in such a course. The northern victory at Antietam, the Emancipation Proclamation, and the skillful diplomacy of Charles Francis Adams, United States Minister to Great Britain, all helped to swing the balance against the South in both of these European nations. British and French recognition of the Confederacy would undoubtedly have been followed by offers of mediation and perhaps of intervention, but by 1863 there was no longer the possibility of such action.

The Confederacy did succeed in building the cruisers *Florida* and *Alabama* in England. After these were then outfitted at Nassau and the Azores, respectively, they went on their destructive way as commerce raiders. But Confederate efforts to obtain in England two powerful ironclads, the "Laird rams," were unavailing. Due to steady pressure by Seward and Adams, which included the threat of war if the rams were permitted to leave England, and in part to the veiled threat that Union privateers would be commissioned to prey on neutral commerce that might be carrying contraband, the British government first seized and then purchased the rams. Thereafter relations between the Confederacy and the European powers became more and more distant.

Politics and diplomacy had their difficulties for the Confederacy, but its greatest problems lay in raising money, in transportation, and in the increasing scarcity of supplies. The South had few banks and only a small amount of specie when the war began. A $15 million bond issue in 1861 was a success; principally subscribed by the banks, it was the chief source of hard money for the central government. Later bond issues were hard to dispose of, despite an 8 per cent interest rate, and bonds were sold for agricultural produce, chiefly cotton. Only a small quantity of this could be disposed of abroad, due to the blockade. The one important foreign loan, contracted with Erlanger and Company of Paris, turned into a gigantic cotton speculation. The Erlangers made enormous profits out of marketing the bonds involved, but the Confederate government received only $2.5 million to $3 million cash and the investors, chiefly English, lost everything they had put into it.

The chief monetary reliance of the Confederacy was the printing press. Paper money issued reached $1.5 billion by 1864; its gold value, at $.90 on the dollar in 1861, reached $.017 by 1865. In addition to the central government, states, cities, and even private corporations issued a variety of currencies, which were made all the more dubious by counterfeiting at home and counterfeit issues poured into the Confederacy from the North. Taxation as a money source was at first slow and ineffectual; as the war went on, it became heavier but was also more and more difficult to collect.

By October, 1864, the Confederate government owed, in bonds and paper currency, a debt of $1.687 billion.

Transportation, next to finances, was the South's next most serious problem. The southern railroads were short lines, mainly owned by local companies; gauges varied, and the equipment came chiefly from northern shops. Under the stress and strain of wartime needs, the service on these roads rapidly deteriorated, immensely complicating the logistical problems of the southern armies. When peace came, the roads that had not been destroyed by the northern troops were nearly useless.

The railroads were not the only means of transport that broke down during the war. Wagon and cart service, which was extremely important in local transportation, also deteriorated. This was partly due to difficulty of replacement, most of these vehicles having been built in the North, and also to impressment for army use. Thousands of horses and mules likewise disappeared, pressed into army service or taken by the Federals.

Supplies became almost as scanty as the means of transporting them. The factories in the South had always been grossly inadequate for the needs of the section. General Josiah Gorgas, head of the Ordnance Bureau, was remarkably successful in supplying the Confederate armies with guns and munitions, but iron was always in short supply and deficiencies in this area became critical as the northern armies moved down into the iron-producing states of the Upper South. Clothing, too, was a problem; the textile factories at first worked night and day and made large profits, but their machinery wore out, raw materials became scarce, and operatives were drafted. The food supplies of the armies became increasingly inadequate as the war went on. Farms and plantations were plagued by the lack of animals and tools, harried by taxation, and bereft of manpower as their white workers became subject to impressment and the slaves sought freedom in the shelter of the Union armies. Finally, medical supplies were largely cut off by the blockade, and southern doctors were hampered by the lack of quinine, calomel, opium, and chloroform; this situation grew worse and worse, despite the trade between the lines.

The truth was that as the war went on, the whole southern economy began grinding to a halt. Economic deficiencies were as important as the lack of manpower in spelling the doom of the Confederacy.

The Cost of the War

What estimate can be given, in monetary terms, of the cost of fighting the Civil War? The national debt increased from $65 million in 1860 to

$2.322 billion in 1866, not to be equaled again before World War I. Down to 1900, the United States paid $2.8 billion in interest on this debt and $2.5 billion in pensions. If to these amounts there be added the cost of monetary inflation and of wartime taxes, it is conservatively estimated that, by 1917, the Civil War had cost, in such items alone, not less than $10 billion. If this figure is enlarged to include the state war debts, the cost of the war to the Confederacy, the destruction of property on both sides, the cancellation of property rights in slaves, the losses in the war panic of 1861, and the waste in the carpetbag governments during the Reconstruction period, the bill could easily be doubled. In comparison, the freeing of four million slaves with the owners compensated at $2,000 each, with the debt amortized by 1900, would have been economical, viewed solely as a financial proposition, though neither North nor South would have accepted such a solution in 1861.

Suggested Reading

The bibliography of all aspects of the Civil War is extensive. For general accounts of the nonmilitary side, see the works by Randall, Cole, Eaton, and Hesseltine cited in the previous chapter. For Lincoln in wartime, Sandburg, *Abraham Lincoln, the War Years* and Thomas, *Abraham Lincoln,* both previously cited, are excellent. The student should also consult J. G. Randall, *Lincoln the President* (4 vols., 1945–1955), the last volume completed by Richard N. Current, and the essays in David Donald, *Lincoln Reconsidered* (1956).

E. C. Smith, *The Borderland and the Civil War* (1927) helps to explain Lincoln's policy toward emancipation. Indispensable for a study of the North's relations with England is M. B. Duberman, *Charles Francis Adams, 1807–1866* (1961). Northern diplomacy in general is covered in G. G. Van Deusen, *William Henry Seward,* previously cited.

The standard work on Lincoln's use of war powers and his interpretation of the Constitution is J. G. Randall, *Constitutional Problems Under Lincoln* (1926), although the works on the Constitution and the Supreme Court by Warren, Swisher, and Haines and Sherwood, previously cited, should also be consulted. J. T. Dorris, *Pardon and Amnesty under Lincoln and Johnson* (1953) is a useful monograph. R. N. Current, *The Lincoln Nobody Knows* (1958) is very useful.

Destructive criticism and Copperheadism during wartime are examined in G. F. Milton, *Abraham Lincoln and the Fifth Column* (1942), and Wood Gray, *The Hidden Civil War* (1942). T. Harry Williams, *Lincoln and the Radicals* (1941) presents one view of their relationship. A revisionist viewpoint is suggested in David Donald, *Lincoln Reconsidered.*

The social and economic side of life in the North is examined in E. D. Fite, *Social and Industrial Conditions in the North During the Civil War* (1910) and in A. C. Cole, *The Irrepressible Conflict* (1934). See also E. P. Oberholtzer, *Jay Cooke, Financier of the Civil War* (2 vols., 1907).

The Homestead Act and its limitations are examined in Paul W. Gates, "The Homestead Act in an Incongruous Land System," *American Historical Review*, XLI (July, 1936), 652–681. In this regard, see also F. A. Shannon, *The Farmer's Last Frontier* (1945).

There is an interesting analysis of the presidential election of 1864 in W. D. Burnham, *Presidential Ballots, 1836–1892* (1955).

The South in wartime is examined on the political, social, and economic side in the volume by Clement Eaton previously cited; in J. C. Schwab, *The Confederate States of America, 1861–1865* (1901); and in a series of useful essays by C. W. Ramsdell, *Behind the Lines in the Southern Confederacy* (1944). See also F. E. Vandiver, *Ploughshares Into Swords: Josiah Gorgas and Confederate Ordnance* (1952). On southern leaders, see B. J. Hendrick's well-written *Statesmen of the Lost Cause: Jefferson Davis and His Cabinet* (1939), Hudson Strode's *Jefferson Davis, American Patriot* (1955), R. R. Von Abele's brilliant *Alexander H. Stephens* (1946), and the two classic works by D. S. Freeman, *R. E. Lee, a Biography* (4 vols., 1934–1935) and *Lee's Lieutenants* (3 vols., 1942–1944).

The standard work on Civil War casualties is T. L. Livermore, *Numbers and Losses in the Civil War in America, 1861–65* (1900).

33 ' Reconstruction

As the war drew toward its close in the winter of 1864–1865, both Congress and the President continued to manifest great interest in the reconstruction of the nation. The former passed the Thirteenth Amendment prohibiting slavery in the United States, which was submitted to the states and was declared ratified on December 18, 1865. Congress also passed a Freedmen's Bureau bill which became law on March 3, 1865, and which was designed to care for the freed Negroes and loyal refugees, utilizing abandoned southern lands for that purpose.

The Martyred President

While Congress sought to clarify the status of the freedmen, the President felt his way cautiously along the road to reunion. He told Confederate commissioners at an abortive peace conference at Hampton Roads in February that peace was only possible on the basis of a reunited country, but that he still would prefer to indemnify the former owners of slaves, perhaps to the amount of $400 million. His second inaugural breathed a spirit of magnanimity and reconciliation:

> With malice toward none, with charity for all, with firmness in the right as God gives us to see the right, let us strive on to finish the work we are in, to bind up the nation's wounds, to care for him who shall have borne the battle and for his widow and his orphan, to do all which may achieve and cherish a just and lasting peace among ourselves and with all nations.

697

In his last public address, on April 11, Lincoln urged acceptance of his plan of Reconstruction then being carried out in Louisiana, a plea that brought quick criticism from some of the radical leaders.

What Reconstruction would have been had Lincoln lived, we shall never know. On the evening of April 14, 1865, he attended a performance of the play *Our American Cousin* at Ford's Theatre. John Wilkes Booth, a brilliant actor but an unbalanced southern fanatic, and a few other conspirators, had formed a plot that had at first been designed to abduct the President, but then turned into a plan of assassination. As the President sat enjoying the play, Booth entered, shot him in the back of the head with a pistol, then leaped upon the stage shouting, *"Sic semper tyrannis."* His left leg was broken by his landing on the stage, but he ran limping to the alley back of the theatre where he had tied his horse, and fled into the night. One of the other conspirators that same evening attacked and seriously wounded Secretary Seward.

Lincoln died at 7:22 the next morning. Gruff Secretary Stanton, coming out of the death chamber with tears streaming down his face, pronounced the martyred President's best obituary—"Now he belongs to the ages." The same day Andrew Johnson took the oath of office as President of the United States.

The New President

Andrew Johnson was born in Raleigh, North Carolina, on December 29, 1808. His parents were poor, and he had no formal schooling. He was apprenticed to a tailor at the age of fourteen and at one time was advertised as a runaway apprentice. In 1826, he moved to Greeneville in eastern Tennessee, and the following year married Eliza McCardle, a Scotch shoemaker's daughter, who helped him to improve his reading and taught him to write. He set up a tailor shop, prospered, and eventually became a well-to-do slave owner.

A certain lack of intellectual assurance on Johnson's part was compensated by obstinacy of opinion, once his mind was made up to pursue a given course. He was apt to take independent positions in politics. He was also ambitious, able, and endowed with great earnestness of purpose, and he had deep convictions about equality of rights for all white men, the necessity of respecting the rights of the states, and the high importance of the Constitution. Willing, even glad, to see the Negro free, he was far from being a fanatical exponent of equal rights for both races.

Neat in appearance, courteous in ordinary social life, a powerful and effective speaker who hated the Tennessee aristocracy as he hated all pretensions to superiority based on wealth or birth, Johnson rose rapidly in the politics of his state. He served at various times in the state legislature and as governor, and in both houses of Congress, where he was a leading champion of homestead legislation. In 1861, he remained loyal to the Union. He was a War Democrat, and the following year Lincoln made him military governor of Tennessee. His nomination for the vice presidency in 1864, prompted largely by a desire for Democratic votes, provoked a fleering comment by Thad Stevens about going down into "a damned rebel province" for a candidate. Now that an assassin's bullet had made Johnson the Chief Executive of the land, the question was, what would be his attitude toward the reconstruction of the South?

Johnson said in his inaugural that his policy would be indicated by its development under his Administration, and his first acts were indicative of vigor and decision. Orders were issued for the trial of those implicated in Lincoln's assassination. The President re-established federal authority in Virginia and on May 29 proclaimed amnesty for those involved in the rebellion, but with sweeping exceptions: all who had left the service of the United States government to serve the Confederacy, all governors of Confederate states and all officials of the Confederacy, all of its high-ranking military and naval officers, and all participants in the rebellion with taxable property worth over $20,000 were exempted. Despite the promise of liberal clemency for those requesting it, this proclamation sounded a stern warning to the South. When, in private, Johnson declared that traitors must be punished, and treason made odious, radical leaders opposed to Lincoln on policy toward the South were much encouraged. "Johnson, we have faith in *you,*" said Ben Wade. "By the gods, there will be no trouble now in running the government."

During the summer and fall of 1865, however, it became evident that Johnson's policy left much to be desired from an extremist point of view. Evidence piled up that the President's ideas on Reconstruction did not differ substantially from those of Lincoln. He issued pardons with a liberal hand. He appointed provisional governors of the erstwhile seceded states, and had them call conventions chosen by "loyal" citizens. The members of these conventions took oath to support the federal Constitution, and then framed new state constitutions and established voting requirements. They abolished slavery and nullified or repealed the ordinances of secession. They did not give the vote to any Negroes, and the President did not insist that they do so. By December, all of the seceded states save Texas had fulfilled the President's requirements, had established their own governments, and had elected members to the federal House and Senate, most of whom had reached Washington by the time Congress convened.

Congress and the South in 1865

When the Thirty-Ninth Congress finally met on December 4, 1865, it represented widely divergent points of view on Reconstruction. The Democrats, a small minority, were enthusiastic about Johnson's course, feeling that it would result not only in a swift reconstruction of the Union but also in a much-needed increase of Democratic party strength. Republican opinion was divided: some Republican radicals agreed with Charles Sumner that the Confederate states had, by secession, committed "suicide"; that federal jurisdiction in these states must be exercised just as though they were territories; that this being the case, Congress, rather than the Executive, must control their reorganization; and that, so far as suffrage was concerned, Negroes and whites should be equal before the law. Other Republicans held, with Thad Stevens, that the southern states had become merely "conquered provinces," quite outside any rights or privileges under the Constitution. Like Sumner, Stevens held that these "provinces" were entirely subject to congressional control, and he proposed a wholesale confiscation of "rebel" property and its redistribution in forty-acre homesteads to the former slaves. He was not a proponent of Negro suffrage, regarding it as a bad political issue in the North.

Of the rank and file of the Republican party in Congress, few men were ready in the winter of 1865–1866 to follow the lead of Sumner and Stevens in assigning to Congress sole responsibility for Reconstruction. They were sure that the southern states should be readmitted as soon as it was safe to do so, and wanted only Congress to have a hand in the conditions that should be laid down. A majority of them were in favor of some form of Negro suffrage in the South, though they were uncomfortably aware that the Negro had the vote in only six northern states and that in one of these, New York, there was a special Negro property qualification. They were not hostile to Johnson and felt that some form of cooperation between Congress and the Executive was both possible and desirable.

There were numerous reasons why the Republicans in Congress should feel it necessary, by December, 1865, to take some part in reconstructing the South. The passions aroused by the war were still high in the North. There appeared to be general approval of the trial by military commission and the execution in July of four members of the Lincoln assassination conspiracy, one of them a woman, and of the similar trial and execution in

November of Henry Wirz, the commandant at Andersonville prison. Hatred of the South rankled in those whose relatives and loved ones had died in battle or in Libby and Andersonville. Many, not so strongly moved, at least felt the need for security, for guarantees against another outbreak by the defeated section, and looked to Congress to provide such protection.

The security demanded did not seem to be forthcoming. While southerners in general accepted the restoration of the Union, many of them did so in bitterness of spirit. Northern travelers in the South during 1865 brought back stories of being treated with hatred and contempt, of the unrepentant spirit of the "rebels," of the indignities suffered by southern Unionists. The South, it seemed, was not sufficiently aware of its need for repentance. It began to appear, also, that the former slaves were not really free.

While more than a million Negroes had been liberated and, to some extent, had become accustomed to freedom during the war, the majority of the colored people had entered upon their new status only after peace was declared. Even for those who had served in the northern armies or had been colonized along the Atlantic coast during the conflict, peace was an unsettling experience. The result was a blind, disorderly movement of the Negro population, especially in the Deep South. Men and women left homes and their jobs, wandering about to enjoy their freedom. There was a good deal of thievery or, as the Negroes called it, "spilin' de gypshuns." Tens of thousands of the freedmen died of disease, and many more became utterly destitute.

The southern whites, faced by this great problem, had felt compelled to take matters into their own hands, and the new state governments in the South undertook to bring some order out of chaos. Black codes were established in Mississippi, Alabama, South Carolina, and other states, setting up apprentice, vagrancy, and contract labor laws. The Negro's right to choose his occupation was limited, and in no case was he given the privilege of voting, holding office, or sitting on juries.

Much of this legislation was well intentioned. Some of it protected the families and property of the Negroes. Nevertheless, the codes bore hardly on the freedmen, and in some states tended to reduce them to a condition of peonage. This was deeply resented in the North, where, coupled with stories of southern outrages against Negroes, it seemed to indicate a determination to keep the blacks in a subordinate and altogether inferior role.

The South not only circumscribed the Negro's freedom; it also affronted the North by its choice of leaders, and sometimes by words and acts. Georgia elected to the United States Senate Alexander H. Stephens, the

Vice President of the Confederacy. South Carolina refused to repudiate its war debt, and Mississippi elected as its first governor Benjamin G. Humphreys, a still unpardoned Confederate brigadier-general. These and other evidences of southern contumacy provoked bitter criticism in the North.

In view of the above circumstances, it was natural for Congress to feel that affairs in the South were not going well under the Johnson plan; that northern opinion would have to be taken into account; and that Congress should take a hand in dealing with the southern situation. Some congressmen were also impressed by the argument that Republican supremacy would be endangered unless something was done about Negro suffrage. When the three-fifths rule for counting representatives in Congress disappeared with slavery, this meant eighteen additional southern representatives in Congress, under the census of 1860, with more to come after the 1870 census, and the frightening specter of a Congress dominated by southern rebels and northern Copperheads emerged.

The Growing Breach Between Congress and President

By December, 1865, Johnson's Reconstruction policy was being loudly praised by the southern whites and by the northern Democracy, and only feebly defended in the northern Republican press. Radical leaders like Stevens and Sumner had vainly tried to get the President's ear, to convince him that something must be done about southern Negro suffrage and about showing the southerners that they must bring forth fruits meet for repentance. A rift was appearing between the President and his party in Congress, one that was destined to become a chasm.

The principal leader on the congressional side in the dramatic struggle which now developed between Congress and the Chief Executive was Thaddeus Stevens of Pennsylvania. Born in Vermont in 1792, Stevens received a good education; he graduated from Dartmouth in 1814, his college record marked by a taste for deviltry that apparently prevented his election to Phi Beta Kappa. Admitted to the bar, he settled in Gettysburg, Pennsylvania, to practice. A successful lawyer, he branched out into iron manufacturing, and also entered politics. He distinguished himself in the Pennsylvania legislature by his ardent antimasonry and by his championship of free schools. He became a Whig, a Free-Soiler, and then a Republican. Always an ardent opponent of slavery and of compromise with it, he served in Congress from 1849 to 1853, and again from 1859

THADDEUS STEVENS
(1792–1868)

Stevens supported some good causes, but he was an extreme partisan and vindictive in his treatment of the South. His sardonic humor stood him in good stead when he rose to speak in the House of Representatives. As a parliamentary leader he has had few equals in American history.

COURTESY OF THE LIBRARY OF CONGRESS

to his death in 1868. His bitterness against the South was at least partly due to the destruction of his iron works at Chambersburg during Lee's Gettysburg campaign.

An intense partisan, by nature vindictive, Stevens was also courageous, forceful in speech, and a parliamentary tactician of rare ability who used effectively a biting and sardonic humor. He was by general report an unscrupulous opponent and of lax moral standards. When James G. Blaine met him one morning outside a gambling house where Stevens had spent the night, a Negro preacher came up soliciting contributions for his church; Stevens pulled out a thick roll of bills and handed over $50, saying to Blaine, "God moves in a mysterious way, his wonders to perform." On his deathbed, he remarked, "It is not my appearance but my disappearance that troubles me." Gambler and teetotaler, this Pennsylvania politician was a strange combination of faults and virtues.

Shortly before Congress met, Stevens and a number of other like-minded extremists caucused in Washington. They determined to push through Congress the establishment of a joint committee of the two Houses on Reconstruction, and this project was approved by the supporters of the Administration. Then Stevens persuaded the Clerk of the House to omit from the roll call of that body the names of members from the reconstructed states. Both Houses agreed to the Joint Committee on Reconstruction—preponderantly conservative in point of view—which was thereupon established.

There was not at this point any powerful, central bloc of radicals that was capable of driving the majority into a definite policy of harsh Reconstruction. Extremists like Stevens, Wade, Sumner, and Boutwell were few in number and not always of harmonious views. Such moderate Republicans as Lyman Trumbull of Illinois and William Pitt Fessenden of Maine, Administration supporters such as Henry J. Raymond of New York and James R. Doolittle of Wisconsin, and the Democrats in Congress were ready to support Johnson, or at least to reach some reasonable compromise with him. Lack of coordination among these elements, the skillful tactics of the extremists, and the mistakes of the President were to transform the radical minority into a majority.

During the winter of 1865–1866, the Joint Committee on Reconstruction heard evidence about the operation of the black codes, southern outrages against Unionists and Negroes, and the general situation in the South. On January 5, Senator Trumbull, after consultation with the President, introduced two bills with, as he understood it, the approval of the President; the Freedmen's Bureau bill extended the life of the Bureau for an indefinite period and gave it representation on military courts set up to protect civil rights in states not yet "fully restored in all their constitutional relations with the United States," and the civil rights bill attempted to confer citizenship status upon the Negro and to protect him in a wide variety of rights and privileges.

After the Freedmen's Bureau bill had passed Congress with practically solid Republican support, Johnson vetoed it on February 19. He found it expensive, inadequate for its purposes, and unconstitutional, not only because of its extension of military power in peacetime, but also because the states it affected were not represented in the Congress that passed the bill; in his judgment, those states were fully restored and should have congressional representation. An effort to pass the measure over the veto failed in the House.

There was considerable critical comment in the North on the veto of the Freedmen's Bureau bill. Distrust of the President increased sharply when, on February 22, he spoke in violent and unseemly fashion to a crowd of serenaders at the White House. He denounced Stevens, Sumner, and Wendell Phillips as traitors, clearly intimating that they were attempting to incite his own assassination, and boasted of his prowess as a tailor and of the purity of his motives. With this speech, he opened a breach between himself and the radicals that the conservative Republican majority had been striving to avoid, and markedly increased the power in Congress of men like Stevens and Sumner.

The Senate now passed a concurrent resolution that the House had earlier approved. It stated that southern senators and representatives should be excluded from Congress until that body declared the southern states entitled to representation. Both Houses passed the civil rights bill. Though it was generally regarded as a moderate measure, and most of the President's friends hoped that he would sign it, he vetoed it as unnecessary, destructive of states' rights, and establishing "a perfect equality of the white and colored races."

After the veto of the civil rights bill, Johnson's conservative Republican support began to drift away. The radicals, after using dubious means to unseat a Democratic Senator from New Jersey, found themselves with enough strength to pass the civil rights bill over the President's veto by the margin of one vote; when the House also summoned the requisite two-thirds majority, the measure became law. On July 16, the resurrected Freedmen's Bureau bill was put on the statute books, despite the President's opposition, and, eight days later, when Congress admitted Tennessee's representatives to its portals, it had virtually announced its assumption of control over Reconstruction.

While these stirring events were taking place, the Joint Committee on Reconstruction had not been idle. It reported that the South had forfeited its constitutional rights, that its state governments were not in proper form, and that Congress and the President must act together in establishing the terms of readmission to the Union. Johnson, however, made no effort to cooperate with the Committee. That body went ahead on its own initiative to frame what became the Fourteenth Amendment to the Constitution; primarily designed as a platform for the fall election, this famous amendment received congressional approval and, on June 16, 1866, was sent to the states.

The Fourteenth Amendment consisted of four main sections: (1) It declared all persons born or naturalized in the United States to be citizens of the United States and of the states in which they reside. No state should pass any law abridging the privileges or immunities of citizens; "deprive any person of life, liberty, or property, without due process of law; nor deny to any person within its jurisdiction the equal protection of the laws." (2) Representation should be apportioned in accordance with the population of each state, but reduced in proportion to the number of those disfranchised. (3) It barred from holding office all Confederates who before the war had taken an oath of office to support the federal Constitution, but provided that Congress by a two-thirds vote could remove such disability. (4) It declared the Confederate debt void and the public debt of the United States valid.

This amendment was a compromise between the radical and conservative congressional Republican wings. Obviously designed to pressure the South into granting some suffrage to the Negro, it was punitive, but not severely punitive. Johnson refused to exert his influence, which was still very considerable, in shaping it and openly disapproved of it when it was drafted; in effect, he told the southern states not to ratify. Moreover, he served notice that he would campaign in the fall elections against those Republicans who opposed him and his policy, and he helped prepare a "National Union" convention designed to start such a campaign.

The National Union convention met at Philadelphia in August, 1866. It was an attempt to organize conservative Republicans and Democrats from both North and South in a movement to support the President. Amid great enthusiasm, the delegates from Massachusetts and South Carolina marched into the convention hall arm in arm; the gathering, however, had little significance, and the radical press covered it with sarcasm, including plenty of references to the animals who came in two by two. Few conservative Republicans joined the movement, and by election time Republican voters regarded the National Union movement as being simply the Democracy in disguise.

There were two main reasons why the National Union movement sputtered and failed. A riot in New Orleans on July 30, occasioned by a radical effort to force Negro suffrage on the state, resulted in some 200 casualties, almost entirely Negroes and white Unionists. The local police were responsible for the bloodshed. The tardiness of the government at Washington in giving orders to the military in New Orleans to keep order occasioned considerable criticism in the North, and a torrent of abuse fell on the head of President Johnson when he failed to condemn the white perpetrators of the outrage, using it as an occasion to attack the radicals in New Orleans and in Congress.

The second factor in the situation was the famous "Swing around the Circle"—the trip that the President undertook on the pretext of dedicating a monument to Stephen A. Douglas in Chicago. Between August 28 and September 15, he spoke in a number of the principal northern cities, but his defense of what the Republicans had begun derisively to call "My Policy" was worse than ineffective. Badgered by hecklers, he frequently lost his temper. The spectacle of the President of the United States exchanging insults with those who baited him revolted popular taste. Radical misrepresentation of his ideas and sedulous propagation of the false rumor that his actions were the result of drunkenness heightened the bad impression that he made in these public appearances. The "Swing around the Circle" swung thousands of the uncommitted voters into the radical camp.

The election of 1866 was a stunning defeat for the President. The Republicans against whom Johnson campaigned were uniformly victorious, sweeping into the governorships of the northern states and carrying all the state legislatures. The delegation of every state represented in Congress had a Republican majority, and Johnson could count on the support of less than one-third of both the House and the Senate.

The President and the South might still have salvaged something out of this defeat by accepting the Fourteenth Amendment. This the President stubbornly refused to do and, acting under his advice, it was rejected by every southern state save Tennessee. The amendment was harsh enough, but what followed was much worse. When Congress met in December, 1866, the fact that the radicals were in control of the situation resulted in the passage over Johnson's vetoes of the Radical Reconstruction Acts of 1867.

Radical Reconstruction and the Impeachment of the President

Radical Reconstruction of the South was provided in the basic act of March 2, 1867, which was passed over Johnson's veto and was supplemented by three subsequent pieces of legislation. The ten southern states (Tennessee was deemed reconstructed because it had accepted the Fourteenth Amendment) were divided into five military districts under Federal commanders. These generals were to direct and supervise the calling of state conventions whose delegates were to be chosen by white and Negro suffrage. The conventions had to frame constitutions which would disqualify Confederate leaders and establish Negro suffrage on a permanent basis, and the constitutions would then have to be approved by Congress and ratified by the people of the reconstructed states. Legislatures elected under these constitutions had to ratify the Fourteenth Amendment.

While Congress was returning the southern states to military rule, it also sought to prevent presidential interference with its drastic reconstruction procedures. Particularly anxious that the military commanders should be unimpeded in their operations, and recognizing in Secretary of War Stanton a valuable ally, Congress passed two significant acts. The Tenure of Office Act made the removal of Cabinet officers subject to the consent of the Senate; such officers, the Act stated, should, unless removed, "hold their offices respectively for and during the term of the President by whom they may have been appointed and for one month thereafter," and violations of the act were made "high misdemeanors." A second measure, the Command of the Army Act, required the President to issue all military orders

RECONSTRUCTION OF THE SOUTH

through the general of the army (Grant), and prohibited his removal. Johnson accepted the second Act under protest, in order not to defeat necessary army appropriations; he vetoed the Tenure of Office Act, however, though two days later it was passed over his veto.

When the President tried to interfere with the effective administration of the congressional reconstruction policy, his wrath fell upon Secretary Stanton, who had drafted one of the supplementary Reconstruction Acts.

There followed an *opéra-bouffe* affair. Johnson suspended Stanton, who refused to resign. Pending a report to the Senate, Grant was appointed Secretary of War ad interim, but the Senate refused to concur in Stanton's suspension; Grant resigned and was angered and humiliated by the ensuing altercation with the President. The Secretary of War proceeded to barricade himself in his office. When the President appointed General Lorenzo Thomas, an aged dandy and something of a sot, as Secretary of War, Thomas tried to storm the War Office but, having had no breakfast and being given two drinks of whiskey by Stanton, left the latter in possession of the field. Stanton clung to his office until May 26, 1868, by which time the final assault on the President had been made and had failed.

Impeachment of the President had been previously suggested by some of his bitter foes. Now, with its indignation heightened by the Stanton-Grant-Thomas affair, the House Judiciary Committee, by a five-to-four vote, recommended that the President be impeached and removed from office. On February 24, 1868, the House voted 126 to forty-seven that the President "be impeached of high crimes and misdemeanors in office."

As provided in the Constitution, Johnson was tried before the Senate. The eleven articles of impeachment were, in general, vague and without foundation. They charged Johnson with "unlawfully" removing Stanton, with intent to violate the Constitution and the Tenure of Office Act, and with having sought to bring Congress into disrepute. The only possible ground for trial was violation of the Tenure of Office Act, but Johnson's lawyers had no difficulty in showing that the purpose of the President in removing Stanton was to test the constitutionality of the Act, and that the Act did not cover Stanton since he had been appointed not by Johnson but by Lincoln. Yet such was the bitterness felt against the President in the Senate, and such was the pressure exerted on wavering Senators, that the issue was highly doubtful. Conviction actually failed by only one vote, thirty-five to nineteen; it might have succeeded had the President not informed an influential Senator that, if acquitted, he would violate neither the Constitution nor the nation's laws. The seven Republicans who joined the Democrats in voting not guilty were savagely denounced throughout the North, and Senator Ross of Kansas, whose vote had been crucial, received a telegram from 1,000 of his constituents telling him that Kansas repudiated him as it did all perjurors and skunks.

President Johnson in his term of office did a number of foolish and stupid things, but none that warranted his impeachment. To have removed him from office would have constituted a precedent that, in future times, might have seriously limited the independence of the executive branch of the government. Taken in conjunction with other radical procedures, it might have jeopardized the entire character of the American political system.

The Legal and Economic Implications of Radicalism

The radicals, in their determination to make effective their Reconstruction of the South, attacked not only the President but also the Supreme Court. In *Ex Parte Milligan*, a judgment handed down in 1866 in the case of a man sentenced to death by a military commission for treasonable activities during the Civil War, the Supreme Court ruled that his trial had been illegal because martial law could not legitimately be enforced where the civil courts were open and in full exercise of their jurisdiction.

"SPOONS" AS FALSTAFF MUSTERING THE IMPEACHMENT MANAGERS

This cartoon by Thomas Worth in 1868 shows Ben Butler and the other leaders of the impeachment proceedings in the House of Representatives. Butler was called "Spoons" because he was accused of having stolen the silverware of southern families in New Orleans. Note President Johnson, with his tailor's shears stuck in his belt and his thumb to his nose.

COURTESY OF THE NEW-YORK HISTORICAL SOCIETY, NEW YORK CITY

Radical denunciation of this decision was violent, in part because it threw doubt on the justice of the trial of Henry Wirz and that of the conspirators in the Lincoln assassination plot and in part because Johnson used the Milligan decision in an effort to dismiss all military trials of civilians in the South. Various Republicans talked about abolishing the Supreme Court, or of "packing" it so that it would uphold the reconstruction policies of the radicals.

Neither of these expedients was utilized, but in July, 1866, Congress passed a law reducing the number of Supreme Court justices to seven, thus preventing Johnson making any new appointments to the Court. In March, 1868, another law, passed over the President's veto, took away from the Supreme Court appeals from the lower federal courts involving the right of habeas corpus; this deprived the Court of handling cases tried before military commissions in the South, cases in which the lower courts generally sustained the maintenance of military law.

Though the Supreme Court had acted courageously in the Milligan case, it bowed to these subsequent congressional attacks upon it and its prerogatives. Pleading lack of jurisdiction, it refused to review case after case involving the constitutionality of radical Reconstruction, and military trials where civil courts were open continued in the South.

Radical Reconstruction changed, to some extent, the character of the American government, and the assaults of the radicals upon the President and the Supreme Court came close to subverting the Constitution itself. In order to achieve its end, Congress drastically increased the powers of the national government, diminishing the role of states' rights and changing the federal system into one which was much more highly centralized than it had ever been before. The radicals also tried to locate the national government's authority in an all-powerful Congress to which the President and the courts would be distinctly subordinate. The successful impeachment of Johnson might have been a long step toward ending the checks and balances provided by the Constitution and creating a governmental system resembling the parliamentary government of Great Britain.

There can be little doubt that preponderant northern public opinion in 1867 favored harsh treatment of the South, as illustrated in the case of Jefferson Davis. In May, 1865, the former President of the Confederacy had been imprisoned at Fort Monroe, where he remained for two years. In 1867, he was released by writ of habeas corpus and brought before the federal circuit court at Richmond for trial on charges of treason. The prosecution was not ready, and Davis was released under $100,000 bond, the money for which was furnished by a number of men, including Cornelius

Vanderbilt and Horace Greeley. Though the *Tribune's* editor meant his act to be a gesture of conciliation, it found small favor in the North; he was overwhelmed by a flood of slanderous vituperation, and thousands canceled their subscriptions to the *Tribune*. Greeley's history of the Civil War, *The American Conflict,* had theretofore been a best seller, but with the signing of the bail bond its sale was ruined. Fortunately for Davis, his trial for treason encountered many legal obstacles, and prosecution was dropped after the President's proclamation of unconditional amnesty on Christmas Day, 1868.

A number of reputable historians in recent years have subscribed to the theory that radical Reconstruction was a successful effort on the part of the business class in the North to use the national government for its own ends. Through the Republican party, so the argument runs, this class established its control over the tariff, the national banks, and the currency; dominant in the party councils, it favored radical Reconstruction as a means of maintaining the Republicans in power, thus leaving the business interests free to exploit the resources of the southern states. It is said that the plan succeeded because President Johnson missed a great opportunity by not launching an attack upon hard money exponents and the tariff, and upon banks and monopolies; this would have found favor in the West, would have split the Republican party from top to bottom and thus would have weakened, perhaps destroyed, the program of the radicals.

Recent scholarship casts grave doubts on this theory of a business-dominated radicalism. Western farmers, it contends, were prosperous in the latter 1860s, and indifferent to the contraction or expansion of the currency. It was not, with them, an effective political issue, and therefore Johnson could not have used it to divide the radicals. The business class cannot be regarded as having had common ideas on financial matters; most industrialists favored high tariffs and a policy of easy money, while financial capitalists were inclined to support hard money and free trade. Bankers and manufacturers had so many divergent interests that the idea of a plot by big business to control either economic legislation or the reconstruction of the South for its own advantage has lost much, if not all, of its validity. This contention is given added force when it is understood that the radical Republicans in Congress were themselves split on financial questions: such powerful eastern Republicans as Thad Stevens and Benjamin F. Butler of Massachusetts opposed hard money and contraction, while radicals such as George W. Julian of Indiana, John A. Logan of Illinois, and George S. Boutwell of Massachusetts were at first for soft money but after 1868 switched to a hard money policy. In the case of this latter group of radicals, their action was governed by considerations of political expediency, rather than being the result of pressures exerted by a monolithic capitalist class.

The Impact of Radical Reconstruction upon the South

What were the effects of radical Reconstruction upon the South? It had a variety of social, economic, and political consequences, a number of which were good. The Freedmen's Bureau under General O. O. Howard furnished food and supplies for the Negroes and needy whites, found land for the former slaves under the Homestead Act, and furnished them protection in their legal rights. It set up a system of Negro education that operated 4,000 primary schools, seventy-four normal schools, and sixty-one industrial schools, thus performing valuable and constructive services.

The so-called black-and-tan legislatures, chosen after the states had complied with the requirements of the Reconstruction Acts, passed a considerable amount of admirable legislation. In the few years of their existence, they did more for the education of the Negro than the South had done in two centuries, and they also markedly improved white education. By 1878, the constitutions of nearly all the southern states contained provisions making tax-supported, free public schools mandatory for both whites and Negroes. These laws were not rigidly enforced, but they represented real progress. In 1860, South Carolina had a total of 20,000 children, white and black, in school and in 1876 there were 59,000 white and 70,000 Negro children in the public schools of the state. It is not without significance that South Carolina and two other southern states passed legislation providing that, ultimately, Negro and white children should attend the same schools.

These same legislatures of the mixed races were concerned with more than education. They sweepingly revised the tax laws on the basis of ability to pay and reorganized voting districts to give better representation to the more populous but less wealthy regions of the states. They reformed judicial systems in the interest of justice and equity, provided relief for the indigent, and built railroads, roads, hospitals, and orphan and insane asylums. There was much that was sound and progressive in the enactments of these radical legislative bodies.

It should also be remembered that the amendments establishing the citizenship of the Negro and "protecting" his right to vote were put in the Constitution during the radical Reconstruction period. Had the South been reconstructed without these amendments being adopted, they would in all probability not be in the Constitution today, and integration would be facing even more difficulties than it does at the present time.

But if radical Reconstruction had its admirable aspects, it also had its darker side. The mixed legislatures were often dominated by combinations of unscrupulous carpetbaggers from the North, equally unprincipled southern scalawags, and ignorant and venal Negroes. Such legislative bodies passed laws that penalized thrift and industry while they lined the pockets of the unscrupulous. The open and unashamed corruption of legislators and state officials is illustrated by many stories of the period. A Negro solon remarked as he pocketed the price of his vote that he had been sold eleven times but this was the first time that he had obtained the profit. The manager of a Georgia railroad, asked how he could amass $20,000 to $30,000 on a salary of $2,000 to $3,000 a year, replied, "By the exercise of the most rigid economy." With the prevalence of such a low state of public morals, it is not surprising that the state printing of South Carolina, which from 1790 to 1868 had cost $609,000, during the next ten years amounted to $1,326,589, or that tax rates shot up 400 per cent in Alabama and 800 per cent in Louisiana. These excesses gave a bad name to Negro suffrage, as well as to the system of Reconstruction engineered by the congressional radicals.

Radical Reconstruction had other evil fruits. It promoted racial animosity, as the whites undertook by force to get out from under the rule of the black-and-tan legislatures and to reduce their black fellow citizens to a condition of subservience. While it did not bring segregation into full flower (that was to come a generation later), some aspects of that practice appeared and were sanctioned by public opinion during this period: the Negroes voluntarily withdrew from the chief Protestant churches and set up their own religious organizations, and segregation in the public schools, in the military services, and in private society did become the order of the day. Radical Reconstruction also produced that unnatural political phenomenon, the "Solid South"; the experiences of these ten years resulted in discrediting Republicanism in the South and making "Democrat" synonymous, or nearly so, with respectability, and a vigorous two-party system an impossibility. Finally, there was the bitterness of feeling in the South when northern armies once more occupied southern soil, and the resentment aroused in the North by what it felt to be southern intransigence in accepting the new order of 1867. The Ku Klux Klan, the Knights of the White Camelia, and other organizations that terrorized the Negroes and drove them into a condition of political and social subservience were viewed with disgust north of the Mason and Dixon line.

The suspicion, disorder, and oppression that were the fruits of radical Reconstruction delayed significant progress toward the re-establishment of national unity. It was not until the close of the century that the United States had again become a united nation, and even then numerous signs of bitterness remained.

Resumption of an Expansive Foreign Policy

The Civil War put an end, for the time being, to the expansionist fever that had been rampant during the antebellum period. With the close of the struggle, however, American foreign policy again showed signs not only of a vigorous interest in affairs abroad, but also of an outward thrust. One of its major emphases concerned the situation that had developed in Mexico during the early sixties.

After the close of the Mexican War, Mexico remained a weak and faction-ridden republic. In 1861, a full-blooded Indian leader, Benito Juarez, overthrew the opposition of a powerful clerical-monarchist party and became the head of the government. His regime was in financial straits and therefore suspended for two years payment on the foreign debt. England, France, and Spain thereupon agreed to collect, by force if necessary, their claims against Mexico, and sent 10,000 troops into the country.

When Juarez made a satisfactory debt settlement, England and Spain withdrew. They were all the more ready to do so since it had become apparent that Napoleon III contemplated something more than debt collection. Napoleon dreamed of establishing a monarchy in Mexico that would be closely associated with France—a monarchy that would be a New World conservative bulwark and would also serve as a barrier against the expansion of the United States into Latin America. Instead of withdrawing, France sent more troops into Mexico and made exorbitant demands upon the Juarez government. These being refused, the French occupied Mexico City and Napoleon III persuaded the Austrian Archduke Maximilian and his charming wife, Carlotta, to abandon Miramar, their beautiful estate on the Adriatic, and become Emperor and Empress of Mexico.

Maximilian and Carlotta arrived in Mexico in 1864 and their regime began its brief and troubled existence. Juarez, with popular support, undertook a system of guerilla warfare, and Maximilian's control extended little beyond the environs of the capital, though even there his main reliance was French bayonets.

The United States government had viewed these proceedings in Mexico with distaste, but, engaged in desperate civil strife, its reaction had been cautious. Secretary Seward continued to recognize Juarez as the legitimate ruler of Mexico and, though he did not mention the Monroe Doctrine by name, made it clear to the French government that the United States regarded French interposition in the affairs of Mexico as an unfriendly act. Backed by American public opinion, Seward's tone became stronger as the Civil War came to an end. He made it clear in November, 1865, that the United States would never recognize Maximilian's government, and a few months later asked bluntly when French troops would be withdrawn from Mexico.

Napoleon III, faced by European complications and aware that the United States had a powerful army at its disposal, had become sick of his venture. He began withdrawing his forces, and by the spring of 1867 the last French troops had left Mexico. Maximilian's regime then tottered to its fall: its unhappy Emperor was captured by the forces of Juarez and shot, and the Empress, who had been vainly importuning the capitals of Europe to intercede for her husband, went mad.

Seward's course in regard to Mexico indicated his high regard for the principles of the Monroe Doctrine, but he was more than an advocate of American supremacy in the western hemisphere. He had a vision of American expansion that might eventually bring the United States and England to grips in the Orient for the mastery of the world. During the Johnson Administration, however, he confined his efforts to the promotion of American expansion in the Pacific area and in the Caribbean. Particularly interested in a Caribbean naval base, he negotiated a treaty in 1867 for the purchase of two islands in the Danish West Indies, only to have it blocked by a Congress that could see no need of spending $7.5 million on such a project. He also wished to acquire Santo Domingo, or at least a naval station on Samana Bay in the Dominican Republic, but these projects also were rebuffed by Congress.

One reason for the cold reception given to Seward's plans in the Caribbean was the amount of money that Congress was being asked to appropriate for the purchase of Alaska. Russia was ready and willing to sell this northern province, an expanse of territory larger than what is now its sister state of Texas, and Seward was anxious to buy. Negotiations began in the winter of 1866–1867. When, one evening in March, the Russian

Minister to the United States, Baron Stoeckl, called at Seward's house to inform him that the Czar had consented to the transaction, and that the treaty could be drawn up the next day, Seward, abandoning the game of whist he had been playing, proposed that they make the treaty that very night; it was drawn up and signed at four o'clock the next morning, March 30, 1867.

The Senate approved the Alaska treaty on April 6, but the purchase price of $7.2 million was not appropriated until more than a year later. This delay was the result of Republican opposition in the House to President Johnson and all the works of his Administration. There is evidence that Baron Stoeckl used some of the $200,000 in the purchase price to bribe influential Republicans, so that the necessary appropriation bill might pass the House of Representatives.

Greeley and other radical Republicans were loud in criticism of Seward's purchase of Alaska, dubbing the territory "Seward's ice-box," and calling the project a "Quixotic land hunt," undertaken at the expense of the American taxpayer. It is strange to read these expressions of opinion today, when Alaska has long since proved its worth in fish, furs, and gold, and when the presence of Soviet Russia on the American continent would be viewed with the utmost alarm.

Alaska was Seward's one great territorial acquisition. He also succeeded in raising the American flag on tiny Midway Island, some thousand miles northwest of Hawaii, in 1867, but his desire to annex Hawaii met the same fate as his plan for the acquisition of Santo Domingo. The Republicans of the later 1860s were not much interested in expansion, and they had little use for the dreams of a Secretary of State who had remained loyal to President Johnson.

Suggested Reading

The story of the Reconstruction of the South has gone through a variety of historical interpretations. The classic older accounts of the period are to be found in J. F. Rhodes, *History of the United States Since the Compromise of 1850,* vols. V and VI (1904, 1906), and in W. A. Dunning, *Essays on the Civil War and Reconstruction* (1904) and *Reconstruction, Political and Economic, 1865–1877* (1907). These accounts are generally critical of Johnson and have little good to say about the radicals or radical rule in the South.

More recent accounts are to be found in J. G. Randall, *The Civil War and Reconstruction* (1937); G. F. Milton, *The Age of Hate* (1930); E. M. Coulter, *The South During Reconstruction, 1865–1877* (1947); L. P. Stryker, *Andrew Johnson* (1929); W. B. Hesseltine, *A History of the South, 1607–1936* (1936); and H. K. Beale, *The Critical Year* (1930, 1958). The general tendency of this group of historians is to be laudatory of Johnson and to paint the radicals as violent, unprincipled men, sympathetic with or perhaps controlled by the northern business class. R. N. Current, *Old Thad Stevens* (1942) is extremely critical of Stevens.

A revisionist movement is now under way. Robert P. Sharkey, *Money, Class, and Party, An Economic Study of Civil War and Reconstruction* (1959); Eric L. McKitrick, *Andrew Johnson and Reconstruction* (1960); and Stanley Coben, "Northeastern Business and Radical Reconstruction: A Re-examination," *Mississippi Valley Historical Review,* XLVI (June, 1959), 67–90, question the validity of the business domination theme. McKitrick is disposed to lay much more blame on Johnson for the successful development of the radical program than are such authors as Stryker and Beale. See also La Wanda and J. H. Cox, *Politics, Principle and Prejudice: 1865–1866* (1963).

A short but useful survey of the Reconstruction period is W. L. Fleming, *The Sequel to Appomattox* (1919), and the student should also consult the *Documentary History of Reconstruction* (2 vols., 1906) by the same author. A recent and well-written account of the period is Hodding Carter, *The Angry Scar* (1959). Two accounts by Negro scholars are W. E. B. DuBois, *Black Reconstruction* (1935) and the more moderate J. H. Franklin, *From Slavery to Freedom* (1947); see also his *Reconstruction: After the Civil War* (1962). Special monographs of value are J. W. Garner, *Reconstruction in Mississippi* (1901) and F. B. Simkins and R. H. Woody, *South Carolina During Reconstruction* (1932). Also see V. L. Wharton, *The Negro in Mississippi* (1947). The student should also read C. Vann Woodward, *The Strange Career of Jim Crow* (revised ed., 1966); P. H. Buck, *The Road to Reunion, 1865–1900* (1937); chapter VIII in C. N. Degler, *Out of Our Past* (1959); and the biographies listed in the bibliography for chapter XXXI.

For the role of the Freedmen's Bureau, see G. R. Bentley, *A History of the Freedmen's Bureau* (1955).

On the Fourteenth Amendment, see Joseph James, *The Framing of the Fourteenth Amendment* (1956).

Seward's role in the political and diplomatic events of the period is portrayed in Van Deusen, *William Henry Seward,* previously cited. The account of the period in J. G. Randall and D. Donald, *The Civil War and Reconstruction* (2nd ed., 1961) is excellent.

34 ⲉ Enter President Grant

B Y THE TIME the impeachment trial of President Johnson was over, the presidential campaign of 1868 was only months away. There were three fundamental problems likely to influence the voters in that contest, and that therefore might reasonably be expected to mold the character of the party platforms and the choice of candidates. One was the

Political Problems in 1868

Reconstruction policy adopted by the Republican party and embodied in the great Reconstruction Acts passed over Johnson's vetoes: should it be endorsed or repudiated? A second, closely linked to Reconstruction, was Negro suffrage: should it be upheld in principle, denounced as bad practice, or simply left to each state to decide for itself? These were the most important problems, but there was also a third issue: should the financial policy of the government support hard money or soft money? Here a word of explanation is necessary.

When Salmon P. Chase resigned as head of the Treasury Department in 1864, Lincoln had appointed in his place William Pitt Fessenden of Maine. Fessenden took the post only reluctantly, and when the Maine legislature elected him to the United States Senate in January, 1865, he promptly resigned from the Treasury. His successor was Hugh McCulloch, an able and conservative Indiana banker who believed that the Almighty had made gold and silver so that they might serve as measures of value and regulators of trade. The only good currency, in McCulloch's eyes, was specie, or paper amply backed by specie. He looked upon the greenbacks with abhorrence, and promptly initiated a policy of retiring this fiat money that had been issued due to the exigencies of wartime.

The country's supply of legal currency in 1865 amounted to a little over $900 million. Of this, $433,160,000 was in greenbacks, and it took $157 in this paper money to buy $100 in gold. McCulloch wanted to wring the water out of the American monetary system by gradually eliminating this "rag money" from circulation—essentially a policy of contraction and deflation.

Congress gave guarded approval to the deflationary policy in 1866, in a law providing that $10 million of United States notes might initially be retired and after that not more than $4 million in any one month. The Democrats supported this bill, while the radical Republicans split on it, Thad Stevens and George Julian being among the prominent radicals who voted against the measure. Geographically, the chief opposition came from the Middle West and Pennsylvania and Maryland.

During the next two years, McCulloch pursued a policy of contraction, the net change in the total volume of the currency being a decrease of some $45 million. Then, in February, 1868, Congress put a stop to further retirement of paper, the reason for this move being an economic recession, accompanied by falling prices, which particularly affected industrial and commercial interests. Significant Democratic gains in the 1867 state elections also helped to swing a number of Republican votes away from a hard-money policy.

By 1868, both parties had abandoned the policy of contraction. A large Republican majority was in favor of stopping it, and so were western and a majority of eastern Democrats. The swing in Democratic sentiment was largely because of the growing support in Democratic circles for the so-called Ohio or Pendleton Idea.

The proposal associated with the name of that versatile and engaging Democratic politician, "Gentleman George" H. Pendleton of Ohio, was simply that the bond issues of 1862 and 1864 which were redeemable in five and payable after twenty years should be paid off in greenbacks. These amounted to some $600 million. Such a procedure would mean a substantial increase in the amount of greenbacks outstanding, and in this way the currency would be inflated and prices would rise. According to Pendleton, these greenbacks would also more and more replace the national bank notes then in circulation, thus decreasing the incomes of bankers, especially those in the East, the center of banking strength. It was a Democratic proposal, but one strongly opposed by such eastern financiers and politicians as August Belmont and Horatio Seymour of New York, who were very influential in the Democratic party. The project was popular in the West, however, and it was thought certain to play an important part in the campaign of 1868.

The Party Nominations

There was only one possible nomination for the Republicans in 1868, but Salmon P. Chase thought there were two. He was now Chief Justice of the Supreme Court, appointed to that post by Lincoln in 1864, but his heart still yearned after the White House. He was known to be an advocate of Negro suffrage, and Greeley and some other prominent Republicans were his supporters for the nomination. But there was a handicap which could not be overcome: Chase had impartially presided over the impeachment of Johnson—too impartially for the radicals—and this, together with the well-founded suspicion that it mattered little to him which party gave him the accolade, prevented the development of anything like a Chase boom in the Republican camp. Even had his strength been greater than it was, his candidacy would have collapsed before the Republican demand for the Hero of Appomattox.

Grant's name was on every tongue. The conviction was widespread that, having won the war, he could also win the peace. Grant could do everything: bring reconstruction to a successful conclusion, settle the Negro problem, balance the budget, solve the currency question, and promote all-round prosperity. The chorus shouting for his nomination by the Democrats faded after his split with Johnson, but that within the Republican party began early and steadily grew.

Grant himself had never been either a politician or much interested in politics. He had voted for President only once in his life, for Buchanan in 1856. He made no effort to achieve the presidency, either during or immediately after the war, though if he had avowed himself early enough, he could in all probability have had the nomination of either party. The radicals, however, began to woo him early, and his quarrel with Johnson at the time of Stanton's removal threw him into their camp. The Grant boom thereupon assumed monumental proportions, and when the Republican convention met at Chicago on May 20, 1868, he was the only candidate put in nomination for the presidency. As his running mate, the convention chose Schuyler Colfax of Indiana, an amiable politician whose reputation of never having made an enemy or lost a friend had earned him the nickname of "Smiler" Colfax. Everybody felt that the vice-presidential nomination was really unimportant; Grant was what counted, and the Democrats were challenged to "Match Him."

The Republican platform approved the congressional Reconstruction policy. It advocated sound money, specifically the redemption of bonds in coin, not greenbacks. It approved leaving the control of suffrage in the North to the states, but took its stand on suffrage for all "loyal" men in the South.

The Democratic convention met in New York on July 4, in a newly built Tammany Hall, with a number of aspirants clamoring for the presidential nomination. Pendleton was Ohio's candidate; a movement for the nomination of President Johnson had assumed modest proportions; and Chase ardently desired the prize. Some delegates were for General Winfield S. Hancock of Pennsylvania, a hero of the Gettysburg campaign, while others preferred Thomas A. Hendricks, United States Senator from Indiana. There was also considerable support for General Frank P. Blair of Missouri, brother of Montgomery Blair in Lincoln's Cabinet, friend of President Johnson, and a stern critic of radical Reconstruction.

The convention elected Horatio Seymour of New York as its permanent chairman. Lawyer and politician, Seymour had been prominent in the New York Democracy for thirty years. He had served as governor of the state, a fearless critic of Lincoln's Administration, but a loyal supporter of the war. He was a hard-money man, no friend of the "Ohio Idea." His candidate for the nomination was the Ohioan, now Chief Justice, Chase. Seymour had been mentioned repeatedly as a presidential possibility, but had consistently refused to have his name put forward.

Twenty-one ballots were cast for the presidential nominee without decisive result. When on the twenty-second ballot, Seymour was put in nomination, he protested against the use of his name for the fifth time during the convention, but this time it was without avail. Eastern Democrats who would not have Pendleton and western Democrats who disliked Hendricks started an irresistible band-wagon rush. Seymour is the one candidate in the history of the presidency who has been nominated in spite of a sincere desire on his part to avoid the honor. As his running mate, the convention put up Frank Blair.

The Democratic platform declared that all bonds not expressly payable in coin should be redeemed in lawful money (the Ohio Idea) and that government bonds should be taxed. It asserted that the question of Negro suffrage should be left to the states, both North and South. And it declared that the "so-called" Reconstruction Acts of Congress were usurpations, "unconstitutional, revolutionary, and void."

The Campaign of 1868

Contrary to general expectations, the state of the currency was not emphasized in the campaign. Seymour being a hard-money man, the Democrats had executed a "straddle" on the question, and no real money issue developed. The contest was fought mainly over the Reconstruction policy and the way in which it had affected the South.

The Republicans spent a good deal of time glorifying Grant as the conqueror of the rebellion. Four lines from a poem by Miles O'Reilly resounded up and down the land:

> And if asked what State he hails from
> This our sole reply shall be,
> "From near Appomattox Court House,
> With its famous apple tree."

They also emphasized southern outrages against the Negro and declared that Blair's expressed desire for the overthrow of radical Reconstruction meant that a Democratic victory would send revolution flaming up and down the land. The Democrats denied being incendiaries. They denounced congressional Reconstruction as a failure, and called for a restoration of the South that would be fair to all concerned.

Both candidates, as was then the custom, at first declined to campaign. Grant remained silent at his home in Galena, Illinois, but Seymour, as his chances darkened, broke precedent with a speaking tour that extended from Buffalo to Chicago and back to Philadelphia. He identified himself as an exponent of hard money and was dignified and restrained in his condemnation of reconstruction by congressional fiat.

The general tone of the canvass, however, was low. Democratic orators denounced Grant as an incompetent general who had needlessly sacrificed thousands of lives, a thief who had stolen a Mississippi lady's silver, and a drunkard. Colfax, they declared, had been a Know-Nothing and was an enemy of all foreigners and Catholics. The Republicans retorted in kind: Seymour was a Copperhead and a coward, who had incited the New York draft riots in 1863. Bryant, of the New York *Evening Post,* used the suicide of Seymour's father as basis for a charge that the Democratic candidate was tainted with insanity, and viewed with horror the probable event of his becoming incapacitated and that firebrand, Frank Blair, entering the White House; the insanity charge was widely circulated.

In the October elections, Pennsylvania, Ohio, Indiana, and Iowa all went Republican—a foreshadowing of the national outcome. Grant carried twenty-six of the thirty-four states, with an electoral college vote of 214 to eighty for Seymour. The popular vote for the candidate from the apple tree at Appomattox was 3,012,833 to 2,703,249 for his rival. The Republicans increased their already top-heavy majority in the Senate and outnumbered the Democrats in the House by over two to one.

The election, however, had not been as one-sided as these figures appear to indicate. Grant had a popular majority of only some 300,000 votes. Since he carried six of the reconstructed southern states, the 650,000 Negro votes there were a substantial factor in producing this majority. The Democrats carried New York and came close to carrying Pennsylvania. They also increased their membership in the House of Representatives from forty-nine to sixty-three. Despite the identification of the Republican party with victory in the war, the two parties were close to being evenly balanced, and, without Grant's enormous personal prestige, the presidency in 1868 might well have gone to the Democrats.

The significance of the Negro vote was not lost on the Republicans. In 1869, Congress passed the Fifteenth Amendment, which forbade the United States or any state to deny the right of voting to any citizen on account of race, color, or previous condition of servitude. This amendment was the last basic pillar of congressional Reconstruction, and subsequent enforcement acts, which we shall examine later on, were passed to implement and sustain this amendment.

President Grant

Grant did not visualize his presidential function as that of a great chieftain who would solve the nation's problems. Rather, like the West Pointer that he was, he looked to Congress for leadership and conceived of his White House role as one of administration. Above and beyond politics, or so he thought at first, he used his wartime staff officers to set up his presidential entourage and establish a "chain of command" that gave the executive mansion some of the aspects of an army camp.

The new President was the representative, and in some ways the symbol, of a generation that was dynamic and imaginative in a material sense but worshipped success and the acquisition of the dollar. It was an era beginning to feel the impact of social Darwinism, one that tended to equate financial difficulties with feeble character. It lavished millions on railroad projects; gave three times as much land to railroad, coal, and land companies as all the homesteaders received by 1876; and gazed serenely on while stock juggling, gold corners, fraud, and corruption abounded in high places. Like

ULYSSES SIMPSON GRANT
(1822–1885)

Grant was a far greater general than he was President. Here he appears in civilian dress, stodgy, with a faintly puzzled and yet determined expression. He never seems to have doubted his fitness to be President.

the great majority of his contemporaries, Grant never understood the forces operating around him and had no interest in battling for reform.

The President had physical courage in abundance and could on occasion be stubborn and unyielding in pursuit of an objective. He was personally honest; a Puritan so far as his personal morals were concerned, he was also modest, unassuming, kind of heart, and he possessed some sense of humor. But his mind and character were limited in many ways. He was incapable of formulating broad policies and was a poor judge of men, trusting completely those who gave him admiration and loyalty. His narrowness of comprehension led him into unwise decisions and dubious friendships. He wanted to see the Union reunited and the Negro treated fairly, but he had no conception of how to go about reaching these objectives. Henry Adams' caustic remark that Grant disproved the theory of evolution because if it had been true, he would have been extinct centuries ago was altogether too harsh; but the country did have a plodding, unimaginative administrator at its head when it needed a leader who combined the skill of the practical politician with the vision of a statesman.

A Fairly Good Beginning

Grant's inaugural stated his approval of the Fifteenth Amendment and of the hard-money doctrine. Other than these points, it consisted of platitudes. He would have a policy to recommend "on all subjects," but there was no outline of such a policy. The announcement of his Cabinet—which came on March 5—took the country, and even some of the appointees, by surprise. Some of those on the list, such as Elihu B. Washburne for the State Department and Adolph E. Borie for the Navy, were without other qualifications than being friends and patrons of the President. A. T. Stewart, a Philadelphia merchant appointed to the Treasury, could not serve because a law of 1789 prohibited the post to anyone engaged in carrying on trade and commerce. Stewart vainly offered to put his business in trust during his term of office, the proceeds to go to charity, but it was all to no avail; the Senate radicals secured in his place George S. Boutwell, whose only qualification for the position was his vindictive partisanship.

The Cabinet, however, was by no means a total loss. Since Washburne had wanted the State Department only for the honor, he resigned after a few days and was made Minister to France. His successor was Hamilton Fish, a kindly, sensible, and sagacious statesman who had been a competent governor of New York and United States Senator from that state and was destined to serve with distinction in the State Department. There were also two other excellent appointments. Jacob D. Cox, a former governor of Ohio known for his interest in civil service reform, became Secretary of the Interior. The genial and witty E. Rockwood Hoar, a Massachusetts judge with high standards of public service, took the post of Attorney General. These appointments gave tone to an otherwise mediocre assemblage of administrative heads.

It was also refreshing to see a resumption of amicable relations between President and Congress. An act providing for payment "in coin or its equivalent" of the five-twenty government bonds was signed by the chief executive, and steps were taken to hasten the reconstruction of Virginia, Mississippi, and Texas by providing for early votes on their state constitutions. For the time being, both ends of Pennsylvania Avenue appeared to be in sweet accord.

The Alabama Claims

A diplomatic achievement of real significance was the settlement of the *Alabama* claims dispute, which had been in negotiation since the Civil War. The United States had begun asking for redress almost as soon as the notorious raider had left the British Isles, and the demands pressed upon Great Britain covered damages caused not only by the *Alabama* but also by the other Confederate warships that had been built in English ports. Progress in the settlement of these claims had been slow, partly because of British unwillingness to give adequate compensation, and partly because of Seward's unpopularity in the Senate. A convention for the settlement by arbitration of all claims against Great Britain since 1853, which had been carefully worked out by Seward, was rejected in the Senate, and Fish inherited the controversy.

By 1869, Britain had become eager to arbitrate, for the European scene was distinctly troubled. France and Germany were on the verge of conflict, and Russia was manifesting an unfriendly disposition toward England. If the latter should become involved in war, it was more than likely that enemy cruisers would be given carte blanche to outfit in American ports, and this was an eventuality that the English government wished to avoid.

But, though Britain was ready to negotiate, the problem was now complicated on the American side. Charles Sumner was chairman of the powerful Senate Committee on Foreign Relations. He had made a speech on the proposed arbitration in which he demanded that the British government pay both direct and indirect damages, and he presented an itemized bill that assessed actual losses at $15 million. Commerce driven from the oceans of the world, the rise in insurance rates, and losses caused by ships leaving American registry came to $110 million. He also estimated that the aid and comfort given by Britain to the Confederacy had prolonged the war two years, and for this the bill was $2 billion. The grand total was $2.125 billion, and Sumner's intention, which became clear in the speeches of other Senators, was that this should be paid by the cession of Canada to the United States.

There was much sentiment in America for the annexation of Canada, and Grant was at first pleased by Sumner's demand. The President had had some thoughts of taking Canada by force. It was obvious, however, that there was no Canadian sentiment for annexation, and that Britain would never accept responsibility for the "indirect" damages. Fish persuaded

Grant that the best thing to do was to arbitrate. After lengthy negotiations, both sides agreed in 1871 to arbitration by a tribunal of five persons, one each to be selected by the President of the United States, the Queen of Great Britain, the President of the Swiss Confederation, the King of Italy, and the Emperor of Brazil.

The arbitration was almost wrecked when the American claims for indirect damages were brought before the court, but British feelings were placated by the tribunal's opinion that such claims were not a good basis for damages. The British government paid the $15.5 million awarded to the United States for losses inflicted by the *Alabama, Florida,* and *Shenandoah,* and relations between the two countries were once more on an amiable footing.

The Legal-Tender Cases

That the *Alabama* claims were settled in satisfactory fashion was largely due to astute handling by Secretary of State Fish. In the legal-tender cases, it was Grant himself who had to make the crucial decision. The law of February 25, 1862, made greenbacks legal tender in payment of all public and private debts, save for duties on imports and interest on the public debt. They were, as we have seen, a depreciated currency, worth considerably less than gold. The question that arose was whether or not they could be used in payment of debts contracted before the passage of the law of 1862. In *Hepburn v. Griswold* (1870), with Supreme Court Chief Justice Chase rendering the majority opinion, the court ruled five to three that they could not be so used. To make them payable for such debts, it declared, would be a clear impairment of contract and therefore would be unconstitutional. Chase's reasoning also cast doubt on the validity of the greenbacks as legal tender for debts incurred after the passage of the 1862 act.

Before the decision in *Hepburn v. Griswold* was made public, Justice Greer resigned, leaving seven justices on the Supreme Court bench—the number that had been specified by Congress during its quarrel with President Johnson. After Grant's election, however, Congress restored the number of Supreme Court justices to nine, and now Grant had two appointments to make. He immediately appointed William Strong of Pennsylvania and Joseph P. Bradley of New Jersey; it was generally understood that both of these men believed that the greenbacks were constitutional in payment of all debts.

When two more cases involving the legal-tender question (*Knox v. Lee* and *Parker v. Davis*) were argued in 1871, the Court reversed itself and by a five-to-four ruling declared that greenbacks could be used in payment of contracts made before as well as after the passage of the Legal Tender Act. The judges who had been in the majority in the *Hepburn v. Griswold* decision were indignant at the reversal, and Chase, by inference, accused Grant of "packing" the Court. Criticism of that body was widespread among conservatives and continued for many years.

Grant had asked for no commitment, nor had he sought any expression of opinion from Strong and Bradley before they were appointed. He had, however, believed that the first decision was wrong, and he had had evidence before him that his appointees would vote to reverse it. To that extent only, had he "packed" the Court. Though the reversal was in accord with congressional and popular opinion, it did injure the reputation of the Court as an impartial tribunal; to put it another way, the decision helped to destroy the fiction that the Supreme Court always renders its opinions in a judicial vacuum in which political and social pressures have no weight.

The Reconstruction Problem

Reconstruction of the South in accordance with the provisions of the radical Reconstruction Acts had now been accomplished, but the resulting situation was far from stable. The southern state governments furnished many examples of gross corruption, and political factions clashed with one another in a mad race for the spoils of office. In Louisiana, South Carolina, and Arkansas, rival governments were set up, and southern public opinion in state after state was affronted by the travesty on popular government that had been imposed from Washington.

Worse than corruption, from the point of view of many southern whites, was the enforced Negro participation in governmental affairs. It did not matter that the worst excesses were committed, not by Negroes, but by white carpetbaggers and scalawags, nor that the Negroes who won some of the higher offices were about as competent as the average white office-holder. Fear of Negro domination, of the destruction of white supremacy, made the situation intolerable from the point of view of the majority of southern whites. They reacted in determined and sometimes in violent fashion.

Even before the worst effects of radical Reconstruction became apparent, protective and revolutionary clubs of white men began appearing in the

South. They bore a wide variety of titles, such as the "Pale Faces," the "Society of the White Rose," and the "Knights of the White Camelia"— but by far the most important was the Ku Klux Klan.

The Klan was started in Pulaski, Tennessee, in the late summer of 1866 by a group of young soldiers returned from service in the Confederate army. They formed a circle, primarily for social diversion, which was called *Kuklos* from the Greek; this was soon corrupted into Ku Klux, and Klan was added for alliteration. As the idea spread, new Klans, usually called "dens," were formed, and a loose federation of "provinces" culminating in an "empire" appeared, with "ghouls," and "cyclops" as local officials, "grand dragons" higher up, and at the top of the edifice ten "genii" and a "grand wizard." The principles of the Klan, outlined at conventions held in 1867 and 1868, included defense of the Constitution and protection of the weak, innocent, and defenseless, with special reference to the widows and orphans of Confederate soldiers. But as the project caught the popular imagination, so did the idea that it might be used as a means of combating carpetbag rule and teaching the Negro his "proper" place in southern society. From this to violence and crime was only a short step.

At first the various dens confined themselves to frightening the Negroes by riding furiously through their settlements at the dead of night arrayed in white sheets and hoods, burning fiery crosses, or rattling chains or bones in front of Negro cabins. Sometimes a hooded horseman would stop before a Negro's abode, call for a drink in sepulchral tones, and then pour down two pails of water into a concealed rubber bag, remarking that it was the best drink he had had since he had dug himself up from the infernal regions after the battle of Shiloh.

But more and more the Klan became a sponsor of lawlessness and brutality. Its early leaders, such as General Nathan Bedford Forrest, withdrew when cutthroats, horse thieves, and rioters invaded the ranks. Beatings, scourgings, mutilations, and murders of both whites and blacks disgraced the organization. By 1869, the Klan had become more an instrument of crime than simply a means of teaching the Negro to be always respectful to whites and to stay away from the polls on election day.

Congress and northern public opinion reacted strongly to reports of these events in the South. Senator John Sherman of Ohio, brother of General William Tecumseh Sherman, said that the rebel flag was once more afloat in Dixie. Charles Sumner branded the Ku Klux Klan a "fiendish organization," and the New York *Tribune* called it a "secession snake." Congress undertook to compel obedience to the Fourteenth and Fifteenth Amendments, President Grant being in full accord with this effort. On May 31, 1870, an Enforcement Act "guaranteed" Negro voting in the southern states, provided fines and imprisonment for obstruction of voting, and put enforcement under federal marshals and federal courts.

The disorders continued, and a new act was passed in February, 1871, providing for supervison of election under federal court authority and more stringent punishment of offenders. Night riders were particularly active in South Carolina, and in March, 1870, President Grant issued a proclamation calling upon disorderly elements in that state to disperse and also asked for further legislation. In response, Congress passed the Ku Klux Act of April, 1871, giving the Chief Executive power to proclaim martial law in any state or portion thereof and to suspend the writ of habeas corpus in the offending area. Grant thereupon put nine counties in South Carolina under the ban, and hundreds of arrests were made by the federal authorities. Under these various enforcement acts, federal troops in increasing numbers moved into the South. Their activities, together with the increasing disgust of responsible southerners with the Klan, broke the power of that organization by the close of 1871.

The Klan had had little to do with the movement toward giving the South home rule, which developed in large part out of the growing conviction in the North that enforcement of Republican rule with the bayonet was impossible. Republican majorities in the southern states shrank with each election, and it is significant that, though the Ku Klux Act of 1871 easily passed Congress, responsible Republican leaders such as James A. Garfield in the House and Carl Schurz and Lyman Trumbull in the Senate viewed it with alarm as a dangerous invasion of local self-government; federal control cost more than it was worth in terms of ballots. Still another factor in bringing home rule to the South was the role played by southern leaders such as Wade Hampton in South Carolina, Benjamin H. Hill in Georgia, and "Marse" Henry Watterson of Kentucky. Working hand in glove with southern bankers and railroad men, and often with northern financial and industrial interests, these leaders organized conservative party movements that obtained control of one state government after another. Tennessee, Virginia, North Carolina, and Georgia were "redeemed" by 1871, and Texas and Alabama soon followed. As the "redeemers" assumed control, there began to emerge the spectacle of a Solid South, safe in the bosom of the Democratic party. This was done, too, without wholesale disfranchisement of the Negro. White control of the state legislatures was assured, but many Negroes continued to vote. It was not until the turn of the century, for reasons that will be explained in the next volume, that Negro exclusion from the polls and subjection to "Jim Crow" laws became the order of the day.

Grant and the Breath of Scandal

Grant stood loyally by the congressional radicals as they vainly tried to keep their Reconstruction policy alive in the South even though it was a policy that, as Greeley said fretfully in the *Tribune*, lost one southern state after another to the Democracy. The President also never wavered in his devotion to friends and associates who, as time went on, proved to be of a most questionable character. He accepted gifts, for which he sometimes returned favors, and put so many of his relatives in government positions that he was accused of nepotism. He loved to drink whiskey, smoke black cigars, talk about horses, and associate with moneyed men. He willingly accepted entertainment from Jay Gould and Jim Fisk, two of the most notorious rascals in Wall Street.

It was on Gould's recommendation that Grant appointed General Daniel Butterfield as head of the subtreasury in New York when he was deep in a plot engineered by Fisk and Gould to corner the New York gold market in 1869. After the conspirators had pushed the price of gold from 132 to $163\frac{1}{2}$, Grant and Secretary of the Treasury Boutwell began a belated sale of government gold. This broke the corner, but not before importers suffered great losses and hundreds of business firms were seriously crippled. (For details of the gold corner, see Volume II.)

The opposition press, by trying to implicate Grant directly in the gold scandal, produced a reaction in his favor. The affair, however, had aroused considerable scepticism about the quality of his leadership, and succeeding events caused this feeling of doubt to grow.

Grant liked the unscrupulous Senator Ben Butler of Massachusetts, for Butler was a consistent supporter of the President. Attorney General Hoar, also from Massachusetts, was a foe of the Senator, and Butler tried hard to force Hoar's resignation. Partly because of this, and partly because Hoar opposed the annexation of Santo Domingo, upon which Grant had set his heart, the President removed Hoar from the Cabinet in the spring of 1870, appointing in his place a nonentity from the South, Amos T. Ackerman, who was supposed to control several Republican votes in the Senate.

A few months later, Grant dismissed Secretary of the Interior Cox, who had incurred the presidential wrath by trying to keep the Indian Bureau out of politics, and by his efforts to keep certain California mineral lands out of the hands of men who had a questionable claim to them but also had the ear of the President. Two of the three strong men in the Cabinet were now gone, and more than once Secretary Fish was on the point of resignation. The Administration was passing under a cloud, and honest men, concerned for the nation's welfare, were becoming more and more alarmed.

Grant and Diplomacy

As his Administration wore on, Grant concerned himself with two diplomatic problems, one involving Cuba and the other Santo Domingo. In 1868, revolt against Spanish rule broke out in Cuba under the leadership of an outstanding planter and lawyer Don Manuel de Cespedes. The Spanish government was in grave difficulties at home, but it moved with what energy it possessed to snuff out the Cuban insurrection. When savage guerilla warfare ensued, with atrocities committed on both sides, Spain sent thousands of troops to Cuba, and the insurgent cause became increasingly desperate.

It was inevitable that the United States become more than an interested spectator of the Cuban struggle. Cuban juntas established in New York and other American cities engaged in vigorous propaganda and in efforts to aid the insurgents by raising funds and by shipments of munitions and supplies. The United States government moved slowly at first in enforcing its neutrality, and Spain protested with vigor. Popular sympathy with the rebellion mounted in the United States, and a clamor arose for recognition of Cuban independence and even for annexation of the island.

Secretary Fish was doubtful of the success of the rebellion and had no interest whatever in annexation. He strove to avoid the danger of war with Spain, as well as the vexing problems that would be involved in any recognition of belligerency or independence, and in this he was backed by Senator Sumner, chairman of the Senate Foreign Relations Committee. At the same time, Fish tried unsuccessfully to get Spain to initiate a reform program in Cuba. He also urged Spain to liberate the island and the Cubans to pay $100 million or more (guaranteed by the United States) to the Spanish government.

Grant's sympathies were with the insurgents. In this he was influenced by Secretary of War Rawlins, a thorough-paced expansionist. At one point, the President signed a proclamation recognizing Cuban belligerency, and gave it to Fish to issue at an appropriate time. While the President wavered on the question of recognition and then became enthusiastic in support of it, months went by without any firm Administration policy on the problem. Finally, in June, 1870, Fish literally forced Grant's support of his own stand by a threat of resignation. The President then turned to another project that commanded his attention, the annexation of Santo Domingo.

Agitation for the acquisition of Santo Domingo was largely due to the efforts of two unscrupulous adventurers, William L. Cazneau and Joseph W. Fabens. As we have seen, the Senate rejected annexation of the Dominican Republic during the Johnson Administration, but Cazneau and Fabens continued to urge their schemes after Grant took office, obtaining fabulous concessions from Buenaventura Baez, the Dominican dictator. Various and sundry New York financiers became interested in what promised to be a financially profitable exploitation of the republic. The Baez government, which was out of funds, favored annexation, and some sentiment for it developed in the United States.

Among those favorable to annexation was President Grant, the advantages of possessing this lush tropical isle having been presented to him in glowing terms by Fabens and his associates. Grant sent his private secretary, Orville E. Babcock, to investigate the situation on the island. Without authority to do so, Babcock signed a treaty of annexation conditioned upon a plebiscite; the price to be paid to Santo Domingo was $1.5 million in gold.

Grant ordered Fish to draft a treaty of annexation based on the paper Babcock had brought back from Santo Domingo, and the Secretary reluctantly did so. On January 10, 1870, Grant presented this document to the Senate. There it encountered strong and mounting opposition, with Charles Sumner as the leader. Many Senators, and much public sentiment, opposed taking over a tropical outpost filled with an ignorant population. Senate jealousy of the executive branch of the government was also a factor. The opposition pointed to the dubious character of the promoters, and this, together with a well-founded rumor that Babcock was financially interested in the project, aroused resentment. Despite Grant's use of the executive patronage and other pressures, the Senate rejected the treaty, on June 30, 1870. After this signal defeat, the President was bitter against Sumner, and instrumental in his removal as chairman of the Senate Foreign Relations Committee. Sumner was furious. Standing in his own front door, across the square from the White House, he would shout his denunciation of the President in tones easily audible in the White House grounds.

The Liberal Republican Movement

During the years between 1868 and 1872, a movement of revolt against Grant and his policies developed in the Republican party. It was chiefly liberal in character, although it early suffered an infusion of practical politics, and its sponsors called themselves Liberal Republicans.

There were a number of specific reasons for the rise of Liberal Republicanism. Some elements in the party favored a lowering of the tariff. After the war, the vast system of internal taxation, including an income tax levied between 1862 and 1872, was swept away, but the high protective duties remained. Efforts made in 1867 and again in 1870 to lower the tariff failed, and the West especially was becoming dissatisfied with a protective system under which only Ohio and Michigan farmers were appeased by the duty on wool.

Grant, like the Congress, was indifferent to the rising demand for tariff reform. Another movement in which he and the radical Republicans had no interest was civil service reform. Stimulated by the abuses of the spoils system and by England's reform of its civil service, demands increased for a system of civil service examinations, together with specified terms of office for government officeholders. Prominent Republicans such as Senators Schurz and Trumbull were ardent supporters of this idea, as was Secretary of the Interior Jacob Cox. But Cox was dismissed, and Grant gave only the most perfunctory support to proposals for a civil service act.

Advocates of a tariff for revenue, and civil service reformers, were becoming more and more dissatisfied with the Administration's indifference to their proposals. Many Republicans, too, became alarmed by Grant's lack of sensitivity in regard to his associates. The gold corner scandal of 1869, Babcock's dubious character, and the President's willingness to be entertained by Jim Fisk (whom he rightly regarded as being destitute of moral character) irritated and disgusted a growing number of people.

Another cause of the liberal movement was the widespread laxity in standards among public officials throughout the nation. Corruption was by no means confined to the carbetbag governments of the South. The governor of Nebraska was tried and convicted of embezzling state school funds. Two United States Senators from Kansas, Pomeroy and Caldwell, were elected only by the grossest bribery. The treasurer of the state of Pennsylvania, William H. Kemble, was convicted of bribery and sentenced to prison; his motto, it appeared, was "addition, division, and silence." There were enormous frauds in the New York customs, and in 1871 the gross thievery and corruption of the Tweed Ring in New York came to light. Everywhere men began asking if something could not be done to bring a higher tone to the public service, and many felt that it was incumbent upon the national Administration to pave the way to reform.

Another fundamental cause of dissatisfaction was the situation in the reconstructed South. As the passions of war cooled, it became apparent that radical Reconstruction could only be maintained by federal bayonets, and that force was not preventing the steady growth of the Conservative-

Democratic movement which was cutting the ground out from under the Republican organizations in the southern states. Important Republican leaders, north and south, were asking if the time had not come for a general amnesty, the return of home rule to the southern commonwealths, and an end to the attempt to force wholesale Negro suffrage on the South.

The congressional elections of 1870 gave point to the movement for reform within the Republican party: the Democrats gained six seats in the Senate and forty-one in the House. Never again were the Republicans to have a two-thirds majority in the latter body, and the situation in Congress had become such that Grant could not be sure of support for his policies in the lower house.

One of the outstanding features of the election of 1870 was the victory of the Liberals in Missouri. There a movement had risen in the Republican party for the removal of loyalty test oaths prescribed in the state constitution. Its leaders were B. Gratz Brown, a versatile politician with flaming red hair and beard, and Carl Schurz, a spare-visaged, eloquent, and energetic reformer who had fled from Germany after the 1848 revolutions there, and whose varied and brilliant career since coming to the United States had brought him to the editorship of a St. Louis newspaper. The Democrats came to the support of Brown and Schurz. The former was elected governor by a 40,000 majority, and Schurz was sent to the United States Senate.

Liberals everywhere were encouraged by the victory in Missouri. In Massachusetts, revolt spread against the domineering ways of Grant's friend, General Ben Butler. In New York, the organizations of Governor Reuben Fenton and Senator Roscoe Conkling were at war with one another, with Greeley and the *Tribune* supporting Fenton while Grant backed Conkling. Similar feuds existed in Pennsylvania and in the Middle West. As Liberalism gathered force, factions annoyed with Grant trooped to the Liberal flag, which meant a gain in numbers. It also meant the presence of more and more practical politicians interested only in victory at the polls and indifferent to reform.

Despite this infusion of practical politics, the Liberal movement gained headway. Sparked by the passionate idealism of Schurz and the tempestuous vigor of Brown, aided by four powerful newspaper editors—Samuel Bowles of the Springfield (Massachusetts) *Republican,* Murat Halstead of the Cincinnati *Commercial,* Horace White of the Chicago *Tribune,* and Colonel "Marse" Watterson of the Louisville *Courier-Journal*—the Liberals began laying plans for a ticket of their own in the national campaign of 1872.

Presidential Nominations in 1872

Early in the year, Liberal leaders issued a call for a national convention to meet in Cincinnati on May 1, 1872. Assembled, it proved to be a heterogeneous gathering of earnest idealists, doctrinaires, faddists, and practical politicians. With difficulty, they built a platform with planks on which were stamped acceptance of the war amendments, universal amnesty, local self-government, and civil service reform, but with no mention of a lower tariff. Greeley had declared that a tariff for revenue plank would forfeit the New York *Tribune's* support, and the reformers were sure that they could nominate a man who would be in sympathy with pushing the tariff downward.

The platform having been constructed, there followed a bitter squabble over the nomination. Politicians led by Fenton and Colonel A. K. McClure of Pennsylvania were determined to nominate Supreme Court Justice David Davis, a man of wealth and no particular political convictions who was nominally a Republican, was popular with conservative Democrats, and whose "radical" views had made him the candidate of a group of labor reformers. When the four newspaper editors—who became known as the Quadrilateral—refused to support Davis, his candidacy faded. Many Liberals wanted to nominate Charles Francis Adams of Massachusetts, but this roused the ire of Brown and his supporters, who then threw their strength to Greeley, the candidate of the New York delegation. The cry arose "Anybody to beat Grant," and on the sixth ballot Greeley was nominated, with Brown for Vice President.

The nomination of Greeley was scarcely a triumph for the cause of reform. The peppery editor had strength in the West because of his long standing advocacy of free land and a Pacific railroad, and many southern Republicans liked him because since the war he had pleaded for universal amnesty and impartial suffrage. But he was volatile and had little political sense. He was also one of the most extreme protectionists living and was lukewarm on civil service reform. Furthermore, since the hope of success in the campaign hinged upon Democratic support, it was scarcely good policy to nominate a man who had warred with that party for thirty years, and who was known to have remarked that, while not every Democrat was a horse thief, every horse thief was a Democrat. Bryant, Godkin of the *Nation,* Schurz, and Gideon Welles, all prominent in the Liberal movement, felt bitterly affronted and supported the ticket only with the greatest reluctance.

The Liberal Conspirators (1872)

United States Senators Schurz, Trumbull, Tipton, and Sumner consider-
ing Greely as a candidate. Horace, grotesquely arrayed in Roman cos-
tume, top hat, and white coat, is apparently absorbed in his New York
Tribune. This is a Thomas Nast Cartoon.

The machine-controlled Republican convention that met early in June
at Philadelphia nominated Grant without opposition, on a platform endorsing the hero and all his works and standing clearly for the radical
Reconstruction policy and for a protective tariff.

The Democrats met at Baltimore on July 9. For them to put up a
separate ticket meant splitting the opposition to the Grant Administration
and certain defeat. In bitterness of spirit, they nominated Greeley and
accepted verbatim the Cincinnati platform.

The Campaign of 1872

The election of 1872 was one of the most dismal political contests in
the nation's history. The Republicans collected large sums of money from
businessmen and officeholders. Their state campaigns were carefully organ-

ized, and in the South they had the support of prominent Confederate leaders like Generals Gideon Pillow and Nathan Bedford Forrest, who could not accept Greeley. Like many others among the redeemers, these men had no love for Grant, but still less for the man whose paper had pilloried the South for years before the Civil War.

The Liberal Republicans and Democrats were not as well organized as the regular Republicans, they did not have as much money, and many of the reforming spirits in their ranks were cool to their candidate.

While Grant stayed at home, Greeley made a spirited campaign. He demanded a "New Departure," saying his administration would stand on universal amnesty, equal rights for all, thrift and honesty. It would lead the way to an era of peace and prosperity, one in which Negro and white would live and work together for a greater American nation.

A large part of the campaign was devoted to vilification, with Greeley the principal target. "Old Chappaquack" (his home was in Chappaqua, New York) was subjected to a torrent of abuse. The Republicans declared that he planned to pay the Confederate debt and pension the soldiers of the Confederacy, and his violent attacks on the Democracy during past years were exhumed and printed. The eminent cartoonist Thomas Nast pictured him as catering to Tweed, and as clasping hands with John Wilkes Booth across Lincoln's grave. Frederick Douglass's *The New National Era,* the leading Negro newspaper in the United States, denounced Greeley as one who had never been a genuine foe of slavery.

The October elections went Republican—omens, as usual, of what would happen in November. When election day came, Greeley carried only six states—Georgia, Kentucky, Maryland, Missouri, Tennessee, and Texas—with sixty-six electoral votes to 286 for Grant. The Liberal Republican candidate had only 43.8 per cent of the total vote, and the Republicans substantially increased their majority in the House of Representatives.

Greeley's defeat ended in personal tragedy. Exhausted by his efforts and by constant watching at the bedside of his dying wife, so overwhelmed by contumely that, as he wrote to a friend, he scarcely knew whether he was running for the presidency or the penitentiary, he emerged from the campaign in a morbid frame of mind. When he found that he was not only in financial straits but had also lost control of the *Tribune,* he sank into a deep despondency and died (November 29, 1872).

The campaign of 1872 had been tragic for Greeley and deeply disappointing for the Liberal Republicans, but it had considerable historical significance. It demonstrated the existence of a ground-swell movement for reform and for reconciliation with the South. This spurred the Republican Congress in May, 1872, to pass a General Amnesty Act which, with some exceptions, removed disqualifications from officeholding on Confederate leaders. It influenced Grant to put in his message to Congress in December, 1872, recommendations for civil service reform. The campaign was also the means by which the Democratic party was put on record as accepting the war amendments, thus eliminating the possibility of any violent overturn of the southern situation. Last, but by no means least, the outcome of the contest demonstrated once more the potential strength of the Democracy. In the fifteen ex-slaveholding states the Republicans received only 50.1 per cent of the vote. Since many northern Democrats stayed away from the polls altogther, rather than vote for Greeley, the narrow Republican victories in such states as New York, New Jersey, and Indiana could only be regarded as ominous for that party. If Republicanism was to remain in control of the nation, it behooved Grant's second Administration to record some substantial achievements.

Suggested Reading

The student of the economic problems of this period should consult D. R. Dewey, *Financial History of the United States* (1934); W. C. Mitchell, *A History of the Greenbacks* (1903); F. W. Taussig, *The Tariff History of the United States* (1923); and R. P. Sharkey, *Money, Class, and Party,* cited in the previous chapter. For the "Ohio Idea," see also C. A. Destler, *American Radicalism, 1865–1901: Essays and Documents* (1945).

C. H. Coleman, *The Election of 1868* (1933) is a useful monograph. See also Duberman, *Adams,* already cited, and Stewart Mitchell, *Horatio Seymour* (1938).

There is no definitive life of Grant. The late Lloyd Lewis' *Captain Sam Grant* (1950) is brilliant, and Bruce Catton's *Grant Moves South* (1960) places the continuation of this study in competent hands. W. B. Hesseltine, *Ulysses S. Grant* (1935) is as good a one-volume biography as is available. The student should not neglect Grant's own *Personal Memoirs of U. S. Grant* (2 vols., 1885–1886).

On Reconstruction, in addition to the books cited in the previous chapter, see C. Vann Woodward, *Origins of the New South, 1877–1913* (1951).

The story of Grant's first term is told, with some bias, in the second and third volumes of E. P. Oberholtzer, *A History of the United States Since the Civil War* (5 vols., 1917–1937). Useful are Hugh McCulloch, *Men and Measures of Half a Century* (1888); John Sherman, *Recollections of Forty Years* (2 vols., 1895), and J. G. Blaine, *Twenty Years of Congress* (2 vols., 1884). Allan Nevins, *Hamilton Fish*

(1936) is an important study which deals especially with diplomatic aspects. The Santo Domingo episode is also examined in C. C. Tansill, *The United States and Santo Domingo, 1789–1873* (1938).

S. F. Horn, *Invisible Empire* (1939) is a sympathetic study of the Ku Klux Klan. The exploits of Gould and Fisk are dealt with in Julius Grodinsky, *Jay Gould: His Business Career, 1867–1892* (1957) and R. H. Fuller, *Jubilee Jim, the Life of Colonel James Fisk, Jr.* (1928).

For the Liberal Republican movement and the campaign of 1872, see, in addition to the works already mentioned, E. D. Ross, *The Liberal Republican Movement* (1919), G. G. Van Deusen, *Horace Greeley, Nineteenth Century Crusader* (1953), and Eric Goldman's opening chapters in *Rendezvous with Destiny* (1955).

35 ' The End of an Era

GRANT REGARDED himself as vindicated by the election of 1872. He thought of that contest, says Allan Nevins, "as simply an impertinence," and his complacency increased when it developed immediately after the election that some of the prominent members of Congress were involved in a disgraceful scandal.

Congressional Scandals

A construction company known as the Credit Mobilier had been organized to finance the building of the Union Pacific Railroad. T. C. Durant, a vice president of the Union Pacific helped to establish this company, and Oakes Ames, a manufacturer of shovels and a member of Congress, was one of its directors. The members of the Credit Mobilier were also promoters of the railroad, and they used their positions with the road to award profitable contracts to the construction company. In one year, Credit Mobilier paid between 340 and 350 per cent dividends. The Union Pacific cost at least $50 million to build, and when completed in 1869 it was on the verge of bankruptcy, while the construction company had made some $23 million in profits.

Building a railroad by means of a construction company was an accepted practice in this period. The huge profits of the insiders, however, could scarcely be justified as in the public interest. The members of Credit Mobilier, moreover, had engaged in some definitely shady practices. The law required that the stock of the road be paid for in cash, but the construction company had evaded such payment for its Union Pacific holdings; inquiry in regard to this would be embarrassing to the men concerned. When it developed in addition that a bill to regulate rates on the Union Pacific was being introduced in Congress, Ames took steps to prevent any investigation of the way in which the road was being built. Starting in December, 1867, he began distributing stock in Credit Mobilier to various Senators and Representatives at its par value, when it was worth at least double that amount. Others who were carried on account were told that they could pay for the stock out of dividends received.

The news of Ames's doings which appeared in a garbled form in the New York *Sun* during the 1872 campaign was apparently discounted as one of the usual election-time lies. As soon as Congress met in December of that year, however, investigating committees were appointed by both House and Senate. They found that among those receiving the Ames largesse were Senator James W. Patterson of New Hampshire, Senator Henry Wilson of Massachusetts, who had just been elected Vice President on the Grant ticket, James A. Garfield of Ohio, and Schuyler Colfax, the retiring Vice President.

Ames had distributed the stock, not as a bribe for the commission of specific acts, but rather with the idea that those who received it would thereafter be guided as legislators by their vested interest in Credit Mobilier. A number of those involved canceled their acceptance of stock before receiving any dividends. Though Garfield took oath that he had received no money, in Oakes Ames's memorandum book he was listed as having received $1,376; the evidence indicates that he either swore falsely, or had an absolutely unreliable memory. When Garfield appealed to his constituents, they supported him, and he remained in public life. Colfax, who was down for $1,200 in the same book, denied receiving the money; the ensuing investigation showed not only that he had perjured himself, but also disclosed that, while chairman of the Post Office Committee in the House, he had been paid $4,000 by G. F. Nesbitt of New York, to whom large contracts for government envelopes had been awarded. Colfax left Washington in disgrace on March 4, 1873, his public career at an end.

The disgust with which upright men regarded the venality of their representatives was deepened when, on March 3, 1873, the Forty-Second Congress passed what became known as "The Back Pay Steal," or "Salary Grab." This, bill increased the salary of the President from $25,000 to $50,000, and raised the pay of the Vice President, the judges of the Supreme Court, the Cabinet, and the Speaker of the House. The ire of the populace was roused by the fact that the same piece of legislation not only raised the salaries of Senators and Congressmen from $5,000 to $7,500, but made this increase retroactive for two years. A furious outcry resulted, and the next Congress repealed all of the increases save those of the President and the members of the Supreme Court.

The Panic of 1873

As the Forty-Second Congress ended its career, rising storm clouds began foreshadowing the end of the prosperity that had so far characterized the post-Civil War era. The panic that descended upon the country in 1873 was world-wide. A series of wars, together with feverish railroad development, had unsettled the European economy. The depression which began in Vienna in May, 1873, and spread through Europe, with London being especially affected, soon involved the United States.

For the past eight years, there had been marked expansion in the American building trades, especially in the building of railroads. The latter had doubled from 35,000 to 70,000 miles, and two-thirds of this had been in the West, mostly in thinly settled regions. Such roads were, for the time being, unprofitable. In the year before the panic began, for example, only one-third of the 350 railroad companies in the United States paid any dividends. The industry was in a dangerously overextended condition.

There was overinvestment also in the iron industry, largely due to the demands of the railways. The debts of western farmers had steadily increased as they bought land and labor-saving machinery, and their dissatisfaction with interest payments and railroad charges was beginning to cast a pall over the economic situation. So, too, did the growing distrust of big business resulting from the Credit Mobilier scandal, and the mounting anxiety caused by the unfavorable balance of trade with Europe that had existed since the Civil War. As European investors, caught in the depression overseas, began to unload their American securities and gold shipments to Europe increased, it became apparent that money was very tight. The country was about to pay the penalty for the exuberant optimism of the business class.

The panic was touched off by the failure of Jay Cooke and Company. This banking firm had become heavily committed to financing the Northern Pacific Railroad, advancing money for the construction of the road and underwriting its seven-thirty bonds at a price to yield nearly 8.5 per cent. After the road, pushing far into the Northwest, was unable to make returns, and its assets had become "frozen," Cooke and Company were unable to market more bonds. During the summer and fall, the money available to the bank was drained to the West to help in seasonal crop shipments, and the situation of the New York branch became desperate. On September 18, 1873, it closed its doors, and the Philadelphia branch followed suit.

Cooke and Company had been regarded as such a financial Rock of Gibraltar that in Philadelphia a policeman arrested a newsboy crying an extra with the story of the bank's failure. Everywhere consternation reigned, and a rush for ready money ensued. Stocks fell, railroads began to go into bankruptcy, and on September 20 the New York Stock Exchange closed for ten days. By the end of the year there had been 5,000 commercial failures in the United States, with liabilities of over $225 million, and eighty-nine railroads had defaulted on their bonds. Railroad construction came to a halt in 1874, throwing half a million men out of work. Bankruptcies multiplied, unemployment grew, and by the winter of 1874–1875 bread lines were a common sight in the great cities. Between 1873 and 1876, mercantile failures amounted to $775 million, and railroad defaults by January 1, 1876, were $779 million. As the American economic machine slowed down, farmers became resentful over sinking markets and continued high railroad rates, and labor was badly hurt. For over five years, the nation's economy remained in a dismal condition.

Jay Cooke's subsequent career showed that he was the child of fortune as well as misfortune. The failure of his banking firm caused his financial ruin. Discharged from bankruptcy in 1876, he still possessed his organizing ability. He supervised the building of a railroad to the Silver Horn mine in Utah and helped negotiate the sale of the mining property. For these services, he received 40,000 shares of the mine's stock, together with commissions. The mine was fabulously rich, and by 1880 he was again a wealthy man, worth close to $1 million. Until his death in 1905, he was in very comfortable circumstances.

Inflation or Deflation?

The onset of the depression produced a renewal of the battle over inflation. Demand rose for the issuance of more greenbacks, and the cry was loudest in the West. The proponents of this policy claimed that it would stimulate prices and encourage the resumption of business activity. Those opposed declared with equal heat that inflating the currency would foster a resumption of speculation, and prevent the "water" of overexpansion from being wrung out of the economic system.

The inflationists were encouraged by two factors in the situation. William A. Richardson—a plodding, unimaginative lawyer and political opportunist, who had replaced Boutwell as Secretary of the Treasury in March, 1873—had during the previous year, while Under-Secretary of the Treasury, re-issued $5 million of the $44 million greenbacks retired by Secretary Mc-Culloch; this had been a political move, designed to help the western Republicans in the election. Taken in conjunction with Richardson's known aptitude for compliance, his appointment seemed to indicate that a policy of inflation was looked upon with favor by the government. This seemed all the more likely, since Grant, himself a westerner and beset by supporters of inflation such as Senators Oliver P. Morton of Indiana and John A. Logan of Illinois, was wavering on the monetary issue.

Richardson, under pressure from the inflationist elements, kept putting more greenbacks into circulation, until by the early part of 1874 he had issued $26 million. That there were now $382 million in greenbacks outstanding was unsatisfactory to the inflationists, who talked of pushing the irredeemable paper issue up to $800 million. Congress, however, was more moderate, and in April, 1874, it passed a bill providing for an increase of the greenbacks outstanding to $400 million, at the same time providing for an increase of $46 million in national bank notes.

Grant wanted to sign this bill, and the country expected that he would do so. Though he wrote a message defending it, finally, influenced by protests from New York City financial leaders and by the stern opposition of Secretary Fish, he tore up his message and vetoed the bill.

Grant's veto was perhaps wise. Deflation was not yet far advanced, and the bill might have been made an opening wedge for extreme inflation. On the other hand, the inflation which the measure proposed was moderate, and Congress was scarcely in the mood for extreme monetary measures. The most that can be said is that the enthusiastic response of businessmen, East and West, to the veto showed that Grant's action had the support of the conservative urban elements.

The elections of 1874 showed, as always, that the country was disposed to blame the party in power for hard times. The Republicans held their majority in the Senate by a reduced margin, but the House Democrats rose in number from 92 to 169 and took over control of the lower chamber. Missouri, Indiana, and Illinois went Democratic, and Alabama moved out from under Republican control and into the camp of the Redeemers.

Despite defeat at the polls, the Republican leadership was determined to nail the party's flag to the hard-money staff. Secretary of the Treasury Richardson, heartily disliked by eastern financiers, resigned in 1874, and in his place Grant appointed Benjamin H. Bristow, a western hard-money man. Partly because of Bristow's insistence, and partly because of that of the President, the congressional Republicans in the "lame-duck" session of 1874–1875 passed the Resumption of Specie Payment Act, which provided for subsidiary silver coins to replace the fractional currency notes then in circulation; its most significant provision, however, was that specie payments should be resumed by January 1, 1879. For each $100.00 in new national bank notes issued, the Treasury was to withdraw $80.00 in greenbacks, and, at the same time, by using surplus specie in the Treasury and by selling bonds for coin, the Treasury was to build up its gold reserve so that the greenbacks still outstanding in 1879 would be backed by specie. The inflationists had been defeated for the time being, but it would not be long before they turned their attention from paper to silver as an inflationary medium.

Cuba Again

While the American people became engulfed in the woes of the depression, the Cuban revolution was continuing its long-drawn-out course. In its first four years, it cost 150,000 lives, and the destruction of property ran into hundreds of millions of dollars. Among those suffering losses were the holders of American estates, which were impounded and often damaged. United States citizens, too, were seized and imprisoned by the Spanish authorities in Cuba, to the mounting ire of the American government, which could only make impotent protest and continue to demand Cuban reforms. The Spaniards, in their turn, made repeated representations in Washington about filibustering expeditions originating in the United States. The Cuban situation presented the one major foreign-policy problem of the Grant Administration's second term.

In its pressure for reform in Cuba that would help pacify the insurgents, and for the abolition of slavery, the Administration moved to the verge of asking Congress to establish discriminatory duties against Cuba, Puerto Rico, and Brazil. This would have been a heavy blow to the Cuban sugar planters, who were opposing all concessions to the guerillas that were harassing the island, and were determined to maintain slavery. The Spanish government did, indeed, free the slaves in Puerto Rico, but no such reform appeared in Cuba, and the establishment of a republic at Madrid in February, 1873, brought only a temporary improvement of relations.

Early in November, 1873, an event occurred which threatened to bring Spain and the United States into open conflict. The *Virginius,* a ship flying the American flag, was notoriously engaged in carrying arms and munitions to the Cuban insurgents. The Spaniards seized the *Virginius* on the high seas off the coast of Jamaica, and the authorities at Santiago promptly court-martialed and shot fifty-three of its passengers and crew. Among a number of Americans thus summarily dealt with was the captain of the ship, Joseph Fry of Louisiana.

The news of the bloody deed at Santiago produced much excitement in New York and other eastern cities. Secretary Fish promptly lodged a vigorous protest at Madrid, and the United States government began making preparations for war. Fish was at first determined to exact a full apology, together with monetary compensation and punishment of the Spanish officials at Santiago. Investigation, however, disclosed that the right of the *Virginius* to fly the American flag was more than doubtful, for the ship was actually owned by the New York Cuban junta and was falsely registered in the name of an American citizen. When Spain surrendered the *Virginius* and its survivors to United States authorities, and paid an indemnity of $80,000 for capturing the ship on the high seas and for the execution of American citizens, the government at Washington was glad to regard the incident as closed. War with Spain had been averted.

Corruption and Lax Administration

The Spanish crisis had been handled in creditable fashion, due largely to Secretary Fish. It constituted the brightest spot in the second Grant Administration. From 1872 to 1877 came a series of episodes which reflected discredit upon the President, the executive departments at Washington, and the nation as a whole.

It speedily developed that James Watson Webb, Minister to Brazil from 1861 to 1869, had pocketed money which he had hectored Brazil into paying on an unjust damage claim; the United States had to make restitution to the Brazilian government. Moreover, the Minister to Great Britain, Robert C. Schenck, a Grant appointee, had sold his name to the promoters of a bogus American mining concern, and the promoters used his endorsement to mulct British investors out of vast sums of money. The American consular service too, which had never been high in character, descended to still lower levels, because of the disgraceful character of some of Grant's selections.

Worse than the scandals in the foreign service were those that involved Grant's official family. When W. W. Belknap, Secretary of War, was impeached by the House of Representatives for the sale of trading posts in Indian Territory, Grant accepted his resignation before his trial: he was acquitted by what amounted to a strict party vote, on the excuse that the

Senate lacked jurisdiction, but he was clearly guilty. William A. Richardson, Secretary of the Treasury, who was involved in a disreputable scheme for extorting money from internal revenue tax evaders, resigned before the House could pass a vote of censure. The Attorney General, George H. Williams, resigned under suspicion of gross laxity, if not corruption, in the conduct of his office. Columbus Delano, Secretary of the Interior, resigned under charges of graft in Indian affairs. It also developed that George M. Robeson, Secretary of the Navy, had been grossly negligent in awarding navy contracts.

Grant was notoriously unwilling to believe evidence of corruption in those who supported him, and in most cases he accepted only with reluctance the resignations of the men under fire. He had implicit faith in his private secretary, Orville E. Babcock—a smooth, ingratiating, and consummate rascal, who was working hand in glove with a Whiskey Ring, centered at St. Louis, that, in the short space of two years, defrauded the government of over $4 million in tax revenue. He was brought to trial with other members of the Ring, and Benjamin H. Bristow, the new Secretary of the Treasury, pushed the prosecution of the criminals. Grant, who had third-term leanings, became convinced that Bristow was anxious for Babcock's condemnation so that he himself might climb to the White House by destroying the President's reputation. In part because of this, but mainly on account of his loyalty to his secretary, the President gave a sworn statement as to Babcock's integrity; this swayed the jury, and Babcock was the only member of the Ring brought to trial who was acquitted. Grant retained him for a few days as his secretary and then replaced him with his own son, U. S. Grant, Jr.

The Southern Situation

Growing evidences of ineptitude and scandal in the Administration at Washington added to Republican woes in the South. There the carpetbagger governments maintained themselves only with difficulty, where they did not slip out from under Republican rule. To all appearances, however, the President remained oblivious to the alteration in his party's fortunes below the Mason and Dixon line, and, even though the Republican hold in the South steadily weakened, his policy there remained unchanged.

The government of Louisiana was under the control of radical William Pitt Kellogg, assisted by carpetbagger S. B. Packard and Grant's brother-in-law, James F. Casey. It was a corrupt rule, maintained only by the presence of federal troops and the support of the government at Washington. The Kellogg clique controlled the returning board, which threw out many Conservative-Democratic returns in the election of 1874 but nevertheless failed to produce a Republican legislature. When the Conservative-Democrats tried to organize the House, Governor Kellogg appealed to General Sheridan, who had been sent down to Louisiana by Grant, and the legislature was forcibly dispersed. This roused such violent northern protests against military coercion of a duly elected state legislature that Grant reluctantly yielded to a compromise. The Conservative-Democrats were allowed to control the Louisiana lower House, on promise not to try to impeach Governor Kellogg.

Grant also wanted to overturn by force the regularly elected Conservative-Democratic government of Arkansas. He gave up the idea when prominent Republicans joined congressional Democrats in protest.

The 1876 Conventions

When the Republicans gathered in their national convention at Cincinnati, on June 14, 1876, they were in sad need of an outstanding candidate for the presidency. Grant had announced, in qualified fashion, that he would not seek a third term; no one wanted him, save those who would profit by continued laxity in high places, and he was not seriously considered. The leading contender for the nomination was James G. Blaine of Maine.

It was often said that the mantle of Henry Clay had fallen upon the shoulders of witty and magnetic Blaine, who was skilled in the arts of political management. He had been a member of the House of Representatives since 1863, serving as Speaker of the House from 1869 to 1875. Classed as a moderate liberal, he was a leader of the Half Breeds (Republicans critical of Grant), as opposed to Roscoe Conkling of the Stalwarts (100 per cent for Grant and his policies), and the two men were sworn enemies. Blaine's followers went to Chicago with nearly 300 sure votes, less than 100 short of the necessary majority.

But all Blaine's popularity and charm had to be weighed against a grave indiscretion. Some months before the convention, an investigation by the Judiciary Committee of the House of Representatives produced evidence that when the Little Rock and Fort Smith Railroad—for which Blaine had at one time acted as a broker—had failed, the Union Pacific had taken some of its worthless bonds off Blaine's hands and had given him $64,000 which had never been repaid. Furthermore, certain letters that Blaine had written to a Mr. Fisher of the Little Rock and Fort Smith

RUTHERFORD B. HAYES (1822–1893)   SAMUEL J. TILDEN (1814–1886)

The presidential rivals of 1876. Both were patriots, reformers, and astute politicians. Tilden was the more brilliant of the two, Hayes steadier and less mercurial in temperament. Had the latter been elected, his policies would probably have been very similar to those of Hayes.

(now in the possession of one James Mulligan) were supposed to contain evidence that Blaine had received the money from the Union Pacific and had promised to be useful to that road.

Mulligan came to Washington to testify before the committee. Blaine called on him, asked to examine the letters, and then refused to give them up. He read parts of them before the House in a dramatic scene, and such was his personal popularity that his colleagues gave him an ovation. When the Republican convention met, he was nominated by the celebrated orator Robert G. Ingersoll, who called him "a plumed knight" who "marched down the halls of the American Congress and threw his shining lance full and fair against the brazen forehead of every traitor to his country and every maligner of his fair reputation." The suspicion of unsavory doings remained, however, and the steady opposition of the reform element and Senator Conkling defeated the nomination of the man from Maine.

During the first six ballots at Cincinnati, the vote for Rutherford B. Hayes of Ohio steadily increased. A Whig lawyer who had turned Republican in 1855, he had served in the Union army and had then been three times elected governor of Ohio. Men regarded him as a mild reformer. Quiet and unobtrusive, his clothes always ill-fitting and his long beard a bit scraggly, he had a commonplace, middle-class appearance that helped to make him a symbol of honesty and good government. He was nominated on the seventh ballot, to the great delight of the reform element, especially those who, like Schurz, had gone back into the regular Republican ranks.

The Republican platform was conservative in tone. It called for enforcement of the war amendments, a tariff protective of "American labor," and sound money. It also spoke of the gratitude owed to Grant for "his immense service in war and in peace." But on these planks stood a man whose record was without a stain.

Two weeks after the Republicans adjourned, the Democrats met in St. Louis, where there were a number of contenders for the nomination. The outstanding one was Samuel J. Tilden of New York, a Democrat of the Jacksonian and Van Buren vintage, who had established wealth and reputation as a railroad and corporation attorney. An economic liberal who believed in the free operation of the law of supply and demand and was devoted to hard money, he was also a fearless opponent of corruption in government. He had risen to national prominence when he took a leading part in smashing the Tweed Ring, and, after being elected governor of New York in 1874, he added to his laurels by destroying the Canal Ring, which was mulcting the public of millions through the repair and extension of the state's canal system. Of medium height, with a round boyish face and a weak voice, often gruff and secretive, a hypochondriac who consumed quantities of patent medicines, he was nevertheless an outstanding symbol of reform. The convention nominated him on the second ballot. The Democratic platform denounced the iniquities of the Grant Administration and also pledged tariff and tax reduction, improvement of the civil service, a sound currency, and the elimination of sectional strife and hatred.

The Republican and Democratic nominees were confronted by two rivals in the presidential race. The expiring Greenback Movement nominated the eighty-five-year-old philanthropist Peter Cooper for President; he polled only some 80,000 votes. Even less significant for the moment was a Prohibitionist party ticket headed by General Green Clay Smith of Kentucky, which demanded a constitutional amendment prohibiting the importation, manufacture, and sale of alcoholic beverages; though Smith received less than 10,000 votes, the ticket symbolized the reawakening of the temperance movement that had been so powerful in the decade before the Civil War.

So far as issues were concerned, there was little to choose between the leading candidates. Both stood for hard money, reform of the civil service, and moderate treatment of the South. Tilden was an advocate of tariff reform, but Hayes had no pronounced opinions on that subject. The campaign centered around the record of the party in power.

The Republicans were on the defensive because of corruption, and the hard times that had continued since the panic of 1873. They tried to counter Democratic charges that they were leading the country down the road to ruin by "waving the bloody shirt," an expression that originated when an impassioned Republican orator in Congress held aloft the blood-stained shirt of a Union soldier. The "bloody shirt" appeal invariably coupled denunciation of southern outrages against the Negro with appeals to northern patriotism.

There was the usual drumfire of personal calumny in the campaign. The relative obscurity of Hayes stood him in good stead here, for almost the only charge the Democrats could find to bring against him was the flimsy accusation that he had drawn the pay of dead soldiers in his regiment. The major abuse fell on Tilden, whom Republican orators and newspapers called a harpy who, in his legal practice, ground the poor into the dust. He was said to be a briber, a hypocrite, a sham reformer, a secessionist, and a man who had falsified his income tax returns during the Civil War. Both sides used the customary pageantry of bands, torchlight processions, red fire, and general hullabaloo.

At first the Republicans exuded confidence, for their victories in the October elections in Vermont, Maine, and Ohio, were happy omens. Then, after Indiana, home of Tilden's running mate, Thomas A. Hendricks, went Democratic, and it became apparent that Tilden was likely to carry New York, the national outcome became very much in doubt.

The Crisis

When the November election was over, Tilden appeared to be victorious. He had carried seventeen states, including New York, New Jersey, Connecticut, Indiana, and most of the South. He had 184 sure electoral votes, one less than the needed majority in the electoral college. The Democratic papers of November 8 confidently claimed a victory, and the great majority of Republican papers admitted defeat. The New York *Times,*

THE ELEPHANT WALKS AROUND, AND THE STILL HUNT IS NEARLY OVER

This Nast Cartoon was published in Harper's Weekly, *October 28, 1876. Nast originated the use of the elephant as the Republican symbol. Here he shows the elephant trampling on the Tammany Tiger and on Tilden. Note the Bloody Shirt and Nativist implications of this cartoon.*

however, declared that the election was still in doubt; it asserted that Oregon, South Carolina, and Louisiana had gone for Hayes and that, if Florida did likewise, Hayes would be elected with 185 votes. That same day, Zachariah Chandler, the Republican national chairman, declared that all of those states had gone for Hayes, and that he was elected. Both parties promptly sent observers to the three southern states, which were still ruled by carpetbag governments.

The Oregon situation was peculiar. The state had clearly gone Republican. It could scarcely be held for Tilden, but one of the three Republican electors, a postmaster, was disqualified since he was a federal officeholder. The Democratic governor promptly appointed the Democratic elector with the next highest number of votes to fill the vacated place, and Abram S. Hewitt, Democratic national chairman, supported this move—his object being to force going behind the official returns, which would then set a precedent for doing the same thing in any contested southern state. This seemed all the more necessary, since in the three southern states Republican governments controlled the returning boards, and Chandler had wired the officials in those states asking them if they could hold them for Hayes.

In no one of the three southern states was there a free and fair election,

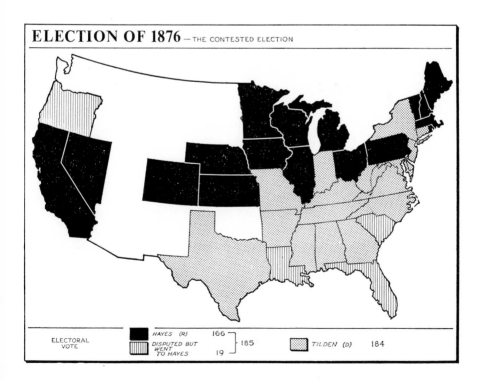

ELECTION OF 1876 — THE CONTESTED ELECTION

ELECTORAL VOTE

HAYES (R)   166
DISPUTED BUT WENT TO HAYES   19 } 185

TILDEN (D)   184

both parties being guilty of dishonest practices. In Florida and Louisiana, the returning boards threw out thousands of Democratic and a relatively few Republican votes, thereby converting what looked like Tilden majorities into victories for Hayes. The South Carolina canvass, according to the returning board there, gave the presidency to Hayes, the governorship and the legislature to the Democrats. The best evidence indicates that Hayes was the victor in South Carolina and Louisiana, and that the four Florida votes should have gone to Tilden; had this been the case, Tilden would have received 188 electoral votes and the presidency. As it was, on December 6, the appointed day, the Republican electors in all three states met and voted for Hayes, while electors with certificates from Democratic state authorities met and cast their votes for Tilden. Both sets of returns were sent to Washington, and on the face of the "official" returns, with nineteen votes from the contested southern states for Hayes, the electoral college stood 185 for the Republican and 184 for the Democratic candidate.

Congress met on December 4 in an atmosphere of growing tension. There were cries of "Tilden or blood," and Republican charges of intimidation of Negro voters and sneers at Democratic "vaporings." Many were alarmed that there might be an outbreak of violence, but there was no agreement as to what action should be taken in meeting the situation.

The Twelfth Amendment states that "the President of the Senate shall, in the presence of the Senate and House of Representatives, open all the certificates and the votes shall then be counted," but it does not say who shall count the votes. The House was Democratic, the Senate Republican, and the temporary president of the Senate, Thomas W. Ferry, was also a Republican. If, as that party demanded, Ferry did the counting, Hayes would emerge the victor, but if the combined Houses acted jointly, Tilden would be declared elected. The Democrats contended that, as neither candidate had a clear majority of the electoral votes, the election should go into the House, but this the Republicans refused because of the Democratic majority in that body. As the New Year dawned, tempers became more heated, and once again, as just before the Civil War, members of Congress began coming to Capitol Hill armed. Some way had to be found out of the impasse, and men both in and out of Congress became involved in the negotiations that ensued.

The Compromise

Hayes had accepted the Republican platform's defense of radical Reconstruction, but privately he had expressed sympathy with a let-alone policy for the southern whites. There is evidence that he hoped for a new political alliance between the conservatives of North and South. Garfield and other men of influence in the Republican party also suggested the possibility of a rapprochement with the Old Whigs of the South, now Democratic-Conservatives, and with Democratic businessmen of both sections. The Republican candidate was more than willing that an effort be made along this line, so long as it did not involve him in hostilities with the radical wing of his party.

Hayes's close friend William Henry Smith of the Western Associated Press, Murat Halstead of the Cincinnati *Commercial,* and Andrew J. Kellar of the Memphis *Daily Avalanche* now began moving in concert with such prominent business leaders as Tom Scott of the Pennsylvania Railroad and Grenville Dodge, formerly chief engineer of the Union Pacific and interested, as was Scott, in railroad development in the Southwest. They found support among the bankers and industrialists of the South, who were eager to see a southwestern railroad constructed, and to open up southern coal and iron mines and develop the manufacturing of textiles, sugar, molasses, and tobacco with the aid of northern capital. This point of view had considerable popular approval in the South, but it found little sympathy among northern Democratic political leaders.

When the Hayes men began to sound out southern Democrats in Congress, they found a considerable number of them not averse to putting Hayes in office if the South received definite promises of "generous" treatment. The aid of these southerners was the more essential because Conkling (who disliked Hayes and believed that Tilden had been elected) was threatening to torpedo the election of the Republican candidate, and the southern carpetbagger Republicans in Congress were suspicious that they were about to be sold out. Such was the situation as Congress came to grips with the problem of handling the disputed election.

In January, 1877, a bill passed Congress setting up a Joint Electoral Commission of fifteen members, to be chosen from both Houses and from the Supreme Court. Three Republicans and two Democrats were to be chosen by the Senate, two Republicans and three Democrats by the House. The bill named two Republicans and two Democrats from the Supreme Court, and left it to them to choose the fifth Justice, assuming that they would select Judge David Davis, an independent. The decision of the Commission on the returns from the four disputed states would be final unless both Houses disagreed with the pronouncement.

Hayes had opposed this bill, and a majority of the Republicans had voted against it, while Tilden had consented to the measure, and an overwhelming majority of the Democrats had voted with the Republican minority to put it through. Then Davis was elected United States Senator from Illinois and declared himself ineligible for the Commission. The Democrats were outraged and claimed foul play. Their disappointment was somewhat assuaged, however, when the fifth Justice chosen was Joseph P. Bradley; it was true that he was a Republican, but he had presided on the southern circuit of the Court and was popular in the South.

The Commission met and examined the returns from the disputed states, beginning with Florida. In this crucial case, the vote was eight Republicans to seven Democrats not to go behind the official returns. Justice Bradley, at first in favor of giving Florida's electoral vote to Tilden, changed his mind between midnight and morning of the day the decision was announced; there is considerable evidence that he yielded to Republican pressure. In the other cases the Commission divided in exactly the same way. If its decision were to be accepted by Congress, Hayes would be elected.

When the Commission's ruling on the Florida returns was announced on February 10, the House Democrats moved a recess, which carried by a strict party vote. This maneuver was repeated on succeeding days, being, in effect, a filibuster that slowed down the electoral count. Both northern and southern Democrats now seemed to be in accord.

Then came a series of events which broke the filibuster. Tom Scott, who had a powerful lobby working for government aid to the Texas and Pacific Railroad, used all the lobby's influence to induce southern congressmen to accept the election of Hayes. The latter, it was made clear by his own statements, favored federal aid for internal improvements in the South. An understanding was also reached that he would appoint a southern Democrat as Postmaster General (a rich patronage plum) and withdraw federal troops from the states where their presence alone supported the Republican-carpetbagger governments. To these factors was added a growing realization that if the filibuster continued and inauguration day came without an election, the country would face a dangerous interregnum. Some thirty southern Democrats deserted the filibuster, and a number of their influential northern brethren, alarmed by the prospect of impending chaos, joined them in voting with the Republicans against any further recess.

With the filibuster broken, the electoral count gathered speed. It was concluded at 4:00 a.m. on March 2, 1877, and Hayes was declared the next President of the United States. Since Sunday fell on March 4, he was privately inaugurated on March 3, the public ceremonies taking place on Monday, March 5.

The elevation of Hayes to the White House ended the crisis precipitated by the election of 1876. To a majority of observers, it seemed apparent that the Republicans had triumphed in the face of the popular will, but more significant than this victory were the revelations made clear by the manner of its achievement. It was evident that the leaders of the Republican party, despairing of retaining their hold in the South by forceful means, were now attempting to achieve the same objective by conciliation of the southern Redeemers who were of a conservative mold. Also apparent was the growing power of big business and the influence which it could wield in political affairs.

One hundred years before, the thirteen colonies, a weak and poorly united band, had declared their independence from Great Britain. Now the United States was fast becoming an industrial giant, and its bankers, railroad men, and industrialists were exerting an influence undreamed of by the petty merchants and struggling farmers of 1776.

The Centennial Exhibition

Despite the fury of political contention in 1876, and the misery of hard times, many Americans were conscious that the year marked the centennial anniversary of the nation's independence. As men reflected on the great development in national wealth and power that had come within little more than three generations, it seemed only fitting to celebrate the centenary in some outstanding fashion. In response to this desire, Congress appointed a Centennial Commission which, in turn, selected Philadelphia as the logical site for a world fair. The Commission raised money by loans and private and state subscriptions, solicited the cooperation of foreign governments, and undertook the erection of the necessary buildings.

The Centennial, as Americans insisted upon calling it, opened on May 10, 1876, and continued for five months. It was the first of its kind in the United States and the sixth of the world fairs held during the nineteenth century. The buildings were spread over 236 acres of ground overlooking the Schuylkill River. Each state of the Union had its own building, and around the huge Main Exhibition Building were grouped some 200 other structures, in which were displayed the arts and crafts, industry, and agriculture of the world. A narrow-gauge railroad carried about the grounds those who came to see and to marvel, and there were restaurants aplenty —with prices that ranged from moderate to the overexpensive tariffs (so thought William Dean Howells) of the Trois Frères Provençaux—furnishing meals for the 10 million visitors, a considerable number of whom came from overseas.

The exhibits from abroad varied widely in quality but were chiefly of a high order of excellence. Great Britain had the largest and the best display; visitors commented particularly upon its fine showing of textiles and the collection of paintings that ranged from Gainsborough and Reynolds to Millais and Turner. The French, German, and Austrian paintings were mediocre, and the German government had the bad taste to send a large canvas representing the French surrender at Sedan, showing a small, solitary Frenchman creeping up a hill at the top of which stood Kaiser Wilhelm I and Bismarck.

As was to be expected, the United States had more exhibits than any other country. The paintings of C. W. Peale and Rembrandt Peale, the American genre as represented by Eastman Johnson's "Corn-husking Scene," and the works of such artists as Winslow Homer and Hiram Powers provided Americans with a sense of their country's respectable contributions in the field of the fine arts. The Women's Pavilion, a pioneer venture, recognized the growing importance of the feminine sex in the American world, for exhibits from the United States occupied three-fourths of the space in this building. While skill in needlework and embroidery was exhibited, the work done by students in the Massachusetts School of Technology, together with a complete and accurate materia medica from the Women's Medical College of Philadelphia, indicated that feminine interests and pursuits were no longer confined to the home.

It was in the Agricultural, Carriage, and Machinery Halls that the American showing was most impressive. The display of reapers, drills, mowers, and other agricultural implements showed American preeminence in this field. There was a display of tobacco from Kentucky, and Iowa demonstrated the depth and quality of its rich, corn-growing soil. From a Cincinnati packing house came large hams, arrayed not in linen cases but in crimson, white, and gold silk. The Carriage Hall contained a notable display of equipages, from lumber wagons to a Pullman sleeping car. In the Machinery Hall, everyone marveled at the great Corliss engine with its double-walking beam, that almost noiselessly supplied the power for running the great number of machines with moving parts. There were multitudes of sewing machines—"a whole half-mile," it seemed to one observer—a variety of planes, lathes, and other machine tools; an extensive collection of looms; and a small watch factory from Waltham, Massachusetts, in full operation.

One of the exhibitors at the Centennial was inventor Alexander Graham Bell (1847–1922), who taught at the Boston City School for the Deaf and who had a little exhibit in the main building. When the judges reached the section where Bell had his display, they were accompanied by Dom Pedro, Emperor of Brazil, who was much interested in North American educational methods and had met Bell in Boston. Since it was a hot day, the judges were weary and had decided that the exhibit just before Bell's would be the last that they would examine that day, but then Dom Pedro spied Bell, who had to go back to Boston that night. As a result, Bell had his opportunity to display and explain his invention, which made a tremendous impression and received an award. So the telephone—symbol of a new era—had recognition. Sir William Thomson (later Lord Kelvin), who was one of the judges, declared it one of the most amazing things he had seen in America. Dom Pedro, too, had been impressed, though the story of his exclaiming "My God, *it talks*" was a later invention.

The Centennial was an education for Europeans, and for a multitude of Americans. It gave the American visitors some conception of the talents and products of their own country, and a glimpse of other cultures as well. Japanese art, Indian and Persian rugs and shawls, to say nothing of the foods prepared by the French and Austrian cooks, afforded new experiences for the great majority of those who came to Philadelphia from all parts of the United States. And kindergarten child training, which occupied two of the buildings, showed methods used in Germany, Belgium, and Switzerland that opened the eyes of American educators.

The Centennial Exhibition was a tribute to American ability in organization. Remarkably free from disorder and wasted effort, it broadened the outlook and stimulated an interest in invention on the part of many an American youngster. Coming as it did in the midst of a great depression, it was an important demonstration of talent and capacity which sent Americans away with renewed faith in their country's future.

Suggested Reading

The second Grant Administration is dealt with extensively in W. B. Hesseltine, *Ulysses S. Grant* (1935); E. P. Oberholtzer, *A History of the United States,* vol. III (1926); and Allan Nevins, *Hamilton Fish* (1936), which ranges beyond an account of Fish's career as Secretary of State.

The panic of 1873 and the subsequent depression may be studied in Rendig Fels, *American Business Cycles, 1865–1897* (1959), and O. C. Lightner, *The History of Business Depressions* (1922) and D. R. Dewey, *Financial History of the United States*

(1934). The best biography of Jay Cooke is Henrietta Larson, *Jay Cooke, Private Banker* (1936).

Three good biographies of political figures in this period are D. S. Muzzey, *James G. Blaine* (1934); A. C. Flick, *Samuel Jones Tilden* (1939); and H. J. Eckenrode, *Rutherford B. Hayes* (1930). Eric Goldman, *Rendezvous with Destiny* (1952) comments briefly on the liberal currents in the Grant era. See also Matthew Josephson, *The Politicos* (1938), and Allan Nevins, *Abram S. Hewitt* (1935).

For some time, the standard work on the disputed election of 1876 has been P. L. Haworth, *The Hayes-Tilden Disputed Presidential Election of 1876* (1906), but it has now been largely superseded by C. Vann Woodward, *Reunion and Reaction* (1951). The student interested in this election should also consult Harry Barnard, *Rutherford B. Hayes and His America* (1954).

The Centennial Exhibition of 1876 is briefly described in Allan Nevins, *The Emergence of Modern America, 1865–1878* (1928). There is a wealth of material on the Exhibition in *Appleton's Annual Encyclopedia,* new series, vol. I (1877); *The Nation,* XXII and XXIII; and W. D. Howells, "A Sennight of the Centennial," *Atlantic Monthly,* XXXVIII (July, 1876), 92–107.

❲ APPENDIX I. ❳

The Declaration of Independence[1]

In Congress, July 4, 1776

THE UNANIMOUS DECLARATION OF THE THIRTEEN UNITED STATES OF AMERICA

W HEN, in the Course of human events, it becomes necessary for one people to dissolve the political bands which have connected them with another, and to assume among the powers of the earth, the separate and equal station to which the Laws of Nature and of Nature's God entitle them, a decent respect to the opinions of mankind requires that they should declare the causes which impel them to the separation.

We hold these truths to be self-evident, that all men are created equal, that they are endowed by their Creator with certain unalienable Rights, that among these, are Life, Liberty, and the pursuit of Happiness. That, to secure these rights, Governments are instituted among Men, deriving their just powers from the consent of the governed, that, whenever any Form of Government becomes destructive of these ends, it is the Right of the People to alter or to abolish it, and to institute new Government, laying its foundation on such principles, and organizing its powers in such form, as to them shall seem most likely to effect their Safety and Happiness. Prudence, indeed, will dictate that Governments long established, should not be changed for light and transient causes; and, accordingly, all experience hath shewn, that mankind are more disposed to suffer, while evils are sufferable, than to right themselves by abolishing the forms to which they are accustomed. But, when a long train of abuses and usurpations, pursuing invariably the same Object, evinces a design to reduce them under absolute Despotism, it is their right, it is their duty, to throw off such Government and to provide new Guards for their future security.—Such has been the patient sufferance of these Colonies; and such is now the necessity which constrains them to alter their former Systems of Government. The history of the present King of Great Britain is a history of repeated injuries and usurpations, all having in direct object the establishment of an absolute Tyranny over these States. To prove this, let Facts be submitted to a candid world.—

He has refused his Assent to Laws the most wholesome and necessary for the public good.

---

[1] Spelling and capitalization follow the parchment copy.

He has forbidden his Governors to pass Laws of immediate and pressing importance, unless suspended in their operation till his Assent should be obtained; and when so suspended, he has utterly neglected to attend to them.

He has refused to pass other laws for the accommodation of large districts of people, unless those people would relinquish the right of Representation in the Legislature; a right inestimable to them and formidable to tyrants only.

He has called together legislative bodies at places unusual, uncomfortable, and distant from the depository of their public Records, for the sole purpose of fatiguing them into compliance with his measures.

He has dissolved Representative Houses repeatedly, for opposing with manly firmness his invasions on the rights of the people.

He has refused for a long time, after such dissolutions, to cause others to be elected; whereby the Legislative powers, incapable of Annihilation, have returned to the People at large for their exercise; the State remaining, in the meantime, exposed to all the dangers of invasion from without, and convulsions within.

He has endeavored to prevent the population of these States; for that purpose, obstructing the Laws for Naturalization of Foreigners; refusing to pass others to encourage their migrations hither, and raising the conditions of new Appropriations of Lands.

He has obstructed the Administration of Justice, by refusing his Assent to Laws for establishing Judiciary powers.

He has made Judges dependent on his Will alone, for the tenure of their offices, and the amount and payment of their salaries.

He has erected a multitude of New Offices, and sent hither swarms of Officers to harass our people, and eat out their substance.

He has kept among us, in times of peace, Standing Armies, without the Consent of our legislatures.

He has affected to render the Military independent of, and superior to, the Civil power.

He has combined, with others, to subject us to a jurisdiction foreign to our constitution, and unacknowledged by our laws; giving his Assent to their Acts of pretended Legislation:

For quartering large bodies of armed troops among us:

For protecting them by a mock Trial, from punishment, for any Murders which they should commit on the Inhabitants of these States:

For cutting off our Trade with all parts of the world:

For imposing Taxes on us without our Consent:

For depriving us, in many cases, of the benefits of Trial by Jury:

For transporting us beyond Seas to be tried for pretended offenses:

For abolishing the free System of English Laws in a neighboring Province, establishing therein an Arbitrary government, and enlarging its Boundaries, so as to render it at once an example and fit instrument for introducing the same absolute rule into these Colonies:

For taking away our Charters, abolishing our most valuable Laws, and altering, fundamentally, the Forms of our Governments:

For suspending our own Legislatures, and declaring themselves invested with power to legislate for us in all cases whatsoever.

He has abdicated Government here, by declaring us out of his Protection, and waging War against us.

He has plundered our seas, ravaged our Coasts, burnt our towns, and destroyed the lives of our people.

He is, at this time, transporting large Armies of foreign Mercenaries to compleat the works of death, desolation, and tyranny, already begun with circumstances of Cruelty & perfidy scarcely paralleled in the most barbarous ages, and totally unworthy the Head of a civilized nation.

He has constrained our fellow Citizens, taken Captive on the high Seas, to bear Arms against their Country, to become the executioners of their friends and Brethren, or to fall themselves by their Hands.

He has excited domestic insurrections amongst us, and has endeavored to bring on the inhabitants of our frontiers, the merciless Indian Savages, whose known rule of warfare, is an undistinguished destruction of all ages, sexes and conditions.

In every stage of these Oppressions, We have Petitioned for Redress, in the most humble terms; our repeated Petitions have been answered only by repeated injury. A Prince, whose character is thus marked by every act which may define a Tyrant, is unfit to be the ruler of a free people.

Nor have we been wanting in attentions to our British brethren. We have warned them, from time to time, of attempts made by their legislature to extend an unwarrantable jurisdiction over us. We have reminded them of the circumstances of our emigration and settlement here. We have appealed to their native justice and magnanimity, and we have conjured them by the ties of our common kindred to disavow these usurpations, which would inevitably interrupt our connections and correspondence. They too have been deaf to the voice of justice and of consanguinity. We must, therefore, acquiesce in the necessity, which denounces our Separation, and hold them, as we hold the rest of mankind, Enemies in War, in Peace Friends.

We, therefore, the Representatives of the united States of America, in General Congress, Assembled, appealing to the Supreme Judge of the world for the rectitude of our intentions, do, in the Name, and by Authority of the good People of these Colonies, solemnly publish and declare, That these United Colonies are, and of Right ought to be, Free and Independent States; that they are Absolved from all Allegiance to the British Crown, and that all political connection between them and the State of Great Britain is, and ought to be, totally dissolved: and that, as Free and Independent States, they have full Power to levy War, conclude Peace, contract Alliances, establish Commerce, and to do all other Acts and Things which Independent States may of right do. And, for the support of this Declaration, with a firm reliance on the protection of divine Providence, we mutually pledge to each other our Lives, our Fortunes, and our sacred Honor.

The foregoing Declaration was, by order of Congress, engrossed, and signed by the following members:

John Hancock

NEW HAMPSHIRE
  Josiah Bartlett
  William Whipple
  Matthew Thornton
MASSACHUSETTS BAY
  Samuel Adams
  John Adams
  Robert Treat Paine
  Elbridge Gerry
RHODE ISLAND
  Stephen Hopkins
  William Ellery
CONNECTICUT
  Roger Sherman
  Samuel Huntington
  William Williams
  Oliver Wolcott
NEW YORK
  William Floyd
  Philip Livingston
  Francis Lewis
  Lewis Morris
NEW JERSEY
  Richard Stockton
  John Witherspoon
  Francis Hopkinson
  John Hart
  Abraham Clark
PENNSYLVANIA
  Robert Morris
  Benjamin Rush
  Benjamin Franklin
  John Morton
  George Clymer

  James Smith
  George Taylor
  James Wilson
  George Ross
DELAWARE
  Caesar Rodney
  George Read
  Thomas M'Kean
MARYLAND
  Samuel Chase
  William Paca
  Thomas Stone
  Charles Carroll, of Carrollton
VIRGINIA
  George Wythe
  Richard Henry Lee
  Thomas Jefferson
  Benjamin Harrison
  Thomas Nelson, Jr.
  Francis Lightfoot Lee
  Carter Braxton
NORTH CAROLINA
  William Hooper
  Joseph Hewes
  John Penn
SOUTH CAROLINA
  Edward Rutledge
  Thomas Heyward, Jr.
  Thomas Lynch, Jr.
  Arthur Middleton
GEORGIA
  Button Gwinnett
  Lyman Hall
  George Walton

RESOLVED, That copies of the Declaration be sent to the several assemblies, conventions, and committees, or councils of safety, and to the several commanding officers of the continental troops; that it be proclaimed in each of the united States, at the head of the army.

〖 A P P E N D I X I I . 〗

The Constitution of the United States[1]

W̶E THE PEOPLE of the United States, in Order to form a more perfect Union, establish Justice, insure domestic Tranquility, provide for the common defence, promote the general Welfare, and secure the Blessings of Liberty to ourselves and our Posterity, do ordain and establish this CONSTITUTION for the United States of America.

ARTICLE I.

Section 1. All legislative Powers herein granted shall be vested in a Congress of the United States, which shall consist of a Senate and House of Representatives.

Section 2. The House of Representatives shall be composed of Members chosen every second Year by the People of the several States, and the Electors in each State shall have the Qualifications requisite for Electors of the most numerous Branch of the State Legislature.

No Person shall be a Representative who shall not have attained to the Age of twenty-five Years, and been seven Years a Citizen of the United States, and who shall not, when elected, be an Inhabitant of that State in which he shall be chosen.

[Representatives and direct Taxes shall be apportioned among the several States which may be included within this Union, according to their respective Numbers, which shall be determined by adding to the whole Number of free Persons, including those bound to Service for a Term of Years, and excluding Indians not taxed, three fifths of all other Persons.][2] The actual Enumeration shall be made within three Years after the first Meeting of the Congress of the United States, and within every subsequent Term of ten Years, in such Manner as they shall by Law direct. The Number of Representatives shall not exceed one for every thirty Thousand, but each State shall have at Least one Representative; and until such enumeration shall be made, the State of New Hampshire shall be entitled to chuse three, Massachusetts eight, Rhode-Island and Providence Plantations one, Connecticut five, New-York six, New Jersey four,

---

[1] This version follows the original Constitution in spelling and capitalization. It was published by the United States Department of the Interior, Office of Education, in 1935.
[2] Replaced by the 14th Amendment.

768

Pennsylvania eight, Delaware one, Maryland six, Virginia ten, North Carolina five, South Carolina five, and Georgia three.

When vacancies happen in the Representation from any State, the Executive Authority thereof shall issue Writs of Election to fill such Vacancies.

The House of Representatives shall chuse their Speaker and other Officers; and shall have the sole Power of Impeachment.

Section 3. The Senate of the United States shall be composed of two Senators from each State, chosen by the Legislature thereof, for six Years; and each Senator shall have one Vote.

Immediately after they shall be assembled in Consequence of the first Election, they shall be divided as equally as may be into three Classes. The Seats of the Senators of the first Class shall be vacated at the Expiration of the second Year, of the second Class at the Expiration of the fourth Year, and of the third Class at the Expiration of the sixth Year, so that one-third may be chosen every second Year; and if Vacancies happen by Resignation, or otherwise, during the Recess of the Legislature of any State, the Executive thereof may make temporary Appointments until the next Meeting of the Legislature, which shall then fill such Vacancies.

No Person shall be a Senator who shall not have attained to the Age of thirty Years, and been nine Years a Citizen of the United States, and who shall not, when elected, be an Inhabitant of that State for which he shall be chosen.

The Vice President of the United States shall be President of the Senate, but shall have no vote, unless they be equally divided.

The Senate shall chuse their other Officers, and also a President pro tempore, in the absence of the Vice President, or when he shall exercise the Office of President of the United States.

The Senate shall have the sole Power to try all Impeachments. When sitting for that purpose, they shall be on Oath or Affirmation. When the President of the United States is tried, the Chief Justice shall preside: And no person shall be convicted without the Concurrence of two thirds of the Members present.

Judgment in Cases of Impeachment shall not extend further than to removal from Office, and disqualification to hold and enjoy any Office of honor, Trust, or Profit under the United States: but the Party convicted shall nevertheless be liable and subject to Indictment, Trial, Judgment, and Punishment, according to Law.

Section 4. The Times, Places and Manner of holding Elections for Senators and Representatives, shall be prescribed in each State by the Legislature thereof; but the Congress may at any time by Law make or alter such Regulations, except as to the Places of Chusing Senators.

The Congress shall assemble at least once in every Year, and such Meeting shall be on the first Monday in December, unless they shall by Law appoint a different Day.

Section 5. Each House shall be the Judge of the Elections, Returns and

Qualifications of its own Members, and a Majority of each shall constitute a Quorum to do Business; but a small number may adjourn from day to day, and may be authorized to compel the Attendance of absent Members, in such Manner, and under such Penalties, as each House may provide.

Each House may determine the Rules of its Proceedings, punish its Members for disorderly Behavior, and, with the Concurrence of two thirds, expel a Member.

Each House shall keep a Journal of its Proceedings, and from time to time publish the same, excepting such Parts as may in their Judgment require Secrecy; and the Yeas and Nays of the Members of either House on any question shall, at the Desire of one fifth of those Present, be entered on the Journal.

Neither House, during the Session of Congress, shall, without the Consent of the other, adjourn for more than three days, nor to any other Place than that in which the two Houses shall be sitting.

Section 6. The Senators and Representatives shall receive a Compensation for their Services, to be ascertained by Law, and paid out of the Treasury of the United States. They shall in all Cases, except Treason, Felony, and Breach of the Peace, be privileged from Arrest during their Attendance at the Session of their respective Houses, and in going to and returning from the same; and for any Speech or Debate in either House, they shall not be questioned in any other Place.

No Senator or Representative shall, during the Time for which he was elected, be appointed to any civil Office under the Authority of the United States, which shall have been created, or the Emoluments whereof shall have been increased, during such time; and no Person holding any Office under the United States shall be a Member of either House during his continuance in Office.

Section 7. All Bills for raising Revenue shall originate in the House of Representatives; but the Senate may propose or concur with Amendments on other bills.

Every Bill which shall have passed the House of Representatives and the Senate, shall, before it become a law, be presented to the President of the United States; If he approve he shall sign it, but if not he shall return it, with his Objections, to that House in which it shall have originated, who shall enter the Objections at large on their Journal, and proceed to reconsider it. If after such Reconsideration two thirds of that House shall agree to pass the bill, it shall be sent, together with the objections, to the other House, by which it shall likewise be reconsidered, and if approved by two thirds of that House, it shall become a Law. But in all such Cases the Votes of both Houses shall be determined by Yeas and Nays, and the Names of the Persons voting for and against the Bill shall be entered on the Journal of each House respectively. If any Bill shall not be returned by the President within ten Days (Sundays excepted) after it shall have been presented to him, the Same shall be a

Law, in like Manner as if he had signed it, unless the Congress by their Adjournment prevent its Return, in which Case it shall not be a Law.

Every Order, Resolution, or Vote to which the Concurrence of the Senate and House of Representatives may be necessary (except on a question of Adjournment) shall be presented to the President of the United States; and before the Same shall take Effect, shall be approved by him, or being disapproved by him, shall be repassed by two thirds of the senate and House of Representatives, according to the Rules and Limitations prescribed in the Case of a Bill.

Section 8. The Congress shall have Power To lay and collect Taxes, Duties, Imposts and Excises, to pay the Debts and provide for the common Defence and general Welfare of the United States; but all Duties, Imposts and Excises shall be uniform throughout the United States;

To borrow money on the credit of the United States;

To regulate Commerce with foreign Nations, and among the several States, and with the Indian Tribes;

To establish an uniform Rule of Naturalization, and uniform Laws on the subject of Bankruptcies throughout the United States;

To coin Money, regulate the Value thereof, and of foreign Coin, and fix the Standard of Weights and Measures;

To provide for the Punishment of counterfeiting the Securities and current Coin of the United States;

To establish Post Offices and post Roads;

To promote the Progress of Science and useful Arts, by securing for limited Times to Authors and Inventors the exclusive Right to their respective Writings and Discoveries;

To constitute Tribunals inferior to the Supreme Court;

To define and punish Piracies and Felonies committed on the high Seas, and Offenses against the Law of Nations;

To declare War, grant Letters of Marque and Reprisal, and make Rules concerning Captures on Land and Water;

To raise and support Armies, but no Appropriation of Money to that Use shall be for a longer Term than two Years;

To provide and maintain a Navy;

To make Rules for the Government and Regulation of the land and naval forces;

To provide for calling forth the Militia to execute the Laws of the Union, suppress Insurrections and repel Invasions;

To provide for organizing, arming, and disciplining the Militia, and for governing such Part of them as may be employed in the Service of the United States, reserving to the States respectively, the Appointment of the Officers, and the Authority of training the Militia according to the discipline prescribed by Congress;

To exercise exclusive Legislation in all Cases whatsoever, over such District (not exceeding ten Miles square) as may, by Cession of particular States, and the acceptance of Congress, become the Seat of the Government of the United States, and to exercise like Authority over all Places purchased by the Consent of the Legislature of the State in which the Same shall be, for the Erection of Forts, Magazines, Arsenals, dock-Yards, and other needful Buildings;—And

To make all Laws which shall be necessary and proper for carrying into Execution the foregoing Powers, and all other Powers vested by this Constitution in the Government of the United States, or in any Department or Officer thereof.

Section 9. The Migration or Importation of such Persons as any of the States now existing shall think proper to admit, shall not be prohibited by the Congress prior to the Year one thousand eight hundred and eight, but a tax or duty may be imposed on such Importation, not exceeding ten dollars for each Person.

The privilege of the Writ of Habeas Corpus shall not be suspended, unless when in Cases of Rebellion or Invasion the public Safety may require it.

No Bill of Attainder or ex post facto Law shall be passed.

No capitation, or other direct, Tax shall be laid unless in Proportion to the Census or Enumeration herein before directed to be taken.

No Tax or Duty shall be laid on Articles exported from any State.

No Preference shall be given by any Regulation of Commerce or Revenue to the Ports of one State over those of another: nor shall Vessels bound to, or from, one State, be obliged to enter, clear, or pay Duties in another.

No Money shall be drawn from the Treasury, but in Consequence of Appropriations made by Law; and a regular Statement and Account of the Receipts and Expenditures of all public Money shall be published from time to time.

No Title of Nobility shall be granted by the United States: And no Person holding any Office of Profit or Trust under them, shall, without the Consent of the Congress, accept of any present, Emolument, Office, or Title, of any kind whatever, from any King, Prince, or foreign State.

Section 10. No State shall enter into any Treaty, Alliance, or Confederation; grant Letters of Marque and Reprisal; coin Money; emit Bills of Credit; make any Thing but gold and silver Coin or Tender in Payment of Debts; pass any Bill of Attainder, ex post facto Law, or Law impairing the Obligation of Contracts, or grant any Title of Nobility.

No State shall, without the Consent of the Congress, lay any Imposts or Duties on Imports or Exports, except what may be absolutely necessary for executing its inspection Laws: and the net Produce of all Duties and Imposts, laid by any State on Imports or Exports, shall be for the Use of the Treasury of the United States; and all such Laws shall be subject to the Revision and Control of the Congress.

No State shall, without the Consent of Congress, lay any duty of Tonnage, keep Troops, or Ships of War in time of Peace, enter into any Agreement or

Compact with another State, or with a foreign Power, or engage in War, unless actually invaded, or in such imminent Danger as will not admit of delay.

ARTICLE II.

Section 1. The executive Power shall be vested in a President of the United States of America. He shall hold his Office during the Term of four years, and, together with the Vice-President, chosen for the same Term, be elected, as follows:

Each State shall appoint, in such Manner as the Legislature thereof may direct, a Number of Electors, equal to the whole Number of Senators and Representatives to which the State may be entitled in the Congress: but no Senator or Representative, or Person holding an Office of Trust or Profit under the United States, shall be appointed an Elector.

[The Electors shall meet in their respective States, and vote by Ballot for two persons, of whom one at least shall not be an Inhabitant of the same State with themselves. And they shall make a List of all the Persons voted for, and of the Number of Votes for each; which List they shall sign and certify, and transmit sealed to the Seat of the Government of the United States, directed to the President of the Senate. The President of the Senate shall, in the Presence of the Senate and House of Representatives, open all the Certificates, and the Votes shall then be counted. The Person having the greatest Number of Votes shall be the President, if such Number be a Majority of the whole Number of Electors appointed; and if there be more than one who have such Majority, and have an equal Number of Votes, then the House of Representatives shall immediately chuse by Ballot one of them for President; and if no Person have a Majority, then from the five highest on the List the said House shall in like Manner chuse the President. But in chusing the President, the Votes shall be taken by States, the Representation from each State having one Vote; a quorum for this Purpose shall consist of a Member or Members from two-thirds of the States, and a Majority of all the States shall be necessary to a Choice. In every Case, after the Choice of the President, the Person having the greatest Number of Votes of the Electors shall be the Vice President. But if there should remain two or more who have equal votes, the Senate shall chuse from them by Ballot the Vice-President.]³

The Congress may determine the Time of chusing the Electors, and the Day on which they shall give their Votes; which Day shall be the same throughout the United States.

No person except a natural-born Citizen, or a Citizen of the United States, at the time of the Adoption of this Constitution, shall be eligible to the Office of President; neither shall any Person be eligible to that Office who shall not

---

³ Superseded by the 12th Amendment.

have attained to the Age of thirty-five years, and been fourteen Years a Resident within the United States.

In Case of the Removal of the President from Office, or of his Death, Resignation, or Inability to discharge the Powers and Duties of the said Office, the same shall devolve on the Vice President, and the Congress may by Law provide for the Case of Removal, Death, Resignation, or Inability, both of the President and Vice President, declaring what Officer shall then act as President, and such Officer shall act accordingly, until the disability be removed, or a President shall be elected.

The President shall, at stated Times, receive for his Services a Compensation, which shall neither be increased nor diminished during the Period for which he shall have been elected, and he shall not receive within that Period any other Emolument from the United States, or any of them.

Before he enter on the execution of his Office, he shall take the following Oath or Affirmation:—"I do solemnly swear (or affirm) that I will faithfully execute the Office of President of the United States, and will, to the best of my Ability, preserve, protect, and defend the Constitution of the United States."

Section 2. The President shall be Commander in Chief of the Army and Navy of the United States, and of the Militia of the several States, when called into the actual Service of the United States; he may require the Opinion, in writing, of the principal Officer in each of the executive Departments, upon any subject relating to the Duties of their respective Offices, and he shall have Power to Grant Reprieves and Pardons for Offenses against the United States, except in Cases of Impeachment.

He shall have Power, by and with the Advice and Consent of the Senate, to make Treaties, provided two thirds of the Senators present concur; and he shall nominate, and by and with the Advice and Consent of the Senate, shall appoint Ambassadors, other public Ministers and Consuls, Judges of the supreme Court, and all other Officers of the United States, whose Appointments are not herein otherwise provided for, and which shall be established by Law: but the Congress may by Law vest the Appointment of such inferior Officers, as they think proper, in the President alone, in the Courts of Law, or in the Heads of Departments.

The President shall have Power to fill up all Vacancies that may happen during the Recess of the Senate, by granting Commissions which shall expire at the End of their next Session.

Section 3. He shall from time to time give to the Congress Information of the State of the Union, and recommend to their Consideration such Measures as he shall judge necessary and expedient; he may, on extraordinary occasions, convene both Houses, or either of them, and in Case of Disagreement between them, with respect to the Time of Adjournment, he may adjourn them to such Time as he shall think proper; he shall receive Ambassadors and other public Ministers; he shall take Care that the Laws be faithfully executed, and shall Commission all the Officers of the United States.

Section 4. The President, Vice President and all civil Officers of the United States, shall be removed from Office on Impeachment for, and Conviction of, Treason, Bribery, or other high Crimes and Misdemeanors.

ARTICLE III.

Section 1. The judicial Power of the United States, shall be vested in one supreme Court, and in such inferior Courts as the Congress may from time to time ordain and establish. The Judges, both of the supreme and inferior Courts, shall hold their Offices during good Behaviour, and shall, at stated Times, receive for their Services, a Compensation, which shall not be diminished during their Continuance in Office.

Section 2. The judicial Power shall extend to all Cases, in Law and Equity, arising under this Constitution, the Laws of the United States, and Treaties made, or which shall be made, under their Authority;—to all Cases affecting ambassadors, other public ministers and consuls;—to all cases of admiralty and maritime Jurisdiction;—to Controversies to which the United States shall be a Party;—to Controversies between two or more States; between a State and Citizens of another State; [4]—between Citizens of different States,—between Citizens of the same State claiming Lands under Grants of different States, and between a State, or the Citizens thereof, and foreign States, Citizens or Subjects.

In all Cases affecting Ambassadors, other public Ministers and Consuls, and those in which a State shall be Party, the supreme Court shall have original Jurisdiction. In all the other Cases before mentioned, the supreme Court shall have appellate Jurisdiction, both as to Law and Fact, with such Exceptions, and under such Regulations as the Congress shall make.

The trial of all Crimes, except in Cases of Impeachment, shall be by Jury; and such Trial shall be held in the State where the said Crimes shall have been committed; but when not committed within any State, the Trial shall be at such Place or Places as the Congress may by Law have directed.

Section 3. Treason against the United States, shall consist only in levying War against them, or in adhering to their Enemies, giving them Aid and Comfort. No Person shall be convicted of Treason unless on the Testimony of two Witnesses to the same overt Act, or on Confession in open Court.

The Congress shall have power to declare the Punishment of Treason, but no Attainder of Treason shall work Corruption of Blood, or Forfeiture except during the Life of the Person attainted.

---

[4] Restricted by the 11th Amendment.

ARTICLE IV.

Section 1. Full Faith and Credit shall be given in each State to the public Acts, Records, and judicial Proceedings of every other State. And the Congress may by general Laws prescribe the Manner in which such Acts, Records and Proceedings shall be proved, and the Effect thereof.

Section 2. The Citizens of each State shall be entitled to all Privileges and Immunities of Citizens in the several States.

A Person charged in any State with Treason, Felony, or other Crime, who shall flee from Justice, and be found in another State, shall on demand of the executive Authority of the State from which he fled, be delivered up, to be removed to the State having Jurisdiction of the crime.

No Person held to Service or Labour in one State, under the Laws thereof, escaping into another, shall, in Consequence of any Law or Regulation therein, be discharged from such Service or Labour, but shall be delivered up on Claim of the Party to whom such Service or Labour may be due.

Section 3. New States may be admitted by the Congress into this Union; but no new State shall be formed or erected within the Jurisdiction of any other State; nor any State be Formed by the Junction of two or more States, or parts of States, without the Consent of the Legislatures of the States concerned as well as of the Congress.

The Congress shall have Power to dispose of and make all needful Rules and Regulations respecting the Territory or other Property belonging to the United States; and nothing in this Constitution shall be so construed as to Prejudice any Claims of the United States, or of any particular State.

Section 4. The United States shall guarantee to every State in this Union a Republican Form of Government, and shall protect each of them against Invasion; and on Application of the Legislature, or of the Executive (when the Legislature cannot be convened) against domestic Violence.

ARTICLE V.

The Congress, whenever two-thirds of both Houses shall deem it necessary, shall propose Amendments to this Constitution, or, on the Application of the Legislatures of two-thirds of the several States, shall call a Convention for proposing Amendments, which, in either Case, shall be valid to all Intents and Purposes, as part of this Constitution, when ratified by the Legislatures of three-fourths of the several States, or by Conventions in three-fourths thereof, as the one or the other Mode of Ratification may be proposed by the Congress; Provided that no Amendment which may be made prior to the Year One thousand eight hundred and eight shall in any Manner affect the first and fourth Clauses in the Ninth Section of the first Article; and that no State, without its Consent, shall be deprived of its equal Suffrage in the Senate.

Article VI.

All Debts contracted and Engagements entered into, before the Adoption of this Constitution, shall be as valid against the United States under this Constitution, as under the Confederation. This Constitution, and the Laws of the United States which shall be made in Pursuance thereof; and all Treaties made, or which shall be made, under the Authority of the United States, shall be the supreme Law of the Land; and the Judges in every State shall be bound thereby, any Thing in the Constitution or Laws of any State to the Contrary notwithstanding.

The Senators and Representatives before mentioned, and the Members of the several State Legislatures, and all executive and judicial officers, both of the United States and of the several States, shall be bound by Oath or Affirmation to support this Constitution; but no religious Test shall ever be required as a qualification to any Office or public Trust under the United States.

Article VII.

The Ratification of the Conventions of nine States shall be sufficient for the Establishment of this Constitution between the States so ratifying the same.

Done in Convention by the Unanimous Consent of the States present the Seventeenth Day of September in the Year of our Lord one thousand seven hundred and Eighty seven, and of the Independence of the United States of America the Twelfth. In Witness whereof We have hereunto subscribed our Names.[5]

George Washington

President and deputy from Virginia

New Hampshire
John Langdon
Nicholas Gilman

Massachusetts
Nathaniel Gorham
Rufus King

Pennsylvania
Benjamin Franklin
Thomas Mifflin
Robert Morris
George Clymer
Thomas FitzSimons
Jared Ingersoll
James Wilson
Gouverneur Morris

New York
Alexander Hamilton

New Jersey
William Livingston
David Brearley
William Paterson
Jonathan Dayton

---

[5] The full names of the signers follow, not the signatures as they appear on the document.

DELAWARE
George Read
Gunning Bedford, Jr.
John Dickinson
Richard Bassett
Jacob Broom

MARYLAND
James McHenry
Daniel of St. Thomas Jenifer
Daniel Carroll

CONNECTICUT
William Samuel Johnson
Roger Sherman

VIRGINIA
John Blair
James Madison, Jr.

NORTH CAROLINA
William Blount
Richard Dobbs Spaight
Hugh Williamson

SOUTH CAROLINA
John Rutledge
Charles Cotesworth Pinckney
Charles Pinckney
Pierce Butler

GEORGIA
William Few
Abraham Baldwin

Articles in Addition to, and Amendment of, the Constitution of the United states of America, Proposed by Congress, and Ratified by the Legislatures of the Several States, Pursuant to the Fifth Article of the Original Constitution[6]

[ARTICLE I.][7]

Congress shall make no law respecting an establishment of religion, or prohibiting the free exercise thereof; or abridging the freedom of speech, or of the press; or the right of the people peaceably to assemble, and to petition the Government for a redress of grievances.

[ARTICLE II.]

A well regulated Militia, being necessary to the security of a free State, the right of the people to keep and bear Arms shall not be infringed.

---

[6] This heading appears only in the joint resolution submitting the first ten amendments.
[7] In the original manuscripts the first twelve amendments have no numbers.

LEARNING RESOURCES CENTER
Circulation Record
STUDENT

CALL NUMBER	DATE DUE

PRINT
BOOK OR
AV TITLE

PRINT
YOUR
NAME

I.D. NUMBER

TECHNOLOGY   QUARTER

DAY ———— EVE ————

NEW ENGLAND INSTITUTE OF
TECHNOLOGY - WARWICK, RI

—

[Article III.]

No Soldier, shall, in time of peace, be quartered in any house, without the consent of the Owner, nor in time of war, but in a manner to be prescribed by law.

[Article IV.]

The right of the people to be secure in their persons, houses, papers, and effects, against unreasonable searches and seizures, shall not be violated, and no Warrants shall issue, but upon probable cause, supported by Oath or affirmation, and particularly describing the place to be searched, and the persons or things to be seized.

[Article V.]

No person shall be held to answer for a capital or otherwise infamous crime, unless on a presentment or indictment of a Grand Jury, except in cases arising in the land or naval forces, or in the Militia, when in actual service in time of War or public danger; nor shall any person be subject for the same offence to be twice put in jeopardy of life or limb; nor shall be compelled in any criminal case to be a witness against himself, nor be deprived of life, liberty, or property, without due process of law; nor shall private property be taken for public use, without just compensation.

[Article VI.]

In all criminal prosecutions, the accused shall enjoy the right to a speedy and public trial, by an impartial jury of the State and district wherein the crime shall have been committed, which district shall have been previously ascertained by law, and to be informed of the nature and cause of the accusations; to be confronted with the witnesses against him; to have compulsory process for obtaining witnesses in his favor, and to have the Assistance of Counsel for his defence.

[Article VII.]

In suits at common law, where the value in controversy shall exceed twenty dollars, the right of trial by jury shall be preserved, and no fact tried by a jury, shall be otherwise reexamined in any Court of the United States, than according to the rules of the common law.

[Article VIII.]

Excessive bail shall not be required, nor excessive fines imposed, nor cruel and unusual punishments inflicted.

[ARTICLE IX.]

The enumeration in the Constitution, of certain rights, shall not be construed to deny or disparage others retained by the people.

[ARTICLE X.]

The powers not delegated to the United States by the Constitution, nor prohibited by it to the States, are reserved to the States respectively, or to the people.

(Amendments I–X, in force 1791.)

[ARTICLE XI.] [8]

The Judicial power of the United States shall not be construed to extend to any suit in law or equity, commenced or prosecuted against one of the United States by Citizens of another State, or by Citizens or Subjects of any Foreign State.

[ARTICLE XII.] [9]

The Electors shall meet in their respective States and vote by ballot for President and Vice-President, one of whom, at least, shall not be an inhabitant of the same State with themselves; they shall name in their ballots the person voted for as President, and in distinct ballots the person voted for as Vice-President, and they shall make distinct lists of all persons voted for as President, and of all persons voted for as Vice-President, and of the number of votes for each, which lists they shall sign and certify, and transmit sealed to the seat of the government of the United States, directed to the President of the Senate;— The President of the Senate shall, in the presence of the Senate and House of Representatives, open all the certificates and the votes shall then be counted;— The person having the greatest number of votes for President, shall be the President, if such number be a majority of the whole number of Electors appointed; and if no person have such majority, then from the persons having the highest numbers not exceeding three on the list of those voted for as President, the House of Representatives shall choose immediately, by ballot, the President. But in choosing the President, the votes shall be taken by states, the representation from each state having one vote; a quorum for this purpose shall consist of a member or members from two-thirds of the states, and a majority of all the states shall be necessary to a choice. And if the House of Representatives shall not choose a President whenever the right of choice shall

---

[8] Adopted in 1798.
[9] Adopted in 1804.

devolve upon them, before the fourth day of March next following, then the Vice-President shall act as President, as in the case of the death or other constitutional disability of the President.—The person having the greatest number of votes as Vice-President, shall be the Vice-President, if such number be a majority of the whole number of Electors appointed, and if no person have a majority, then from the two highest numbers on the list, the Senate shall choose the Vice-President; a quorum for the purpose shall consist of two-thirds of the whole number of Senators, and a majority of the whole number shall be necessary to a choice. But no person constitutionally ineligible to the office of President shall be eligible to that of Vice-President of the United States.

[Article XIII.] [10]

Section 1. Neither slavery nor involuntary servitude, except as a punishment for crime whereof the party shall have been duly convicted, shall exist within the United States, or any place subject to their jurisdiction.

Section 2. Congress shall have power to enforce this article by appropriate legislation.

[Article XIV.] [11]

Section 1. All persons born or naturalized in the United States, and subject to the jurisdiction thereof, are citizens of the United States and of the State wherein they reside. No State shall make or enforce any law which shall abridge the privileges or immunities of citizens of the United States; nor shall any State deprive any person of life, liberty, or property, without due process of law; nor deny to any person within its jurisdiction the equal protection of the laws.

Section 2. Representatives shall be apportioned among the several States according to their respective numbers, counting the whole number of persons in each State, excluding Indians not taxed. But when the right to vote at any election for the choice of electors for President and Vice-President of the United States, Representatives in Congress, the Executive and Judicial officers of a State, or the members of the Legislature thereof, is denied to any of the male inhabitants of such State, being twenty-one years of age, and citizens of the United States, or in any way abridged, except for participation in rebellion, or other crime, the basis of representation therein shall be reduced in the proportion which the number of such male citizens shall bear to the whole number of male citizens twenty-one years of age in such State.

Section 3. No person shall be a Senator or Representative in Congress, or elector of President and Vice-President, or hold any office, civil or military, under the United States, or under any State, who, having previously taken an

---

[10] Adopted in 1865.
[11] Adopted in 1868.

oath, as a member of Congress, or as an officer of the United States, or as a member of any State legislature, or as an executive or judicial officer of any State, to support the Constitution of the United States, shall have engaged in insurrection or rebellion against the same, or given aid or comfort to the enemies thereof. But Congress may by a vote of two-thirds of each House, remove such disability.

Section 4. The validity of the public debt of the United States, authorized by law, including debts incurred for payment of pensions and bounties for services in suppressing insurrection or rebellion, shall not be questioned. But neither the United States nor any State shall assume or pay any debt or obligation incurred in aid of insurrection or rebellion against the United States, or any claim for the loss or emancipation of any slave; but all such debts, obligations, and claims shall be held illegal and void.

Section 5. The Congress shall have the power to enforce, by appropriate legislation, the provisions of this article.

[ARTICLE XV.] [12]

Section 1. The right of citizens of the United States to vote shall not be denied or abridged by the United States or by any State on account of race, color, or previous condition of servitude—

Section 2. The Congress shall have power to enforce this article by appropriate legislation.

[ARTICLE XVI.] [13]

The Congress shall have power to lay and collect taxes on incomes, from whatever source derived, without apportionment among the several States, and without regard to any census or enumeration.

[ARTICLE XVII.] [14]

The Senate of the United States shall be composed of two senators from each State, elected by the people thereof, for six years; and each senator shall have one vote. The electors in each State shall have the qualifications requisite for electors of the most numerous branch of the State legislature.

When vacancies happen in the representation of any State in the Senate, the executive authority of such State shall issue writs of election to fill such vacancies: *Provided,* That the legislature of any State may empower the executive thereof to make temporary appointments until the people fill the vacancies by election as the legislature may direct.

This amendment shall not be so construed as to affect the election or term of any Senator chosen before it becomes valid as part of the Constitution.

---

[12] Proclaimed March 30, 1870.

[13] Adopted in 1913.

[14] Adopted in 1913.

[ARTICLE XVIII.][15]

After one year from the ratification of this article, the manufacture, sale, or transportation of intoxicating liquors within, the importation thereof into, or the exportation thereof from the United States and all territory subject to the jurisdiction thereof for beverage purposes is hereby prohibited.

The Congress and the several States shall have concurrent power to enforce this article by appropriate legislation.

This article shall be inoperative unless it shall have been ratified as an amendment to the Constitution by the legislatures of the several States, as provided in the Constitution, within seven years from the date of the submission hereof to the States by the Congress.[16]

[ARTICLE XIX.][17]

The right of citizens of the United States to vote shall not be denied or abridged by the United States or by any State on account of sex.

Congress shall have power to enforce this article by appropriate legislation.

[ARTICLE XX.][18]

Section 1. The terms of the President and Vice President shall end at noon on the 20th day of January, and the terms of Senators and Representatives at noon on the 3d day of January, of the years in which such terms would have ended if this article had not been ratified; and the terms of their successors shall then begin.

Section 2. The Congress shall assemble at least once in every year, and such meeting shall begin at noon on the 3d day of January, unless they shall by law appoint a different day.

Section 3. If, at the time fixed for the beginning of the term of the President, the President elect shall have died, the Vice President elect shall become President. If a President shall not have been chosen before the time fixed for the beginning of his term, or if the President elect shall have failed to qualify, then the Vice President elect shall act as President until a President shall have qualified; and the Congress may by law provide for the case wherein neither a President elect nor a Vice President elect shall have qualified, declaring who shall then act as President, or the manner in which one who is to act shall be selected, and such person shall act accordingly until a President or Vice President shall have qualified.

Section 4. The Congress may by law provide for the case of the death of any of the persons from whom the House of Representatives may choose a President

---

[15] Adopted in 1919.
[16] Repealed by the 21st Amendment.
[17] Adopted in 1920.
[18] Adopted in 1933.

whenever the right of choice shall have devolved upon them, and for the case of the death of any of the persons from whom the Senate may choose a Vice President whenever the right of choice shall have devolved upon them.

Section 5. Sections 1 and 2 shall take effect on the 15th day of October following the ratification of this article.

Section 6. This article shall be inoperative unless it shall have been ratified as an amendment to the Constitution by the legislatures of three-fourths of the several States within seven years from the date of its submission.

[ARTICLE XXI.][19]

Section 1. The Eighteenth Article of amendment to the Constitution of the United States is hereby repealed.

Section 2. The transportation or importation into any State, Territory, or possession of the United States for delivery or use therein of intoxicating liquors in violation of the laws thereof, is hereby prohibited.

Section 3. This article shall be inoperative unless it shall have been ratified as an amendment to the Constitution by conventions in the several States, as provided in the Constitution, within seven years from the date of the submission thereof to the States by the Congress.

[ARTICLE XXII.][20]

No person shall be elected to the office of the President more than twice, and no person who has held the office of President, or acted as President, for more than two years of a term to which some other person was elected President shall be elected to the office of the President more than once.

But this article shall not apply to any person holding the office of President when this article was proposed by the Congress, and shall not prevent any person who may be holding the office of President, or acting as President, during the term within which this article becomes operative from holding the office of President or acting as President during the remainder of such term.

This article shall be inoperative unless it shall have been ratified as an amendment to the Constitution by the legislatures of three-fourths of the several States within seven years from the date of its submission to the States by the Congress.

[ARTICLE XXIII.][21]

Section 1. The District constituting the seat of Government of the United States shall appoint in such manner as the Congress may direct:

A number of electors of President and Vice President equal to the whole number of Senators and Representatives in Congress to which the District

---

[19] Adopted in 1933.
[20] Adopted in 1951.
[21] Adopted in 1961.

would be entitled if it were a State, but in no event more than the least populous State; they shall be in addition to those appointed by the States, but they shall be considered, for the purposes of the election of President and Vice President, to be electors appointed by a State; and they shall meet in the District and perform such duties as provided by the twelfth article of amendment.

Section 2. The Congress shall have power to enforce this article by appropriate legislation.

[ARTICLE XXIV.][22]

Section 1. The right of citizens of the United States to vote in any primary or other election for President or Vice President, for electors for President or Vice President, or for Senator or Representative in Congress, shall not be denied or abridged by the United States or any State by reason of failure to pay any poll tax or other tax.

Section 2. The Congress shall have the power to enforce this article by appropriate legislation.

[ARTICLE XXV.][23]

Section 1. In case of the removal of the President from office or of his death or resignation, the Vice President shall become President.

Section 2. Whenever there is a vacancy in the office of the Vice President, the President shall nominate a Vice President who shall take office upon confirmation by a majority vote of both houses of Congress.

Section 3. Whenever the President transmits to the President Pro Tempore of the Senate and the Speaker of the House of Representatives his written declaration that he is unable to discharge the powers and duties of his office, and until he transmits to them a written declaration to the contrary, such powers and duties shall be discharged by the Vice President as acting President.

Section 4. Whenever the Vice President and a majority of either the principal officers of the executive departments or of such other body as Congress may by law provide, transmit to the President Pro Tempore of the Senate and the Speaker of the House of Representatives their written declaration that the President is unable to discharge the powers and duties of his office, the Vice President shall immediately assume the powers and duties of the office as acting President.

Thereafter, when the President transmits to the President Pro Tempore of the Senate and the Speaker of the House of Representatives his written declaration that no inability exists, he shall resume the powers and duties of his office unless the Vice President and a majority of either the principal officers of the executive department or of such other body as Congress may by law provide,

---

[22] Adopted in 1964.
[23] Adopted in 1966.

transmit within four days to the President Pro Tempore of the Senate and the Speaker of the House of Representatives their written declaration that the President is unable to discharge the powers and duties of his office.

Thereupon Congress shall decide the issue, assembling within 48 hours for that purpose if not in session. If the Congress, within 21 days after receipt of the latter written declaration, or, if Congress is not in session, within 21 days after Congress is required to assemble, determine by two-thirds vote of both Houses that the President is unable to discharge the powers and duties of his office, the Vice President shall continue to discharge the same as acting President; otherwise, the President shall resume the powers and duties of his office.

Presidents, Vice Presidents, and Cabinets, 1879-1877

President	**GEORGE WASHINGTON**	**1789–97**
Vice President	JOHN ADAMS	1789–97
Secretary of State	THOMAS JEFFERSON	1789–94
	EDMUND RANDOLPH	1794–95
	TIMOTHY PICKERING	1795–97
Secretary of Treasury	ALEXANDER HAMILTON	1789–95
	OLIVER WOLCOTT	1795–97
Secretary of War	HENRY KNOX	1789–95
	TIMOTHY PICKERING	1795–96
	JAMES McHENRY	1796–97
Postmaster General	SAMUEL OSGOOD	1789–91
	TIMOTHY PICKERING	1791–95
	JOSEPH HABERSHAM	1795–97
Attorney General	EDMUND RANDOLPH	1789–94
	WILLIAM BRADFORD	1794–95
	CHARLES LEE	1795–97
President	**JOHN ADAMS**	**1797–1801**
Vice President	THOMAS JEFFERSON	1797–1801
Secretary of State	TIMOTHY PICKERING	1797–1800
	JOHN MARSHALL	1800–01
Secretary of Treasury	OLIVER WOLCOTT	1797–1801
	SAMUEL DEXTER	1801
Secretary of War	JAMES McHENRY	1797–1800
	JOHN MARSHALL	1800
	SAMUEL DEXTER	1800–01
	ROGER GRISWOLD	1801
Secretary of Navy	BENJAMIN STODDERT	1798–1801
Postmaster General	JOSEPH HABERSHAM	1797–1801
Attorney General	CHARLES LEE	1797–1801
	THEODORE PARSONS	1801
President	**THOMAS JEFFERSON**	**1801–09**
Vice President	AARON BURR	1801–05
	GEORGE CLINTON	1805–09
Secretary of State	JAMES MADISON	1801–09
Secretary of Treasury	SAMUEL DEXTER	1801
	ALBERT GALLATIN	1801–09
Secretary of War	HENRY DEARBORN	1801–09
Secretary of Navy	BENJAMIN STODDERT	1801
	ROBERT SMITH	1801–05
	JACOB CROWNINSHIELD	1805–09

Postmaster General	JOSEPH HABERSHAM	1801
	GIDEON GRANGER	1801–09
Attorney General	LEVI LINCOLN	1801–05
	ROBERT SMITH	1805
	JOHN BRECKINRIDGE	1805–07
	CAESAR RODNEY	1807–09
President	**JAMES MADISON**	**1809–17**
Vice President	GEORGE CLINTON	1809–13
	ELBRIDGE GERRY	1813–17
Secretary of State	ROBERT SMITH	1809–11
	JAMES MONROE	1811–17
Secretary of Treasury	ALBERT GALLATIN	1809–14
	GEORGE CAMPBELL	1814
	ALEXANDER DALLAS	1814–16
	WILLIAM CRAWFORD	1816–17
Secretary of War	WILLIAM EUSTIS	1809–13
	JOHN ARMSTRONG	1813–14
	JAMES MONROE	1814–15
	WILLIAM CRAWFORD	1815–17
Secretary of Navy	PAUL HAMILTON	1809–13
	WILLIAM JONES	1813–14
	BENJAMIN CROWNINSHIELD	1814–17
Postmaster General	GIDEON GRANGER	1809–14
	RETURN MEIGS	1814–17
Attorney General	CAESAR RODNEY	1809–11
	WILLIAM PINKNEY	1811–14
	RICHARD RUSH	1814–17
President	**JAMES MONROE**	**1817–25**
Vice President	DANIEL D. TOMPKINS	1817–25
Secretary of State	JOHN QUINCY ADAMS	1817–25
Secretary of Treasury	WILLIAM CRAWFORD	1817–25
Secretary of War	ISAAC SHELBY	1817
	GEORGE GRAHAM	1817
	JOHN C. CALHOUN	1817–25
Secretary of Navy	BENJAMIN CROWNINSHIELD	1817–18
	SMITH THOMPSON	1818–23
	SAMUEL SOUTHARD	1823–25
Postmaster General	RETURN MEIGS	1817–23
	JOHN MCLEAN	1823–25
Attorney General	RICHARD RUSH	1817
	WILLIAM WIRT	1817–25
President	**JOHN QUINCY ADAMS**	**1825–29**
Vice President	JOHN C. CALHOUN	1825–29
Secretary of State	HENRY CLAY	1825–29
Secretary of Treasury	RICHARD RUSH	1825–29
Secretary of War	JAMES BARBOUR	1825–28
	PETER B. PORTER	1828–29
Secretary of Navy	SAMUEL SOUTHARD	1825–29

Postmaster General	JOHN McLEAN	1825–29
Attorney General	WILLIAM WIRT	1825–29
President	**ANDREW JACKSON**	**1829–37**
Vice President	JOHN C. CALHOUN	1829–33
	MARTIN VAN BUREN	1833–37
Secretary of State	MARTIN VAN BUREN	1829–31
	EDWARD LIVINGSTON	1831–33
	LOUIS McLANE	1833–34
	JOHN FORSYTH	1834–37
Secretary of Treasury	SAMUEL INGHAM	1829–31
	LOUIS McLANE	1831–33
	WILLIAM DUANE	1833
	ROGER B. TANEY	1833–34
	LEVI WOODBURY	1834–37
Secretary of War	JOHN H. EATON	1829–31
	LEWIS CASS	1831–37
	BENJAMIN BUTLER	1837
Secretary of Navy	JOHN BRANCH	1829–31
	LEVI WOODBURY	1831–34
	MAHLON DICKERSON	1834–37
Postmaster General	WILLIAM BARRY	1829–35
	AMOS KENDALL	1835–37
Attorney General	JOHN M. BERRIEN	1829–31
	ROGER B. TANEY	1831–33
	BENJAMIN BUTLER	1833–37
President	**MARTIN VAN BUREN**	**1837–41**
Vice President	RICHARD M. JOHNSON	1837–41
Secretary of State	JOHN FORSYTH	1837–41
Secretary of Treasury	LEVI WOODBURY	1837–41
Secretary of War	JOEL R. POINSETT	1837–41
Secretary of Navy	MAHLON DICKERSON	1837–38
	JAMES K. PAULDING	1838–41
Postmaster General	AMOS KENDALL	1837–40
	JOHN M. NILES	1840–41
Attorney General	BENJAMIN BUTLER	1837–38
	FELIX GRUNDY	1838–40
	HENRY D. GILPIN	1840–41
President	**WILLIAM H. HARRISON**	**1841**
Vice President	JOHN TYLER	1841
Secretary of State	DANIEL WEBSTER	1841
Secretary of Treasury	THOMAS EWING	1841
Secretary of War	JOHN BELL	1841
Secretary of Navy	GEORGE E. BADGER	1841
Postmaster General	FRANCIS GRANGER	1841
Attorney General	JOHN J. CRITTENDEN	1841
President	**JOHN TYLER**	**1841–45**
Secretary of State	DANIEL WEBSTER	1841–43

	HUGH S. LEGARÉ	1843
	ABEL P. UPSHUR	1843–44
	JOHN C. CALHOUN	1844–45
Secretary of Treasury	THOMAS EWING	1841
	WALTER FORWARD	1841–43
	JOHN C. SPENCER	1843–44
	GEORGE M. BIBB	1844–45
Secretary of War	JOHN BELL	1841
	JOHN MCLEAN	1841
	JOHN C. SPENCER	1841–43
	JAMES M. PORTER	1843–44
	WILLIAM WILKINS	1844–45
Secretary of Navy	GEORGE E. BADGER	1841
	ABEL P. UPSHUR	1841–43
	DAVID HENSHAW	1843–44
	THOMAS GILMER	1844
	JOHN Y. MASON	1844–45
Postmaster General	FRANCIS GRANGER	1841
	CHARLES A. WICKLIFFE	1841–45
Attorney General	JOHN J. CRITTENDEN	1841
	HUGH S. LEGARÉ	1841–43
	JOHN NELSON	1843–45
President	**JAMES K. POLK**	**1845–49**
Vice President	GEORGE M. DALLAS	1845–49
Secretary of State	JAMES BUCHANAN	1845–49
Secretary of Treasury	ROBERT J. WALKER	1845–49
Secretary of War	WILLIAM L. MARCY	1845–49
Secretary of Navy	GEORGE BANCROFT	1845–46
	JOHN Y. MASON	1846–49
Postmaster General	CAVE JOHNSON	1845–49
Attorney General	JOHN Y. MASON	1845–46
	NATHAN CLIFFORD	1846–48
	ISAAC TOUCEY	1848–49
President	**ZACHARY TAYLOR**	**1849–50**
Vice President	MILLARD FILLMORE	1849–50
Secretary of State	JOHN M. CLAYTON	1849–50
Secretary of Treasury	WILLIAM M. MEREDITH	1849–50
Secretary of War	GEORGE W. CRAWFORD	1849–50
Secretary of Navy	WILLIAM B. PRESTON	1849–50
Secretary of Interior	THOMAS EWING	1849–50
Postmaster General	JACOB COLLAMER	1849–50
Attorney General	REVERDY JOHNSON	1849–50
President	**MILLARD FILLMORE**	**1850–53**
Secretary of State	DANIEL WEBSTER	1850–52
	EDWARD EVERETT	1852–53
Secretary of Treasury	THOMAS CORWIN	1850–53
Secretary of War	CHARLES M. CONRAD	1850–53

Secretary of Navy	WILLIAM A. GRAHAM	1850–52
	JOHN P. KENNEDY	1852–53
Secretary of Interior	ALEXANDER H. H. STUART	1850–53
Postmaster General	NATHAN K. HALL	1850–52
	SAM D. HUBBARD	1852–53
Attorney General	JOHN J. CRITTENDEN	1850–53
President	**FRANKLIN PIERCE**	**1853–57**
Vice President	WILLIAM R. KING	1853–57
Secretary of State	WILLIAM L. MARCY	1853–57
Secretary of Treasury	JAMES GUTHRIE	1853–57
Secretary of War	JEFFERSON DAVIS	1853–57
Secretary of Navy	JAMES C. DOBBIN	1853–57
Secretary of Interior	ROBERT McCLELLAND	1853–57
Postmaster General	JAMES CAMPBELL	1853–57
Attorney General	CALEB CUSHING	1853–57
President	**JAMES BUCHANAN**	**1857–61**
Vice President	JOHN C. BRECKINRIDGE	1857–61
Secretary of State	LEWIS CASS	1857–60
	JEREMIAH S. BLACK	1860–61
Secretary of Treasury	HOWELL COBB	1857–60
	PHILIP F. THOMAS	1860–61
	JOHN A. DIX	1861
Secretary of War	JOHN B. FLOYD	1857–61
	JOSEPH HOLT	1861
Secretary of Navy	ISAAC TOUCEY	1857–61
Secretary of Interior	JACOB THOMPSON	1857–61
Postmaster General	AARON V. BROWN	1857–59
	JOSEPH HOLT	1859–61
Attorney General	JEREMIAH S. BLACK	1857–60
	EDWIN M. STANTON	1860–61
President	**ABRAHAM LINCOLN**	**1861–65**
Vice President	HANNIBAL HAMLIN	1861–65
	ANDREW JOHNSON	1865
Secretary of State	WILLIAM H. SEWARD	1861–65
Secretary of Treasury	SALMON P. CHASE	1861–64
	WILLIAM P. FESSENDEN	1864–65
	HUGH McCULLOCH	1865
Secretary of War	SIMON CAMERON	1861–62
	EDWIN M. STANTON	1862–65
Secretary of Navy	GIDEON WELLES	1861–65
Secretary of Interior	CALEB B. SMITH	1861–63
	JOHN P. USHER	1863–65
Postmaster General	HORATIO KING	1861
	MONTGOMERY BLAIR	1861–64
	WILLIAM DENNISON	1864–65
Attorney General	EDWARD BATES	1861–63
	TITIAN J. COFFEY	1863–64
	JAMES SPEED	1864–65

President	**ANDREW JOHNSON**	**1865–69**
Secretary of State	WILLIAM H. SEWARD	1865–69
Secretary of Treasury	HUGH McCULLOCH	1865–69
Secretary of War	EDWIN M. STANTON	1865–67
	ULYSSES S. GRANT	1867–68
	LORENZO THOMAS	1868
	JOHN M. SCHOFIELD	1868–69
Secretary of Navy	GIDEON WELLES	1865–69
Secretary of Interior	JOHN P. USHER	1865
	JAMES HARLAN	1865–66
	ORVILLE H. BROWNING	1866–69
Postmaster General	WILLIAM DENNISON	1865–66
	ALEXANDER W. RANDALL	1866–69
Attorney General	JAMES SPEED	1865–66
	HENRY STANBERRY	1866–68
	WILLIAM M. EVARTS	1868–69

President	**ULYSSES S. GRANT**	**1869–77**
Vice President	SCHUYLER COLFAX	1869–73
	HENRY WILSON	1873–77
Secretary of State	ELIHU B. WASHBURNE	1869
	HAMILTON FISH	1869–77
Secretary of Treasury	GEORGE S. BOUTWELL	1869–73
	WILLIAM A. RICHARDSON	1873–74
	BENJAMIN H. BRISTOW	1874–76
	LOT M. MORRILL	1876–77
Secretary of War	JOHN A. RAWLINS	1869
	WILLIAM T. SHERMAN	1869
	WILLIAM W. BELKNAP	1869–76
	ALPHONSO TAFT	1876
	JAMES D. CAMERON	1876–77
Secretary of Navy	ADOLPH E. BORIE	1869
	GEORGE M. ROBESON	1869–77
Secretary of Interior	JACOB D. COX	1869–70
	COLUMBUS DELANO	1870–75
	ZACHARIAH CHANDLER	1875–77
Postmaster General	JOHN A. J. CRESWELL	1869–74
	JAMES W. MARSHALL	1874
	MARSHALL JEWEL	1874–76
	JAMES N. TYNER	1876–77
Attorney General	EBENEZER R. HOAR	1869–70
	AMOS T. ACKERMAN	1870–71
	GEORGE H. WILLIAMS	1871–75
	EDWARD PIERREPONT	1875–76
	ALPHONSO TAFT	1876–77

President	**RUTHERFORD B. HAYES**	**1877–81**
Vice President	WILLIAM A. WHEELER	1877–81
Secretary of State	WILLIAM M. EVARTS	1877–81
Secretary of Treasury	JOHN SHERMAN	1877–81
Secretary of War	GEORGE W. McCRARY	1877–79
	ALEXANDER RAMSEY	1879–81

Secretary of Navy	RICHARD W. THOMPSON	1877–81
	NATHAN GOFF, JR.	1881
Secretary of Interior	CARL SCHURZ	1877–81
Postmaster General	DAVID M. KEY	1877–80
	HORACE MAYNARD	1880–81
Attorney General	CHARLES DEVENS	1877–81

[APPENDIX IV.]

The Population of the United States, 1790-1870[1]

	1790	1800	1810	1820	1830	1840	1850	1860	1870
ALABAMA	.....	.....	.....	127,901	309,527	590,756	771,623	964,201	996,992
ARKANSAS	.....	.....	1,062	14,273	30,388	97,574	209,897	435,450	484,471
CALIFORNIA	.....	.....	.....	.....	.....	.....	92,597	379,994	560,247
COLORADO	.....	.....	.....	.....	.....	.....	.....	34,277	39,864
CONNECTICUT	237,946	251,002	261,942	275,248	297,675	309,978	370,792	460,147	537,454
DELAWARE	59,096	64,273	72,674	72,749	76,748	78,085	91,532	112,216	125,015
DISTRICT OF COLUMBIA	.....	14,093	24,023	33,039	39,834	43,712	51,687	75,080	131,700
FLORIDA	.....	.....	.....	.....	34,730	54,477	87,445	140,424	187,748
GEORGIA	82,548	162,680	252,433	340,989	516,823	691,392	906,185	1,057,286	1,184,109
ILLINOIS	.....	.....	12,282	55,211	157,445	476,183	851,470	1,711,951	2,539,891
INDIANA	.....	5,641	24,520	147,178	343,031	685,866	988,416	1,350,428	1,680,637
IOWA	.....	.....	.....	.....	.....	43,112	192,214	674,913	1,194,200
KANSAS	.....	.....	.....	.....	.....	.....	.....	107,206	364,399
KENTUCKY	73,677	220,955	406,511	564,317	687,917	779,828	982,405	1,155,684	1,321,011
LOUISIANA	.....	.....	76,556	153,407	215,739	352,411	517,762	708,002	726,915
MAINE	96,540	151,719	228,705	298,335	399,455	501,793	583,169	628,279	626,915
MARYLAND	319,728	341,548	380,546	407,350	447,040	470,019	583,034	687,049	780,894
MASSACHUSETTS	378,787	422,845	472,040	523,287	610,408	737,699	994,514	1,231,066	1,457,351
MICHIGAN	.....	.....	4,762	8,896	31,639	212,267	397,654	749,113	1,184,059
MINNESOTA	.....	.....	.....	.....	.....	.....	6,077	172,023	439,706
MISSISSIPPI	.....	8,850	40,352	75,448	136,621	375,651	606,526	791,305	827,922
MISSOURI	.....	.....	19,783	66,586	140,455	383,702	682,044	1,182,012	1,721,295

794

Nebraska								28,841	122,993
Nevada								6,857	42,491
New Hampshire	141,885	183,858	214,460	244,161	269,328	284,574	317,976	326,073	318,300
New Jersey	184,139	211,149	245,562	277,575	320,823	373,306	489,555	672,035	906,096
New Mexico							61,547	93,516	91,874
New York	340,120	589,051	959,049	1,372,812	1,918,608	2,428,921	3,097,394	3,880,735	4,382,759
North Carolina	393,751	478,103	555,500	638,829	737,987	753,419	869,039	992,622	1,071,361
Ohio		45,365	230,760	581,434	937,903	1,519,467	1,980,329	2,339,511	2,665,260
Oregon							13,294	52,465	90,923
Pennsylvania	434,373	602,365	810,091	1,049,458	1,348,233	1,724,033	2,311,786	2,906,215	3,521,951
Rhode Island	68,825	69,122	76,931	83,059	97,199	108,830	147,545	174,620	217,353
South Carolina	249,073	345,591	415,115	502,741	581,185	594,398	668,507	703,708	705,606
South Dakota								4,837	11,776
Tennessee	35,691	105,602	261,727	422,823	681,904	829,210	1,002,717	1,109,801	1,258,520
Texas							212,592	604,215	818,579
Utah							11,380	40,273	86,786
Vermont	85,425	154,465	217,895	235,981	280,652	291,948	314,120	315,098	330,551
Virginia	747,610	880,200	974,600	1,065,366	1,211,405	1,239,797	1,421,661	1,596,318	1,225,163
Washington								11,594	23,955
Wisconsin						130,945	305,391	775,881	1,054,670

Geographic Divisions

New England	1,009,408	1,233,011	1,471,973	1,660,071	1,954,717	2,234,822	2,728,116	3,135,283	3,487,924
Middle Atlantic	958,632	1,402,565	2,014,702	2,699,845	3,587,664	4,526,260	5,898,735	7,458,985	8,810,806
East North Central		51,006	272,324	792,719	1,470,018	2,924,728	4,523,260	6,926,884	9,124,517
West North Central			19,783	66,586	140,455	426,814	880,335	2,169,832	3,856,594
South Atlantic	1,851,806	2,286,494	2,674,891	3,061,063	3,645,752	3,925,299	4,679,090	5,364,703	5,853,610
East South Central	109,368	335,407	708,590	1,190,489	1,815,969	2,575,445	3,363,271	4,020,991	4,404,445
West South Central		77,618	167,680	246,127	449,985	940,251	1,747,667	2,029,965
Mountain							72,927	174,923	315,385
Pacific							105,891	444,053	675,125
TOTAL	3,929,214	5,308,483	7,239,881	9,638,453	12,866,020[2]	17,069,453[2]	23,191,876	31,443,321	39,818,449

1 According to the Bureau of the Census.
2 Includes persons on public ships in United States service, not credited to any geographic division or state.

〖 A P P E N D I X   V. 〗

Presidential Elections, 1789-1876

Year	No. of States	Candidates	Party	Electoral Vote	Popular Vote
1789	11	GEORGE WASHINGTON		69	
		John Adams		34	
		John Jay		9	
		Others		26	
		(Not voted)		12	
1792	15	GEORGE WASHINGTON		132	
		John Adams		77	
		George Clinton		50	
		Others		5	
1796	16	JOHN ADAMS	Federalist	71	
		Thomas Jefferson	Democratic–Republican	68	
		Thomas Pinckney	Federalist	59	
		Aaron Burr	Democratic–Republican	30	
		Others		48	
1800	16	THOMAS JEFFERSON	Democratic–Republican	73	
		Aaron Burr	Democratic–Republican	73	
		John Adams	Federalist	65	
		C. C. Pinckney	Federalist	64	
		John Jay	Federalist	1	
1804	17	THOMAS JEFFERSON	Democratic–Republican	162	
		C. C. Pinckney	Federalist	14	
1808	17	JAMES MADISON	Democratic–Republican	122	
		C. C. Pinckney	Federalist	47	
		George Clinton	Independent–Republican	6	
		(Not voted)		1	
1812	18	JAMES MADISON	Democratic–Republican	128	
		DeWitt Clinton	Federalist	89	
		(Not voted)		1	
1816	19	JAMES MONROE	Republican	183	
		Rufus King	Federalist	34	
		(Not voted)		4	
1820	24	JAMES MONROE	Republican	231	
		John Q. Adams	Independent–Republican	1	
		(Not voted)		3	
1824	24	JOHN Q. ADAMS	*No distinct party designations*	84	108,740
		Andrew Jackson		99	153,544
		Henry Clay		37	47,136
		W. H. Crawford		41	46,618
1828	24	ANDREW JACKSON	Democratic	178	647,286
		John Q. Adams	National Republican	83	508,064
1832	25	ANDREW JACKSON	Democratic	219	687,502
		Henry Clay	National Republican	49	530,189
		William Wirt	Anti-Masonic	7	
		John Floyd	Nullifiers	11	
		(Not voted)		2	

Year	No. of States	Candidates	Party	Electoral Vote	Popular Vote
1836	26	MARTIN VAN BUREN	Democratic	170	762,678
		Wm. H. Harrison	Whig	73 ⎫	
		Hugh L. White	Whig	26 ⎬	735,651
		Daniel Webster	Whig	14 ⎭	
		W. P. Mangum	Anti-Jackson	11	
1840	26	WILLIAM H. HARRISON	Whig	234	1,275,016
		Martin Van Buren	Democratic	60	1,129,102
		James G. Birney	Liberty		7,069
1844	26	JAMES K. POLK	Democratic	170	1,337,243
		Henry Clay	Whig	105	1,299,062
		James G. Birney	Liberty		62,300
1848	30	ZACHARY TAYLOR	Whig	163	1,360,099
		Lewis Cass	Democratic	127	1,220,544
		Martin Van Buren	Free Soil		291,263
1852	31	FRANKLIN PIERCE	Democratic	254	1,601,274
		Winfield Scott	Whig	42	1,386,580
		John P. Hale	Free Soil		155,825
1856	31	JAMES BUCHANAN	Democratic	174	1,838,169
		John C. Frémont	Republican	114	1,341,264
		Millard Fillmore	American	8	874,534
1860	33	ABRAHAM LINCOLN	Republican	180	1,866,452
		J. C. Breckenridge	Democratic	72	847,953
		Stephen A. Douglas	Democratic	12	1,375,157
		John Bell	Constitutional Union	39	590,631
1864	36	ABRAHAM LINCOLN	Republican	212	2,213,665
		George B. McClellan	Democratic	21	1,805,237
		(Not voted)		81	
1868	37	ULYSSES S. GRANT	Republican	214	3,012,833
		Horatio Seymour	Democrat	80	2,703,249
		(Not voted)		23	
1872	37	ULYSSES S. GRANT	Republican	286	3,597,132
		Horace Greeley	Democrat and Liberal Republican	See note 1	2,834,125
		(Not voted)		17	
1876	38	RUTHERFORD B. HAYES	Republican	185	4,036,298
		Samuel J. Tilden	Democrat	184	4,300,590

[1] Democratic electors scattered votes after Greeley's death.

⟦ A P P E N D I X V I. ⟧

The Admission of States to the Union, 1787-1876

		Date of Admission [1]	Area in Square Miles
1.	DELAWARE	Dec. 7, 1787	2,307
2.	PENNSYLVANIA	Dec. 12, 1787	45,126
3.	NEW JERSEY	Dec. 18, 1787	8,222
4.	GEORGIA	Jan. 2, 1788	59,265
5.	CONNECTICUT	Jan. 9, 1788	4,965
6.	MASSACHUSETTS	Feb. 6, 1788	8,266
7.	MARYLAND	Apr. 28, 1788	12,327
8.	SOUTH CAROLINA	May 23, 1788	30,989
9.	NEW HAMPSHIRE	June 21, 1788	9,341
10.	VIRGINIA	June 25, 1788	42,627
11.	NEW YORK	July 26, 1788	49,204
12.	NORTH CAROLINA	Nov. 21, 1789	52,426
13.	RHODE ISLAND	May 29, 1790	1,248
14.	VERMONT	Mar. 4, 1791	9,564
15.	KENTUCKY	June 1, 1792	40,598
16.	TENNESSEE	June 1, 1796	42,022
17.	OHIO	Mar. 1, 1803	41,040
18.	LOUISIANA	Apr. 30, 1812	48,506
19.	INDIANA	Dec. 11, 1816	36,354
20.	MISSISSIPPI	Dec. 10, 1817	46,865
21.	ILLINOIS	Dec. 3, 1818	56,665
22.	ALABAMA	Dec. 14, 1819	51,998
23.	MAINE	Mar. 15, 1820	33,040
24.	MISSOURI	Aug. 10, 1821	69,420
25.	ARKANSAS	June 15, 1836	53,335
26.	MICHIGAN	Jan. 26, 1837	57,980
27.	FLORIDA	Mar. 3, 1845	58,666
28.	TEXAS	Dec. 29, 1845	265,896
29.	IOWA	Dec. 28, 1846	56,147
30.	WISCONSIN	May 29, 1848	56,066
31.	CALIFORNIA	Sept. 9, 1850	158,297
32.	MINNESOTA	May 11, 1858	84,682
33.	OREGON	Feb. 14, 1859	96,699
34.	KANSAS	Jan. 29, 1861	82,158
35.	WEST VIRGINIA	June 19, 1863	24,170
36.	NEVADA	Oct. 31, 1864	110,690
37.	NEBRASKA	Mar. 1, 1867	77,227
38.	COLORADO	Aug. 1, 1876	104,247

---

[1] For the original thirteen states, the date given is that of the ratification of the Constitution.

[APPENDIX VII.]

Justices of the Supreme Court, 1789-1876 [1]

	Term	Years
JOHN JAY (*N.Y.*)	1789–1795	6
John Rutledge (*S.C.*)	1789–1791	2
William Cushing (*Mass.*)	1789–1810	21
James Wilson (*Pa.*)	1789–1798	9
John Blair (*Va.*)	1789–1796	7
James Iredell (*N.C.*)	1790–1799	9
Thomas Johnson (*Md.*)	1792–1793	½
William Paterson (*N.J.*)	1793–1806	13
JOHN RUTLEDGE (*S.C.*) [2]	1795–1795	
Samuel Chase (*Md.*)	1796–1811	15
OLIVER ELLSWORTH (*Conn.*)	1796–1800	4
Bushrod Washington (*Va.*)	1798–1829	31
Alfred Moore (*N.C.*)	1800–1804	4
JOHN MARSHALL (*Va.*)	1801–1835	34
William Johnson (*S.C.*)	1804–1834	30
Brock. Livingston (*N.Y.*)	1806–1823	17
Thomas Todd (*Ky.*)	1807–1826	19
Joseph Story (*Mass.*)	1811–1845	34
Gabriel Duval (*Md.*)	1811–1835	24
Smith Thompson (*N.Y.*)	1823–1843	20
Robert Trimble (*Ky.*)	1826–1828	2
John McLean (*Ohio*)	1829–1861	32
Henry Baldwin (*Pa.*)	1830–1844	14
James M. Wayne (*Ga.*)	1835–1867	32
ROGER B. TANEY (*Md.*)	1836–1864	28
Philip P. Barbour (*Va.*)	1836–1841	5
John Catron (*Tenn.*)	1837–1865	28
John McKinley (*Ala.*)	1837–1852	15
Peter V. Daniel (*Va.*)	1841–1860	19
Samuel Nelson (*N.Y.*)	1845–1872	27
Levi Woodbury (*N.H.*)	1845–1851	6
Robert C. Grier (*Pa.*)	1846–1870	24
Benjamin R. Curtis (*Mass.*)	1851–1857	6
John A. Campbell (*Ala.*)	1853–1861	8
Nathan Clifford (*Maine*)	1858–1881	23
Noah H. Swayne (*Ohio*)	1862–1881	19
Samuel F. Miller (*Iowa*)	1862–1890	28
David Davis (*Ill.*)	1862–1877	15
Stephen J. Field (*Calif.*)	1863–1897	34
SALMON P. CHASE (*Ohio*)	1864–1873	9
William Strong (*Pa.*)	1870–1880	10
Joseph P. Bradley (*N.J.*)	1870–1892	22
Ward Hunt (*N.Y.*)	1872–1882	10
MORRISON R. WAITE (*Ohio*)	1874–1888	14

[1] Chief Justices in small capitals.
[2] Appointed and served one term, but not confirmed by the Senate.

Index

Literary Landmarks

1. WASHINGTON IRVING, *The Sketch Book (1819–1820)*. Delightful tales of the Hudson River Valley that fostered patriotic interest.

2. JAMES FENIMORE COOPER, *The Leatherstocking Tales (1823–1841)*. Romantic novels about Indians and the frontier that were immensely popular.

3. RALPH WALDO EMERSON, *Essays (1841–1844)*. These were the outstanding expressions of Transcendentalist thought.

4. NATHANIEL HAWTHORNE, *The Scarlet Letter (1850)*. An outstanding depiction of life in Puritan New England.

5. HERMAN MELVILLE, *Moby Dick (1851)*. The saga of the white whale and its pursuit of Captain Ahab. One of America's great novels.

6. WALT WHITMAN, *The Leaves of Grass (1855)*. Carl Sandburg calls this poem "The most wildly keyed solemn oath that America means something and is going somewhere that has ever been written."

7. GEORGE BANCROFT, *History of The United States (1834–1866)*. These nine volumes were a paean of praise for American democracy.

8. FRANCIS PARKMAN, *Pioneers of France in the New World (1865)*. This brilliant study in the history of New France went far toward establishing the author's reputation as an outstanding American historian.